A History of Finnish Literature

A HISTORY
OF
FINNISH LITERATURE

BY

Jaakko Ahokas

Published for
The American-Scandinavian Foundation
by Indiana University.
Research Center for the Language Sciences

Copyright © 1973 by Indiana University

Textual editing by Lee Zacharias

ISBN: 87750-172-6

Library of Congress Catalog Card Number: 67-65319

Printed in the United States of America
Cushing-Malloy, Inc., Ann Arbor, Michigan, Printers

To Lauri Viljanen, my fatherly friend, who knows so well to apply the old adage, *Fortiter in re, suaviter in modo.*

Contents

Preface

A book that deals with history up to the present is always left with a number of loose ends. This one is no exception; for various reasons, independent of everybody's will, its publication has been delayed for a rather long period, and, as the literary scene in Finland has witnessed a lively activity during the last years, the final chapters are not what they would be like should I write them today. Young writers who seemed very promising do not develop further and others acquire an unforeseen importance, but I shall not make myself odious by telling whom I should have dropped from the book or ingratiate myself by announcing whom I should have included. At any rate, the biographical data in the book are as up to date as possible. The following authors have died during the editing and composition of this book: Martti Haavio/P. Mustapää, 1973; Huugo Jalkanen, 1969; Alex Matson, 1972; Martti Merenmaa, 1972; Timo M. Mukka, 1973; Oiva Paloheimo, 1973; Marko Tapio, 1973; and Einari Vuorela, 1972.

Due to the peculiar conditions in which the book was produced, with the author and editor traveling and settling in different places in the U.S., it has some minor technical deficiencies for which I feel I must apologize. The translations of Finnish and Swedish texts presented in the book are by myself, unless otherwise indicated. For some of the poems quoted, I give a translation which attempts to reproduce the meter, the rhythm and all the artistic qualities of the original. For reasons relating to production and printing considerations the original texts and certain quotations from which translations are made are not always presented side-by-side, but the placement should not unduly inconvenience the reader. In addition the translation of titles is in some cases omitted. If the translation of a title does not appear in the text, it is given in the Index.

I wish to thank the Finnish publishers Kirjayhtymä Oy., K. J. Gummerus Oy., Otava Oy., Tammi Oy., Werner Söderström Oy., the Swedish publishers of Finland Söderströms & Co. Förlags Ab., and Holger Schildts Förlags Ab., and the Press Bureau of the Ministry for Foreign Affairs of Finland for the photographs kindly given for this work, and the same publishers for the right to quote the texts published by them (although they all indicated in their answers that such authorization is not required under Finnish law). I also thank the Finnish Writers' Guild for the biographical information provided about its members. The American-Scandinavian Foundation has kindly included this book in a series of works sponsored by it, thus partly making its publication possible.

Temple University, Philadelphia　　　　　　　　　　Jaakko A. Ahokas
June 1973

A History of Finnish Literature

The General Background

NOT LONG AGO, FINLAND celebrated the fiftieth anniversary of her Declaration of Independence, passed on December 6, 1917, as a bill of the government presented to Parliament, assembled for its normal session. We notice that before independence the country had a government and Parliament. The bill passed one hundred to eighty-eight, the minority social-democrats not opposed to independence but in favor of a different form.

> Parliament, having been presented by the Government a Bill providing for a new Constitution under which Finland shall be an independent Republic, approves, as the holder of the supreme executive power, this principle and decides further that, in order to secure the recognition of Finland's political independence, the Government shall take the measures it has declared necessary to that effect.

The apparent anomaly of the legislative organ declaring itself the holder of supreme executive power is explained by the fact that, at the news of the Bolshevik *coup d'état* in Russia, the Finnish Parliament had decided to assume this power which had previously been vested in the czar and various governments following him.

Conspicuously missing from this document are the expatiations on the inalienable rights of free men, the Law of Nature, decrees of the Supreme Being, hate for tyrants, and love of the native country to be found in the Declaration of Independence of the United States or the *Déclaration des Droits de l'Homme* of France. The directness of the Declaration, however, is in keeping with the realistic, critical, and perhaps earth-bound nature of Finns, who are not easily seduced by fancy terms. These Finnish characteristics are reflected in their literature (whether written in Finnish or Swedish) as well as other manifestations of their public and private lives.

After independence was proclaimed, the country endured a socialist *coup d'état*, a civil war, the election of a German king by conservative groups, and renewed proclamation of a republic before it became the parliamentary democracy it has been since the Constitution of 1919, which has survived in nearly original form.

The existence of the government and Parliament before independence was due to the kingdom of Sweden's rule over Finland until 1809, the Swedish constitution then in force remaining by permission of Alexander I when the Russians annexed Finland. Until Nicholas II, Alexander's successors respected it. Throughout the nineteenth century Finland had a Parliament, a cabinet (called Senate), a national civil service and judiciary (no Russian could be appointed to office), a Bank of Finland and monetary unit of her own, Finnish stamps, state railways, and a small army—everything an autonomous country needs except a chief of state, independent foreign relations, a flag, and a national anthem. However, the Russian autocrats ruled Finland as constitutional monarchs because the Swedish constitution gave the ruler wide powers. The Parliament, the Estates General of the Grand Duchy of Finland, a very archaic organ, met only if summoned by the monarch. Although Parliament's approval was needed for new taxes, custom duties could be modified by the emperor's will. As freedom of the press was limited in Sweden at the beginning of the nineteenth century, the Russians were able to submit to severe censure any writing intended for publication in Finland. In 1850 an imperial decree forbad the publication in Finnish of anything not dealing with religion or agriculture, the exemption including "old poems, songs, and tales," thus leaving folklorists, historians, and linguists free to pursue their work. Although the field of application was limited in 1854 and the decree formally revoked in 1860, with the exception of a brief period under the liberal Alexander II, censorship was enforced until the end of the Russian domination. The Russian emperor had the support of Finland's ruling class, the Swedish-speaking aristocrats, civil servants, and conservative, patriarchal magistrates. Most members of this ruling class did try to improve the material conditions of the country: during the first half of the nineteenth century, new land was cultivated, the population was increased considerably, roads and canals were built, and modern industries were begun; but the authoritarian and restrictive spirit of the ruling power was still evident. No new measures could be taken unless approved or (better) initiated by the ruling power. In contemporary documents the limitations on all publications in Finnish are often justified as protective of workers and the rural population, supposedly the only people who read Finnish, against the harmful influence of nonreligious or nonutilitarian literature, which could only make them less willing to work. The decree contained no provisions on works written in Swedish (or any other language) because the allegedly greater spiritual maturity of the educated classes enabled them to resist the enticements of false social and political theories.[1] A remnant of this protective spirit was recently still evident among the Finnish ruling class, although it is now largely Finnish-speaking. Although there is no censorship, authorities were quick to prosecute and condemn works considered immoral, especially when pointed out by members of the established church, but only if they were original productions or translations in Finnish. After 1964 or so, the situation radically changed; practically anything can now be printed, publicly displayed, and sold.

The fiftieth anniversary of Finland's independence in 1967 could be considered the hundredth anniversary of literature in Finnish. Between 1864 and 1870 Aleksis Kivi, the first genuine writer and poet to use that language, published his major works. A century earlier (between 1766 and 1778) educated classes in Finland first became interested in the amazingly abundant and varied folk poetry of the country. During that period Henrik Gabriel Porthan, professor at the University of Turku, published his *De Poësi Fennica*, the first modern scholarly work on Finnish folklore.

Although this volume will not deal at length with folklore (in Finland now included in literature as "oral" or "unwritten" art), folklore is discussed because of its great influence on the spiritual life of the country and its illustration that, in spite of the near total lack of literary production before the nineteenth century, the Finns possessed creative instinct. Under Swedish rule, from the invention of printer's art, approximately two thousand works, most nonliterary, were published in Finland, whereas by now more than one and one-half million lines of folk poetry have been collected.

It is traditionally accepted that between 1150 and 1160 the Swedes began expeditions which eventually led to the conquest of Finland. The Finns, who had settled in their country near the time of Christ's birth, were then grouped in small independent communities with a level of civilization comparable to that of the Germans or the Celts at the time of the Roman conquest. They knew iron, copper, and bronze, the main cereals, and the most important domestic animals; they made skillfully decorated weapons and jewelry and sailed in ships in which the bodies of chieftains were burned after their deaths. The forcefulness and violence of this period, corresponding to the last days of Rome, the inroads of the Barbarians, and the raids of the Vikings, is reflected in epic poems, especially in the cycle of Kaukamoinen or Ahti Saarelainen, whose main character is a warrior ever ready to sail to foreign countries for adventure and plunder, to abduct women (by force if they are unwilling), and to fight single-handedly to defend his honor. This cycle is a small part of the vast number of epic compositions sung by folk poets and transcribed by Elias Lönnrot and his successors.[2] At the end of the nineteenth century, an Italian scholar discovered among them very archaic elements,[3] reflecting the primitive magic rituals and beliefs of the shamans, who sought the magic words among the dead or even in the body of another

3

shaman, as does Väinämöninen, one main character, with Antero Vipunen.[4] Also included are the universal myths, e.g., the creation of the world from an egg, the representation of (perhaps) the Milky Way as a gigantic tree extending across the sky, and the mysterious *Sampo,* possibly the world pillar supporting the starry vault above the earth. As these myths were not transcribed until the nineteenth century, they had been considerably obscured in time and were not entirely understood even by the folk singers who maintained the old traditions. One of the foremost contemporary folklorists, Professor Matti Kuusi, has declared that he would not even try to determine the original meaning of the *Sampo* myth and that it would be much more profitable to classify the poems referring to this myth according to typological criteria, in order to define their relative chronology and mutual relations.[5] Thus, the interpretations to which we refer are perhaps the most widely accepted, but not absolute.

Besides these myths Finnish folklore comprises motifs more familiar and found in folk poetry of many West European countries, though Eastern, mainly Russian, elements also occur,[6] both appearing in ballads dealing with courtly life, such as *The Song of Inkeri and Lalmanti*, the story of a maid faithfully waiting for her betrothed, who is fighting in a war abroad; *Elina's Death*, supposedly based on a historical incident, which depicts the slaying of an innocent wife by her jealous husband; *The Song of the Virgin and the Dragon*, a free interpretation of the legend of Saint George;[7] *The Creator's Song*, a bold, original transposition of the life, birth, death, and resurrection of Christ; or *The Song of Saint Henry*, a pious legend about the life and martyrdom of this English-born saint, the first apostle and patron of Finland. These poems represent a successful attempt to combine old forms with new subjects. Whether courtly or Christian in content, their form is always the old Finnish meter, a trochaic tetrameter of eight syllables appearing in two distinct types: the dipodic trochaic line with a caesura and the so-called broken line, used in both epic and lyric poetry. Except *Elina's Death*, for which there was a manuscript, the more recent poems were sung by folk poets, then transcribed, but it seems probable that they were originally written for the Finnish nobility of the Middle Ages, who were undoubtedly faithful subjects of the Swedish crown but had not yet adopted its language. Perhaps in the sixteenth and seventeenth centuries the old meter was forgotten in the west, but, in eastern Finland and the Finnish-speaking areas beyond the Russian border, it was still used at the beginning of this century. Old poems were passed from generation to generation, and new ones, of poorer quality, were composed. Although folk poems were still sung in western Finland, they were similar to the Scandinavian and West European ones in meter, stanza division, the use of rhyme and choruses, and subjects.[8] Love was treated more often in a stereotyped manner: a fair maid and a young man meet in the same setting, "under the green tree," "on a flowering meadow," the conventional *locus amoenus* of poetry from antiquity; they swear fidelity but are separated by adversities or death, though one returns to exact the terms of or free the other from the oath. Like the broadsheet ballads of England, these songs were widely printed and sold. They included soldiers', sailors', and lumberjacks' songs; narratives about wars, fires, other calamities, highwaymen, and murderers; and satirical, humorous compositions in which quick-witted country people ridicule their neighbors and their small misfortunes. This modern folk poetry was long ignored by scholars, who were overwhelmed with the beauty of the old poems; the more recent songs were not systematically collected until 1950.

In addition to great epic poems sung by men, the folklorists have discovered a vast field of lyrical poetry belonging specifically to women. Except lamentations, improvised and sung at funerals and on mournful occasions, these poems were composed in the epic meter reflecting by their structure and motifs traditions of antiquity. But, they are surprisingly modern in sentiment and closer to our contemporary poetic sensibility than the narrative poems or the more recent West European folk poetry. A fleeting moment, an evanescent feeling, a human destiny appear in condensed, forceful, vivid imagery consisting of everyday words depicting ordinary gestures and objects, which acquire new meanings and unexpected intensity. Seldom do we find joy, happiness, or love in these songs; anger sometimes appears, but most often they are pervaded by dreamy melancholy, expressed by the old poets: *Soitto on suruista tehty / murehista muovaeltu* ('Songs are made of sorrows / poems wrought of woes'). Alliteration was so characteristic of ancient Finnish poetry that it became an almost conventional device, although the best of these unknown poets used it with taste. In the lyrical poems the bird was often used as a symbol—Professor Kuusi speaks of a "poetess of the birds"[9] whose personality is outlined by certain compositions—of the freedom as well as the misery of a homeless wanderer perpetually looking for shelter and food in a bleak, inhospitable world. The following poem is considered one of the oldest because of the simple, almost primitive structure used for expression.[10] In the last two lines the conventional alliteration is dropped, underlining their importance:

> Alahall' on allin mieli
> uiessa vilua vettä
> alempana armottoman
> käyessä kylän väliä
> syän on kylmä kyyhkysellä
> syöessä kylän kekoa
> vilu vatsa varpusella
> juoessa viiua vettä
> kylmemp on minun poloisen
> kylmemp on minun sitäkin

Sad is the seagull
when swimming in wintry waters
sadder still the homeless
wandering in the wide world
unhappy the heart of the dove
when picking a foreign pittance
throbbing the throat of the sparrow
when drinking icy droplets
colder am I and wretched
colder still than that.

Another poem expresses simply and briefly sorrow and its effect on the human spirit and is close to a modern poet's direct vision of closely intertwined spiritual and material images, e.g., Robert Frost, *My November Guest* ("My sorrow, when she's here with me / Thinks these dark days of autumn rain / Are beautiful as days can be...."), Carl Sandburg, *Four Preludes on Playthings of the Wind*, I ("The woman named Tomorrow / sits with a hairpin in her teeth / and takes her time / and does her hair the way she wants it...."), T. S. Eliot, *Preludes* IV ("His soul stretched tight across the skies / That fade behind a city block...."), Edith Sitwell, *Early Spring* ("... The cold wind creaking in my blood / Seems part of it, as grain of wood...."). In this poem feeling is intensified by lack of explanation:

Miun on huolet kolminaiset
murehet monennäköiset
apeat erinomaiset.
Yks on huoli pääni päällä
toinen alla jalkojeni
kolmas keskellä syäntä.
Jok on huoli pääni päällä
sen mie silkillä sitelen
panen kassapalmikoille;
jok on alla jalkojeni,
sen mie pauloilla panisin,
taluksilla talloaisin;
jok on keskellä syäntä,
tuo minut manalle viepi,
Tuonelahan torkuttavi
Manalan matojen syöä,
tuonen toukkien kaluta.

Great are my griefs
Several my sorrows
Threefold my throes
High on my head is one
Fallen under the feet the other
Hidden in the heart the third
The one that is high on the head
I secure with silken ribbons

6

I bind it with my braids
The one fallen under my feet
I snare in my shoestrings
I tread it to the turf
The one hidden in my heart
Will draw me into death
Will haul me to Hell
To the devouring worms of Death
The mouth of the maggots of Hell.

Although contemporary Finnish poets have a similar vision of the world, they almost never use their ancestors as models. Occasionally a poet has used the old meter, e.g., Helvi Juvonen, but others, such as P. Mustapää or Larin-Kyösti, drew inspiration from modern folksongs. The only great Finnish poet to revive the old folk meter was Eino Leino, who used it in his *Helkavirsiä* ('Holy Songs'), short narrative poems of a more lyrical than epic character. As do *Räikkö Räähkä*, in which Räikkö Räähkä is forced to become a traitor, in *Ylermi* and *Tuuri* (names), whose main characters are destroyed by pride, or in *Tumma* (name, lit. 'The Dark One'), whose main character is tortured by demons born of his own soul, these poems describe briefly the fate of men at critical moments in their lives.[11] Though Leino wrote much during his short life and his works vary in form and content, he is the only poet to have used successfully the old meter and motifs in modern poetry.

Prose writers who have drawn inspiration from folklore are still fewer, although a significant number of prose folkloric texts have been collected — tales, legends, stories, proverbs, and riddles. Not one important work in Finnish literature deals with subjects from the old epic, except, perhaps, A. Kivi's play *Kullervo* (main character), not his most important work, however. In his great novel *Seven Brothers*, on several occasions the characters tell each other typical ghost stories, but they often begin their stories with statements indicating their disbelief in them.[12] Heikki Toppila has, perhaps, used folkloric motifs most consistently, but his novels and stories are basically narrations from the lives of country people who believe in the supernatural and accept it as part of everyday life. His characters often undergo evolutions which give them more rational attitudes, e.g., in the great novels *Päästä meitä pahasta* ('Deliver Us from Evil,' 1932) and *Tulisilla vaunuilla* ('On a Chariot of Fire,' 1935). In 1897 Juhani Aho wrote *Panu* (main character), a novel about the fight between dying paganism and victorious Christianity, in which the information on pagan beliefs and practices is ultimately taken from folklore though the plot is not. Arvi Järventaus did the same in some stories on the Lapps. In one of his first works, the novel *Laulu tulipunaisesta kukasta* (1905; tr. *The Song of the Blood-Red Flower*, 1920), somewhat unfortunately translated into several foreign languages because the book is not typical of Finnish literature and very uneven, Johannes Linnankoski attempted a rhythmic prose based on the patterns of the old meter. Clauses such as *lämpimään syliinsä otti, koko rinne riemuitsi, tulta silmän tuikkehessa* reproduce the trochaic line of the old poems. In addition, he used gods and fairies of old Finnish mythology in a contemporary setting, but in his later works discarded these devices, which were received with mixed feelings by the critics. It was easy to parody this style; in Joel Lehtonen's novel *Putkinotko* (2 vols., 1919 and 1920) we find: "But who is following them now, unseen? Is it a blue fairy of the ancient forests of Finland? No, it is Saara. . . ." The reader already knows that Saara is a sturdy, unromantic country girl.[13]

A reader familiar with Finnish literature and folk poetry may wonder why the *Kalevala*, the great Finnish epic, has not yet been mentioned. The *Kalevala* is not genuine folk poetry. When Lönnrot found, mainly in the Finnish-speaking regions beyond the eastern frontier of Finland, these epic poems, he sincerely believed that they were the fragments of a great masterpiece similar to the *Iliad* or the *Odyssey*. In his equally sincere attempt to restore it, he unintentionally composed a work which is not genuine, though almost entirely made up of genuine materials.[14] Lönnrot had formal scholarly training and wrote an M.A. dissertation on Väinämöinen. He took a degree in medicine and arranged his appointment as district physician at Kajaani, in the northern part of the country, to be able to travel in the regions of old poetry. He discovered the areas of richest tradition, although another physician, Z. Topelius the elder (1781-1831), had spoken of them and of transcribing and publishing the poems in the form he thought most accurate. The *Kalevala* immediately met such enthusiasm and admiration in Finland that criticism was unthinkable. Scholars studied it as pure folk poetry, and a project of collecting further epic poems was formed to complete the *Kalevala* or prove that Lönnrot had done unalterable work.[15] However, the new materials eventually revealed that the *Kalevala* was Lönnrot's composition and not a folk epic.

The *Kalevala's* immediate effect among the educated classes, who were chiefly Swedish-speaking or bilingual, as was Lönnrot, was a feeling of self-confidence and a belief in the possibilities of Finland as a nation. Almost no significant literature had been published in Finnish, and, although the book never became commercially popular, it is considered the mark of awakening national spirit in Finland. After 1860, when Alexander II, the Russian emperor, liberalized his rule, Finnish was made one of the official languages of Finland; from that time hostility developed between the two linguistic groups. Finnish has always been the language of the majority of inhabitants, and recently this majority has grown stronger (in 1880 14 percent of the population was Swedish-speaking; in 1960 less than 8 percent); for a long time Finnish has been the predominant language in all fields. Not only did the *Kalevala* give the Finns confidence in their own language, but it also supported their belief in the creative powers of the Finnish nation and in this way contributed to the development of Finnish literature, although direct influence on individual works has not been important.

Shortly before and after 1900 there was great interest in the *Kalevala* and the Finnish past. Eino Leino wrote his *Helkavirsiä*, and Akseli Gallen-Kallela painted vast compositions on subjects from the *Kalevala* which were much admired at his time, though often for other than artistic reasons. In the same period Jean Sibelius composed on *Kalevala* motifs, although the majority of his work is without specific literary reference.

Literature in Finnish before the Nineteenth Century

WHILE FINLAND WAS PART OF THE KINGDOM of Sweden, there had been only a very modest literature in Finnish. It originated between 1542 and 1552, when the first Protestant (Lutheran) bishop of the country and one of the reformers of the church, **Mikael Agricola** (ca. 1510-57), translated the New Testament, part of the Old, and the Psalms into Finnish. The son of a farmer, Agricola took his Latin name in the fashion of the humanists when he began his studies. He was born in the village of Torsby in the district of Pernaja, on the Gulf of Finland, west of the present town of Loviisa. He first went to school in Viipuri, then worked in Turku, where in 1531 he became acquainted with Luther's works. Between 1536 and 1539 he studied at Wittenberg in Germany under Luther and his friend Melanchthon. When he returned to Finland, he was again active in Turku as a chapter member of the cathedral and principal of the school where future ministers received training. He was appointed bishop of Turku in 1554 and died soon afterwards on his return journey from Moscow, where he had been sent to represent Sweden at peace negotiations.

Some anonymous manuscripts written between 1530 and 1540 indicate that at the same time others were attempting to use Finnish in writing, but Agricola's were the first Finnish works printed and widely used. We know that Agricola had finished his translation of the New Testament in 1543, but his first published work was a primer, *ABC-kiria* (1542), followed the next year by a book of prayer, *Rucouskiria Bibliasta*. The New Testament appeared in 1548, followed by approximately one-fourth of the Old, i.e., the Psalms of David, on which other translators had collaborated, the "Songs and Prophecies Collected from the Law of Moses and the Prophets" (both 1551), and the prophets Haggai, Zechariah, and Malachi (1552). He also wrote a "Manual on Baptism and Other Christian Ceremonies," the "Mass or Holy Supper," and "The Passion, Resurrection, and Ascension of Our Lord Jesus

Christ, Assembled from the Four Gospels" (all 1549). He provided many of his works with prefaces in Finnish verse. That appended to the Psalms has become famous, as it purports to list the pagan deities of the Finns and the Karelians, the latter eastern Finns mostly under Russian domination at that time. As it is the first information of its kind, it has been widely studied by Finnish scholars, but with conflicting and sometimes inconclusive results.[16]

Agricola was not a creative writer; his works were for the spiritual and practical needs of the church and the faithful, but, as the first to publish texts in Finnish and one of the founders of the new church, he had wide and lasting influence on the development of literary Finnish. As he lived and worked in Turku, where there probably was some tradition in the use of literary Finnish, he naturally followed such tradition and based his language on the dialect of the Turku region and southwest Finland. This city remained the administrative and cultural center of Finland until 1812; thus this tradition prevailed for almost three centuries, until, after the publication of the *Kalevala* and discovery of the folk poetry of the East, adopting the eastern dialects as a basis for literary Finnish became an issue. **Reinhold von Becker** (1788-1858) first discussed this question in 1820, when he published in *Turun Viikko-Sanomat*, the Finnish newspaper edited by himself, articles advocating reform and purification of the Finnish language on the model of northern and eastern dialects. Von Becker also taught at the University of Turku (moved to Helsinki after 1827); the resulting polemics, sometimes called the "Battle of the Dialects," lasted approximately twenty years. Under the moderating influence of Lönnrot, a former student of von Becker, and the linguist **Gustaf Renvall** (1781-1841), a compromise was reached. The phonology and morphology of old literary Finnish were kept, but, greatly due to Renvall, the spelling was modified, and a number of new words were introduced, many from the eastern dialects. Because of the changes in spelling and vocabulary and because Agricola himself was inconsistent in his clumsy spelling and followed his original texts so closely that he used non-Finnish constructions, Agricola's work is difficult for a modern reader to understand. (Agricola's use of non-Finnish constructions was so extensive that there has been speculation whether his native tongue might not have been Swedish— Torsby is now and has long been a Swedish-speaking community.)

Agricola had a more specific influence on Finnish poetry. His translations of psalms and hymns and the verse introductions to his works were not written in the old Finnish meter (perhaps it seemed too pagan; the reason is unknown), but in a rhymed meter he had learned in Sweden and Germany, where it was called *knittel* and used, e.g., by Hans Sachs. Rules for that type of poetry were not yet fixed, and Agricola was definitely not a poet; his efforts are almost unreadable, but he established a pattern: Finnish poetry was to be modeled on foreign—mainly German and Swedish—rhythmic patterns and rhymed, one might say, at any cost. As a consequence, almost every characteristic of the Finnish language was ignored; in a Finnish grammar published in 1649 by **Eskil Petraeus** (1593-1657), permission is given to ignore the quantity of syllables in Finnish prosody, and, to accomplish the necessary rhyme, words may be shortened or lengthened with various suffixes. According to these rules Agricola's successors wrote what they called poetry, mainly, as they were almost all ministers, hymns for the faithful. In the middle of the seventeenth century and thereafter, scholars again attempted to write poetry in the old Finnish meter. But, hardly anything of artistic value was written in the Western meters before the nineteenth century.

Agricola's immediate successors as composers of hymns were **Jacobus Finno** (Finn. Jaakko Suomalainen; ca. 1540-88) and **Hemmingius Henrici** (Maskun Hemminki, a name derived from his place of origin, Masku, in western Finland; ca. 1550-1619). In 1583 Finno published a collection of one hundred one hymns including translations or adaptations from Swedish, German, Latin, and Greek and approximately ten original compositions. In his preface he attacked the Catholic church, which did not allow its members to sing hymns in their own language, and stated that, as human beings have a natural desire to sing,

> They started to practice ungodly, shameful, lewd, and ridiculous songs / sang them at their feasts and during their travels to pass time and rejoice themselves / ... And so the Devil, the source of all wickedness / aroused his poets and minstrels / into the minds of which he inserted / and for the mouths of which he fabricated words fitting enough / so that they put together and made songs quite nimbly and quick / which were also then learned and remembered by the others sooner / than Godly and Christian songs are now learned and memorized.

Fortunately, Finno said, Luther and other God-fearing men then began to write hymns in the languages of their own countries, and so would he do himself, "rhyming them in the fashion of other Christian countries." Views like Finno's were, of course, widely held; in England at almost the same time, Sternhold, Groom of the Chamber to Henry VIII, versified (1549) fifty-one Psalms to be sung "in private houses, for Godly solace and comfort and for the laying apart all ungodly songs and ballads," and John Baldwin wished that his *Ballads of Solomon* (1549) "might once drive out of office the bawdy ballads of lecherous love, that commonly are indited and sung by idle courtiers in princes' and noblemen's houses."[17]

In 1605 Hemmingius published a new edition of Finno's hymnal, adding one hundred forty-one new religious songs, mainly translations from Swedish, German, and Latin; his own hardly exceed ten. He also translated a collection of medieval Latin hymns sung in Finland, *Piae Cantiones*, first printed in 1582 in Greifswald, Germany. It contains sixty-seven poems from the Middle Ages and twenty-four from the Reformation. Fourteen of the medieval ones are of French and German origin, but no foreign counterparts have been found for the fifty-three others.[18] Although they were not necessarily composed in Finland or Sweden, they show that spiritual life was alive there in those early times. Hemmingius's translation is not based directly on the Greifswald edition; he used manuscripts no longer extant and added some of his own poems. Although, for the same reasons, they are approximately as poor as Finno's (the rhythm is often halting and the rhymes clumsy), they have a natural simplicity which is appealing. Hemmingius was freer in his translations than was Finno, sometimes achieving more satisfactory results. A translation from the *Piae Cantiones, In Vernali Tempore* ('In Springtime'), which he titled *Keväst ja kesäst* ('On Spring and Summer'), is among his best-known works, beginning:

> Kylmän talven taucoman
> Päevän penseys soima
> Vilun valjon vaipuman
> Auttap auringon voima
> Kevä käke kesän tuoma
> Hengetöin hangidze vircoman
> Covan callon alda
> Meri maa ja mandere
> Orghod kedhod kans cangared
> Toevovat Suven valda.

> The icy winter is retreating
> Before the warmth of brighter days
> The might of sun is now defeating
> The dreary cold, pierced by its rays
> The spring will soon the summer call
> The dead spring up beneath the snow
> The sea the earth the countries all
> The valley field and lush green meadow
> Are waiting for the reign of Summer.

Daniel Juslenius (1676-1752) merits inclusion here although he wrote no fiction, poetry, or drama. He was the first avowed Finnish patriot. He did not express his patriotism in political terms, however, and he did not have difficulties with the Swedish authorities. He was professor of Greek and Hebrew at the University of Turku, and near the end of his life bishop of Skara in Sweden, where he died. In his works he followed the example of a famous contemporary scholar, Olaf Rudbeck of Sweden, proclaiming his love for his native country in Latin dissertations, considered highly learned in the seventeenth century but recognized as products of fantasy in the eighteenth. According to Juslenius the Finns descended from Japhet, son of Noah, and were once a mighty and powerful nation (*Aboa vetus et nova*, 1700;

Vindiciae Fennorum, 1703), whose language was related to both Greek and Hebrew (*De convenientiae linguae fennicae cum hebrea et graeca*, 1712). He was one of the first people in Finland to collect old folk poems, from which he included passages in his works as evidence on Finnish history, and he translated a Swedish catechism into Finnish. In 1745 he published *Suomalaisen sana-lugun coetus*, a Finnish-Swedish-Latin dictionary which had more than fifteen thousand entries. In the introduction he gave the first accurate, though short, description of the traditional Finnish meter used in folk poetry.

In the seventeenth and eighteenth centuries, the fashion of writing hymns and occasional poems in Finnish was maintained by the ministers of the established church, who were almost alone in their interest in intellectual pursuits. Slowly in the eighteenth century this situation changed, as the Enlightenment and the interest in natural sciences and their application to practical life spread to Finland. The age's ideas were acceptable to members of the church because they came to Finland via Germany,[19] not France, where they often had an irreligious or anticlerical bias. **Johan Brovallius** (1707-55) first studied theology and became a priest, but developed an interest in physics and obtained a professorship in physics at the University of Turku, then returned to theology, taught that subject at the same university, and finally became bishop of Turku. **Carl Fredrik Mennander** (1712-86) also studied theology, then natural sciences, became professor of physics at Turku, then professor of theology, bishop of Turku, and finally archbishop of Sweden. He was also the first teacher of statistics as a science in Finland. **Anders Chydenius** (1729-1803) was incumbent of various parishes in northern Finland all his life, but also published extensively on economics and other practical questions and several times won election as representative of his region's clergy to the Swedish Parliament, where Finland, like all parts of the kingdom, had seats. In several pamphlets and a book (1765) Chydenius advocated free trade as the source of all wealth more than ten years before Adam Smith's *An Inquiry into the Nature and Causes of the Wealth of Nations*. Chydenius also supported freedom of the press and freedom of religion. Although he was violently attacked for these ideas by his colleagues, a bill establishing limited freedom of worship was passed in 1781.

As no artistic fiction was written in Finland before the nineteenth century, scholars, scientists, and practical writers like Chydenius and Porthan are vital to the history of Finnish literature, although they actually had no influence on it. Men like Mennander and Chydenius clearly felt that Finland, their country, was a separate entity within the kingdom of Sweden. Before he was appointed bishop of Turku, Mennander was supported by a Finnish party against a Swedish candidate. Their loyalty did not, however, prevent their being faithful subjects of the Swedish crown, accepting high offices in Sweden, or election to the Academy of Sweden, or receiving Swedish orders.

14

LITERATURE IN FINNISH BEFORE THE 19th CENTURY

Before 1809 *Sweden* and *Swedish* indeed referred to Sweden proper and all of its dominions, Finland included.

We have mentioned that poems in Finnish, Swedish, Latin, and occasionally even Greek were written during this period at the University of Turku, founded in 1640. For approximately a century this institution was merely a theological school for future ministers. Professors and students wrote learned, even pedantic, poems for birthdays, marriages, deaths, and other occasions in the lives of friends or superiors. Public events, coronations, births of heirs to the throne, and victories over the realm's enemies were also celebrated. Natural catastrophes, portents, plagues, or similar calamities were not forgotten; the famous Lisbon earthquake was recorded in 1756 in a poem by **Abraham Achrenius** (1706-69). A few of these authors of solemn and elaborate platitudes might have been poets. But, the audience for those who wrote in Finnish was so limited that their writings were hardly more than pastimes for small groups of friends. Those who wrote in Swedish had a wider audience and, with the established traditions of Swedish, did not have to grope for correct form of expression. Although poetry written by Swedish-speaking Finns in the seventeenth and beginning of the eighteenth centuries is generally mediocre, it flows more smoothly than the poetry of the same period in Finnish. Still, some poets who wrote in Finnish showed genuine depth of feeling: Matthias Salamnius, Juhana Cajanus, and the brothers Simo and Henrik Achrenius, nephews of Abraham Achrenius, whose son Antti also wrote some verse. The pseudo-Latin names were the result of the fashion for classical denominations prevailing among German and Scandinavian scholars; the family of Cajanus, e.g., came from the region of Kajaani in northern Finland.

Those scholars of the seventeenth century who wrote in the old folk meter did so nearly by accident. Their intent was to model their poetry on West European standards, but, as the Finnish language was incompatible with them, their compositions took a form much like that of the old folk poetry. By that time this poetry was disappearing from western Finland, as the scholars living there found it more difficult to reproduce correctly the old folk meter than those in contact with the northern, central, and eastern Finnish population did. **Laurentius Petri** (ca. 1608-71), a minister who published thirteen sermons in Finnish, wrote in 1658 a Finnish Chronicle (*Ajan tieto Suomen maan menoist. . . .*) in verse containing lines of distinctly popular sound. **Eerik Justander** (1623-78), the first professor of prosody at the University of Turku, wrote poems with such titles as *Imitatio Antiquorum Tavvast-Finnonicorum Runorum* (1654, on the marriage of King Charles X Gustavus; the poem in Finnish) or *Gratulatio. Tavast-Runico-Finnonica Extemporanea* (1667, to a friend). *Tavast* refers to the Finnish province Tavastland (Swed.; Finn. *Häme*) and *runorum, runico* not to *runes*, but to *runo* 'poem' (Finn.). Petri and Justander were western Finns to whom

15

the old folk meter was no longer natural, but Olaus Lauraeus, who originated in the northwest section of the country, wrote in 1679 a poem using the old meter almost without fault.

Ilo-Laulu Jesuxesta ('Song of Rejoicing in Jesus,' 1690; new limited ed., Helsinki 1962) by **Matthias Salamnius** (ca. 1650-91) is generally considered the best Finnish poem from the time of Swedish domination. It follows numerous similar poetic composition from Germany and Sweden in the same period. A simple narration of the birth, life, passion, death, and ressurection of the Savior as presented in the Gospels, the poem is artless in its simplicity and, unlike others poems of the time, unmarred by excess rhetoric and scholarship. Perhaps because Salamnius lived between 1680 and 1686 in Ingria, a province at that time purely Finnish and owned by Sweden (Leningrad is now located there), his use of the folk meter is smooth and almost faultless (fewer than 50 of 2265 lines are incorrect). As a wealth of folk poetry was collected in Ingria, Salamnius probably was acquainted with such poems as *The Creator's Song*. His poem became very popular; sixteen editions were published within a brief period, and later poets, such as Simo Achrenius and Jaakko Juteini, were influenced by it. A few lines from it even appear in the *Kalevala*—an indication that folk singers had inserted the lines in the old poems Lönnrot collected.

Juhana Cajanus (1655-81) is known for his only poem, written, according to tradition, on his deathbed in the spring of 1681 to fortify himself against the approaching end. It is known by the first line, *Etkös ole ihmis parca aiwan arca* ('How art thou fearful, Man, poor wretch' [approximately]). It was later included in the Finnish hymnal although it is a philosophical meditation rather than a religious song. Cajanus was a minister's son, born in north Finland, but he went to the University of Uppsala in Sweden to study theology, languages, and philosophy. His M.A. dissertation on the world-soul, *De Anima Mundi*, was noticed especially because it was thought to be influenced by the ideas of Descartes, which both Protestants and Catholics considered subversive. However, when he returned to Finland, Cajanus enjoyed protection and favor from Count Per Brahe, a powerful Swedish nobleman appointed governor general of Finland and chancellor of the University of Turku, which had been founded on his initiative. Brahe secured Cajanus a professorship of philosophy, although, because of faculty resistance, as supernumerary, not as regular member. Cajanus's untimely death was reportedly caused by an excess of work.

The poem, consisting of twenty-three stanzas of four long and two short lines, is mainly a description of the invincible power of death. All creatures, not only man, must die or be destroyed: animals, plants, rocks and iron, even the starry heaven. The revolving movement of heaven, described with six different verbs, seems influenced by Descartes' theory of vortices. Man must not lament because he is subject to the law of nature, but should think of the bliss of Heaven awaiting him; indeed, as death is the only means of reaching this bliss, he must accept it gladly. Except the structure and rhyme pattern, taken from Lasse Lucidor (pseudonym of Lars Johansson; 1638-74), a Swedish poet, the poem is an independent work of art. In Cajanus's poem, the third and sixth lines of every stanza are longer than the corresponding lines in Lucidor's poem; each has eight syllables arranged in a trochaic pattern, an arrangement close to the Finnish folk meter. Salamnius was the best poet to use the old folk meter before the nineteenth century, Cajanus the most skillful writer to wield other rhythmic patterns.

Simo Achrenius (1729-82) was a minister of the church who showed early signs of insanity and after much suffering died in an asylum. He began his literary career in 1758 by writing a poem on the birchbark canoes made by the natives of North America (*Runolaulu tuohiweneestä*). He was supposedly *compos mentis* at the time and intended his didactic poem to teach the Finns to make such useful vehicles. Also in 1758 he published a poem composed for a funeral, a poem typical of his entire production. Its most striking section is a description of Death personified, with blue wings, snow-white garments, a scythe on his shoulder, a "darkly burning" candle in one hand and an hourglass in the other, spreading a mournful odor of decay. The visual fancy, vivid to incoherency, a marked preference for colors and smells, morbid predilection for physical aspects of destruction wrought by Death, skulls, bones, putrescent flesh, maggots, and the smell of decay, all are typical of his later poems. In 1766 he published his major work, a poem in seven cantos, *Uudet Hengelliset Runot Läsnä olewaisista Ja Tulewaisista Tiloista* ('New Spiritual Poems on [Our] Present and Future State'). In the first canto there is almost no logical connection between the images crowding the lines which describe with breathless violence all sins man can commit. The second and third cantos, descriptions of the life of Christ and his piety, are more subdued, and the fourth, a vision of Hell, is both coherent and impressive. The fifth, devoted to the Last Judgment and the bliss of Heaven, does not reach the same level—the poet was best with gloomy, terrifying subjects, like the torments of Hell, to which he returned in the sixth canto. He concluded, in the seventh, with a description of Heaven as a luxuriant, beautiful landscape. This poem, like all he wrote (except one dedicatory poem in imitation of Latin hexameter), is in the folk meter.

Henrik Achrenius (1730-98) was in all respects unlike his brother Simo. Almost the first Finnish writer who did not belong to the clergy, he studied law, but did not take a degree and passed his life as justice of the peace of Kalajoki, in northwestern Finland. He wrote poems regularly from 1754 to 1792, although his poems show no deep feeling or thought, for he was a cheerful man who preferred subjects fitting his temperament. He used the Finnish meter and was also the first to apply successfully Western rhythmic patterns to the Finnish language; he had taste and considerable technical skill.

17

His first poem, *De Echo* ('On Echo'; only the title is Latin), opens with the description of a peaceful landscape in which the poet walks, plucking flowers and stopping to sing and listen to the echo of his voice. He enjoyed writing poems for the marriages of his friends and other merry occasions and often indicated that they should be sung to well-known tunes, sometimes taken from compositions of his contemporary, the most famous Swedish poet of his age, Bellman. He was probably the first to translate into Finnish one of Bellman's poems, which was then printed as a broadsheet and sold. When he chose more serious subjects, as in the poem for the occasion of the consecration of the church of Sievi or in *Katoowaisuus* ('The Ephemeral Nature [of Everything]'), the expression of his feeling was sincere, but the feelings were conventional. He was more at ease in *Wiinasta Walitus Wirsi / Runo raukan kuolemasta* ('Lament on John Barleycorn / A Poem on His Death') written when the government passed a law restricting the manufacture of spirits.[20]

He also produced several translations; he published thirty-two fables in the Finnish meter in 1775 and later an elegy by Ovid, in which he emphasized the erotic more than Ovid had, and a Finnish version of the *Marseillaise*. He can appropriately be called the last and perhaps best representative of the first period of Finnish literature, preceding the great national revival of the nineteenth century.

The Beginnings of Swedish Literature
in the Seventeenth and Eighteenth Centuries

IN FINLAND NO LITERATURE WAS WRITTEN in Swedish before the end
of the sixteenth century. The religious works of Agricola, Finno, and
Hemmingius were sole evidence of the country's spiritual activity. The
adoption of Swedish as the only language of the educated class in Finland did
not begin until the seventeenth century; it was completed in the eighteenth.
The eventual literature written in Swedish and published in Finland might be
confused with Swedish literature, but the Swedish-speakings Finns were
indeed Finns (as the English-speaking Americans are Americans and the
French-speaking Belgians Belgians), seldom actually coming from Sweden.
These Finlandswedes (*Finlandssvenskar*, their present name for themselves)
referred to themselves as Finns (*Finnar*) well into the nineteenth century,
when this name was restricted to the Finnish-speaking inhabitants of the
country. Even the Swedish critics and literary historians have admitted that
all Finnish authors, regardless of their language, had a common way of viewing
the world and reacting to it. Insisting that this shared trait made Finnish
writers different from Swedish writers, these critics and historians have tried
to analyze the common Finnish characteristics.

The first literary works written in Finland, both in Swedish and in
Finnish, were poems; literature in most countries evolved in this manner,
fiction being a rather modern form. Although little of artistic value was
published before the eighteenth century, a few names provide a background to
the later development. **Sigfrid Aronus Forsius** (also **Helsingforsius**; he was born
in Helsinki, Swed. *Helsingfors*; ca. 1555-1624) was one of the foremost
writers in the kingdom of Sweden in his time. He was a true Renaissance man
with a wide variety of interests, especially in natural sciences. He wrote on
astronomy and astrology and taught these subjects at the University of

19

Uppsala between 1608 and 1610, published several almanacs, on which he had a royal monopoly, did practical surveying in Lapland, wrote about physics and mineralogy, was a church minister with an inclination to mysticism, and a poet. In spite of his scholarly activities and position with the church, he was also somewhat bohemian. In 1610 he moved to Stockholm and in 1613 became incumbent of the Finnish parish there; in 1615 he was suspended from office for disrespect to his superiors, drunkenness, quarreling with his wife, and continual arguments with his colleagues. In the same year a friend was killed in a brawl in front of his house. From 1615 through 1621, according to his own words, he lived in a hovel on the outskirts of Stockholm and worked like a slave, writing and translating for a living, for "to make shoes or cut clothes I have not learned, to dig I have no forces, and of begging I am ashamed." According to his own wish, he was eventually made incumbent of the parish of Ekenäs (Finn. *Tammisaari*) in southern Finland, where he died peacefully.

Although his scientific works contributed no original information to science and are full of superstitious beliefs, their style has literary merit. *Physica Eller Naturlighe tings Qualiteters och Egendomars beskrijfuelse* ('Physica, or A Description of the Qualities and Properties of Natural Objects,' manuscript dated Stockholm, 1611) was intended to be a translation of *Physiologica peripatetica* by Johannes Magirus, a German scholar from Marburg,[21] but poetic inspiration and admiration for the works of God in nature caused Forsius to write in a solemn, rhythmic prose:

O Lord our Lord, how powerful, great, and marvelous is thy name in the whole world!

Thy marvelous works praise thy powers, thy wisdom is to be seen in all thou hast made.

Thou hast given the air its own place and thou makest the heavy cloud dwell in the midst of it.

Thou makest it fly like a bird, like a ship thou makest it sail.

Thou makest the air, the water, and the earth bear wonders so that the creatures must tremble in front of them.

O Lord, Lord of Heaven, how wonderful is thy name on the Earth!

The book ends with a twenty-three stanza poem which the author called a praise of the Creator and a summary of the book's contents. It contains quaint descriptions of the animals and monsters of the sea and ends with a lofty invitation for all creation to sing the praise of God.

Although neither author nor exact date are known, Forsius is generally considered the author of *Andelige Psalmer och Wijsor* ('Spiritual Psalms and

Songs'), probably published in 1614. It, too, consists mainly of translations of German hymns of penance and mortification which reveal considerable poetic talent. They have been highly praised by Swedish scholars, including one who thought he had discovered in them a "typically Finnish" inclination toward mysticism and occultism.

Forsius titled his next work, a translation of a Danish book, *De Vita Hominis*, published in the early sixteenth century, *Speculum Vitae Humanae. Om Menniskionnes Leffuerne Från thet första hon födhes in til hennes dödzdagh, och then ytterste Domen* ('A Mirror of Human Life. On the Life of Man from His Birth to the Day of His Death and on the Last Judgment,' Stockholm, 1620). He added translations of the medieval Latin *Piae Cantiones* and modified the original text. The book's images (death as the mirror of life, the ages of man, and the dance of death)[22] gave many motifs to the poets of the late seventeenth century in Sweden.

The last important literary work attributed (somewhat uncertainly) to Forsius appeared in 1621. It was the story of Reynard the Fox, so popular in the Middle Ages,[23] translated from German. Written in fluent and elegant Swedish verse, it is considered among the best nonreligious works of the period. While in Sweden, Forsius also translated Agricola's poem about the pagan gods of the Finns and the Karelians into Latin distichs and wrote a rhymed *Finnish Chronicle* no longer extant.

After Forsius there is a gap in the history of Swedish literature in Finland. Occasional poems were written at the University of Turku; **Jacob Chronander** (b. ca. 1620, d. after 1669), a Swede who spent eight years in Finland, wrote two comedies performed by the students at Turku. An isolated acrostic poem extant in only one copy from 1651 spells with the initial letters of the twenty-nine stanzas the authoress's name, **Christina Regina von Birchenbaum**, alias **Börkenbohm**. She was married to Axel Pauli Liljenfeldt, a major in the Swedish army who died in the Thirty Years' War. The autobiographical poem tells that she was born in Karelia, lost her father at the age of three, at an early age met the man she would eventually marry, and later received the message that her husband had disappeared in the war in Germany. She then traveled in that country to find him, but was eventually forced to believe that he was dead. After seventeen years of widowhood, she met a young man of noble birth and married him, but this union proved bitterly disappointing. In the last lines she tells that she is again alone and bids farewell to the world.

Johan Paulinus-Lillienstedt (1655-1732) is, among the many occasional poets at Turku, very typical of his time. His works were read and admired even later and can be enjoyed today, since the style of the sixteenth and early seventeenth centuries is no longer branded mannerism and affectation. The son of a Finnish clergyman, Paulinus studied at Turku, then made a brilliant career in Sweden, where he held many high administrative positions, was sent on diplomatic missions, received the titles of baron and count, and ended his life as president of the high court of Wismar in the part of north Germany then belonging to Sweden. Soon after his arrival in Sweden, he wrote a discourse in verse for an academic function at the University of Uppsala, titled in Latin *Magnus Principatus Finlandia, epico carmine depicta,* but composed in classical Greek hexameters. The poem has several hundred lines of faultless Greek, expressive of genuine love and attachment for the author's native country. Paulinus is also credited with the introduction to Swedish poetry of the sophisticated elegance and witty elaboration of the baroque period created in Italy and Spain by Marini and Góngora. He also translated parts of Guarini's *Il Pastor Fido,* a pastoral poem of enormous European popularity, thus introducing that genre to his country. He wrote in his youth, between 1675 and 1691, but Guarini had died in 1612, Marini in 1625, and Góngora in 1627, and French classicism, which dominated literary taste in Europe for more than a century, had already fully developed with Corneille, Racine, and Boileau. However, in the seventeenth century new ideas and fashions spread slowly to the extreme north of Europe, where literary and artistic life in a modern sense was only beginning to develop. Besides purely geographic obstacles to the spreading of cultural developments, a formidable barrier was created by bitter hostility between Catholic and Protestant churches.

Paulinus published only one work during his life, a three-canto poem titled in Latin *Christus nascens, patiens et triumphans* followed by a Swedish translation ('The Born, Suffering, and Conquering Christ,' 1686; new, enlarged ed. 1694), which was similar to a work by the well-known German poet of the early seventeenth century, Martin Opitz. Paulinus's style is no doubt rhetorical, but he used it with great skill and good taste, achieving graphic effects:

> Den alltings fader var, är född een son på jörden;
> Den evigheeten skoop, är sielf nu skapad vorden.
> Han, hvilkens opsyn förr var blixt och lågand eld,
> Är gråt-ögd, ynckelig, i trählehamn förstäld.

> A Father He, now born as Son on earth
> Creator of Eternity, created now in birth.
> Appearing once as burning fire, and lightning bright,
> Now seen tear-eyed, feeble, a slave so slight.

The poet used the Passion for dramatic effects:

> Kom, ach, så kom doch, jord, kom, himmel, hit att gråta!
> Kom, alla himlars här, fast ynkelig at låta,
> Kom, lufft, och sucka, kom J elementer all,
> Och qvijda, kom, häf op ett sorg- och jemmer-skall.

> Come all, come all, come, Heaven, Earth, to weep,
> Come, Host of Heav'n, thy sorrow shall be deep,
> Come, Air, to sigh, come elements ye all,
> Lament ye, come ye, sound a mournful call.

A description of the Resurrection and Ascension form a resplendent finale to the work:

> Ja, stiernor gifva rum. Och fästets högsta ort
> Haar längst af skön saphir reest op en seger-port,
> Där han nu genom går, där han sin fahrt framsträcker
> Och en osäijlig frögd i vijda himlen väcker.

> The stars now step aside and, made of sapphire bright,
> An arc of triumph crowns the castle in its might
> There goes He now, there follows He His glorious road
> A boundless joy arousing in Heaven wide and broad.

Posterity more admired a smooth love poem in which Paulinus lamented the departure of his beloved Iris (conventional name) in the manner common to that period. Not printed before 1820, it is a perfect work of art, written with good taste and skill, but it lacks genuine feeling. Still, a nineteenth-century Finnish scholar, J. J. Tengström, said that its "simple, peaceful, and harmonious ... atmosphere" expressed "the natural characteristics of Finnish national poetry itself."[24]

In the seventeenth century Sweden had become a great military power under Gustavus Adolphus and his successors; she had won many victories in the Thirty Years' War and had conquered vast provinces around the Baltic Sea. But material and human resources were overtaxed by her success, and under Charles XII, the "mad Swede" of Pope's and Dr. Johnson's writings, her armies, first victorious, were crushed in a terrible war of more than twenty-year duration which left her devastated and impoverished. The Baltic provinces were lost forever, and Finland was occupied. Although Finland was restored to Sweden in the 1721 peace with Russia, the southeastern province of Karelia and Viipuri, the town over which Finns, Swedes, and Russians have fought for centuries, were lost.

Almost nothing was written in Finland during that period. At the initial Swedish victories, poems celebrated the king's triumphs, but after 1710 both Finnish and Swedish lamentations replaced them. They have little artistic interest; the best is **Bartholdus Vhaël's** (1667-1723) *Waikia walitus-runo, runo raudalla rakettu* ('Sad Poem of Sorrow, a Poem Wrought with Iron,' 1714), which rises to some extent above the level of mere enumeration of the miseries of war.

At this time, however, **Jacob Frese** of Viipuri (1691-1729), who later became one of the best Swedish poets of the period, was growing up in

Finland. The son of a wealthy German merchant, he matriculated at the University of Turku at the age of twelve (not entirely unusual at that time). After Viipuri was seized in 1710, he fled the country and settled in Stockholm, where he spent his life as a transcriber of the King's Chancery. He considered himself a poet and wrote verse throughout his life; even when bedridden by the long illness which eventually killed him, he read and corrected his printed works. Like Henrik Achrenius of the Finnish writers, Frese can be called the first Swedish writer conscious of his artistic vocation. His talent was recognized early, although he never received material reward for his writings. In 1715, when Charles XII returned to Sweden after a long absence spent in foreign wars, a solemn reception was organized in Stockholm, and Frese (then twenty-four) was given the task of writing in verse a congratulatory address to the king and reading it at the celebration. As lines in one of his poems and his letters and documents show, Frese considered himself a refugee from Finland. Perhaps for that reason he was asked to write the address, as a discreet reminder to the king that, while he fought abroad, the country was being invaded and destroyed by her enemies, and that his subjects, while rejoicing in his return, hoped that he would assist them in their distress. The king, however, undertook one more fruitless campaign, during which he died; afterwards he was mourned and worshiped as the greatest Swedish hero.[25]

Frese's poem, modeled after other works written for official functions, contains much of a song published in 1702 by one of his teachers at Turku, Torsten Rudeen. Frese used Rudeen's idea of describing the blessings of peace, but presented it in different circumstances. Fourteen stanzas were devoted to the memory of Viipuri. Since Paulinus's *Magnus Principatus Finlandia*, this was the first work in which a Finn expressed his patriotism and love for his native country. It is the best of Frese's numerous occasional poems, which were modeled on those of his predecessors. His style was more refined; he refrained from the coarse jokes common to wedding poems and replaced them with prayers for the newlyweds. Many such poems were written for the merchant class, to which Frese's father had belonged, and he praised their virtues, honesty and thrift, known even abroad; by so doing he perhaps foreshadowed the eighteenth century, in which middle-class ideals and morals acquired increasing importance compared to the life style of the aristocracy. Frese also wrote some conventional love poems under the influence of Johan Runius, an acquaintance and poet well known in his time.

Soon after his arrival in Sweden, Frese contracted his terminal illness, a recurrent fever, probably tuberculosis, which greatly influenced the major part of his production, *Andelige Och Werldslige Dikter* ('Spiritual and Worldly Poems,' 1726), a series of prose writings *Kårta Sede-Läror och Sede-Tillämpningar* ('Short Teachings in Morals and Applications of Morals,' 1726), a long poem *Passions-Tankar* ('Thoughts on the Passion,' 1728), and a last collection *Nagra Poëtiske Samblingar* ('Some Poetic Collections,' 1728). His *Spiritual and Worldly Poems* are marked by suffering and his sense of approaching death. His illness attacked him most severely in spring, and he contrasted awakening nature with his own misery, though never bitterly. Although he occasionally despaired, he found consolation in his faith and in the contemplation of God's creation. In 1727, "when a long and grievous illness had pursued me the whole year," he wrote:

> Förgiäfwes ömsa sig höst, winter, sommar, wåhr,
> Ty idell, idell natt ä' alla mina åhr.

> Throughout the year Spring, Summer, Autumn, Winter vainly range
> For only nights and nights cover my years and never change.

Near death one year later, he wrote his last poem to spring:

> War hälsad, där du ren en liuflig wåhr bebådar,
> Du skiöna nechtergahl, som än min ängslan skådar!
> O huru gläder mig din stämmors gälla liud,
> Hälst jag upmuntras at tillika prisa Gud.

> Hail thee, o nightingale, early herald of sweet spring,
> Who comest to see once more how pains to me still cling!
> I am so pleased to listen to thy clear voice rise,
> That courage enough I also find our Lord to praise.

Death, a stern, terrifying apparition to remind men of their sins in poems of many earlier poets, was a *liuflig* 'sweet' friend to Frese, who called upon him to free his soul from his tormented body, and upon the earth, a loving mother appearing in his *Epitaph to Himself* (1724), to take him into her arms again. The influence of pietism, a religious movement begun in late seventeenth-century Germany stressing individual piety and feeling as opposed to religion's formalities emphasized by the Protestant churches, is often noted in Frese's religious thinking. *Passions-Tankar,* indeed, contains passages, e.g., Christ's blood and wounds as a source of world blessing, reminiscent of pietist hymns, a Swedish collection of which was published in 1717. But, in Frese's last work, *Poëtiske Samblingar,* a long poem titled *Betraktande af Guds allmakt och godhet, alle tings fåfäng- och förgängelighet, Döden, och den tilkommande roligheten* ('Consideration on God's Might and Benevolence, the Vanity and Perishability of All Things, Death, and the Future Bliss') reveals him in many respects as a man of the past, formally as well as religiously, for the meter of the work is not the fashionable French alexandrine, but rhymed classical hexameter. The poem's concern is man, the world, and God, motifs dear to Frese—not individual feeling. It opens with a description of the beauties of spring and nature, where God's might and wisdom can be seen, but the mood shifts when the author shows that all must perish and decay.

The expression of equality in death—"Who can distinguish in the grave the scepter of the king and the staff of the beggar?"—and man's frailty—"He is like a dream, a stream, a grass, a glass, a flower"—is typical of the seventeenth-century poetry that influenced it,[26] but the ending is typical of Frese: death, however fearful, is sweet for those who trust in it; it is the death of the body but the salvation of the soul.

In the same collection one of Frese's best nonreligious poems, *The Shepherd's and the Countryman's Pleasant Life*, appears in the style of earlier pastorals, but there is conspicuous absence of the erotic. Frese's "Arcadia" is a land of peace, freedom, and hard work in the fields, rewarded by abundant harvests and good health.

Frese was also one of the foremost Swedish prose writers in Finland before the nineteenth century. His *Short Teachings in Morals* is a collection of aphorisms in which his idea is conveyed by a vivid picture as often as by a well-formulated saying. Some are nearly small prose poems: "I saw the rolling of the sea and the foaming of the waves, once they rose up against the heaven, once they fell to the lowest depths, but the end of their rage was some loose and floating froth." This work, too, ends in an epitaph to himself: "Thou who treadest on my grave do not mock my dust, what thou art, I have been, and, what I am, thou shalt be. / He rests here whose soul rests in the Lord."

In the spirit of the eighteenth century, intellectual interest in Finland was directed at practical rather than artistic matters, and, although many scholarly works of great interest were published at the University of Turku, a great part of the century was dead in the history of Finnish literature. Besides Chydenius, a notable scholar was a pupil of the great Linné, **Pietari (Pehr) Kalm** (1716-79), who journeyed to the British Colonies in North America, was reportedly the first white man to describe Niagara Falls, and published a travel account in Swedish, translated into English and printed in London in 1770 and 1771, *Travels into North America* "containing its natural history and a circumstantial account of its plantations, with the civil, ecclesiastical and commercial state of the country, the manners of the inhabitants, and several curious and important remarks on various subjects" (3 vols.; there are also later editions).

The only literary figure of the period before Porthan and especially Franzén, Count **Gustaf Philip Creutz**[27] (1731-85) might even be considered part of the history of Swedish literature proper. During his life he was recognized as one of the greatest poets in all Sweden, and his place in his country's literary history is secure, although his erotic and pastoral poems are not exactly in vogue today. He studied at the University of Turku during 1749 and 1750, then settled in Stockholm; he was received in the literary circles in which he soon became famous, was made gentleman-in-waiting to a prince of the blood and appointed ambassador to Paris, then Madrid. At

Ferney he saw Voltaire, who reputedly enjoyed his company. He ended his life as president of the King's Chancery and member of the King's Council. The famous nineteenth-century Swedish poet, Esaias Tegnér, and others have found Finnish traits in his works and have called him a Finnish poet. A Swedish essayist and art critic of the eighteenth century, Carl August Ehrensvärd, who whimsically classified authors by their noses, declared: "The only Swedes to have taste all had hooked noses. . . . The man Creutz was a Finn, and his was upturned."

Like Paulinus, who renounced poetry after embarking upon his official career, Creutz wrote in his youth, between 1754 and shortly after 1760. His work only comprises approximately a dozen short poems and the long pastoral *Atis and Camilla* (ca. 1760). In Stockholm he joined the *Tankebyggarorden* ('Order of the Thought Builders'), a society of lofty ideals like many of the eighteenth century; Mrs. Hedvig Charlotta Nordenflycht and Gustaf Fredrik Gyllenborg, two of the best Swedish poets of that time, were members, but Creutz soon dominated all Swedish poetry of his age, because he not only followed the by-laws of the Order, according to which all works were to be "in conformity with the strictest rules of Swedish grammar and prosody," but also expressed sincere feelings in spite of the artificial form. Members of the Order had pseudonyms; Creutz chose *Mellanväg* ('Midway'; more freely 'The Golden Mean'), a most appropriate name; he was a man of moderation and good taste. Almost all his poems are erotic and contain much eighteenth-century frivolity, but they are never improper or even elegantly indecent, as were so many others at that time. His, instead, constitute a hymn to sensuous love, the highest law of nature, not unlike Rousseau's worship for nature and unrestricted feelings.[28]

Creutz's first six poems, published in 1754, are mediocre, but in *Fråga* ('A Question'), a common erotic situation is treated with discretion. The narrator tells his friend Alexis that he once surprised a beautiful shepherdess sleeping under an aspen tree, crept closer in order to steal a kiss, and bent to the mouth with the divine smile. The poem ends: "But say, Alexis, say! May anybody try for more?" Another, *Guda-Saga* ('A Tale of Gods'), contains a curious, but not uncommon, mixture of classical and old Norse mythology. Minerva, goddess of wisdom, undertakes the education of Astrild, god of sensuous love, by giving him maid Modesty as a companion. Modesty soon sighs and cries and almost dies, and Minerva, remembering that "children are most frightened by ghosts," declares to Astrild "whenever thou takest a heart / *Weariness* shall enter thine," an unexpectedly sad truth in the playful verse.

Creutz's first mature poem, *Sommar-Qväde* ('A Summer Song'), written in 1756, is a series of idyllic scenes among which the author wanders, proclaiming his satisfaction at leaving the false life and artificial luxuries of the city and dreaming of the sensuous happiness of shepherds and shepherdesses in the forests and of butterflies, flying two together from flower to flower. He rapturously bends to kiss the earth, which surrounds him with soft grass, and his only regret is that man cannot enjoy life as fully as do the butterflies, but must look for suffering amidst felicity. These contrasting feelings beyond the conventional dream are typical of Creutz. The landscape is surprisingly realistic and northern. There are alders, elms, spruces covered with moss, wild strawberries, a sea with a thousand islands past which a sail glides, an angling boy whose float bobs on the waves and goes under, drawn by a fish, which is then pulled onto the grass where it lies twitching, and, an intimation of coming romanticism, a "Gothick" building destroyed by winds and time.

Daphne and *Atis och Camilla* are both Creutz's main and last works. *Daphne* is a short narrative in verse, a *conte* in La Fontaine's style, though more refined. The subject is slight: a young girl's—a debutante's—first experiences, hesitations, fears, first love, and first kiss. Again love is the highest feeling, which uplifts man and prevents his destruction by the empty life of society: life is like death when it does not know love. The poem concludes with a half-serious exhortation to follow nature and love instead of society, for the only honor in repressing feelings is boredom.

A semiconventional landscape, a northern scene, is the setting of *Atis och Camilla*, hailed as a masterpiece upon publication. Creutz was the first poet in Sweden to describe nature consistently at some length in his works; the sunrise in the first canto has been much admired. Again the poem's emphasis is love, sensuous, idealized love. Atis, a young hunter, is in love with Camilla, Diana's priestess, who has made a vow of chastity but returns Atis's love. In the second canto Camilla asks Diana if nature is not as holy as her law, and in the fourth, when threatened with death, she declares that the instinct of love will survive her. Finally Diana releases Camilla from her vow. The ending has sometimes been called an easy solution, but Creutz was obviously interested, more than in the conflict itself, in (again) showing love as the highest power through Diana, who states: "To love is not an instinct which debases the heart / I do not know of any virtue which is unnatural."

Creutz's poetry had little direct influence in Finland during his life. After 1770 intellectual life, which had remained active at Turku, centered around **Henrik Gabriel Porthan** (1739-1804) and his friends, grouped for a few years in a literary and scholarly society called *Aurora* (1770-78). From 1771 to 1778, they published a periodical, *Tidningar Utgifne af et Sällskap i Åbo* ('Tidings Published by a Society in Åbo'), known simply as *Åbo Tidningar*, continued under other titles by Porthan and others from 1782 to 1785, 1789 to 1791, 1791 to 1799, 1800 to 1809, and later until 1861. Porthan was a scholar, a historian, and in a scholarly spirit he collected, published, and studied folk poetry; in that respect he was the first literary historian in Finland and perhaps one of the first in the world. He also wrote about the aesthetic qualities of this poetry and had a general interest in literature.

Among Porthan's students, later his colleagues, was **Frans Mikael Franzén** (1772-1847), the last great poet who wrote in Swedish during the union with Sweden and one of the foremost writers of Sweden. Franzén's parents were of Finnish origin and belonged to well-to-do families of merchants and shipowners in Oulu, a seaport in northwest Finland on the Gulf of Botnia. Franzén was precocious as both poet and scholar; he matriculated at the University of Turku at age fourteen and took his M. A. four years later (1789). In part due to Porthan's friendship and protection, his academic career progressed smoothly; he was made reader of rhetoric at the university in 1792, librarian in 1795, professor of literary history in 1798, and professor of general history and practical philosophy in 1801. In 1808 he was elected to the Royal Academy of Sweden. He moved to Sweden in 1811, after Finland had become part of the Russian Empire in 1809. This loss of Finland and the death of his first wife after seven years of marriage were the only tragedies in his life. He had taken the orders in 1803, and in Sweden, besides serving as secretary of the Academy, a post to which he was appointed in 1824, he was the incumbent of several parishes until he was made bishop of Härnösand on the northeast coast of Sweden, where he died.

Throughout his life he remained a man of sedate habits and rational mind and combined poetry and respectability without difficulty, reminding us of Dryden, who wrote: "Great wits are sure to madness near allied / And thin partitions do their bounds divide," but was far from madness himself. However, especially in his youth Franzén was considered a bold innovator who broke all rules and wrote with breathtaking audacity. In a period when literary taste and love for formal refinement had reached such a high degree, any changes in accepted patterns were immediately noticed. Classical French taste was still prevalent in Sweden and Finland to the point that parts of Macpherson's *Ossian* poems were translated into Swedish from the French translations by Johan Henrik Kellgren,[29] but both England and Germany were becoming more influential in all fields of science and letters. Franzén journeyed to England and Germany and found the literatures of these countries more to his taste than the French. While teaching practical philosophy at Turku, he basically followed Kant's system, although it was criticized by Porthan and the older generation as too abstruse in both terminology and thought. Near Aachen he visited the ruined castle of Falkenberg and declared that it was a good place to read Young and to melancholize" [sic] and possibly to throw oneself into the river, but added "I had either too little courage or too much love for life to drown myself voluntarily." Paris disappointed him, for none of France's great eighteenth-century writers remained, and those of the nineteenth had not yet appeared. He preferred Diderot and Beaumarchais, but attended classical tragedies to see, as he wrote, "the best theater in the world performing the best plays of the greatest authors of the country," which fell short of his expectations. He did not, however, see the best plays of Racine and Corneille, but Voltaire's *Alzire* and *Brutus.* He admired the English actors for their naturalness (he saw Mrs. Siddons and John Kemble) and wrote enthusiastically about Shakespeare.

In 1792, when the king was shot in Stockholm, the first notice received in Turku indicated that he was recovering, and Franzén was requested to write a poem expressing the joy of his subjects, his first poem. When news arrived that the king was dead, Franzén was asked to rewrite the poem for the official function to be held. In 1793 he had some of his poems published in Stockholm, including *Människans anlete, ode till Selma* ('The Human Face, an Ode to Selma'). The same year he added more works, among them *Den gamle knekten* ('The Veteran'). His now well-established fame was crowned when the Swedish Academy awarded him one of its prizes. After his journey to the continent and England, he won the Grand Prize of the same institution for *Sång öfver Gustaf Philip Creutz* ('Song on . . . ,' 1797). On this occasion Franzén's views clashed most violently with those of the Academy, especially its chairman, Carl Gustaf af Leopold, a poet of the classical school. According to Leopold, terrifying or sensuous descriptions could make a deep impression on readers, but they belonged to periods in which philosophical enlightenment had not yet progressed, not to poets like Horace, Pope, or Voltaire. Their proper place was old Scotland or other primitive countries although "some German poets" were using them again. Franzén rewrote the poem, depriving it of much of its original strength, but not without protest. He claimed that the Academy could not expect him to write a philosophical poem, for he found it easier to find a picture than a thought, and quoted one of Leopold's poets, Horace, who said in *Ars Poetica* that "poetry is like a picture." In addition to the imagery, the Academy criticized Franzén's technical innovations, e.g., the many *enjambements* and the short line ending the stanza with its three rises.

Like a true panegyric, the poem is exaggerated in its praise of Creutz, but it is an interesting example of the new literary taste appearing in Sweden. Compared to previous literature, parts were wild and terrifying indeed. It is a description of the progress of letters and civilization in Sweden. The pagan times had a savage majesty; when Christianity was introduced, the old songs disappeared; the Renaissance failed to conquer the far North, and attempts in Queen Christina's time to spread enlightenment there were only partially successful; it was Creutz who first definitively secured his native country a place in the realm of Hellenic ideals and classical spirit. The same mixture of classical and Nordic elements that appeared in Creutz's works is found again, but local color is stronger. Many landscapes are purely Finnish, especially in the unrevised version. In his description of heathen antiquity Franzén broke most decisively with the prevailing taste; the influence of Ossian is notable in the Bard:

Ingen Erato på Manhems fjällar
Gratierna böd till dans. Der klang
I dess stormbebodda hällar
Ingen Lesbisk sång. Blott Rota sprang
Tjutande på heden, och i spåren
Döden flög från rad till rad.
Barden stod på klippan nära, håren
På hans hjessa reste sig; han qvad:
Såsom nordanvinden skarpa
Stormade hans ljud: och på hans harpa
Från de slagne Kämpars tropp
Bloden stänktes opp.

On Manhem's hills no Erato found
The Graces dancing. The scowling
Crags were not echoing the sound
Of Lesbian songs. But Rota, howling,
Roamed the heath and bleak
Death with her for prey was vying.
Standing on a nearby peak
Sang the Bard; his hair was flying:
Like a gust from North, so sharp,
Rushed his words: and on his harp
From the host in death arrayed
Blood was sprayed.

Franzén did not consider this poem important; he is best remembered as the author of shorter pieces which better expressed his dreamy idealism and love for nature. The poems published in Sweden in 1792 and 1793 are often dedicated to Selma, a fictitious name designating a young lady with whom he was in love at that time, but who eventually married another man. The idealistic, dreamy feeling expressed by the poet is often combined with religious and philosophic speculation, as in *Ode to Selma* or *Det nya Eden* ('The New Eden'). *Människans anlete* in the title of the first poem is quoted from Milton's *Paradise Lost*; his words, "The human face divine," are a motto at the beginning.[30] A description of the world on the sixth day of creation before the appearance of Man is first. Then, when he "raises his face from the dust," all the world bows before him. Next follows an attack on materialism, referred to as the ideas of "those who exclaim: there is no soul," who are refuted by an invitation to reexamine the human face and judge whether or not all lofty thoughts and feelings reflected therein do not prove the contrary. The poem ends with a description of Selma's beauty, which will not be destroyed in death, but which the poet will see again "in the vales of Elysium."

The New Eden, first published in 1794, was extensively changed in later editions. The first is an ecstatic description of the dwellings of the blessed, where the soul rises to ever higher spheres and is finally allowed contemplation of God, as in Dante's *Paradiso*, whereas later editions are more didactic. Each time man allows himself to be led by his better feelings, pity, charity, humility, he gains sight of the new Eden, more beautiful than the old, where his heart did not have to master itself. The poet then returns to a description of Heaven, ending in a promise of highest bliss in the contemplation of God.[31]

Like others of his youthful poems, *The Veteran* appeared in several versions. Though uninteresting in itself, it was an inspiration to Runeberg in his cycle on the 1808-09 war. It is evident in the different versions that Franzén consistently wavered between a realistic and an idealistic view of the world. In one version the old soldier is individualized in clothing, appearance, and environment; in another he is a roughly sketched human type representing typical thoughts and feelings.

While Franzén was in Turku, directing the publication of *Åbo Tidningar* from 1794 to 1795 and 1797 to 1799, he wrote for the paper many light poems praising life's joys and pleasures. Such poems as *Champagne vinet* ('Champagne Wine') or *Lifvets njutning* ('The Pleasure of Life') were long popular.

Without hostility to Sweden, he loved Finland and thought it quite different from Sweden. He expressed his love in an occasional poem for the Finnish Economic Society, *Finska Hushållningssällskapet* (originally *Kuninkaallinen Huoneen Hallitusseura*, now *Suomen Talousseura*), founded by Porthan and his friends in 1797. The poem, *Finlands uppodling* (lit. 'How Finland Was Cleared for Cultivation,' more freely 'Finland's Progress'; 1800), reveals a fascination with the wild, savage past of his country. In the first stanzas he wonders if the Finns were not happier in pagan times than after Christianity's introduction into the country:

> Med dina sångers eld, et utbrott af naturen;
> med dina ordspråks skatt, et fynd af sinnrikt wett;
> . . . .
> war du ej wis och säll, o fordne Scythers son?
>
> Did not thy songs, sprung from the very Nature,
> Thy proverbs not, a find of fertile mind
> . . . .
> Provide thee bliss and wit, o son to Scyths of yore?

The Scyths are the result of an eighteenth-century literary fashion created by speculations on the origin of the Finnish language which were started by Leibnitz.[32] The poem then describes how the author "already sees in the mirror of hope his native country the equal of proud Albion, ordering a stream of her products to every bay teeming with ships" and "Finland, lifted up on the side of Sweden, admired by a world which had forgotten that she existed."

As secretary of the Academy, Franzén was required to take active part in the literary life of his new homeland. Among his official writings are no less than thirty biographies of distinguished personalities in various fields, of which *Porthan's Life* contains the most genuine warmth. Continuing Porthan's interest in Finnish folk poetry, Franzén wrote in 1837 a letter to a friend containing a lengthy discussion on its metric qualities. Without success he tried to write Swedish poems in the Finnish meter; when the *Kalevala* was published, he considered translating it into Swedish, though nothing came of the plan.

At the death of his second wife, he wrote a series of poems dedicated to "Fanny," and, as a minister, he composed approximately thirty hymns for the Swedish hymnal of 1819. He also tried historic compositions, e.g., the poems *Julie de St. Julien eller Frihetsbilden* ('Julie de St. Julien or The Image of Liberty,' 1819), a love story set in the French Revolution, and *Svante Sture eller mötet vid Alvastra* ('Svante Sture or The Meeting at Alvastra,' 1829), whose subject was from Swedish history, but they added nothing to his fame. He is remembered for the works of his youth in Finland, dreamy and ecstatic in their love for nature, in which God and thoughts and feelings of man are reflected. In these works a lofty, sometimes naive idealism is combined with love for humble, ordinary life and people of modest condition and simple virtues, both described with loving and warm realism.

Besides Kellgren, who introduced Franzén to the Swedish public, another Turku contemporary of Franzén was **Abraham Niklas Clewberg** (1754-1821), who moved to Sweden in 1783 and had a brilliant career there. Second director of the Royal Theater, member of the Royal Academy and the Academy of Sciences, Baron Edelcrantz, builder of a new optic telegraph, owner of a linen manufacturing concern, president of the Academy of Agriculture, and chairman of the Board of Trade, he first taught at the University of Turku, where he also wrote poetry. One poem, written at Queen Lovisa Ulrica's death in 1782, contained a lengthy, loving description of Finland, its history and its progress under the reigning king. Franzén admitted that it gave inspiration to his own patriotic works.

Jacob Tengström (1755-1832) was also Porthan's friend and a university man. He taught philosophy, then theology at Turku, became bishop of Turku in 1803 and archbishop of Finland in 1817. He was politically active, sat in Parliament under Swedish rule and was instrumental in securing Finland's new position within the Russian Empire after 1809. He wrote poems, light verse, hymns, biographies, historical sketches, didactic works, and children's stories, and edited *Åbo Tidningar* from 1781 to 1783. He was a member of committees entrusted with re-editing the catechism, hymnal, and other books used by the church of Finland. He attempted both a tragedy in the classical French style, *Zelis*, and a ballad in the romantic German style, *Skräbböle hög* ('The Mound of Skräbböle,' 1807). All his works are smooth and faultless, and comform to the taste of his time without notable depth of feeling or strength of expression.

One other true poet besides Franzén who belonged to the Aurora Society was **Mikael Choraeus** (1774-1806). The dreaminess of some of his poems and his brief life, ended by tuberculosis, have surrounded him with romantic shimmer. On the beautiful island of Ruissalo near Turku, the "Poet's Well" is still shown; Choraeus supposedly composed his works near it. Franzén aided him especially by publishing his poems in *Åbo Tidningar*. Eventually they were printed in Sweden and noticed by the Swedish Academy, which granted him its prize in 1801. His award-winning poem, like Franzén's, celebrated the memory of a well-known personality, Field Marshal Count Augustin Ehrensvärd, a Swede who lived and worked many years in Finland, which he loved and where he was buried in 1772.[33] Choraeus took the opportunity to praise his native country in the poem. Other works are marked by his sense of impending death, but his satires show a sharp pen and lively spirit. His contemporaries admired him greatly, but now he is considered a good, second-rate poet who might have developed further had he lived longer. Runeberg, who then lived at Bishop J. Tengström's home, expressed esteem for him in *Färd från Åbo* ('A Journey from Åbo' [Turku], 1828).

Swedish Literature in the Nineteenth Century
from the Turku Romanticists,
Runeberg and Topelius, through Wecksell

THE CHANGE BROUGHT TO FINLAND by the Russian conquest in 1809 was a beneficial one. The Finnish part of the Swedish army supported by some Swedish units won a few battles, but, badly led, trained, and equipped, it lost the war. During the conflict, a kind of Finnish Parliament or Diet met at Porvoo and swore allegiance to Alexander I as their new ruler, although Sweden did not recognize this oath until the peace treaty between herself and Russia was signed. The emperor eased the transition in rule for his new subjects; Swedish currency, for example, was legal tender in Finland until 1840.[34] With a few exceptions, the members of the Finnish ruling class, conservatives in their views and loyal subjects of the Swedish crown, transferred this loyalty to the new ruler.[35] During the long union with Sweden, Finland had become spiritually and socially a Scandinavian country, which she remains. Russia was alien in spirit, tradition, and social structure, as well as overwhelmingly powerful. Very few Finns considered reuniting Finland with Sweden; some moved to the old mother country, but most of the ruling class accepted the change and felt that they had secured for their country a very advantageous position in the Russian Empire. They also felt that Finland should remain inconspicuous in order to live under the old Swedish Constitution and laws, now her own, with the social order unchanged. However, a few young radicals thought that "they were not Swedes, they could not become Russians, so they must be Finns,"[36] and considered it dangerous that the country be ruled by a relatively small group whose language was not understood by the majority of the population. Therefore, they argued, Finnish must be made the language of law, administration, education, and all spiritual life. Their program was too advanced for its time. Not until 1861, when Parliament met for the first time since the union with Russia, were any political and social changes enacted.

In 1812 Helsinki became the capital of Finland, and the university moved to that city after a fire almost totally destroyed Turku in 1827. Briefly, however, Turku had retained power as the intellectual center of the country long enough to name a literary group, the Turku Romanticists. Although this group included no remarkable writers and had little direct influence in the country, it introduced new ideas, and the first Finnish nationalists to advocate the use of the Finnish language, although they wrote in Swedish, were among its members. They had close contacts with Sweden, especially at the University of Uppsala, where they were acquainted with a group of Swedish romantic writers, the Phosphorists. Chiefly through the Phosphorists contemporary German philosophic and aesthetic ideas were transmitted to Finland. Also at Uppsala three Finnish students met H. R. von Schröter, a German scholar, in 1819 and helped him in the translation of a selection of Finnish folk poetry into German. It was von Schröter's German imitation of the Finnish folk meter that Longfellow adopted for *Hiawatha.*[37]

Adolf Ivar Arwidsson (1791-1858) was the most prominent of the Turku Romanticists as well as the most radical. Because of his writings in *Mnemosyne*, a periodical published by his friends Linsén and Bergbom in Turku from 1819 to 1823, and in *Åbo Morgonblad*, the newspaper he tried to issue himself in 1821, he was dismissed from the university, where he had taught history, and exiled from Finland. He then lived in Sweden, where he became head of the Royal Library in Stockholm and maintained active interest in Finnish affairs. Allowed to revisit Finland, he died in Viipuri on a journey during which he had been well received by the authorities. At Turku he regularly wrote poetry, but was critical of his own efforts and included in his collected works, published in 1832, only 29 of the 166 poems he had composed. The first were light and idyllic, somewhat in Franzén's vein, but he then explored subjects related to the natural philosophy of the German Romantics and wrote about the cosmic forces and elementary spirits which govern and animate the world. In *Kettil Okristen* (name) he followed the taste for old Norse subjects then prevailing in Sweden. He also wrote patriotic verse. A popular patriotic composition, *Sång* ('Song'), may have contributed to the authorities' suspicion of him. In Sweden he published some scholarly works on the history of Finland and two pamphlets on the political position of the country.

Axel Gabriel Sjöström (1794-1846), another Turku Romanticist, collaborated with Arwidsson in the publication of a short-lived periodical (only two issues appeared, 1817 and 1818), *Aura*, the name of the river on which Turku is located. Their relations were not always friendly, and

Sjöström published some rather personal criticism of his colleague which led in part to the dispersion of the group intended to support *Aura*. In 1827, after the fire, Sjöström moved to Helsinki, where he published a newspaper until 1831, and in 1833 he became professor of Greek at that university. He wrote poetry all his life and translated German and Greek poetry into Swedish. He composed light, elegant poems which show the influence of Franzén and the German Romantics. Although he was much admired during his life, acclaim proved fatal to his talent; he continued producing with great facility verse little more than elegant word play, "romantic" in an unflattering sense.

Johan Gabriel Linsén (1785-1848), one of the founders of the *Aura* and *Mnemosyne*, had a career similar to Sjöström's; he taught Latin at the University of Turku, then in Helsinki, and wrote poetry which even his contemporaries found lacking in depth and strength. *Den Finska Fosterbygden* ('Finland, [Our] Native Country') reflects his patriotism. He, known as a mild, dreamy man, not the fiery Arwidsson, made the most radical proposal to adopt Finnish as the sole language of the country in all fields of public and private life.

Still another Turku Romanticist, **Gustaf Idman-Idestam** (1802-51), published several poems in *Mnemosyne* before choosing the career of lawyer and civil servant. His works are often more subjective and emotionally stronger than those of the friends who were publicly recognized as great poets; these qualities do not weaken his writings. One, *Till min fosterbygd* ('To My Native Land'), is more personal and warmer than Linsén's composition of similar title, written in accordance with the established tradition.

The Turku group also consisted of a few poets who composed Finnish verse, but they will be discussed more thoroughly later. K. A. Gottlund, who later wrote in Finnish, published a few Swedish poems in 1817 and 1818, but his main work was not in literature. **J. J. Tengström** (1787-1858), nephew of the archbishop, taught literature and later philosophy at Turku, then Helsinki, where many of the time's leading personalities met in his home, and published in *Aura* articles advocating the study of the Finnish language, the collecting of folk poetry, and similar nationalistic activities. We have already mentioned him as an admirer of Paulinus-Lillienstedt's poems.

An important fact about the first half of the nineteenth century, to approximately 1860, is that normal political, social, and intellectual activities could not be carried on in Finland. Alexander I had granted the country an autonomous position under influence of the liberal ideas he admired in his youth. Although he later became a mainstay of the Holy Alliance, he remained favorably inclined toward his new subjects. In 1811 the provinces conquered from Finland in 1721 and 1743 were reunited with Finland, which the emperor visited four times, seeing on his last journey in 1819 even its

37

most remote sections. Although his successor, Nicholas I, did not directly interfere much in Finnish affairs and generously granted funds for the building of the new capital and the institutions housed there, including the university, his practised ideal was absolute monarchy. In Finland, as in Russia, political, social, and economic questions could not be publicly discussed, and a kind of *ancien régime* was maintained for approximately sixty years. At that time the majority of the population was rural (7.5 percent lived in urban areas in 1870), traditionally conservative, and loyal to the crown, so that a need for political or other reform was not felt. Although there were plans in the Crimean War for Sweden to side with England and France and reconquer Finland, Finnish units fought the Anglo-French fleet bravely and were rewarded by the emperor.

However, one aspect of public life in early nineteenth-century Finland was resented by the whole Finnish speaking population. It was the exclusive use of Swedish in all official matters, and complaints from representatives of the rural population interested in public affairs soon began to appear. In his newspaper Reinhold von Becker published two poems by a village blacksmith, Paavo Tuovinen, expressing concern over the position of the Finnish language, and in 1840 Lönnrot printed in his paper, *Mehiläinen* ('The Bee'), a similar composition by another folk poet, Pietari Makkonen.[38] Runeberg translated the latter into Swedish. All social and political problems became connected with the language question. Among the Swedish-speaking upper classes, the hallmark of liberalism was an interest in Finnish and its development as a medium for culture.

Examining the philosophy of the Finnish educated classes of that period more closely, however, we find much of the bourgeois respectability, smug morals, and religiosity typical of the age (often thought best represented in Victorian England). It is probable that, even if not ruled by Russia, Finland in the nineteenth century would have been much the same. The sedate, stale idyll of the period is strikingly exemplified in Runeberg's house at Porvoo, which has been maintained as it was in his lifetime. The house looks like what it was, the home of a small-town schoolteacher who won fame as a poet, but nevertheless remained a small-town schoolteacher.

Still, though limited to fields permitted by the authorities, vigorous intellectual activity also took place in nineteenth-century Finland. Runeberg and Topelius wrote; Snellman composed his treatises on Hegel's philosophy, the theory of government, and nationalism; Lönnrot collected the materials for the *Kalevala*; M. A. Castrén began the scientific study of Finno-Ugrian languages; J. Gadolin, whose work actually belongs to an earlier period, was a chemist of European fame; J. J. Nervander, also a poet, became well known for his research in electricity. Although little had previously been done in the fine arts, painting, sculpture, music, and architecture greatly developed at that time in Finland. It was truly a classical age without deep conflict:

religion was not criticized and not yet challenged by science; revolutionary social theories, though extant, were seldom discussed, even in private. The era was characterized by lofty, naive idealism based on belief in the goodness of human nature and backed by solid classical studies; a harmonious synthesis was believed to have been achieved between Christianity and humanistic ideals.

The happiest period during the Russian rule was the reign of Alexander II (1855-81), a liberal, benevolent czar who granted the Finns almost all reforms they requested by making sessions of Parliament regular and independent of his will and by approving the acts it passed. Elementary education was instituted, the decree forbidding the use of Finnish abolished, and Finnish was made an official language of the country. Local rural and urban administration was put on a new basis, the country's finances were reorganized, and the Bank of Finland was authorized to issue a Finnish currency separate from the Russian (the same used today), and general military service was introduced. The established church formally requested a law to secure the position of dissenters. Due to primitive economic and technical conditions, there was a terrible famine in 1867 and 1868, but it gave an impulse to improve the situation, especially by the building of railroads.

After the death of Alexander II, resentment against Finland's privileged position grew in Russia, and systematic attack against Finland soon began. Finland's internal harmony was broken at approximately the same time: Darwin's theories were studied by scientists and opposed by churchmen; socialism and trade unions were new goals of the workers growing more numerous with development of modern industries; naturalism and realism were introduced to literature. Hostility developed between the Finnish- and Swedish-speaking groups of the population, specifically the middle and upper classes. The Social-Democrat party openly condemned linguistic quarrels among its members, and none have appeared within its ranks or in the trade union movement.

In autumn, 1822, Lönnrot, Runeberg, and Snellman matriculated at the University of Turku. Receiving tuition from Runeberg, Topelius attended the same institution after it had been moved to Helsinki. Thus, the four greatest literary figures of the mid-nineteenth century in Finland began their adult lives together, but soon separated. Lönnrot went to Kajaani as a physician to collect folk poems, Runeberg settled in Porvoo to teach at a secondary school, Snellman, after many vicissitudes, ended in Kuopio in the same position, and Topelius remained in Helsinki. Without Runeberg, who remained in Porvoo, they met again in Helsinki in the 1850s, all now famous men: Lönnrot the compiler and publisher of the *Kalevala* and professor of Finnish; Snellman a professor, then a statesman, Secretary of Finances and member of Parliament (the old Diet of the Four Estates); Topelius a professor of history and well-known writer. They were showered with honors, awards, medals, decorations, titles, and official positions. Snellman was knighted by the emperor in the Finnish nobility, always strictly separated from the Russian; Runeberg and Topelius were officially honored in Sweden and all of them were elevated to the rank of great men in Finland.

Runeberg, Snellman, and Lönnrot were of modest origin. Runeberg's and Snellman's fathers were captains of the merchant marine, Lönnrot's a village tailor, and Z. Topelius the elder, Topelius's father, was a country physician (mentioned in connection with the collecting of folk poetry). As students in Helsinki, Runeberg, Snellman, and Cygnaeus shared an apartment to which Snellman brought a chair and Cygnaeus his books, which were piled on the floor. Runeberg and Cygnaeus slept in the same bed, Snellman on three chairs pushed together. Indirectly and without knowledge of it, they represented the lower middle class who were then asking for a share in political and social power in many countries.

While studying in Turku in 1826 and 1827, Runeberg, Snellman, and Cygnaeus belonged to a group of students named for its leading personality, Nervander's Group. At their informal meetings they discussed all subjects, especially philosophy (that of Hegel, the "Sartre" of the time) and literature, and scorned the conservative professors. When the university moved to Helsinki, Runeberg and Nervander founded a more formal circle, which became famous as *Lauantaiseura* 'Saturday Society,' named for its Saturday meetings. Snellman, M. A. Castrén, J. J. Tengström, and, near the society's end, Topelius were members; Lönnrot was sometimes a guest. The purpose of this literary society was to promote Finnish civilization and awaken national spirit. Its results were a newspaper, *Helsingfors Morgonblad*, edited by Runeberg until 1837, published between 1832 and 1844; a secondary school, *Helsingfors Lyceum*, more liberal and humane than corresponding state institutions; and the Society for Finnish Literature, *Suomalaisen Kirjallisuuden Seura*.[39] The newspaper and school were Swedish and no longer exist, but the society for literature still flourishes, though mainly as a folklore society. It published the *Kalevala* and has guided almost all the collecting and publishing of folk poetry.

Johan Ludvig Runeberg (b. 1804 in Pietarsaari, Swed. *Jakobstad* [sic], on the Gulf of Botnia, d. 1877) accepted while at the university tutorial positions in wealthy families, as did other poor students. At Saarijärvi in north central Finland (northwest of Jyväskylä) and at Ruovesi (north of Tampere), he became acquainted with and soon loved the interior of Finland and its Finnish-speaking population, which he often later described in his works. At Parainen, near Turku, where he lived in Archbishop Tengström's family, he associated with highly cultured, kindly persons in whose company he widened his experience and lost some of the timidity due to his modest condition. Although he wrote poetry early, he matured late. Critical of his first compositions, he did not publish a collection of poems before 1830, the year of his marriage.

Runeberg's first poems contain the motifs which later dominated his work. Although love is more conspicuous in the earlier works, patriotic poems, descriptions of popular life, and meditations on man and nature appear. Happy love is described in the 1828 *Odes to Frigga.* The torments of love are the subject of a five-canto poem, *Nights of Jealousy*, which ends in the death of the beloved and suicide of the narrator; this work contains an affinity to many romantic love poems, including Goethe's *Young Werther* and Byron's *Manfred.* Runeberg's early poetry was also influenced by Franzén, whose pupil Linsén had been his teacher at Turku, but Runeberg was more robust and tormented than his mild predecessor. In 1828 he read a collection of Serbian folksongs in German translation which greatly impressed him. He published a Swedish translation of them in 1830, and their influence is evident in the *Idylls and Epigrams* included in his first collection. He seems to have been uninterested in Finnish folk poetry, and in answer to a critic of his Serbian songs, he stated that his interest in folk art was due to theoretical considerations which had their origin in German thought. The simpler, more direct form and feeling of *Idylls and Epigrams*, in which love is happy and playful or tragic and violent, is influenced by the folksongs, as is the simplicity and majesty of *Bonden Paavo* (Finn. *Saarijärven Paavo* 'Farmer Paavo' or 'Paavo from Saarijärvi'), whose main character has become a proverbial representative of the Finns. This character represents Runeberg's view of simple people; other writers have consciously opposed characters to this strongly idealized, hard-working, honest, generous, and God-fearing man.[40] Soon afterwards Runeberg published two poems in which his interest in the military past of his country first appears, *Graven i Perho* ('The Grave at Perho,' 1831) and *Molnets broder* ('The Brother of a Cloud,' 1834). Both foreshadow his cycle of poems on the 1808-09 war, *Fänrik Ståls Sägner* ('The Tales of Ensign Stål'); in fact, it contains *Molnets broder.*

He was also a lover of nature, outdoorsman, and hunter. At Turku he had written two short narrative poems, *Vargen* ('The Wolf,' after 1823), a harmless parody of majestic epic style, and *Älgjakten* ('The Moose Hunt,' 1826), a technical description of the subject. He was also influenced by German poems, e.g., Goethe's *Hermann and Dorothea,* with its idealized, sentimental description of middle-class life. In 1827 he wrote a similar composition, *Midsommarfesten* ('The Midsummer Feast') also reminiscent of the happy, simple home life of Goldsmith's or Dickens's works. Like the German models, these poems imitated classical hexameter.[41] These elements combine in his first epic poem, *Älgskyttarne* ('The Moose Hunters,' 1832). The hunt, less important than the characters, was eliminated from the final version. Its contents are a love story ending in happy betrothal, humorous episodes introduced by Karelian peddlers,[42] and the tragic life story of Aaron the beggar, poor but dignified, who relieves his tale with his half-humorous mishaps in a big city. Though idealistic, Runeberg did not romanticize the common people, and some critics reproved him for being too realistic. Strindberg, in his autobiographic novel *Tjänstekvinnans son* ('A Woman Servant's Son,' 1886; the action is twenty years previous), introduces one character to whom *The Tales of Ensign Stål* are "realism and barbarism" and another who, speaking of *The Moose Hunters*, says that "Runeberg . . . formally a strong realist, overstepped sometimes the limits of brutality when he tried to be classically simple."[43]

After another person had been appointed professor of Latin and Greek at the university, the post Runeberg had hoped for, he had to abandon all plans for an academic career. It was then that he became a teacher at Porvoo, where he remained until his death. Before moving there, he published his second collection of lyrical poems in 1833, *Hanna*, a short epic, in 1836, miscellaneous writings, a small comedy, and short stories. The best-known of the latter, *En julkväll i lotskojan* ('A Christmas Night in a Pilot's Cabin,' 1832) and *Lurendrejaren* ('The Smuggler,' 1834), indicate how well Runeberg knew the life of the inhabitants of the islands off the Finnish coast. Simple in form, the lyrical poems are occasionally reminiscent of English or Scots ballads, often describing thoughts and feelings of a maid-servant, a boy from a humble cottage, a fowler, a sailor's sweetheart, or others. This, to Runeberg, was sound and natural poetry, which contrasted with the egocentric character of romantic art. He often projected human emotions and moods into nature or linked natural and psychic processes, e.g., in the poems *Hvem styrde hit din väg?* ('Who Showed You the Way Here?), in which a girl compares her beloved and herself to two brooks running apart, two trees growing on opposite sides of a meadow, two birds nesting in different groves, and *Vid en källa* ('By a Spring'), in which he compares his soul, brightened and obscured by joys and sorrows, to a spring's surface, lit and darkened by the reflections of passing clouds. In this latter poem's last stanza, Runeberg's feeling of intimate union with nature is strikingly demonstrated: the components of the metaphor, the spring and the soul, finally blend—the light and darkness of the mirror (soul) depend upon the empty clouds on its surface. Then follows: "O spring, when shall this play come to an end / When shall thy waves find a rest?"

Hanna, in the vein of *The Midsummer Feast*, describes a young girl, her first love, and an old fisherman's peaceful, pious death. Scenes from Finnish nature contrast the Swedish seacoast and Finnish inland. Idealized young love is the power by whose means the soul refinds its innermost self. It was this poem that made Runeberg famous in both Finland and Sweden. In Sweden reaction had slowly been growing against the excessively ornate, obscure poetry of the romanticists, especially the Phosphorists; Runeberg's simple verse was hailed there as the sign of a new period. In 1839 a young poet, B. E.

Malmström, advised his readers to study "the *Iliad* or *The Moose Hunters*, the *Odyssey* or *Hanna*."[44] The same year Atterbom, an author of established fame, coined the laudatory epithet "poetic realist" for Runeberg. There was renewed interest in Franzén, whom Runeberg had warmly praised.

In 1832 Runeberg attacked violently in *Helsingfors Morgonblad* Sweden's prevailing school of poetry, which he found obscure, lacking in true depth and idealism, and, worst, too individual and egoistic. He was deeply religious, though his faith was influenced too much by his aesthetic ideas and Platonism to be truly orthodox; law and order in nature and society were his highest values. The family, nation, and universal civilization represented eternal truths; individuals sinned in rebelling against them. A poet rather than philosopher, he was inconsistent in practicing his own ideas. A strong revivalist movement emphasizing individual piety, strict morals, and personal communion with God had spread among Finns from the beginning of the nineteenth century in part due to the activity of Paavo Ruotsalainen, a farmer and preacher who became famous throughout the country. Although it attracted educated persons, students, and ministers, the church officially opposed it; members taking part in formally illegal meetings were removed from office and laymen fined. A special act against unauthorized religious assemblies, the so-called Conventicle Placard, had been passed in 1726 and was not abolished until 1869. The movement, known as *herännäiset* 'the awakened' or, more disparagingly, *körttiläiset* (reference to a kind of dress its members affected), gathered strength in spite of persecution, which was not harsh. In the regions where revivals took place, North Savo, Karelia, Kainuu (east and northeast Finland), and later especially Ostrobotnia (northwest and west Finland), drinking, gambling, loose sexual relations, and fighting, for which Ostrobotnia particularly was known, diminished. The converts were puritan fundamentalists, intolerant and intent upon suppressing worldly diversions, from playing cards, dancing, and colorful clothing to art and literature. Lönnrot criticized the movement, and, when Lars Stenbäck, a poet and teacher, wrote an article rejecting all fiction, even that written for religious edification, Runeberg answered in *Den gamle trädgårdsmästarens brev* ('Letters from an Old Gardener'), a poem published in *Helsingfors Morgonblad* in 1837. He compared man to a plant whose roots are as important as the flower and said that the revivalists were so concerned with the soul that they ignored or despised all else in life. Stenbäck's answer called the old gardener's worship of nature paganism and an adoration of idols alien to the true spirit of Christianity. The polemic was inconclusive; the movement never conquered the country or the church, but the church began to tolerate it not long afterwards, and the movement has endured and is still influential in some parts of the country.

As an essay *Är Macbeth en kristlig tragedi?* ('Is *Macbeth* a Christian Tragedy?') written in 1842 and his collection of poems published in 1843 indicate, Runeberg remained preoccupied with religious problems. It contained some whose subjects were extracted from Christian legends. *Kyrkan* ('The Church') and *Chrysanthos* dominate the collection. Reflecting again Runeberg's love for simple people and belief in God's presence in nature, *Kyrkan* tells of a poor man, refused a horse to ride to church, who takes a boat instead, is lost in the early mist on the lake, and, alone, must worship on a small island. In the last stanza the rising of the sun can be considered representative of the appearance of truth. Although the poem's spirit could be called pantheistic, its core can be found in Acts of the Apostles 7:48-49:

> Howbeit the Most High dwelleth not in temples made with hands; as saith the prophet, Heaven is my throne, and earth is my footstool: what house will ye build me? saith the Lord.

or 17:24:

> God that made the world, and all things therein, seeing that he is Lord of heaven and earth, dwelleth not in temples made with hands.

In *Chrysanthos* Runeberg expresses his belief in the possibility of combining the ideals of classical antiquity and Christianity into a harmonious whole. Chrysanthos is a Greek (in Christian antiquity) who has been converted to the new faith but does not eschew the world, performing gladly his duties as a citizen who loves his native city, Athens, Greece and its language. The image of the world as a beautiful garden of flowers lovingly tended by Christ is related to the philosophy of *Letters from an Old Gardener*.

Runeberg wrote almost no lyrical poetry after 1843 except in the years 1853 to 1857, when he composed a proposal for a hymnal of the church of Finland. (As a secondary school teacher he was obliged by existing regulations formally to take the orders, although he was never active as a minister.) Sixty of the hymns were by him, many still popular, but he often bitterly saw his texts altered by the publication committee, since his verse was considered too artistic for the simple taste of the faithful. By 1841 he had published two narrative poems, *Julkvällen* ('A Christmas Night') and *Nadeschda* (name); *Kung Fjalar* ('King Fjalar,' 1844), the first part of *The Tales of Ensign Stål* (1848), a collection of short stories (1854), the second part of *Ensign Stål* (1860), a short comedy *Kan ej* ('Can't,' 1862), and *Kungarne på Salamis* ('The Kings of Salamis,' 1863) followed these.

His fame had grown steadily. In 1839 he was granted a state pension for his literary merits and awarded the gold medal of the Swedish Academy. In 1858 a national collection donated seventy-two thousand marks to him. In 1863 he suffered a stroke, but lived for fourteen more years, a patriarch venerated by the entire nation. His sons distinguished themselves in their fields; Walter Magnus, a sculptor well known in Scandinavia, made the statue of his father unveiled in Helsinki in 1885.

Runeberg's popularity rests mainly in *The Tales of Ensign Stål*, unfortunately, for his merits, complex personality, and philosophy are to be found elsewhere in his works. With Aleksis Kivi he was undoubtedly the greatest writer of his time in Finland and perhaps even Sweden. However, as Finland's national consciousness developed in the nineteenth century, the educated classes succumbed to the temptations of glorifying her history, and these poems which praise the Finnish army (officially part of Swedish defense forces, whose officers and rank and file came from Finland) met the popular demand. Some of the poems were published separately before the first volume was issued (December 14, 1848), and one, *Vårt Land* ('Our Land') was set to music by Fr. Pacius. At the students' traditional spring festival on May 13, 1848,[45] Cygnaeus made a stirring speech which, unfortunately, has not been preserved, and immediately afterwards *Our Land* was sung amidst "indescribable enthusiasm." Topelius, who was also present, candidly revealed later, in a letter to his wife and in *Helsingfors Tidningar*, that the indescribable amount of alcohol consumed on the occasion had something to do with the enthusiasm.[46] Nevertheless, the song was thereafter, unofficially under Russian rule and officially after independence, the national anthem. Like the rest of *Ensign Stål*, it was soon translated into Finnish, and the entire collection enjoyed large and lasting popularity. That the publication of patriotic poems about a war against Russia did not arouse hostile reaction in Russia shows how good the relations between the two countries were. Later, when, as a result of Russian attacks on Finland's autonomy, bitter hostility developed between them, *Ensign Stål* became a catechism to the aggressively nationalistic and militaristic educated classes and is still widely used as a textbook in Finnish (and Swedish, as Finland is officially bilingual) classes in elementary schools. The shibboleth of patriotism in Finland was for a long time admiration for Runeberg, i.e., *Ensign Stål*, and, to some extent, it still is. When, in 1954, Väinö Linna published his novel on the 1941-44 war, *Tuntematon Sotilas* ('The Unknown Soldier'), in which his characters misquote *Ensign Stål* and make fun of the quotations, he was charged with being unpatriotic. However, as the novel was successful and the characters are good, courageous fighters, Linna was cleared; Jahvetti (pseudonym of Yrjö K. Kilpeläinen) stated in *Suomen Sosiaalidemokraatti* that "Linna's *Unknown Soldier* is the *Tales of Ensign Stål* of the last war."[47] Among citizens with less warlike ideals, the worship of *Ensign Stål* has produced a total rejection of Runeberg as an author, but also appeals for a more comprehensive study of his works.

For historical background Runeberg relied heavily upon Gustaf Montgomery's *Historia öfver kriget emellan Sverige och Ryssland 1808 och 1809* (1842), but his work is only loosely related to the war and not a piece of historical research, as some admirers believed, even trying to identify his characters.[48] *The Tales* is not an epic but a series of poems about different events or persons, supposedly related to the poet by a war veteran. Like *The Charge of the Light Brigade*, its events are not necessarily militarily important; a similar poem in *The Tales* is *Löjtnant Zidén* ('Lieutenant Zidén'), whose hero was so eager to be the first in an attack that he and all his men were fatally shot before reaching the enemy, a feat the poet found admirable. Many of the poems rely on strongly dramatic effects, for example, *Döbeln vid Jutas* ('Döbeln—the general—at the Battle of Jutas'), in which the appearance of the main character is carefully prepared:

> At Jutas mid the battlefield's confusion
> There was a lull where death's dread scythe had passed.
> Broken, dispersed, with desperate resolution,
> Expecting but to fall, the Finns stood fast.
> . . . .
> A gloomy silence reigned, as when in heaven
> A mighty thundercloud, by whirlwinds driven,
> Returns above the region whence it fled.
> . . . .
> But silence, hark! What's this? A loud ovation
> Rolls heavenward, as a rider looms in sight.
> . . . .
> 'Tis he, himself. No fever blast could shake him.
> That bandaged forehead—no one could mistake him.
> Our noble general's here, and all is well.
> . . . .
> From all the line rose sudden jubilation:
> "Forward to death or victory!" it rang.
> . . . .
> And Döbeln rode ahead with sword upreared.
> Before the shades of evening had descended,
> The Russians were flung back, their threat was ended.[49]

Sandels, another general, appears equally impressive in the poem bearing his name. He is lunching when informed of enemy attack, but refuses to be disturbed until he hears that he is suspected of cowardice. He rides to the breastworks and remains there in sight of the enemy until the moment to order a counterattack. The soldiers share the glory; Sven Duva, the laughingstock of the company, misunderstands an order and, instead of retreating, attacks, withholding the enemy singlehandedly on a narrow bridge until his comrades arrive. The most sympathetic trait of *The Tales* is Runeberg's understanding for the common soldier and description of the democratic, straightforward spirit of friendship between the officers and the rank and file. Runeberg referred to himself in the second poem as a Finn and gave the same epithet to his heroes; a general is shown giving the highest possible praise to a private by saying simply, "He was a Finn."

Among his last works are *A Christmas Night* and *Can't*, idyllic descriptions from contemporary middle-class life much like *Hanna* and *The*

Midsummer Feast. In *A Christmas Night* two characters, the major and an old, faithful soldier, Pistol, are much like those of *Ensign Stål. Nadeschda* is exceptional among his works because of its Russian subject, chosen, perhaps, because Runeberg had met Jakov K. Grot, professor of Russian language, literature, and history at the University of Helsinki. Grot, who was very interested in Finland and Sweden, translated *Nadeschda* and *The Moose Hunters* into Russian. At the same time Runeberg admired a well-known Swedish poet, Almquist, especially for his ease in treating exotic subjects. Certain metric peculiarities in *Nadescha* and, later, *King Fjalar* reflect Almquist's influence. Reminiscent of well-known folktales, the plot of *Nadeschda* involves two brothers of high birth, one fair and good, the other dark and evil, who are in love with a girl of humble origin, Nadeschda. The good brother marries her, but the couple is separated through family pride and, after many vicissitudes, reunited through the empress's intervention, much as in Pushkin's *The Captain's Daughter.* Though ever ready to side with the poor and oppressed, Runeberg was uninterested in political democracy; in *Nadescha* it is love and a benevolent ruler who unite young lovers of different social origin.

The Kings of Salamis, a tragedy in verse unsuccessful on stage, tells, in classical setting, of a conflict between duty and filial love. Leiokritos, the king of Salamis, is a usurper whose son Leontes allies himself with Eurysakes, the son of the lawful king, because he values justice. Unable to rebel against his father, he arranges to be killed by him by exchanging arms with Eurysakes, who eventually recovers his rightful position. The emphasis on moral conflict and sense of duty is a similarity to classical French tragedies, especially Corneille's *Héraclius*, although there is no evidence of direct influence. Since the play is almost barren of human emotion, it has understandably left its readers cold.

King Fjalar is certainly the most interesting of Runeberg's epic poems. Its subject is reminiscent of classical Greek tragedies, and its setting is taken from old Norse sagas and Macpherson's *Ossian*, both passé as literary motifs by that time, but Runeberg obviously found the latter congenial to his mood at that moment. He called the poem "a song to the gods, a small epic, the theme of which is their greatness and their grace."[50] Professor Lauri Viljanen, a Runeberg expert, considers it a Christian poem, but admits that it is difficult to explain the "grace," because Fjalar's goal, peace on earth, is in conformity to Christian ideals, but he is punished by the death of his two innocent children. Runeberg's mention of "the gods," not God, is significant; we feel that the poem is not Christian in spirit, although Runeberg himself said the contrary. This statement was no doubt necessary for a man in his position, but, once again, he was trying to find a synthesis between Christianity and the ideals of pagan antiquity.

The poem's outline recalls the story of Oedipus: King Fjalar is told that his son and daughter will marry each other one day; he has the girl thrown into the sea. Rescued, she grows up in another country, to which her brother eventually travels. He wins her hand in competition against many rivals, but her identity is discovered when he brings her home, and both die. The major theme is the Greek concept of blind Fate, superior to the gods, against which struggle is vain; the introduction of love as an active force seems modern, but Euripides had used it in his time. Runeberg's thought of love as fateful and destructive was personal. During his outwardly sedate marriage, he fell deeply in love more than once and had his sentiments returned. His attachment to his wife and his environment prevented those relationships from developing further.

When Runeberg died, **Zachris Topelius** the younger was, by popular opinion, expected to uphold Runeberg's tradition, and the two of them indeed dominated literary life in their time. In writing Topelius disappointed no one. With the greatest facility he continued to produce in astounding quantity poetry, fiction, drama, criticism, scholarship, newspaper articles, fairy tales, letters, and detailed diaries which provide valuable information and gossip about his time. Gentle, friendly, and lovable, he was also naively idealistic, so that, in Finland, *Topelian* is synonomous with that idealism, which made him narrow-minded about new trends in art and literature.

Topelius was born in 1818 near the small town Nykarleby (Finn. *Uusikaarlepyy*) on the Gulf of Botnia. He was successful relatively early, graduating from secondary school at age fifteen, taking university degrees, teaching history in a Helsinki secondary school, editing *Helsingfors Tidningar* from 1842 to 1860, becoming professor of Finnish history in 1854, of Finnish, Russian, and Scandinavian history in 1863 and of general history in 1876. He was vice-rector (vice-president) of the university from 1872 to 1875 and rector from 1875 to 1878, chairman, member, and honorary member of many (Finnish and foreign) learned and literary societies, knight and commander of a Swedish order, recipient of the prize and grand prize of the Swedish Academy and holder of honorary title of Counsellor of State.[51] On his eightieth birthday, citizens organized huge festivities in his honor, thus killing him with kindness, for he actually died of the effort of participating in them.[52]

The best-known work in his production is perhaps *Läsning för barn* ('Readings for Children,' 8 vols., 1865-96; Finn. *Lukemisia lapsille*, 1874-1905; also several English editions).[53] It includes not only fairy tales from international folklore, e.g., "Sleeping Beauty," but also stories about children in contemporary setting, boys' pranks and adventures, descriptions of nature and personified natural phenomena, and stories loosely intended to teach simple virtues of charity, honesty, and others. The educational intent was seldom pointed; Topelius once wrote that he disapproved of writers who "crammed the poor children with moral rubbish."[54] Read ever since, these stories have become in Finland and Sweden as popular as Andersen's tales, and unlike some of Andersen's, Topelius's stories were intended for children. For instruction to children, Topelius wrote *Naturens bok* ('A Book on Nature,' 1856; Finn. *Luonnon kirja*, 1860) and *Boken om vårt land* ('A Book about Our Country,' 1875; Finn. *Maamme-kirja*, 1875); the latter is still used in Finland's schools.

Topelius's poetry is more superficial than Franzén's and Runeberg's, but it is no less sincere in its expression of sentimental, pure love, childlike religiosity, and warmhearted patriotism which often invites the reader to admire the natural beauties of the country. As newspaper editor and historian, he was also interested in public affairs, and, in his idealism, he approved of the liberal and revolutionary movements in Europe. In 1848, inspired by the French Revolution, he wrote *Våren 1848* ('The Spring of 1848'), a poem in which he spoke of a spring storm, renewing all, approaching Finland's coasts in the form of rain and sunshine. These images from nature were congenial to Topelius, but dictated by prudence, which he never lacked.[55] Nineteenth-century Finnish minds were generally discreet: while longing for more freedom and admiring nations which fought foreign oppression, they remained unwilling to displease the authorities. In 1830 some students, including Runeberg, drank success to the Poles who had risen against the Russian rule. However, there was an informer in the group, and authorities threatened action against all who had been present. The affair was smoothed over, and Runeberg, like others, was annoyed at having been involved in the incident. In 1831 the Finnish Fusilier Battalion of the Imperial Bodyguard commanded by Baron Anders E. Ramsay[56] helped suppress the Polish rebellion, and the emperor awarded the unit the colors of St. George for gallantry. In a speech Ramsay said that the highest civic virtues for the sons of Finland were love for duty and honor, fidelity to the ruler and the country, and, in the poems *Morgonstormen i våren* ('A Storm on a Spring Morning,' 1846), *Den blå randen på havet* ('A Strip of Blue on the Sea,' 1847), *Studentvisa* ('The Students' Song,' 1852), *Islossningen i Uleå älv* ('The Break-up of Ice in Uleå River'; Finn. *Oulunjoki*, 1856), and *Saima kanal* ('The Canal of Saimaa,' 1856), Topelius expressed the hope that, no matter what tempests might rage throughout the world, Finland might enjoy peaceful progress under the benevolent emperor. During the Crimean War Topelius openly sided against England and France, and when attacks against Finland began, he wrote a poem of indignation, *Den första bloddroppen* ('The First Drop of Blood,' 1854). In Sweden it was openly hinted that he was courting the ruler's favor, and, almost in confirmation, he was at that time appointed professor (the University of Helsinki was and is under government control, and appointments are formally made by the chief of state).

During this period Topelius also wrote lyrical poetry. He published his first collection, *Ljungblommor* ('Flowering Heather'), in 1845, and in the 1850s he composed *Vintergatan* ('The Milky Way') and the cycle *Sylvias visor* ('Sylvia's Songs'). The smooth, melodious quality of his poems invited composers to set them to music, and in this form many are still popular, like Runeberg's. However, Topelius's great facility for writing was sometimes harmful to the quality of his prose and verse; often his stanzas are crowded with images to the point of incoherence, e.g., *A Strip of Blue on the Sea*, in which the wind rushes to the sea, galloping wildly like a boy going out to the world, and a solitary drift of snow, consumed by tears, weeps its- / (him-, her-) self to death under the loving gaze of the sun. In *En sommardag i Kangasala* ('A Summer Day at Kangasala'), popularized by the music of S. Gabriel Linsén (son of the poet), the writer says that he is "only a little bird with small and weak wings," but, should he be "an eagle in the clouds," he would fly to the throne of God Almighty and "twitter thus my tune"; the twittering eagle is left out of the Finnish translation, in which he simply sings in a "humble and low voice."

Many of his historical novels were published as serials, an explanation of some of their incoherence. His readers loved his narratives, and he gave them those which they (and he) wanted: cloak-and-dagger stories, sinister plots, assassinations, poisonings, ghosts, black magic, spiritualism, alchemistry, ruined castles, and similar romantic extravaganza made popular in England by Sir Horatio Walpole and Mrs. Radcliffe. Of all this, we prefer *Konungens Handske* ('The King's Glove,' 1863), a simple story about the war of Gustavus III against Russia in 1788 and the Anjala conspiracy,[57] during which a young man saves the king, although his own family is involved in the plot; at his death he asks the king to pardon his relatives. A subplot of innocent young love and some comic interludes are added, and the book combines the best of Topelius in a charming whole. His popular historical novel, *Fältskärns Berättelser* (4 vols., 1853-64; Finn. *Välskärin kertomukset*, 1867-80; several English translations titled *The King's Ring* and *The Surgeon's Stories*), provides an entertaining panorama of Finnish and Swedish history ranging from the Thirty Years' War to the time of Gustavus III. It is not too romanticized, except for the mysterious king's ring which brings fortune and success to its owners until they commit perjury (constant fortune and success make them overbearing so that they do commit perjury). The passing of the ring from father to son in an aristocratic family gave Topelius the opportunity to show his dislike for the nobility and love for the humble, though these feelings never reached a social or political level. It seems typical of Topelius that he was at his best when he did not try to do anything special, as in *The King's Glove*. His novel *Planeternas skyddslingar* (3 vols., 1886; Finn. *Tähtien turvatit*, 1890-92; sometimes known as *Stjärnornas kungabarn* 'The Royal Children of the Stars') was intended as a profession of his religious faith and an attack on contemporary anti-religious trends which had by then reached Finland. He purported to show that intellectual pride, lust for power, and egoism lead humans to perdition. A believer in goodness of heart, charity, humility, and love, Topelius was often anti-intellectual, disliking mainly the eighteenth-century French philosophers, especially Voltaire, and the realistic or naturalistic writers and positivistic or agnostic scientists of his own time.[58] To illustrate his thesis, he created three persons born simultaneously so that they have the same horoscope (the title can be roughly translated 'Under the Protection of the Planets' and refers to astrology): Queen Christina of Sweden and two poor children in Finland. The queen ends her life, we know, a lonely convert to Catholicism in Rome; the children, a boy and a girl, grow up with unbelievable adventures which take them all over Europe (and to the seraglio of the sultan in Istanbul) and have a miserable end. The girl, however, renounces her pride and devotes herself to charitable works. The message is all but lost among the fantastic incidents, and the lives of the main characters are far too exceptional to be a convincing proof of anything except the author's vivid fantasy.

Among his few plays, *Regina von Emmeritz* (name, 1854; Finnish version 1899), based on an episode in *The Surgeon's Stories*, is still occasionally performed when light, colorful, historical entertainment is called for. *Kung Carls jakt* ('King Charles's Hunt,' 1852) and *Prinsessan av Cypern* ('The Princess of Cyprus,' 1860), in which characters from the *Kalevala* mingle with ancient Greeks on Cyprus, later became the librettos of the first two Finnish operas, by Pacius, both now forgotten.

His historical scholarship is almost nonexistent; the suspicion that he obtained his professorship for other than scholarly merits was perhaps not unfounded. He wrote one work on a subject connected with the secondary school of Vaasa (1845), his Ph.D. thesis on the old marriage customs in Finland (1847), and one work on whether or not Finland had a history (1845). The Turku Romanticists had already discussed the problem. Tengström and Linsén had already concluded that, as long as Finland was part of Sweden, there was no Finnish history; Topelius came to the same conclusion, which Nervander shared. As Finland was geographically, if not politically, different from Sweden, a separate treatment of its events seems desirable for practical reasons, but in Topelius's time the question was not merely practical.[59] According to German romantic thought, states and nations were higher organisms, and individuals reached full development only as parts of them. To deny Finland theoretical existence as such an organism was to place Finns on a level lower than that of citizens of independent countries. The problem was an emotional one, and Topelius was sharply criticized, especially by Cygnaeus, who made use of the opportunity to ridicule Topelius's appointment as professor of a subject the existence of which he denied. Not a great scholar, Topelius was, however, one of the first in Finland to stress geography as an independent science and its importance for historical research, an inclination in keeping with his many descriptions of the beauties of Finnish nature.

One reason, besides literary merit, that led to Runeberg's and Topelius's domination of the Swedish literature of their time in Finland was the lack of significant writers during that period. Although J. V. Snellman (1806-81) influenced the course of Finnish history with his work, his major activities were not related to literature except through his propaganda for the use of Finnish. After taking degrees at the university, he was an administrator there and was appointed lecturer. However, he announced in 1837 that he would lecture on academic freedom, involving himself in a long litigation that resulted in his dismissal. He then went to Sweden, where he participated in literary life and had an argument with the famous writer C. J. L. Almquist, who had advocated free love in his short story *Det går an* ('It Will Do'). Snellman wrote a continuation to the story to prove that it wouldn't do. Two years later, after a lengthy journey to Germany, he published *Fyra giftermål* ('Four Marriages'), a collection of short stories intended to demonstrate that love alone is not enough for a happy marriage, but Snellman himself admitted that the stories were artistic failures.

While in Germany and Sweden, he published several textbooks on philosophy and logic and two scientific works, *Versuch einer spekulativen Entwicklung der Idée der Persönlichkeit* ('Essay on the Speculative Development of the Idea of Personality,' 1841) and *Läran om Staten* ('Theory of the State,' 1842). As Snellman was influenced by Hegel, who, according to Sir Bertrand Russell (and others), is "the hardest to understand of all the great philosophers,"[60] his scholarly works, especially the *Essay*, are not easy to read. Nor are they original contributions to philosophy, theory of knowledge, psychology, or sociology, but expressions of Snellman's views on contemporary questions, dressed in Hegel's abstruse terminology. Their basis is that only the universe as a whole: the state, the nation and the family are meaningful entities and the individual can reach full development only as part of them. A parallel theory is that language is all-important as the expression of thought; indeed, thought is possible only in words, so that thinking and its verbal expression are identical. The system of knowledge inherited from former generations is expressed in the heir's native language, as are traditions, customs, and laws, the entire national civilization. As Snellman conceived of states and nations as organisms, he could not accept a country with two languages and concluded logically that Finland's language must be Finnish. This linguistic theory was the most original part of his works and did not entirely conform to Hegel's system.[61] Later he wrote to younger generations that "every Swedish word used by you from now on is practically wasted,"[62] but he wrote these words in Swedish.

He returned to Finland in 1843 and became principal of the lower secondary school (similar to a U. S. junior high) at Kuopio, where he began to publish two newspapers, one, *Maamiehen Ystävä* ('The Farmer's Friend'), in Finnish, the other, *Saima* (from Lake Saimaa), in Swedish. His open criticism of the country's situation and propaganda for the use of the Finnish language made many enemies, private and official,[63] and the censure surpressed the latter newspaper in 1846. He then obtained authorization to publish another paper, *Litteraturblad för allmän medborgerlig bildning* ('Literary Journal for the General Instruction of the Citizens'; the clumsy name was probably chosen to convince authorities that it was not subversive), which he edited for approximately two years and later from 1855 to 1863. He moved to Helsinki, hoping to be appointed professor of philosophy to replace J. J. Tengström, but, although the university would have accepted him, another person was appointed. Until approximately 1856, when the political situation in Finland changed, he lived in difficult circumstances; he then became professor of ethics and philosophy of science and soon after began his public career. Despite apparent radicalism, he was basically conservative and, like Topelius, believed that Finland's best future was in peaceful development of her civilization in union with Russia. During the Crimean War, when some Finnish emigrees supported reuniting Finland with Sweden and hinted that efforts to make Finnish Finland's official language was a Russian plot to weaken resistance by disuniting Finns, Snellman violently protested against these charges in an article (1858) that cost him some popularity; in Sweden he was openly called a traitor courting Russian favor. In 1863, when the rebellion in Poland stirred hope in Sweden that Finland would follow the example to become independent, Snellman again protested; his protests made partially possible the subsequent reforms in Finland.

Besides the fiction he wrote in his youth, Snellman wrote literary criticism[64] in which he was consistent with his philosophical and political theories. Although he did not reject all Swedish writing in Finland, he felt that the best literature was that which reflected the spirit of the time and the national feeling of its country. He admired the French poet Béranger's patriotic compositions on Napoleon's wars, but Shakespeare left him cold because he had captured nothing of the spirit of English national feeling in his time (one cannot help wondering how much Snellman knew about Shakespeare).[65] He did not appreciate Runeberg's *King Fjalar* as he considered the theme a conflict between family and state, but was enthusiastic about *Ensign Stål*. He criticized *Vårt Land* for containing too much of Finland's natural beauties and too little of the spirit that moves a nation to great deeds, but he admired very much *Döbeln vid Jutas* for an unknown reason. Perhaps he was attracted not because the poem conformed to his ideals but because it appealed to his emotions. While in Germany and

Sweden, Snellman had become involved in discussions on religion. Some of Hegel's followers, called leftists, maintained that his system was atheistic; although Snellman did not support these extreme ideas, he declared that he belonged to the "moderate left."[66] Von Döbeln claims to be a freethinker in his battlefield monologue, although in actual life he was not known as such:

> I'm called freethinker, and I count it glorious;
> Freeborn I am, and so my thought is free.
> . . . .
> The slave may court his god with genuflection;
> I cannot cringe and grovel for protection,
> I seek no favor, ask for no reward.
> I would but stand here happy in Your presence,
> With fervent heart but yielding no obeisance;
> That prayer a free man's soul may still afford.
> . . . .
> How shall I speak to You? My God, my brother,
> Giver of victory, my thanks to You![67]

Snellman was not an atheist, but he wanted freedom to criticize the established religion; moreover, he had an abrupt character, attacked opponents violently, made many enemies, and became involved in polemics to the end of his life.

His lasting influence was not as a scholar but as a journalist and a statesman, and the reforms he originated in this capacity are still remembered. One is the decree establishing Finnish as one of the official languages, published by the emperor in 1863.

Fredrik Cygnaeus (1807-81), although he wrote poetry, is mainly known as a literary critic, scholar, and supporter of Aleksis Kivi. He was a decided original, sporting bushy whiskers and an ample cloak which he used for dramatic effect when orating; once, when he had mislaid the cloak, he refused to speak until another was found. His appearance was often caricatured. Runeberg, referring to the slowness of his studies, published *The Last Graduate*, a humorous imitation of *The Last Skald* by E. G. Geijer, the Swedish poet. R. W. Ekman, a painter well known in his time, drew a picture in which Minerva and Apollo play battledore and shuttlecock with his head,[68] an allusion to his hesitations in deciding whether to devote himself to history or literature. Somewhat priggish at times, Cygnaeus did not always appreciate such jokes, but he was a kind and intelligent person who had both wide knowledge of and good taste in literature and literary theories of his time. While still studying at Helsinki, he taught at the Officers' School of the Finnish Army[69] and, after graduation (1839), at various secondary schools in Helsinki. He was lecturer at the university. From 1843 through 1847 and in 1850 he journeyed to Germany, France, and Italy. In 1848 he became professor of history, in 1854 professor of comparative literature (the Finnish title was and is "aesthetics and modern [not classical] literature"), from 1865 to 1866 he acted as vice-rector of the university, and he received the titles of doctor *honoris causa* (1860) and Counsellor of State (1867).

He began his life work by publishing some historical research on Hannibal (Latin, 1839), on the war of 1741-42 in Finland (1843), and, after his journey abroad, information on North European history found in foreign archives and libraries (1848). Thereafter he published only two biographical articles on Finnish officers who participated in the 1808-09 war and devoted himself to literature, though his interest in history is apparent in his works in this field. In 1853, just before he was appointed professor of literature, he published a work on Eric XIV, king of Sweden, as a dramatic character, sustaining that literature must always be solidly based on history. In his first public lecture after the appointment, he spoke of the "rights and duties of historic drama toward history itself" and sharply criticized inaccuracies he had found in the works of Topelius and others. He did admire Runeberg and *The Tales of Ensign Stål*, but he explicitly noted that the work was not and should not be criticized as a historical document. He concluded that *The Tales* were dramatic rather than epic in character, an implied evaluation. Hegel and Vischer considered drama the highest form of literature, a view shared by many in Finland, e.g., Runeberg, Snellman, Topelius, and Cygnaeus. Cygnaeus, consequently, attempted to find dramatic qualities in every literary work he liked, including the *Kalevala*.

As it was then fashionable to define the national spirit of every people, Topelius decided in 1851 that the Finnish national spirit was "deeply epic," but a few months later, after reading the *Kullervo* episode of *Kalevala*, he was no longer sure. He found Kullervo a tragic personality comparable to the heroes of Aeschylus and the episode "a tragedy in an epic form."[70] Cygnaeus agreed and then wrote his own analysis of the Finnish national character, which appeared in *Det tragiska elementet i Kalevala* ('The Tragic Element in *Kalevala*,' 1853). He contended that the national character and, consequently, Finnish poetry were not epic in essence. He found lyric traits in the national character, but stressed especially the violent contrasts found in the poetry and nature of Finland, which-were reflected in the dramatic elements of the *Kalevala* (the *Kalevala* was then considered genuine folk poetry arranged for publication by Lönnrot). Cygnaeus found Kullervo vastly superior as a character to Job or the heroes of the Greek tragedies; only Shakespeare's creations equalled him. During the entire nineteenth century Europe was plagued with this mania for grading authors and works and for lofty, meaningless disquisitions into Supreme Good, Truth, Spirit of History, Progress, Tradition, National Spirit, etc.; Cygnaeus, with his love for rhetoric, was a natural victim of this fashion. That he still made many penetrating observations about his subjects is a credit to his intelligence. Also, Finland, intoxicated by the pace and significance of her development after the 1850s, bestowed exaggerated praise indiscriminately on all its newly flourishing intellectual and artistic activities, an attitude disturbingly in evidence well into this century.

Although he considered drama the highest art form, Cygnaeus appreciated lyrical qualities in Runeberg's poetry, his descriptions of Finland's natural beauties and simple folk life. He added this peaceful, idyllic trait to the national character, finding it in the works of Franzén, Creutz, and Frese. Calling Frese the most Finnish of all the poets who wrote in Swedish, Cygnaeus composed one of his best poems to his memory (1859). He understood Aleksis Kivi's genius and assisted him financially as well as in other ways. In 1865 he published favorable criticism of Kivi's comedy, *The Cobblers on the Heath*, and was instrumental in securing the government's literary prize for it. At the Society for Finnish Literature, he praised *Seven Brothers*, recommending it for publication; later he defended it against Ahlquist's attacks.

Cygnaeus's numerous poems were often based on literary subjects, addressed to Schiller, Byron, the Swedish poet Geijer, Frese, Runeberg, the Polish hero Kosciuszko, Victor Hugo, and others. The good ones are exceptional, for most show his love for rhetoric and often whimsical word play. His contemporaries, beginning with Runeberg, criticized them sharply, but Cygnaeus ignored them.

His great appreciation for drama led him to express the wish for the foundation of a Finnish theater, but he did not believe that it could soon be done. His hope, however, was fulfilled earlier than he expected, in 1872.

Johan Jakob Nervander (1805-48), who was the center of student gatherings in Turku and, with Runeberg, a founder of the Saturday Society, was primarily a scientist. His father had died and left a poor family when Nervander was quite young. As a student, he had financial difficulties but was a brilliant scholar who passed his examinations with the highest marks. After working as a tutor in wealthy families at Tampere and other places (like Topelius, he wrote a poem on Kangasala's natural beauties), he was appointed lecturer in physics at the University of Helsinki (1829), associate professor (1832), acting professor (1838), and professor (1845). Founder and director of the university's magnetic and meteorological observatory, he was well known abroad for his discoveries in electricity and was invited to teach at Jena (Germany). He preferred to remain in Finland, however.

Maintaining an active interest in literature and art, he published poetry regularly, and his conversational talents made him the center of the Saturday Society. His private life was unconventional. While still a tutor, he fell in love with a young woman of good family, with whom he lived in a secret, common-law marriage for many years before wedding her in the church.[71] It was an unhappy union because of the wife's jealousy; Nervander fell in love with another young woman who returned his feelings but broke with him when she discovered his marriage. They remained friends, met at the Saturday Society, and wrote poetry to each other (the girl had seemingly real literary talent). Nervander was ever tormented by contrasting emotions and was, despite his success, often unhappy, bitter, and sarcastic. He suffered from an ailment Runeberg thought common among Ostrobotnians and called "the Ostrobotnian tapeworm" (envy).[72] Near the end of his life he quarreled bitterly with Snellman about the language question and Finland's political situation. Snellman had been a close friend since they had both studied at Turku and deeply regretted the argument. After Nervander's untimely death, due to smallpox, Snellman wrote warmly of him in his newspaper and two years later provided Nervander's *Selected Works* with a biographical notice.

Nervander's poetry reflects his life's difficulties, sometimes happy and mildly sensuous in its praise of love and invitation to enjoy life while it lasts, e.g., *Morgonhelsning* ('A Greeting in the Morning'), sometimes expressive of sadness at parting or love's sufferings. In 1830 he translated the works of Ludwig I, king of Bavaria, known as a protector of arts and letters, whose torn, unhappy personality appealed to him. In 1840 he published *Jephtas bok. En Minnes-Sång i Israel* ('The Book of Jephthah. A Memorial Song in Israel'), a long poem whose subject was taken from the Bible (Judges II); in its postface he expressed regret that old Hebrew poetry had not been studied from an artistic viewpoint. This interest was due in part to his previous acquaintance with Professor Jakob Bonsdorff, a specialist in Oriental languages who had translated sections of the Bible directly from Hebrew into Swedish verse. Nervander's complex poem adds Oriental pomp and color to the Old Testament story. It compares the life of a man and woman to the river Jordan and the brook Cedron, which flow into the Dead Sea and gives the daughter of Jephthah a passionate love for freedom. As a cycle of poems, this work won the lesser gold medal of the Swedish Academy in 1832; Nervander later added prose passages to connect the poetic sections. The subject of a short poem by Nervander, *Dödens vaggsång* ('The Lullaby of Death'), is from Finnish folklore, the same motif that Kivi later used in *Sydämeni laulu* ('The Song of My Heart'). As he devoted more and more time to scientific work, Nervander gave up poetry. He is reported to have remarked to Cygnaeus, when Runeberg published *The Moose Hunters*, that Finland was too poor to keep more than one poet at a time. Indirect recognition of his friend's superiority appears in the parable *Den talande stenen i Mekka* ('The Speaking Stone in Mecca'); the stone praises Mohammed when he is despised but remains silent when he has become the leader of his nation.

Lars Jacob Stenbäck (1811-70), who adopted the ideas of the revivalist movement, was actually ordained a priest in 1842, after experiencing a religious conversion while studying humanities at Helsinki. As the revivalist movement was opposed by the church, he met with many difficulties. In 1839 he became editor of a religious weekly that was suppressed in 1841 and was refused appointment as university lecturer. When the church was reconciled with the movement, Stenbäck became headmaster of the lower secondary school in Vaasa (1846) and spent one semester as professor of education and pedagogics at Helsinki (1855). In 1856 he was made incumbent of the parish of Isokyrö in Ostrobotnia, where he remained until his death from tuberculosis, before which he was partially paralyzed and totally blind.

Much like John Bunyan,[73] he was continually tortured, without reason, by the feeling that he was utterly sinful and worthless, and then exalted by the conviction that God had given him His grace to save him. Convinced that all art was sinful, he decided never to write any poetry; but on the university's two hundredth anniversary, in 1840, his friends urged him to publish a collection of his poems; Nervander's *Book of Jephthah* appeared on the same occasion. Stenbäck began each of the collection's two sections with a new sonnet, the second ending with the self-reproach that, "although the poet is in Christian garments clad, the heathen is still dwelling in his heart."[74] In the third edition of his poems in 1868, he again condemned poetry as the enemy of religion and wrote in the *Epilogue*: "Yet one I know far higher on this earth than the song of the poet, it is the majesty of God's truth. . . ." From 1853 he worked on the committee appointed to compose the Swedish hymnal for the church of Finland. Hoping to earn enough money to build a school in his parish, he published a proposal including five of his own hymns, but neither the church nor the public appreciated it. It was Topelius who brought this difficult task to an end.

Despite his inner conflicts, Stenbäck gave great care to the form of his poems; in this respect he was perhaps the most accomplished artist of his time in Finland. He often chose elaborate regular patterns like the sonnet or the Arab ghazel, which the Finnish poets knew from the works of Fr. Rückert, a German scholar and poet. Stenbäck often used as a stylistic device the repetition of a line throughout the poem, especially in those composed as ghazels, in which the same rhyme recurs from beginning to end, giving a musical character to the works. Such devices stressed the poem's central idea. *Den väcktes suck* ('The Sigh of the Convert') is built on a three-word rhyme scheme in a pattern varied in each stanza. Such a *tour de force* could not be very long; this poem has only twelve lines, but gives a powerful, moving picture of Stenbäck's spiritual struggle: "My heart is a heap of smoking ruins (*ruiner*), over which a storm is howling (*hviner*) and, sometimes the sun also shining (*skiner*); the storm is sin, the sunshine is the grace of God; and, although I tremble at the howling of the storm, although I rejoice, perhaps in the sunshine, I love but the smoking ruins." Other poems are more resigned, such as *Till Sorgen* ('To Sorrow'), in which "mild mother sorrow" is invoked at each stanza's end to carry suffering humans through this world to heaven; some are even joyful, e.g., the first from the series *Accorder* ('Chords'), opening *Guds barn jag är;* / *o, saliga ro och glädje* ('I am God's child; / O, blissful peace and joy'), and the second, built on two rhymes, ending "I rest on my Jesus' breast (*bröst*), I rest by his heart (*hjerta*), He gives me life and light and solace (*tröst*), he takes away all pain (*smärta*)." On the occasion of his polemic with Runeberg in connection with the revivalist movement, each translated some poems by the German L. Th. Kosegarten, *Legends*, to support his views. Runeberg selected those showing God's presence in nature and his love for all creatures; Stenbäck chose those expressing self-denial and rejection of the world.

Although **Josef Julius Wecksell** (1838-1907) was younger than these authors, his active life ended in 1862, when he was committed to a mental hospital. After Frese he was the first real Swedish poet in Finland (just as Kivi was the first Finnish poet), that is, a poet by profession who had no other career. This kind of writer had long been common in West European countries, but all Finland's previous poets, though some possessed great talent, were professors, bishops, statesmen, or men of some other profession. In his brief career Wecksell produced a large quantity of work, not all of the best quality, of course. He realized that and chose carefully the poems he published in a collection in 1860. He was born in Turku, where he first went to school, and began writing at age thirteen or fourteen. Although his age was not absolutely exceptional, the freedom with which he wrote about humorous, erotic subjects surprised and even shocked later critics. These writings were not published, but, when he was sixteen years old, his light comedy, *Tre friare* ('The Three Suitors'), was produced in Turku and then in Helsinki; six years later, several performances were given in Stockholm. A Finnish critic and essayist has pointed out that it was unfortunate that Wecksell was born in mid-nineteenth-century Finland with its strict morals and precise ideas about what and how a poet should write.[75] Wecksell followed the model of poetry set by Runeberg and Topelius, but, with his keen sense for the tragic and ironic, he greatly admired Byron and Heine, and his poetry consequently reflects his inner tension. Contemporary critics complained that he often destroyed his descriptions of delicate feelings with parodic remarks, and one warned him that Byron's demoniac, disharmonic philosophy, to become sublime, needed social conditions far more developed than those Finland offered, a surprising statement in an age of official idealism.[76] Wecksell also admired the more harmonious Schiller, to whose memory he wrote a poem in 1859, but *Don Juans avsked från livet* ('Don Juan's Farewell to Life'), inspired by Byron, is far more interesting. The hero sums up his life in bitter maxims and concludes that life is empty and absurd. Still more original is the monologue *Almquist* (named for the Swedish poet who in 1851 had become involved in an affair of embezzlement, blackmail, and poisoning and fled to the United States). He is presented preparing the poison and considering the consequences of his planned act in light of the world's standards for morals and action. The poem offers no conclusion except that the individual's conscience determines the morality of an act. Though brief, the poem has many contrasts and finally expresses the poet's yearning for innocence and purity, a pale, lilac blue flower, under which there is, however, a thought "lascivious, bestial like Messalina's." His shorter poems are more conventional, frequently expressing contrast between love and the impossibility of its fulfillment, attended frequently by tragedy. In *Fågeln* ('The Bird') a bird flies over the sea toward the "gates of gold and ruby" of the sunrise, only to sink into the waves. In *Demanten på marssnön* ('The Diamond on the Snow in March') the diamond, an ice crystal on the snow, melts and vanishes under a sunbeam's loving kiss. In *När och fjerran* ('Near and Far Away') two lovers feel that they are close to each other even if forests, lakes, and mountains separate them, but, when they meet, they see endless desert between them. In *Stjernorna* ('The Stars') two stars, millions of miles apart, love each other and see their brightness, not knowing that they are both darkness and dust.

Wecksell's best-known work is the tragedy *Daniel Hjorth*. He was present at its first performance in 1862 in Helsinki, but his mind was already clouded, and he was unable to enjoy its success. It is occasionally performed today; stripped of its romantic paraphernalia, the subject should have strong appeal in the contemporary world of civil wars, rebellions, social strife, and foreign intervention. Daniel Hjorth actually lived in Finland at the time of the play's action, but, except for the name and general setting, Wecksell freely invented the incidents. In the late sixteenth century there was a war in Sweden and Finland between the lawful ruler Sigismund, also king of Poland, and his nephew Charles, who eventually won and became King Charles IX (his son was the great Gustavus Adolphus). The Finnish nobility, led by Admiral Klaus Fleming, supported Sigismund, but the country population, aroused by Charles's agents and irritated by Fleming's harsh rule, revolted. They were rapidly crushed and their leaders executed; Charles later won and took a merciless revenge on the Finnish nobility, many members of which were beheaded. This uprising became known as the War of the Maces, because the rebels were supposed not to have had other weapons, and has often been treated by Finnish scholars and writers. Cygnaeus wrote two plays, *Claes Flemings tider* ('The Times of Klaus Fleming,' 1851) and *Hertig Johans ungdomsdrömmar* ('Duke John's Dreams in His Youth,' 1854). Others were Gabriel Lagus's *Klubbhövdingen* ('The Leader of the Rebels,' 1869) and K. R. Malmström's *Erik Fleming* (1867; about Klaus Fleming's father), but none of these had lasting value. In Wecksell's play Daniel Hjorth, a young man whose home has been burnt and father beheaded on Fleming's order, has been brought up in Fleming's family. Charles's troops are besieging the castle of Turku, the last stronghold of the Finnish nobility, and Hjorth plans to deliver it into the hands of the enemy because he feels despised and slighted in his aristocratic surroundings due to his low birth. However, he recognizes his debt of gratitude to Fleming and has sworn loyalty to King Sigismund. Added is the story of his unhappy love for a girl of high birth whose death reproduces almost to every particular Ophelia's end in *Hamlet*, but the play's chief interest lies in Hjorth's moral and political conflict.

In the nineteenth century it was customary in Finland to publish poetic "calendars" or "albums," i.e., collections of poems written by well-known poets, less-known poets, and would-be poets; some became well known through these albums, others never outgrew them, but there was such a constant flow of these publications that in Finland a word has been coined to designate poets who wrote mainly or only for them, *albumirunoilijat* 'album poets.'[77] A few of their poems have remained popular, especially those set to music, e.g., **Emil von Qvanten's** *Suomis sång* ('The Song of Suomi,' 1844; music by Fr. Pacius), in which the Finnish name for Finland, *Suomi*, is used in a Swedish text. Von Qvanten (1827-1903) was one of the few Finns who hoped that Finland would be reunited with Sweden, and, consequently, he had to leave his country. He settled in Sweden and wrote continuously about Finland for newspapers; he also lived in other European countries, including Italy, where he died.

Besides Topelius there were few noteworthy Swedish prosaists in nineteenth-century Finland, except two women, Runeberg's wife and Sara Wacklin. **Fredrika Runeberg** (*née* Tengström; 1807-79) had a strong, independent character and a sharp eye for the defects and hypocrisies of her time. She resented the dependent position of women in that period, but, rather than express her feelings in direct attack on existing institutions, she used irony as her weapon. She assisted her husband in publishing *Helsingfors Morgonblad* and, with his encouragement, wrote essays and short stories, a collection of which was published in 1861 titled *Teckningar och drömmar* ('Drawings and Dreams'). It includes a group of stories, *Facetter ur kvinnans liv* ('Facets out of Woman's Life'), in which positive examples show that women in her time were denied the opportunity to learn or practice a profession, but the authoress often preferred more romantic settings, as the titles indicate: *Salik Sardar Khans maka* ('The Wife of Salik Sardar Khan'), *Kvinnan på Tongatabu* ('The Woman of Tongatabu'), *Kuhinanuis dotter* ('The Daughter of Kuhinanui'), and so forth; the reader travels from the East to Polynesia and even the arctic tundras, everywhere meeting the same women with proud hearts, strong emotions, and compassionate minds. *De vackra orden* ('Beautiful Words'), however, is much more prosaic and demonstrates the effectiveness of her irony. A boy falls into an ice-covered river; a young man laments to the bystanders in "beautiful words" his sad fate and the terrible loss to his parents, but another, swearing at the boy who is endangering his own and others' lives, rescues him at personal risk, spanks him soundly to teach him to be more careful, and departs, leaving everyone shocked at his brutality. By the end of the story the authoress passes to more general considerations and criticizes the superficiality of her time. Good manners, she says, forbid enthusiasm; therefore, Beethoven's music is considered nice, the crash of the sea driven by a tempest against the rocks charming, and Shakespeare's tragedies quite pretty. She also wrote two historical novels, *Fru Catharina Boije och hennes döttrar* ('Lady Catharina Boije and Her Daughters,' 1858) and *Sigrid Liljeholm* (name, 1862). The latter is set during the War of the Maces, and even Daniel Hjorth is among the characters.

Sara Wacklin (1790-1846) was born in Oulu, the home town of Franzén, where Snellman also went to school. Her father died when she was young, and she earned her living as a tutor and teacher. She saved enough money to journey to Paris to study education, and she had hopes of being appointed teacher at a government-supported girls' school, but, embittered by her difficulties, she moved to Stockholm in 1843. There, encouraged to write about her life, she published three volumes titled *Hundrade minnen från Österbotten* ('Hundred Memories from Ostrobotnia') in 1844 and 1845. The book was a success—such memoirs were very popular then in Sweden—but she did not live long enough to enjoy her achievement. The stories describe life in a small town (Oulu, despite its small size, was an important commercial center with shipowners and merchants who conducted a lively trade with all parts of the world), its everyday incidents, its inhabitants—important and unimportant—and the great events which disturbed its quiet life. Sara Wacklin was neither naive nor sentimental and unhesitatingly portrayed the foibles of her contemporaries without regard to their social status. Resenting the dominant position of men in her society, she described women with strong wills and sharp tongues who knew how to put their lords and masters in their places. Her good-natured irony extended to public matters; she told of the dutiful eagerness with which Oulu's inhabitants received important person- alities who visited their town, including the king of Sweden, Russian generals and dukes, and even Emperor Alexander I, and vividly pictured the terrible fire which destroyed the greatest part of Oulu in 1822. Her descriptions of life and customs in another age are historically interesting, of course, but also reveal her own intelligent, attractive personality.

Literature in Finnish from the
Beginning of the Nineteenth Century through Kivi

LITTLE WAS WRITTEN IN FINNISH before the nineteenth century except the occasional poems mentioned in Chapter II and the Bible translations. After Agricola had published his New Testament and parts of the Old, many church members and official committees labored to translate the Scriptures, which were finally printed in 1642; a new edition appeared in 1685, a third in 1758, and a fourth, slightly modified, in 1776. The latter was reprinted several times until 1852, but a complete, new authorized version was not issued until 1938. A development of literary Finnish through the seventeenth and eighteenth centuries, though slow and inconspicuous compared to that in the nineteenth century, especially the second half, can be followed in these Bible translations.

Agricola, who lived and worked in Turku, fashioned his language not on the dialect of that city, but on the dialect of southwest Finland in general, and thus established a tradition for his followers. However, as this dialect differs even from its immediate neighbors,[78] persons with another linguistic background gradually discarded forms typical of it, improved Agricola's uncouth spelling, and modified his syntax, often reminiscent of Swedish and German. Consequently the eighteenth-century Bible eventually took on an appearance sometimes not unlike the Finnish of today.

Antti Lizelius (1708-95), a minister who wrote the 1758 and 1776 editions, also published in 1776 the first Finnish newspaper, *Suomenkieliset Tieto-Sanomat* ('A Newspaper in Finnish'; Lizelius himself coined the word *tieto-sanomat*, today *sanomalehti*). It appeared twice a week and contained mainly practical advice to farmers, instructive and moral writings, and so on. There was little actual news—in February readers were informed that "last November, the Americans have won two forts from England."[79] Despite

Lizelius's position it contained no religious writings, and Martti Rapola has suggested in *Kirjallisuus* II this lack as a possible reason that it did not last longer. The revivalist movements, already in existence in the eighteenth century, and even part of the clergy had made the people so suspicious of the secular that nonreligious writing was rejected, regardless of its content. Lizelius participated in many practical activities and had the minutes of his parish council written in Finnish, an act without precedent in his time, but his efforts passed almost without notice. In 1811, when Gustaf Renvall praised *Suomenkieliset Tieto-Sanomat* for its good, pure Finnish, he did not know who the author was.

Besides Lizelius, a few other church members in the eighteenth century wrote Finnish prose which was important in the history of the language and widely read in its time. **Kristfrid Ganander** (1741-90) composed practical works on medicine, collected folklore, from which he published one volume of riddles (*Suomalaiset arwotuxet vastausten kansa*, 1783) and one of tales (*Uudempia uloswalituita satuja*, 1784), and left the manuscript of a Finnish dictionary (*Nytt finskt lexicon*), which, because of its numerous quotations, is a valuable source of materials for linguists and folklorists. **Juhana Wegelius** the younger (1693-1764), whose father was one of the first ministers in Finland to be influenced by the pietist movement in Germany, published a collection of sermons called *Se Pyhä Ewangeliumillinen Walkeus* ('The Holy Light of the Gospels,' 2 vols., 1747 and 1749), which were long popular.[80] Three editions were published in the nineteenth century, the last in 1896, and many of its metaphors are still familiar to members of the revivalist movement, e.g., the life of Christ and the faithful as a flight of stairs, each of which must be climbed before the next can be reached. **Johan** (Abrahaminpoika) **Frosterus** (1720-1809), who worked in his youth as a tutor in Count Carl Creutz's family with the future poet as one of his pupils, is often mentioned in Finland as the author of instructive works, especially the first treatise in Finnish on natural history.[81] This treatise was published in 1791 as *Hyödyllinen huwitus luomisen töistä, yxinkertaisille awuxi Jumalan hywyden tundoon ja palwelukseen* ('A Useful Entertainment on the Works of Creation, to Help the Humble to Recognize and Worship the Benevolence of God'); following the title are the words of the Bible: "And God saw everything that he had made, and, behold, it was very good " (Gen. 1:31). The work proposes to teach as much religion as science and is somewhat reminiscent of Forsius's *Physica*, for descriptions of natural phenomena are always followed by praise to God, whose might and benevolence are therein demonstrated to mankind. Frosterus is reputed to have been moved to compose his work possibly by the influence of a similar treatise written by an Englishman, William Derham, and published in Swedish translation in 1760, *Physico-Theologie Eller Til Gud ledande Naturkunnighet* ('Physico-Theology or a Natural History Leading to God'). This work professed to be a defense of

Christianity against atheism, but its general plan is different from that which Frosterus followed. In any case, such apologies were rather common at that time; in France Bernardin de Saint-Pierre published *Études de la Nature* in 1784 and Châteaubriand *Le Génie du Christianisme* in 1802—both use the same kind of argument. Saint-Pierre was perhaps a better writer, but Frosterus was certainly a better scholar. Whereas the Frenchman tried to disprove well-known scientific facts with his own fanciful inventions, Frosterus accepted up-to-date knowledge, which he knew well and explained accurately. He described the size of the earth, its distance from the sun and fixed stars, knew that wind is caused by variations in atmospheric pressure, was familiar with the law of conservation of matter, pointed out that all natural phenomena have natural causes and are not "ghosts," but he concluded that they were an invitation to man to recognize and worship the power and greatness of God. The book had considerable success; three editions were issued in the author's lifetime, and the ninth was issued in 1850. It is considered the best prose work written in Finland during Swedish rule.[82] It was still used in 1830 as a textbook for Finnish at the University of Helsinki.

Although the Russian conquest of Finland in 1809 was politically important, it left the daily life of the people almost untouched. They could even feel that, in the phrasing of Alexander I, Finland had been elevated to the rank of a nation, and this idea led to the desire for a national language. We have already discussed the formulation of this program by the Turku Romanticists, but they, like many after them who shared their ideas, wrote and spoke in Swedish. A few writers, however, used Finnish: Samuel Berg, Abraham Poppius, Jacob Judén, (who has been mentioned), and Carl Gottlund. Berg and Poppius, who wrote poetry, and Gottlund, who was a folklorist, were in contact with the Turku Romanticists, whereas Judén (Finn. Juteini) lived in Viipuri.

Abraham Poppius (1793-1866) belonged to the group of Finns who studied at the University of Uppsala in Sweden. While still at Turku, where he studied history and Finnish from 1813, he collected folk poetry and was one of the first in Finland also to transcribe melodies to which it was sung. While studying he wrote the poems for which he is remembered, although later, when he became a minister of the church, he published some in newspapers. They number scarcely more than twenty. The first ones appeared in *Mnemosyne* and a short-lived paper edited by Arwidsson. Poppius was influenced by the Swedish romantic poets, the well-known Danish author Oehlenschläger, and classical Greek models; approximately five of his poems are taken from Anacreon. The subjects he chose in his youth are typical of the sentimental, romantic school and include *Perhoisen synty* ('The Birth of the Butterfly') and *Rakkauden synty* ('The Birth of Love'). *Laulu* ('The Song') speaks of the soul's yearning to be freed from the fetters of the body, and both *Horjutessa* ('Wavering') and *Sala-itku* ('Secret Tears') treat unhappy love. He wrote many of his poems in the Finnish folk meter, which he tried to vary by inserting a half line of four syllables between the full eight-syllable ones; he also skillfully used metrical patterns from the poetry of other countries. His later poems are quite different, often written in a humorous vein. His artistic taste was sure, and he wrote faultless, melodious Finnish, but his works were too few in number to make him really influential in the literary life of his country.[83]

Much the same can be said of **Samuel Gustaf Berg** (1803-52), known in Finland under his pseudonym **Kallio** (Finn. translation of his real name). After taking a law degree at the University of Turku, he held a post at the Court of Appeals of Vaasa for a while. His eyes were very weak, and, though he spent a long time in Sweden and Denmark seeking a cure, he eventually became blind. He died as a children's teacher in Finland. He published only six poems during his life, but they are six very good poems. Although two were obviously inspired by Goethe, one has classical overtones, and one is the familiar fable of the ant and the grasshopper, they are new and individual. Its setting is entirely Finnish, and no moral is emphasized; instead, we feel that the poet's sympathy is with the careless and gay singer.

Sirkka lauloi lystiksensä
oman intonsa ilosa,
huviksensa hyräeli,
mättähällä mesisellä,
simakukkien keralla.

Päivä paistoi. Nurmen nunnut,
kukat kullaset, keolla,
kattelivat, kuuntelivat
kun hän laulella liritti.

"Mitä laulat laiska roisto,
hullutuksia hyräilet?
Teehän työtä; eihän vatta
täyvy tyhjistä loruista;
raipat selkään semmosille,"
toru muuan muurahainen,
ylen itara itikka
sirkan syytöntä iloa.

Sirkka lauloi lystiksensä,
oman intonsa ilosa,
huviksensa hyräeli,
mättähällä mesisellä
simakukkien keralla.

The grasshopper gay
Was a-singing, was a-sitting
Was a-humming for fun

On a dewy little hillock
Where the honey-flowers grew.

The bright sun was shining
The golden little flowers
On the meadow were listening
To his chirping so gay.

"You lazy little beggar
You shameless singer
Had better start working
It's not just empty music
That can fill up your belly"
The ant was a-grumbling,
A miserly crawler,
At the other's merry song.

The grasshopper gay
Was a-singing, was a-sitting
Was a-humming for fun
On a dewy little hillock
Where the honey flowers grew.

Like many other Finnish poems, this one is popular as a song. In three others Kallio deals with unhappy love in a subdued, dreamy manner; in both *Ystävälleni* ('To My Friend' or, perhaps better, 'To My Beloved') and *Runo* ('A Poem'), the changing seasons serve as background for the poet's feelings, and both achieve musical effect by repetition of the same motif. In *Ystävälleni* the description of changing seasons is accompanied by repetition of *Muistan sua* ('I remember you') at the beginning of each stanza and *Millon muistelet minua? Millon?* ('When do you remember me? When?') at the end. *Runo* tells first of the vanishing summer—*Pois meni merehen päivä, / poijes kullana keränä, / läntisille lainehille; / meni kevät, meni kesä* ('The sun sank into the sea / sank as sphere of gold / into the western waves / the spring vanished, the summer vanished')—and then states that they will all return, but the poet's beloved will not. This poem, too, is well known as a choral composition. *Oma maa* has a classical exordium, *Vallan autuas se...*, reproducing the *Beatus ille* of Horace's well-known poem, rendered by "Happy the man..." in Pope's version or *Heureux qui, comme Ulysse* in Joachim du Bellay's sixteenth-century poem. It is written in the classical elegiac meter, which Kallio applied to the Finnish language with far greater skill than many later poets, and reflects Kallio's feeling of irretrievable loss at impending blindness and his nostalgia for Finland during his long stay abroad, ending with two oft-quoted lines:

Huoleti kiitelkööt muut Alppein seutuja kauniiks';
kauniimpi, kalliimpi on mulla mun syntymämaa.

67

> Well may the others give praise to the Alps and their beauty so mighty
> Fairer and brighter to me is my own country of birth.

As long as the upper classes in Finland were Swedish-speaking, a person of Finnish origin who attained a social position spoke Swedish and took a Swedish name. Classes at the university were given in Swedish only. When, under the influence of nationalist ideas, a counter-evolution began in the nineteenth century, Finnish names were reassumed or new ones invented. In 1906, on the one-hundredth anniversary of Snellman's birth, perhaps one hundred thousand persons changed their names to show their patriotism. Thus a number of figures in Finnish literary history are known under two names, e.g., Juhani Aho (Brofelt), Ilmari Kianto (Calamnius), Eino Leino (Lönnbohm; his brother Kasimir kept the old name), Maila Talvio (Winter), and Jaakko Juteini (Judén). Juteini was aggressively Finnish and always signed his works with his assumed Finnish name, not the Swedish Jacob Judén, his official designation.

Jaakko Juteini (1781-1855) came to the University of Turku in 1800 to study theology, which he dropped for humanities and Finnish. Porthan oriented his interests toward Finnish folklore, and Franzén advised him on the writing of poetry. He never completed his studies and, after holding various small posts in different parts of the country, came to Viipuri, where he was appointed secretary of the city council and notary public. He spent the rest of his life there. His outlook was typical of the rational, enlightened eighteenth century; he absorbed almost nothing of the romanticists except their interest in the Finnish language. Little in his works is of interest to contemporary readers, except from a historical viewpoint, whereas Poppius's and Kallio's poems—and even earlier ones—are still enjoyable. He was humane, well-meaning, and eager to help the poor and the suffering and had a passion for education and enlightenment. He resented the dependent position in which the Finnish-speaking population was kept by the Swedish upper classes. In 1804 he began literary activity by writing a poem to the memory of Porthan. He gave advice in verse on curing measles or malaria and praised Alexander I for his benevolence to the Finns. Between 1810 and 1819 he published no fewer than eleven volumes of verse and a long poem, on the history of Finland, the noble qualities of the Finns, and the use of Finnish in poetry, against loose living, superstition, excessive drinking (though he also wrote poems in praise of wine), envy, slander, greed, and other vices. His many attacks against grasping priests, corrupt judges, and incompetent officials made many enemies, but he never mentioned specific individuals. Although he became less aggressive after 1820, he clashed with the authorities over *Anteckningar af Tankar uti Varianta Ämnen* ('Thoughts Written Down on Various Subjects,' 1827), a prose work he wrote in Swedish, in which he expressed tolerant, liberal views on religion displeasing to the church authorities. He was indicted for spreading views contrary to the Evangelical-Lutheran confession, fined, and his book publicly destroyed, although a Court of Appeals later reversed the sentence.[84] The church, however, attained its goal; Juteini did not publish another book in sixteen years and carefully avoided controversial subjects in the few poems he sent to newspapers. With Poppius and others he edited a weekly publication, *Sanan Saattaja Viipurista*, for a while. Near the end of his life, Snellman's activity inspired him to write more verse, and the public recognized his merits when the University of Helsinki conferred on him the title of doctor *honoris causa*. Besides being almost alone in using Finnish for poetry and prose at that time, he produced a significant quantity of both and is always discussed in histories of Finnish literature, but there is hardly a better example than he that good intentions and industriousness do not make a poet. One of his poems, *Arvon mekin ansaitsemme* ('We Are Worth Respect Too'), set to a catching tune, has remained popular and is probably often considered an anonymous folksong.

Kaarle (Carl) **Aksel Gottlund** (1796-1872), best known as a folklorist, was a notorious original. He studied at the University of Uppsala and did his first scholarly works in folklore with great accuracy and care at a time when, for example, Lönnrot did not always indicate from where or under what circumstances he had transcribed the old poems he published. Gottlund found in the Dalarna province in central Sweden descendants of Finnish settlers who had arrived there in the sixteenth and seventeenth centuries and had preserved their old traditions, and in Finland he later found at Ritvala, a village in the district of Sääksmäki, southeast of Tampere, an old festival, probably dating from the Middle Ages, celebrated annually with songs and processions, which he described. This practical work is the best in Gottlund's activities; he was less successful in attempting to find the religious and philosophical background of Finnish folk poetry, but he was following the theories of German natural philosophers and metaphysicians greatly admired in Scandinavia at that time. His remarks about Ilmarinen, the mythical blacksmith who appears in a poem he discussed—"Here, *Ilmarinen* means the absolute god, but only from a certain point of view, that is, as an absolutely-subjective subject-objectivity. The *smithy* corresponds more or less to the concept of empty space. The *ashes* mean chaos, matter, or the lowest subject-objectivity, and, when Ilmarinen kindled the fire in the ashes with his breath, it meant that the Creator put his stamp on nature, in other words, that nature was lifted to the level of intelligence . . ."[85] —were less strange then than they seem today. He was the first to think that the Finnish epic songs were fragments of a great epic poem, which scholars should reconstruct. He became more and more eccentric and decided that the dialect of the province of Savo should be the basis for literary Finnish. The Battle of the Dialects was then going on, but most scholars were seeking a satisfactory compromise between old literary Finnish and the eastern dialects, not the composition of a completely new language based on an unremarkable dialect. Gottlund persisted in writing in it, however, or in a kind of Gottlundese, for he never fully mastered the form of speech he advocated. In 1831 and 1832 he published the first of the so-called literary albums in Finnish, *Otava eli Suomalaisia Huvituksia* ('Otava or Finnish Pastimes'), for which he translated several poems, including some by such classical Greek authors as Homer, Anacreon, and Sappho, trying to use a variety of new meters in Finnish. His oddities prevented him from attaining a settled position, and he was embittered; but he continued writing on several subjects, mainly Finnish history and language, though he also published some poems and short stories. He criticized the *Kalevala* violently when it appeared, for, although he approved of the idea, he thought Lönnrot's methods incorrect. Modern folklorists agree with his conclusion, but not for his reasons. Gottlund was in many respects a failure, but his practical work in folklore is still valuable; his descriptions of his journeys in Sweden to collect materials were published in Finland in 1928 and in Sweden in 1931.

Although no great author or poet wrote in Finnish in the first half of the nineteenth century, more and more works were in Finnish, and newspapers in that language also began to appear. In addition to von Becker's *Turun Viikko-Sanomat*, Pietari Ticklén and two friends started *Oulun Viikko-Sanomia* (1829-41, 1852-71), which published some of Ticklén's poems and some by F. P. Kemelli, Lönnrot edited *Mehiläinen* from 1836 to 1837 and worked for *Oulun Viikko-Sanomia* from 1852 to 1853, Snellman had *Maamiehen Ystävä* (1844), and Pietari Hannikainen controlled *Kanava, Sanansaattaja Viipurista* from 1845 to 1847. In Turku **Juhana Fredrik Granlund** (1809-74) rose from shop assistant to owner of an important printing press and published poetry, first popular and humorous, later religious. One poem, *Koto-maamme* ('Our Home Country'), has remained popular; Väinö Linna even borrowed its first line as a (half-ironic) title for one of his novels, *Täällä Pohjantähden alla* ('Here Under the Polar Star'), aware that the allusion would not go unnoticed in Finland.

The most influential Finnish writer of the period was **Elias Lönnrot** (1802-84), whose work is so significant to the language and spiritual life of Finland that he cannot be omitted from Finnish literary history though he wrote few original works. While a physician in Kajaani from 1833 to 1852, he made eleven long journeys to various parts of Finland, eastern Karelia, Estonia, and Ingria to collect folk poetry which he rearranged and published as the *Kalevala* (1st ed., 1835, 2nd ed. enlarged, 1849). We have mentioned his method—assembling lines from different popular poems (he rarely followed the same for more than ten lines) and thus creating a new work of almost all old materials, since he wrote only a few connecting passages.[86] In his sincere belief that he had reconstructed a genuine, old epic, he openly explained his methods. *Kalevala* was a success, and not until 1885 did Julius Krohn declare that it was "not at all fit to be taken as a basis for scholarly research."[87] It also attracted the attention of foreign scholars: M. A. Castrén, the Finnish linguist, translated the 1835 edition into Swedish in 1841; L. A. Léouzon le Duc made French translations of that edition in 1845 and of the 1849 edition in 1867; Karl Collan published a Swedish translation of the 1849 edition from 1864 through 1868, A. Schiefner a German one in 1852, F. Barna a Hungarian in 1871, M. Crawford an English in 1888, L. B. Belski a Russian in 1889, I. Cocchi an Italian in 1909, which was immediately followed in 1910 by P. E. Pavolini's and in 1912 by F. Di Silvestri-Falconieri's. Many others have also been published.

Besides the *Kalevala* Lönnrot published other folklore works, the *Kanteletar* ('Old Songs and Ballads of the Finnish People,' 1840-41),[88] a collection of proverbs (1842), a collection of riddles (1844), and a collection of magic formulas and incantations (1880). The *Kanteletar* was composed by the same method used for the *Kalevala*, with the same results: although the materials are genuine, it contains poems, such as the first one, *Eräskummanen kantele* ('The Marvelous Kantele'), which have no counterpart in folk poetry.[89] However, it received as much admiration as did the *Kalevala*, and Lönnrot himself, Runeberg, Snellman, and others soon translated many of the poems into Swedish.

Folklore was only part of Lönnrot's activity, which covered many fields, but was basically linguistic. Perhaps more than anyone else, he influenced the evolution of the Finnish language in the nineteenth century and supported the idea that the new form of expression should not be based on any one dialect, but on a combination of the old western literary tongue and elements from various popular forms of speech. He explained his views in theoretical articles and put them to practice in his writings and numerous translations, in which he coined Finnish words for many scientific and technical terms. He translated parts of the *Iliad* and the *Odyssey* into Finnish as well as some of Runeberg's poems, discussing in this connection the laws of Finnish prosody. He wrote a *History of Finland* (1839) with J. F. Cajan and a *History of Russia* (1840) with Kustaa Ticklén, a practical handbook on medicine (1839), a book on Finnish plants, *Flora Fennica—Suomen Kasvisto* (1860), and translated a handbook of law into Finnish (1863). He wanted Finnish equivalents for all foreign words, even those common to several European languages. This policy has been followed to the present, so that Finnish has become perhaps even more Finno-Ugric and less Indo-European than it need be. Many words used in most European languages have Finnish equivalents (e.g., 'electricity' *sähkö*, 'oxygen' *happi*, 'medicine' *lääketiede*, 'telescope' *kaukoputki*, 'science' *tiede*, 'telephone' *puhelin*, 'thermometer' *lämpömittari,* 'restaurant' *ravintola*). Even recent inventions and discoveries receive Finnish names, such as 'radar' *tutka* and 'plastic' *muovi*. However, this practice is not consistent, for 'philosophy' is *filosofia,* 'logic' *logiikka,*

71

'physics' *fysiikka*, 'music' *musiikki*, and so forth. The culmination of Lönnrot's linguistic activities was publishing, with A. Warelius, G. Cannelin, and others, a Finnish-Swedish dictionary (1880) of more than two hundred thousand words, of which he wrote the largest part, a gigantic effort. He was professor of Finnish at the University of Helsinki from 1853 to 1862, a founder of the Society for Finnish Literature and its chairman from 1854 to 1863, honorary member of many Finnish scientific and literary societies, doctor *honoris causa* of the University of Helsinki, knight of several Russian and foreign orders, and Counsellor of Chancery. Although he, too, received the veneration felt for the *Kalevala*, he remained modest and unassuming, with simple habits and little taste for public life.

Pietari Hannikainen (1813-99), publisher of *Kanava, Sanansaattaja Viipurista*, attended a school at which pupils were forbidden to speak Finnish. His name was there changed to Petter Hanén, but he later insisted on using the Finnish form. The humanities attracted him during his studies at the university, but, as his modest origin forced him to begin earning his living quickly, he chose the practical career of surveyor and worked in that capacity for many years. Interested in journalism and literature, however, he published his newspaper for approximately three years, until financial difficulties and continual harassment by the authorities caused him to discontinue it. Still, he managed to issue a periodical for farmers from 1849 to 1851 and a children's paper from 1856 to 1859; he was also chief editor of *Suometar* in Helsinki from 1863 to 1866. He died on his estate in Parikkala, in the eastern part of the country.

He was the first to write in Finnish plays actually staged. Although a retired major of the old Swedish-Finnish army, **Jaakko Fredrik Lagervall** (1787-1865) had published in 1834 an adaptation of *Macbeth* titled *Ruunulinna* and in 1847 biblical plays on Cain, Joseph and Judith. His work, for lack of merit, could not be considered seriously.[90] Hannikainen's works were all light, popular comedies ridiculing the foibles of the time, especially the fashion of adopting Swedish names. In 1845 Hannikainen published in his newspaper *Silmänkääntäjä* ('The Conjurer'), which was performed by amateur groups in two provincial towns in 1846 and 1847; in 1858 a drama group of Helsinki students played it in the capital. Snellman and Topelius praised it, but Cygnaeus was critical, for the plot is slight: a man who, by taking a resounding Swedish name and pretending to be a conjurer, swindles credulous country people and escapes. *Sukuylpeys* ('Family Pride'), *Joululahjukset* ('Christmas Presents'; *lahjukset* also means 'bribes'), and *Anttonius Putronius eli Antto Puuronen* (a pseudo-Swedish name and its Finnish equivalent) were also published in 1845 and 1846; the latter, an adaptation of a comedy by the famous Norwegian-Danish author Holberg, was performed in 1858 by the Helsinki students. The main character common to these plays is an honest farmer opposed to a conceited gentleman, who is a butt of ridicule.

72

Hannikainen also translated several plays, short stories, and poems by Shakespeare, Holberg, Cervantes, Schiller, Goethe, and Oehlenschläger and wrote literary and dramatic criticism, the first in Finnish. His production includes scores of short stories, often on historical subjects, such as *Salojärven kukkanen* ('The Flower of Salojärvi') set during the War of the Maces. They often bear the mark of hasty journalism and are chiefly based on thrilling, improbable incidents following each other in quick succession. He was an industrious writer rather than a great artist, but he was a pioneer in many fields, especially drama, and encouraged others to follow him.

In spite of all that has been written about artistic genius, there is no general definition of this term; a literary genius seems to be a figure read in several countries and considered a genius by his readers. Thus, an author of a small nation not widely read outside his native country cannot be proved a genius. Consequently the efforts of Finnish critics and scholars in that direction on behalf of **Aleksis Kivi** (officially **Aleksis Stenvall**, 1834-72) have been useless, and we must simply state, with certainty, that he was one of the greatest Finnish authors,[91] if not the greatest, not only in his lifetime (only Runeberg can be compared to him) but up to the present. He was also the first real author to write in Finnish (that is, author only by profession and not author and something else). By a mere reading of his works, one should be convinced of his strength of vision and depth of feeling, of his need to communicate with his fellow men through writing. His biography confirms his inner compulsion to write, for writing cost him whatever fortune he had, his physical and mental health, and his life—he died at the age of thirty-eight, insane.

In spite of the romantic impression these facts give, of misunderstood genius and proud spirit conquered in an unequal struggle with a prosaic world, Kivi remained until the last years of his life a strong, healthy, genial country boy who liked to roam the forests with his rifle on his shoulder, to swim, and to fish. He once wrote that he considered man's highest quality humor, "And, when I mention humor," he said, "I mean a fresh and natural one, not such as springs from a shipwreck suffered on the sea of life. I mean a sense for the comic, the ultimate foundation of which, after all, is a good but strong and healthy heart,"[92] but he often found that the only source of mirth in life's difficulties was alcohol, which hastened his death. He seems most like Robert Burns; both came from the country, were of modest origin but acquired education, were accepted, then rejected by society, could not find a stable position, drank too much, and died at almost the same age. More important is their attachment to their native soil, its traditions and its speech, less conspicuous, however, in Kivi than in Burns as far as the form of the language is concerned.

The son of a village tailor from Nurmijärvi, approximately twenty miles north of Helsinki, he never forgot his childhood environment and often located his works there, magnifying his memories with fantasy into vast, wild forests, swamps, and rugged mountains overrun with bears, wolves, and lynx. Actually Finland still is a thinly populated country, and quite close to the capital many species of wild animals were found at the beginning of the nineteenth century, although one of Kivi's characters remarks that the beasts of the forest are becoming more and more scarce. When he was twelve, his parents sent him to school in Helsinki with the hope of making him a gentleman. He literally went hungry during his studies, and his health was probably permanently injured then; he did not finish secondary school but managed, through private studies, to pass the university matriculation examination in 1857.[93] Desultorily he followed lectures by, among others, Cygnaeus, who influenced him most deeply, and Lönnrot, but he never took a degree. There was nothing desultory about his literary activities, however. He read widely: contemporary Finnish authors, like Runeberg, Topelius, and Cygnaeus; Swedish, such as Stagnelius, Atterbom, and Tegnér; classics in Swedish translation, e.g., Shakespeare, Cervantes, Dante, Homer, Virgil, and Aristophanes; and *Ossian*, which had an amazingly long popularity in Finland. He was familiar with the dramatist Holberg, who was greatly admired in Finland in the nineteenth century, and, at the Swedish theater of Helsinki, he saw plays by Molière and Schiller.

He wrote almost all of his works—three five-act tragedies, two long comedies, five short plays, five others either lost or not completed, approximately thirty poems, and a great novel—between 1860 and 1870, partially pressed by the ever-present need for money, although, except for occasional drinking sprees, he led a very frugal life. He often had to borrow money from friends, and the little money he earned with his writings went for payment of his debts. Between 1863 and 1870 he benefited from the hospitality of a woman several years older than he, Charlotta Lönnqvist, who took motherly care of him. Although there is no evidence that their relationship was unchaste, Kivi was chagrined by gossip and irritated by his dependent position. In his works, especially *Seven Brothers*, he describes with admiration strong, energetic men who conquer position through their own efforts. As Miss Lönnqvist did not live far from Helsinki, Kivi was able to go to the capital, visit friends, and even see one of his plays performed in 1869. (This year is considered the beginning of a Finnish theater in Finland.) Nevertheless, he continued to struggle financially, and his health gave out. At the end of 1870, the first symptoms of insanity appeared; early the next year he entered a mental hospital, and he died at the end of 1872.

Although influential persons, like Snellman, Lönnrot, Topelius, and Cygnaeus, gave him help and advice at the beginning of his career and Cygnaeus remained faithful to him, Kivi's relations with them were marked by stiffness and awkwardness. He most liked Cygnaeus, who was a solitary original somewhat like himself, and called him in letters, "the old man," but he remained aloof from the others, in spite of similarities in background to Lönnrot especially. He first planned to write in Swedish, but Cygnaeus and Snellman, to whom he showed an original short comedy, advised him to use Finnish, and he soon developed radical pro-Finnish views. Even in secondary school he sided with the Finns, and he became acquainted with a group of young people with various interests, including Emil Nervander, the son of J. J. Nervander, also known as a writer. At the university he met the poet and folklorist Julius Krohn (alias Suonio) and his two closest friends at the end of his life, Th. Rein and Kaarlo Bergbom, the founder of the Finnish theater. Bergbom was also among the founders of the Finnish-oriented periodical *Kirjallinen Kuukausilehti* published between 1866 and 1880, in which many of Kivi's works appeared. At the university students were grouped in organizations according to origin.[94] Kivi belonged to one with a majority of Swedish-speaking members, but he voiced his opinions there without hesitation. He remained a radical throughout his life; in 1869 he wrote to Rein that, instead of waiting, as some had recommended, in the matter concerning the foundation of a Finnish secondary school in Helsinki, a "strong and stern" article should be written for it and a newspaper founded to support the Finnish cause (though printed in Swedish; such a newspaper was created). He was too individual, however, to accept without protest all that was done for the Finnish cause; in a letter to Bergbom in the same year, he called its leaders fools and idiots and their language "a swill without any spirit or fire, tasting of wood."[95] He always wrote in a language influenced by the dialect of his native region and somewhat more like old literary Finnish than the modern tongue which was developing. (No one with a knowledge of modern Finnish should have difficulty in understanding him, however.)

He never married, though it is certain that he was in love at least twice. Even before he was a student, he asked for the first girl's hand, but her father, a well-to-do craftsman, disapproved. He wrote the second girl, an innkeeper's daughter, several letters, but the relationship never progressed further. Other letters hint bitterly at the cheap kind of sexual adventures he had. Significantly, we find in his works characters who are at odds with their neighbors and surroundings, find adjusting to society difficult, and have unhappy love affairs. He liked to describe simple country people realistically and wished to have an optimistic or, as he said, humorous philosophy. Some of his works are broad comedies or farces, such as *Kihlaus* ('The Betrothal,' 1866) or *Nummisuutarit* ('The Cobblers on the Heath,' 1864), and there are many comic elements in *Seitsemän veljestä* (*Seven Brothers*, 1870) as well. But, in spite of the slapstick humor in *The Betrothal* and *Cobblers*, one finds in them a message that is, if not tragic, at least pathetic; in each play the main character seems ridiculous because he wants to marry a woman who will not have him and has to accommodate himself to the situation in the best possible way, to remain a bachelor. A similar incident occurs near the beginning of *Seven Brothers.* A purely humorous, almost nonsensical comedy is *Olviretki Schleusingenissä* ('The Beer Expedition at Schleusingen,' 1866), whose subject was suggested by an actual incident of the Austro-Prussian War in the same year. A Bavarian detachment occupied the small town of Schleusingen and drank an unbelievable quantity of beer in a few days. Kivi turned the event into an uproarious farce with a humorous effect underlined by the characters' ludicrously serious remarks about the state of the world and life. It was not published in his lifetime (it would have been perhaps more damaging to his reputation than *Seven Brothers* was) and was not presented until after 1920.

Kivi experienced, however, deep emotions and considered love a dark, destructive force or a dreamy feeling which could not be fulfilled in this life; many of his love stories end in death and destruction. An early work, *Kullervo,* which won the prize of the Society for Finnish Literature in 1860, is a five-act tragedy based on a canto from the *Kalevala,* one of the most coherent in the book although Lönnrot composed it from different folk poems. It deals with the fate of a man who feels he must avenge the death of his parents but, in doing so, brings death and destruction to the innocent. Eventually his parents are discovered, not dead, but hiding from their enemies. However, he has previously committed unwitting incest with his sister, who kills herself when she discovers their sin; when his parents die of the sorrows he has brought upon them, he takes his own life. The action closely follows that of the original poem, which centers on hate and revenge, although it might be said that it is the criminal relationship with the sister which prevents the hero from finding a place in society. *Karkurit* ('The Fugitives,' 1865, printed in 1867), another full-length tragedy often said to have been inspired by Shakespeare's *Romeo and Juliet,*[96] actually has little in common with the English play besides the circumstances of young lovers whose families are feuding and who die at the play's end. In *Karkurit* the tragic ending seems contrived, for the enemies are near reconciliation and the couple near marriage when the unmasked, dying villain shoots the hero fatally and the bride dies of sorrow. *Canzio* (1868), set in Italy, has an improbable and complicated plot although its core is simple: Canzio, a young nobleman returning home to his family and fiancée after a long absence, falls in love with an adventuress (who is respectable insofar as her late husband's and her own republican ideals have brought her to that position) and thus sets off a series of incidents ending in his killing his best friend, driving his sister insane and his fiancée to a cloister. Despite the artificial mechanics of the end, poison and a duel, obviously inspired by *Hamlet,* the play is not inadequate in its analysis of the destructive force of love. His characters also discuss the problem of atonement and the soul's immortality, concerns which reappear in other works, e.g., *Lea.*

Although the major part of *Seven Brothers* deals with the main characters' free and adventurous life in the forests, love is treated in both the beginning and the end and appears in two tales or legends told by one of the brothers. These stories, unrelated to the action, are introduced only to relate events which occurred at the place where the characters are at that point. The first is about a father who murders his stepdaughter and her beloved, whom he has forbidden her to see, when he surprises them together, then kills himself;[97] the second, entirely supernatural, concerns a maid carried away and imprisoned by a monster,[98] but ultimately rescued by the young man she loved in life—both appear at the end in the form of radiant, heavenly spirits. The tales are built on motifs from the folklore of various nations—the first is most reminiscent, perhaps, of the Greek myth of Acis and Galatea, the second of the many legends of virgins threatened or abducted by monsters and rescued by young heroes, beginning with Perseus and Andromeda—but their style and incidents are far too literary and refined for the circumstances in which they are told. This discrepancy is emphasized by the contrast to other stories of a popular nature, about ghosts, giants and memorable hunting expeditions to Lapland, for example. They obviously reflect problems which were so vital to the author that he had to express them even in an inappropriate context.

He speaks of unhappy, destructive love in two poems, one exclusively devoted to it, *Nuori karhunampuja* ('The Young Bear Hunter,' in the collection *Kanervala*, 1866; also called *Ensimmäinen lempi* 'First Love'). Kivi produced several works about hunting bears, the largest and most dangerous game in Finland. This poem opens with a brief description of the beast's killing, then tells that the young man, coming home, finds that the girl to whom he was engaged is celebrating her marriage to another man and kills himself, a tragic version of the situation treated humorously in *The Cobblers on the Heath*. The other poem, *Mies* ('The Man,' same collection), describes a man who loses his property, crops, and house, but is comforted by the thought of his faithful beloved. When she proves untrue, he momentarily considers suicide, but eventually submits to his destiny and lives thenceforth as a pious hermit.

Other poems of his deal with love as a dreamy, almost mystic feeling he does not even attempt to fulfill. Not even a kiss is described. We see only the lovers standing on a mountain, united in a pure embrace, watching the scenery before their eyes. This motif of a mountain and its view recurs many times in Kivi's works, for example, in the poems *Onnelliset* ('The Blissful') and *Sunnuntai* ('Sunday'), both written before the publication of *Kanervala*. Two often quoted are *Keinu* ('The Swing') and *Anianpelto* (place), both in *Kanervala*. The typical opening in which the narrator stands on a high hill or walks in smiling valleys is followed by the description of a noisy, merry market at Anianpelto[99] and a beautiful maid who stands in the crowd with "an earnest brow, with smiling lips" but then disappears, leaving her image forever in the viewer's mind. *The Swing,*[100] which repeats the lines *Heilahda korkeelle, keinu, / Ja liehukoon impeni liina / Illalla lempeäl.* ('Swing high, swing, / Wave, my maid's kerchief / In the mild evening.'), at the end of each stanza, is like a folksong of the West European type, also known in Finland,[101] and the "maid with the white kerchief" has become proverbial in mentioning Kivi. A strong erotic undercurrent, however, is expressed in the swing's movement, in the image of flying together to a faraway country (fourth stanza), and in the last lines of the poem, *Seisahda, heiluva keinu, / jo kelmenee impeni poski / Illalla lempeäl.* ('Stop swinging, swing, My maid is growing pale / In the mild evening'). *Helavalkea* ('The Whitsuntide Fire')[102] and *Ruususolmu* ('A Knot of Roses'), both from *Kanervala,* are even more like folksongs. The first is a description of folk life, showing without further dramatization young men and girls dancing at a country feast. The second centers on a universal symbol of love, the rose, used by a young woman to mark her affection toward her suitor.

Another frequent motif in Kivi's poems is the mother-child relationship, often with tragic undertones. Many times this motif is blended with that of wandering, lost but found again. *Lapsi* ('The Child') is the simple description of a child's coming home to his loving mother, but in *Hannan laulu* ('Hanna's Song'), a three-stanza poem from *Karkurit,* the child is briefly lost, then finds his mother, who has a "waving kerchief," and sleeps happily in her lap. The image of the road of golden sand frequent in Kivi's works also appears in this poem; it is not an imaginary road in fairyland, but a simple road along which walking in the sunshine is pleasant. Even his visions of another world are constructed of elements from daily life and Finnish nature. Kivi ultimately followed the development initiated by Creutz and Franzén by creating a dreamworld that is completely Finnish. *Kaunisnummella* ('On Kaunisnummi'; the name means 'the beautiful heath,' 'Fairheath') is a further development of the same subject, a child lost in a forest and found by his mother. *Paimentyttö* ('The Shepherd Girl') describes a small girl sent to watch cows, who is lost in the forest but in the end finds her way home again. *Äiti ja lapsi* ('The Mother and the Child') is the most tragic poem; a dying mother is forced to send her child to beg and, hearing the wolves' howling outside, prays for God to protect him—her prayer is answered, for the child freezes before the beasts reach him.[103]

The Song of My Heart, already mentioned in connection with Nervander's *Lullaby of Death,* is close to folksongs having the same motif found in Finland, Estonia, Ingria, and Russia.[104] The contents of both Kivi's poem and the songs may seem startling: a description of the land of death (not paradise) as a beautiful, quiet place to which the mother says she is sending, or would like to send, her child. The names for death and the land of death used by Kivi and in some of the folk poems, *Tuoni, Tuonela,* are (at least today) poetic and unusual, leaving a different impression than does the usual word, *kuolema*. Kivi's poem is sung by an exalted, visionary woman at the end of *Seven Brothers*, but the motif is found in a wide area.

A more conventional yearning for death appears in the poem *Ikävyys* ('Spleen,' 'Sadness,' or 'Dejection,' not the present translation 'boredom'; 1866), although its form is personal. It reveals that Kivi was already capable of deep depression although he was in his best creative period and two years later was still explaining his philosophy of humor to Bergbom; perhaps his many writings in those years were an attempt to ward off the impending doom he sensed. In the poem he expresses a wish to escape from the "pain of knowledge" to the "silent emptiness" and asks his friends to build him a house of death (*Tuoni*) and leave him forever under the "dim willow tree" in an unmarked grave so that no one might know his resting place.

One of his most original poetic creations is his vision of another world, a dreamland or Isle of the Blessed, somewhat like the age-old myth in Homer, Hesiod, Pindar, or the life of St. Brendan, though still very personal and Finnish. It appears in *Kesäyö* ('A Summer Night'), *Lintukoto* (name), and *Kaukametsä* ('The Faraway Forest'), for which Kivi perhaps found inspiration in contemporary Swedish poets like Atterbom and Stagnelius,[105] although he includes motifs from Finnish folklore. Influence from world literature is perhaps most clearly seen in *The Summer Night*, in which the poet sees a rocky island or mountain floating in the air over a meadow on a summer night. It is reminiscent of both Virgil's "pleasant greenery of the fortunate forests and blissful seats"[106] and Dante's Limbo; the voice of an angel explains to the poet that it is the "island of peace of the pious heroes whose lives' morning was lit, whose day, pure of the clouds of sin, was spent before the rise of the star in Bethlehem, before they heard the joyful message,"[107] where they "wait for the great day on which the voice of the trumpet shall call them to their home." Kivi, less rigorous than Dante, admits thus that the souls of great men born before Christ's coming will be redeemed at the Last Judgment; he adds that this island is an abode of joy, whereas Dante says that Limbo's inhabitants had a countenance "neither sad nor gay."[108] The Finnish description reminds us more of Virgil's heroes, who dance in choirs and recite poems.[109]

To understand fully the poem *Lintukoto* (lit. 'The Home of the Birds,' but no birds appear),[110] one must have a knowledge of Finnish folklore, although the same motif appears in many other parts of the world.[111] It is actually a combination of two myths: according to the first, somewhere in the ocean is an island on which migratory birds spend the winter which they find by following the Milky Way, called *Linnunrata*, 'Track of the Birds'; according to the second, people living near the edge of the world, where heaven and earth meet and there is, consequently, little space, are dwarfs like the pygmies in Greek mythology. The story of their wars with the birds, especially cranes, told, e.g., in the third canto of the *Iliad*, appears in Finnish folklore. Kivi expects his readers to know the Greek myth; he says at the beginning of the poem that the inhabitants of Lintukoto are beautiful, innocent small beings, not ugly trolls "as in many tales." He describes their abode and life, which have no reference to a Christian heaven and simply represent a dreamland of eternal bliss. The island is not, however, ethereal: it has forests, meadows, fields, and a flowery mound on which there is a castle made of the wood of birdsongtree,[112] taken from Finnish fairytales. The island people engage in real activities: men plow the fields, women weave cloth, they have meals together and sometimes sail around their home. Still, at times a vague sadness overcomes them, and they remain gazing at the grass, not knowing why, for "they do not seek and do not find the answer," but the sadness is without pain and soon fades away like the morning dew. The poem ends with a few lines again describing their life, underlining its perennial character.

Without literary reminiscences, *Kaukametsä* is the simplest of the three poems, an unadorned description of a child's dreamland. The poet seems to say that he wishes to go to a country reminding him of his native place instead of a resplendent, glorious heaven:

Alas kalliolta lapsi riensi,
Äitins luoksi riensi hän,
Lausui loistavalla katsannolla:
Nähnyt olen taivaan maan.

"Mitä haastelet, mun pienoseni,
Mitä taivaan kaukamaast'?
Missä näit sä autuitten mailman?
Sano, kulta-omenain."

Vuoren harjanteella kauan seisoin,
Katsahdellen koilliseen,
Siellä näin mä nummen sinertävän,
Honkametsän kaukasen.

Puitten kärjill' näin mä kunnaan kauniin,
Armas päivä paistoi siell'
Ylös kunnaan kiirehelle juoksi
Kultasannotettu tie.

Tämän näin ja sydämmeni riutui,
Kyynel juoksi poskellein,
Enkä ymmärtänyt miksi itkin,
Mutta näinhän taivaan maan.

"Ei, mun lapsein; sineydess' ylhääll'
Taivaan korkee sali on,

80

Siellä lamput, kultakruunut loistaa,
Siell' on istuin Jumalan."

Ei, vaan siellä, missä ilmanrannall'
Kaukametsä haamottaa,
Siellä ompi onnellisten mailma,
Siellä autuitten maa.

The child came from the slopes of the high hill
To his mother came he, saying,
Turning blissful eyes toward her:
I have seen the land of heaven.

"What say'st thou, my beloved,
What about a country far away?
Where didst thou see the bless'd and their land?
Say, golden apple mine."

On the rock near our own fields
I was, the northeast watching
There I saw a pale blue heath
And pine trees, all so wonderful.

A hill rose from among the trees,
The sun shone bright upon the hill,
And to the highest summit went
A road with golden sand bestrewn.

This I saw, and felt my heart a-burning,
Tears a-running on my cheeks
Could not understand my crying,
But Heaven it was I saw.

"No, my child! In the blue, high up,
Is the lofty hall of Heaven
There the lamps and golden crowns are shining,
There the Lord had raised his seat."

No, but where the skies are ending,
Where the forest faraway is looming,
There the blissful have their home,
There the holy have their land.

Kivi seldom speaks of formal religion or of man's relation to God. He never experienced a religious crisis, but he doubted the truth of certain dogmas, especially the immortality of the soul; these doubts appear in some of his letters. He seems to have accepted in general the traditional views of the church, but even in 1870 he wrote to Bergbom, "Could I believe with certainty in something about life beyond the grave. . . ."[113] Canzio is an

81

agnostic who discusses with his friend Claudio the soul's immortality; Claudio, who defends the religious ideas, has the better arguments. Kivi usually gave his characters his own straightforward, quiet attitude toward an acceptance of religion, but he could also depict religious ecstacy. A typical character in the second respect is a young girl or woman who proclaims eternal truths with a force and exaltation not of this world. Anna Seunala, wife of one of the seven brothers, Selma of *Karkurit*, Liisa in *Yö ja päivä* ('Night and Day,' 1867), and Margareta in the play with the same name (1870) are such characters.

Lea is built entirely on a subject from the New Testament, although Kivi expanded it far beyond the few words of the Gospel. Of all the characters, only one appears in St. Luke (19:1-8), Zacchaeus, the publican who climbed up into a sycamore tree to see Jesus and promised to give half of his goods to the poor. Insofar that almost no outer action takes place onstage, and only the changes in the minds and hearts of the characters are shown, the play follows closely the rules of classical French tragedy. The play has been and is admired greatly in Finland, more, possibly, for sentimental and religious reasons than for artistic merits. The language is beautiful, and Kivi inserted a few half-humorous interludes, which are irrelevant to the plot; but the play is like an oratorio in which each character sings about his rapture at the sight of Christ and about his conversion. These conversions, however, are brought about through supernatural intervention of the Savior, not by inner struggle. Some action is introduced by the secondary plot, in which Zacchaeus first wants to marry his daughter Lea to a Pharisee, Joas, who is later revealed a hypocrite interested in Zacchaeus's money, then gives her to Aram, a young Sadducee (agnostic), who is converted by Lea after she is converted by Jesus.

The most often translated[114] work of Kivi, *Seven Brothers*, is also the work for which he is best known in Finland, with *The Cobblers on the Heath* and *The Betrothal*. Its dialogue is play-like, without explanatory remarks such as "he said" or "answered the other"; the speaker's name merely precedes each line. Consequently, it was easily adapted to the stage, a version which added to its popularity. The popularity came late, however; at its initial publication, August Ahlqvist-Oksanen, then professor of Finnish language and literature at the University of Helsinki, strongly criticized it, in fact, tore it to pieces with senseless violence, heaping abuse after abuse upon it and the author, certainly thereby hastening the outbreak of Kivi's illness. Although Kivi had friends, especially Cygnaeus, who had secured him the Literary Prize of the government in 1865 for *The Cobblers on the Heath*, had written a preface completed by Snellman to *Seven Brothers* and one to *Margareta* (Kivi's last play), and later published a moving obituary of him, *Ett farväl* ('A Farewell,' *Morgonbladet*),[115] Ahlqvist's opinion was accepted for many years. He charged that the book was immoral, brutal, coarse, and formless, a shame to Finnish literature, and a nasty caricature of Finnish people; we can find no such elements in it. Nevertheless, not before the beginning of this century was Kivi really appreciated. Volter Kilpi wrote an article favorable to him in 1900, O. Manninen in 1901, and Eino Leino in 1909, but, even in 1928, in his preface to Kivi's selected works, J. V. Lehtonen explained on several pages that "to a person who examines it impartially, it is the best proof of Kivi's pure intentions, his morally *constructive* ideas, and his bright philosophy of life."[116]

Kivi described the book as a "merry tale,"[117] and almost none of its scenes, no matter how tragic, are without comic elements. Several later Finnish authors, e.g., Lehtonen, Kianto, Sillanpää, and Haanpää, have also sympathetically described people struggling with hardship while seeing that suffering does not necessarily ennoble man and that pity does not require blindness to its object's defects. Kivi described the seven brothers as sturdy country boys like his childhood friends and himself. They occasionally quarrel and fight with their neighbors (a feature especially shocking to Ahlqvist), drink more than they should, make unrefined jokes and indulge in boisterous fun and games. They are represented almost free of superstition; Simeoni says, when listening to a horned owl's hooting in the forest: "It announces fires, bloody fights, and murders," but adds "as old people say," and Tuomas retorts, "It's his job to hoot in the forests, and it doesn't mean a thing." Kivi never introduced folk customs, beliefs, or practices in his works to make them more thrilling or attractive, and he never acquired the city dweller's interest in the quaint manners of the country people. What violence, terror and brutality he depicted were unadorned. The Finns have been accused occasionally of lengthy brooding over real or imaginary wrongs ending in sudden eruptions of destructive violence; Kivi describes this temperament in his characters. A long-standing hostility between the brothers and boys of the neighboring village leads to three neither gentlemanly nor heroic fights of senseless brutality which almost result in murder.[118] Among themselves some of the brothers also have fits of sudden anger, and they experience the surrounding world as hostile. They react with hate and near panic, but their most destructive actions make them see the dangers in their way of life and help them to become law-abiding citizens. A central episode, combining realism and fantasy in a way typical of Kivi, concerns the brothers' adventure on the Devil's Stone, a rock on which they are besieged by forty oxen from a neighboring manor. After three days and three nights without food, they shoot their way to freedom with the rifles they have with them as they were originally on a hunt. The scene is described from the point of view of the characters, and, to underline its importance as a turning-point in their lives, the author builds the noise and smoke of the rifle fire, the bellowing and rushing of the stampeding animals and a breaking thunderstorm into a terrifying cataclysm. Next they must face the owner of the oxen,[119] and, though they first spurn his threats, they eventually agree to pay a reparation, for which they must cultivate the ground to find the necessary means, the first step on their road toward an orderly life. They meet difficulties due to their own character, and Kivi gives a simple but penetrating description of their mental struggles, both conscious and unconscious, in reaching a well-balanced attitude toward the world, which some of them never achieve. Their psychological development is motivated partially by external factors, partially by the workings of their subconscious, expressed in dreams and delirious visions, which are attributed to excess drink. Kivi projects in the brothers, especially with the vision, many of his own mental sufferings, but his mastery in combining realism and fantasy is evident in the presentation of the difficult motifs of dream and vision. They are not too literary, beautiful, or romantic, but are composed of realistic and even humorous details; nevertheless, they produce an unreal impression of sadness, dejection, and wild terror. In the dream one brother sees himself transformed into a mole; in this form he forces his way through the rotten core of a pine tree to its top for a look at the world. There he sees "the steep mountain of Impivaara, but at an immeasurable, heart-breaking distance, he sees there, in the midst of the forests, in the evening, the melancholy little house, and (he sees also) his dear brothers . . . on the misty, resounding heath."[120] Eventually the brothers are carried away in a cloud by a whirlwind raised by the rector of their parish, who has warned them in vain against their ungodly lives; then the dreamer wakes. In the vision one brother sees himself carried by the devil to the moon and there taken to a tower made of boot leather,[121] from which he can see the whole world and its ultimate destruction, which he takes as a warning for his brothers and himself to better their ways.

By far Kivi's most popular work besides his comedies, *Seven Brothers* has been printed in many editions illustrated by well-known Finnish artists.[122] It alone does not give an altogether one-sided picture of his work, for it does not reflect only the optimistic side of his creations. Nevertheless, as often happens when a book is "officially" recommended for general admiration, an official idea about it is easily accepted; in this case, the book is considered an edifying, optimistic, and humorous tale, a view which obscures its tragic conflicts, lyrical beauties, and psychological depth. The many descriptions of nature, hunting expeditions, and the farmer's work are realistic, but they contain something of an epic majesty and breadth, which give an impression of a remote, almost mythological past, although the scenes are composed of familiar, everyday elements. Kivi's language, which offended Ahlqvist and made even Bergbom say that his poems were like "gold that had not been minted into coins,"[123] gives the same impression; it seems age-old, archaic, and solemn, though it is used to tell the most ordinary incidents in a way understandable even today. We might compare Carlyle's English to it, but Kivi had none of Carlyle's conscious oddities; he simply wrote in a manner influenced by the speech of his native region and old literary Finnish (especially the Bible translation) at a time when other writers and linguists were developing a different form, which Kivi could not accept. His thoughts and their expression are so intertwined that whether the subject matter or the style makes his works cannot be judged; perhaps it is this total equation of form and content that best marks a great writer.[124] His works give a full and vivid picture of the Finnish man in his Finnish surroundings, but also of Man in human surroundings, and, as such, should be foreign to no member of the human race.

Literature in Finnish in the
Second Half of the Nineteenth Century
Realists and Folk Writers

DURING THE HAPPY PERIOD between 1860 and 1880, when reforms were rapidly modernizing Finland, the church willingly relinquished much of its control over civil life. Local administration had been supervised by the church,[125] but in 1865 it was given to special bodies elected by the inhabitants of each of the country's districts. Education became independent of religious authorities in 1866,[126] and the new Church Law of 1869, besides instituting many liberal reforms, granted all Finnish citizens the right not to belong to the established Lutheran church, though lack of a Dissenter Act long prevented its being implemented. The great clash between traditionalists and modernists—between the churches and Darwin, the conservatives and liberals, both of them and Marxists, writers who represented the old ideals and realists or naturalists—which was to shake the spiritual life of all Europe, came slowly to Finland and remained almost unnoticed until the eighties. The peculiar social and political conditions of that country and the strict censure imposed by the authorities prevented the inhabitants from following closely the events abroad. As Finland was largely agricultural, social problems already created in Europe by the development of modern industry had not yet appeared there. Finns felt that existing problems were being resolved by the reforms enacted in quick succession; in the seventies many even felt a need to slow down, and, aside from a growing tension between the Finnish- and Swedish-speaking groups, this period was rather tame. The spiritual leaders of the forties and fifties were old men: Lönnrot had published his great works, Runeberg was silenced by illness, and Snellman was an official personality preaching moderation to the young. Topelius was to carry on the literary tradition of Runeberg; with no one to dispute the position, he marked the period with his naive and sentimental idealism. Although Kivi had been admired and defended in his lifetime, Ahlqvist-Oksanen's criticism had spiritually killed him so thoroughly that no one used him as a model—indeed, Kivi was too individual to be followed; he was too realistic for contemporary idealists and too idealistic for future realists, and his language was against the trend of the evolution.

A fairly large group of nineteenth-century writers are known as folk authors or poets in Finland.[127] Men of modest origin, they never acquired significant formal education, although, through individual efforts, some accumulated a fair amount of knowledge about the world. In occupation they varied from wandering craftsmen and laborers to wealthy farmers who occasionally even sat in Parliament for their native regions,[128] but the subjects they chose were almost invariably the same: great natural catastrophes[129] or other events; accidents; the building of churches or other noteworthy structures, such as dams, canals, and others; satire and personal attack; times of dearth and bad harvest; criticism of contemporary customs and fashions; warnings against excessive drinking and smoking; attacks on superstition; war, peace, and the country's rulers; and so forth. They provided a kind of chronicle, a straightforward registering of remarkable facts, accompanied by edifying and moralizing observations on life, but more personal and lyrical subjects are not absent from their production,[130] which includes poems on the coming of spring, love, sorrow at the death of a small child, and the difficult life of the poet himself. Two folk poets who wrote on the position of the Finnish language and were noticed in educated circles have already been mentioned.[131] These poets also adapted and translated, almost always from Swedish, ballad-like poetry, which was often printed, like their other works, in broadsheets and sold by peddlers, organ grinders, and other such characters, especially at markets, where eager customers were always found. The great period of this ballad-like literature arrived relatively late in Finland, approximately between 1870 and 1900,[132] and publications of this kind appeared even in this century. Many internationally-known poems were also given a Finnish form, such as Matthew "Monk" Lewis's *Alonzo the Brave and Fair Imogene* ("the worms they crawl in and the worms they crawl out") titled *Aalonksi ja Emueli*.[133] *Sweet William's Ghost*, first published by Percy in 1765, was translated by Finnish immigrants in the United States in the 1890s, then printed in their home country in 1902.[134]

In many West European countries it was fashionable in the second half of the eighteenth and first half of the nineteenth centuries to admire such folk poets, who included, in Scotland, Burns, Robert Tannahill, a weaver, James Hogg, a shepherd who could neither read nor write until the age of thirty, and John Leyden, the son of a shepherd;[135] in France, Pierre Dupont, one of whose collections contains a laudatory preface by Baudelaire. In

Finland there was vivid interest in folk poetry from the time of Porthan, which poets such as Franzén, Runeberg, and Topelius promoted with their romantic and sentimental admiration for the humble. Porthan presented in *De Poësi Fennica* two poets from Iisalmi, Matti and Paavo Remes, and Gottlund patronized Kustaa Paturi. Some needed no help and introduced themselves to the world, e.g., Pietari (Petter) Väänänen from Nilsiä, who under the Swedish rule represented his home region in Parliament. In 1800 he wrote a poem on the coronation of King Gustavus IV Adolphus, in 1802 one on the king's journey to Germany, and in 1805 another on his homecoming. He was at the Diet of Porvoo, where he produced a metric composition honoring Alexander I, in which he showed unusual knowledge of public affairs for a man of his social position; the poem was later sent to the ruler in St. Petersburg. Antti Puhakka, from Kontiolahti in Finnish Karelia, who was illiterate until he was twenty-one, wrote nearly twenty thousand lines of poetry, became a member of the Society for Finnish Literature, purchased many books, read newspapers regularly, and was elected to Parliament four times after 1862. Others, such as Pietari Makkonen and Olli Kymäläinen, remained in their original surroundings. They were admired, praised; their portraits were painted, and they were received by well-known personalities like Runeberg, who reportedly said to Kymäläinen, "If you, Olli, could but write, you would become a much better poet than I am."[136] Jaakko Räikkönen was born in Ingria, which had been conquered by Peter the Great but had remained almost completely Finnish in spirit. He remained a serf until serfdom's abolition in Russia in 1861,[137] but he learned to read and write both Finnish and Russian, attained several posts in the administration of his village and region, helped found the Finnish elementary school there, read Finnish newspapers regularly and published his poems in them. Like the inhabitants of Finland, he was also a loyal subject of the Russian crown and was awarded by the emperor a silver medal in 1868. Also interested in foreign events, he wrote at times on unexpected subjects, such as the temporal power of the pope. In *Mietteitäni* ('Thoughts of Mine') he claims that all material wealth wasted in preparation of wars would be better used in building factories and all idle intellectual effort better directed toward useful inventions such as cement or concrete (probably the meaning of "houses made of clay"), harvesting machines, and railway engines. His conclusion is an ironic thrust at religion: he pretends to lament that he is thinking of such vanities instead of laying up for himself treasures that thieves do not steal and rust doth not corrupt.[138]

Some folk writers produced works which can be appraised independently, without regard to the circumstances in which they were written. This statement applies especially to Pietari Päivärinta, Heikki Kauppinen, and Heikki Meriläinen. Although the latter two do not really belong to the chronological period now under discussion, their mental outlook and artistic expression are very typical of it. Because of the simple form and moral content, their works were extremely popular in their lifetimes, but they did not court the readers' favor with sentimental or thrilling stories with happy endings. Finnish critics and literary historians have, in general, given just treatment to their works without unduly emphasizing the authors' backgrounds, but the great popularity of **Pietari (Pehr) Päivärinta** (1827-1913) resulted in a listing of him as one of three or four Finnish authors worth mentioning in foreign encyclopedias and other reference works, which often said little, if anything, about Finland and still less about Finnish literature. Päivärinta was also translated not only into Swedish and Estonian, but also into Norwegian (one of the three translations was published in 1888 in Chicago), German (1890, 1892, second edition 1919), and Russian (1886, 1887, 1903, 1904, 1905, 1911, 1924; by 1910 there were eight editions of the 1887 translation, by 1912 there were two of the 1904, by 1930 six of the 1924). His short story *Puutteen Matti* ('Matti of the Misery,' after 1877; *Puute* 'misery' or 'want' is also the name of Matti's farm) was especially popular in Russia. Although the author was neither a socialist nor communist, the story was interpreted as a good picture of the sufferings of the proletariat in a precapitalist society, for even a German translation was published in Moscow in 1930.[139] The dates of the translations indicate that, as long as Ahlqvist's curse lay upon Kivi's works, Päivärinta was considered a better representative of Finnish literature.

The son of a poor farmer, Päivärinta had to beg in his childhood, but through his own efforts he was able to purchase a farm, which he successfully cultivated. He had a good voice and acquired the modest education necessary for a precentor in his home parish, and, after the age of fifty, when he had become a well-known writer, he was elected to Parliament several times. His first story, *Elämäni* ('My Life,' 1877), was autobiographical and won the prize of the Society for Popular Education (*Kansanvalistusseura*) and six hundred markkas in copyrights, a considerable sum at the time. His many short stories and novels fall mainly into two groups: those which deal with individuals like him, who, in spite of difficulty, achieve success through their energy and effort, and those which deal with people who, through no fault of their own, are destroyed by adversities such as hunger and cold. The former includes *Tintta-Jaakko* (name, 1883), *Torpan poika* ('The Son of a Tenant,' 1883), and *Oukkari* (name, 1889); the latter *Pikakuvia 1867 katovuodesta* ('Sketches from the Famine of 1867,' 1893), *Puutteen Matti, Kontti-Anna* (name, in the collection *Elämän havainnoita* ['Observations from Life,' 10 vols., 1879-89]), and *Rouhu* (name, in the "Sketches" from 1867). Although each of Päivärinta's works has a moral, he does not point out; the meaning is evident, but not expressly stated. This technique is especially conspicuous in the sad stories, which occasionally achieve considerable tragic force through their simple description of life's adversities. *Rouhu* probably inspired a modern author, Veijo Meri, to write the short story *Kalkki* ('The Lime'); Rouhu, who has seen his wife and children starve during the great famine of 1867, chokes to death when, half-mad with hunger, he tries to eat flour mixed with straw from an open sack. Päivärinta's characters never rebel against fate, God, society, or the authorities, not even the protagonist in *Puutteen Matti* who meekly pays tithes to the rector of his parish in spite of his utter misery, for, as Matti thinks, "He has a hard job and a heavy responsibility for our souls." The undertone, however, is satirical, as in the description of Matti's burial, at which the rector quotes a hymn saying: "What are goods and fortune? / But dirt and dust that disappear." In his modest way, Päivärinta represents the transition from idealism to realism which took place in Finnish literature during his life.

Heikki Kauppinen (known under his pseudonym **Kauppis-Heikki**, a popular form of his official name; 1862-1920) was more a writer and less a moralist than Päivärinta; Professor Rafael Koskimies calls him "a pure artist."[140] He was born in the eastern part of the country, near Iisalmi, where he was a farm hand, but he was fortunate to work for a minister of the church, H. G. Theodor Brofeldt, whose son, known as Juhani Aho, became perhaps the most famous Finnish author of his time. Aho and his brothers were lifelong friends of Kauppinen and helped him in every way; Kauppinen later met another well-known writer, Minna Canth, in Kuopio and received advice as well as material assistance from her. After acquiring the necessary instruction, he worked as an itinerant teacher, director of a reformatory, and elementary school teacher, publishing novels and short stories fairly regularly. The atmosphere of his works is often sad and subdued, except in the short stories describing humorous popular types from his native region, the province Savo, whose inhabitants are known for their fondness of jokes and tales. Anaski, the main character in a collection of short stories bearing his name (1911; new, enlarged edition 1923), is a good-natured thief and remarkable liar; similar comic individuals appear in other collections, such as *Savolaisia* ('People from Savo,' 1912) and *Tarinoita* ('Tales,' several vols., 1886, 1897, 1900-1906).

His novels often deal with individuals who overreach themselves attempting to achieve wealth or better social position or whose dreams are shattered by reality. They are melancholy or ironic, seldom bitter, somewhat like the works of Chekhov, which Kauppinen hardly knew. The morals in his works are obvious: people who build their lives on false premises and have misdirected ambitions fail miserably and dreamers must learn to accept reality, but, like Päivärinta, he implies rather than states the moral. His first novel, *Mäkijärveläisiä* ('People from Mäkijärvi,' 1887), was in the humorous vein, but the next, *Viija* (1889), reveals his deep insight into a woman's soul. Viija, daughter of a well-to-do farmer, has many suitors but makes the wrong choice; a similar situation occurs in the next novel, *Kirottua työtä* ('Accursed

Work,' 1891). It is the story of a man, Risto Malinen, whose scheming for a better position and contempt for others' feelings destroys their lives and his own. He tries to arrange a good marriage for his pretty daughter, who is in love with a poor man, by whom she has an illegitimate child. Malinen tries to poison the child, who dies in circumstances leaving the cause doubtful, and the girl must marry a man who was earlier thought not good enough. The husband is a drunkard and an idler, so that Malinen sees his fortune, his life, and his daughter's life disintegrate before his eyes. In spite of their tragic destinies, the characters are not very exceptional, and the author does not emphasize the sordid or dramatic aspects of the story. His next work, *Laara* (1893), is the most dramatic of his works.

Laara is an active, energetic woman who uses her attractiveness to men for advancement. A servant, she marries an elderly farmer who dies and leaves her mistress of the house. She has affairs and eventually marries a man for whom she has a sentimental attachment, though he proves a weak, worthless drunkard and causes her accidental death. Obviously, there is a moral in each of these novels. Those who act wrongly are punished, but the punishment is fully psychologically motivated. It is more a melancholy philosophy of life that Kauppinen presents than a didactic mode of conduct for his readers.

Although Kauppinen remained a modest man, he was recognized as a writer of quality and had friends in literary circles. He followed the world's events and was, to some extent, influenced by changes in artistic taste that took place during his life. The two novels just discussed follow, more or less, the theory of dispassionate observation of realism or naturalism, but in the next novels the outlook is more idealistic, due, it has been supposed, to the influence of Tolstoy and, more directly, his Finnish disciple, Arvid Järnefelt.[141] The first of these, *Aliina* (1896), is the story of a young woman from the country who struggles to acquire the education necessary for a schoolteacher. Her father, whose immoral life creates many difficulties for her, is an obstacle to her efforts, but Aliina forgives him as she has decided to work to help others, her family first. The book contains many passages about women's rights and their new opportunities, reflecting the evolution then taking place in Finland.

The second of these novels, *Uran aukaisijat* ('The Trail Blazers,' 1904), is in part autobiographical. The two main characters are men of modest origin who have devoted their lives to educational activities and have become schoolteachers in the country. (The movement for free popular education, started by Grundtvig in Denmark, had spread quickly to the other Scandinavian countries in the second half of the nineteenth century; the purpose was to give persons who did not have an opportunity for formal education a wider knowledge of the world. Students and other educated people volunteered to give lectures, organize courses, arrange meetings and festivals, and publish textbooks; on a local level people of more modest standing collaborated with them. The chautauquas in the United States were a similar form of voluntary work for the spreading of enlightenment.) In this book Kauppinen concentrates on a great summer festival, at which important people from Helsinki deliver speeches and lectures. The description is not idealized, for the author sees clearly the slightly comic aspects of such a function, as well as plans for personal advancement and profit which some of the participants try to carry out. One main character is involved in a more humorous than wily scheme; it is a hard blow to him that all his efforts to improve his position come to nothing. In the end he accepts his fate with resignation.

The third novel, *Savolainen soittaja* ('A Musician from Savo,' 1915), opens with a description of the life of a poor country boy, in which Kauppinen shows masterful insight into the sufferings of a lonely child and his experience in the adult world. The end of the book may seem less credible, for the boy becomes a well-known musician and plans to leave his money to a philanthropic foundation whose purpose is to help illegitimate children like himself. Actually Kauppinen borrowed these details from the life of a person he knew.

Near the end of his life, he planned a romantic biography of his benefactor, Rector Brofeldt, part of which was published with a preface by Juhani Aho.

Kauppinen's main defect is his style, for he never reached a mastery of literary expression, but his humane, unprejudiced philosophy and his ability to understand psychological conflicts and place them in proper social context more than compensate for this defect. Indeed, too refined an artistic form would not have been appropriate for his subjects.

The least prominent of the three writers is **Heikki Meriläinen** (1847-1939). He was discovered by a lady with literary interests. Päivärinta was already well known, Kauppinen had begun to write, and people hoped for more folk geniuses like them. As Meriläinen was gifted at telling stories, he was urged to put them on paper. The result was an autobiographical story, *Korpelan Tapani* (name, 1888), other novels and stories like *Pietolan tytöt* ('The Girls of Pietola,' 1892), *Kahleeton vanki* ('A Prisoner without Fetters,' 1898), *Huutolaistyttö* ('The Beggar Girl,' 1899), and many more. Even after 1920 he published five volumes, one of them his *Life* (1927). His strength was his lively, colorful language, full of words and expressions from his native dialect, but it is the only remarkable part of his works. He became interested in folklore and made several long journeys to collect it, traveling even to Lapland and Russian Karelia to find magic formulas and incantations, which especially attracted him.

Although these folk writers are only an episode in Finnish literary history, they illustrate some facets which have not changed. Among the Finnish-speaking population people of modest origin have so often written and become well-known authors that the denomination of "folk writer" has become obsolete. To some extent the term described the quality of the works composed by the persons so designated, but it is much more descriptive of an attitude among those who used it. The educated class of the nineteenth century admired the common people for all their real or imaginary good qualities and bestowed praise upon their intellectual achievements, with the reservation that the writings of the common people could never be on the level of those of the educated class. This distinction is difficult to maintain in the case of Kauppinen, and in the twentieth century this preconception has been proven thoroughly false by some of the greatest Finnish writers, e.g., Sillanpää, the Nobel Prize winner of 1939, Lehtonen, Pekkanen, or Linna. As a consequence, writers have been classified for a long time only according to the artistic level of their work. Still, in general, these authors have remained true to their origins because they mainly describe the people and surroundings they know best—farmers, workers, craftsmen, small officials, and others at their everyday tasks—although their works are not all similar and do not carry specific social or political messages. With few exceptions Finnish authors exclude such questions from their books and concentrate upon individuals, who move in a social setting and may have political opinions, but who are seen as individuals, not as representatives of any particular group. The authors, too, are individuals, creative artists, each with his own view of man and the world, reflected in his style; in our opinion style and content are two sides of the same thing: the philosophy of life and the conception of man.

Members of educated families have also become writers in Finland—many more among the Swedish-speaking group than among the Finnish, however—but even they have described popular life as often as their own surroundings. It was in the nineteenth century that the sharpest distinction was made between folk writers and writers. However, it is still meaningful today to differentiate between authors who take their subjects from popular life and those who do not. In the nineteenth century the development of Finnish literature accompanied the development of the Finnish language, and the educated class felt that everyone should work to make the language as elegant, rich, and flexible as possible, capable of expressing everything that had been said in countries with long cultural traditions. Correctness of form and expression were emphasized, an emphasis which, though necessary, resulted in a lack of appreciation of an original genius like Kivi. There were and still are authors who did write according to rules for correct literary expression and work to make the language more flexible and expressive, such as Juhani Aho, Eino Leino, Maila Talvio, V. A. Koskenniemi, Mika Waltari, or Olavi Paavolainen. However, another group, perhaps not consciously in opposition, has worked on quite different principles. This group is formed by those who prefer popular motifs, and for that reason their language reflects the way of feeling, thinking, and speaking of their characters. They do not write in the local dialects—only a few humorists have done that—but they use a word or two of dialect when they feel that it expresses their thoughts better than a literary phrase. The form of their works is the result of a conscious artistic effort to reproduce the various aspects of primitive minds, not of an inability to write correctly. Another characteristic these writers share is the sympathy with which they describe their characters, although they often do not idealize them. The characters of Lehtonen and Ilmari Kianto, for example, are almost caricatures, but we do not feel that the authors condescend to them; rather, we feel that human weaknesses in general are caricatured.

Although Kivi had no influence on his contemporaries or even his successors, after the efforts of such pioneers as Arwidsson, von Becker, Juteini, Lönnrot, and Snellman, the use of the Finnish language in spiritual and intellectual life progressed steadily.[142] More and more works were written in Finnish—literary, scientific, scholarly, political, and other; everyone had an opportunity to be the first to publish something in Finnish in some field. **Rietrikki Polén** (1823-84), who gave his first name, Fredrik, a popular Finnish form, was the first to present a Ph.D. thesis in Finnish, *Johdanto Suomen kirjallishistoriaan* ('An Introduction to the History of Finnish Literature,' 1858), and **Georg Zacharias Forsman** (also **Yrjö Sakari Koskinen** and **Yrjö Sakari Yrjö-Koskinen**; 1830-1903)[143] was the second with *Nuijasodan syyt ja alku Pohjanmaalla* ('The Causes and the Beginning of the War of the Maces in Pohjanmaa,' 1858). The latter was part of a work in two volumes, begun in 1857, which he later enlarged, completed, and published in 1877. To be appointed professor at the University of Helsinki, he needed to publish some additional works, and he wrote *Tiedot Suomen suvun muinaisuudesta* (' / Our / Knowledge on the Past of the Finnish Race,' 1862).[144] However, it was suggested that this work should not be accepted as proof of the author's scholarly capacities because it was written in Finnish; eventually the opposing opinion was accepted, and he was appointed in 1863. Although active in politics, as a founder and leader of the Finnish party (also called the Old Finnish party after 1880, when a Young Finnish party had been founded), member of Parliament and of the cabinet, he wrote several historical works, newspaper articles, a few literary compositions, and contributed regularly to papers he had founded with his friends. Two poems, set to music, have remained popular, *Suomeni salossa* ('In the Forests of Finland'), simple and melodious as a folksong, and *Milloin Pohjolan nähdä saan* ('When Shall I See the North'), expressing patriotic feelings. His short story *Pohjanpiltti* (name, which sounds like 'The Child of the North'; 1859),[145] on a historical subject, is one of the first of its kind in Finland, but is not a remarkable literary work. It is full of thrilling incidents, fights, and conspiracies and also contains a love story, but the author was unable to blend these elements into a coherent whole.

We have mentioned, when speaking of Kivi, **Karl August Engelbrekt Ahlqvist** (1826-99), also known under his pseudonym **Oksanen**. He was the illegitimate son of a country servant in Kuopio, but became a well-known scholar and poet. While still young, he met Snellman in his home town and later Lönnrot and Runeberg. As a student he had already made several journeys to collect folklore. When he had taken his M. A., an important scholarship enabled him to travel almost without interruption five years among the Finno-Ugric tribes of northern Russia and Siberia (1854-1859). He became a Finno-Ugric scholar and professor of Finnish literature and language, succeeding Lönnrot in 1863, although his friends had hoped that he would chose a literary career. He did write poems and literary criticism and also published a treatise on Finnish prosody, *Suomalainen runousoppi kielelliseltä kannalta* (1863). This work and his poetic activity considerably influenced Finnish poetry. He wished to give strict rules to every form of linguistic expression and to make Finnish as elegant and precise as the European languages with long artistic traditions.[146] It has been said that, especially in poetry, by so doing he forced his native tongue into an unsuitable mold and ignored the old folk meter's beauties. Especially among the post-World War II generation of writers and critics, it was for awhile fashionable to attack all poetry written from the time of Ahlqvist to roughly 1920 or 1930, when the first experiments in free poetic form were made, because it was rhymed and followed fixed metric patterns.[147] Actually Ahlqvist knew the old folk meter in which he composed some fairly good poems, but he felt that attempts should also be made to write Finnish poetry in other patterns, as had been done before his time. The old folk meter had become so closely connected with the subjects of the folk poems that its use by contemporary writers sounded anachronistic.[148] Eino Leino was almost the sole modern poet to use the folk meter successfully, mainly in poems with historical or mythical subjects. His other poetic works are written in several European meters, which many of his greatest successors have used well although some practical problems have never been completely solved.

In a discussion of the use of West European meters in Finnish poetry, a distinction must be made between classical Greek and Roman meters and those that evolved during the Middle Ages and the Renaissance. We have already mentioned, when speaking of Runeberg, the attempts to reproduce the classical meters, especially the hexameter and the elegy, in Swedish, after German models.[149] These meters were based on the quantity of syllables, but that factor is much less important in German and Swedish (and English), so that the poets arranged not long and short but stressed and unstressed syllables into patterns to which they gave classical names. For example, a line of eighteen (or seventeen) syllables in which the first, fourth, seventh, tenth, thirteenth, and sixteenth syllables were stressed was called a (catalectic) dactylic hexameter, although it was very different from such a line in a classical poem. As the quantity of syllables and sounds is of primary importance in Finnish,[150] (as well as in Estonian and Hungarian), writing poems in pure classical meters in that language seems possible, if not easy. Not only has it been attempted, but the problem has also been believed solved, the solution presupposing, of course, that there is no doubt about the relative length of the syllables. Finnish grammarians and linguists agree on syllable length,[151] but poets do not always compose according to rigorously-observed patterns of long and short syllables. Instead, they have relied upon alternation of stressed and unstressed syllables, as in Swedish and German. Professor Kohtamäki says that in Ahlqvist's first poems one is disturbed because the meter is based on quantity, and adds that later Ahlquist took stress into consideration and rightly predicted that in the future Finnish poetry would be composed exclusively according to stress.[152] Ahlqvist's idea was based on a faulty analysis of the folk meter; he wrote that "Those who say that the meter of our poetry is based on the quantity of syllables make a big mistake";[153] his statement contradicts all known facts and reminds us of Petraeus's old grammar.[154] He did not realize fully that in the old Finnish meter there are two kinds of lines, one which the Finnish scholars now call the dipodic trochaic line with a caesura and the other the broken line.[155] The first has a regular succession of trochaic feet, although the first syllable may also be short, with the stressed syllables in the word corresponding to the rises in the meter,[156] whereas in the second a short syllable bearing the main stress in the word may be put in a fall, and an untressed syllable in any word may appear in a position corresponding to a rise in a dipodic line. The following is a dipodic trochaic line:

pănĕn / aĭtăn / / părvĕn / păāhăn

and this a broken line:

sĕlvi / ă si / nă i / kănä

(stressed syllables in the words *selviä sinä ikänä*), in which every syllable except the first is short. One can see that Ahlqvist, assuming the old Finnish meter to be trochaic but finding recurring lines such as the second, concluded that the quantity of syllables was not observed.[157]

Another factor which has caused difficulty to Finnish poets appears in this example: the relation between the rises in the metric pattern and the stressed syllables in the words. In classical Greek and Roman poetry the *ictus* did not coincide with the stressed syllables, and, as, according to a tradition followed by many scholars and teachers, the syllables bearing the *ictus* were to be stressed when the poetry was read aloud, the syllables normally unstressed were emphasized.[158] Consequently, when Finnish poems were written in strict observance of classical rules, stressed syllables were placed in unstressed positions at times and vice versa; although this phenomenon has always been considered un-Finnish, Professor Kohtamäki finds this disturbing in Ahlqvist's poems, and it often makes an unintentional comic impression, e.g. in these lines by Ahlqvist:

lĕhtŏ jŏ kĕllăstŭū, sўўs hŏpĕŏitsĕvi māan

tắlvĕă ĕnnŭstăā tăvĭĕnki jă tĕlkkĭĕn lắhtŏ

or in these by Paavo Cajander:

lĕntŏhŏn pўў pўrăhtăā, kăhĭlĭstŏssă ăantăvĭ sŏrsă

tŭŏllă kĭmĕltăĕn sĕisŏvĭ vŭŏri jă săarĕt nĕ tŭŏllă.

Berg's (Kallio's) poem *Oma Maa* is so enjoyable because the stress in the words corresponds to the *ictus,* and he even respects the classical rules of quantity.[159] After Ahlqvist, however, and as long as classical (pseudo-classical) meters were used, there was great confusion among Finnish poets, who talked of iambs, trochees, dactyls, anapests, and so forth, although these names mainly designated arrangements of stressed and unstressed syllables, not, as the names originally had implied, long and short. Poets of other countries do the same, but in Finland it was often assumed that quantities were somehow taken into account as well, although it is not exactly clear how. V. A. Koskenniemi writes of "dactyls," "short closed syllables," in his own poetry and prides himself on having consistently followed for spondees the classical quantitative pattern, never having put a trochee in a spondee's place, but quotes from his own work:

sắmmŭttăā sĕ ĕi vŏi, kŭŏlĕvă, sŭn jănŏas

in which the diphthong *ei* is counted as short and the next, *voi,* as long.[160] This confusion has persisted as long as poets have been interested in classical and regular modern meters, but, since 1920 and especially World War II, they have found it not worthwhile to cut or untie this Gordian knot and have begun writing by now almost exclusively free verse.[161]

They have also disposed of another problem inherent to the old type of poetry, the use of lengthened or shortened forms of words to force them into the metric patterns. For example, *mä* and *sä* might be used for *minä* and *sinä, tuun* for *tulen, oon* for *olen, taloss'* for *talossa,* and *talohon* for *taloon*; verb forms like *tuleepi, saapi* for *tulee, saa;* and all kinds of meaningless suffixes like *−han, -hän, -kin, -pa,* and *-pä* might be added to words.[162] In fact this practice takes us back to Petraeus's prosody! Some of these forms are colloquial, some archaic, and some dialectal, but the poets used them indiscriminately for convenience in following the metric patterns or rhyming. These lines by Kaarlo Sarkia are a good example:

käsivarsillas levännyt oon

. . . .

tämän lauluni todistakoon

Käsivarsillas should be *käsivarsillasi* and *oon olen*, which would not rhyme with *todistakoon.* Another example is in the following by V. A. Koskenniemi:

Iltarusko jo sammunut on,
nukutin lapseni kehtohon.
pitkät on tunnit aamuhun-
suruni, milloin ma nukutan sun?

in which *kehtohon* stands for *kehtoon, aamuhun* for *aamuun, ma* for *minä,* and *sun* for *sinun* (or, rather, *sinut*).[163] As we said, contemporary poets no longer feel compelled to use such devices, and good, traditional poets, like Koskenniemi and Sarkia, generally avoided using them too often. However, these substitutions were quite common for a long time, and we cannot criticize a poet because we find them in his works; other formal and aesthetic criteria must be applied when one judges their quality.

Ahlqvist practiced his theories by writing a number of poems and translating poetry. The first of these appeared in Snellman's *Saima,* while he was still at school. The first poems he translated into Finnish were by Runeberg, Franzén, and two Swedish poets, Tegnér and Stagnelius. In 1845 he published Runeberg's *Idylls and Epigrams* in Finnish, a rather unsuccessful effort, it is said, and he was the first to translate poems from *The Tales of Ensign Stål.* Strongly patriotic, he urged that all Runeberg's works be published in Finnish. At a time when Finnish nationalism, represented by Yrjö-Koskinen, for example, was becoming progressively more anti-Swedish and anti-Finnish feelings were developing among the Swedish-speaking group, Ahlqvist was one of the few public personalities to advocate conciliation between the two language groups. In the poem *Valtiollista* ('On Politics,' 1865), he insisted that the Finns and Swedes had, in the past, fought together so often that they must be forever united. He saw in Russia a threat to Finland, an unusual attitude in his time, and felt that Finland could not afford to sever its ties with Swedish culture and Western Europe, although he never formulated these ideas practically. He did work constantly to improve the position of the Finnish language, and, as the rector (president) of the University of Helsinki, he delivered the speech at the beginning of the academic year in Finnish for the first time in the history of that institution. He had a querulous character and was often at odds with almost everyone he knew; he was one of the founders of the newspaper *Suometar,*[164] on which Yrjö-Koskinen also collaborated, but the two never agreed, and Yrjö-Koskinen soon left to found his own paper. Ahlqvist also edited a linguistic and literary paper, *Kieletär*, and Yrjö-Koskinen had one titled *Kirjallinen Kuukauslehti*, in which they had continual opportunity to disagree.[165]

In the first issues of *Suometar*, Ahlqvist published an "ethnographic dream,"[166] *Satu* ('A Saga' rather than 'A Tale'), in which he predicted that Finland would one day be independent; by mere chance it escaped the attention of the censure. His other patriotic poems include *Savolaisen laulu* ('The Song of Savo,' 1852),[167] *Suomen valta* ('Finland's Power,' 1860), and *Sotamarssi* ('The War March,' 1889), all set to music and long popular. *Savolaisen laulu* is the first in a series of poems by various authors praising the old Finnish provinces, their nature, history, and inhabitants, later set to music and sung at local festivals. Such poetry meant for public consumption was not, of course, on a very high artistic level, only more or less conventional. In Ahlqvist's poem the military qualities of the Finns (or the inhabitants of Savo) were praised almost for the first time in Finnish poetry. Even without the example of *Ensign Stål*, Ahlqvist's aggressive nature might have inspired this kind of verse, a more typical example of which is *The War March*, commemorating the victory of Porrassalmi in the war of 1788-90. It calls all Finns from Savo, Ostrobotnia, and Karelia to rise against the enemy (who is not named) and suppress "violence" or "unjust domination"; the allusions are thinly veiled, and the poem was avowedly written to celebrate the Swedish and Finnish victory over the Russians.[168] That such a poem could be written and published and the author not only unharmed but also awarded the usual honors for public personalities (in addition to his post at the university, he was made first Counsellor of Chancery, then Counsellor of State) is a good illustration of the peculiar relations then existing between Finland and Russia.

Suomen valta, written in praise of the Finnish language and its speakers, calls them to take their country's destiny into their own hands, as they have alone cleared the land for cultivation and defended it against the enemy. This last assertion implies the criticism often voiced in Finland that under Swedish rule the country was left to fight its enemies alone, without aid from Sweden.[169] The last stanza indicates the proper extension of Finland's power: from Lake Onega (Äänisjärvi) to the Gulf of Botnia, from the banks of the Aura (where Turku is located) to the mouth of the Dvina (*Wienansuu*) on the White Sea.[170] Since both Lake Onega and the Dvina have been in Russian-controlled, though Finnish-speaking, territory throughout history, Ahlqvist's dream was so mad that only a scholar and poet like himself could have thought of it. However, as the nationalist spirit grew among the Finns, they hoped for present victories, not only celebrations of those past, and as Karelia, especially the Russian-dominated section, due to its amazingly rich folklore, was considered a dreamland where the last remnants of a glorious Finnish past were preserved, more and more Finns and, eventually, nationalistic politicians claimed that Karelia should be liberated from Russia and united with Finland, after the country had become independent, of course. After Finnish guerillas had fought in Russian Karelia and Ingria during the troubled years immediately following the Bolshevik Revolution, many patriotic organizations continued to proclaim that it was the sacred duty of every Finn to liberate his brothers beyond the border,[171] and in 1941 the country went to war against the Soviet Union on the side of Hitler's Germany, after having been badly provoked and frightened by the Russians in 1939-40. When conquered, Karelia proved a rather bitter disappointment although public statements could not be made about this. An out-of-the-way corner of the Russian state, it was backwards in many respects, and its inhabitants had become as Russian in their way of living during their long union with Russia as the Finns of Finland had become Swedish during their union with Sweden.[172]

The best-known poem among Ahlqvist's nonpolitical or nonpatriotic poetry is his ballad *Koskenlaskijan morsiamet* ('The Ferryman's Brides,' 1853),[173] set to music by Sibelius. It is of the supernatural type often found in Germany, and Ahlqvist was perhaps moved to write it by the tale of Lorelei. It tells of a mermaid dwelling in a river who falls in love with a young ferryman unaware of her love. When he takes his human bride with him on his boat, the mermaid lifts a stone from the bottom of the river, which upsets the vessel, and the lovers drown. At his best Ahlqvist was not a bad poet, and the fact that there are few poems of this type written by real artists in Finland, and Sibelius's music, explain its long popularity. As the language has changed considerably in the last hundred years, the poem sounds even more quaint than was intended, just as one would expect a traditional ballad to be.

In 1854 Ahlqvist wrote the first Finnish sonnet, *Suomalainen sonetti* ('A Finnish Sonnet'). Although it was admired at the time, it has no considerable artistic value. He was accordingly a well-known poet when, in 1860, he published his first collection of verse, *Säkeniä* ('Sparks'). It was considered one of the events marking the beginning of a literature in Finnish. A new edition was printed three years later, and a new collection, called *Säkeniä, toinen parvi* ('Sparks, Second Flight') was issued in 1868. Both were republished with additions and modifications in 1874, 1881, and 1898, after the poet's death. Many of the poems had been previously published, and there were many translations among them, from Swedish, German, and classical Greek, as well as free adaptations of other works. They reflect accurately Ahlqvist's character and his inability to express finer feelings, a lack he admitted, saying once that his verse was only an attempt to adapt Finnish to a variety of meters in the hope that others would be encouraged by his example to try the same. In the title poem of his collections, *Säkenet* ('The Sparks'), he says so metaphorically and directly; after the description of a smithy from the chimney from which sparks fly as the blacksmith works and the assertion that sparks are soon extinguished but can kindle a fire if they meet the proper material, the poet says that his works are but sparks which he hopes will kindle poetic fire in the breasts of other Finns.

He rarely built a poem on subjective feelings alone, but almost always added general considerations, as in *Syksytoiveita* ('Hopes of Autumn'). After describing the coming autumn and winter, the poet finds consolation in knowing that the harvest has been good and the grain for next year has been sown, then states that approaching death is like autumn, which a man need not fear if he has worked well and planted the seeds of the future. Besides a few love poems, among which *Etelälle* ('To the South') and *Eräs nuorukaismuisto* ('A Memory from My Youth') are best known, *Mun kesäni* ('My Summer') is perhaps most personal. The poet, after having toiled all spring like a slave and having waited for the summer in order to be free, sees the summer glide away and autumn come nearer without any change in his condition. He concludes that this songless spring and mirthless summer are a picture of his life; Ahlqvist obviously did not trust his readers to draw the right conclusions and supplied them himself. In *Sydämeni asukkaat* the author confesses that an angel and a devil have always dwelt in his heart and the devil has usually won. *Kerran viinikellarissa* ('Once in a Wine Cellar') is almost his only poem with a more humorous outlook; it is a bacchic praise of wine, which brings joy to our short lives and helps us see that the world, a "tumbling-place of fools," is but a soap bubble, which we may ignore when, thanks to the "old strength of sherry-juice," we see beauty and truth.

Ahlqvist's literary criticism was always rather strict and pedantic, although he did recognize talent (but not genius, e.g., Kivi). We really do not know why he abused Kivi's works. Like Kivi, he was of very modest origin, but reached a high position through hard work, intelligence, and good luck. Perhaps Kivi reminded him of what he might have become himself, a man who never cared to finish his studies, who lived almost on charity, was always in debt, and wrote works whose form seemed to Ahlqvist sloppy.[174] Emotionally unbalanced as he was, Ahlqvist was likely to reject with disgust and fear the idea of sharing these weaknesses, punishing Kivi for having them. Whatever his motives, he established a pattern in Finnish literature, for not until the twentieth century did authors see and describe the world in a manner similar to Kivi's.

From the time of Kivi and Ahlqvist, literature and poetry in Finnish developed steadily, although among their immediate contemporaries there were no great authors. They did help establish a literary tradition, which scarcely existed among the Finnish-speaking group, some of their works became quite popular, and all made efforts toward perfection of form and style, which they partially achieved. One poet who worked with this aim was **Julius L. F. Krohn** (1835-88, also known under the pseudonym of **Suonio**), the son of a well-to-do merchant from Viipuri. He chose an academic career, became professor of Finnish literature at the university in 1885, and a well-known folklorist. He developed the so-called historical and geographical method of research, perfected by his son Kaarle Krohn, and made Finnish folklore research known abroad. An outdoorsman and sailor, he drowned on his yacht in the Gulf of Viipuri.

His parents were German, private tutors taught him Russian and French, and he went to a Swedish school, but out of idealism and patriotism, like so many others in his time, he decided that he would become a pure Finn. He studied Finnish at the university and among country people he met at his father's estate near Viipuri, where the island of Suonio, which gave him his pseudonym, is located.[175] As a schoolboy he had written poems in German and Swedish, but he first gained notice in 1859, when he translated Schiller's ballad *Der Taucher* ('The Diver') into Finnish (*Sukeltaja*) on the hundredth anniversary of the poet's birth. Ahlqvist presented a Finnish version of Schiller's *Die Glocke* ('The Bell') and praised Krohn's work. Subsequently he followed his younger colleague's progress, encouraging and criticizing him. Krohn considered poetry for himself a pastime and was modest about his compositions. In *Varpunen* ('The Sparrow') he says that the sparrow, who has sung in winter, must remain silent in spring, when better singers return from the south. Typically, for himself and his time, he did not leave the metaphor simple, but added religious and patriotic considerations: a sparrow's voice will not carry to heaven, but, if he were a nightingale or a lark, he could tell his sorrows to God,[176] who would perhaps see Finland and let his sun shine on its dark forests.

Such self-pity has been common among all Finns, not only poets, from the nineteenth century almost to the present; Finland has been represented as an exceptionally unhappy country, devastated by wars, plagues, and famines, attacked by the Russians and neglected by the Swedes, denied a culture in its own language, and ignored by the rest of the world.[177] The inner, eastern, and northern parts of Finland were until the nineteenth century more or less a wilderness, slowly cleared by settlers who struggled against hard soil, harsh climate, bad harvests, and wild animals, but; in the southwestern, western, and southern parts of the country, a fairly prosperous civilization developed steadily from prehistoric times. A sharp contrast existed between the developed and underdeveloped areas in the country; in fact large quantities of grain were at times exported from the west while the population went hungry in the east and north.[178] Like that of the American West, the life of the underdeveloped parts of Finland is often used to represent the country as a whole. But, as Finland is sparsely populated and out-of-the-way, largely unnoticed by the rest of the world, its inhabitants try to compensate for their feeling of inferiority by assuring everyone that their inconspicuous position in the world is due to the Russians, the Swedes, poor soil, hard climate, famines, and acts of God. The greater the odds against the Finns appear, the greater is their glory in coping with them.[179] In another poem, *Virsi kotimaan*

102

puolesta ('A Hymn for Our Country'), which has remained very popular, Krohn also says that "our nation is small and worthless in the eyes of the world."

Krohn's poetry was, in general, sweet and melodious, so much so that Kivi, his friend, once said that he was "such a la-di-da."[180] However, his love for outdoor life and exercise is reflected in such poems as *Suksimiesten laulu* ('The Skiers' Song')[181] or *Purjehdusretki* ('Sailing'), but again moral and patriotic considerations are included. When the enemy invades Finland, the skiers will take sharp irons in their hands to retaliate, and the sailor struggling against the waves is like a strong man struggling against evil. Between 1873 and 1880 he also published a magazine, *Suomen Kuvalehti*,[182] which was one of the first of its kind in Finland, wrote poems for children published with illustrations, which enjoyed long popularity, composed symbolic fairy tales, *Kuun tarinoita* ('Tales of the Moon'), sometimes called his best work, and did many translations, of Walter Scott and Hans Christian Andersen, for example. At his initiative four other poets and translators met to translate *The Tales of Ensign Stål*; this translation was later revised by Paavo Cajander and is generally credited to him.[183]

Paavo Cajander (1846-1913) was born in Hämeenlinna, the son of a tanner. He took his M.A. at the University of Helsinki, worked for Yrjö-Koskinen's *Kirjallinen Kuukauslehti* and *Suomen Kuvalehti*, was lecturer in Finnish at the university from 1886 until his retirement in 1912, was chairman of the Finnish Writers' Guild[184] between 1901 and 1908, and received the title of doctor *honoris causa* in 1907. He occasionally wrote poems published in newspapers and periodicals, but was very modest about them. Although asked to collect his verse, he never did so; a collection appeared only after his death, in 1914. Some of his poems have remained popular; *Vaipuos, vaivu, synnyinmaasi helmaan* ('Sink, o sink, into the bosom of thy country'), written for Aleksis Kivi's funeral, is often sung at the last services for the deceased,[185] and his patriotic poems, e.g., *Vapautettu kuningatar* ('The Liberated Queen'—the queen is Finland) and *Maljanesitys isänmaalle* ('A Toast to Our Country'),[186] which, set to music by Cajander's friend Sibelius, have been, since they were written, standard features of public functions. They are rhetorical, especially the *Toast*, but rather good rhetoric, as Sir Winston Churchill's great speeches during the last war are good rhetoric. The *Toast* is not an appeal to war and conquest, does not express hate, fear, or contempt for anyone or declare Finland superior to other nations; it simply reminds the reader that love for one's country can be a mighty power and help in time of distress.

Cajander's main work, as a translator, began in 1869 with a story by the Norwegian Björnson. He then translated many works by the Swedish authors of Finland, e.g., Runeberg's *Hanna* and *Christmas Night* in addition to his part in *Ensign Stål*, Topelius's *Readings for Children* (Volumes I-III), *The*

Book of Our Land, and *The Book of Nature*, and Wecksell's *Daniel Hjorth.* His major translation is that of all of Shakespeares's plays, completed between 1879, when he published *Hamlet*, and 1912, when he finished *Titus Andronicus.* He also did a Finnish version of part of the *Sonnets.* Because there is so little verse drama in Finnish, his translations are almost unique, and, because the Finnish language has changed a great deal since his death, they now have the same slightly archaic flavor of the originals. It is greatly due to Cajander that Shakespeare has become one of the foreign authors most performed in Finland[187] and has had great influence on Finnish literature, though indirectly.[188] Nowadays Cajander's texts are not considered quite satisfactory.[189] Another poet, Yrjö Jylhä, published his versions of some Shakespearean plays, but the older translations are still used, possibly slightly revised, for the other plays.

Arvid Oskar Gustaf Genetz (1848-1915), known as **Arvi Jännes**, was a scholar like Ahlqvist, under whom he studied. He published numerous important works in his field of Finno-Ugric languages, among them a phonology, morphology, and prosody of Finnish in which he stated the theories he practiced as a poet. He loved his native Finnish Karelia. Like Ahlqvist, he dreamed of Finland's future greatness and was one of the few poets, besides Leino, who introduced figures from old Finnish mythology in his works, e.g., in *Väinölän lapset* ('The Children of Väinölä'), in which he laments that the children of Väinölä—his name for the country where Väinö or Väinämöinen once lived—are dispersed, that great Finland is torn and its people shattered. The ghost of old Väinämöinen sings that, were there but a spirit of kinship[190] among them, they could be reunited and a new day would dawn for the unhappy nation. As in Ahlqvist's *Suomen valta*, the great Finland includes Vepsä, Aunus (in Russian Karelia), and even Estonia. Another patriotic poem, *Herää, Suomi!* ('Awaken, Finland!') was set to music by his brother Emil Genetz and was long popular. *Karjala* ('Karelia') and *Kalevala, Suomen kruunu* ('Kalevala, the Crown of Finland') are of the same type. He also translated some Hungarian poems and short stories and Runeberg's *The Moose Hunters,* and occasionally wrote literary criticism. He was also once elected to Parliament and appointed a member of the cabinet for four years.

Kaarlo Robert Kramsu (1855-95) had a personality totally unlike those of the writers just mentioned; he was a man whom we can think of only as a poet, although he did not produce many works in his brief life. He was born in Oulu, the son of a sailor, and in 1874 went to study in Helsinki. At the university Ahlqvist and Yrjö-Koskinen influenced him, and he took a decidedly Finnish standpoint on all linguistic and political questions. His first poems won a prize awarded by a students' organization, but he never completed his studies. To earn his living he worked as a journalist in small towns, but he was poor and suffered from illness and depression, eventually becoming insane. He was taken to a hospital in 1891, released for a short time, but was soon readmitted; he died there soon afterwards.

His poetry, unlike the idealistic, patriotic, and rhetorical work of his contemporaries, is deeply personal, expressing his ingrained pessimism. Even when treating patriotic subjects, it reflects his somber mood rather than appeals to his fellow citizens. His best-known poems deal with the War of the Maces. As he sided with the rebellious peasants, there is a social and national message, but it is hardly more than a protest on behalf of the oppressed, without a definite program or hint of a better future. They do give a true picture of the war, even though such may not have been Kramsu's intent.[191] They also contain some grim humor, or, in modern terms, a feeling of life's absurdity, especially *Ilkka*, named after the leader of the rebels. The first stanza says "Ilkka's deeds will perhaps live long still on the lips of the people; he lived like a man of Finland and died on the gallows." The next (and last) says, "Great deeds bring glory but may also take you elsewhere; and Ilkka they took the shortest way to the gallows."[192] In *Santavuoren tappelu* ('The Battle of Santavuori')[193] a rebel dying on the battlefield pronounces words of revenge and hope for a better future "with the pallor of death on his face, with a mocking smile on his lips." *Tarina* ('A Tale') and *Huokaavat kentät* ('The Fields That Sigh') have a more directly patriotic appeal. Four lines in the latter express a hope, however slight; the poet calls the fields of his country, "full of memories, full of sorrows, to sigh until all the mists have cleared away, until the heart of Finland starts beating, until the blood starts running, until the ice of centuries melts." *Jaakkima Berends*, named for a tyrannic nobleman,[194] describes the resistance, by patient work, of a farmer he oppresses and ends with four lines stating, "It has always been the husbandman's work in Finland to rebuild what the gentleman destroyed." *Hannu Krankka* is the only genuinely humorous poem in Kramsu's production; Krankka, a historical character who survived the War of the Maces and was a prominent figure in his home region, wins a skirmish against the regular troops and takes the fur coat worn by the enemy's leader to wear. Mistaken for the original owner, he is beaten by his own men before the error is discovered. *Uusi aika* ('The New Time') expresses Kramsu's disbelief in reform or change. It vaguely alludes to his own time, stating that old beliefs are tottering and what was once holy is disappearing, that ideals are clashing, heroes dying, and slaves shaking off their fetters. The mood is not hopeful but ironic in its prediction of the new society. When the best of nations have fallen, when warriors are tired and their ideals debased, those who did not struggle but were biding their time come forward to heal the wounds. New laws are made by small spirits, and a new society built like the old, merely more polished on the surface. A new order is created, new fetters wrought for the human spirit, and then a new tempest lashes out to destroy all.

Kramsu's poems on more personal subjects reflect similar feelings and thoughts as well as doubt about his identity, perhaps a premonition of the coming disintegration of his personality. One might call it a slip of the pen in *Ensimmäinen leivo* ('The First Lark'; the simile of this bird was much favored in Finland). The first lark announces the coming of spring although the nights are still cold and dark and the ground covered by snow. The author then wishes that he, too, could hope for sunshine and green fields, forgetting the frost's destruction and the terror of nothingness—this last phrase is out of place because the image of coming spring and receding winter is maintained throughout the poem. *Haihtumaton muisto* ('A Memory That Will Not Vanish') is about the presence of a memory which follows the poet through his life. Although he does not know whether the memory is sad or happy, he does not wish to be separated from it because it is something that belongs to him alone. *Vanha lauluni* ('My Old Song') states that, when the poet found an old song in which he had expressed his innermost feelings, he did not recognize it because his own heart was no longer familiar with its old self. *Vanhat tuttavat* ('Old Acquaintances') adopts the old theme of two friends who meet again but hardly recognize each other; Kramsu's peculiar humor appears in the last stanza: "we spend our evening / like dear friends / and pretend to believe / that we are acquaintances."

In other poems Kramsu formulates a grim philosophy, a desperate protest against the meaningless suffering inflicted on man by the world. In *Onnensa etsijä* ('Seeking One's Luck') he describes himself, hurrying toward his luck along a stony path and through stormy weather, knowing his time to be short, like that of all others going in the same direction. No one reaches the goal, but all must hurry, for he who rests is dead while alive. *Miksi naurat?* ('Why Do You Laugh?') addresses its question to an anonymous person laughing as if in childish joy in the midst of the pain and miseries of the world, but the poet says that he has finally discovered that the laughter expresses dark scorn and rebellion. Juhani Aho later said that students liked to quote *Mustalainen* ('The Gypsy') to express their contempt for traditional values.[195] Although different in many respects, it is reminiscent of a short prose poem by Baudelaire, *The Stranger*,[196] with which Kramsu was certainly unfamiliar. In both the main character declares that he has no friends, no family, no country and that he loves only one thing: in Baudelaire's poem "the clouds, the marvelous clouds that pass far away"; in Kramsu's work pleasure, which ends in death, though not unhappily, for no one would want to live forever.

Among the rather conventional Finnish poets of the nineteenth century (Kivi, of course, excepted), Kramsu stands alone. In form he followed the rules of Ahlqvist and Genetz, giving his poems regular rhythmic pattern and rhyme scheme; he did not use the classical meters. Even the greatest of Finnish poets at times seem to have been as interested in the formal beauty of their works and the choice of subjects thought suited for poetry as in essential human problems. Of those who followed Kramsu, Eino Leino used elements from a mythic Finnish past, Koskenniemi was interested in classical antiquity, and the generation of the 1920s looked for romanticism in exotic, faraway countries. Only a few poets, like Kramsu, concentrated on basic moral and metaphysical problems—Siljo, occasionally Kailas, and Hellaakoski—and, like he did, they reduced their poems to essential elements.[197] Kramsu's compositions sometimes seem almost uncouth and clumsy, but also rough and powerful. He stated his interest in certain basic human problems in a simple and forceful manner, with everyday words and phrases, giving them elemental fullness and depth of meaning.

In addition to Kramsu, Kivi, and other poets previously discussed, there were a few writers who should be classified as album poets.[198] Among their many poems a few have survived, often as songs whose authors have been forgotten. In Finland, as in all Scandinavian countries, singing has always been very popular,[199] and composers have written numerous *lied*-type songs and choral compositions for poems, the simple, melodious form of which lent itself easily to music.

Like Ahlqvist, Krohn, and Genetz, **Bernhard Fredrik Godenhjelm** (1840-1912) was a university man. Born into a Swedish-speaking family and educated in a Swedish school, he chose Finnish as his language. He was active in many fields of education, was elected to Parliament, and taught German at the University of Helsinki. He took part in translating *The Tales of Ensign Stål* into Finnish, published a textbook on literature and another on poetry for the schools, a German-Finnish dictionary, and a large treatise on poetry and prosody, *Runous ja runouden muodot* (Part I, 1885; Part II, posthumously, 1914). His poems were collected and published in the latter work; among them *Kaupin linna* ('Kauppi's Castle'), written on a folk motif, is best known. It deals with God's punishment to a haughty nobleman who showed contempt to a beggar.

Aleksanteri Rahkonen (1841-77) had a short, active life. He wrote to newspapers, collaborated in translating *Ensign Stål*, translated poems and plays, and wrote verse. Among his poems, *Leivo* ('The Lark') survives as a song. His death was due to lung tuberculosis, once a widespread illness which killed so many young writers in Finland that Professor Kohtamäki calls it the "poets' disease."[200] The two small volumes of poems he published between 1865 and 1867 are titled *Sääskiä* ('Moths'), a name explained in the title poem. The poet says his works are like moths flying on a summer evening and scattered by a gust of wind the next morning; when a greater poet appears, he will be forgotten. This attitude of self-deprecation also appears in Ahlqvist, Krohn, and other nineteenth-century Finnish poets.[201] They felt they had a duty to write so that their country might have a literature in its own language, but they were modest about their achievements and, failing to recognize the greatness of Kivi or Kramsu,[202] hoped for a genius to appear.

Isa (Louise) Asp (1853-72) also died of tuberculosis, at the age of nineteen. She was from a Swedish-speaking family, and most of her more than one hundred poems are in that language, but she changed to Finnish when she began studies at the Teachers' College of Jyväskylä (now a university). Her production is not especially mature, but, with her letters and diary, shows lyrical talent and depth of feeling. Her best-known poem is *Aallon kehtolaulu* ('A Lullaby to a Wave') in which the free, irregular rhythmic pattern is notable.

Besides translating numerous German, Spanish, Hungarian, and other poems into Finnish, **Uno Gabriel von Schrowe** (1853-81) wrote some himself. *Morsian* ('The Bride'), in the ballad tradition, tells a tragic story of unhappy love. *Ensi kerran* ('The First Time') has remained popular as a song. He, too, died of tuberculosis.

Antti Törneroos (1835-96), known under his pseudonym **Tuokko**, was a friend of Aleksis Kivi. He took a university degree and worked as a teacher, journalist, and writer, but, like Kivi, he fought many difficulties, including illness and drink, and was insane at the time of his death. He was among the first to translate English poems into Finnish, publishing some works of Thomas Moore in 1861, and continued this activity throughout his life.[203] His collection *Leivonen* ('The Lark,' 1877) contained more than one hundred Finnish versions of poems by Uhland, Bürger, Franzén, Tegnér, Runeberg, and others. One of the most active members in the group which produced the Finnish text of *Ensign Stål*, he also translated approximately fifty plays and opera libretti. His most important work, a blank verse tragedy titled *Saul* (1868), was the first Finnish tragedy after Kivi's *Kullervo*. Both Cygnaeus and Bergbom praised the lyrical beauty of the language, but pointed out its weaknesses: the loose composition, excessive length of some passages, and superficiality in the characters' description. It was never performed and is hardly even read today; what has survived of his production is a poem, *Työväen marssi* ('The Workers' March' or 'The Workingmen's March'—to use an archaic English word), set to music and still sung at public functions and festivals arranged by politically and socially organized labor.[204]

Although Finland had remained quiet and isolated until 1880, after that date new ideas appearing abroad were quickly noticed in Finland and studied in the original works or translations.[205] The authors whose works drew the most interest were, in general, those who influenced the world's thinking: Darwin; Herbert Spencer and John Stuart Mill; Hippolyte Taine and Renan; Zola, Flaubert, and Maupassant; Ibsen and Björnson; Strindberg; and Georg Brandes, who was widely read in Scandinavia in his lifetime. Some authors acquired even more importance abroad than in their own countries:

Henry Thomas Buckle's *History of Civilization in England* was considered epoch-making in Finland, and the American economist Henry George often represented socialism for Finnish writers, instead of Marx and Engels.[206]

Writers in Finland chose that which was congenial to them in their readings and absorbed the atmosphere of the time instead of following ready-made formulas.[207] Brandes once complained that pure naturalism never gained a foothold among Scandinavian authors because of their basically sentimental and idealistic outlook. Buckle's conviction that the course of human affairs is "permeated by one glorious principle of universal and undeviating regularity"[208] was not shared even by those who read and admired his works. Minna Canth, for example, was most attracted to Buckle by his criticism of the church, clergy, and army, the three institutions she considered opposed to progress. Actually much of Finland's literature was realistic even before 1880. The term was often applied to Runeberg's descriptions of folk life, and Kivi was frequently thought of as a naturalist. In his case, as in many others, the term had a disparaging connotation.

In literature Norway had the greatest influence on Finnish writers—one might say, half-seriously, that Finland began to feel its impact in Ibsen's thoughts at the moment when the curtain went up for the first presentation of *A Doll's House* at the Finnish Theater in Helsinki in 1880, not more than a year after the play had been produced in Norway and eleven years before a British audience would see his works. The shock initiated long and violent discussions, first about the play and its character—the question was whether or not Nora had a right to leave her home and husband—and then about the position of woman, family, morals, religion, and society in general. For approximately ten years Norwegian influence on Finnish literature was so strong that, according to a popular saying, Finland was a literary colony of Norway. As Juhani Aho said, "We loved Norwegian literature as much as our own, and to some extent it superseded the Swedish. Norwegian was a language of civilization for us, and we even deciphered patiently a strange popular dialect in Garborg's books."[209] Besides the great authors Ibsen and Björnson, others such as Jonas Lie, Alexander Kielland, Arne Garborg, and Kristian Elster were read. Although these authors differed, they shared a sharply critical attitude toward existing society. Kielland, a rather aristocratic radical, wrote in faultless and elegant language, often satirizing violently both the established church and dissenters. Garborg, less refined, gave frank descriptions of young artists' and students' lives in Oslo, with an undercurrent of deep pessimism, often considered by the leading writers the only possible mood in the sick, stagnant society of the period. Elster was much like Garborg, but Lie was less radical, although a hidden criticism of his days' life can be found in his novels. Strindberg, whose writings produced such passionate discussions in his own country and eventually abroad, was much less influential in Finland than the Norwegian authors because his violent, disharmonious personality was not congenial to the calmer, more contemplative Finnish writers. Even the most radical, Minna Canth, as a woman, could not share his views on women and marriage.

During the last years of the nineteenth century, when Alexander III ruled Russia, relations between that country and Finland remained good. Parliament, still the old Diet of the Four Estates, met regularly every third year and received the right to propose new bills. A new criminal law, considered very progressive at that time, and a law on dissenters were passed. The official use of Finnish was extended, many private Finnish schools were taken over by the government,[210] and new railroads were built. However, the Russian government did publish in 1890 an imperial manifesto which placed the Finnish postal service under the control of Russian authorities, though Finnish stamps were not suppressed until 1901. With the revival of political life after 1860, parties appeared, first the Finnish party, led by Yrjö-Koskinen and his friends, and the Swedish party. Near 1885 a group of young writers, poets, and artists, including Juhani Aho, Minna Canth, J. H. Erkko, Santeri Ingman, Arvid Järnefelt, and Kasimir Lönnbohm (Leino), formed a group called Young Finland (*Nuori Suomi*), formally organized as a party in 1894. From that moment the Finnish party, corresponding to the conservative parties in other countries, was called the Old Finnish party; the Young Finnish party was more or less the equivalent of a liberal party. The Swedish party grouped almost all of the Swedish-speaking population. A Workers' party, founded in 1899, adopted a socialist platform and the name Social-Democrat party in 1903. When, in 1906, an Agrarian party (*Maalaisliitto*) had been founded, the major political groupings, (which, favored by the proportional vote used in the elections, still exist) had organized themselves. Although the names have been changed for some, the organizations remain basically the same. In the 1930s there was an extreme right-wing party with fascist tendencies, now forbidden; the Communist party, forbidden until the end of World War II, is now legal and working.

Among the writers who introduced new ideas and actively took part in discussions on political, social, religious, and moral questions, **Minna Canth** (1844-97)[211] proved with her own life that women did not need to be treated as legal minors, as was the case all over the world. Her father, an intelligent and energetic worker who eventually became a draper in Kuopio, sent his daughter in 1863 to the newly founded Finnish Teachers' College at Jyväskylä. Instead of becoming a teacher, she married the professor of sciences at the institution, J. F. Canth, and, when he died in 1879, she had seven children and experience in raising a large family with modest means. Her marriage had been happy; it was not from her own experience that she wrote her many descriptions of unhappy family life. She returned to Kuopio and took over her father's shop, which she managed successfully. Eventually she became a renowned author, specifically a playwright, and met many well-known personalities. At times she had almost a literary salon in Kuopio, where persons of different origin and education, united by intellectual pursuits, met, including the talented wife of General and Governor Alexander Järnefelt, *née* Baroness Clodt von Jürgensburg, and her gifted sons, especially Arvid; the Swedish-Finnish author Karl August Tavaststjerna, also of an aristocratic family; the former farm hand Heikki Kauppinen; Elias Erkko, brother of the better-known poet J. H. Erkko; Juhani Aho; and the director of the Finnish Theater,[212] Kaarlo Bergbom.

Minna Canth had her "period of innocence"[213] in the years near the 1880s, when she wrote her first short stories and the two comedies *Murtovarkaus* ('The Burglary,' 1883) and *Roinilan talossa* ('At Roinila Farm,' 1885).[214] At Jyväskylä she had already written a few short stories for a local paper edited by her husband; when the Finnish Theater visited the town between 1876 and 1878, she felt more attracted to drama. She was, however, deeply religious, very far still from the woman who would one day vehemently attack the established church, and she felt pangs of conscience at having written something as frivolous as a play. In a letter she says that she was happy that her play was met with sharp criticism because it would humble and purify her,[215] but whether she meant that all theater was sinful or that her own play was not serious enough is not clear.

As there had been no Finnish theater before 1872 and Swedish dramatic art did not have much longer traditions in Finland, melodrama as a genre was unknown there. Nevertheless, Minna Canth's early plays can be aptly described under that heading—even her later plays are reminiscent of it. However, she had a talent for plot and dialogue that allowed some of the weaknesses and improbabilities of the action to pass unnoticed, and in her serious plays she presented deep social and moral problems that made the audience forgive or forget their artistic defects. Of course, as those problems became unimportant, interest in the plays subsided. Technically she is one of the best, if not the best, Finnish playwright; there are in fact only two other writers whose dramatic works can be considered seriously: Kivi and Hella Wuolijoki, who wrote immediately prior to World War II, a surprising fact as the Finns have an extraordinary passion for the theater.[216]

Murtovarkaus and *Roinilan talossa* have basically the same plot: two young people from the country are in love, but their parents oppose the marriage; the young man is unjustly suspected of a crime; when his innocence is proved, the lovers are united. The good people are very good, the villain very bad, and a humorous character makes the audience laugh occasionally. Kuopio is in Savo, which we have mentioned as a region of jokers; Minna Canth had opportunity to observe many popular types, and she represented the comic ones well, thus demonstrating her talent as a playwright.

After *Murtovarkaus* she had suggested to Bergbom that she might try something more serious, but he wanted her to keep the subject of "the merry life of Finnish youth in the summer,"[217] and so she composed *Roinilan talossa.* By then she had been reading about important foreign authors and had become ardently interested in social and moral problems. In a letter of 1884 she expressed enthusiasm for a work by Henry George: "Socialism, just pure socialism. It is the best I have read so far. Excellent." In another from 1886, she told of her search for materials at the Kuopio poorhouse and among the workers building the Savo railway; these last, she said, had been so angered by a construction engineer that they had planned to kill him, but calmed themselves when she promised to write about conditions at the working places.[218]

She also became interested in the controversy about sexual morals which marked the gradual breakdown of the Victorian attitude in all European countries and spread to Finland in the 1880s. The complex question had many aspects, treated both together and separately.[219] One was the fight against prostitution, coupled with the protest that prostitutes and unwed mothers were despised and punished while the men who had put them in those positions went free. The discussion often turned to the double moral standards of society and then to the value of sexual love. The most conservative opinion defended prostitution on the grounds that good women felt no desire but men had shameful lusts which they must satisfy with bad women in order to preserve the purity of thier homes.[220] The extreme opposite view was that men and women should be equal, equally free to enjoy sex without restraint, whereas, according to what can be called the progressive but moral view, men and women should be equal, equally chaste, and should practice intercourse only in marriage for the procreation of children, as sex in itself was sinful.[221] Still another variant was that sex was holy and wonderful, to be enjoyed equally by men and women only in marriage.[222]

Although Minna Canth's marriage was happy, she apparently never experienced any pleasure of the senses and considered sex repulsive. While still living in Jyväskylä, she said that "every marriage is not chaste, many shameful acts are committed in them."[223] Later, in a letter from 1882, she told a friend that, as man and woman were spiritually different, they should make each other more perfect in marriage, so that "a spiritual collaboration, freed from the bond of senses, would reduce the excesses in the characters of both the sexes. ... The sexes would learn to know each other as *human beings*, not as cocks and hens."[224] In 1887 she stated, again in a letter, that erotic love is an illusion, marriage a prosaic reality. In 1890 she wrote about an article published by a writer who had traveled in the eastern parts of the country and expressed admiration for the country girls there, so different from the emancipated women who despised men and themselves, that it was disgusting to see an old man so infatuated with young girls and that one had to thank God that there were also healthy people in the world, i.e., those not like men.

Besides claiming equal rights for women, she insisted that men must follow the same moral rules in sex that women follow; she was criticized for both views. In 1885 the Bishop of Kuopio wrote that the emancipation of women was against God's order and would be the undoing of society and women. Less stringent morals were argued, too, and Gustaf af Geijerstam, a Swedish writer who came to Helsinki in 1887 to lecture on the subject, presented the argument that men were basically different from women, that he did not condone immorality and prostitution, but recommended that women try to understand men rather than condemn them so that, through a long, slow process of development and education, man would reach woman's level of purity. His opinions were violently attacked by many women crusading for their sex and public morality, including Minna Canth.[225] Among his defenders was Juhani Aho, until then Minna Canth's friend, who in the newspaper *Savo* opposed her; he was ironic not only about her opinions, but also about her appearance and age. One article in which he presented his arguments was *Juorun jumalatar* ('The Goddess of Gossip').[226] Despite the use of a pseudonym, Minna Canth knew his identity, and, although their relationship was mended after a few years, they followed different roads from that moment. Her most powerful argument for higher morality, which has never been rebutted, was that, if men were to be allowed a certain amount of immorality, what of the necessary partners in that immorality, the prostitutes and "bad" women and the brutal, humiliating treatment society reserved for them?

Työmiehen vaimo ('The Wife of a Worker'), written between 1883 and 1884 and first produced in Helsinki at the Finnish Theater on January 28, 1885, was her first serious play. It was a sensation and produced violent discussion of its moral qualities, not of its artistic and literary merits. In the last respect it has many weaknesses, for she felt other considerations to be secondary to her message and, besides the good authors she had studied, she had read many inferior works, trashy and sentimental German novelettes and such.[227] After the play's presentation, she wrote to a friend that she was not satisfied with it, but because it did not contain the "truth of life."[228] She attacks in it the dependent position of women, the irresponsibility of men, and the indifference of society to these facts, and she also mentions the evils of alcohol. In 1882 an act giving legal protection to the earnings of married women had been proposed in Parliament, but the proposal was killed; its failure greatly angered Minna Canth and other leaders of the feminist movement and moved them to protest publicly. *Työmiehen vaimo* shows that a wife is completely at her husband's mercy, even if he is an idler and a drunkard. Before his marriage Risto, a worker, has had a relationship with the gypsy girl Homsantuu,[229] whom he leaves when he meets an honest girl with some money. After marrying her, he drinks all her savings and earnings, reminding her as he takes her money that he has the right to do so, for the law gives a husband the right to all of his wife's property. Homsantuu appears at the end and tries to shoot Risto; when taken away by the police, she shouts, "Your law and order . . . That's what I ought to have shot at," terrifying the audiences of the time. In spite of her negative attitude toward sex, Minna Canth displays an unconscious attraction to characters with few sexual inhibitions, like Homsantuu or the peddler Kauppa-Lopo in a short story, who are not depicted unsympathetically; indeed, she was charged with condoning sin.[230] True to the sense of humor she possessed, she also introduced a comic character in the play, Risto's drinking companion Toppo, who jokes in defense of drink. Still other secondary characters make less inoffensive remarks and criticize sharply the hypocrisy and backwardness of the church and believers. Upper class persons appearing in the play are depicted as unpleasant and even stupid, so the play had something to anger everyone. Conservative critics accused the author of trying to undermine the foundations of law and society, and differences of opinion on the play's moral and social implications obscured differences of opinion on the play.

It is still difficult to form an exact opinion of it, as of all Minna Canth's works. Professor Koskimies says that three-quarters of a century have sufficed to answer who was right or more right,[231] implying that during that time social legislation has progressed in Minna Canth's direction, but does not indicate whether or not the play is good. It has all the general defects of her works, a schematic division of mankind into good and bad individuals, improbability of plot due to a decision to prove the point at any cost, and artificiality of dialogue. Some characters, however, are fuller; Homsantuu and Toppo, for example, are really neither good nor bad. It is perhaps wrong to judge her plays according to the criteria of the realistic drama based on the psychological analysis of the characters. Through her readings and Bergbom's advice, she had become convinced that that was the best form of theater, in which she tried to express herself, but her view of the world and the subjects she chose did not fit that type of drama. Even Ibsen, whom she admired, and Strindberg, whom she did not admire, moved in their later plays from realism toward more symbolical forms of expression, but her way of seeing the world was neither symbolic nor mystic. Her interest was in social situations, expressed by typical characters rather than finely drawn individuals; her best dramatic medium probably would have been something like the epic theater of Brecht and Piscator, but she could deviate only so much from the standards of her time. However, should a stage director consider her plays from that point of view, the approach would perhaps be more refreshing and rewarding than the usual one of considering them slightly stuffy realistic drama from the 1880s.

Her second and last politically radical play, *Kovan onnen lapsia* (perhaps best translated 'Hard Destinies'), was first performed at the Finnish Theater in 1888 and cancelled after the first night by order of the Board of Trustees. (*The Wife of a Worker* had been a huge success, performed no less than nine times, the normal number of performances for a play at that time being two or three.)[232] After that she was effectively silenced as a writer of plays with social messages. Not only conservatives, but even the so-called radical and realistic writers of the Young Finland group, whom she had admired, attacked her and thought that she had overstepped, if not the limits of decency, at least those of moderation and good taste.[233] She was comforted by the workers' movement, then developing, which considered her a champion of the proletariate—as she thought of herself; *Hard Destinies* was often performed by amateur groups within it, at Tampere and Helsinki in 1892.[234]

The workers' movement has always been culturally oriented in Finland, as in Scandinavia; its aim was not only to organize trade unions, improve working conditions, ask for higher salaries, and have a political party to support such claims, but also to sweep away what the workers considered the whole rotten capitalist culture. The political and economic programs have had remarkable success in all the Scandinavian countries;[235] Finnish literature in particular has been greatly enriched by works written by persons of working-class origin, although they have been more individually than ideologically oriented.[236] The workers' movement has achieved the greatest artistic success in the theater because many theaters, officially called Workers' Theaters, were founded by members of the movement and are still active as professional institutions. The foremost, the Tampere Workers' Theater (*Tampereen Työväen Teatteri*), is also preeminent in the entire country.[237]

It is often hard to understand why certain literary works caused such scandals when published, and it is especially hard to understand why a moral, sentimental melodrama like *Hard Destinies* created such a disturbance. Minna Canth was well acquainted through experience with the living conditions of the working class and described them accurately and at length in her letters.[238] Professor Koskimies says that Bergbom gave the final touches to the play, so that its improbabilities are perhaps due to him as much as to the author.[239] The main character is Topra-Heikki (a modern Robin Hood or Karl Moor, from Schiller's famous play, better known in Finland), who takes from the wealthy to give to the poor. In the first act he comes with some friends to the house of a fellow worker, whose child is dying of hunger and inadequate care. After criticizing a society which allows such things to

115

happen, he promises to find help, through crime if necessary. In the second act, as the leader of a band of outlaws in the forests, he attacks a wealthy house, sets it on fire, and sends the stolen money to the sick child's parents. He also has to shoot one of his own men who threatens to denounce the band to the authorities; for an unclear reason that man had become insane, not a traitor. In the third act the hero and his followers have returned to the house of the child, who has died because help did not come in time. The mother reproves the men for their crimes; they repent and, without resistance, let the police take them. Except the vague protest against existing society, the ideology does not seem oriented toward the workers' movement, although Minna Canth called it "socialistic."[240] It could be called a premonition of the events of and after 1918, when the radical elements in the Social-Democrat party tried to seize power by violence but were crushed in the Civil War, whereafter the moderates rebuilt the party and eventually carried through many social and political reforms in collaboration with other progressive political groups.

After the condemnation of *Hard Destinies*, Minna Canth no longer wrote "socialistic" plays. The educated class had plainly indicated that they were not interested in the ugly problems of the working class, an attitude which may partially explain the explosion of the workers' movement in 1918 as well as the lack of good plays in Finland. A playwright's hesitancy in writing problem plays in an atmosphere of disapproval is understandable. Another obstacle is the noncommercial structure of the Finnish theaters—the general manager of a theater depends upon the board of trustees, city and government money for the working of his institution. Foreign plays enjoy fewer restrictions; Finnish theatergoers seem to feel that such plays do not directly concern them. However, though works by Sartre, Anouilh, Ionesco, Beckett, Pinter, Albee, Williams, and Miller have been performed without difficulty, a stage director who produced Genet's *Le Balcon* was immediately dismissed.[241]

Although radical elements now disappeared from her plays, Minna Canth in 1889 founded *Vapaita aatteita* ('Free Thoughts'), a periodical which lasted only a year, in which she discussed contemporary problems and introduced several foreign writers to the Finnish public.[242] She was assisted in the editorial work by A. B. Mäkelä, a student later conspicuous in the workers' Party, and N. R. af Ursin, an aristocrat who was one of the few from the educated classes to be active in that same party. af Ursin's articles about the history of Christianity were critical. Most of the materials were by Minna Canth, however. She attacked conservative church representatives and traditional theology and chose for translation short stories reflecting those ideas. In Tolstoy, for example, she found a "practical Christianity"[243] aimed at improvement of living conditions for the poor and suffering rather than at performance of worn-out rites. She wrote popular articles on evolution, the philosophy of progress, and contemporary psychology, although the official censure forced her to be careful.

Her next play, *Papin perhe* ('The Family of a Clergyman'), first performed in 1891 at the Finnish Theater, was an immediate success, hailed as a masterpiece by the critics. Some became hysterical about it; Juhani Aho wrote a personal letter to the author in which he said that he had wept when seeing the play, that he could not understand how she could be so good, that he recognized her as the greatest writer in Finland and the greatest female writer in Scandinavia.[244] With a literature Finland had also acquired writers and the coteries, slandering, backbiting, public quarrels and reconciliations, educated insults, turgid praise, and declarations of admiration—everything that the literary world in more advanced countries has had for centuries. *Papin perhe* is an excellent example of the kind of play Finnish audiences like when they want something serious about contemporary problems. A problem is mentioned, and the beginning of a personal conflict between the characters built around it. However, the play ends happily; the problem is neatly disposed of, and all, even the author, are able to feel that it has been solved or never existed. The play is presented in good faith, and the author and audience feel that Finland is a nice country where ugly questions never arise. (Should they, the theater is not the proper place for discussing them.) *Papin perhe* is about the family of a clergyman who publishes a conservative newspaper. His children do not share his ideas; his son works for a liberal paper, and a daughter runs away to become an actress, a terrible disgrace in those days even though, because of the noncommercial character of dramatic art in Finland, the theatrical profession was from the beginning considered more respectable there than in many other countries. The opinions of father and son clash vigorously enough to seriously upset the audience, and things look bad, but news that the runaway daughter has had great success on the stage arrives, and the family members fall weeping into each others' arms in joy and reconciliation. The play has had continual success in Finland. Professor Koskimies praises it highly, notes that all the exaggerations of the proletarian plays have been omitted, and mentions that a well-known Finnish actor was very successful in the role of the father.[245]

Minna Canth once more showed her old spirit in her next play, *Sylvi*, which shocked the Finnish public. It was written in Swedish and first performed at the Swedish theater of Helsinki in 1893 although there was already a deep rift between the Finnish- and Swedish-speaking groups. She disliked the conservative Bergbom (it was a mystery that he had ever produced her plays) and thought that the new stage director of the Swedish theater would better understand her. She also happened to meet K. A. Tavaststjerna, a Swedish author of Finland who was contemplating writing a play in Finnish. When Juhani Aho heard of her plans, he published them in his newspaper as though they were definite, and she carried them through. We find in the play an implicit plea for freer divorce laws or a more liberal attitude toward divorce, but Finnish critics and scholars do not share that opinion. Sylvi, a young girl, is married to an elderly man whom she treats like a father; after becoming acquainted with a charming young man, she suspects that marriage with a young husband might be more pleasant than with an old one. However, she discovers that divorce, although permitted by law, is made almost impossible by society. *Sylvi*, like a short story by Minna Canth in which a young wife betrays her husband with a seducer, ends in tragedy: the heroine poisons her husband, but her act is discovered. The young man declares that he will have nothing to do with her, and she is sentenced (not to death; capital punishment, though legal until recent times, has not been effected for more than a century). In the last act, set in court, she delivers a long, somewhat rhetorical speech against society, its laws, and the position of women in it. V. Tarkiainen, whose views have been generally accepted, called Sylvi a completely unbelievable character, a monstrosity, a brainchild of Minna Canth without counterpart in reality.[246] However, the play was based upon an incident which took place in Finland at that time, and literary antecedents might be found in *A Doll's House* or *Madame Bovary*. Parts of the play are even reminiscent of the authoress's personal experience. Another approach to the play was taken by O. E. Tudeer, who said that the heroine was originally a child of nature, pure and free, but unfavorable circumstances made her a criminal; this view is shared by Professor Koskimies, who insists that, after losing her innocence, she becomes an unlikely character.[247] We feel that Minna Canth, in spite of her negative sexual attitude, was still fascinated by sex and could understand its effects on behavior although she saw only its destructive nature. She displays this fascination in both this play and her last, *Anna Liisa* (1895) and, perhaps unconsciously, illustrates that the education given to girls of her time, which suppressed sex but did not replace it, left them with no other preoccupation for the formation of their personalities.

Anna Liisa, considered her best play, though not by us, has provided scholars with an interesting problem of literary history, whether or not she was inspired by Tolstoy's *The Power of Darkness*. It now appears that she had not read this work before she wrote her play,[248] although she had been interested in Tolstoy's philosophy from the late 1880s. The question is rather academic; it is the spirit of the play, its philosophy of repentance and forgiveness, which reminds us of the Russian master. Although she had often attacked the established church,[249] she was deeply religious and in time became more understanding toward the official faith. In *Papin perhe* the father, a minister, is reconciled with his rebellious children, and in *Anna Liisa* it is a person in the same position who finally shows a spirit of understanding and forgiveness. A country girl, Anna Liisa, is about to marry, but the memory of a crime still tortures her. She once bore an illegitimate child, killed it, and hid the body. At last she feels compelled to confess, and she does so dramatically, before the people gathered for her marriage. The priest declares that she has found the grace of God and the right road, everyone should rejoice, her sins will certainly be remitted, and she may go in peace. The play's popularity is understandable, for it deals with the individual problem of an exceptional character with whom the members of the audience cannot identify; they feel more like the clergyman who nobly pardons the miserable sinner. Again Minna Canth analyzed the feelings of a woman who had sinned and tried to solve her problems, but her fighting spirit was broken by the time she wrote this play, for her answer now was that she should place herself at the mercy of society and hope for the best.

From the beginning of her literary career, Minna Canth also wrote short stories reflecting the ideas of her plays, and, as they were not intended for the stage, she could voice her opinions more freely. Two problems are prominent: the position of workers and the poor and the position of women; occasionally they are combined, as in *Lain mukaan* ('According to the Law,' 1889). She was always tempted to make her characters as miserable and unfortunate as possible, but social and economic conditions in Finland were bad in her times. In 1867 and 1868 a famine had killed thousands of people, and, as the country was still largely agricultural, there remained the possibility of a recurrence. For several reasons there was an excess rural population in Finland at that time,[250] and all could not find work in agriculture. The luckiest worked as farm hands, others found occasional jobs, and the rest lived as beggars and vagrants. As modern industry began to develop, many, accepting any work under any conditions for any salary offered, drifted to the cities and factories. Some of the early capitalists were foreigners attracted to the country by its abundant supply of cheap, unorganized labor. Social consciousness had not yet developed, and no legislation protected the workers who often were treated no better by their countrymen.[251]

Minna Canth had gathered first-hand information about the living conditions of the workers, and, although the accumulation of miseries in some of her stories may seem excessive, they were very real miseries. Professor Koskimies says that *Köyhää kansaa* ('Poor People,' 1886), for example, is "a description of poverty painted in black and grey."[252] During the building of the Savo railway, the workers' salaries were often below the level needed to keep a man and family alive. Public funds were granted irregularly for this work, and long periods of unemployment occurred. Minna Canth and Juhani Aho, then a young newspaperman, protested with others on behalf of the workers against "eighty pennies (cents) an hour," the lowest wages paid. In *Köyhää kansaa* a laborer on the Savo railway, Holpainen, is without work for a while. His child dies of hunger, and his wife breaks down and is taken to an asylum. Eventually he is rehired, a broken, unrebellious man. While other workers criticize society and jeer at him because of his meekness, he continues working, his eyes fixed on the asylum. A physician and a minister of the church, representing the upper classes, discuss social and economic questions. The physician has Minna Canth's sympathy; she describes him as a man with radical views on reform, but the minister as a man helpless when confronted with misery, rather than as an aggressive conservative. The doctor remarks that the weak and incurably ill should be disposed of in a quick, painless way. When the pastor, horrified, protests, he retorts:

> If you would preach like that when wars are declared, I would agree with you. But that's just what you don't do. According to the good old custom, anybody may then kill and cripple crowds of healthy, strong men without any qualms of conscience. People aren't even ashamed of asking God's benediction for the "weapons," and maybe at the same time they are telling others to love their neighbors like themselves. They don't think that the people they are going to kill are neighbors, too.

Minna Canth never trusted her readers to reach the correct conclusions for themselves. The tone of the story, however, is subdued, in keeping with the personality of the main character.

Although Minna Canth combined her interests of the position of women with the position of the workers and the poor, she was primarily interested in women. But, although in public discussions she sided with her sex and represented its members as the victims of men's immorality, in her writing she realized that women were not always guileless. *Lain mukaan* is the psychological analysis of a woman who allows herself to be seduced because she unconsciously wants to and she desires the money her seducer is ready to give her for fine clothes. The young woman, Maria, is married to a worker, Ville, whom the seducer, a businessman, sends on a long journey so that his plans will be undisturbed. The husband returns unexpectedly because he has been badly wounded in a fight with gypsies, an episode irrelevant to the story, and surprises the guilty couple. He beats the seducer, but, as he sees that his wife is not innocent, refuses to defend himself when charged with assault and battery. He is sentenced "according to the law" to three years in prison. As they are in many Minna Canth stories, the events are somewhat overdramatic. We are not certain that legal proceedings would have taken the form described, even at that time.

Kauppa-Lopo (1889) does not deal directly with a social or moral problem. Its presentation of a thoroughly bad character caused the guardians of morals to protest, and the person who gave inspiration for the story, a woman who sold small goods at the market of Kuopio, sued the author for libel. The clue to Minna Canth's reason for choosing a character given to drink, men, and theft, for which she is eventually sentenced to life imprisonment, is in the story: she wanted to show that human character is often composed of contrasting elements and urges. Kauppa-Lopo tries to help, to the limits of her understanding, those in trouble, but they do not always appreciate her efforts, especially those directed at people who are socially above her. The author uses the opportunity to criticize the middle class, whose members she describes in many of her stories as selfish, callous, and unpleasant. The origin of her attitude is in her background. She was the daughter of a worker and a Finnish-speaking Finn, and at that time an immense distance separated the Swedish-speaking better society from a Finnish-speaking shopkeeper. *Kodista pois* ('Away from Home,' 1893) is about a young girl whose parents do not consider education important and want her to make a good marriage as soon as possible. She, however, is as unhappy about the vulgarity of her parents, social upstarts who do not know how to behave in society, as about their domineering attitude. In her stories Minna Canth often pointed out that the heartless, egoistic middle class spoke Swedish. The sentimental *Lapsenpiika* ('The Nursemaid,' published in a collection in 1892) describes a very young girl who comes from the country to a good family in town. The young housewife forces her to work excessively hard, keeping her up until midnight to wash party dishes and waking her at four to care for the baby. The maid never rebels, but considers herself a bad girl for being unable to cope with all the work.

She also wrote short stories about middle-class life, such as *Hanna* (1886), *Salakari* ('The Sunken Rock,' 1887), *Lehtori Hellmanin vaimo* ('Mr. Hellman's Wife,' 1890), and *Agnes* (1892). *Salakari* gives the subject of *Lain mukaan* another setting: a young, intelligent woman of good family allows herself to be seduced by an experienced man, again because she unconsciously wants to.[253] The author described the psychological process with an intuition that reveals her to be more than the moralist and preacher she sometimes appeared, but the moralist in her punished the adulteress with illness and death. *Hanna*, concerned with the life of a young girl of good family, provided her an opportunity to criticize openly the education then given to young girls. Without dramatic incidents, the sufferings of Hanna consist mainly of the endless dreariness of her daily life, the fault of her tyrannical father, a drunkard and philanderer. She can neither resign herself nor rebel, and, though the story ends while she is young, we understand that she will never marry. The directness with which Minna Canth spoke of men's sins shocked the critics, and Elis Bergroth, a minister of the church, wrote her that she was undermining the morals of the Finnish-speaking population. He admitted that the Swedish-speaking upper classes were already depraved, but maintained that the Finnish-speaking group had preserved its purity, which her writings now threatened.[254] *Lehtori Hellmanin vaimo* ('Mr. Hellman's Wife'; *lehtori* is the title of a secondary school teacher) is apparently auto-biographical but it is generally believed that her own marriage was happier than that in the story.[255] We conclude from her writings, her interest in normal sex as sin, and her grievances on the position of women, that she felt, perhaps unconsciously, that marriage to an older man at an early age and the arrival of seven children on a modest income had deprived her of life's simple joys, which a more congenial marriage might have brought her. *Agnes*, another study on the dangerous consequences of love, is the most worldly she ever wrote. A young woman who knows the world because she has lived in St. Petersburg, the capital of the empire, comes to Kuopio, where she conquers all the gentlemen, including Antti, the innocent young husband of Liisi, a naive young wife. The story concentrates on psychological analysis of the jealousy suffered by Liisi and is one of the best short stories of that time. Professor Koskimies remarks that there are few writers of good short stories in Finland, where the genre has been considered offhand writing to be done when one was too tired for serious work.[256] Minna Canth was at her best in theater, and, though some of the problems in her plays are no longer of interest, they contain more than that. She had a natural talent for drama, but even other writers saw in her work only the message, not the art or technique. No one succeeded her as a playwright, and for a long time Finnish dramatic literature remained on a modest level.

Juhani Aho (first **Johannes Brofeldt**, 1861-1921), the son of a minister influenced by the revivalist movement, grew up in a strict, religious atmosphere tempered by his father's cordial spirit and humor, which had opportunity for development in their native region, Lapinlahti and Iisalmi in northern Savo, north of Kuopio. He remained attached to this area, its nature and its people, which he often described in his works. It is a barren, sparsely populated district where it is difficult to earn a living by agriculture, and Aho spoke of its inhabitants with compassion. His character was dreamy, melancholic, and sentimental, and he seldom directly attacked existing conditions. This trait, coupled with his somewhat naive idealism and love for Finnish nature, made him in some respects similar to Topelius. He strove to make his language refined and elegant, developing a very personal style which accurately reflected his conception of life but occasionally became a mannerism, just like that conception. In his very short stories or sketches (he called them *lastuja* 'shavings' which dropped from his bench while he was shaping his greater works), he often described a mood or a landscape reflecting a mood, never dramatic, but always sad, subdued, and dreamy. He had the artistic taste not to prolong this word-music, but at times his works still seem too pretty and affected. He made a great effort to write simply and naturally but did not always succeed.

He went to secondary school in Kuopio. The school was ready to become completely Finnish although educated persons still spoke Swedish; Aho naturally sided with the Finns. The pupils read Runeberg, Topelius, and the *Kalevala*, which he found congenial to his taste. He wrote a composition on the "poetic character of the *Kalevala*." Later, in a story called *A Youthful Dream*, he tells that he used to dream with his friends about their country's great future.[257] In his fancies we find a motif common in patriotic Finnish literature, the idea that Finland was similar to old Greece. The Finns identified with the "Hellens" (a more unusual and nobler word than "Greeks") because Finland was a small and, they proclaimed, highly civilized nation with a big, uncivilized neighbor whom they fought to protect Western civilization, just as the Greeks did when they fought Persia. This likeness led to the conclusion that the Finns were just as intelligent, clever, refined, and artistic—or even more so—than the Greeks, for was not the *Kalevala* superior to the *Iliad* and the *Odyssey*? Aho and his schoolfellows did not hesitate to answer yes, for Homer's heroes fought for a woman and destroyed a city, whereas the *Kalevala's* conquered Sampo, the purveyor of wealth and prosperity, and fought with words and wisdom, not with swords and sinews.[258] Unlike most people who in their youth dream of things which soon after embarrass them and eventually receive indulgent smiles, Aho and many Finns never became ashamed or amused at their own fancies.

After graduating from secondary school in 1880, Aho studied for approximately four years at the University of Helsinki without taking a degree. He soon began to publish short stories and worked for many years as a newspaperman, first for the conservative *Uusi Suometar* in Helsinki (1882), then for *Keski-Suomi* at Jyväskylä (1886), *Savo* at Kuopio (1887), the illustrated review *Uusi Kuvalehti* (1892-1903), and *Päivälehti*, the organ of Young Finland (1890s). In 1906 he was granted a state pension for authors and the degree of doctor *honoris causa* by the University of Helsinki in 1907.

Besides his dreaminess, Aho also had a gift for satire and irony apparent in some of his writings. With his Young Finland friends he represented the liberal current of thought, critical of all conservative, oppressive, narrow-minded, and oldfashioned in art, literature, politics, religion, and morals. He learned several foreign languages, read widely, traveled in Europe, closely followed the intellectual and artistic life on the continent, and became something of a man of the world. This superior and blasé attitude was rather superficial in him, and he remained attached to his home country and its people. The irony in his works is mild and understanding, somewhat like that of Chekhov. He liked energetic outdoor activities, fishing, hunting, mountain climbing, long walks, and ski trips in the forests, but, in one of his short stories, he expresses disgust at the senseless slaughter of wild animals by a hunting party; the disgust takes the form of mild irony.[259]

In some short stories, especially *Yksin* ('Alone,' 1890), he shocked the Finnish public with his frankness in erotic matters, but little was needed to shock the Finnish public of his time. Two years later moralists were outraged because Akseli Gallen-Kallela painted a picture containing a nude on a subject from the *Kalevala*, and Aho wrote an ironic story about *The Painter Who*

Painted a Woman without Any Clothes. His irony about Minna Canth's moralizing has already been mentioned. He had a few passionate love affairs. When visiting the Järnefelt family in Kuopio as a young student, he fell in love with Mrs. Järnefelt, an attractive, intelligent, cultivated married woman more than twenty years his senior. Circumstances and age prevented the love from developing further, but it was no less ardent. Later, after he had married Venny Soldan, a well-known painter, his wife's sister attracted him, and a passionate relationship developed between them. The sisters eventually agreed to share him; this rather unusual outcome was somehow typical of Aho, who, rather than make a decision, accepted the women's solution.[260]

His first stories are half-humorous descriptions of country people. His intent does not seem comic; he describes usual situations which are, from his point of view, somewhat humorous. He lived during the period when "modern times" came to Finland, and some of his stories deal with simple people confronted with new inventions, such as *Siihen aikaan kun isä lampun osti* (1883; tr. *When Father Brought Home the Lamp*, 1893)[261] or *Rautatie* ('The Railroad,' 1884). As they are nice stories, fit for all, they have become standard in textbooks and have been read, analyzed, and hated by all Finnish schoolchildren. We must admit that we cannot understand why literary historians in Finland describe them as small masterpieces.[262] Both stories are good examples of Aho's efforts to write simply and naturally. In his endless observations of nature, imitations of popular speech, and his attempts to understand simple people, he gives the impression of a person who forces himself to use a kind of babytalk because he believes that it is the way his characters think and speak, and thus condescends to them.

Other early stories show his satirical but understanding view of life: *Kello* ('The Watch') is about a young boy, an apprentice in Helsinki who saves his earnings to buy a watch, which is stolen when, slightly drunk for the first time, he walks the city streets proudly and happily; *Kievarin pihalla* ('In the Courtyard of the Inn,' 1884) describes a lazy, insolent innkeeper who does not think it worthwhile to treat politely two young students who stop at his place until he discovers that their father is a high official who might revoke his license. *Muudan markkinamies* (tr. *A Man at the Market*, 1885)[263] is a longer, more complex story into which the author put some of his own experiences, especially his love for Mrs. Järnefelt.[264] The main character is a folk singer who goes from market to market performing his compositions;[265] he is an unhappy bohemian who could do better but has not the strength of character to pull himself together. He is in love with a farmer's daughter, a good girl with whom he cannot associate. He is unable to resist revealing his feelings at her wedding, and this event ends everything. The story is not a direct rendering of Aho's life, but certain passages, such as that in which the poet feels himself an unwanted guest in a strange house which he cannot leave because his beloved is there, contain thinly veiled allusions to his own situation. Other early stories, *Hellmanin herra* (1886; tr. *Squire Hellman*, 1893)[266] and *Helsinkiin* ('To Helsinki,' 1889), are dispassionate observations of fundamentally unpleasant characters. Squire Hellman, a typical wealthy landowner, greedy and coarse, enjoys good food and drink with friends like himself. Antti Ljungberg, of *Helsinkiin*, is a snob, a student coming to the university in Helsinki with the conviction that he is a man of the world; Aho may have put some self-irony into the character. After a description of Ljungberg's journey and relations to the people he meets, the story ends with some views of the seamy side of student life in Helsinki.

Also among Aho's early works are *Papin tytär* ('The Daughter of a Clergyman,' 1885), a short novel and its sequel, *Papin rouva* ('The Wife of a Clergyman,' 1893). They perhaps represent the best of Aho's writings; in them all that is typical of his art appears in its positive aspects. Although his time's fashion of writing about women's sufferings in contemporary society influenced both novels, their psychological analysis of a young woman is penetrating and sensitive. An ordinary life is described from childhood, through the school years, to the time of the girl's marriage to a young clergyman. She is dreamy and unsatisfied, always waiting for an undefined lucky event to change her life. Oppressed by the narrow atmosphere of her home, she feels freer in town, where she attends school, but each time she thinks she has achieved her dream she experiences disillusionment. At the end of *Papin tytär*, she meets a charming, gay, somewhat egotistic student. He reappears in *Papin rouva*, when she is the wife of a young clergyman. They fall in love but do not consummate their relationship; the circumstances and their characters are stronger than their passion. Seemingly inconclusively, the novel ends with a scene on a hill where they stand together enjoying the panorama before them, deeply feeling its beauty. Rather than in events, the novels' interest is in the minute analysis of subdued emotions.

In 1889 Aho lived briefly in Paris where he acquainted himself with its life and French literature. He was already familiar with the works of such authors as Zola, Maupassant, and Daudet; now he read Bourget, Huysmans, and Edouard Rod, who are credited with fortifying Aho's conviction that naturalism had not answered all literary problems and that a penetrating psychological analysis was a more adequate way of studying life. The unerring security with which many Finnish authors who made the customary pilgrimage to the intellectual Mecca of Europe chose only the great authors of the day, who would soon be forgotten as the younger generation rebelled against them, is somewhat sad, but Aho had sufficient greatness to avoid imitation. He read that which he liked and could easily find. Later he said that this stay had been important for him, for it enabled him to understand naturally, without effort, what art and style really were. He discovered that "everyone of us has two native countries (*isänmaa, patrie*), our own country and France."[267] It was while he was in Paris that he wrote *Yksin*, a brooding, melancholy analysis of the feelings of a lonely man in Paris and his relationship to a woman, not his mistress. The aforementioned scandal was in the character's visit to the *Moulin Rouge* and a prostitute.

During Aho's stay in Paris, his Young Finland friends had founded *Päivälehti*,[268] now, under the name *Helsingin Sanomat*, the largest paper in the country. Although it became a typical daily paper with news and political articles, it had literary and artistic beginnings. Besides Aho and the other writers who founded it, several young painters, such as Akseli Gallen-Kallela, Eero Järnefelt, Pekka Halonen, and Louis Sparre, and the composer Jean Sibelius were connected with it; Eino Leino, too, later worked for it. As the Old Finnish paper *Uusi Suometar* had somewhat neglected literary and artistic questions, the young liberals were eager to show interest in them, both Finnish and foreign in concern. The groups and their organs developed progressively opposing political and social views. *Päivälehti* gave Aho an outlet for the publications of short stories, sketches, and "shavings."

He published several collections in 1891, 1892, 1896, and five more between 1896 and 1921. Their material varies from his contemplative philosophy of nature to realistic sketches and political pamphlets written after 1899, when Russia began its attack against Finland's autonomy, but his patriotism was unaggressive, and the struggle between the two nations was generally nonviolent. He praised the beauties of Finnish nature and the honesty, thrift, and patience of the Finnish people and professed his belief that, in the struggle between right and might, right would prevail in the end. His idealistic view was shared by many of his countrymen and even by a large number of the intellectuals of most Western countries.[269] Aho stood for nonviolence and coined in a sketch a phrase that remained popular in patriotic writings, even more militant ones; a collection of stories published in two volumes, 1899 and 1900, bears the phrase as its title: *Katajainen kansani* ('My Juniper People,' a literal and meaningless translation).[270] In many countries trees have traditionally symbolized strength and resistance, e.g., the hickory in the United States; Aho utilized this symbol. He saw the juniper, which never grows very high in Finland, as a humble, but tough, plant which could be bent and crushed but would never break, and this quality he saw in the Finns. Aho was one of the Finnish writers who thought Finland an unfortunate nation which had suffered more than any other,[271] and his frequent, compassionate descriptions of poor country people, pioneers, and settlers such as he had seen in his native region stressed the patience and humility with which they endured great hardships. *Uutisasukas* ('The Settler,' in *Lastuja*, first collection), typical in this respect, gives in a few lines two episodes from the life of a young couple who leased a small tract in the forest instead of living as farmhand and maid in the vicarage. They plan for their future on the new farm in the first episode; in the second the exhausted husband is taking his wife's body for burial at church. Debts, many children, and their solitary efforts to clear the forest have overcome them. The purpose of the story is to arouse pity and respect for the characters, but the point is overemphasized. In the last lines Aho tells the reader that "we must not forget these victims of the first settlement" and "we cannot raise monuments to them, for they are counted in thousands, and we do not know their names."[272]

Kannikka ('A Piece of Bread,' *Lastuja*, second collection) is very similar; Aho, posing as the narrator, describes a poor man who travels with him in a railway carriage. Trying to picture the other's life (a frequent Aho device), the narrator imagines that it must have been endless suffering in trying to make a living in the forests. The man replies, when asked his destination, that he is going to prison because he was unable to pay his taxes.

At the end of the nineteenth and beginning of the twentieth centuries, relations between agricultural tenants, who leased their estates from wealthy landowners, and these landowners became tense and sometimes developed into open conflict. In 1906 the tenants of a great landlord at Laukko (south of Tampere) disagreed with him on the terms of lease and struck. The owner sued them for breach of contract and legally evicted seventy-seven tenants and their families (approximately four hundred people). Several details dramatized the incident and gave it an ugly character: the owner was a Swedish-speaking aristocrat, and the tenants belonged to the Finnish-speaking population; the strike leaders were sentenced to prison; the eviction was effected in the coldest period of the year, and the doors, windows, and fireplaces of the tenants' houses were broken; the police and soldiers who carried out the law were Russian. Even Finns not interested in the conditions of the tenants were indignant at the insult to national feelings.[273] Eleven years later, when civil war broke out, approximately thirty houses belonging to landowners were looted and burned at Laukko, the great manor included.[274]

This agricultural question was treated not only in newspapers and political pamphlets, but also in fiction sympathetic to the tenants when by Finnish-speaking writers. Aho favored the tenants but warned in *Helsingin Sanomat* that they would not improve their position by violence. The humorous Finnish paper *Tuulispää* caricatured him in academic garb addressing a group of tenants being herded like cattle from their broken homes by whip-swinging Cossacks.[275]

Although faithful to his liberal friends, Aho was basically a conservative who loved the good old times and watched with regret their disappearance in the face of progress. His nostalgia is apparent even in *When Father Brought Home the Lamp* and *The Railroad,* but in *Vanha valkama* ('The Old Haven,' *Lastuja*, first collection) he openly expresses dislike for the steamships and piers which have replaced the old landing places. Still, he ironized people who lived in the past only, e.g., in *Vanha laulaja* ('The Old Singer,' *Lastuja*, first collection), a sketch describing a man living in memories of the wonderful days when he was a student singing in a choir (an activity greatly enjoyed by Scandinavians; think of an American who dreams of the days when he played quarterback for his college). Aho liked to depict typical characters, such as the man in *Mallikelpoinen* ('A Model of Virtue,' *Lastuja*, first collection) who thinks only of the fine career he has decided to have. *Sasu Punanen* (name, *Lastuja*, second collection) is a humorous sketch about a man whose only passion is the *sauna*, the enjoyment of which he has developed into a fine art. *Maailman murjoma* (best translation perhaps 'The Outcast,' 1894), a lengthy short story, is the analysis of an exceptional individual and a description of the conflict between old and new times. The main character is a dour, unsocial pioneer whose house and fields are taken from him because a railroad is built in their place. He cannot or does not understand and considers it an injustice. Here Aho shows understanding of the violent, primitive sides of human nature, which he describes impartially. Although he disapproves of the man's actions, he demonstrates that they are a logical consequence of the situation and his mentality. A Finnish critic pointed out French influence in the story when it was published; Aho might have found the idea for its end, in which the main character throws an enormous rock at the first train passing on the line, from Zola's *La Bête Humaine*, although the plots are different.[276] In 1894 he published a collection of short stories, *Heränneitä* (lit. 'The Awakened'), in which he described the revivalist leaders as they had lived and worked. The work is reputed to be historically accurate and shows Aho's capacity to render feelings and motivations alien to him, for the Finnish revivalists were no dreamy mystics, but energetic, robust reformers, intent upon changing the world and fighting evil with all their strength.

His most typical sketches describe scenery reflecting his thoughts and feelings. Finnish landscapes are known for their melancholy, dreamy, and intimate impression. They are not magnificent, bold, or majestic, and one cannot admire them from a distance but must walk in the forests, across the meadows, along the brooks and lakeshores. Aho did just that and expressed his reactions in short sketches like *Kosteikko, kukkula, saari* ('The Fen, the Hill, the Island,' *Lastuja*, first collection), *Salaperäisin* ('The Deepest Mystery,' sixth collection, *Tyven meri* ['The Quiet Sea']), and *Lumoissa* ('Spellbound,'*Lastuja*, seventh collection, 1917). Dreams in nature are not uncommon in literature, but they are usually parts of longer stories.[277] Aho left them as they were, long prose poems. His feelings in the presence of the Finnish landscapes were not esoteric; in this respect he is very Finnish, like Aleksis Kivi, for example. But, so melancholy were Aho's emotions that he wrote *Alakuloisuuden ylistys* ('The Praise of Melancholy,' first collection). Aho's sketches defy description; to give an accurate impression, we have translated an excerpt from *Lumoissa*:

I am still sitting in my boat although I am not angling any more. I have pulled up the anchor. The angling rod leans drowsily against the gunwale. I ought to leave, but I cannot pull myself together enough to take the oars.

I am in a small strait between two rocks out on the sea. Behind me there is a small enclosed gulf, and, at its end, the mainland, a thin line of trees appearing against the evening sky which has not yet grown dark. In front, there is the open, boundless sea with a few rocks rising still above the water level, which, as the dusk grows deeper, melts with the sky so softly that their limit cannot be seen. Where the land is, a few noises can be heard from a village of fishers, the sudden low of a cow, the barking of a dog, the oars of an unseen boat—and all this is already over.

Nothing is seen on the sea either except the sea itself, not a sail, not a wisp of smoke, and nothing is heard either. Once, a dull report was heard in that direction, very far. There is a war, indeed, and nobody may sail there, nobody, except the Russian fleet, which does not sail. . . .

This is still the old familiar feeling which has often come over me and left me during the many summers the war has lasted. I have often been under its spell when the night was taking the place of the evening, I have felt myself gliding, half-awake, from the one to the other, I have dwelt an instant in it, shuddered in myself at something threatening and strange, pulled myself out of it, weighed the anchor, and rowed home.

Now, I cannot awaken myself from it, although I am trying— weakly, it is true.

This is no longer reality, although it looks like it and although the world around me has all of its familiar features. I have the same feeling as when I was a child and stood in the courtyard on a summer night, looking at the gate, the road and the smoke from the fire made to keep the flies away from the cows, which was rolling toward the lake. Under it and beyond it there was something else, something mysterious which I could not understand, but it could be there, I was not afraid of it and did not marvel at it. I did not know how to ask for the reason of it, and I did not fear it either. Now, this duality is somehow oppressing, and I would like to know why, but I cannot bring myself to ask the question loud enough to make someone come to answer it. I am unable to answer myself, and I have a feeling of constraint and oppression in my breast.

There is a splash somewhere, there, where the low, sunken rock is, and a flash of foam, which does not disturb the silence, however. On the contrary, it makes it even deeper, like a sudden gust of wind in a forest which barely moves a leaf and dies at the same moment. Everything is still more unreal than a moment ago. I wish I could flee, but in front of what and where? Am I growing insensible and loosing my strength? Am I drifting away from this place and going over to some other? From my summer to the autumn and still along the same road from the autumn to the winter?

Am I going away? But I have a rock here—unless it is also drifting with me, and this whole region with it, and the sky, and the sea?

So this is what it was, this life? What was it? A confused train of sensations no one of which can be distinguished from the others, no one is more remarkable than any other. Did I ever achieve anything? Was I of any help or joy to anybody? Was I not trying, whenever I did my duty, to fill, before all, a kind of emptiness in myself, the bottom of which was, nevertheless, also shining? Nothing so far, perhaps, so why should I go on still after this? Would I still want to go on, even if I were allowed to, if someone came and helped me to land? I would perhaps flee from him, when he would try to free me, like one who is trying to drown himself flees from his rescuer. I am on an ice floe which is falling apart, which the wind is driving to the sea, and I only wave my hand to say farewell. . . . In fact, I want to leave, I have wanted it a long time, only I have not dared. If someone tried to stop me, perhaps I would dare to do it better.

The narrator finally does pull himself together, rows home, and meets his wife, with whom he exchanges a few meaningless words, though he knows that the spell will come over him again on the following day. Buried in these melancholy dreams is a gibe at the Russian fleet, which did not or could not fight the Germans in World War I. There is something ominous in the fact that this story was written only four years before Aho's death. Although he says "I want to leave," he did not commit suicide, but World War I and the Finnish Civil War were terrible shocks to his pacific, humane, sensitive mind.

In 1916 he wrote *Rauhan erakko* ('The Hermit of Peace'), a short story about a man who, in protest of the horrors of the war and the brutality of the world, lives as a hermit in the Tyrolian Alps and finds comfort in the contemplation of nature. Although the strongest protest against the world Aho could imagine was flight, he did not flee himself. He could have retired to a faraway place in his native region, but he was a newspaperman, a public figure, and a well-known author who expressed his opinion on many questions, and that he continued to do. Especially the Civil War, which lasted from the end of January to the middle of May, 1918, shook him, for it showed with ruthless clarity that the Finnish people were not so meek, humble, honest, and God-fearing as he and so many others had believed. The country had become independent immediately before this conflict, called the War of Independence by the victors, but Finland long after remained torn by dissensions, hate, fear, and suspicions roused by that clash. In 1918 and 1919 Aho published three volumes of the diary he had kept in the spring of the first year titled *Hajamietteitä kapinaviikoilta* ('Stray Thoughts from the Weeks of the Rebellion'), in which his sufferings and hesitation are apparent. Happy that his country was independent, he condemned the brutalities committed by the rebels. He admired the victorious army, but rejected the violence with which the repression was conducted and the antidemocratic tendencies among the victors. All who were full of energy and faith in the future could not understand Aho's waverings, when they noticed them. Using a cliché, we might say that the old writer did not die, but slowly faded away during his last years.

In a full description of Aho's life, personality, philosophy, and work, his several translations, especially from Swedish, and his many novels in addition to *The Daughter of a Clergyman* and *The Wife of a Clergyman* must also be mentioned. *Panu* (1897) was written when admiration for the *Kalevala* had developed into general interest in the mythical past of the Finnish people. As it was fashionable for young artists to go to Finnish or Russian Karelia in search of something to use in their works for the re-creation of old Finnish civilization and in expression of the movements of the primitive Finnish soul, Aho made the pilgrimage in 1892. He embodied some of his experiences and readings in pagan Finnish religion in *Panu*, but the result was a peculiar mixture of his mildly ironic rationalism and pessimism and of folkloric and ethnographic materials rather than a re-creation of the mythical past. The action is set in the seventeenth century (A.D.). Without supernatural incident, the novel tells of the struggle between a minister intent upon eradicating the last remnants of paganism and superstition from his parish and a sorcerer and magician, Panu, who resists him. In accordance with history, Panu is defeated; he represents the negative aspects of the old religion. Another character, Jorma, however, incorporates the positive side as Aho imagined it: a love, respect for, and feeling of communion with nature, illustrated at the end, when Jorma, who cannot forsake the old religion and accept the new one, retires deeper in the forests, where he can live according to his ideas.[278]

Kevät ja takatalvi ('The Spring and the Late Frosts,' 2 vols., 1906) again shows Aho's interest in history and the revivalist movement, the subject of his short stories, *Heränneitä*. The work presents a panorama of Finnish life in the second half of the nineteenth century, and real characters like Lönnrot, Snellman, and Paavo Ruotsalainen, a famous popular leader of the movement,[279] appear with fictitious individuals including a variety of human types. There is an aristocratic official, a conservative professor, an honest but uninspired minister of the church, young students, and country people against a background of north Savo landscapes, Aho's native region over which he still felt the spirit of the *Kalevala* lingering. He alludes to *Panu*; the setting of both is the same, and a character in *Kevät ja takatalvi* is a descendant of one in *Panu*. *Kalevala* and the Finnish past were still fashionable when Aho wrote this book,[280] and he must have felt it should mention them, but, in fact, both are irrelevant to the action, which centers on the conflict between the clergyman and his son. The father is a very ordinary person who performs his duties faithfully but is unable to arouse religious ardor in his congregation. His son, converted to the revivalist movement, attempts to reform the world without regard for the feelings of his neighbors. The ending is undramatic: the characters go on living, each according to his own ideas, in a world where they simply have to tolerate each other.

Juha (1911) is often called Aho's best novel, but we are not in agreement with that judgment. The style is an uneven mixture of Aho's peculiar style and the trend which had developed in Finnish literature at the beginning of this century, which Professor Koskimies calls impressionism.[281] A short-lived fashion, it makes much of what was written at that time almost unreadable today. The purpose of the style is conciseness; action is merely suggested and the reader allowed to supply the details. Occasionally it gives dramatic strength and vivacity to a narration, but more often it is artificial, especially when unusual word order is used. This latter feature can only seem calculated to make prose as different from speech as possible. The book's action is a mixture of Aho's dispassionate realism and ornate folklore. It is situated in a not-too-faraway past and contains no mythical or supernatural elements. A penetrating psychological analysis of an ordinary erotic situation, it loses its effect in the stylistic oddities and ethnographic ornaments with which it is overloaded. Juha is a middle-aged man, a settler in Finland's forests who has a young, beautiful wife. She elopes with a more attractive, younger man who, due to his Russian Karelian origin, has an exotic charm.[282] Eventually the seducer grows tired of her, and she allows her husband to take her home. He has always believed—or wanted to believe—that she was carried away by force. Later she admits that she left home willingly, and he leaves his boat adrift in the river rapids; the motif of the boat gliding toward annihilation reappears in *Lumoissa*. This common plot is often the pretext for a funny story in which the betrayed husband is ridiculed by the young lovers. Although Aho is not the only writer to have seen this situation from the serious point of view of the husband, he does belong to a minority. The erotic side of the story was not the most important to him; of more concern was the feeling of helplessness before approaching old age and decay and the realization that nothing can bridge the gulf separating the generations. Juha is good and honest, as is his wife; they cannot live together because the difference in their ages is too great. *Juha* contains a similarity to Minna Canth's *Sylvi*, another example of a usual erotic situation treated seriously.

We think that *Omatunto* ('The Conscience,' 1914), written slowly during the years when Aho was a member of the Board of Trustees of the Finnish National Theater, is a better book; it, *The Daughter of a Clergyman*, and *The Wife of a Clergyman*, are among his best novels. It is a simple story about ordinary people, and the style, though unmistakably Aho's, is straightforward. The narration neither dwells on moods and landscapes nor reaches for special effects. It moves from beginning to end simply but in a broadly descriptive and half-humorous character. Although not a funny story, it is one of Aho's gayest, gently ironic and full of understanding for human weaknesses. It takes place among the fishers of the islands in the Gulf of Finland, where Aho liked to spend his free time. The members of a poor family constantly think of possible ways, even dishonest ones, to improve their condition. They take an opportunity to keep some goods from a shipwreck instead of declaring them to the authorities, but they become afraid of the consequences and the difficulties in disposing of the loot. Their minister praises them for following their conscience, but they receive his words with feelings that can be aptly rendered by the phrase "And a lot of good that will do us." Aho's impartial view of man, his both sad and humorous vision of life, and his penetrating though humane realism are nowhere better evident than in the ending of this book, which one might or might not consider a happy one.

During the period of Russian oppression Aho wrote a play, *Tuomio* ('The Judgment,' 1907), as well as patriotic short stories. Forbidden by the authorities, it is full of allusions to the events of the time, but it does not contain a patriotic message or an appeal to resist the oppressors. Its analysis of a situation which could have developed in Finland at that time is not inadequate, but the description of the sufferings of those caught in it is without conclusion, save an artificially violent end almost unrelated to the play. The picture of Aho and his inability to adjust to a situation in which both violence and nonviolence seemed wrong is clear; arguments for and against both attitudes are presented, but Aho was obviously unable to decide which side should have the moral victory. During the Russian oppression attempts to organize an armed underground movement were made. However, no action resulted, and Finnish retaliation was mainly limited to passive resistance. Finnish officials refused to carry out orders given by Russian authorities or to follow laws and ordinances which they deemed illegal because they violated the rights of autonomous Finland. These officials were dismissed and occasionally exiled, whereafter Russian officials replaced them. Another group of Finns, mainly conservatives in the Old Finnish party, argued that Finnish officials should protest against illegal Russian measures but submit to them in order to keep the administration in Finnish hands. The groups clashed bitterly, but it is interesting to note that, while Russia conducted an aggressive policy against Finland, the best methods of resistance could be openly discussed by Finns. In the play these developments appear in the form of very civilized conflict; a Finn, exiled to Siberia because of his resistance to the Russians, has died there, whereas his brother has submitted to the authorities and is in a position in which he can decide whether or not to bring the body home for burial. The widow, who shares her later husband's ideas, must apply for authorization. The key scene is in the discussion between widow and brother-in-law, which expresses both views. It is discovered that the deceased did not remain staunchly patriotic but submitted a request for pardon to the emperor. However, as his reasons are never explained, the action seems to be used as a device to sustain the play. The dead man's son kills his uncle, whom he considers a traitor and a Russian agent. When he hears that his father was not a hero to the end of his life, he kills himself. Aho was not a playwright, and the play reflects his inability to take a position although he sympathized with the Young Finns and passive resistance; it describes the situation but implies that there is no resolution. It is an accurate representation of the desperation felt by many Finns who felt that, whatever they did, the Russians would prevail.

Aho's last work is *Muistatko* - ? ('Do You Remember - ?,' 1920), an autobiographical novel or highly romanced autobiography. Its elements are from his life—landscapes he had seen, people he had met, thoughts he had had—but it is not an account of his life, and there is no hint of his authorship. The narrator, after telling of his childhood, concentrates on his religious and moral doubts, quoting from Kramsu's *Mustalainen*, and then moves to his love and marriage. His account of these does not correspond completely to Aho's life; the narrator's first wife soon dies, and he marries a woman who is like a reincarnation of the first wife, although she is never described as such. Aho, who occasionally doubted church teachings, had even less confidence in metaphysical or esoteric speculations which, during certain periods of his life, were fashionable in Finland. The tale of the two women in the narrator's life is a more harmonious version of Aho's entangled love life and reminds us somewhat of Poe's *Eleonora*. The book's mood is sentimental, too sentimental for today's taste; childhood and youth are a happy dreamland. The philosophy is based on the same principle: "Think that unhappiness does not exist when you won't let it exist. . . . Do not care about the miseries you see, and you won't see them. Deny the facts, and you won't have them. Learn how to smile when your sorrows are deepest."[283] These words of wisdom are carried to such extremes that they appear to be half-ironic paradoxes although they are not. By the time that he wrote this book, Aho had turned from the world to his memories; it might well be called his farewell to life.

Although Aho and Minna Canth dominated literary life at the end of the nineteenth century, other writers deserve mention here. **Teuvo Pakkala** (originally **Theodor Oskar Frosterus**, 1862-1925) is foremost among them. Like Aho, he lived well into the twentieth century, but his works reflect the spirit of an earlier period, and he published little in his last fifteen years. His family had reached a certain social status as early as the eighteenth century; Johan Frosterus, author of *Hyödyllinen huwitus luomisen töistä. . .* , was his great-great grandfather.[284] By 1862 the family's social standing was somewhat lower; Pakkala's grandfather was a foreman and his father a goldsmith who sometimes deserted his wife and children, who lived in actual poverty in the outskirts of Oulu.[285] At times he was accompanied by his son, who thus had a chance to become acquainted with rough, outdoor life and picturesque popular characters like lumberjacks, tarmakers, and boatmen along the Oulujoki River whom he later described in his works. In the same region, at Paltamo, the boy knew the Lönnbohm family, whose sons became the poets Eino and Kasimir Leino. He went to school and studied at the university, but never took a degree. Afterwards he worked for several newspapers in various towns, for a publisher in Helsinki, and as a traveling salesman for a rope factory. In 1907 he became a successful French teacher in a secondary school; he had studied the language from his youth and had journeyed to Paris in 1896. In 1921 he wrote and directed a film, *Sotapolulla* ('On the Warpath'). Like his father, he was emotionally unstable, and literary work strained his nerves. In 1920 he left the school and changed residence two or three times before his death at Kuopio.

His first works are descriptions of folk life; in a letter from 1888, he said that he wanted only to write about that, not to resolve a problem or to become a great writer.[286] *Lapsuuteni muistoja* ('Memories from My Childhood,' 1885) describes his early life, freely using local dialect and popular speech, which were his own although he of course knew literary Finnish. His childhood had not been happy, and these memories are not exclusively gay. Social issues are not treated, but upper-and middle-class representatives are generally depicted as heartless and egotistic. *Oulua soutamassa* ('Rowing on the Oulunjoki River,' 1885), a description of boatmen who take a load of tar along the river from the inland, also reflects the author's early life.[287] Written in the same naive and humorous vein as Aho's *Rautatie*, it, too, avoids social problems. He also wrote two plays of the same type,[288] *Tukkijoella* (best translated perhaps 'The Lumberjacks,' 1899) and *Meripoikia* ('Sailors,' 1915). Oskari Merikanto and Toivo Kuula, both well-known composers, wrote music for the respective plays. Both were first performed at the Finnish National Theater, and *Tukkijoella* is still popular as summer-theater entertainment.[289]

Pakkala published his first serious works, *Vaaralla* (lit. 'On the Hill'; it is part of Oulu which is indicated)[290] and *Elsa* in 1894. The first is subtitled *Pictures from the Outskirts of a Town* and is more a series of loosely connected sketches than a continuous narrative. It describes the lives of various persons living in the same neighborhood. Pakkala's own experiences had taught him that they could expect little happiness, and his conviction was most likely confirmed by his readings in contemporary realist literature (he had already translated some Norwegian works), often directed at unveiling the world's wrongs and sufferings. In *Vaaralla* the son of a poor family is adopted by good-hearted people. He has the opportunity to study and becomes a priest, but his real father gets drunk at the good news, falls asleep in the snow, and freezes to death. Some of Pakkala's characters humbly accept their fate and trust in God, others are rebellious and bitter, but the author stresses that priests and believers generally do not live according to His law. Minna Canth, who had written similar stories in the 1880s, before her conversion, wrote a letter to Pakkala, praising his work but warning him that he was committing her error in allowing his sympathy for the oppressed to foster hate and desire to wrong others.[291]

Elsa uses the characters of *Vaaralla*, but, more carefully planned, it focuses on the unhappy life of Elsa, an innocent girl engaged to a sailor. Seduced in his absence, she has a child; meanwhile her fiancé has forgotten her and married another woman. On his return he need not even repudiate her, for she dies of an illness caused by sorrow. The callousness of the seducer is underlined: he is the welfare official who in the end places his own child in a strange family, but the book is more an analysis of Elsa than a social protest.

Another play, *Kauppaneuvoksen härkä* (the title can only be translated 'Mr. So-And-So's Ox,' because there is no English equivalent for the main character's title), first performed in 1902, satirizes small-town life and self-important, wealthy upstarts. Pakkala attempted to make the play a broad, satirical farce but was unsuccessful.

Pakkala was best at describing irrational people moved by their imagination and feelings rather than by reason. Elsa is such a person, as are children, and he wrote many delightful short stories about them published in the collections *Lapsia* ('Children,' 1895) and *Pikku ihmisiä* ('Little People,' 1913). These stories are rather pleasant, and the ugly happenings of disillusioned modern stories, *Lord of the Flies*, for example, are absent. Only in *Jumalanmarjat* ('God's Berries,' in *Lapsia*) is there a similarity: children, after picking berries in the woods, sacrifice some on "God's stone"; but the story's end is moral: the inventor of this ceremony, who took the berries, repents and confesses her scheme, which she had developed innocently. Pakkala understood the workings of children's subconscious and fantasy, which blend with reality until they become indistinguishable, but he aimed at the development of a more rational attitude through love and understanding. However, he loved children too much to moralize or present educational systems in his works, which are half-humorous, simple descriptions from the daily lives of children in the modest surroundings in which he had grown up.

His most ambitious work is the novel *Pieni elämäntarina* ('The Modest Story of a Life,' 1902). Differing from his other works, it contains no folk humor or dialect, and the style is intentionally sharp and lively, impressionistic in the same meaning as in Aho's *Juha*. The style was partially due to Norwegian influence, especially that of Hamsun, whose *Viktoria* Pakkala translated in 1899, as was the choice of the main character, a young woman of enigmatic, unpredictable reactions and emotions, although her type of personality had always interested the author. We might say that it foreshadowed literary expressionism, but, though true, the words are only partially adequate. The main character is, in her apparent illogicality, an example of a neurosis resultant from an excessive attachment to her father. Her mother died when she was quite young, and her father raised her, but he marries again and rejects her violent outbursts of passion. She spends the rest of her short life in search of a substitute father, but chooses suitors and admirers inferior to her, thus proving that no one is superior to her father and humiliating herself as punishment for being unworthy of him. The scenes are short and dramatic (perhaps over-dramatic) and follow each other without transition; as they often present contrasting thoughts and moods, the impression is sometimes that of a hastily written, unplanned book. However, even though Pakkala did not completely master his subject or style, the seeming incoherencies mostly reflect the mental conflicts of the main character. This feature can be considered expressionistic if we define expressionism as a way of representing the world in the form of a projection of the author's (or character's) mind rather than objectively; still other particulars in Pakkala's novel are reminiscent of typically expressionistic works. Some of the secondary characters are decidedly unrealistic; they are expressions of the destructive forces in the mind of the main character as projected into the world. After this novel Pakkala did not proceed further in this direction, however, but published his stories about children and his play about sailors. Although his life and work remained in a sense unfinished, they are no less interesting.

Another contemporary of Aho was **Santeri Alkio** (originally **Filander**, 1862-1930; the family name was really Lyyski, but the author's father took a more erudite denomination because he used thread, Latin *filum*, in his work as a tailor). In *Kirjallisuus* he is treated in the same chapter in which Kauppis-Heikki and "other folk writers" are discussed.[292] The label is misleading in general, and its application to him is even more so since he was a political leader and public figure of first rank. He received little formal education and began a career of shopkeeper, but turned to journalism and worked in that field for almost forty years as well as participating in numerous other activities. He was a founder and leader of the movement for free popular education,[293] for fifteen years a member of Parliament, and during Finland's independence Minister of Social Affairs (welfare), member of the committee appointed to write a new constitution in 1905 and 1906, a founder and leader of the Agrarian party, and so forth. In addition, he wrote more than thirty volumes (fiction and nonfiction) between 1885 and 1928, almost all now forgotten unless consulted by scholars interested in the history of the Agrarian party or the movement for popular education. One novel, *Puukkojunkkarit* (1894), has remained a small classic and has introduced or at least given national recognition to the word *puukkojunkkari*. In Ostrobotnia (Finn. *Pohjanmaa*), Alkio's native region, there were knifemen or knifeslingers (*puukkojunkkari*), like the gunmen or gunslingers of the American West.[294] The other name for these knifemen, *häjyt*, can be translated 'bad men.' They were not necessarily criminals, but young men grouped under leaders known for strength and courage who indulged in rough games, drinking, and fighting with similar groups; a favorite pastime was crashing big parties or weddings and, if admittance was refused, tearing down the place of festivity. The fighting was with knives (*puukko*) as well as fists and sticks, and there were occasional fatalities. Some of these characters also became robbers and ended in jail. They were the subjects of popular ballads which are still sung,[295] but the spread of the revivalist movement, education, new customs which replaced most of the old ones, and the efforts of energetic officials made law and order prevail. Alkio describes this enforcement from the viewpoint of the popular educator and temperance worker although he shows understanding for the comradeship, courage, and pride of the knifeslingers. *Murtavia voimia* was intended as a continuation of *Puukkojunkkarit* but is weaker in conception and somewhat spoiled by the author's reflections on the philosophy of history. He was best when he confined himself to his home region, in the novels *Jaakko Jaakonpoika* (1913) and *Patriarkka* ('The Patriarch,' 1916), for example. *Keisaririkos* ('The Crime of the Emperor,' 1923) and *Karuliinan poika* ('Karuliina's Son,' 3 vols. published under the pseudonym Iiska Heikkiläinen, 1925-26) are romanticized popular history in which well-known characters like Yrjö-Koskinen and Juhani Aho appear.

Santeri Ivalo (pseudonym of **Herman Alexander Ivalo**, originally **Ingman**, 1866-1937) is the author of several historical novels. He took a Ph.D. in history and wrote several scholarly works and biographies on Finland's past, but worked for most of his life as a newspaperman for *Päivälehti* and *Helsingin Sanomat*, of which he was at times chief editor. He was elected to Parliament and the City Council of Helsinki and was chairman of the Finnish Writers' Guild, the Finnish Newspapermen's Guild, and the Finnish PEN Club. His first two novels, *Hellaassa* ('In Hellas,' 1890; Hellas is the name of a restaurant in Helsinki) and *Aikansa lapsipuoli* ('The Stepchild of His Time,' 1895), are descriptions of Helsinki in his time with attention to politics, morals, and other contemporary problems. His first historical novel, *Juho Vesainen* (1894), tells the life and deeds of this Finnish guerilla leader of the sixteenth century, who guided men of his region in plundering expeditions to Russian Karelia and defended his country against similar attacks from the other side. Ivalo continued publishing similar works on Finnish history, in which kings, generals, men of the church, farmers, and soldiers appear. He had more interest in action and historical events than in analysis of individuals, but he took his authorship seriously, never thinking that he was providing mere entertainment for his readers. Though simple and artless, his works are deftly written; for their kind they were the best of the time.

Gustaf Adolf von Numers (1848-1913) is the only Finnish playwright of importance in the late nineteenth and early twentieth centuries besides Minna Canth. He is one of the few writers who used both Finnish and Swedish in their works; he belonged to a Swedish-speaking, aristocratic family and wrote most often in that language. Kaarlo Bergbom, leader of the Finnish Theater, helped him write his Finnish works, especially *Elinan surma* (it is said that both could be called the authors of this play).[296] Impractical and interested in literature and theater, he soon lost his properties, but obtained a position in the Finnish State Railroads and worked as station master in various places to the end of his life. At regular intervals he published plays which were performed, several of them in both languages. He read drama, from Shakespeare to Ibsen, Björnson, and Strindberg, and his works reflect his readings. He had an inclination for romantic historical subjects, which Bergbom encouraged, but contemporary drama with its realistic psychological analysis also attracted him. As a result his characters sometimes seem to be from his own time but dressed in historical costumes and performing romantic acts such as lute playing, singing, or sword fighting. His contemporary comedies are harmless, but well written and entertaining.

His tragedy *Elinan surma* ('Elina's Death,' performed in Swedish and Finnish in 1891; *surma* implies violent death) and the comedy *Kuopion takana* ('Beyond Kuopio,' performed in Swedish and Finnish in 1890) have remained popular. The former is based on a medieval ballad in dramatic form, whose manuscript Lönnrot found and copied while a student at Laukko.[297] The simple original is about a husband who is made jealous of his young, innocent wife. He kills her and their child, then commits suicide. The situation is much like that of *Othello*, and Iago's function is performed by a woman, the husband's housekeeper, with whom he has had relations before his marriage. The outline of the poem is preserved in the play, but the characters are greatly changed and some irrelevant scenes added to give a more romantic and historical atmosphere and even to introduce the author's (perhaps Bergbom's) ideas on contemporary issues, e.g., some clumsy attacks on the Catholic church.[298]

Kuopion takana—the implication of the title is that the action occurs in an out-of-the-way place in the country—is innocuous, although its subject, the position of women in society, was timely. Von Numers had been scolded by Minna Canth for his "excessive interest in young girls,"[299] and the play can be interpreted as his answer. In it he satirized both sides of the ideological quarrel of the period, which he refused to consider seriously. Pastor Jussilainen, a conservative minister with the most traditional ideas about men, women, and society, clashes with a young woman from Helsinki with progressive ideas when they meet at his vicarage beyond Kuopio. The end shows that a hectoring male can be overcome by feminine guile and that women more easily achieve their goals with charm and flattery than with recitations of social theory.

Another playwright is **Robert Kiljander** (1848-1924), postmaster of Jyväskylä. His father, a minister of the church, translated some of Runeberg's works into Finnish, and his mother was a talented pianist. He dreamed of an artistic career himself and achieved sufficient skill at the piano to appear as an accompanist at concerts, but had to earn his living in the mail service, a source of some bitterness to him. His plays are light comedies in which small-town characters appear in small-town situations and are now seldom presented by other than amateur groups. *Sanny Kortmanin koulu* ('Sanny Kortman's School,' 1902) is probably most popular among them. There are more satire, bitterness, and reflections on the difficulties he encountered in Kiljander's plays than is usually supposed,[300] but these qualities are forgotten or ignored.

By the end of the nineteenth century, literary life in Finland had developed enough to produce, as well as a few well-known authors, a number of minor writers worth brief mention here. **Kaarle Jaakko** (Karl Jakob) **Gummerus** (1840-98) is best remembered as founder of the important publishing company bearing his name, still active in Jyväskylä. He taught in schools and published several widely read periodicals for popular entertainment and instruction. He also wrote novels and short stories with moral tendencies and happy endings, full of colorful characters and thrilling incidents as well as terrifying, supernatural elements from folktales, e.g., the story *Sovitus haudalla* ('Reconciliation on the Grave'). Ahlqvist-Oksanen compared his novel *Ylhäisiä ja alhaisia* ('The Mighty and the Meek,' 1870) to *Seven Brothers*; he thought that the former had more taste and refinement but was equally deficient in language and style. **Theodolinda Hahnsson** (*née* Limón, 1838-1919; wife of Yrjö-Koskinen after the death of her first husband) is known as the first Finnish woman to produce literary works. Despite changes in literary fashion, she wrote in the idealistic, patriotic, and religious manner prevailing in her youth until 1911. Bergbom was using the same energy and courage that resulted in the Finnish Theater to urge almost all writers to produce plays; such authors as Kivi, Minna Canth, and von Numers were successful, but cases such as Theodolinda Hahnsson, where talent was missing, produced discouraging results. Three of her plays were performed but almost immediately forgotten. Her even more long-lived daughter, **Hilja Haahti** (1874-1966), was one of the founders of the Finnish Writer's Guild. Almost until her death she published novels, similar to those of her mother, which were popular among a solid group of readers. **Evald Ferdinand Jahnsson** (1844-95), a newspaperman, teacher, and minister of the church, was the first author of historical plays in Finnish, plays which were performed successfully in 1873 and 1874 at the Finnish Theater. He also wrote the historical novel *Hatanpään Heikki ja hänen morsiamensa* ('Heikki of Hatanpää and His Bride,' 1884), which, though not intended as such, became a boys' classic.

At that time the first purely humorous writers appeared.[301] They established for themselves a pattern still prevalent: writing short stories rather than longer narratives, avoiding impropriety and profanity, describing country or small-town characters, and using a pseudonym. **Karl Gustaf Samuel Suomalainen** (1850-1907), whose translations from Russian and West European languages we have mentioned, wrote as Samuli S., publishing between 1876 and 1905, short stories set in small towns in which humor occasionally gives way to sentiment. He also wrote memoirs of his life in St. Petersburg, which provide an interesting view of Finnish society there, and of Russian life, which he criticized. **Aksel Wilho Soini** (originally Hoffrén, 1854-1934), who wrote under the name **Pii**, printed between 1877 and 1899 a few short stories and, at Bergbom's request, some light comedies which were performed at the Finnish Theater. They are reputed among the best of what was written between 1870 and 1880, an otherwise rather empty period in Finnish literature. The collection *Kirjavia kuvia pölkkyjen historiasta* ('Various Stories from the History of Logs,' 1877; the reference is to logging and lumberjacks) inspired one of its many readers, Juhani Brofeldt (later Aho), to write similar stories based on folk life. Soini was another founder of the Finnish Writer's Guild, but after becoming a member of the Board of Trustees in a large Helsinki bank, he stopped writing, and people have forgotten his authorship. His daughter **Elsa Soini**, a well-known writer in her time, wrote a biographical article on him for an anthology. **Gustaf Adolf Heman** (1855-1917), whose pseudonym was **Kah**, was a minister entrusted with many important ecclesiastic duties and was elected to Parliament. His writings, small humorous and instructive stories for newspapers, were published between 1883 and 1888 in three collections. Mysterious events and romantic narrations about robbers and highwaymen are included. He was from Häme, as was Kivi, whose influence can be seen in his works. His admiration for Kivi was unusual for a man of his position and time. He also translated some texts by Kierkegaard and published a collection of serious short stories, *Kysymysmerkkiä* ('Question Marks,' 1885); one of the subjects is his own life and its religious and ideological conflicts. Johannes Linnankoski said that the book had inspired him to become a writer. **Juho Reijonen** (1855-1924), also a minister, signed his works -ijo-. His works all depict the nature and people of his native north Karelia. His language and style, influenced by the north Karelian popular speech, are colorful. The best of these small humorists, he attempted more than these sketches, though he was better at them. Mild social satire appears in his works in his invariable siding with the common people against the wealthy and the educated, whom he ridiculed. Like the other humorists, he first wrote stories for magazines, e.g., Krohn's *Suomen Kuvalehti*, and later published collections. He also composed religious works.

Two late nineteenth-century poets are generally called realists, but they did not write realistic descriptions of daily life to unveil society's injustices and miseries although they were aware of them.[302] Their works are more general and idealistic. One of them, **Juhana Heikki Erkko** (1849-1906),[303] wrote an aphorism refuting realistic art:

> Art is not an imitation of nature, for nature as such does already exist, art is a continuation and development of nature in a human spirit; it

is the creation of something new from the foundations of nature and humanity.[304]

His declaration contains a philosophy of art similar to the tenets of French classicism at the end of the seventeenth century, whose theoreticians insisted that truth and nature be followed, but represented in an idealized form. Also in harmony with this conception was the other "realist" poet, **Kasimir Agathon Lönnbohm** (1866-1919), better known as **Kasimir Leino**, brother of the more famous Eino Leino. It should be emphasized, however, that, except for a few poems which touch upon the principles of freedom, progress and fraternity, actual French influence in their works is negligible.

Erkko's father was a well-to-do farmer at Orimattila, south of Lahti. Minna Canth's circle considered one of his brothers, Elias, a promising poet, but he died young. His other brother, Eero, was a lifelong newspaperman who eventually worked for *Päivälehti* and *Helsingin Sanomat*. Erkko's childhood was old-fashioned and rural: he watched the cows and did other farm work until he went to school at the Finnish Teachers' College at Jyväskylä, where Minna Canth also studied. After 1872 he taught and held public offices in the towns in which he lived. After approximately 1896 he was able to devote himself exclusively to writing.

Erkko published his first poems in newspapers or periodicals and collected them between 1870 and 1904. He also wrote short stories and plays, but his reputation rests on his lyrical works. Some were set to music, often by Oskari Merikanto, a well-known but insignificant composer, and have remained popular due to their catchy tunes and simple words. Some of these songs were patriotic poems, e.g., *Hämäläisen laulu* ('The Song of [the People of] Häme') and *Kansalaislaulu* ('The Citizen's Song'), not similar to the *Marseillaise*. Except the songs his poetry is now forgotten although he was popular in his time. Nevertheless the *Helsingin Sanomat* continues to eulogize him on every suitable occasion.

His initial poems were simple, naively sentimental, and bucolic, like those of Topelius; despite his later development, he wrote similar works until his death. He naturally produced children's poems, and many homes still sing *Jouluaatto* ('Christmas Eve'), also set to music, at the proper time. Some of his composition, e.g., *Tuutiessa* (best translated perhaps 'Lullaby'), are in the old folk meter. Critics have mentioned Runeberg's influence, but Professor Koskimies points out that they actually underline Erkko's inferiority to his great model. Erkko had only simple charm but was also clumsy, because he obviously paid little attention to the form of his works.

As Erkko's poems became known, he met other artists, journeyed abroad, read the standard foreign authors of the time, became more worldly, and worked for *Päivälehti*. He was influenced by the Unitarian church and the works of Edouard Laboulaye, a French writer whose work on freedom of religion he read in Swedish translations. These developments are noticeable in his poems, especially in those from the collections *Havaittuani* ('After I Had Awaked,' 1886) and *Kuplia* ('Bubbles' or, better, 'Froth,' 1890). In the poem *Havaittuani* he tells that he was born free but with the mind of a slave and the fear of God, whom he sees as an Oriental tyrant, ruling with an iron scepter. However, God has in reality made man free and capable of perpetual progress. His spring is coming, Truth will be our liberation, Love our strength, and this faith will overcome all obstacles. In *Käynti kotikylässä* ('A Visit to the Native Village') he protests against those who complain of the new generation's destructiveness; he admits that the rotten is pulled down but points out that it is replaced and adds that in time this generation's works will be renewed by another. Erkko's radical period did not last long beyond 1890. He published some poems on materialism and idealism and *Työkansan marssi* ('The Working People's March,' 1893),[305] but basically he reverted to his earlier interest in love and the beauties of nature. Occasionally he also wrote patriotic verse. He never married, but he often fell in love and honored each woman with a series of poems.

Erkko's plays, all in verse, are built on ideological problems with messages for the audience and reader. *Tietäjä* ('The Prophet,' 1887), written in blank verse, is about the biblical figure Balaam, who represents the new man in search for a new religion, a synthesis of the old polytheism of Moab and the new monotheism of Israel. Erkko really criticized as polytheism the dogma of the Holy Trinity. The hero is unsuccessful but still confident that life will progress and humanity reach a higher spiritual level. This play and his others were performed at the Finnish Theater.

His next plays are based on the *Kalevala* and written in its meter. With the exception of Eino Leino, he is the only writer in Finland to show a definite influence of Lönnrot's epic. He used these subjects to express views on contemporary problems; the results were sometimes unintendedly humorous, for example, *Aino* (1893). In the *Kalevala* Aino is a young girl who drowns herself rather than marry an old man. In Erkko's play she represents the emancipation of women. In *Kullervo* (1895) the tragic hero of the *Kalevala* was better suited to symbolize by his revolt the workers' movement of the nineteenth century and its attacks on society. Considerations of the opposition between conservatives and liberals, which Erkko viewed as evil, and the necessity of the moral improvement of man also appear in the play. Erkko was successful in adapting the old folk meter for the stage, but he was far too lyrical and dreamy for drama.

His last play was written for the formal reopening of the Finnish Theater as the Finnish National Theater in 1902, after Russian oppression had begun. The verse, considered his best, shows the influence of Eino Leino's early works, but the list of *dramatis personae* is incredible.[306] Among them are herds of shepherds, shepherdesses, singers, musicians, riders, and pseudomythological beings, such as Hallatar, Usvatar, Ilmatar, etc. Creation of goddesses and semigoddesses is easy in the old folk verse: addition of the suffix -*tar* (or -*tär*) to and capitalization of the initial letter of any noun, e.g., *halla* 'frost,' *usva* 'mist,' or *ilma* 'air,' creates the "Frostess," "Mistess," or "Airess." This device is observed even in genuine folk poetry.[307] The play's message is a call for national unity and strong resistance in the face of the Russians; the play's title, *Pohjolan häät* ('The Wedding at Pohjola'), refers to the *Kalevala* episode of momentary reconciliation between Kalevala and Pohjola, the eternal enemies. Erkko's plays were admired at the time, mainly for patriotic reasons, but are now forgotten.

Kasimir Leino's philosophical ideas were natural to him, for he had scholarly training. He wrote a Ph.D. thesis on Prosper Mérimée, an essay on Minna Canth's drama (1897), and the biography of a Finnish painter Aleksander Lauréus (1908), as well as numerous newspaper articles and translations of Daudet, Maupassant, Mérimée, Ibsen, and others. He was an original collaborator on the *Päivälehti*, Bergbom's assistant at the Finnish Theater, and manager of two other theaters, but near the end of his life he earned his living by writing only, doing criticism for the conservative *Uusi Suometar* rather than for *Päivälehti.* He has been called a highly talented man who could not choose a career,[308] but Aho was active in almost as many fields; it is more likely that his achievements fell short of greatness for lack of talent.

Many of his poems seem sloppily written, for, like many Finnish poets, he felt that rhyme, regular rhythm, and melodious words were the elements of poetry and that, to achieve them, many liberties could be taken with vocabulary and syntax. In the European lyrical tradition a poet is not usually permitted to alter the length or form of his words merely to make them fit his chosen rhythmic pattern.[309] The collection *Ristiaallokossa* ('Among the Breaking Seas,' 1890) contains many poems expressing the poet's will to be free at the expense of peace. Such images as the stormy sea, the courageous sailor, or *Myrskylintu* ('Stormy Petrel,' a poem still known as a song) appear, but the effect is often spoiled by bad grammar and lack of taste in the formulation of the poet's thoughts and feelings. His poor grammar is not so much the result of a poet's feeling that in his expression of deep truths he should go beyond rules of ordinary speech as of a failure to fit his conventionally-patterned sentences to poetic schemes. Mediocre poets have been published in all countries, but in Finland almost anything containing beautiful words and expressing beautiful feelings was acceptable due to lack of criticism of poetry's formal and technical qualities. We, too, wholeheartedly support Leino's ideals: love of freedom, courage to fight for it, hate for all oppression and narrow-mindedness, and respect for the individual, but Leino's expression of them is formally faulty and factually shallow.

He satirized his opponents but also expressed doubts in the validity of a purely intellectual approach to life's problems. In the collection *Väljemmillä vesillä* (1893) he included *Elämän laulu* ('The Song of Life'; a volume of selected poems by his brother Eino, published posthumously in 1947, also bears this title), a long poem which, although no more remarkable that his other works, shows better mastery of form, especially when he approaches usage of the old folk meter, anticipating the works of Eino. Attempting to present a general philosophy, it begins modestly enough, Professor Koskimies says, with the creation of the world,[310] but its interesting rhythmic pattern is skillfully built and closely adapted to the contents. The chaos from which God created the world is described in a few iambic lines, heavy and monotonous (*kun kaaoksesta kaikkeuden / loi luoja maailmoita*); transition is provided with two short trochaic lines with an vanacrusis, *ja (ja vuoret nousi / ja uomat uurtui)* which lead into a section depicting the beauties of the new world and their development in a different trochaic meter interspersed with dactyls as melodious and buoyant as the scenery. Such passages hint that Leino (and Erkko) lacked self-discipline and friendly criticism more than they lacked talent. Contemporary criticism was often destructive rather than constructive, and Leino also wrote satirical poems about conservative critics, narrowly academic and hostile to all not conforming to moral, not artistic standards. One reaction to this criticism was disdain for all rules. Finland was not alone in experiencing this situation, but, in a country almost without literary tradition, opposition was sharper than in countries where such differences were accepted.

Literature in Finnish in the Twentieth Century from 1901 to the Independence

CONVENIENTLY, FOR THE HISTORIAN, THE TURN of the century in Finland marked a great change in all fields, not only art and literature: in the relations with Russia, the year 1899 was the landmark for the beginning of an open attack against the autonomous position of Finland;[311] in Finnish politics the Workers' party, which soon after adopted the name of Social Democrat party, was founded the same year—the Young Finnish party had been organized only a few years earlier, in 1894; in art and literature a new generation with new aesthetic theories and a new philosophy appeared. Simultaneously the old generation disappeared; Minna Canth and J. H. Erkko died, Kasimir Leino was overshadowed by his younger brother Eino, and Pakkala went rather unnoticed. Juhani Aho remained the only older writer of some consequence and became a patriarch among young radicals.

In Finland, as in the rest of Europe, the trend was away from realism and naturalism toward romanticism or symbolism—in Scandinavia the term "neoromanticism" is often used.[312] Foreign models were not lacking: Selma Lagerlöf, Verner von Heidenstam, Oscar Levertin, Strindberg and Ibsen (in the last symbolic plays of these latter two), and Knut Hamsun in Scandinavia; Verlaine, Maeterlinck, and Nietzsche in Europe. Nietzsche found enthusiastic followers, but the Finns rarely indulged in the decadent and morbid aspects of symbolism. Some found them attractive, but not congenial; Eino Leino once wrote about Heine: "I was downright angry and impatient when seeing myself mentally and physically healthy. I would have liked so much to be a pale, emaciated moonlight poet like Heine, with his ironic smile on my lips. But it wouldn't do, it would't do at all. . . . What could I do when the mirror gave the opposite testimony and showed a most flourishing and red-cheeked country boy?"[313]

There was little need for imitation of foreign models, for romantic inspiration existed at home. Finns had just rediscovered the beauties of the *Kalevala* and the ancient folk civilization still in existence in the easternmost parts of their country and in Russian Karelia. Artists went there first, and a "national romantic" style developed in architecture. A prime example is an insurance office in Helsinki lined with enormous stone blocks decorated with carved birds, squirrels, foxes, pine twigs, and grinning faces of Finnish peasants.[314] Fortunately, this style, out of place in modern settings, soon died, but not before it made the point that not all art need follow established, classical patterns. Thus, one can say that in many fields modern art in Finland began at that moment.

Unfortunately, however, this fashion presented a most inaccurate image of Finland among foreign nations. One of the most illustrious victims of this distorted view is Jean Sibelius, who is represented as the bard of the great forests in the North who composed mysterious legends on folk motifs. Actually, he was the son of a physician living in the western part of the country; he studied in Helsinki, Berlin, and Vienna, traveled widely, spoke several languages, and met many of the foremost personalities in music. Sibelius himself once said that there was not one bar of folk music in his works. Still, the legend persists, even in Finland.[315]

The first ten or fifteen years of this century can be called the period of national romanticism in Finnish literature, or even the period of **Eino Leino** (originally **Armas Eino Leopold Lönnbohm**, 1878-1926).[316] His father, a surveyor, who was originally called Mustonen, belonged to the generation whose members acquired Swedish names with education. Although many other writers began their careers approximately when he did, none equaled him as a poet, and the great novelists of his generation wrote their major works later. He typified in his poems, short stories, novels, plays, criticism, and newspaper articles[317] the mood of the times, the yearning for something higher and more beautiful than reality, for heroic deeds, and for outbursts of burning passion, as well as a general feeling of vanity and the doubts in all human effort. Such feelings degenerate easily into theatrical attitudes and rhetoric, neither of which is lacking in Leino or his contemporaries. Many factors made Leino's production uneven. He had a great facility for writing, composed verse as a schoolboy, and published his first collection *Maaliskuun lauluja* ('Songs in March,' 1896) when only eighteen, but his brother Kasimir had already introduced him to the literary circles of Helsinki. A comic paper published a caricature in which Kasimir was shown kindling the flame of Eino's genius with a pair of bellows.[318] The younger brother soon proved far superior to the older in all genres, superior, in fact, to all poets of his time; later his power declined. His untimely death was largely due to the rather sordid bohemian life he led, but even at that time his works bore the unmistakable mark of genius.

Despite Leino's description of himself as a healthy country boy, there were but few gay, careless, and happy songs among his works, and his first poems which did not reflect his personal conflicts were in the rhetorical and ornately patriotic tradition initiated by Ahlqvist-Oksanen and Genetz-Jännes. He was able, however, to create good poetry about his own problems, and only after 1910 did the first signs of his coming breakdown appear in his art and his life. The great problems recurring in his works can be classified as the relationship between dream and fulfillment, the opposition between life and death, and the opposition between good and evil.[319] Leino's poems, however, are about characters, not abstractions, except in a few cases, as in the section *Ajan kirja* ('The Book of Time') of the collection *Talvi-yö* ('The Winter Night,' 1905). His heroes are self-defeating; they either meet destruction in a struggle against superhuman enemies or receive ambiguous oracles which leave them unsatisfied. Artistically this description of man's eternal struggle for truth is more rewarding than a presentation of cut-and-dried answers to human problems.

His second collection followed the first within the same year. Called *Tarina suuresta tammesta ym. runoja* ('The Tale of the Great Oak and Other Poems'), it takes its name from an obscure myth in folk poetry,[320] which Lönnrot incorporated in the *Kalevala*. The contemporary fashion of admiring the *Kalevala*, old folk poetry, and Karelian folk art is evident; even the first collection had poems written in imitation of old and new folk meters. Soon after, in 1897, Leino made the pilgrimage to Karelia which so many artists and writers undertook at that time.[321] Although he met no old bards there, his observations are reputed to have made a deep and lasting impression on him; subjects from old poetry and from Karelia recur in his poetry.[322] Occasionally these subjects seem little more than pretexts for writing colorful, romantic descriptions of the past, as in the legends[323] *Luojan leipä* ('The Bread of God,' in *Helkavirsiä* I,[324] originally in *Kangastuksia* 'Mirages,' 1902), *Sininen risti* ('The Blue Cross'), and *Impi ja pajarin poika* ('The Maid and the Son of the Boyar,' both in *Helkavirsiä* I, 1903). Some build a metaphysical conception of life, *Väinämöisen laulu* ('Väinämöinen's Song,' in *Kangastuksia*), *Aika* ('Time,' same collection), and *Kouta* (name, in *Helkavirsiä* I). Some gave the poet the opportunity to analyze his own soul, *Tumma* (name, in *Helkavirsiä* I), *Tuuri* (name, same collection), *Iku-Turso* (name, in *Talvi-yö*), and *Turjan loihtu* ('Turja's Spell,' in the collection *Halla*, 'The Frost,' 1908).

Despite Leino's precociousness as a poet and facility for writing, recognition was not immediately given to his works, in which many critics saw only faults and oddities.[325] After his first two books he continued producing from one to two collections a year: *Yökehrääjä* ('The Nighthawk,' 1897; poems), *Sata ja yksi laulua* ('Hundred and One Songs; 1898, poems), *Tuonelan joutsen* ('The Swan of Tuonela,' 1898; poem; Tuonela is the Hades of old Finnish mythology), *Ajan aalloilla* ('On the Waves [or Sea] of Time,' 1899; poems), *Hiihtäjän virsiä* ('Songs of the Skier,' 1900; poems), *Johan Wilhelm* (name, 1900; play), *Sota valosta* ('The War about Light,' 1900; play), *Kivesjärveläiset* ('The People of Kivesjärvi,' 1901; poem), *Pyhä kevät* ('The Holy Spring,' 1901; poems), *Kangastuksia* ('Mirages,' 1902; poems), *Suomalainen näyttämötaide* ('Dramatic Art in Finland,' 1902; essay), and the first collection of *Helkavirsiä* ('Holy Songs,' 1903; poems) generally considered his foremost work, that which made his reputation and superseded all his other works in the mind of the public.

During these first years as an artist, Leino had met another poet, Otto Manninen, quite different from himself, with whom he established a lasting friendship after a few brushes due to Manninen's severe but just criticism of Leino's youthful works.[326] After noting the weaknesses in, e.g., *Sata ja yksi laulua* and *Kivesjärveläiset*, Manninen fully recognized *Kangastuksia*, in which he believed Leino had reached a mastery of expression which, he hoped, would make possible the attainment of a higher level of perfection in Finnish poetry, not only for Leino, but also for poets who followed his example. Critics, somewhat bewildered by *Helkavirsiä* I,[327] tended to view the collection negatively until Manninen, in a long article published in *Valvoja*,[328] gave a penetrating analysis and placed it in the context of Finnish poetry. According to Manninen, until then there had been a rift in Finnish poetry, literature, and art between the followers of the old Finnish tradition and those who took their models from Western Europe, but Leino had combined both into a harmonious whole. Manninen maintained that the meters of old Finnish and new European poetry must remain separated, but that in Leino's works, especially *Helkavirsiä*, a Finnish and European way of seeing the world and expressing feelings were happily united.[329] Other poets used the old folk meter before Leino, but almost no one used it after him, and the subjects from Finnish mythology or the legendary past were also discarded, both as reconstructions of a lost world and as expressions of modern thoughts. Thus, Leino's work did not mark the beginning of a new era; it was more the culmination of an old one, if not an era in itself. National romanticism, the resurrection of the Finnish past and the creation of a new civilization from its elements and the modern world, of which Juhani Aho and his friends dreamed when they went to school, was at best a dream of intellectuals and artists. Although attempted at the beginning of this century, the entire myth was so short-lived that even its creators soon turned away from it. Finnish poetry, literature, and art remained individual variants of the Scandinavian type of West European civilization, perhaps touched by a faint East European strain. If they were specifically Finnish, it was because they reflected the Finnish realities of their time.

There is considerable difference in the treatment of the subjects from Finnish mythology and past in Leino's earliest collections and *Helkavirsiä* I.

In *Laulu suuresta tammesta* the myth about a gigantic oak which over-shadowed the whole world until an unknown, small, weak-looking man felled it, is treated superficially. Parts of the poem are reminiscent of the patriotic compositions that Genetz-Jännes and other scholarly poets wrote for public functions, with all the romantic paraphernalia of Finno-Ugric geography, Viena and Valdai, Kainuu, Karelia, the mouth of Ruija, the shores of Väinä, and so forth. Väinämöinen is no longer spiritual leader of the nation; only an unknown old man sings of the great deeds of the past and predicts a better future, when a hero will fell the gigantic Swedish oak. The poem is really only an argument in the quarrels between the two linguistic groups in Finland. In *Tuonelan joutsen* the mythical motif already expresses something deeper. The *Kalevala* episode tells the story of Lemminkäinen, who, to win the hand of a maid, must perform seemingly impossible deeds, the last consisting of killing the swan of the underworld; he perishes in the attempt, but is revived by his mother.[330] In his effort to represent allegorically the quest of man for the ultimate truth, the mystery of life and death, Leino followed this outline rather closely. He did not state all of the metaphysical implications in the poem, but, in a letter to Maila Talvio, he indicated that Lemminkäinen's defeat and death were due to the fact that he was a mere sinful human being. Only Christ, Leino concluded, can bring hope and solve the mystery of death for mankind, who lives and suffers in fear of it.[331]

The collections that followed, *Yökehrääjä, Sata ja yksi laulua, Ajan aalloilla, Hiihtäjän virsiä,* and *Pyhä kevät,* were not remarkable. *Ajan aalloilla* is directly inspired by the Russian oppression, and the others, though some have remained popular as songs,[332] show mainly that Leino had a great facility for writing light, melodious verse; he was duly criticized for these compositions. Although they contain a few poems based on subjects from the Finnish past, only the play *Sota valosta* is based on an episode in the *Kalevala.* Again, Leino was attracted by an episode largely composed for the epic by Lönnrot, in which original materials did not have a great part: the sun and the moon were kept in a mountain by the enemy of the *Kalevala's* major heroes, who then set them free.[333] In Leino's poem each of the heroes represents a human type: Väinämöinen is the leader of the nation, bringing it light and knowledge, Ilmarinen the artist, Lemminkäinen the warrior; but Pohjola, the enemy country, is a pure symbol of the negative side in human nature:

> Pohjola on siellä täällä
> vesissä ja vetten päällä
> maassa, puussa, kuolleen luussa,
> itse ihmisen lihassa.

> Pohjola is here and there
> On the waters, under them,

In the earth and in the wood
In the bones of all the dead,
Even in the flesh of Man.

Leino alluded again to the political situation in Väinämöinen's proclamation of faith in the power of light and the human spirit, which will remain even after the Swedish conquerors and Christianity rob the heroes of the *Kalevala* of their strength. Leino's admiration for Nietzsche is often seen in the manner in which he describes his characters, reminiscent of the German writer's superman. Neither Leino nor his contemporaries considered this work of much value, but Bergbom, who died in 1906, produced it at the National Theater.

Leino's next collection, *Kangastuksia*, is introductory to *Helkavirsiä* I, so much so that Leino included two of its poems in the later collection. It still contains "some of everything," including an epic poem in twelve cantos, *Perman taru* ('The Saga of Perma'),[334] in a meter typical of modern Finnish folksongs which he had also used in the earlier *Kivesjärveläiset*.[335] As this meter is closely connected for Finnish readers with folk motifs and melodies, the difficulties of writing other poetry with it have kept its use infrequent; Leino progressively discarded it in his later poems. Seemingly exotic subjects in some of the compositions in *Kangastuksia* were used by Leino to express views on questions of general interest, for example, *Tahtoisin nähdä mä Kartagon naisen* ('I Wish I Could See a Woman of Carthago'), *Imatran tarina* ('The Tale of Imatra'),[336] or *Temppeliherra* ('The Templar'), which exalt freedom and the fight for it. In *Temppeliherra* the concept of freedom includes any high ideal, expressed as "the man who lived for an ideal / is but sleeping, he cannot die / his sword is striking from beneath the ground." This philosophical vein is further pursued in some poems inspired by Finnish mythology, such as *Väinämöisen laulu*, in which the bard and hero is presented as an ideal for mankind with the warning that even the hero is not eternal—what endures is the ideal, the spirit, man himself. A complex pattern of interwoven motifs and ideas, reflected in Leino's life, appears in *Aika*. Time, which Leino identifies with death, is an evil against which all heroes are called to fight, but the fight is purely spiritual. These heroes, "the stepping stones of their own ideals," are victorious only when doing "deeds of the spirit, which shall not disappear, even if all nations vanish." Here is Leino's basic fear of death, which reappears throughout his works though he tried to overcome it by philosophic and metaphysic considerations, the most common being that mankind does not disappear even though the individual is destroyed, and that great spiritual deeds live forever. The problem of good and evil, stated more clearly in *Helkavirsiä*, is here apparent insofar as Leino insists that it is not by warlike deeds and violence but by spiritual struggle that ultimate victory can be achieved. His hidden fear of the opposite sex is expressed in the personification of time as a Gorgon, a hideous monster, "half a lizard, huge and scaly, half a woman with lips burning red like flames," which devours its victims.

Leino's fame as a poet and bohemian earned him the reputation of an irresistible lover,[337] but in fact he often disappointed women; both of his marriages were resounding failures. In his love poems and love letters an uncertainty, distrust of the future and of himself, often lurks behind the ecstasy and sensuousness.[338] In a letter to the poetess L. Onerva, he laments his difficulties, expresses his fears and his suspicion of himself, and begs her to be kind, to help him.[339] He matured considerably between his first collections and *Helkavirsiä* I; with its publication he reached his full development as a poet. Two years later he married and now seemed ready to assume the full responsibilities of man and citizen, but his maturation caused him to doubt his powers more and more; life was no longer to be taken into the arms of the young poet, and the power of spirit, the words he could arrange in ever new patterns, were not enough to sustain him in the struggle for daily bread. He wanted help and comfort rather than companionship and love from the other sex. Although he would not admit defeat and maintained that the ideals of his poetry were enough to take a man through life, something in him was broken. He still produced great works, wrote for newspapers and periodicals, and was a familiar figure in the literary circles of Helsinki; he fell in love more than once and married a second time, and each love seemed to fill him with new energy and buoyancy, but his life really decayed slowly and steadily. When he died, there was not much of the brilliant poet or man of the world left in him. Perhaps he achieved success too quickly and too young, though not without merit. His downfall came mainly, if not entirely, from within.[340]

In *Helkavirsiä* I there are but few compositions on mythical and metaphysical problems, and no transpositions of motifs from the *Kalevala*, like *Sota valosta* or *Tuonelan joutsen*. Leino seems not to have been inspired by myths to treat them in verse, but to have been inclined to use them as metaphors for his own problems. The poems include ballads and legends, and it is in the first ones that his problems, or those of man as an individual, are presented by means of historical or mythical motifs. The main character of *Ylermi* is vaguely defined a medieval nobleman, a proud knight who defies God and is punished. Ylermi is a kind of Byronic hero, a Don Juan,[341] and a Nietzschean superman, but he directs his rebellion not against God or a specific religion as much as against the slavish spirit of men who fear death; the hero hopes for a later generation, sterner than his, that will not bow to death or crawl on its way to the underworld.[342] The poem, not a lengthy narration of his life and deeds, presents him only as a proud man who defies God, declares, when his house is burned, that he will build a new and better one and, when his wife dies and son goes mad, that he will have new and better ones, rides into the church, throws down his gauntlet, and speaks a few proud words before flames erupting from below the ground swallow him. There is little Finnish mythology in *Kouta*, although its subject seems to be taken from it; Leino admitted that he had thought of describing the main character, Kouta, as a shaman, but that he eventually gave him more individuality and a yearning for the highest truth.[343] He possesses all the knowledge of the gods and men, but not the ultimate wisdom, described as "binding the blue fire / opening the treasure troves." (According to Finnish beliefs mysterious blue flames burn over hidden treasures, which can be found if the flame is "bound.") Later the ultimate wisdom consists in the unveiling of the secrets of Death, held by the goddess of Time, Ajatar; the motifs of *Tuonelan joutsen* and *Aika* again appear here. Kouta eventually descends to the underworld and meets the goddess, who announces that he must be ready to sacrifice his own life to be allowed to partake of the deepest mystery; he declares his readiness and learns the words of wisdom. It is obviously dangerous for a poet to declare that he knows the ultimate secret of the universe, and Leino made his statement oracular enough to allow speculation on its meaning among Finnish scholars: *Elon huoli huomisesta / Mana mennyttä manaapi* ('Life's sorrow is about tomorrow / Death is conjuring the past').[344] Hardly mysterious, they seem to be a warning by Leino to himself not to brood about death, but to turn to life and the future.

The heroes of some of the other ballads, which are neither so metaphysical nor solemn as these two, though still tragic, are more ordinary human beings, caught in forces larger than their immediate experiences. *Tuuri's* main character is only a wealthy farmer (*goodman* or *husbandman* suggest the archaic character of the poem), but at a time when gods are still walking among men and admitting them to their feasts. Tuuri rashly asks for immortality, which is granted, but in a manner that shows him his imprudence. When the feast is over, he discovers that it has lasted longer than one life and that his family and friends are dead.[345] The last scene is otherwordly only in the presence of the supernatural driver of the sleigh of Death, in which Tuuri leaves his empty home:

Istui Kuolon korjasehen
kuului kulkusten helinä
hämärässä talvi-aamun;
kuului vielä viittatieltä
jäälle järvien hävisi.

He sat in the sleigh of Death
The silver of the bells was sounding
In the dawn of the winter day
Sounding on the snowy road
Fading on the frozen lake.

153

Tumma has still less mythology; supernatural beings are embodiments of individual subconscious fears rather than objects of actual worship. Tumma ('dark, somber') is "frightened from his birth on"; on ordinary errands in the forest or on the lake, he sees demons and spirits everywhere and wishes to be freed from this life. His dead father warns him not to try to reach the underworld before his due time, for it is a place of empty, hopeless nothingness—Väinämöinen expresses the same idea in *Sota valosta*. At the end of the poem, Tumma lives, sad but no longer frightened, taking days as they come—an obvious attempt for Leino to solve his own problems, this time in a simple, subdued manner. Among his poems this one is closest to the realities of his time and contemporary psychology, though with a trace of mythology remaining.

Some of the poems classified as ballads in *Helkavirsiä* I are not at all supernatural or mythological and give only stirring, tragic, or violent descriptions from the past without implication of a deeper meaning. *Räikkö Räähkä*, named for the main character, gives a few essential facts from the story of a traitor. "He showed the road to the enemy on a dark autumn night between two cliffs, he did it because his life was threatened," but his neighbors do not retaliate directly; they only reject him, and he hangs himself. Although it was written during the Russian oppression, when some Finns were traitors and others, who thought they could prevent the worst by collaborating with the Russians, were branded as such, Leino was probably not using these facts in his poem, whose events could happen anywhere. *Mantsin laulu* ('The Song of Mantsi'), another story of old wars, is set in Finnish Karelia and tells of young men taking arms in vengeance upon their enemies, who have abducted a maid; *Orjan poika* ('The Son of a Slave') is set in Lapland. Leino did not consciously imitate, but he recreated closely the atmosphere of old folk poems about border wars, feuds, and plundering expeditions, familiar in every country with a violent past. In *Orjan poika* the leader of a Finnish plundering expedition in Lapland carries away a Lapp boy and later kills him, fearing his evil eye—Lapps have always been considered great magicians and sorcerers. The murder is accomplished while the victim sleeps; a vision of his home country, experienced at the moment of death, closes the poem:

> Puikoivat punaiset pulkat
> punaisilla kukkuloilla,
> siukoivat siniset petrat
> sinisillä virran-suilla,
> jolui joutsenet hopeiset,
> käet kukkui kultahiset,
> käet kukkui, linnut lauloi,
> vihannoivat viidat kaikki
> Lapin suuressa suvessa,
> yössä päivän paistamassa.

Red sleighs were sliding
On high red hills,
Blue reindeers were running
On the banks of blue brooks,
Silvery swans were swimming,
Golden cuckoos were calling
Cuckoos calling, birds warbling,
Blooming the green groves
In the sweet summer of Lapland
In the night of sun and light.

This vision, in the style of folk poetry, marks a slight break with the beginning of the poem. It is more the voice of Leino than that of an anonymous ballad singer by whom, we imagine, the first part of the story was told. The same break occurs in *Räikkö Räähkä*. It begins—*Tuo turilas, Räikkö Räähkä / Neuvoi tien viholliselle* ('That varmint,[346] Räikkö Räähkä / Showed the road to the enemy')—in an almost popular or familiar tone, but ends with a highly poetic vision, supposedly of the main character, about to hang himself, but actually of Leino: *Elo kaunis kangastihe / askar autuas inehmon / maan kovalla kannikalla* ('He saw as in a sight / life so light and fair / the blessed burden of Man / on the hard crust of Earth').

The quotation from *Orjan poika* is typical of the ornate verse written in imitation of old folk poetry. In descriptions of the wealthy and sumptuous or wonderful and supernatural, the old folk poems employed a set of colors, mainly blue, red, gold, and silver, the latter also metals; this device was conventionally applied, colors being assigned to objects for the alliterative effect common in Finnish folk poetry.[347] For example, *Ihmemaa* ('Wonderland'):

Souda, souda tuolle maalle,
souda tuolle rantaselle,
kussa puut punalle paistoi,
puut punalle, maat sinelle,
kellalle petäjän kerkät,
hopealle hongan oksat,
kullalle kanervan latvat.
Siell' on sillat silkin pantu,
Sillat silkin, maat sametin,
veralla vetelät paikat. . . .

Row, row, to that land,
row to that shore,
where the trees are shining red,
the trees red, the ground blue,
yellow the cones of the fir,
silvery the twigs of the spruce,
golden the heads of heather.
There the bridges are sheathed in silk,

> the bridges in silk, the ground in velvet,
> the muddy places with cloth. . . .

The trees are red (*puu* 'tree' *punainen* 'red'), the twigs of the spruce (or pine) silvery (*hopea* 'silver' *honka* 'pine'), the bridges covered with silk (*silta* 'bridge' *silkki* 'silk'), all for alliteration. This excerpt also has the rhetorical figure called *limikkäiskerto* by Finnish scholars, 'repetition by overlapping' or 'enjambement,' i.e., the repetition in a line of a group of words appearing in the preceding line. Interestingly, Leino used the same device in *Orjan poika* (*käet kukkui*), a composition on a vaguely medieval subject; according to Finnish scholars these devices were introduced into Finnish folk poetry in the Middle Ages.[348] No doubt his use was instinctive, for Leino never studied folk poetry as a scholar and considered the *Kalevala* as good a source for inspiration as genuine folklore.

The poems classified as legends in *Helkavirsiä* I deal with Christian subjects, also treated in old Finnish folk poems.[349] Leino often set the action in orthodox Karelia, giving himself the opportunity to describe colorful, magnificent churches and monasteries topped by gilt cupolas, where priests in glittering chasubles performed the divine service under icons encased in precious metals amidst clouds of incense, and holy men and hermits performed miracles. He was attracted by the superficial exoticism which appealed to so many Westerners who discovered old Russia and which had no counterpart in the austere Lutheran church of Finland. Although Leino does not express deep emotional or religious involvement, he found more in the orthodox creed than mere outer pomp: the simple, childlike faith with which its believers accepted miracles, the direct intervention of the supernatural in everyday life, and the spirit of almost cheerful mysticism with which they approached their God, all banned by the more rational Protestant church[350] and alien to the practical spirit of Finland proper. *Sininen risti* ('The Blue Cross'), typical of Leino's poems in this respect, tells of a young girl called by God to preach Christianity to the heathen Karelians; she proves her supernatural calling by walking through the closed gates of a monastery forbidden to women, is blessed by the monks, and sets out on her mission. When a man attempts to rape her, God changes her into a blue cross. *Ihalempi* (name) is a transposition in Finnish setting of the Annunciation story, whereas Leino invented *Tyyrin tytti* ('Tyyri's Maid'), which tells that Christ, an unknown young man, gives the maid a flower, which she finds changed into gold the next morning, for it was a recognition of her purity and humble spirit. *Impi ja pajarin poika* ('The Maid and the Son of the Boyar') is a tragic love story without specific religious implications, save the motif of atonement; when the lovers are separated forever, the young man, who has killed his brother, is sent to do penance in a monastery. *Kaleva* again contains Leino's conception of woman as temptress. It has motifs from Wagner's

HENRIK GABRIEL PORTHAN,
painting by J. E. Hedberg
Werner Söderström Oy. Publishers

FRANS MIKAEL FRANZÉN,
painting by Fredrik Westin
Werner Söderström Oy. Publishers

ELIAS LÖNNROT, painting by Bernhard Reinhold
Werner Söderström Oy. Publishers

JOHAN LUDVIG RUNEBERG,
painting by Johan Knutson
Werner Söderström Oy. Publishers

ZACHRIS TOPELIUS JR.,
painting by Albert Edelfelt
Werner Söderström Oy. Publishers

ALEKSIS KIVI, pencil drawing by a friend
The Finnish National Museum

MINNA CANTH
The Finnish National Museum

ARVID MORNE
The Finnish National Museum

JOHANNES LINNANKOSKI,
painting by A. Gallen-Kallela
Werner Söderström Oy. Publishers

JUHANI AHO,
painting by Albert Edelfelt
Werner Söderström Oy. Publishers

HJALMAR PROCOPÉ, drawing by Albert Gebhard
Holger Schildts Förlags Ab. Publishers

ILMARI KIANTO, painting by Viljo Kojo
Werner Söderström Oy. Publishers

VOLTER KILPI,
painting by Edvin Lydén
Werner Söderström Oy. Publishers

BERTEL GRIPENBERG,
painting by Albert Edelfelt
Werner Söderström Oy. Publishers

AINO KALLAS
Otava Oy. Publishers

EINO LEINO
Press Bureau,
Ministry for Foreign Affairs of Finland

MARIA JOTUNI
Otava Oy. Publishers

V. A. KOSKENNIEMI

L. A. Pietinen and the Press Bureau, Ministry for Foreign Affairs of Finland

GUNNAR BJÖRLING,
sculpture by K. G. Elfgren
Söderström & Co. Förlags Ab. Publishers

JOEL LEHTONEN
Otava Oy. Publishers

Tannhäuser (or the original German legend), such as the supernatural enchantress who induces King Kaleva to commit sin with her, for which he does penance by a pilgrimage to the Holy Land.

Often an author's best-known work is misleading in its representation of his art and personality; such is the case with Runeberg and *The Tales of Ensign Stål* and even with Kivi and *Seven Brothers.* Eino Leino, known in Finland as the author of *Helkavirsiä* I, does not suffer that misconception. *Helkavirsiä* I is so rich and complex in content and so perfect in form that it alone gives a not inadequate picture of its author and his art.

The years between the publication of *Helkavirsiä* I and the end of his first marriage in 1908 were the most stable in Leino's life; during that time he wrote some of his best poems, contained in the collections *Talvi-yö* and *Halla.* As the titles suggest, they are neither cheerful nor optimistic. The title *Eyan kirja* ('Eya's Book'), a section of *Talvi-yö*, is an allusion to his wife, Freya. Many of its erotic and sensuous poems have sumptuous and fantastic oriental settings indicated by the titles: *The Children of Nineveh, The Song of the Caravan, The Bayaderes,* in keeping with the current fashion, both abroad and in Finland. Not particularly personal, they are shadowed by insecurity and sadness behind the pictures of inebriating pleasure, and Leino's handling of the various verse forms is masterful. In *Atlantica*, in which Eya appears, the fabled continent Atlantis is presented as a land of bliss and happiness, doomed in a world for which it was too perfect; the poet himself did not trust his luck, and future events soon proved these premonitions true.

The other poems are meditations on the destiny of man, more specifically, the poet. They contain little mythology, although many are written in the old folk meter as used by Leino.[351] *Talvi-yö*, the title poem, is basically pessimistic. It opens with an impressive description of a winter night: everything is dead, frozen, and snow-covered except a waterfall, roaring, free and alive amidst silence, under which an icy swan swims. Here we have, as in *Tuonelan joutsen* and other poems by Leino, this poetic bird par excellence, dear to so many symbolic artists and writers, whose role in Leino's art is the subject of a special study in Finland.[352] The power of the spirit is like the waterfall which is free and alive in the dead landscape, but Leino's faith in the power of the spirit was obviously wavering. The lines in which the ephemeral character of all human efforts is described seem confused, as do other parts of the poem, because the author appears to have been unable to coordinate his thoughts and feelings: *Pursuu puhki jäästä, yöstä / hetken kupla kultainen: / vaahto vaan jää urhon työstä, laulu tiestä laineiden.* ('The bubble of a golden instant bursts forth from ice and night: / only foam remains from the deeds of the hero, [only] a song from the way of the waves.') The parts of the metaphor are fused in the first two lines; a golden, happy moment in life is represented as a bubble bursting through the ice in the waterfall. In the second two there is a curious confusion, for we expect a song to remain from the deeds of the hero and foam from the way of the waves (this would be metrically correct in Finnish). Although Leino was using alliteration moderately, the simplest explanation was that the words were transposed for alliterative effect. Other possibilities are that the personality and its material symbol are blended, as in Runeberg's *Vid en kvälla*, in which the spring and the poet's soul eventually fuse, or that the foam emphasizes the ephemeral nature of a hero's deeds.[353]

In *Tuulikannel* ('The Eolian Harp,' or 'kantele', also 'kannel') a poet's fate is described with the assertion that he must create, compose, sing like a harp played by the winds, even against his will. In *Iku-Turso* (a mythological sea monster) the monster raises its head from the waves and stares at a star shining on the heaven, a not unusual representation of the Beauty and the Beast, a yearning for an unattainable beloved or ideal, but then the monster "defeats" the star, which falls so that he can "drink" it "like a swan." The shifting moods are easier to follow if we consider the monster female, like the monster "half a lizard, huge and scaly, half a woman" who personifies time in *Aika* and "attracts her lover in her horrible embrace." Woman is the representative of the earthbound, sensuous nature of mankind, the seductress who attracts man from the heights of ideals, absorbs, and destroys him. The poet (the narrator) also appears as a falling star in another poem in the collection *Halla, Yksilön murhe* ('The Sorrow of the Individual'): *Ma sammua tahdon / kuin tähdenlento / tien viitaten erämaan lampeen* ('I want to be extinguished / like a falling star / showing the way to a mere in the forests').

The publication of *Halla*, which reflects, even more than *Talvi-yö*, his depression, coincided with the end of Leino's first marriage. He felt that his ideals were shared by few, if any, and, although he was careful to say that this fact made him feel neither sad nor proud,[354] it did not encourage him. However, his spirit was not yet broken (even later he almost never admitted that); his poems contain much of the Nietzschean superman, who proclaims that I, the ego, the poet's self, is the highest being; transposing the words of the Gospel, he stated in one of the four short poems commonly titled *Minä* ('I'):

> Minä oli alussa
> Minä
> kasvoi luona Kaikkivallan
> ja kaikki oli se minä
> Itseys on ihanin mahti,
> minkä sait sa syntymässä:
> älä anna pois ikinä!

> At the beginning was I
> I
> grew close to the Almighty
> and that I was all

Your Self is the most wonderful power
which you received at your birth:
Never give it away!

In *Yksilön murhe*, previously quoted, as in *Tuulikannel*, Leino insists that the poet's fate cannot be avoided, though others are free to choose, but in *Keskiyön kuoro* ('The Midnight Song' or 'Choir')[355] the fulfillment of all dreams is defined as the doom of mankind: "The doom of Man will be there when the maddest fancies come true, when life is more beautiful than dreams, and nature fairer than the white snow of songs." "The white snow of songs" gave Leino an easy rhyme (*unta-lunta* 'dream-snow'), but he probably felt that at that time his art was cold and dead, like snow.

Leino's next collection of poems, *Tähtitarha* (best translated perhaps 'The Starry Meadow'),[356] was published in 1912. By that time he had married again (and was soon to divorce) and was in love with the poetess L. Onerva, to whom he wrote several love poems and who, after his death, published his (in part their) biography.[357] It is in *Tähtitarha* that he gives the best expression to his love, but even there it is not pure happiness. In *Loukatut* ('The Wounded' or 'Hurt') he speaks of himself and his beloved as "two slaves, fettered together with the irons of love." In *Runokirje* ('A Rhymed Letter') he says that she may be merciless, cruel, and even unfaithful; he will accept all although he once felt that he should die when hearing of these things.

Other types of poems appear in the collection, including patriotic verse, such as the famous *Karjalan kannas* ('The Isthmus of Karelia'), which remained a standard feature at patriotic functions until 1944, when the Soviet Union took the whole region and a new era of better relations between Finland and Russia began. There are signs of an artistic breakdown in some of the poems, which are incoherent, not because of the poet's contrasting emotions, but because they are sloppily written, for example, *Vaeltaja* ('The Wanderer'), in which many verbs are strung together without other connection than rhyme, or *Nuori Nietzsche* ('The Young Nietzsche'), in which "children" are called to raise against "the hordes of darkness, against the lion of human night." The following two collections, *Painuva päivä* ('The Setting Sun,' 1914) and *Elämän koreus* ('Gaudy Life,' 1915), are hardly better, although they still bear the mark of a great poet.

In 1916 Leino published the second collection of *Helkavirsiä*, which, like the first, contains some of his best poems and is much better than all else written near the end of his life. At that time, although he did not strictly adhere to that creed or apply it to his art, he was influenced by theosophical thinking, which was popular in Finland at the beginning of this century. In 1916 he and some friends edited a weekly paper called *Sunnuntai* ('Sunday') to which many well-known writers and artists contributed. It was devoted to art, literature, and related subjects, not theosophy. These metaphysical preoccupations appear in Leino's poetry in the form of vast cosmic visions, not always among his best writings. In *Helkavirsiä* I the legends with Karelian setting are simple, naive, and colorful, whereas in *Marjatan poika* ('Mary's Son'; Marjatta is a popular form of Maria applied to the Virgin in old poems), for example, included in *Helkavirsiä* II, the coming of Christ is announced by cosmic cataclysms, comets, "the blue flames of electricity,"[358] and a multitude of noises produced by the Savior's chariot and by heaven itself: the horses neigh, the axletree squeals, the air roars, the vaults of the sky echo. His material representation of heaven is not peculiar to him and could have been based on classical examples. The poem *Bellerophon*, published a few years later, shows his interest in classical mythology. The mention of a chariot is reminiscent of the myth of Phaethon and its treatment by, e.g., Ovid,[359] a comparison rather disadvantageous for Leino. These cosmic poems are more turgid than majestic although, or perhaps because, the sun, the moon, and the stars are introduced as characters in a setting of timeless astral space. A somewhat morbid eroticism appears for the first time in Leino's poetry in the description of a female demon, a temptress, and her lover in *Ukon lintu ja virvaliekki* ('The Bird of God and the Ignis Fatuus'; note the Finnish word used for the Latin in English): they are twined around each other "like blue snakes," "burn against each other like two coals," and bring death to each other "like a poison in their veins." In *Auringon hyvästijättö* ('The Farewell of the Sun') the Sun takes farewell of the Earth, his mistress, another instance of eroticism in cosmic scope; the "sparks of electricity" appear again.

This collection does contain some simpler, less ambitious compositions reminiscent of Leino's best poems. *Mennyt manner* ('The Continent That Was') takes up the myth of Atlantis, treated in an earlier work; *Syvärin impi* ('The Maid of Syväri') and *Arja ja Selinä* (names) are short, lyrical, slightly melancholic love poems. *Ukri* (name) is about a man, like *Ylermi*, who defies the world and the gods and who, though destroyed, remains proud and unbending. *Ukri* suggests *Ugric* (of *Finno-Ugric*), mainly the Hungarians; without precise references to time or place, the description of a nation of horsemen and warriors who, led by their ruler, invade the steppes to kill and conquer but instead are conquered is partially relevant to Hungarian history. Although the end is not applicable, warlike deeds and glory, as well as death and destruction, were on everyone's mind during World War I.

Although he was reported to have lived alternately in a hotel, a hospital, and at friends' homes during his last years, Leino continued writing and, as was the fashion, was often invited to write poems for public functions; such poems form a large part of his later collections, e.g., *Leirivalkeat* ('The Campfires,' 1917), *Kodin kukka ja uhrikuusi* ('The Flower of the Home and the Sacrifice Tree,' 1920), *Vanha pappi* ('The Old Priest,' 1921), and *Pajarin poika* ('The Son of the Boyar,' 1922). Many of his compositions were published posthumously, such as *Manamansalo* (name), directly inspired by a modern folksong motif also found in other countries, on which Bürger in Germany wrote his famous ballad *Lenore*. The effect of Leino's poems is largely due to the repetition of these lines, appearing in the original Finnish folk song:

> Kuuhut paistaa heliästi,
> Kuollut ajaa keviästi,
> Etkös kultani pelkää?

> The moon is shining bright,
> The dead is driving light,
> Fearest thou not, my love?

Among Leino's last collections two stand distinctly above the others: *Bellerophon* and *Juhana herttuan ja Catharina Jagellonican lauluja* ('Songs of Duke John and Catharina Jagellonica'), both published in 1919 with three other works. By that time V. A. Koskenniemi, quite unlike Leino, was beginning his wide, lasting popularity; Leino reportedly felt challenged to write on classical and historical subjects as well as his colleague could and produced these two volumes.[360] Readers tended to notice the extraordinary virtuosity with which rhyme and rhythm were wielded rather than the content of *Bellerophon,* a very complex work. Leino used the framework of the classical myth and filled it in with his own materials; he was successful in creating a well-balanced whole which is reminiscent of the great romantic, metaphysical-philosophical poems such as Goethe's *Faust* and Byron's *Cain.* Bellerophon, a typical Leino hero, is related to the characters in the early poems, Lemminkäinen in *Tuonelan joutsen,* for example; he is the man in quest of the ultimate truth who is taken through heaven, hell and earth, and eventually reaches a state beyond human joys and sorrows when the Moirai announce to him that he will be changed into a star. At the time when the other collection was written, Leino was in love with Aino Kallas, an authoress, and he used the colorful story of Duke John (later King John III of Sweden) and his Polish-born wife Catharina Jagellonica, who resided in Turku in the second half of the sixteenth century, bringing the pomp and splendor of Renaissance courts to a city which never again saw anything like it, as a basis for love poems, which contain more elaborate rhyme-play and ornate phraseology than real feeling.

Besides Leino's prolific production of poetry, he wrote drama, fiction, essays, a *History of Finnish Literature*, biographies of Finnish writers, a film script, newspaper articles (as a columnist he used three pseudonyms, all names of characters in Kivi's works), criticism, and much miscellaneous prose; for a while he was also one of the best chess players in Finland. Leino's best nonpoetic works are his dramatic ones, some in verse. *Johan Wilhelm* (1900), one of the first, is unremarkable although superficially original. The play is not connected with Johan Wilhelm Snellman; Leino's reason for using his well-known first names is a mystery. The main character, who is insane, does not appear on stage, but his existence influences the action, for his brother is in love with his wife and her sister. These erotic, somewhat incestuous complications never lead anywhere; at the end of the play, Johan Wilhelm dies, still offstage, and his wife dies from the shock of the news of his demise.

After 1905 Leino published his plays in six collections called *Naamioita* ('Masks,' 1905, 1907, 1908, two in 1909, and 1911; the name contains no allusion to Renaissance masques). In the preface to the fifth volume, he revealed his theory of drama, not unlike those of Gordon Craig, Appia, Reinhardt, Copeau, Meyerhold, or Evreinov, who were beginning to lead European theater away from realism and naturalism. Leino's aim was to stylize drama, carry the simplification of artistic means to extreme, render the theater beautiful to the eye and pleasant to the ear, and make the stage again a home for poetry, not only bourgeois taste and literary handicraft. Of Leino's plays, we might say that good intentions do not make good art, but some are still performed in Finland, especially those dealing with Finnish history. In 1912 he and some friends founded an open-air theater for the performance of his own adaptations from the *Kalevala*, but it was a failure. An experienced actor in the company suggested that the repertory also include more commercial plays, but Leino rejected this idea.[361] His dramatizations of the *Kalevala, Kalevala näyttämöllä* ('*Kalevala* on the Stage,' 1911), and the play on a Finnish mythological subject published in *Naamioita* I are unremarkable.

Characters from Finnish history appearing in Leino's plays are usually proud, violent, cruel, and perhaps ultimately defeated because of weaknesses within themselves. *Lalli* (second collection) is about the half-legendary pagan Finn who, according to a medieval chronicle and folk poems, killed the first Christian missionary in Finland, but was justly and miraculously avenged by God. *Ritari Klaus* ('Knight Klaus,' third collection), whose main character was perhaps suggested by the folk ballad on Elina's death and von Numers' tragedy, shows a proud, violent, cruel nobleman conquering a lady's heart through those very qualities and losing her as he becomes more humane, or weaker. *Tuomas piispa* ('Bishop Thomas,' fifth collection) is about a warlike Catholic prelate of the Middle Ages who is torn between his violent nature and his Christian duties. *Simo Hurtta* tells of an eighteenth-century nobleman, Simo Affleck, nicknamed *Hurtta* ('The Bloodhound') by the inhabitants of the district he was sent to govern because of his conduct there; he admits that a weakness in himself brought about his downfall. Leino also wrote two poems (1904 and 1919) about this character, who lived near Leino's birthplace. The most-performed of Leino's plays is *Maunu Tavast* (third collection), a peaceful play whose disturbances are in the memories of

162

the main character, a great churchman of Catholic Finland who sinned in his youth but had a happy, successful life afterwards.

The dramas on classical subjects also deal with men who are reminiscent of the Nietzschean superman but ultimately fail, such as *Tarquinius Superbus* (fifth collection) and *Alkibiades* (fourth collection). *Alkibiades*, one of his most interesting and personal plays, was written in 1908 during a long journey abroad. Alkibiades lives in exile, speaks contemptuously of his home country, and declares himself a citizen of the world who feels most happy wherever he can fulfill his dream of individuality and enjoy the highest sensuous pleasures, but he also speaks of a mysterious world spirit with which man will one day be reunited. At the time of writing *Alkibiades*, Leino's first marriage had collapsed, and he felt ill at ease in Helsinki and Finland, which at various times he, like other Finnish writers, found small and paltry, full of little intrigues and slandering, a feeling also applied to politics. He maintained regular contact with public life and expressed his political opinions as a newspaperman for the liberal *Päivälehti (Helsingin Sanomat)*. In *Alkibiades* and in letters written from Rome, where he was living at that time, Leino expressed his belief in the right of the individual to taste all pleasures and in the superior interest of the decadent and sick over the healthy.[362] However, his sense of the precarious nature of such a philosophy is indicated in the play by a secondary character speaking to Alkibiades: "Truly, Alkibiades: you may drain the cup to the dregs, but never . . . fill it again."

Some plays with contemporary setting are more symbolic than realistic, e.g., *Melankolia* ('Melancholy,' second collection), a mere conversation between characters designated as the Man, the Woman, and the Friend, and *Ilotulitus* ('The Fireworks,' sixth collection), in which a pyromaniac is pushed to new crimes by a (real) character appropriately named Lucifer. In *Shakkipeli* ('A Game of Chess,' fifth collection), set in medieval surroundings, only one player is present; the other makes his moves but is away, dying. Others have more conventional plots, but often show that traditional moral values do not consistently resist the impact of contemporary life; whether he intended to criticize these values seriously or to satirize their supporters, the conservatives and the church, with whom he feuded all his life, is not clear. In *Pentti Pääkkönen* (first collection) a wealthy farmer whose ambition is to be elected to Parliament has been successful because of a crime, for which an innocent man has suffered, but his children die one by one. Pentti Pääkkönen addresses God as an equal, asking for the life of his lastborn. When it is granted, he expects to lose the elections as payment, but he wins, is ever after a success, and no one believes him when he tries to confess his old crime. Bewildered, he says, "This world is getting stranger and stranger every day." In *Kirkon vihollinen* ('An Enemy of the Church,' sixth collection) a man with a technical education (representative of a modern civilization, already called American) clashes with a clergyman over his desire to marry the clergyman's daughter; the minister unexpectedly ends the argument by giving in, saying that he must not oppose the general evolution of the world. *Maan parhaat* ('The Country's Best,' same collection) is a light, satirical comedy on political and literary life containing easily recognizable caricatures of well-known contemporary personalities.

Leino's novels reflect his activities as a journalist rather than his poetic gifts. They are breezy, lively descriptions of contemporary life in Helsinki, but they are written in the fashion of the period, the "impressionistic" technique that Leino carried to extreme, often using an unnatural word order. The Helsinki of Leino's novels, like the Helsinki of Finnish or Swedish authors in Finland contemporary to Leino, was a great, sinful city where people lost fortunes overnight in business or gambling; passionate, illicit love affairs went on; one could become addicted to vice and ruin his health; and something interesting—operettas, balls, cabarets, circuses—was always going on. Helsinki at that time had barely over one hundred thousand inhabitants, it is true, but, in a sense, it could be compared to some Swiss cities, which, though not large, have intensive cultural lives.[363]

Tuomas Vitikka (name, 1906) and *Olli Suurpää* (name, 1908) are the most superficial novels and are hardly more than Leino's observations on political life in Finland, the struggles between parties and linguistic groups, the Russian oppression, and so forth. *Jaana Rönty* (name, 1907) is more concerned with the characters; Jaana is a poor country girl who comes to Helsinki, where she is debased and eventually attracted into the company of revolutionary socialists. At the end of her story, a description of the armed riots in Helsinki of 1906 in which socialist and nonsocialist vigilantes, the Red and White Guards, clashed for the first time, she appears as Fury, dressed in red and dancing among the dead.

For good reason critics dealt roughly with Leino's novels, but he continued to produce them. Between 1911 and 1913 he produced a tetralogy of "slave" novels: *Työn orja* ('The Slave of Work'), *Rahan orja* ('The Slave of Money'), *Naisen orja* ('The Slave of Woman'), and *Onnen orja* ('The Slave of Luck'). It is the very romantic, improbable life (often based on Leino's own) of a Ph.D., who is also a socialist, successful businessman, and writer. He lives in Helsinki, Berlin, London, and Rome, loves, marries, and divorces many women, eventually tries to kill one of them in the Catacombs, cannot do it, voluntarily enters a hospital, emerges a broken old man, and spends the rest of his life as a hermit in the mountains. In these works Leino's peculiar prose style was most developed and, consequently, his worst.

Nuori nainen ('A Young Woman,' 1910), which suffers least from his twisted style, is considered his best prose work. It is spicy and even reminiscent of *Decamerone*, as four gentlemen from Helsinki tell stories to each other in a restaurant, but its observations on love and the nature of men and women are penetrating:

A loving woman always wants to be absolutely honest, share the joys and sorrows, the pains and sufferings, preferably just the latter, for only then she will feel a necessary being in the universe. But it is just this which, before long, will make her love so irritating to a man. . . . But women will never learn to stand on their own feet or to pay just casual visits to a man's heart. They want to snuggle up in a cozy place near the fire like cats, and they want to make a home in every smallest nook in their hearts. . . . But a man's true home is only that part of his soul in which he is alone and will remain alone forever.

Pankkiherroja ('Bankers' or 'Financiers,' 1914) is the most typical period piece in Leino's production—a description of high life in Helsinki, big business, love, marriage, divorce, and parties, now taking on the romantic shimmer of a past era. *Paavo Kontio, lakitieteen tohtori* ('Paavo Kontio, LL. D.,' 1915) verges on the detective story, but there is more emphasis on the character relations than the whodunit, and the crime remains unsolved. *Mesikämmen* ('Honey-Paw,' a popular name for a bear, 1914), *Musti* ('Blackie,' a common name for a dog, 1916), and *Ahven ja kultakalat* ('The Perch and the Goldfishes,' 1918) are loosely allegorical stories without depth but attractive in their simplicity.

In 1917 Leino published *Alla kasvon Kaikkivallan* ('Before the Face of the Almighty') and the tragedy *Karjalan kuningas* ('The King of Karelia'), his last great works, greater perhaps in conception than in execution, however. The subtitle of the first indicates that it consists of "thoughts, confessions, and distant visions." Aaro Hellaakoski, a young critic later to become perhaps the greatest poet after Leino, wrote ironically about it, saying that it showed the unfortunate influence the theosophical group of *Sunnuntai* had had on him.[364] In the book Leino sought answers to vast philosophical and metaphysical problems (or pseudoproblems), which he was not equipped to cope with. As a picture of his own personality and philosophy, however, it is not without interest. Unfortunately, he chose an artificial, pseudoarchaic style imitative of the *Kalevala* and folk poetry, for there was no tradition of artistic prose in Finnish folklore. *Karjalan kuningas*, a somewhat confused tragedy in verse, is set in a vague, half-mythological past with human, not divine or semidivine, characters. The young hero Lemmes, destined to become king of Karelia, falls in battle against the enemies of the country; Helka, his betrothed, drowns herself, and a man of peace, the old sage Turo, becomes ruler. As in Leino's earlier poems, a man reaches his highest goals only through self-sacrifice. Obviously, the poet was reflecting, as were more and more Finns, that the country should one day secure independence from Russia; but when thinking of an armed conflict with the ruling power, the poet was torn between his instinctive abhorrence for violence and his natural desire to see his country free.

As a translator Leino produced Finnish versions of works by Topelius and Runeberg, such as *Nadeschda* and *Kung Fjalar* (1903), and Racine's

Phèdre (1907, Corneille's *Le Cid* (1917), Anatole Frances's *La rôtisserie de la Reine Pédauque* (1910) and *Les opinions de l'abbé Coignard* (1920) in collaboration with Eino Palola, Schiller's *Wilhelm Tell* (1907), Goethe's *Iphigeneia auf Tauris* (1910), and Dante's entire *Divina Commedia* (1912-14), though not in *terza rima* and attenuating in places the language of the original. Though his habits in his last years were not conducive to regular literary production, he produced in incredible quantity and had the love and respect of the entire country. After his death Uuno Kailas wrote a commemorative poem of warm, respectful homage and high artistic quality, unlike so many similar works.[365] Although it doesn't imitate Leino's poetic style, its symbolism is much like his, a blend of realistic pictures and supernatural visions. The beast of the forests, the grizzly,[366] is dead; he has gone to his lair to lick the wounds made by the hunter, Fate, and with him the whole race of the grizzlies has perhaps died, for we see frozen tears in the mossy hair of the pines. He left a red streak of blood behind him, but it does not lead to his lair; it is splashed across the sky, for he took the well-known road toward blue space.

Some of Leino's contemporaries, without imitating him, drew their inspiration from the same sources, and their art was, in some respects, similar to his. Best known among them was his friend and beloved **L. Onerva** (pseudonym of Hilja Onerva Lehtinen, later married to the well-known composer L. Madetoja; 1882-1972). She studied French and art history at the University of Helsinki, taught in a secondary school, traveled widely in Europe, and wrote both literary and theater criticism for newspapers. She did translations from French, but, like many Finns with an interest in France, she mainly translated authors of the generation immediately preceding hers, including Musset, Baudelaire, Verlaine, Benjamin Constant, Balzac, Bourget, France, Hippolyte Taine, and Joseph Bédier (not Apollinaire, Max Jacob, Pierre Reverdy, or the surrealists). After publishing in 1904 her first collection of poems *Sekasointuja* ('Confused Sounds'), she produced until 1927 one or more volumes of verse and fiction a year, still a few in the 1930s, including the famous *Biography of Leino*, and three more after world War II; her *Selected Works* appeared in 1956. Her similarity to Leino lies in their interest in the exceptional individual above everyday morals, exotic and colorful motifs, and the erotic, sometimes in decadent and perverse form. Though not really very decadent or perverse, her work was rather audacious in Finland, especially for a teacher at a girls' school, which she soon left. She was contemptuous of petty, stuffy, gossiping Helsinki and yearned for more interesting surroundings; her characters are ever traveling and living in Paris, Berlin, or Rome, where they can fully mature. Her exoticism and cosmopolitanism are now outdated; what remains is the image of an exceptional, gifted, courageous individual who openly declared her contempt for traditional values in her attempt to find new ones, though her quest proved deceptive.

Nietzsche's most faithful follower in Finland may have been **Aarni Kouta** (first Arnold Elias Candolin, 1884-1924), who translated, in addition to works by Swedish authors, including Strindberg, *Also sprach Zarathustra* (1907), *Antichristus* (1908), and *Dionysos* (1909) into Finnish. He worked throughout his life for publishers, wrote criticism for newspapers, and published, besides essays and short stories, nine volumes of poetry between 1905 and 1923. His titles are indicative of the contents: *Tulijoutsen* ('The Fiery Swan'), *Jäiset temppelit* ('Icy Sanctuaries'), *Uhriliekki* ('The Flame of the Sacrifice'). We find in them warriors with crowned heads of the race of heroes, cold as death, standing in icy sanctuaries among the snow of the highest summits, under the eternal stars. Warm, normal, earthly life is held contemptible, and the hero is always identified with ice, snow, and death. The poems in the adapted old folk meter, like Leino's, are artistically respectable, but those in new European meters are less satisfactory. After 1915 he wrote more humanely about the simple joys of home and family life and other everyday subjects.

A poet of a different nature, **Larin-Kyösti** (pseudonym of **Karl Gustaf Larson**, 1873-1948) represents the romantic trend that marked the first years of this century. Between 1897 and 1924 he wrote forty volumes, mostly verse, but little after that. His historical ballads are not unlike Leino's. His parents were from Sweden, but he was born in Hämeenlinna. He always wrote in Finnish, though often taking open inspiration from Swedish poets, especially in his first collections. Bellman, whom Henrik Achrenius had translated, and the contemporary Gustaf Fröding were among his models. Like Fröding, Larin-Kyösti eventually used the language and form of the modern folksong to express his own feelings, and, although he never reached the emotional strength and depth of his Swedish colleague, his poems are not only a sincere expression of his personality but also have high artistic merit.

Often the setting of his poems is the west Finnish countryside, its fields, meadows, pastures, brooks, groves, villages, and old towns, not the vast, mysterious wilderness of Karelia and east Finland. West Finland's traditional civilization stretches back to the Middle Ages and further,[367] and Larin-Kyösti's descriptions of merry country life have a general similarity to such English poems, for example. The title of his first collection, *Tän pojan kevätrallatuksia* ('Merry Springtunes by This Here Fellow,' 1897; the colloquial title is not easily translated),[368] expresses the character of the poems, often pure descriptions of quaint or amusing places or situations, e.g., *Sunnuntai* ('Sunday'), a description of an old church ornamented with dusty statues of saints and shaded by maples, in which the old pastor preaches as the congregation, dressed in Sunday best, does or does not listen; the boys look at the girls, and the girls return stealthy looks when their mothers are not watching. Later, in the cycle *Musta hepo* ('The Black Horse,' 1904) and the collection *Meren maininkeja* ('The Swell of the Sea,' 1905), the poet used another characteristic region, the coasts of the Gulf of Finland, full of islands, reefs, and rocks, an area not often described by Finnish-speaking writers who felt that the interior of the country was more typical of Finland, but used by the Swedish poets in Finland who came from the coastal region. There is a Scandinavian tradition of sea poetry not unlike the English, in fact.

Soon after 1900 Larin-Kyösti began writing more personal poems, often landscape descriptions reflecting moods or sensations of an unidentified "I," not necessarily the poet. At the same time he began composing long narrative poems like *Kuisma ja Helinä* (two names, 1902), a romantic story from a time when Cossacks were quartered in Finland, and *Musta hepo* ('The Black Horse,' 1904), a more realistic description of life on the islands of the Gulf of Finland. He continued publishing ballad-like poems in the collection *Ballaadeja* ('Ballads,' 1913), in which we find motifs typical of this style; of these *The Last of the Moors* is situated in Spain, *Aslak Smaukka* is about an old Lapp sorcerer by that name, the hero of *Otto Rud* is a Danish soldier and adventurer of the late fifteenth century, and the main character of *Kurkijärven Pusa* ('Pusa of Kurkijärvi') is a "wild dark man" living somewhere in Finland.

Only two works do not fall into any of these categories, the collection of poems *Vuorivaeltaja* ('The Wanderer of the Mountains,' 1908) and the play *Ad Astra* (1906). His depression during a journey to Italy in 1906, when he fell seriously ill and required hospitalization, is reflected in *Vuorivaeltaja. Ad Astra* is a typical symbolist play, a form used at that time across Europe by such geographically diverse writers as Maeterlinck, Strindberg, Leonid Andreev, Arvid Järnefelt, and Eino Leino. The action is in a dream, and the characters include the Artist (or the Virtuoso, *Taituri*), a Woman in Grey, the Stepsister, the Stranger or the Dark Physician. The Artist is torn between vice (the Woman in Grey) and virtue (the Stepsister), he alternates between happiness and dejection, health and sickness, but he eventually "reaches the stars," and the temptress loses her hold on him.[369]

Larin-Kyösti also wrote comedies about country people, children's plays on fairy-tale motifs, descriptions of the lives of sailors and fishermen on the Gulf of Finland, memoirs, and sketches of his contemporaries. He translated into Finnish Scandinavian authors including Strindberg and Fröding. Although his kind of art is not appreciated now, judged amidst its own, it is quite good; his prosody, for example, is on a very high level.

The period had several lesser poets. The poems of **Valter Juva** (pseudonym of **Valter Juvelius**, 1865-1922) are largely forgotten, but one has remained popular as a song, *Jo Karjalan kunnailla lehtii puu* ('On the Hills of Karelia, Leaves Are Already Opening on the Trees'). He translated Heine, including the *Buch der Lieder*, Goethe's *Faust* (Part I), and several Swedish authors. His work, with that of Leino and Manninen, is reputed to have contributed greatly to the development of Finnish poetic style and prosody.[370] **Severi Nuormaa** (first **Nyman**, 1865-1924), a journalist active in adult education, published a few collections of poems between 1895 and 1922. **Yrjö Weilin** (1875-1930), who used the pseudonym of **Weijola**, composed romantic ballads in the manner of Leino and Larin-Kyösti, and formally faultless sonnets, perhaps the best of his works.

The most typical prosaist of the romantic period at the beginning of this century was **Johannes Linnankoski** (1869-1913), officially **Johan Viktor Peltonen**, a very common Finnish name which he changed to something more romantic and euphonious. Such a move speaks for his character, for pseudonyms are generally used in Finland only to replace Swedish names. He was born the son of a farmer in south Finland, near Porvoo, not far from Erkko's birthplace. Like the older poet and Minna Canth, he studied at the Teachers' College in Jyväskylä, but, dismissed from the institution, took up journalism, and became chief editor of the newly founded paper *Uusimaa* in Porvoo, where he worked from 1894 to 1899. Through his writings he acquired some influence; reportedly it was to a large extent due to him that a Finnish school and a Finnish Club were founded in Porvoo, a traditionally Swedish-speaking town. It was Runeberg's hometown, and the home for retired Swedish writers of Finland is there. But, in 1900, to the astonishment of those who knew him, he suddenly disappeared from public life and lived in various places in southwest Finland, doing miscellaneous literary work for a publisher. He had decided to become a great writer and felt that he must study for that career; he compiled a tremendous list of literary masterpieces, works on history, science, philosophy, etc., which he then read in Finnish, Swedish, and German translations. The result was a tremendous play, the tragedy *Ikuinen taistelu* ('The Eternal Struggle,' 1903),[371] describing the conflict of good and evil, God and Lucifer, giving glimpses of the world from the beginning to the future. From 1903 to 1909, he edited a work of popular science, *Keksintöjen kirja* ('The Book of Inventions'), and in his instructions for the production of the play he indicated that moving projections should be used (he was not yet familiar with films), but there is little science fiction in the play. The main character, Cain, wants but doesn't really expect to know the ultimate meaning of life and the nature of God. Byron's Cain and Milton's Lucifer are frequently linked with Linnankoski's work. Linnankoski's Lucifer is not unlike Milton's, but Cain is treated quite differently by Byron and Linnankoski.[372] As the majestic, mysterious, and mythological had wide appeal in art at that time, the play was a sensation in Finland, though eventually the public was not interested. The play is prose interspersed with verse printed like prose, neither good, due partially to Linnankoski's immaturity and his convulsive attempts to be solemn and awe-inspiring and partially to the trend of the time. He is a good example of the fateful influence of misdirected ambitions on a writer, but he matured considerably during his career and eventually wrote quite differently on subjects from everyday Finnish life until a sudden illness carried him to an untimely grave.

Linnankoski's next work, the novel *Laulu tulipunaisesta kukasta* (1905; tr. *The Song of the Blood-Red Flower* by W. Worster, London, 1920), was no better. Set in contemporary Finland, partly among lumberjacks and timber-floaters, traditionally rough, manly, gay, and careless (i.e., romantic) characters in Finnish literature, it consists largely of the love affairs of Olavi, who eventually reforms and marries. The style is in keeping with the story, colorful and lively, sometimes imitating the rhythms of old folk poetry; the trees, woods, hills, lakes, and all nature often listen, watch, smile, whisper, or speak. From the beginning critics were dubious about this book, but the Swedish movie of it probably unleashed it abroad.[373] Often foreign visitors to Finland, anxious to seem knowledgeable about the country, mention that they have read the masterpiece of Finnish literature, *The Song of the Blood-Red Flower*, to the annoyance of the Finns.[374]

In 1905 Linnankoski also published *Taistelu Heikkilän talosta* ('The Fight over Heikkilä Farm'), a tragic short story in a rural setting. It is more realistic and simpler in style than *Blood-Red Flower*, but we feel, contrary to popular opinion in Finland, that it reveals an extremely unpleasant attitude toward life. Although the main characters are arrogant, cruel, and callous, the author has consistently indicated that these qualities are to be admired at least in the wife of a worthless drunkard, owner of Heikkilä farm. In order to reform him, she beats him with a leather strap, but forces the servants to treat him as master. These facts are all told in earnest, for Linnankoski had little sense of humor. One almost pities the husband and feels it only fair that he kills his wife. The crime is discovered, in part through supernatural apparitions, the murderer is punished; and the reader is relieved that the world is free of two nasty individuals.

In 1908 Linnankoski published his best work, the novel *Pakolaiset* ('The Refugees' or 'Runaways'). The title refers not to political refugees, but to people running from their own consciences for moral reasons. It is known that Linnankoski based it on life.[375] An elderly man marries a young woman and moves with her family to a new district ostensibly because a farm is to be purchased profitably there. Actually the woman is pregnant by another man, with whom a marriage could not be arranged; no one should inform the husband in the new surroundings. When he discovers the deception, he admits, after a lengthy mental struggle, that he can consider it a punishment for his pride in his cleverness at finding a young wife and a farm; he decides to ask forgiveness rather than forgive and to continue living with his new family. In an exclusive concentration on psychological analysis without dramatic events, written in simple straightforward language, the book tells more of basic human problems than Linnankoski's more ambitious works.

Linnankoski wrote three more plays: *Kirot* ('The Curse,' 1907), *Simson ja Delila* ('Samson and Delilah,' 1911), and *Jeftan tytär* ('Jephtha's Daughter,' 1911). Even in the most friendly descriptions of Linnankoski's works, *Kirot* is all but skipped; it is an elaborately allegorical description of political life and the struggle against Russification in Finland, set in half-mythological surroundings among imaginary Finno-Ugric peoples, and conveys an appeal to national unity before the aggressor. Although slightly similar to *The Eternal Struggle* in style, the two biblical plays do not return to its metaphysical grandness, for they realistically describe, in an exotic setting, exceptional individuals who struggle against fate to find meaning in their lives. Love is more conspicuous than in the Bible stories, but, especially in *Simson ja Delila*, its role is not unjustified. Samson's mother comforts her son after he has lost his strength and lies in fetters, but he admits that his defeat is a just punishment for his sensuous love for Delilah; Delilah later repents and tells Samson that his strength has returned so that he can pull down the temple of Dagon. The love story is irrelevant to *Jeftan tytär* and does not appear in the Bible. There is as little conclusion as in the original story: the characters submit to the will of the Lord, trusting that whatever happens happens because He has ordered it to happen.

In addition Linnankoski published a collection of *Sirpaleita* ('Fragments,' 1913), in which the short story *Hilja, maitotyttö* ('Hilja, the Milkmaid') is the most interesting. He also wrote extensively on subjects of political and general interest, but this particular activity is not really relevant to the study of literature.

Maila Talvio (pseudonym of **Maria Mikkola, née Winter**, 1871-1951) published most of her important works during this same romantic period, although her last work appeared in 1949. She is probably remembered as the author of three historical novels about Helsinki: *Kaukaa tullut* ('Coming from Far,' 1929), *Hed-Ulla ja hänen kosijansa* ('Hed-Ulla and Her Suitors,' 1931), and *Hopealaiva* ('The Silver Ship,' 1936), later published under the collective title *Itämeren tytär* ('Daughter of the Baltic'). They are typical family novels in which marriages, births, deaths, and everyday life in general are set in a historical framework intended both to add interest and provide entertaining information about the past. *Linnoituksen iloiset rouvat* ('The Merry Wives of the Fortress,' 1941), the title adapted without reason from Shakespeare, is of the same type; it is about the war of 1808-09 and its effect on the lives of Helsinki's inhabitants.

Although energetic and active, Maila Talvio sometimes lacked discretion and judgment. Her father, a minister, died when she was young, and for a while the family lived simply in the country. She became convinced that anything plain and Finnish was good and anything refined and Swedish bad. After marrying a well-known linguist, Professor J. J. Mikkola, and moving to the still largely Swedish-speaking Helsinki, she pretended not to know

Swedish and demanded public documents in Finnish. The Swedish-speaking society was amused, and she was briefly the favorite victim of cartoonists,[376] but the Swedish-speaking bureaucrats would not tolerate her conduct and distrained her (husband's) properties when she refused to pay taxes unless her receipt were in Finnish. Eino Leino described her as one of "the country's best" in the play *Maan parhaat*. She also expressed her opinion on the question of agricultural tenants, with which many, including Juhani Aho, were concerned, alluded to it in one of her novels, held a literary salon in her home, directed a literary club for students and appeared at patriotic meetings and functions organized in protest of the Russian oppression. She is seen in a photograph fantastically costumed as the Goddess of Liberty with a white robe and sash (probably blue) in a theatrical pose before a badly stuffed tiger. There is a lion on the Finnish coat of arms, but, not finding one, the organizers apparently thought any big cat would do.[377] Her opinions were conservative though her nationalism was radical. She was later proud to be honored by the Third Reich, for, like many conservatives, she saw Hitler only as an energetic conservative statesman who treated communists, socialists, trade unionists and others as they deserved. Several of her books were translated into German,[378] and she was awarded a literary prize; she joined the (so-called) European Writers' Guild in 1942. Disturbingly, *Suomen Kirjallisuus*, often quoted here, displays a half-page photograph in which she, dressed as a Finnish country girl, serves Finnish foods to a seemingly appreciative Alfred Rosenberg![379]

Her first works, which appeared in the nineties, reflect some of her art's distinctive characteristics. They are naive, small novels (*Haapaniemen keinu* ('The Swing of Haapaniemi,' *Aili*, name, and *Kaksi rakkautta* 'Two Loves') in which healthy, traditional country life is opposed to the temptations of the city and sensuous love, which are finally defeated after the characters go through a severe mental struggle. In her first important novel, *Pimeänpirtin hävitys* ('The Destruction of Pimeäpirtti,' 1901),[380] she described incest, unwittingly committed; sensuous love interested her throughout her career, although she considered it evil. Her intent in this novel seems unclear; she mixes the story of a father's incest with his illegitimate daughter with an exposé of the social and economic conditions in the country and the exploitation of the Finnish-speaking tenants by the Swedish-speaking landlords. The love story tends to dominate; after the seduction the girl goes to town and leads a sinful life until her grandfather arrives and kills her.

After this novel and until 1929, when the first part of *Itämeren tytär* appeared, Maila Talvio wrote many novels, short stories, and plays. Her plays, which never attracted much attention, are now forgotten, as are her other works although they are individual in approach and style and give a colorful picture of life in Finland at that time. The novel *Juha Joutsia* (name, 1903) is about an honest, industrious, successful farmer opposed by characters showing the evil effects of drinking and other sins. *Louhilinna* (name, 1906) is another attempt to develop more than one subject: one story is about a young woman who loses her family estate in the country and marries a city lawyer, thus seeing how corrupt and unnatural urban life is, another about a farmhand who becomes a socialist leader and agitator. The author attempts to understand the workers' political aspirations, but she inherently regards them as dangerous. In *Tähtien alla* ('Under the Stars,' 1910) descriptions of Helsinki as a great, dangerous, sinful city are the background for a love story in which a healthy young country woman arrives there and takes part in the customary pleasures of her middle-class surroundings. Her relations to a student whose mental sufferings and obsessions both repel and attract her are dangerous to her peace of mind, but she eventually resumes her normal life, matured by this experience. The short stories of the collection *Hämähäkki* (1912) are about exceptional, neurotic individuals; the main character of the novel *Yölintu*,[381] published in 1913, is similar, but the action consists of romantic and improbable incidents, involving similar characters rather than psychological analysis. It should be remembered that the prevailing literary trend was away from realism and naturalism; after symbolism's popularity had waned in Europe, expressionism appeared in Germany and futurism in Italy. The possible influence of expressionism on Maila Talvio has been discussed.[382]

Niniven lapset ('The Children of Nineveh,' 1915), not unlike some of Leino's novels (e.g., *Pankkiherroja*), describes Helsinki's businessmen, journalists, and artists and their favorite haunts, cafés, and restaurants, where a lascivious dance, the tango, has just become fashionable. The book's events are seen by two characters: a young man indignant at the corruption he sees around him and a wealthy old misanthrope who despises the corruption but watches it with half-benevolent indifference; he sees no sin, only unhappiness: "The Nineveh of old is ashes and dust, and ashes and dust shall every new Nineveh be. For pleasure is written on the front of every Nineveh, but the end of all pleasure is ashes and dust." Although few Finnish writers expressed such feelings, several Swedish authors of Finland, known as "men-about-town" or *flâneurs (dagdrivare)* in literary history, shared this trait at the same time. Among them Ture Janson and Erik Grotenfelt shared her violent and shrill patriotism, as the hope that Finland might one day become independent appeared, and later, after the Civil War. However, they took their elegant contempt toward established values seriously, whereas she remained firmly idealistic.

Elämän kasvot ('The Face of Life,' 1916) is her most unrealistic book. Real individuals move in a real world, but their appearance and actions are deliberately exaggerated and stylized in order to express more than the outer facts. Mrs. Karell, who terrorizes and mistreats her unmarried daughter Liina in an evil and witchlike way, dominates the first part; the second part, in which the daughter frees herself by marrying a dreamy, philosophical musician, is more unreal. The musician has achieved harmony through awareness that all is vanity, but death real:

> Behold, all these people think that they can lengthen their lives by making use of every moment that is given to them. They are mistaken, for the noise of the world which surrounds them also consumes them, their senses and their feelings, all that is human in them. And the life they are chasing flees before them at a speed the fastest express train could not match.

Silmä yössä ('An' or 'The', 'Eye In the Night'; the peculiar structure of Finnish makes both equally possible; 1917) purports to be an analysis of the effects of heredity on two powerful families ruined by inherent personality flaws. However, the main character, Dr. Cairenius, is an observer, a voluntary hermit and dreamer, whose separation from the world is underlined by his dwarfish stature. Living in a house surrounded by a beautiful garden, he has developed a philosophy not unlike some Oriental metaphysical systems; existence is but a dream, death a passing from the domain of smaller dreams to a greater one, and beauty the only element of life to be enjoyed. Inspiration for this work may have come from Calderón's play *La Vida Es Un Sueño.*[383] However, Cairenius also has compassion and pity and adopts a small child.

The novels, short stories, and other works that followed this one are interesting only as evidence of her development and the mood of the time. The short stories in *Näkymätön kirjanpitäjä* ('The Unseen Bookkeeper,' 1918) and the novel *Kurjet* ('The Cranes,' the birds that fly away in autumn and return in spring, 1919) are full of contemporary events, strikes, riots, black market deals, and the Civil War; the same motifs recur in *Kihlasormus* ('The Engagement Ring,' 1921) and *Kirkonkello* ('The Churchbell,' 1922), a family chronicle covering four generations which in structure foreshadows the trilogy *Itämeren tytär.* Her temporary pessimism was influenced by the country's mood, for Finns felt that the country would be crushed under the Russian oppression. When this danger was past, her fundamental optimism prevailed.

Arvid Järnefelt (1861-1932) belonged to the generation of Aho, Pakkala, Alkio, and Kauppis-Heikki, but he did not publish until he was past thirty and wrote several important works after 1920. Since most of his contemporaries died before he did, near the end of his life he was left alone in a world entirely different from the one of his youth.[384] However, he was a nearly unique person able to live successfully in society while rejecting its values (Thoreau was not nearly so lucky). His father was from a family well known in Finland; he was an officer in the Russian army, then returned to his native country, where he occupied high posts in the administration and was finally a cabinet member (at a time when relations between the two countries were still good). In St. Petersburg he married the daughter of Baron Clodt von Jürgensburg, a nobleman of Baltic German origin and one of the best Russian sculptors of the time. The entire family was highly talented, intelligent, and reputedly eccentric; Mrs. Järnefelt's children inherited many of these qualities. Arvid's brother Eero became one of Finland's best-known painters in his time, his brother Armas became an equally renowned conductor and composer, and their sister married Jean Sibelius. Arvid first prepared for a career in the administration and took a degree in humanities and law at the University of Helsinki, but, as he was ready to begin work as a junior official at a court of appeals, he suddenly broke with his former life. He had been converted to Tolstoy's ideas and decided to apply them. He learned the shoemaker's and blacksmith's arts, bought a small farm, and lived there quite well. He continued to visit Helsinki, lectured there, and published books, mainly fiction, in which his ideas were reflected. He married and with his wife personally educated his children, who led ordinary lives, one eventually becoming an ambassador in the diplomatic service of independent Finland.

Personally, he was modest and unassuming. Although he lectured publicly and offended many with his ideas, even, in the troubled times of 1917, preaching his beliefs in a church (which resulted in prosecution; he refused to appear in court because laws, according to him, were only the expression of the will of the ruling class),[385] he seems to have been intent first on following his own truth and only second on convincing others. The apparently autobiographical short story *Hiljaisuudessa* ('Without Ceremonies,' 1913; included in the collection of the same title) tells of his provision for the burial of his small daughter. Faithful to his own code, he had not had her baptized, but the family, though loyal to him, would not have her "put away like a dog" outside the cemetery.[386] Fearing his reception, he goes to the vicarage, but his treatment is courteous, and the church representatives agree to bury his child "without ceremonies." However, when he returns home, his family has changed its mind, and they bury the child on their own ground, without ceremony, but the birds sing in the trees around them, "and that was a far better ceremony than the church could ever have provided." The story is told in a calm, subdued manner. Järnefelt applied his eccentric ideas stubbornly, calmly, and in an almost business-like manner; one might almost say that he inherited his artistic gifts and wild ideas from his German-Russian mother and his practicality and quiet approach from his Finnish father. We wonder, however, if he ever thought about the different turn his life might have had if his father had not been General, Governor, and Senator Alexander Järnefelt.[387]

His writings are often autobiographical and deal with recurring problems: the relation of man to God, social questions—especially the ownership of land and agriculture—and sexual morals. Spiritually he belonged to Minna Canth's generation; he found sexual desires evil and felt that marriage should be based on pure friendship. (He did have children with his wife, however.) His first novel, *Isänmaa* ('My Country,' i.e., the Fatherland, 1893), describes the life of a student who comes to Helsinki from the country; such a subject gives the author opportunity to describe university life, the political, social, and intellectual problems discussed among young and old at that time, and to expound his own ideas. Those ideas center on nationalism and love for one's country, called good, positive feelings, but it is also stressed that they are but part of all that God has given to man and that he must strive to broaden the scope of his devotion. *Heräämiseni* ('My Awakening,' 1894), openly autobiographical, belongs to the genre of confessions, though not on the level of confession masterpieces, e.g., Rousseau's or Tolstoy's.[388] The short stories of *Ihmiskohtaloita* ('Human Destinies,' 1895) show that seemingly successful persons can build their success on false foundations, for politics, worldly success, or formal religion cannot give true happiness, only Tolstoy's teachings.

Veljekset ('The Brothers,' 1900) is a lengthy novel concentrating on the psychological problems of four minister's sons who find truth after struggle and difficulty. One studies sciences and philosophy to answer his doubts, but is unsatisfied. Another becomes a minister, but is also unsatisfied and resigns. Another becomes a railroad engine driver. The fourth, a successful politician, learns that there are values other than those upon which he has built his career. Although these characters are portraits of himself as a young man, they are also individual. We feel the characters' internal struggles rather than listen to an exposition of Järnefelt's (or Tolstoy's) ideas, and there are touches of humor. The first two brothers eventually become farmers living by their own work. Through the fourth Järnefelt expressed his opinion on the language question. The Finnish and Swedish groups were in opposition, and after 1899 hate and fear for the Russians also developed in the country. Järnefelt's character, a speaker of Finnish, accepts Swedish as a means of communication and even goes to Russia to learn Russian.

In *Helena* (1902) a young woman of good society is engaged to a young officer, whom she leaves when she discovers truth in socialism. Later, she rejects socialism and, in Tolstoy's spirit, devotes herself to charitable work among prisoners. This is the first book in which Järnefelt's ideas are fully developed. He rejects socialism and insists upon sexual abstinence for both parties before a marriage based on mutual understanding can be concluded. War, the military, and the church are criticized, and land ownership is again questioned.

Near 1900 Järnefelt also wrote a few plays: *Samuel Croëll* (name, 1899), centering on the problem of nonviolence, *Orjan oppi* ('The Teachings of a Slave,' 1902), rewritten, expanded, and republished in 1910 as *Tiitus* ('Titus'), and *Kuolema* ('Death,' 1903). In *Tiitus* (or *Orjan oppi*), which was quite successful on stage in its time, a slave tells the emperor that to do good he must resign, for a man holding power cannot achieve anything positive.[389] *Kuolema*, one of the few symbolist plays of Finland, has some effective scenes, e.g., that in which a dying woman dances with imaginary partners, the last of whom is Death, carrying her away to the tunes of *Valse Triste*. (Sibelius wrote the incidental music containing that piece which has contributed so much to the false impression of his art abroad.)[390]

In 1899 Järnefelt published a description of his visit to Tolstoy, whose radical program of land reform attracted him, and he later studied the writings of Henry George, whom Minna Canth and others much admired at that time in Scandinavia. The results of his readings on this subject appear in the novel *Maaemon lapsia* ('Children of Mother Earth,' 1905), in which the Finnish agricultural problem is viewed by three characters: a poor tenant who has been evicted from his home, a wealthy landowner driven from his estate by the Russians, and a radical young aristocrat intent on enacting reforms, another self-portrait of Järnefelt. The style of the book, reputedly one of his best, is no longer tense and solemn but simple and familiar, the character descriptions are touched with humor, and the varying reactions to the same events by persons of different social positions are rendered with insight. During the strike at Laukko, about which Juhani Aho (and almost everyone in Finland) wrote, Järnefelt journeyed to the scene and published a pamphlet titled *Maa kuuluu kaikille. Matkoiltani Laukon lakkomailla.* ('The Land Belongs to Everyone. From My Journeys to the Strike-Torn Region of Laukko,' 1907). *Veneh'ojalaiset* I-II ('People from Veneh'oja,' 1909) also describes people from Laukko, but not in relation to the agricultural problem. The novel is set in the slums of Helsinki—the seamy side of the brilliant, gay life described by Eino Leino, Maila Talvio, and the contemporary Swedish writers. It is an unusually frank, unadorned picture of a half-criminal society in which a son of a former farmer in Laukko has become wealthy by keeping horse cabs, selling liquor, and protecting prostitutes. He would like to give his son, who is not interested, a good education; the son is eventually involved with Russian revolutionaries and shot in an abortive rebellion of Russian soldiers in Finland. Another member of the family has become a Russian officer but later sides with them; he fails to carry out his mission for the rebels and escapes to the United States. There was, really, in Helsinki a rebellion of Russian soldiers in which the socialist Red Guards were involved (Eino Leino also wrote about it in *Jaana Rönty*), and a Finn who had been a Russian officer became commander of these Guards and later fled to the United States, protesting publicly his treatment in Järnefelt's work.[391] The implication, never openly stated, is that individuals who lose contact with their home region and their land become corrupted; neither Järnefelt's nor Tolstoy's philosophies are put in evidence.

Between the publication of *Veneh'ojalaiset* and *Greeta ja hänen Herransa* ('Greeta and Her Lord,' 1925), Järnefelt published *Manon Roland* in

1913 (a play, also performed), a collection of short stories and a play titled, like the short story previously mentioned, *Hiljaisuudessa* ('Without Ceremonies,' 1913), an autobiographical novel *Onnelliset* ('The Happy Ones,' 1916, under the feminine pseudonym Hilja Kahila), his speeches in a church (*Kirkkopuheita*, 1917), *Nuoruuteni muistelmia* ('Memories from My Youth,' 1919), all works of no special interest; equally uninteresting is the novel *Minun Marttani* (1927) based on an actual sensational murder and love affair.

In *Greeta ja hänen Herransa* the author describes the life and conflicts of a family without expressing his own ideas. Greeta, the mother, turns to her lord (the book implies that he is not the God of the official church) simply and naturally for help in all difficulties. Her lord does not always tell her she is right, and she accepts his answers without rebelling. A description of simple country life in a prosperous region in which an industrial center is developing, between a Finnish- and a Swedish-speaking region, the story is simple and undramatic. It has passages on traditional life in a large, prosperous Swedish-speaking village which seldom appear in Finnish literature,[392] but the emphasis is on the relationships among members of the family, who, from a Swedish-speaking region, have adjusted without much difficulty to their Finnish surroundings. One unusually sensitive son marries a Finnish girl, and, as conflicts arise over inheritance, rights, and titles to properties, he commits suicide. This mother, in a dialogue with her lord, concludes that he was too good for this world.

Järnefelt ended his literary career by publishing *Vanhempieni romaani* ('A Novel about My Parents,' 2 vols., 1928 and 1930), a perhaps not entirely reliable but honest description of his parents and himself. Although it contains all his preoccupations, the novel is also a delightful narration about a certain period in Finland and some highly intelligent and cultivated persons. Even here Järnefelt retained his sense of humor, e.g., in the situation in which his mother comes from imperial St. Petersburg, the home of the world-famous Russian writers, composers, and artists and the residence of one of the world's mightiest and most pompous courts, to Kuopio, a small Finnish town very aware of its own importance, and in the scene in which the ladies of good society in Helsinki (including his mother) request that their husbands take steps to suppress brothels, one of which their sons pass daily when going to school; the husbands ask in reply what would happen to their daughters then. Brothels have since been outlawed, but Järnefelt's own solution was to educate boys not to have sinful desires. Although discussing social and moral questions of great importance to him, in this book and in his entire production, Järnefelt was never heavy or pompous.

Although **Algot(h) Untola**, alias **Tietäväinen** (1868-1918; he also used the pseudonyms **Maiju Lassila**, **Irmari Rantamala**, and **J. I. Vatanen**) belongs chronologically to this period, it is not easy to categorize his works artistically. The son of a farmer, he was born at Tohmajärvi in the eastern part of the country, southeast of Joensuu; his father died, his stepfather lost his fortune, and he worked as a farmhand, but eventually went to the Teachers' College at Sortavala.[393] Little is known about the years 1900 through 1904, when he went to Russia after teaching elementary school. He hinted that he met both revolutionaries and aristocrats; after returning to Finland, he worked first for a socialist, then a conservative paper, began publishing literature in 1909, rejoined the Social Democrats in 1916, worked for their newspaper *Työmies* until the end of the Civil War, and refused to leave Helsinki when it was threatened by the Whites. He was taken prisoner, sentenced to death, and shot while trying to escape in May, 1918. His sudden changes in life and opinions account for the difficulty in classifying his work; a Finnish scholar, considering his origin and political activities, calls him with some reservations a "proletarian writer."[394] Although he wrote many humorous works, to call him a humorist would be misleading.

Three well-defined periods can be distinguished in his production. The first is marked by a novel in two parts and six volumes (three thousand pages) titled *Harhama* and *Martva* (names; *Harhama* also means 'delusion' or 'mirage'; 1909), neither readable. They are decadent, symbolistic, erotic, political, and moralistic; avowedly he intended to denounce contemporary society's corruption in a Christian spirit, but he described vice more than he chastised it. He antagonized the liberals, including Eino Leino, who declared that neoromanticism had been pushed to absurd extremes and that he was disgusted even by the covers, adorned with serpents, skulls, meditative nudes, and so forth.[395] Such a gigantic enterprise would have required a greater talent than Untola for success; he merely pushed some of the period's characteristics to their extreme conclusion.

He next adopted the pseudonym Maiju (Mary or Molly) Lassila and published funny stories about the inhabitants of his native region, traditionally considered great jokers like all eastern Finns. In a complete reversal from his original, exaggerated ambitions, he said, "I do not think it would be good if so-called better people would buy my products, for it is best that everyone stays within his own trousers."[396] More than likely, Untola was not merely reproducing here the language familiar from his native region, but also inventing some. "Better people," however, did buy these books, read and liked them, e.g., V. A. Koskenniemi, Volter Kilpi, and Kyösti Vilkuna, all well-known writers who will be discussed at greater length later, the first two rather refined and aesthetic. His works have been read by "better people" ever since; an academic dissertation has been written on him,[397] one of his novels has been structurally analyzed by a well-known contemporary poet and essayist in Finland,[398] an emminent Finnish scholar has published two essays on him,[399] and he has also received much other academic attention. His humor is his appeal, and it is its mad perfection which has attracted common readers and scholars alike. The main characters of his novels, e.g.,

Tulitikkuja lainaamassa ('Going to Borrow Matches,' 1910), move endlessly from place to place and become involved in ever new incidents; Tuomas Anhava calls them "novels of wandering" and compares them to *Don Quixote, Tom Jones, The Pickwick Papers, Huckleberry Finn,* and *Dead Souls.*[400] Untola's tales, however, contain no social criticism (others of his works do).

Avuttomia ('Helpless,' 1913, under the pseudonym J. I. Vatanen) describes the miseries and suffering of agricultural tenants, *Kuoleman rajoilla* ('On the Border of Death,' 1916, under the pseudonym Irmari Rantamala) is the story of a strike in which the character's problems have equal importance, and *Turman talo* ('The House of Destruction,' 1917) is a half-fantastic narration about a riot on a large country estate. *Kuolleista herännyt* ('Risen from Death,' 1916, under the pseudonym Maiju Lassila) is half serious, but the humor is macabre; the comic effect is achieved too heavily by repetition. A character, half longshoreman half tramp, supposedly dies two or three times, but reappears to terrify those who knew him, and to this development is added a complicated plot in which he swindles some wealthy people. It is marred by Untola's chief weakness, his inability to retain the effect of his fresh, lively humor, caused by adding too many incidents. *Liika viisas* ('Too Much Wisdom,' 1915) is satirical of some follies of his time, amusing because of the complex manner of presentation. A simple country man is inspired by a religious experience to preach, according to St. Paul, that all worldly wisdom is folly, giving the author the opportunity to criticize both the church and conservatives hostile to science and progress as well as contemporary fads, the sports craze that invaded Finland at that time, the interest in the mysteries of Finnish folklore (one character is a Ph.D. who has gone crazy when trying to solve the problem of the Sampo),[401] the debate about women's rights and sexual morals, and so forth. Unfortunately Untola gave it a conclusion totally irrelevant to the story, of the type which is called in films a "chase."

Tulitikkuja lainaamassa is considered Untola's masterpiece, and his other stories and plays about country life are on the same level. The plays, *Kun lesket lempivät* ('When Widows Are in Love';—*leski* is both feminine and masculine—1911), *Kun ruusut kukkivat* ('When the Roses Are Blooming,' 1912), *Mimmi Paavaliina* (name, 1916), *Ikiliikkuja* ('The Perpetual Motion,' posthumous), are realistic in their humor. It is possible to see social satire in *Mimmi Paavaliina*, in which Mimmi, officially asked to name the father(s) of her six illegitimate children, lists a police chief, the substitute minister, a sexton, and so forth. He also wrote two inferior sentimental comedies, *Nuori mylläri* ('The Young Miller') and *Luonnon lapsia* ('Children of Nature'). He was not basically sentimental and was more successful in ridiculing sentiment; he was, after all, an educated man and not the simple country boy he pretended. As Professor Ojala points out, marriage is popularly supposed to be based on love; so, it is either comical or unpleasant if material and economic considerations influence marriage.[402] In many of Untola's works, *Kun lesket lempivät*, for example, the humor is produced by the suitor's open declaration that he wants to marry a wealthy widow for money.

Untola's long stories, *Tulitikkuja lainaamassa* and *Pirttipohjalaisia* (name, 1911), and most of his short ones defy description, both in substance and style. Their humor is mainly due to the seemingly rational behavior of the characters and the nonsensical results, but Untola was humorous without inventing unusual events. His characters have legitimate errands, borrowing matches from a neighbor's house or asking for the hand of a wealthy widow (a favorite Untola motif), but they are unable to resist impulse and to distinguish between important and unimportant matters, and are always led astray from their original missions, becoming involved in chain reactions of incidents, misunderstandings, and mix-ups which, though seeming to follow with logical necessity, are as improbable as Alice's adventures in Wonderland, an improbability both hidden and underlined by Untola's absolutely consistent outer realism.

Untola is not at all unique in his humorous descriptions of country people; Kivi, Aho, and the minor humorists of the late nineteenth century preceded him, but his complete lack of sentimentality or moral considerations is very personal to him, as is the perfection of his nonsensical logic. Although in this respect he is alone in Finnish literature, his works mark a transition from the earlier period to the great writers who followed him or were his later contemporaries, e.g., Lehtonen and Kianto.

Literature in Finnish
between the Two World Wars

THE PROCLAMATION OF FINLAND'S INDEPENDENCE in 1917 did not signify the immediate appearance of a new generation of writers since literary periods do not necessarily correspond to great historical events. Almost all great novelists whose works dominated the period between the two wars had begun to write between 1900 and 1910 approximately—Ilmari Kianto, Joel Lehtonen, and Volter Kilpi; Sillanpää followed a few years later; Heikki Toppila belongs to the same generation, but he published his first works late. The most productive period in their lives was more or less between 1905 and 1935, and their personalities and opinions were fully formed by the time the greatest event in the modern history of their country occurred. Finns had long lived in an almost independent country, with most institutions needed by a sovereign state, and the last ties with Russia were broken almost casually, with the Bolsheviks' consent. However, after a few weeks the socialists proclaimed a socialist republic, opposed by nonsocialists; the conflict led to a bitter civil war (War of Independence) won by the nonsocialists (Whites) with the help of young Finns who had secretly gone to Germany, then at war with Russia, for military training, and a German division requested by the White government. The victorious side elected, by slender majority in a Parliament without socialist representatives, a German prince the king of Finland, but he never actually ruled, for by November 11, 1918, he and even his most convinced supporters in Finland had decided that it was, perhaps, a poor idea for the country to have a German ruler. In 1919 a newly-elected Parliament, in which the socialists were the largest group, accepted by overwhelming majority a republican constitution still, without significant amendment, in force today. The liberals and moderates then built up an independent, democratic, and, eventually, prosperous Finland.

These political and historical events are reflected in literature, though not always directly. Works celebrating the victory of the Whites were forgotten as quickly as they were written; later the great authors of the time treated these events in a very different mood, though not siding with the Reds or Whites or even writing books specifically about the Civil War. Finnish literature in general deals with individuals rather than types or social classes and is remarkably free from political and social propaganda—remarkably because many of the great Finnish authors were of modest origin and had sympathies for their original class even after attaining middle-class status. They freely expressed their political and social opinions in writing, but not in fiction or poetry. Sillanpää's novel *Hurskas kurjuus* (tr. *Meek Heritage*) is about a man who, at the end of the Civil War, is shot as a rebel by the Whites, but most of the book is about his previous life, which did not include political or social activities. There are similar works in which the characters are involved in the Civil War because they live at that time, but the authors intended to picture fully their lives, in which the war and political events are but a part.

Finnish writers are aware of the contrast between their modest origins and their attitude of dispassionate observation and have written about this discrepancy. In Sillanpää's first published short story, a character says that he is like a man stuck in a trapdoor between two floors, which represent the lower class into which he was born and the upper to which he is trying to rise; he can see the beauties of the upper but cannot get there or go back; he is a bother to the members of both.[403] In many of Joel Lehtonen's works, people of modest origin acquire education and better position, as the author did, but he criticizes their loss of contact with the lower classes and their blindness to real social problems caused by the naively romantic picture of the common people prevalent among the educated classes. Allusions to this same problem appear again and again in the texts of Toivo Pekkanen, a metal worker whose first books appeared in the twenties. In the short story *Elämän puu* ('The Tree of Life'), the main character tells himself that "a man cannot read literature for ten years and still remain a good mechanic." In the novel *Tehtaan varjossa* ('In the Shadow of the Factory'), a worker says of the main character: "You are like a badly shaped brick which won't fit into any building made by people for themselves, you are not a capitalist and not a socialist either." The faculty of seeing themselves objectively is combined in these authors, especially Lehtonen and Sillanpää, with an impartial view of their characters; the authors have understanding and sympathy for them, but do not overlook their weaknesses. In fact Lehtonen especially seems to have exaggerated his characters' defects in order to contrast them as much as possible with the idealistic conception of common people prevalent among earlier Finnish writers, e.g., Aho. The spirit of these more realistic writers is not irony or superiority—any satire in their works is directed at those who pride themselves in superiority, failing to see that human nature is the same everywhere. In this respect, they are reminiscent of the Russians, e.g., Gogol, Dostoyevski, and Chekhov, who often describe repulsive or ridiculous characters but clearly indicate that these characters, like everyone, are human.

These authors share a stylistic feature natural to them as a result of their decision to write simply and to render faithfully the words and thoughts of their characters. We are not alluding to their giving these words and thoughts a realistic form, with the uncouthness, hesitation, and repetition of speech, or to their occasional use of local words and phrases,[404] but to a deeper structural factor in the narrative. This trait is not specifically Finnish, and scholars of many countries have studied it. In Germany, where it has perhaps been most researched, it is called *erlebte Rede,* for which there is no accepted English equivalent, although Dorrit Cohn's "narrated monologue" seems adequate. In other countries scholars have often considered this trait a sophisticated device used by authors who have discarded traditional forms and experimented with new ways of expressing themselves, [405] but it has never received much notice in Finland,[406] and Finnish authors have apparently considered it a means to give a familiar, unaffected tone to their works. We have a distinct feeling that in Finland, when a writer tried to write in a highly literary style, he avoided this type of narration. In France it has been discussed in connection with *le roman nouveau* ('the new novel'). Nathalie Sarraute, who has used it in her own works, thinks that the forms of the narrative must be radically renewed and believes that this renewal can be partially reached by the use of this stylistic device.[407]

To clarify that the apparently careless style of these Finnish authors is partly the result of an attempt to present a definite view of the world in which the subject of the narration is dominant and no clear limit is drawn between his consciousness and the surrounding world, we cite a few examples from their works. Lehtonen's short story *Herra ja moukka, eli mitä kylvää, sitä korjaa* ('The Gentleman and the Boor, or What You Sow Shall You Reap') begins with an intentionally naive, thorough description:

> Aapeli Muttinen's estate is called Putkinotko. He has a sharecropper there.... That man is called Juutas Käkriäinen.–It is an early summer morning.

Later the narration changes. Almost imperceptibly the character's thoughts intrude without the use of a formal device to introduce them. In the following we have italicized those parts which seem to represent his inner monologue:

> ... *now he ought to build, construct, and raise a wall of stones, there, on that spot.... He ought to roll the stones from the heap back there, farther*

184

off. *This in order to protect the currant bushes of the owner, Muttinen, Mister Muttinen, to be sure, the currant bushes and also the apple trees, which are all dead for reasons Käkriäinen knows quite well.* There they stand, black against the sky. *But Mr. Muttinen has planted new bushes under them, and they ought to be taken care of now. And those lilacs then, which grow up there against the wall of the summer house; you can be sure that they will make it rot down.* Juutas Käkriäinen hates to see. . . .

And later:

. . . that's how Muttinen has got this piece of real estate so cheap, and besides, he also knew to buy it when everything was cheap anyway.

And then he built himself this summer house. *Just in the midst of the biggest heap of stones. . . . Wasn't there any other place to be found? He wanted to have a nice view, all right; but then he lets the lilacs grow in front of his windows! After that, he got it into his head to have an orchard made there. In the stoneheap again. A fine place, that, to grow something.* When Muttinen had finished building his summer house. . . .

Sillanpää uses this device even more freely. In his texts the shift from the normal prose to the narrated monologue can occur in the middle of a sentence, as it does in this excerpt from the story *Huhtikuinen tanssiaisyö* ('A Dance on an April Night'):

Through the half-open door, the ticking of the alarm clock was heard in the master's room. It was as if it had always been repeating the same word, and, after Silja had been listening to it for a while, she noticed that the rhythmic noise had become a part of her thoughts. It was trying to explain them in its own way, and, at that moment, something unpleasant, which should have been rejected, crept into Silja's mind. It was, however, a thing of the past, *and what could I do against him, a guest of the family. I couldn't well start calling for help in the middle of the night, and after all, the mistress came then just at the moment when, maybe, I was in need of help. And then he left next morning, and nobody saw anything, except for the mistress, and how could she start telling things like that about somebody from the family.* To Silja the whole story was like one of those dreams. . . .

At times in Sillanpää's texts the individual whose thoughts are represented is not even defined. In the same story we find:

The dance begins first very quietly, but then becomes more and more animated, quite a party, in fact. At first, toward the end of the week, it is just a vague rumor going around, and nobody knows who started it. It may even happen that the owners of the house hear about it from somebody else and are quite surprised to be told that, at their place, there will be a dance on Sunday. *Nobody has come to ask me, anyway, if they could dance in the big room of the house.*

185

We know only that the unidentified "me" is someone from the house. Further into the book is:

> First after a couple of hours some faces, which are examined more closely, are seen next to the door. *So that one is here too. Seems to have been drinking a little; better to watch him closely.*

Again someone from the house is talking to himself, but the author provides no further clues to his identity. The result is a description of the atmosphere at a gathering, made up of the actions, words, and thoughts of the individuals present. Such writing leads to considerable extension of time: to describe all the fleeting thoughts which can crowd a person's mind in a few seconds may take pages. The action in Lehtonen's 531-page novel *Putkinotko* takes place in little more than twelve hours. Volter Kilpi's *Alastalon salissa* ('In the Living Room of Alastalo'), a novel describing a group of wealthy farmers who discuss in a few hours the building of a ship, has 924 pages. This discussion immediately brings to mind Joyce and Proust, but Lehtonen, who wrote *Putkinotko* before 1919, could not have been familiar with them. Kilpi, a librarian, knew of Proust, read some of *A la recherche du temps perdu*, and admitted a similarity in style between them, but said that their aims were different (we do not entirely agree). Kilpi also tried to read Joyce but found his knowledge of English insufficient.

Another feature typical of many Finnish authors, especially these, is their intentional avoidance of sentimentality and rhetoric. In Kianto and Lehtonen it is in conscious opposition to the idealization of common people and the excesses of neoromanticism. At first both wrote a few works in that vein, but Lehtonen later, in some of his characters, made fun of himself and what he considered the errors of his youth. In Sillanpää and Haanpää, however, the lack of romanticism and sentiment in outlook was natural, no longer in protest against a prevailing literary and social trend, and Kilpi, who began his career as a high-strung idealistic and aesthetic writer, managed to combine these qualities (more the idealism than the aestheticism) with realistic descriptions of country people in ordinary situations.

In fact, Finnish literature contains many passages which introduce a false note to the narration when the authors seem afraid of becoming too sentimental. One does not find this type of writing in Kivi, however, for, although he often describes nature and the work of the farmer in a broad, epic tone, he does not omit the familiar details, as this excerpt from chapter 9 of *Seven Brothers*, showing the clearing a field in the forest with the help of fire, demonstrates:

> They put fire to the dry branches, a mighty flame rose roaring toward the sky, and great billows of brown smoke were soon rolling near the clouds. The fire went forward, reducing the clearing to ashes in the bright sunlight.

But the dry sticks and the trees in the clearing were not enough for it, and, at the end, it rushed with a roar into the pillared halls of the pine forest. Frightened, the brothers ran then to resist with all their might the unfettered element; they swept and beat the heather-covered ground, and their brooms, made with branches of spruce, whistled and glittered in the air, falling with heavy, dull thuds on the sandy ground. The furious flames were, however, not to be conquered in this manner and went blazing still further. Eventually, Juhani shouted in a mighty voice: "Take your trousers in your hands, everyone, dip them in the spring, and beat the fire with them!" So they ripped their trousers off, dipped them into the gently rippling, cool spring and began to slap and beat the burning ground on the heath.

Kianto had an eye for the humorous, and in his works these sudden changes in mood are intended. In chapter 16 of *Punainen viiva* ('The Red Line'), when writing about the 1907 elections, in which for the first time all Finnish citizens could vote, he quotes from an imaginary socialist newspaper:

The upper classes have always oppressed this nation and want to go on oppressing it. Down with the power of the few, down with the exploiters of labor! Justice to the oppressed! The election days must be holidays in the whole country. Tomorrow we shall go! Take your spectacles with you!

The passage is a good example of the not always good jokes Finnish authors sometimes use to suppress emotion. Sillanpää, in the previously quoted *Huhtikuinen tanssiaisyö*, says that, when Silja comes home in the spring morning, a wagtail is shaking its feathers in the first rays of the sun, on, however, the roof of the pigsty. In the short story *Merimiehenleski* ('The Widow of a Sailor'), Kilpi presents a poor old woman who thinks of her dead husband, of her life, and of God, complains at times about His harsh laws, but repents and prays for His mercy. Kilpi uses the appropriate tone and, we think, manages here as well as in other works to express in a simple yet deep and moving way thoughts about essential questions which seem natural to the character. The widow also thinks, however, of small, everyday events from her past, of some funny remarks her husband made, and so forth. Even when she remembers how she was told that her husband's ship had foundered, these thoughts come to her mind:

The rector even took her hand and looked her for an instant steadily in the eyes, before he began to speak, still holding that poor hand. "I read yesterday night in the Turku paper that, according to news from Sweden, the *Esmeralda* has been wrecked off Gotland. The ship has been lost with all its crew, except the captain and the cook." ... a moment went before she could ask: Was it said there about Kustaa that Kustaa had also been drowned? Her lips were ice cold, and her eyes were widening more and more. "Kustaa had also a Bible in his sea chest, I put it under the shirts so that God would protects His book and Kustaa." The Bible had sunk into the sea and the sea chest had sunk and Kustaa had sunk; in the chest there were also six pair of new socks. "What does God need the socks I have been knitting and Kustaa's shirts for?" said her mindless lips. . . .

Ilmari Kianto (1874-1970) was born at Pulkkila, approximately sixty miles southeast of Oulu, near the birthplaces of Heikki Toppila and Pentti Haanpää. Oulu, its surroundings, and all of northern Ostrobotnia have provided an impressive number of good writers, including Franzén, Sara Wacklin, Kramsu, Pakkala, V. A. Koskenniemi, Aaro Hellaakoski, Martti Merenmaa, Matti Hälli, Pentti Holappa, and Antti Hyry. Kianto's original name was Calamnius; the family, most of whose members were ecclesiastics, has been known by that name from 1610. **Gabriel Calamnius** (1695-1754) wrote *Suru-Runot Suomalaiset* (Finnish Laments,' 1734), a poem on the war of 1700-21 not unlike Bartholdus Vhaël's Waikia walitus-runo, and the first collection of worldly poems in Finland, *Wähäinen Cocous Suomalaisista Runoista* ('Small Collection of Finnish Poems,' edited by his son, 1755).[408] Although his father was a Lutheran minister, Kianto eventually became violently anticlerical and held views in total opposition to the teachings of the official religion. His funeral, however, was held with great pomp in a church; the president of the republic laid a wreath on his bier. One of Kianto's sons, a minister, officiated and quoted from a kind of testament left by his father: "It was out of respect for the convictions of my forefathers that I, the offspring of an ecclesiastic family, left the church. I did not want to insult that which my fathers and mothers had believed in. I always recognized the principles of the Christian religion and respected the true believers. I confess to a faith which is realized in life and in deeds. And I left the church because I could not find in the church devouts the good deeds of life which Christ is requesting." His son added that it is a hard faith.[409]

Emphasizing Kianto's many oddities and antics, we might easily write a humorous biography of him, and he would probably not have minded, for to a great extent he did so himself. In addition to descriptions of his travels in Finland and abroad, he has published more or less openly autobiographical works and pamphlets on a number of questions. The first, *Auskultantin päiväkirja* ('The Diary of a Teaching Associate,' 1907), was published under the pseudonym Antero Avomieli, which might be translated 'Oscar the Openhearted.' During Finland's period of prohibition, he wrote in protest *K.H.P.V. eli Kohtuullisen Hutikan Pyhä Veljeskunta* ('H.F.O.M.D. or The Holy Fraternal Order of the Moderate Drunks,' 1925). He began his adult life a normal, middle-class young man, although in 1893 he served in the famous Fusilier Battalion of the Finnish Guards, an action unnecessary under the draft law then in force which made him, toward the end of his life, one of the last veterans of the old Finnish army. While studying in Helsinki, he published several volumes, *Soutajan lauluja* ('Songs of the Boatman,' 1897), *Hiljaisina hetkinä* ('Quiet Moments,' 1898), *Lauluja ja runoelmia* ('Songs and Poems,'

1900), and others; these are reportedly no worse than the average poems of that time, and a few have remained popular, especially those set to music, e.g., *Suomussalmi–surunsalmi* ('Straits of Suomus–Straits of Sorrow'). Kianto later settled in Suomussalmi, a village in northeast Finland where he built a house which he named Turjanlinna ('Turja Castle') and where he was buried; afterwards he often referred to himself as *Korpikirjailija* ('Writer of the Woods'). In some of his poems he reproduced successfully the form and spirit of modern Finnish folksongs, like those of Larin-Kyösti or the early works of Eino Leino.

After deciding to become a Russian teacher, he received a scholarship and studied in Moscow between 1901 and 1903; later he published Finnish translations of Pushkin's and Lermontov's poems, Nemirovich-Danchenko's short stories, Leo Tolstoy's *Death*, Gushev-Orenburgskiy's *Young Russia*, and Goncharov's *Oblomov*. He did teach Russian and Russian literature at the Kajaani high school between 1904 and 1905, but in Helsinki he had met the young radicals of the time, Eino Leino, Larin-Kyösti, Otto Manninen, and Maila Talvio, founders of the Finnish Writers' Guild, who, with the Järnefelt family, had a decisive influence on his spiritual development.[410] He proclaimed his anticlerical convictions again and again in his books and in the pamphlet *Vapaauskoisen psalttari* ('The Psalms of the Freethinker,' 1912). When he married for the first time in 1904, he wanted a civil cermony, not legal then in Finland, and so he and his fiancée went to Sweden, where that kind of wedding could be performed.[411] He was an individualist; although he was hostile to religion and had radical ideas on sexual morals, he was not a pacifist or internationalist, but a violent patriot who advocated civil disobedience against Russian oppression. These activities brought him into conflict with the Kajaani authorities, and he resigned from the school, tried journalism, and eventually became a freelance writer. After Finland's independence he again expressed his patriotism. During the first troubled years of the Russian revolution, a movement to make Russian Karelia a part of the country had begun, receiving unofficial support from beyond the western border. Kianto had traveled in Karelia, the fabled land of the *Kalevala*, and had written descriptions of it before 1917, *Vienan virroilta, Karjalan kankailta* ('On the Rivers of Viena, on the Heaths of Karelia,' 1915; he often called the region Viena). Between 1918 and 1920 he made speeches and wrote works asking for its liberation and union with Finland, but the Finnish government knew that carrying through such plans was an impossibility because the Soviet government had no intention of relinquishing the territory.

On the question of sexual morals, Kianto went much further and took a direction quite apart from that taken by Järnefelt, for example. In his many novels, more or less about himself, e.g., *Nirvana* (name, 1907), he confesses that he had many difficulties in establishing satisfactory contacts with the other sex. When he overcame these problems with the help of kind, understanding women, he concluded that salvation lay in complete freedom of love and that sex was a holy, wonderful force which the church and traditional morals had debased. Initially he was able to combine his ideas with a lasting form of marriage. He said that young men and women should remain chaste until they met the right partners with whom to establish permanent relationships, but later he decided that, if love were wonderful and almost holy, it was so every time and could appear several times in one person's life. He declared himself polygamous in the novel *Avioliitto* ('Marriage,' 1917)—his own marriage disintegrated in the same year—and in a series of public lectures in 1921. Meanwhile he lived according to his principles.[412]

These facts are relevant to not only Kianto but also to literary life in his time, but it is not for these activities that he is still remembered, read, and respected. For a long time he was the patriarch of Finnish literature, and in 1957 the University of Helsinki conferred upon him the title Doctor of Philosophy *honoris causa*. His attacks on morals and religion were quite serious, and he was opposed, criticized, and attacked at the beginning of the century, but after 1920, Finns became interested in other things, and his works have since been read as literature. He is now known mainly as the author of only two books, the novels *Punainen viiva* ('The Red Line,' 1909) and *Ryysyrannan Jooseppi* (name, 1924). Both are about the inhabitants of the region known as Kainuu, where Kianto's Turjanlinna is located, on the eastern border of the country, approximately as far north as Oulu. It is beautiful country with high hills, vast forests, picturesque lakes, and rivers with waterfalls, but the climate is harsh, the soil poor, and making a living difficult. So many writers have subsequently described the region, even after 1950, that Matti Kuusi has invented the name "Kainuuist" for them. Although reasonably prosperous people also live there, Kianto represented only the miserable, and he made them not only as miserable, but also as dirty, ragged, lazy, and ignorant as possible, like the characters of *Tobacco Road* or *Cannery Row*—descriptions of picturesque rural misery in Finland and in the United States share several characteristics, including moonshining.[413] The books are humorous,[414] but they were not written by an ironic aristocrat trying to show social reform, suffrage, education, and welfare wasted on the naturally lazy, stupid, unalterable poor. The author was not a social or socialist propagandist determined to show the sufferings of the rural proletariate and to ask for reform. It is true that Kianto closely identified with his characters. Once, when he tried to buy some land for a house and the Forest Services would not let him have the exact plot he wanted, he became furious and wrote *Metsäherran herjaaja* ('Telling One's Mind to the Forest Lord,' 1912), in which he expressed his opinion of the high and mighty authorities who would not let a poor man build his cabin where he wanted,[415] but this novel was just an outburst of temper, as were many of his books. Basically he was an educated man observing people at a distance, though with sympathy and understanding. Because the works of Finnish authors like Kianto were in opposition to the idealistic trend prevalent in literature before them, they emphasized their protest and demonstrated that idealism was false by exaggerating the unidealistic and taking pleasure in shocking their opponents. They also pointed out that an idealistic view of common people prevented people from seeing the real social problems of the time. However, they grew fond of their own characters and admired the patience, strength, and cunning with which these figures struggled against overwhelming odds and lack of support from so-called better people. There is evidence of a similar attitude in earlier Finnish authors, such as Kivi, Päivärinta, Kauppis-Heikki, Minna Canth, and Aho; they understood the poor, criticized the upper classes, and even suggested reform, but their outlook was more objective than Kianto's, for he, like his contemporaries, examined only one side of reality and often magnified it for his own purposes. In that respect he was quite different from his predecessors.

The plots of *Punainen viiva* and *Ryysyrannan Jooseppi* are hardly more than descriptions of everyday life in the backwoods, but *Punainen viiva* is also about the first modern elections in Finland. Before 1906, when the emperor granted Finland the right of a new electoral law and Parliament, an estimated 10 percent of the adult male population could vote. Afterwards all citizens over twenty-four years of age, men and women, had the franchise and used it; in 1907, 70 percent of the electorate cast ballots, which were marked with a red pencil line next to the name of the candidate for whom a vote was cast.[416] The book is about the lives of two simple people, Topi Romppanen and his wife Riika, with the electoral campaign and voting day interwoven. Nothing special happens in the course of these events, but the characters feel them to be of tremendous importance, for they had never dreamed that they would have some influence, even if small, on the fate of the entire country. In the elections the proportional system applied then as now allowed several parties Parliamentary representatives. Although the socialists were the largest group, they did not have a majority; this fact and Finland's membership in the Russian Empire prevented the expected socialist paradise from materializing.[417] The resulting disappointment and bitterness led in part to the Civil War, but Kianto did not include the war in his book. Topi dies fighting a bear, an obvious sign that the best-thought schemes of men fail when confronted with fate and nature, and his blood flows in a red line across his throat.

Ryysyrannan Jooseppi, written much later, does not refer in this way to public matters, although the problems of prohibition, during which it was published, appear. Jooseppi begins moonshining when he can find no other means to support his large family. Although the sheriff and the deputy are willing to close an eye to his activities, he does not fare well, for his misery is due as much to his own incapacity as to outside factors. Eventually Jooseppi and the roof of his cabin, which he was trying to repair, are carried away by a strong wind. He appears in front of the Lord in heaven and tells Him what he thinks about His management of the world, a motif which appears in other Finnish authors.[418]

Kianto did describe some of the upper classes in his home region, in the novel *Patruunan tytär* ('The Master of the Ironworks and His Daughter,' 1933), for example. It is perhaps the most carefully written of his works, but it lacks the intensity of his descriptions of popular life. His last works are mainly memoirs, but not tame or conventional ones.

Joel Lehtonen was, in one sense, more a writer than Kianto, for he wrote much real poetry and fiction, not containing arguments on comtemporary problems or attempts to unravel his own entanglements. He was born the illegitimate son of a country servant girl at Sääminki, south of Savonlinna, in 1881. Kind people helped him through secondary school, and he began studies at the university, but soon started writing. His works were published, read, and appreciated without bringing him lasting happiness. Recognizing his inner disharmony, he tried to achieve a better balance. He traveled in France, Spain, Italy, and North Africa, wrote interesting, personal accounts of his journeys, learned French well enough to translate several works into Finnish, and did a Finnish version of Boccaccio's stories. His great dream seems to have been a house in the country—even as a schoolboy he designed fantastic, castlelike structures amidst trees and flowers.[419] He bought a small estate near his birthplace where he built a summer house, described as Putkinotko in that novel.[420] The book, an unglossed representation of country life, like Kianto's novels, angered his relatives, who threatened a libel suit. Eventually he sold the place and bought another in west Finland, not far from Hämeenlinna, naming it Lintukoto from Finnish mythology or Kivi's poem with that title, in which it means 'The Island of the Blessed.' *Lintukoto* is the title of a half-autobiographical work he published in 1929, and he called his last one, a collection of prose and poetry, *Jäähyväiset Lintukodolle* ('A Farewell to Lintukoto,' 1934; he committed suicide the same year).

Lehtonen began his literary career as a romanticist, in the current fashion; later he made fun of himself and other romanticists.[421] He admired Volter Kilpi, also an aestheticist at the beginning of his career, and used such expressions as "the pure, faraway bird," which moves, trembling, its wings "in the misty aether, in the shining azure of the sky," when saying that only he could write properly about love.[422] His romanticism, however, was robust and sarcastic, fantastic and terrifying. He eagerly listened to folktales of his home region (new ones; the old were no longer to be heard in Finland proper) and published two collections of them, *Tarulinna* ('The Fabled Castle,' 1906) and *Ilvolan juttuja* ('Tales of Ilvola,' mainly animal stories, 1910). His works always contained something disharmonious and strident; he ironized sham idealism and all that was too nice or genteel and opposed them to real life, as he saw it, with its imperfections, dirt, and ugliness, but he yearned for peace and happiness while aware that neither would be reached in this world. In his early stories he described a noisy beer tavern under the title *The Green Hell*[423] and made disrepectful adaptations of the Bible in *The Parable of the Rich Man, Lazarus, and the Dog,* but also wrote dreamy descriptions of a happy childhood, more or less his own, in a kind foster family. He read romantic writers, Hugo, Pierre Loti, contemporary Scandinavians, especially Selma Lagerlöf, and Nietzsche, a must at that time in intellectual circles. He was very interested in Gorki, who was most popular in Finland because of his declared sympathy for that country and his opposition to the czarist government. Lehtonen could not accept initially Gorki's proud individualism, but eventually concluded that courage and daring are the highest qualities required in the world and that complaining of life's difficulties is ridiculous; it is better to fight and perish than submit. In this spirit he wrote three novels, *Paholaisen viulu* ('The Devil's Fiddle,' 1904), *Villi* ('The Savage,' 1905), and *Mataleena* (name, 1906), and an epic poem, *Perm* (name, 1904). *Perm* is the only work in which Lehtonen takes the mythical Finno-Ugric past seriously, and it is more colorful, violent, and romantic than even Eino Leiro's poems. Villi is to a great extent autobiographical: it is about a poor country boy sent to school who, urged by his proud, rebellious spirit, composes "ungodly poems," reads atheistic authors and Darwin as well as romanticists, dreams wild dreams, falls in love and suffers. The best of these works is *Mataleena;* the story of Mataleena begins with her miserable old ages, contrasts it to her proud, passionate youth, and is basically pessimistic. All Lehtonen's early characters know that they fight overwhelming odds and cannot shape the world according to their will, that they will be overcome and will find the freedom they desire only in heaven—but they do not believe in heaven.

From 1907 to 1914 approximately Lehtonen's life and production were in transition. He traveled in Switzerland, Italy, France and Spain, wrote newspaper articles about his experiences, and published books about the places he visited. *Myrtti ja alppiruusu* ('The Myrtle and the Rose of the Alps') is not an ordinary travelogue, but a series of short stories which he rewrote several times and did not publish until 1911, four years after the journey to Switzerland and Italy. Italy was for Lehtonen, as it was for many other northern Europeans, a revelation of overwhelming beauty and serenity. In the long process of writing the book, however, some first impressions were modified: he originally intended *Orjantappura ja kruunu* ('The Thorn and the Crown') to be an appreciation of the Roman Catholic faith, but it eventually represented the opposite view.[424]

During these travels he learned to love and understand the literatures of the Latin countries, especially the Renaissance masters; of them and Tolstoy, one of the characters in *Putkinotko* says:

They are not a mirroring of themselves, like Ibsen, not skeletons of theories, like Rolland, not clouds of humbug words thrown on your eyes, like Hamsun. No, they are broader . . . always merry. And those books . . . no heroic nonsense, no outward glitter. They are full of smile and kindness.[425]

The step from the 1903 newspaper articles in which Lehtonen expressed admiration for Gorki by saying that "man must reach freedom through courage" was a long one. Courage was the war cry, the motto Gorki used to arouse those who whine about the miseries of life. *Putkinotko* was not published until 1919, and Lehtonen had time to experience the long process of moral reevaluation through which he rejected "heroic nonsense." He had to admit that most of the world did not think as he did, a great source of the bitterness apparent in his later works.

Before beginning work on *Putkinotko* and works spiritually connected with it, he published a few collections of poetry and a book on a journey to Paris, *Punainen mylly* ('Le Moulin Rouge,' 1913), similar to *Myrtti ja Alppiruusu*. The poems, published as *Rakkaita muistoja* ('Dear Memories,' 1911) and *Markkinoilta* ('At the Market,' 1912), are almost unique among their kind (Viljo Kojo later wrote a few somewhat similar)[426] in Finland, where poetry, unless directly satirical, was long expected to be noble and refined, fiery and patriotic, or dreamy and nostalgic, never broadly humorous, descriptive, and realistic. Lehtonen's poems are reminiscent of some by Larin-Kyösti, but the latter describes slightly quaint people and events, whereas Lehtonen takes his subjects directly from contemporary folk life. The collections *Nuoruus* ('Youth,' 1911) and *Munkkikammio* ('The Cell of a Monk,' 1914) are more conventional; several poems in the second reflect bitter disillusionment with love, probably related to events in the author's life. *Punainen mylly* is mysterious because the reason for Lehtonen's disenchantment with Paris and with life has not been discovered.[427] Except one Rabelaisian story, *Madame Maquerelle* ('The Madam'), the entire book expresses not simply the peevishness of a traveler who has not found the city of his dreams exactly as he had imagined it, but a deep depression, a loathing of all human, in which he sees only ugliness, stupidity, and nothingness. Why Lehtonen had this fit of depression in Paris is not known (Larin-Kyösti had one in Italy), but it is evident in his life and works that he was subject to them. His last collection of poems was published as *Puolikuun alla* ('Under the Crescent,' 1919), an allusion to his travels in North Africa.

In 1905 Lehtonen had bought the farm he was to call Putkinotko, but he left it under care of his mother and his half-brother with his large family. He did not remain there long himself until the period between 1914 and 1920. The result of his stay was a series of four books describing the region and its people, the novel *Kerran kesällä* ('Once in Summer,' 1917), the collection of short stories *Kuolleet omenapuut* ('The Dead Apple Trees,'

1918), and the two novels *Putkinotkon metsäläiset* ('The Backwoodspeople of Putkinotko,' 1919) and *Putkinotkon herrastelijat* ('The Fine People of Putkinotko,' 1920), later published in one volume as *Putkinotko*. He puts the humor and kindness he could find in his life in these books, but the humor is often satirical, and his smile is resigned rather than truly happy. More than once his characters think of their pasts, of that which has or might have been, and realize that all is past and will not return. The really comic parts of the books are those in which the author draws portraits or caricatures of human types from the country and a small town easily recognizable as Savonlinna.[428] His jokes are often Rabelaisian, and he freely describes body functions not usually mentioned in polite conversation, with the exception of sexual ones, about which he is reticent. Perhaps he felt that country people do not talk about sex as much as townspeople think they do, was shy about them himself, or allowed himself, consciously or otherwise, to be controlled by public morals.

The various individuals depicted by Lehtonen are to be found everywhere: small-town businessmen proud of the money they have earned (in Finland as in other countries, World War I gave opportunity for easy profits), country people who are perhaps cheated by them or who in turn cheat their own neighbors, and intellectuals more honest than the others, but impractical, naively idealistic, and incapable of seeing the dishonesty of others or acting upon it. One of these, the bookstore owner Aapeli Muttinen, is a caricature of Lehtonen, who was as critical of himself as of any other character. Muttinen, although of modest origin, is an educated man who has read and traveled, but he is impractical, fumbling, and cowardly. He thinks first of his comfort and good food, which has made him enormously fat, but he appears to be aware of his own defects and even exaggerates them. As Lehtonen's alter ego, Muttinen also has a sharp eye for the comic sides and weaknesses of his fellow men, and we see quite a collection of them. Konsta Könölin, a wealthy businessman who belongs to the generation that regards everything Swedish better than anything Finnish, has changed his homely name Könönen to Könölin and married a Swedish woman who, everyone knows, was a waitress; she does not make her husband happy. Mr. Kikka, a barber, fancies himself a great poet and man of the world (some of his poems are parodies of Koskenniemi's contemporary compositions); he is delighted when he can discuss literature with Muttinen and borrow from him "Bokkakkeeo's" naughty stories. Mr. Bongman, M. A., is an outrageous caricature of the *Kalevala*-crazy educated Finns.[429] He quotes and misquotes the epic on all appropriate and inappropriate occasions and dreams of a time, soon to come, when all Finnish art will be "national" in spirit, i.e., inspired by Karelian folk art. Tommola, a lawyer, is characterized by his passion for sports and physical exercise, which Untola had already ridiculed in *Liika viisas*.[430] Lauri Falk contains much of Lehtonen: he is a young man who believes, as do all who know him, that he has a brilliant career as an artist in front of him, but fails to live up to expectations, though not through his own fault. His fate is neither romantic nor exceptional. In writing about it, Lehtonen expressed a belief that the worst tragedies are not the great ones, for in great tragedies the victims have consolation in the overwhelming majesty of their sufferings, but the dreary, everyday ones in which everything slowly goes wrong and no one, not even fate, can be held responsible. Lauri Falk's fault is Aapeli Muttinen's, the excessive enthusiasm and idealism of youth which blinded him to the defects of the world and its inhabitants, for he fails to see that, although the world might be friendly to a gifted young man with good manners, it would soon forget him if he had nothing else to offer.

The public and the critics consider *Putkinotko* Lehtonen's major work. It is his most harmonious book, besides *Lintukoto*, which is about a similar haven of peace he had hoped to find. Vilho Suomi has written about the influence of an author's childhood on his feelings toward nature in an attempt to demonstrate a positive correlation between a happy childhood and love of nature and vice versa. According to him, Kivi, Aho, Lehtonen, and Sillanpää are examples of a positive attitude toward nature, whereas Kauppis-Heikki and Toivo Pekkanen are the opposite.[431] The accuracy of the theory might be questioned, but we find much truth in it and feel that it is applicable to Lehtonen, especially in *Putkinotko*. The numerous descriptions of panoramic scenery and small, secluded spots are treated in the book with love; Lehtonen was a highly visual person, and this visualization at times threatens to dissolve his narrative into a disconnected series of optical impressions.[432] Color and light predominate:

> The rounded hillocks on the fields, covered with lush potato plants, or rye, which is turning yellow, or smooth soft oats, or barley, greener and shinier still, cast dark shadows over the hollows between them everywhere on the small clearing. The shadows of the willows, the bird cherries, and the rowan trees are enormously lengthened on the meadow. . . . On the shore of the pond, above the mist, there is a blue and reddish shine in the air. A much thicker fog is rising from the pond than from the lake. There, in the deep blue air, the clear rays of the sun glitter like bright wires of steel. At places, silvery circles appear on the surface of the pond. . . .

These lines contain another characteristic of Lehtonen's style, especially noticeable in *Putkinotko*—his passion for detail, a compulsive urge to transcribe everything. It is very evident in segments of the narration dealing with hypothetical situations, that which might have happened in given circumstances, as though even the most careful recording of facts were not enough. Often the description of scenery is first presented impersonally, but a mainly imaginary onlooker is soon introduced; this pattern is followed in the opening paragraphs of *Putkinotko*. A strait is described as so narrow that a boat must be pulled through by force if one would rather take a short cut than row around a cape. From that point the hypothetical navigator, referred to as a "rower," continues to appear in the text. He can turn to the right and left, for there are straits and bays on every side. Later it is said that in the evening one will notice that the lake is bluish grey if one is rowing on it. After a description of a farm and its buildings, seen from the lake, it is said that, if the rower comes to shore and climbs up from the edge of the water, he will see them in a different shape. At times this obsession for accuracy has unintentional humorous results. When speaking of a small wooden box, he says that it is made of *birch*wood, that it is provided with a *sliding* lid—like the *pencil case*—of a schoolboy—or a *schoolgirl*; in describing a landscape viewed from a ship, he says that "the travelers on the deck—mostly better people, for the lower one is reserved for the commoners—have admired, while drinking their coffee, *if there were someone like that among them*, the shore. . . ." About a girl sitting in a conjurer's tent at a market, he explains that "there, in the corner of the tent . . . an acquaintance of Saara would recognize, *if she were there*, and *perhaps* there is a waitress from the ship or an idle woman from the slum at the place, she would recognize slowly, *when her eyes became accustomed to the dimness*, Saara from Putkinotko." (All our italics and dashes.) This meticulous transcription seems to reflect the author's half-conscious desire to capture completely and reproduce fully a single happy day in his life.[433] He appears to have believed that, if the necessary words and gestures were exactly repeated, he could achieve the desired result, a quest for that which has been lost, a Proustian aim, without Proust's directness.[434] Although Lehtonen reconstructs with infinite patience the image of a place, the people living there, its sounds, smells, and sights, the variations in sunlight, color of the sky, rustling of the leaves, chirping of the birds, and splashing of the fish, there are indications that it is an ephemeral creation which carries the germs of its own destruction. In *The Repetition* Kierkegaard describes, in order to illustrate the futility of such action, an attempt to reenact the past; according to him the uselessness is due to old age. The more one advances in years, the less one is capable of satisfaction, unless one becomes childlike, for children, who unconsciously renounce effort and put their trust in God, can recreate through faith the highest experiences of life.

Lehtonen, decidedly nonreligious, could not find comfort in faith or in God's presence, and the only shield against a hostile, indifferent environment he could devise was hedonism. However, as he grew older, he realized that this protection would not last. Lehtonen was not older than thirty-eight when *Putkinotko* was published; the main character is eight years older than he was, but it is still an early age for a man to begin thinking of death, the vanishing pleasures of life, and the futility of everything. However,

Lehtonen's health began to fail early,[435] and he was more acutely aware of passing time than others were. His physical sufferings, the hedonistic reaction against them, and his love for Cervantes and Rabelais remind us especially of Laurence Sterne, who, like Muttinen, did not agree with his wife, like Lehtonen himself, traveled in France and wrote a book about his journey, was indecent in a childish rather than vulgar way, and carried the art of digression to unprecedented heights. Sterne, too, attempted to recreate the past, an imaginary childhood in *Tristram Shandy*. He and Lehtonen seem so afraid of an early end that Sterne's hero is not born for a large part of the book and Lehtonen's day in the region of his childhood is not over before more than five hundred pages are written. In *Putkinotko* Lehtonen says:

> Nothing could make Muttinen nod his head more thoughtfully than the looks he casts toward the bay and the path! Nothing could make him grasp more eagerly the fleeting instant than the passing of time! Time is sinking away under Aapeli's feet ... the ground, with its smell of earth and of wine, too, is sinking away.

Muttinen reflects:

> Perhaps, now, when you grow older, you also grow poorer, so that you can understand others? You think that you can really understand and love. When you grow poorer, you grow wealthier; you learn to love others, not only yourself.

Here, obviously feeling that he was becoming too sentimental, Lehtonen introduces one of the incongruous jokes we have mentioned:

> ... (the woman) at whose feet he fell here, slumped down in the moonlight of autumn. The moon was shining straight over the middle of the bay, a golden, glittering moon. She became then his wife. But soon they started quarreling. . . . She was too refined for him, a son of country people. They could not understand each other, after all.
> And once she poured buttermilk down Aapeli's neck.
> People's feelings grow older, too, and fade away.

The plot in *Putkinotko* is not prominent; its purpose is apparently the description of a poor family, remarkably lazy, dirty, and disorderly, except, perhaps, for the mother, their activities on the small farm they cultivate as tenants, and their encounter with the estate owner. In the course of the narration the personalities of the twelve members of the Käkriäinen family, their social and economic background and their origins are revealed. Muttinen, the owner of the estate, has, out of generosity, given them land on easy terms to help them out of poverty, but they do not understand his motives and regard him a city sucker, a softy from whom they should profit. They vaguely suspect that the whole deal is a trick, shirk even the modest obligations incurred under the lease, and, rather than work, make illegal liquor and sell it. (Lehtonen, in imitation of old novelists, gave his works explanatory subtitles; *Putkinotko's* is "A Tale about a Lazy Moonshiner and a Foolish Gentleman.") Muttinen, who was an idealist and believed that poor people prove honest, hard-working, and eager to improve their living conditions if they are helped, describes his discovery of the real situation and his submission because, after struggling to change it, he recognized that it was partially his fault since he could not understand them or win their confidence. Lehtonen, was, of course, criticizing the idealistic view of the agricultural problem held by Aho and Järnefelt, for example. The question was not solved until 1922, when a radical land reform made independent landowners of all former tenants. In the end Muttinen decides to give the part of the estate cultivated by the Käkriäinens to them, but the reader already knows that this act will neither help them nor reconcile them with Muttinen. Beneath the boisterous humor and sunny descriptions of a country summer, the book is a narrative of human failure. All tasks the Käkriäinens undertake fail. Their last decision is to build a permanent still and make liquor on a large scale; besides its illegality, this activity brings them in contact with a former criminal who says he will help them but will obviously use them for his own profit. The still is being built in a hideout, an underground cave, and in the last scene the men crawl in, symbolically renouncing all rational adult activities.

Lehtonen again described the characters of *Putkinotko* in the collection of short stories *Korpi ja puutarha* ('The Garden and the Wilderness,' 1923). *Putkinotko* was published after the Civil War although its action takes place before the conflict, so that forebodings of coming catastrophe in it are not genuine from the author's viewpoint. *Korpi ja puutarha*, however, is concerned with the period after the war. By then Lehtonen had sold the estate he described as Putkinotko and found the one he would call Lintukoto; as a farewell to the former, he tells in one of the stories that the Käkriäinen family is dispersed in the war and the father killed like a trapped animal in the forests. The stories, nevertheless, are mainly a search for peace and harmony, as is *Onnen poika* ('The Happy Mortal,' 1925), in which the author returns to childhood memories, the happy, sunny time protected by kind foster parents. The story contains all the standard features of such narratives, e.g., the slightly fantastic story teller, old Pikkari, a cabinetmaker. *Lintukoto* (1929) is in the same vein; it is a description of the small island where he had his summer house, with observations from nature, plants, and animals mixed with considerations of life and man and quotations from French writers. Near 1920 Lehtonen had come in contact with the November Group, founded by radical young painters including Sallinen and Ruokokoski; his criticism of society was in line with their ideas, and his visual way of representation helped him to understand their way of working. Viljo Kojo, a member of the group who became better known as a writer, illustrated an edition of

Lintukoto. Lehtonen is said to have given inspiration to and been inspired by the group.[436]

In 1927 he wrote *Rai Jakkerintytär* ('Rai, Daughter of Jakker'), a book in which his dog, Rai Jakkerintytär, has many human characteristics and partially represents the author. He expresses his misanthropy, caused by World War I and the Civil War, but attempts to escape from this negative attitude through self-criticism. He says that, when one hates strongly enough, one eventually becomes so tired of everything that he cannot even hate anymore and feels his own worthlessness. The author hopes to find salvation in the spirit of humility, modesty, and poverty of St. Franciscus, among the "quiet, small, unseen" people,[437] but in the twenties he also wrote books in which his pessimism and misanthropy are unmitigated by moral or philosophical considerations. The first of them is titled *Rakastunut rampa eli Sakris Kukkelman, köyhä polseviikki* ('The Love of a Cripple or Sakris Kukkelman, a Poor Bolshevik,' 1922; Sakris Kukkelman is a slightly comical Swedish name, and *polseviikki* is a popular Finnish pronunciation of Bolshevik). The book is not funny; it is humorous in a grotesque way, with caricatural characters and situations expressing pain, suffering, and humiliation. The result is an impression of complete despair, as though the author were forcing himself to laugh in order not to collapse completely. The main character is a cripple, a man of dwarfish stature who can do some work and take care of himself, but the author does not describe him with sympathy or even dispassionate objectivity; he makes fun of the wretch. The fact that he is hunchbacked and so short that at times he must crawl like an animal is treated with amusement, as are his mental oddities: he is vain of his appearance and long hair, which should give him Samson-like strength and success with women; he reads and admires Nietzsche, but he professes to be a communist and dreams of a future Marxist paradise on earth. The setting is analogous to the character—crippled. Lehtonen had lived in a suburb of Helsinki called Huopalahti, which he named Krokelby in his books; it is a half-destroyed countryside or a half-built city with the worst features of both. From this environment, Kukkelman's romantic dreams, and his admiration for Nietzsche, it is not difficult to surmise that he is another of the caricatures Lehtonen drew of himself,[438] a projection of his tormented mind. Nevertheless the book is one of Lehtonen's more carefully written works. The sentences are short and direct, and the narration is not fragmented by a maze of details. Professor Sarajas speaks of the expressive quality of the landscapes,[439] also found in the paintings of Sallinen and Ruokokoski. We find the novel expressionistic in conception and in its mixture of the grotesque and the horrible. Expressionism need not be grotesque and horrible, of course, but the German expressionists especially had a predilection for such subjects. The book's climax is worthy of the rest: after two prostitutes swindle Kukkelman out of his small savings, he hangs himself in a shed, and some children, finding the body swinging on the rope, play with it, pushing it back and forth and singing to it.

At the same time that he published *Korpi ja puutarha* and *Onnen poika*, Lehtonen wrote a great novel in two parts, *Sorron lapset* ('The Oppressed,' 1923) and *Punainen mies* ('The Red Man,' 1925), which describes the atmosphere of corruption that prevailed in the country before the Civil War.[440] As we mentioned, numerous profiteers and swindlers, satirized by many writers, appeared during World War I.[441] In addition Lehtonen attacks the social and political antagonisms tearing the country, but the book is not a political or social pamphlet, for he neither analyzes the causes nor suggests a solution; he simply describes the situation with contempt. The main part of the novel is a love story in which there is little happiness. The lovers are exceptional, even morbid characters, the man contemplative and passive, torn from his quiet life by passion, the woman, another man's wife, tortured by her feeling of guilt, trying to find comfort in mysticism and yearning for death. The surroundings of Helsinki, which symbolized the negative to Lehtonen (they reappear in *Henkien taistelu*), and a small town on the coast (not Savonlinna) form the background.

In 1927, in addition to *Rai Jakkerintytär*, Lehtonen published *Sirkus ja pyhimys* ('The Circus and the Saint'), a novel in some ways not unlike his early, romantic stories. Characters from the circus world appear in *Villi, Onnen poika*, and briefly in *Putkinotko*, but here the entire narrative is set among them. Wandering jugglers, clowns, and circus artists have long been favorite characters among romantic writers, but Toulouse-Lautrec, Picasso, Rouault, expressionists, Ingmar Bergman, and Federico Fellini have also used them. The plot is simple: in a small town a young man of good family runs away with a circus because he falls in love with one of the artists, but returns, disillusioned. He comes back not because the woman is coarse or interested in his money, but because she is devoted to her art to the extent that she cannot experience truly human feelings. The grotesque and horrible reappears in the description of the dwarf, Señor Muñeco, who is torn to pieces in view of the audience when he improvises a number with performing cats, as large as tigers in proportion to him.

Lehtonen's last novel, *Henkien taistelu* ('The Struggle of the Spiritual Powers,' 1933), is another criticism of his time's Finland. It is a series of loosely connected pictures from everyday life; only the background story is exceptional. God and the Devil discuss whether or not a completely good, pious man can be forced to lose faith, and the Devil sets out for the earth to prove that he can. In the Prologue he describes his plans:

> I intend to show him what people, not without a kind of pride, call life, as
> if in a film visited by the scissors of the censure, only with the difference
> that I shall cut out the *harmless* parts, the quiet, nice people, and shall

> direct a blinding light from the projector on the corrupt sides of the
> average citizens and even the exemplary ones. I shall represent it all,
> intentionally, as largely disconnected episodes; the result, I hope, will be
> confused and imprecise, like the time in which the world is now living.[442]

It is remarkable that Lehtonen knew so much about the technique of
filmmaking; moreover, the result he describes is close to contemporary
literature and the theater of the absurd. As a man of his generation, Lehtonen
could not live with the idea that the world was absurd; only since World War
II have writers been able to accept or bear this thought.

Before the action begins, the Devil has himself corked in a bottle like
another djinn with "Kill me quick" written on the label. An innocent Finn
opens it in Paris (where Lehtonen had experienced deep depression), and an
innocent-looking but limping Finn, le diable boiteux, appears to take the
victim to various places in Finland where the corruption of the time and
loathsome qualities of man are revealed. Finally the good man does lose his
faith, but he does not begin to live as sinners do. Despairing of God and the
world, he seeks death, which he finds in an undignified manner when a tramp
kills him almost without reason. After the story begins, however, it is not
supernatural or even especially horrible. The general stupidity, narrow-
mindedness, selfishness, greed, and complacency of a part of mankind are
shown. Lehtonen's satire is more effective when it is less conspicious; a
middle-class party with small talk and gossip is a devastating picture of a type
of middle-class mentality.

When Lehtonen wrote this book, the political, economic, and social
situation in Finland was far from satisfactory. The depression was producing
unemployment, misery, and unrest everywhere; communism, seen as the only
remedy or a threat to society, was polarizing people throughout Europe. In
Finland, where the wounds of the Civil War were not yet healed—the losers
were bitter, and the winners felt that victory had slipped through their
hands—a fascist, right-wing movement appeared, threatening all it branded
communists, i.e., a few members of the Communist party, socialists, trade
unionists, and individuals with liberal views. In literature, theater, and art, an
unofficial but very effective censure acted upon all productions not conforming
to the most narrow-mindedly conservative, religious, and moral standards; to
a lesser extent this censure existed later. Initially the authorities viewed with
alarming leniency the right-wing extremists' activities because of their
allegedly patriotic aims, and the Communist party was officially outlawed.
Later, however, an armed rebellion organized by the rightists failed to find
support among the people, and the government banned the movement behind
it with the law used against the Communist party, for its terms were that all
groups conspiring to overthrow the legal order of the country by force were
illegal. The group reorganized as a political party, but never won wide support

among the electorate; the Social-Democrats, who consistently had the largest number of representatives in Parliament, obtained Cabinet seats after Lehtonen's death.

Since the violence began in 1929, Lehtonen had ample time to observe it before he published his book. It is not merely a study in individual morals and behavioral patterns, for, although not directly political, it contains criticism of Hitler and fascist-leaning politicians in Finland. In it the author had reached the depths of his experience; because he could find no consolation in religion and the world seemed hopelessly corrupt, he left it. In 1915 Eino Leino had compared him to Strindberg,[443] but Lehtonen did not criticize society as violently as the Swedish author did. He drew inferences from his observations, but did not seek refuge in mysticism; instead, he took the ultimate action in accordance with his conclusions. His art is not in the mode appreciated today, and his restlessness sometimes interfered with the form of his works, but we find in them a breadth of scope and deep insight into the problems of the individual and society which make them some of the most interesting in Finnish literature.

Heikki Toppila (1885-1963) was only four years younger than Lehtonen, but he did not publish until 1920. He was born in Paavola, not far from Oulu. Between 1908 and 1924 he was an elementary school teacher mainly in Oulu, did some newspaper work and collected folklore. He did not often leave his home region and was not a member of literary circles except in the mid-1920s, when he belonged to the May Group.[444] He displayed no interest in contemporary problems, but slowly, painstakingly wrote his works, which were published in Helsinki, noticed, and appreciated. Although the last ones show marked decline in his creative power so that he was somewhat forgotten at the time of his death, the best are remarkable, if not unique. They exhibit the influence of folklore; in fact, most comprise many superstitious beliefs, folktales, and ghost stories. His aim, however, was not merely to rewrite and edit folklore for the general public; his novels and stories are about real people from his home region to whom ghosts, the devil, and other supernatural apparitions were part of everyday life, experienced and spoken of naturally, though with terror. He did not write to provide entertainment for horror story lovers; the supernatural and the terrifying are not the essential elements, for the works deal with the lives and problems of individuals who sometimes come in contact with apparitions. Toppila has nothing of the artistry of Poe or other writers of "Gothick" tales, for his works are not set in wild, beautiful, faraway places, but are about normal country people who live and love, marry and have children (or just have children), and quarrel about wills, real estate rights, and stolen cows. Toppila's folklore was of a contemporary nature, tales about something that happened to the narrator or another character; a farmer's wife on her way to feed the pigs meets in the yard the spirits of the dead coming from the cemetery on their way to her neighbor's house.[445] Toppila followed the Finnish tradition of building the supernatural with materials from the ordinary, as Kivi did. Toppila's native region, northern Ostrobotnia, is a low marshy area with winding rivers and forests in which trees fall and rot without reaching full growth. There are no hills or lakes, and the inhabitants experience a long, dark fall and winter. They react against this atmosphere of melancholy, gloom, and terror with drinking or religious experiences expressed in the revivalist movement; Sallinen recreated this atmosphere in some of his famous paintings, e.g., *Hihhulit* ('The Revivalists')[446] and *Jytkyt* ('The Country Dance').

Toppila's art contains not only horror and violence, but also humor. In the story *Valkolan vaarin jouluviinat* ('Old Valkola's Christmas Liquor,' 1923), Valkola, who cannot accept prohibition, makes some liquor for Christmas at home, as in the old days, but apparently dies before he can enjoy it. However, two travelers who come to the house that day are served a few drinks. Pitying the dead, they pour some liquor down his throat, both reviving him and terrifying the unaware household.

Toppila also wrote some rather sentimental stories, for example, *Sokea-Sanna* ('Blind Sanna') and *Ruoti-Reeta* ('Charity Reeta') from his first collection *Helvetin koira* ('The Hound of Hell,' 1920). Both are descriptions of the lives of poor old women unveiled by their memories and in conversation. The technique of moving back and forth in time during the narration and slowly building a portrait from odd remarks and apparently disconnected details is peculiar to Toppila, and he used it with great skill. Both stories, like still others, not only describe humble people who have suffered but remained good and kept their faith, but also reveal without embellishment their sins and errors, which consist of illicit love and illegitimate children, as in other stories. An additional motif, also found in Finnish folklore, is that of the pregnant girl who hides her condition, secretly gives birth, kills the child, and hides the body, but is later tortured by her conscience or the ghost of the innocent.[447] The following excerpt from *Peräpirilän Annakaisa* (in *Helvetin koira*) is an example of Toppila's slow, hesitating style and method of composing horror stories in which blood, death, and detailed dismemberment play an important part. The story begins with a description of the vision of a sinner, who sees her future punishment in hell; the vision is explained as a bad dream, although the dream motif is not typical of Toppila, who usually presents the supernatural as real and tangible.

> ... On that same dancing floor, on a beautiful Midsummer Night Eve, she had carried on with the accordion player, and later, when the night was drawing closer, she had fallen into the sin which she still saw her sinful shadow committing. When the accordion player disappeared, she had to carry alone that seed of sin, which she somehow managed to hide from people, but which she had to suppress at the end with violent means in

order not to be discovered. . . . And it was not discovered. She was still walking around as a maiden, although on a dark autumn night she had put her child on the railroad tracks. . . . While she was thinking about this, she came to a dark and slippery gully, where she stumbled at every step on slimy stones. While she was fumbling around a rock that was higher than the others, she felt in her hand something wet, from which a warm liquid was running. While she was wondering what it could be, her eyes slowly grew accustomed to the darkness, and she saw that she was holding in her hand the white leg of a child, still warm, from which blood was flowing freely. She looked at it, terrified, and, when she understood how that leg had come there, she tried fearfully to find a place to put it down, but stopped at the same moment, for the well-known cries of a child pierced her ears, coming, it seemed, from the bottom of the cave. She hurried toward the voice, fumbling around the wet stones upon which she was stumbling at every moment, and arrived finally, wet and with bloody knees, holding in her hand the leg of the child which had just broken off and was still warm, at the bottom of the cave where she found the child, without its leg, crying on the bloody railway tracks. Annakaisa tried to comfort her crying child and at the same time to put the leg back, but this seemed difficult to do. . . .

Just then she heard the roar of a train which was coming nearer and nearer every moment.

Toppila's novel *Auringon nousun maahan* ('To the Land of the Rising Sun,' 1926) employs the technique of *Sokea-Sanna* and *Ruoti-Reeta*; the images of two main characters develop slowly through the speech and thoughts of a group of people on a farm. One of them, Vesi-Maija, is present, but her beloved, Mikko, is hardly seen although he is equally important to the story. Dark, terrifying elements appear in the form of old tales related by those present, but the atmosphere of the book is dreamy and melancholy, somewhat sentimental. Two lovers who could never be joined in life will meet after death in the "land of the rising sun," as Vesi-Maija, an old woman at the time of the narration, believes. Her belief is confirmed by a vision when Mikko dies. In keeping with Toppila's style, the vision is not poetic and beautiful, but follows the popular tradition in which the spirits of the deceased carry away the dying. In this excerpt Totan Ulla is the ghost of a woman said to appear in a house to those who are going to die soon:

Maija goes to the upper part of the storehouse. . . . There, on the second floor, is Totan Ulla, dressed in a light blouse and skirt, her face white like snow, her chin pointed, her nose long, and only black holes in the place of her eyes. . . . From the upper floor, where Totan Ulla was moving a while ago, strange people appear. They come one after the other, Totan Ulla first and then all the others, one old woman, for example, carrying her head on the palm of her hand. . . . Who are these people again? asks Vesi-Maija herself. There they are, this strange, whitish crowd, on the floor of the storehouse, close to Mikko's feet. . . . They have probably come to greet Mikko, to wish him good luck in the land of the rising sun, where they are also living, far away from here. And Maija was not at all afraid of them, it was almost nice to see the departed now, when they were about to leave with Mikko. That's where you are coming from? said Maija, curtseying to the crowd, and the whitish crowd answered, humming strangely:

> There we come from, therefrom, therefrom,
> By the woods and by the church.

... Maija looked at the crow of the departed, and they stared at her with their hollow eyes.... Finally she managed to stammer: Still another time, a second time? A deep song was heard as if from under the ground:

> Still another, still with you
> Wait, wait, with you.

There they were all standing together, the old departed of the Tukala family, looking at Maija with their hollow eyes.... Hullavee! Hullavee! screeched the dead together. Maija shall have him, Vesi-Maija shall have her darling Mikko ... and the whole crowd took off through the door with a noise like birds flying in the air, so that Maija's heart shrank together. Whistling like the wind, the whitish crowd went away toward the church.[448]

Although Toppila's stories do not take place in the past—several, in fact, have details indicating that they deal with the World War I period or an even later one—most of his characters look toward the past, a time when the spirits of the dead, ghosts, trolls, and devils walked among people. Toppila was aware of the contrast, and at times a rational attitude toward life dominates in his work. Even in the story *Helvetin koira* the beast which terrifies the women at a revivalist meeting is only a big dog. In *Veden emännän lehmä* ('The Water Lady's Cow' in *Valkolan vaarin jouluviinat*), two poor people perform magic for the possession of a mysterious animal which proves to be only a neighbor's cow of a new, foreign breed, which had strayed from the herd. In *Auringon nousun maahan,* a story about a troll who promised to act as the godfather of a child and gave him three shovelfuls of gold coins is only an old tale told for centuries in the family. As an educated man and schoolteacher, Toppila had, in a sense, a duty to spread enlightenment and fight superstition, but he usually kept his work apart from his literary activities. His books have no moralizing or instructive tendency and remain remarkably on the level of the characters and free from conspicuous artistry. Literary influence in his works shows only indirectly. In the story *Kuoleman Siiveri* ('Death Siiveri,' 1928)[449] the scene in which one man kills another, and then sees his victim and himself as one being with four arms and four legs moving on each side of the body might have come from the episode of Cianfa in Canto XV of the *Inferno*, which Eino Leino finished translating in 1914; in the same narrative the great battlefield on which bodies are reduced to bloody pulp might have been suggested by descriptions from the trenches of World War I. In *Auringon nousun maahan* a comparison is implied between people who enjoy stories of fighting and killing and Romans who watched gladiator fights in an arena—they are "like those who watched the war games of olden times, who followed with harsh expressions on their faces the desperate fights of men sentenced to death against bloodthirsty beasts." The words *Roman, gladiator,* and *arena* are not used.

Kuoleman Siiveri is Toppila's best story and highest artistic achievement. The first line explains the contents: "On the borderland of life and death, many people are wandering aimlessly about, sick people, destroyed by illnesses, moving like ugly, repulsive carcasses. The sting of death has set its mark on their stinking corpses, although the sinful soul is still yearning toward the sunny meadows of life." A description of a purgatory follows, a seemingly endless repetition of the sinful acts committed by Siiveri, a man nicknamed Death Siiveri for his crimes and the fact that he was thrice sentenced to death and pardoned.[450] The crimes are killing, fighting, robbing, and leaving a girl with an illegitimate child; in only one does Toppila indulge his taste for the horrible. Some cows and a horse find a vat of fermenting wort, drink it eagerly, then fall as if dead; although flayed, they rise and walk again. It is not clear whether these events are to be considered bad dreams, the delirious visions of a man about to die, or a purgatory unknown in protestant theology but used in folklore.[451] In a novel Toppila's style can become tiring—*Auringon nousun maahan* is fortunately short—but in a short story it creates an obsessive sensation of horror with merciless repetition of slightly varied motifs of physical torture. The exacting realism in their description reminds us of Dante,[452] and both writers combined normal, orderly private lives with nightmarish excesses of imagination in their works. In the collection *Kuoleman Siiveri,* a cycle of stories about a place where criminals were publicly flogged (the stories are from the past)[453] gave Toppila an opportunity for a detailed description of the effects of the punishment and the reactions of the onlookers, whose fragmented conversations slowly reveal the criminals' personalities and deeds.

In the thirties Toppila wrote two great novels, *Päästä meitä pahasta* ('Deliver Us from Evil,' 1931) and *Tulisilla vaunuilla* ('On a Chariot of Fire,' 1935), followed by a third, *Siernaporin kuningas* ('The King of Siernapori,' 1937). In them an evolution predictable from his earlier works takes place. In some of his earlier stories the supernatural is really due to natural causes or dreams. He had humor and sentiment; he led an apparently quiet life, was well balanced and able to convert the darker aspects of his mind to literature so that they did not interfere with his work or personal life. This therapy succeeded so well that eventually no resource of terrors was left in his soul, and the artist in him was dead. He published a few more novels, but they are almost without interest.

Päästä meitä pahasta and *Tulisilla vaunuilla* picture a period of transition in Finland, the period between 1870 and 1920, when there, as everywhere, the threshold between old and new times was crossed. Motor cars and airplanes in Toppila's books very effectively destroyed the world he had until then described. Each novel is over six hundred pages long—we have mentioned that his style was best in shorter works. *Päästä meitä pahasta* is still an impressive work relating the life of Lusikka-Lassi, a drunkard who has lost his farm and fortune but pulls himself together and builds a new home near the marsh of Muurrepää. The first part, with descriptions of his delirious visions due to drink and illness, written in Toppila's peculiar manner, has all the suggestive force of his earlier stories. In visions of the great marsh as the symbol of all evil, the evil appears in the form of female demons inhabiting the marsh, obscenely ugly, fat old women who spawn illnesses to fly around the world and torture people. In the second half, however, Lusikka-Lassi, as an honest, hard-working farmer, is much less interesting.

Tulisilla vaunuilla relates the life of Lassi's son, Kykyrä-Joope, first a successful farmer, but in his old age a harmless, dim-witted dreamer whose great desire is to build an airplane; as a whole, the book is disappointing. Although Toppila was masterful in describing people oppressed by supernatural terrors or neuroses, he was unable to treat successfully other attitudes or social problems, and his style, perfect for the obsessive atmosphere of nightmares and visions, was meaningless with brighter subjects, where repetition of motifs had no function.

Siernaporin kuningas, somewhat better and shorter, is a nice fairytale for adults. A story told about the king of Siernapori is parallel to the life of the main character, a young man who leaves his native region and the girl he loves, has many adventures at sea and in faraway lands, but eventually returns home. Occasionally the tale and the novel's reality overlap when fantastic elements, such as a talking cow, appear. The two lovers meet again and live happily ever after. The author's purpose was obviously to retell an old story in a modern setting, and he was almost successful, although the book lacks the force of his great works. His last novels *Onnen kultamoukari* ('The Golden Sledgehammer of Luck,' 1941), *Ja niin tuli kevät taas* ('And Spring Was There Again,' 1945), and *Nuoruuden kujanjuoksu* ('The Trials of Youth,' 1949) are similar. The golden sledgehammer, a magic object bringing luck to its owner, appears in an old tale, then materializes in the form of a modern factory bringing wealth to the region surrounding it, but the symbolism is too superficial to be convincing.[454] *Ja niin tuli kevät taas* is a tale of adventures, obstacles to be overcome, and difficulties to be fought. *Nuoruuden kujanjuoksu* describes a journey to Lapland undertaken by a few young men who desire the sort of adventures their fathers once had there; it is the best of his late novels and has some of the bright dreaminess of *Auringon nousun maahan*. After this work Toppila did not publish for almost fifteen years, until his death. He was almost unknown to the younger generations, undeservedly, for his early works are masterpieces of their kind and perhaps the only works of that nature in the world.

LITERATURE IN FINNISH BETWEEN THE TWO WORLD WARS

The period between 1910 and 1940, from Kianto to Sillanpää, has been called the period of great descriptions of popular life in Finnish literature. Lehtonen, Toppila, Kilpi, Sillanpää, Pekkanen, and Haanpää often represented people from the social class of their origin, i.e., farmers, tenants, agricultural laborers, lumberjacks, and, for Pekkanen, industrial workers. However, many of them also wrote about the middle class, and even when their characters were "common" people, they concentrated on individuals rather than class. A common fallacy among the few abroad interested in Finnish literature is that it describes the life and work of the proletariat (rural and urban). It is a less incorrect assumption than the one that all Finnish literature is related to the *Kalevala*, for a large part of the literature does describe members of the proletariat, but it describes their personal problems. This phenomenon seems largely due to the peculiar structure of Finnish society, in which it is relatively easy for a person of modest origin to attain high position in every field. Biographical data are not emphasized in Finland because rising through the classes is not unusual. A consequence of the easy access to the middle classes is a general acceptance of middle-class values, including respect for education. Kivi and Lehtonen took the national examination required for entering the university as though it were a writing license. The authors we have mentioned who have treated apparently similar subjects are so different from each other because the belief that literature is about individuals and their problems is also of middle-class origin, as Pekkanen observed. Once the artist has accepted this idea, he describes individual characters from his own point of view, not a class point of view.

Volter Adalbert Kilpi (1874-1939) was born into the lower middle class. Like Runeberg's and Snellman's fathers, his father was a captain of the merchant fleet,[455] and his ancestors were all connected with the sea as captains, shipowners, or pilots in the district of Kustavi, on the west coast of Finland, north of Turku. The original family name was Ericsson, and the one of Kilpi's three brothers who followed family tradition by becoming a captain kept it. The two other brothers who used the name Kilpi became an actor in the Finnish National Theater and a professor of chemistry at the University of Helsinki. Volter took his M.A. in 1900 and worked for the rest of his life as a librarian, eventually as the head of the library of the Finnish university at Turku, opened in 1922. He knew German, English, French and some Italian, and translated several books, mainly from German, which he knew best, e.g., Goethe's *Die Leiden des jungen Werthers* and Emerson's *Representative Men*, which he titled *Ihmiskunnan edustajia* (lit. 'Representatives of Mankind'). He read great authors of the past and modernists. At the beginning of the century he was considered one of the foremost representatives of Nietzsche's thought in Finland; Schopenhauer, however, seems to have made a greater impression upon him.[456] His youthful works are deeply pessimistic; he distinguished between "exterior" and "interior" life and declared that, once art had revealed to man the full richness of interior life, he was indifferent to the demands and duties of the exterior world.[457] For him art was an essential part of interior life, an intricate whole consisting of experiences and sensations which released and activated the highest feelings in man.[458] The awakening from this ecstasy was bitter; *Antinous* (1903) is essentially a series of impressions and thoughts experienced by the main character, who states that the best way out of this painful oscillation is to commit suicide at one of the most rapturous moments, as did the historical Antinous, of whose life there is little in the book; his relationship to Emperor Hadrianus, for example, is not alluded to.

Kilpi's first work, *Bathseba* (1900), subtitled *David's Conversations with Himself*, expresses through King David a philosophy of the Nietzschean superman, the idea that feelings, especially love, are higher than all else and that an attempt to dictate laws to them is presumptuous, for it would be dictating laws to Nature itself—"In the bosom of Nature, there is great laughter when it hears such foolish orders." Kilpi had chosen this Biblical story because he was in love with another man's wife, although the book was the only result of his feelings. His David is more a dreamer than a man of action: he thinks of forceful deeds by which he could prove his superiority, but he cannot carry them out. The last chapter, "Beelzebub's Dream," is a meditation on the inability of humans to communicate with each other. For Kilpi this problem was very real, not merely philosophical or metaphysical, for he was hard of hearing even in his youth and his condition grew worse as he aged until he was almost totally deaf. His first books were written in a very peculiar style which became absolutely unique in the last ones. This development has been credited to his ailment;[459] his language is called a "deaf's language," just as Beethoven's last compositions are called a "deaf's music"—the assertions seem equally irrelevant.

The third book of his youth was *Parsifal* (1902). He maintained an interest in German art and had probably read Wolfram von Eschenbach's medieval poem, but gave it a new meaning. Again the aesthetic was more important to him than the ethic. His Parsifal is a knight who wins fame through his courage and deeds, but he is first found worthy of adding glory and shine to the Holy Grail when he has been touched by love, a pure love for his wife Konviramur. Kilpi represents the Grail as a chalice,[460] the symbol of Beauty; the hero and his consort, contemplating it in ecstasy, are the soul of the world, throughout which this ecstasy is diffused. In relation to Wagner's opera, Kilpi said that his work was a "musical fantasy," a position supported by Professor Suomi, but Professor Koskimies sees the book as a visual rather than auditory creation and points out that, apart from his hearing problem, Kilpi had little understanding for music although he often expressed admiration for it. Koskimies believes that many of Kilpi's images are inspired by the English Pre-Raphaelite painters; even when Kilpi describes musical impressions, visual elements tend to dominate,[461] e.g., "Parsifal feels in his soul the veiled kneeling of the virgins around him," "the music falls like gold over the shining waters," "the pillars murmur up." Kilpi's style reaches full development in *Parsifal*, and he uses it in subsequent works, even those on other subjects. It is partially made up of simile, metaphor, and other common figures of speech, for example, the "veiled kneeling of the virgins,"[462] but Kilpi goes further, as evidenced by the shape of the pillars, first seen as a movement which is then transformed to a sound. Another stylistic peculiarity in all his works is the use of unusual compound words, most self-coined, such as *kaipaussilmä* 'longing-eyed' and *sinikirkkoinen* 'blue-churched,' according to common models, e.g., *sinisilmäinen* 'blue-eyed.' In the text he speaks of a maiden with "sea-moist" eyes and "sea-green hair"; the second, ordinary adjective was obviously used as the model for the first.[463] Kilpi might not have used this construction if it were possible to convey the same idea elegantly and briefly in Finnish, as it is in English by use of *with*. Finnish poets have found another way around this difficulty, but linguists and grammarians consider it incorrect.[464] *Suomen Kirjallisuus*, in fact, calls these three books "prose poems."[465]

At the beginning of the century, Kilpi also wrote essays in which he discussed art and literature. They appeared in 1902 in one volume, *Ihmisestä ja elämästä* ('On Man and Life'). The title is as overambitious as it seems; Kilpi did not attempt a detailed analysis of his subjects, but preached his aestheticism and prophesied monotonously and solemnly about Life and the Spirit of Man. Before all, Great Art was "wondrous," "powerful," or "everlasting." Perhaps best among the essays, *Katsomuksen ihanuudesta* ('On the Beauty of Contemplation') describes the relation of man to nature in a spirit typical of the neoromanticism prevailing in that period of Finnish literature. Koskimies detects its influence in several writers of the time: Eino Leino, Larin-Kyösti, Maila Talvio, Linnankoski, and especially Lehtonen.[466] Another, *Taiteesta ja siveydestä* ('On Art and Morals'), denies relationship between art and morals, then claims that art is moral in itself, that it awakens a feeling of higher morals in man, and that morals are only the sensations produced in man by art. Kilpi wrote on all topics with great veneration; he had none of Wilde's frivolous skepticism or Nietzsche's aggressive amoralism. In this respect he is more like the nineteenth-century English aestheticians.

His essay *Nykyaikaisista taidepyrinnöistä* ('Contemporary Trends in Art,' 1905) summarizes his writings thus far, giving another general picture of world literature and art at that moment. He did know contemporary painting well, and, at a time when even the earlier impressionists were scarcely mentioned in Finland and painters did not show their influence, he spoke of not only Manet, but also van Gogh, Gauguin, and still later artists. Although he showed impressive scholarship, he again overreached himself. Following the contemporary idea that a new romanticism was modifying the world, he called the spirit of this romanticism Germanic—or Teutonic—in essence, using *Germanic* in a broad sense. Among the early romanticists he placed emphasis on Goethe, but also discussed Byron, Shelley, Keats, Musset, Hugo, and Leopardi, and analyzed the contemporaries Ibsen, Hamsun, Verlaine, Maeterlinck, Strindberg, Nietzsche, and d'Annunzio, for example. His theories on art are vague; in attempting to define the Germanic spirit, he wrote: "Wherever the Germanic spirit has undertaken to extract beauty out of reality, it has always, so to say, musicalized it, given it through its touch a quality which will produce deep inner vibrations in the soul."[467]

Between 1905 and 1933 Kilpi wrote nothing except two social and political pamphlets, *Kansallista itsetutkistelua* ('A National Self-Examination,' 1917) and *Tulevaisuuden edessä* ('Facing the Future,' 1918), and a scholarly work on early editions of books in Finnish (1924). The pamphlets attracted attention but are unimportant; in both he asks for the strictest standards of quality for all works in art and literature and attacks the facility of authors and laxity of critics. He touches on almost all questions of interest to the public at the time, criticizes the profiteers who made fortunes dishonestly during the war and attempts to portray the ideal businessman, analyzes the causes of the Civil War, and sketches a conservative political future for his country—he wanted a monarchy, a bicameral parliament,[468] and an alliance with Germany. When, after nine years of work, *Alastalon salissa* appeared in 1933, it seemed a complete reversal of all he had written before, but it is actually a further development of his earlier works. Artistic and aesthetic theories are not discussed, the characters are not romantic or mythical figures from faraway lands and times, and the practical action is described in Finnish surroundings in the second half of the nineteenth century, but the language is unchanged. This and the subsequent books can properly be called linguistic works of art, for their language makes them—if it seems too presumptuous to say that through language he builds a world of his own, we might say that through his use of language Kilpi reveals his view of the world.

His writing had become both simpler and more complex. In *Alastalon salissa* and later novels he no longer describes characters with highly refined feelings or elaborate philosophical or aesthetic theories, but he complicates his style by recording not only every word and action but also every thought and feeling of his characters with the same accuracy and detail that marks the earlier works. There is little action. His humor is apparent in the later works, in accordance with their contents. He often gave his chapters lengthy titles; the sixth chapter of *Alastalon salissa* is headed: "A chapter which may conveniently be left unread, as nothing more happens in it than in the others." Kilpi insisted that his style was natural to him, that he never tried to be odd or original, although he admitted that he made "superhuman efforts" when writing in order to achieve the best possible results, even if his readers and critics would have been satisfied with less.[469] In calling his language unaffected, he meant that it expressed accurately what he had to say. If his vision of the world were complex—he called it "plastic"—its linguistic representation had to be complex. Nevertheless he believed that his language was less the result of planned composition than the product of an unconscious process in which he acted as medium.

Alastalon salissa begins with an author's preface he called a "prechapter" (*esiluku*); it is the text of an address read in 1933 at the one hundred fiftieth anniversary of the building of the church at Kustavi, his home parish. In highly emotional style it evokes the past generations of the region: "Days of the past, days of the past brightened by the gold of memories, people of the past, venerated people whom we long to see at the height of your past, let the fleeting memory of a painful and rapturous moment appear to my loving eyes!" It indicates that in the novel Kilpi intends to resuscitate the past and its people, to describe the "good old days." Unlike Kianto, Lehtonen, and Sillanpää, Kilpi represents honest, hard-working, successful characters living when life was relatively prosperous in western Finland, near 1860. *Alastalon salissa* can be dated by its references to the Crimean War.

The book has some similarities to *Seven Brothers*. Both are in a language much closer to the west Finnish dialects than the standard literary form; the language is appropriate since both books are set in the western part of the country, but it is also due to the authors' familiarity with the Bible, which was more western than normal Finnish.[470] Both books seem to be didactic stories about honesty and hard work, but are really much deeper. Kilpi's and Kivi's books are descriptions of a golden age, a dreamland of perfect bliss which never existed, as is Lehtonen's *Putkinotko*; Kai Laitinen, a contemporary critic, considers these three novels the best in Finnish.[471] Another trait these authors share is that, despite a few lyrical, dreamy passages, they remain close to reality. In spite of Kilpi's aestheticism and idealism, his descriptions of west Finnish farmers, sailors, captains, and shipowners are frank, and his late style combines florid, elaborate form with earthy vocabulary reproducing the words and thoughts of his characters. The similes Kilpi was so fond of are taken from their lives, especially the sea, and his vocabulary contains oaths and other words avoided in polite conversation to a point uncommon in the prudish Finnish literature of the thirties.[472]

The discussion among the farmers in *Alastalon salissa* results in a signed document by which all agree to contribute their share for the building of a ship. Here Kilpi describes the life of his forefathers. As early as the Middle Ages farmers and fishermen from the coastal regions of Finland sailed to Sweden and Estonia to sell their products, in spite of the protests of the city merchants, who considered it an infringement on their rights and privileges. In the eighteenth century this right was formally granted to the coastal inhabitants, and in the nineteenth it was extended to include the entire Baltic Sea. Eventually all limitations were abolished so that, in the last great age of sailing ships, vessels built by local carpenters from timber grown in the Finnish countryside and manned with local crews went to Lübeck, Hamburg, Hull, London, Antwerp, and even farther. Sea life appealed to both the pragmatist and dreamer in Kilpi, and in this novel he combined both inclinations. He divides the characters into two groups representing opposite qualities: men who dream of new ventures, bigger ships, and longer journeys and are able to realize their dreams, and the cautious, who are convinced by the others to invest at least their money in the common venture.[473] Kilpi describes their weaknesses: one is stingy, another too clever to be careful, another deeply in debt. In general the negative qualities appear in thoughts and form an accompaniment to the energetic, gay conversation.

Some sailors' yarns are related, such as the one about the overbearing customs official who was twice fooled by the country people to whom he considered himself so superior, and one about Vaasa Ville and his ship. The latter is the tale of a man who invested all his money and more in a ship which was believed lost by everyone except the owner, for it disappeared for seven years, but finally returned with a load of coffee and big chests stuffed with gold coins and banknotes in the captain's cabin. The captain, who had been chosen for his stinginess, had starved himself and the crew almost to death, did not maintain the ship, and never wrote the owner about her journeys. Eila Pennanen points out that this half-fantastic tale, in which an episode of fabulous wealth suddenly bestowed upon a poor man is treated in a manner reminiscent of the *Arabian Nights*, is almost a parody of the novel itself.[474] Kilpi does not pretend that his characters are engaged in noble, unselfish activity, but in a realistic business venture in which they hope to profit greatly. By caricature, although good-natured and with an exaggerated happy ending, he draws the reader's attention to the ignoble sides of the undertaking.

Shipbuilding and navigation brought prosperity to many in the coastal areas, and Kilpi dwells with slightly childish pride in descriptions of its outward symbols, which he considered the well-earned results of hard work. His farmers and shipowners drink Jamaica rum and French brandy served in crystal decanters, they smoke Dutch tobacco in elaborately decorated German pipes, have English china and sterling silver on their tables, bring their furniture from Stockholm, and their wives and daughters have Sunday dresses of silk and satin. Alex Matson has found the quiet opulence of Dutch still life paintings in the book.[475] Kilpi's detailed descriptions extend to the objects, always seen in relation to man, as extensions of his body and projections of his mind. The manner in which they were purchased or made also speaks of the owners; a long passage about pipes at the beginning is, in fact, about their owner.

214

Kilpi's later works also have a social character unstressed by critics and literary historians. He gives a full, varied, and complex picture of human relations within a group, from social and economic to individual and emotional. He does not interpret them, but through the characters' actions, thoughts, and words we discover their motives, hopes, fears, ambitions, hidden antagonisms and jealousies, all the mental, social and material factors which bind a group together or tear it apart. We consider this technique one of his art's most original traits.

Near the end of the twenties, Kilpi wrote several short stories, published in 1934 as *Pitäjän pienempiä*. They are about the humble and contain more bitterness and pessimism than the novel. The first story, *Ylistalon tuvassa*, is almost a full-length novel, which Kilpi called "a description parallel to *Alastalon salissa*,"[476] telling in a humorous spirit what simple sailors were doing in a neighboring house while captains and shipowners were discussing important matters at Alastalo. The humor is partially in the narration's praise of laziness, for sailors considered time spent on land as holiday; accordingly, there is even less action than in *Alastalon salissa*. The other stories have little humor and are often about people who, through bad luck and their own fault, have ruined their lives. In *Kaaskerin Lundström* a captain who once ran his ship aground when drunk and must remain home the rest of his life, Lundström from Kaaskeri, goes over again and again in his mind the causes of his ruin; his coffin is ready for him in his room. In *Jäällävaeltaja* ('The Wanderer on the Ice') the journey of a man over the frozen sea symbolizes his life, made empty and bitter by his stubborn refusal to forgive a minor offense of his son and see him again. The motif of *Merimiehen leski* is lonely old age. The widow, who has no children to brighten her days, is comforted only by the imaginary presence of her dead hunband in memories and by religion, which is more a mental struggle against her rebellious spirit which rejects the injustices of the world than a meek acceptance of God's will.

Kilpi's descriptions of his home region culminate in *Kirkolle* ('On the Road to the Church,' 1937). All inhabitants of the small island community appear together, prepared to go on a holy day to a holy place for a holy ceremony. The trip is made in a community boat (called "church boats" in Finland) carrying "three short of one hundred" persons. The gathering of the churchgoers, journey in the boat, and arrival at the church form the action, which takes place in three hours. Again the descriptions of the individuals, their thoughts and feelings, is primary, as is the picture of surrounding nature on a beautiful summer day. Much of the ecstatic contemplation of Kilpi's early works appears in *Kirkolle*. His style is pushed to its limits in expressing every shade of light and color, every sound and movement in nature in order to recreate completely one brief, happy moment. Kilpi is present in the form of the boy Albert (a shortened form of his middle name), who makes the journey with his parents, a loving portrait of Kilpi's mother and father. He identified so completely with this character that Albert gives an oath to Beauty consistent with Kilpi's ideas but out of context. The novel is built on the contrast between the happiness and the ephemerous character of the moment. Albert expresses the only philosophy which can comfort man against the realization that he, like all else, must soon disappear. Although the destination is a Christian church, the philosophy is basically not Christian.[477] The boy thinks of his parents and grandparents, and his mother tells him about future generations. In this manner a feeling of life's continuity is established in opposition to the passing character of the individual.

Suljetuilla porteilla ('At Closed Gates,' 1938) is known as a "book of meditations," although Kilpi called it poetry. Approximately one-fourth is in verse, though verse of a rather clumsy nature. The book is reputed his most forbidding to the point that critics and scholars can scarcely describe its contents. It reverts to the preoccupations of his youth and demonstrates that he should not have grappled with philosophical problems, just as Eino Leino did near the end of his life, and that his creative power, unsurpassed in description of apparent and hidden movements of the mind and human relations within a group, should not have dealt with abstracts. The book has two parts, Beelzebub näkee unta ('Beelzebub is Dreaming,' a reference to his earlier work Bathseba) and Gethsemanen mies ('The Man of Gethsemane'). The first is critical of the contemporary world—it might be understood as a confession of faith by an agnostic; the second seems to stress the impossibility of communication between man and God.[478]

Before the end of his life Kilpi began writing one more book, a continuation of Gulliver's Travels, Gulliverin matka Fantomimian mantereelle ('Gulliver's Journey to the Continent of Fantomimia'), which was published posthumously in 1944, although he did not finish it. He changed his style so much that he marveled at it himself;[479] it is simple and straightforward, like that of any other adventure story. His purpose was to move Swift's hero from the seventeenth to the twentieth century—his ship is caught in a gigantic whirlpool near the pole and, moving faster than the earth's rotation, displaced in time—so that he could criticize the future society, but Kilpi did not live long enough to carry the project very far.

To a great extent it was Kilpi's chosen fate to be read and understood by few. His social and political opinions were conservative, and his aestheticism was not an ideology acceptable to artistic radicals. Still, an influential conservative critic and writer, Eino Railo, attacked him,[480] whereas the most revolutionary writer and critic of Finland, Elmer Diktonius, admired him; Kilpi wrote letters to him to discuss matters of style and contents.[481] Aaro Hellaakoski, a Finnish poet neither politically nor socially radical though he published works opposed to the accepted poetic tradition, analyzed Kilpi's style and works and tried to dissipate the preconceived idea

216

of potential readers that the books would not be enjoyable.[482] Kilpi will probably never gain popularity, but we find Hellaakoski's advice sound. Kilpi's works can be read by all those who appreciate well-written descriptions of people in all aspects of their relations with each other, their thoughts and feelings, work and activities, and surroundings.

Frans Eemil Sillanpää (1888-1964) was awarded in 1939 the only Nobel Prize Finland has received, a prize which places him in a category with such immortal writers as R.F.A. Sully-Prudhomme, Paul Heyse, Ivan Bunin, Grazia Deledda, and Pearl S. Buck, above Tolstoy, Rilke, Proust, Kafka, or Joyce, for example, who were not recipients. He was the Finnish author best known abroad before 1939, principally for two works, *Hurskas kurjuus* (1919; tr. *Meek Heritage* by Alex Matson, New York, 1938) and *Nuorena nukkunut* (1931; tr. *The Maid Silja* by Alex Matson, London-New York, 1933; the untranslatable title is usually replaced in foreign languages with the name of the main character).[483] These books were translated into many languages, and, though we have no way of knowing how often they were actually read, we do know that twelve or more editions of *Nuorena nukkunut* were printed in Swedish.[484] A superficial description of *Hurskas kurjuus* indicates that it is about the Civil War and events which led to it, written in protest against the brutality of the victors.[485] *Nuorena nukkunut* is about a girl who remained pure in the midst of life's brutality and died young of consumption, the romantic illness *par excellence*.

Sillanpää was the son of a small farmer at Hämeenkyrö, west of Tampere. Receiving financial aid from those who had noticed his gifts, he completed secondary school and began university studies. He had first considered becoming a physician, but his literary interests took precedence, especially under the influence of the Järnefelt family, whose importance in literary circles was considerable. Sillanpää's conception of man as a biological being first of all is credited to his studies in science and medicine, but his philosophy, like that of any artist, was not fundamentally scientific. At that time there was great interest in the irrational forces of the mind; Bergson was discussed in Finland and Hamsun widely read. Sillanpää developed a strong liking for Maeterlinck, whom he later translated, although their works seem very different.

One consequence of this period in his life was an inferiority complex, to which he openly alluded, and which almost had fateful results in his life and art. In an article which he frankly titled *On Alcohol—That Too, For Once* (1935), he wrote:

> But, from the very beginning, my life has been an impossible collection of disconnected whims, and now I live by seeing sights—other people pay for being able to see them conveniently under my guidance. Deliver me from a thousand annoyances, as alcohol—treacherously, it is true—is delivering me,

> give me the joy of life which alcohol is so treacherously giving me—and
> I—shall submit, at this age already, and lead a quiet, even abstemious
> life.[486]

The age to which Sillanpää refers is forty-seven, almost the same age at which *Putkinotko's* main character complains that life is slipping from his hands, that old age and death are approaching. Although there are similarities between the early lives of Lehtonen and Sillanpää, Lehtonen believed more firmly in his vocation as a writer; from the beginning of his career he regularly produced poetry and prose. Sillanpää had a difficult struggle before he began literary activities. He returned to his home region, where he lived as a farmer, and married a country girl. The marriage was happy, but she died early, one of the causes of his partial mental collapse in 1940. The urge to write was ever present, and he eventually published again—a few of his short stories had appeared in newspapers and periodicals when he was a student. The critics received favorably his first novel, *Elämä ja aurinko* ('Life and the Sun,' 1916), and, encouraged, he collected his short stories and titled them *Ihmislapsia elämän saatossa* ('The Procession of Life,' 1917; a literal translation is more solemn, speaking of 'Human Beings' or 'The Children of Man [in the Procession of Life]').

Elämä ja aurinko is very different from all works published in Finland before that time and demonstrates the author's considerable literary talent. The attention and praise it received are deserved but have resulted in the inaccurate picture that Sillanpää's art is totally unrelated to all that was written before it.[487] Tuomas Anhava has called Sillanpää a romanticist,[488] and, vague as the term is, it does help us to understand the nature of his art. He believed in mysterious forces that govern man's destiny against his will, saw in every human being something unique, considered the inner man, the soul, more important than the body, and asserted that this soul remains pure no matter how much the body decays. He often animated nature, making it observe and take part in human actions. Earlier romantic writers such as Linnankoski and Aho often used this last device, but it seldom adds meaning to a narrative. When combined with deliberate effort to write in an artistic, refined style, it most often produces unpalatable results, although many readers and even specialists in literature consider the purple patch the highest achievement of a writer. Sillanpää also had a tendency to overuse metaphors and similes; the trait was natural to him, but reinforced by the examples of earlier writers. He often begins with a vague, ill-defined comparison, assimilating a mood or feeling to an object, then describes the object at length, losing contact with the original idea. In *Elämä ja aurinko*, for example, something called the "poetic character of Midsummer night" first "keeps hold of the courtyards" and "softens the lines of everything visible," then "looks at flowers, birches, roofs" (et al.), "sees the low window of a small house," "settles close to it," and "looks into the room." On the same page the rays of the sun arrive near some birches and start a merry little conversation, waiting for the edge of the sun itself to appear on the horizon, all in the worst Linnankoski manner. Later the "community of all human souls" is compared to a huge mountain honeycombed with numberless caves, the individual souls, and the author speaks of a magic bandage one must put over his eyes to enter them, explaining that they are narrow at first but then widen and send ramifications in every direction, and so forth. Not only does the author lose contact with the original idea, but also this idea has no meaningful relation to the rest of the book. In *Hurskas kurjuus* the main character sees at one moment that life is "like some sour and dull stuff, and man is given much more of it than he can handle, so that he is always half-exhausted because of it, always almost suffocated by it."[489]

Another of Sillanpää's peculiarities is apparent in *Elämä ja aurinko*: his habit of intruding in the story, interrupting the narration to tell the reader what it is about, that, although the events described may seem unimportant, they are connected with the deep rhythms of life and the universe (or something similar), without a trace of humor. In *Elämä ja aurinko:*

> Two differentiated parts of nature stood there opposite each other in silence: the eternal, timeless forest, in the countless cells of which primeval life, swelling under the effect of an unseen spring, was streaming; and a child of man, whose blood was also throbbing and repeating unconsciously the beats of thousands of past generations. When man stops like this, the forest and man look each other in the eyes, beyond all past eras during which they have progressed far, far away from each other and their original unity.[490]

In the following the entire narrative is symbolized:

> You may analyze the flower of a veronica down to its last cell, you may sink into its small blue world, you will find veins and vessels there, humors also, and dust. The form and contents of such a small flower are a perfect small blue stanza to be put as a motto to a growing summer day's green story about the sun and life.

In many of his works Sillanpää meditates about time;[491] his premise is that there is no objective measurement of duration, only the biological rhythm of living organisms, the result being that an interval said to be of definite length can be experienced quite differently by various observers or organisms. In *Elämä ja aurinko* a young man pushes an insect in a flower (both the insect and flower reappear in the book):

> But is not it a marvelous thing too, if you watch it from some higher pedestal, that the same lapse of time seems so different, so much longer or

shorter to the caught and to the catcher? It will give you doubts about the justification of the concept of time. Or, should there be as many times as there are experiences of it?

A passage often quoted from the short story *Aamusta iltaan* ('From Morning to Evening' in *Rakas isänmaani* 'My Beloved Country,' 1919) seems to contradict this idea. The writer asserts that there is but one morning on the entire earth; this morning is, however, not an astronomic phenomenon but a being which moves over the world:[492]

> A morning like this is a being which lives its life here in the universe—on the earth, there is but one morning, which is eternally progressing on its surface. . . . When I look through the window at those fences, those lakes, and those houses, I can distinctly see that there is something in them which was not there a moment ago, that they have gained freedom, that they have expanded. . . . The morning of Polynesia is the same morning as this here.

It is not without relevance to note that during Sillanpää's life books were written about the sun that also rises and bells that toll. In the literature of the twenties and thirties there was a distinct taste for the deeply philosophical and majestic, combined with descriptions of very simple, primitive individuals in like surroundings which reflected the primeval truths of life. Robert Sherwood's play *The Petrified Forest* reflects this spirit in its gangsters, small-town people, and wealthy travelers thrown together by chance at a country store, where they bare their souls and a wandering poet underlines the philosophical implications and points out the symbolic importance of the petrified forest nearby. Sillanpää received the Nobel Prize because he reflected the spirit of his time; other representatives of the period, Hemingway, Steinbeck, Faulkner, received the same award later.

Kai Laitinen, a Finnish critic and essayist, has divided Sillanpää's novels into two groups, the first characterized by predominance of plot, action, and characters, the second by equality or predominance of nature and environment.[493] *Hurskas kurjuus, Hiltu ja Ragnar,* and *Nuorena nukkunut* belong to the first classification, *Elämä ja aurinko, Miehen tie,* and *Ihmiset suviyössä* to the second. The first works are tragic or at least melancholy, ending in the main characters' deaths, whereas the latter are happy or less pessimistic. Vilho Suomi includes Sillanpää in the authors whose love for scenery correlates with a happy childhood.[494] That which we have here noted does indicate that there is a general connection between the extent of nature description and the author's emotional state. Like *Putkinotko* and *Kirkolle, Elämä ja aurinko* describes a brief interval—a few summer days—and emphasizes its overwhelming, exuberant beauty, dwelling at length on the elements which contribute to this quality, with an awareness of the ephemeral nature of the happy circumstances.

In this novel a young man, not unlike Sillanpää, who is a student from the country, returns to his home in the summer and has short love affairs with a girl of his own background and a young woman of a superior social position. He is willing to marry the girl, but she rejects him after hearing of the other incident. In fact, Sillanpää's women are often more conscious of their duties toward life, i.e., life in the biological sense as the author understands it, not society. According to him the ruling force of all human life is love or sex, although neither of these terms is accurate as a description of the motivations behind the behavior of his characters, who, though unconsciously, distinctly feel right and wrong. In *Elämä ja aurinko* it is right for the girl to surrender to the young man, for that is why nature made her, but it is also right for her to reject him when she hears of his other, simultaneous affair, which proves him unworthy of her. The importance Sillanpää gives to the reproductive instinct, love or sex depending upon point of view, and his insistence that it has moral values which are unconnected with social rules, has suggested a comparison to D. H. Lawrence; Lauri Viljanen calls him "the Lawrence of Satakunta,"[495] his home province. However, Sillanpää does not aggressively assert the importance of sex, as Lawrence does; his characters submit to the forces of nature rather than act voluntarily, and he is so discreet in describing the act of love that the reader might be uncertain that anything happens. For example, the same young man and girl enter her room, and the door remains closed for two hours; another love scene is described from the point of view of the insect the young man has pushed into the flower. Sillanpää also uses natural phenomena as sexual symbols. In the short story *Nocturno* (in *Erään elämän satoa* 'The Harvest of a Life,' 1948), a girl admits a young man to her room at night, the door closes, and it starts to rain:

> The drops flowed with a rapturous violence over thousands of buds, beat them the whole night, and penetrated their softest tissues, giving them new life and making them swell. ... On their leaves the rays of the sun still found drops of water, like bright tears. They had certainly welled up from the flowers themselves at the moment when the felicity of opening was sending its powerful vibrations through their tender bodies.

The symbolism is clear, but the author is seldom more explicit. His discretion is due to his lifelong faithfulness to his origin. Though he stresses the importance of sex, he believed in ideal love as pure, even in its physical form. He knew that country people do not have chaste expressions for it, so that any reference to love in those surroundings had to take the form of a coarse joke—some can be found in his works, but not many.

Ihmislapsia elämän saatossa, his next work, is interesting only as a human document; many of the stories describe students of modest origin like Sillanpää who can neither find their place in society nor readjust to their original surroundings. These problems obsessed the author almost to the end of his life.

Hurskas kurjuus, published soon after the Civil War, is very different from both earlier works. It concentrates entirely on the life of the main character, contains no lyrical nature descriptions and few philosophical considerations; those few are placed at the beginning and end, to give the reader the meaning of the book and help him draw conclusions from it. Sillanpää was not a religious man and never spoke explicitly about faith or the church, but he believed in the uniqueness of each human being and the existence of an essential part in man which remains pure even if the body is degraded, and some passages in *Hurskas kurjuus* seem to express faith in the immortality of soul.[496] A section at the beginning which refers to the end, when Juha (Jussi) Toivola is shot by representatives of the Civil War victors, is awkward and confused in its general, abstract expression of the author's ideas, but at the end the description of an unreal but graphic scene conveys his message forcefully:

> Very soon, after the fighting, there may arrive a moment at which an individual human soul will no more stop, even if it should so want, at the irrelevant surface of things, at the efforts of the body, the dirt, the hunger, and the violence, but will irresistibly see deeper, where everyone seems to remain, unmoved and silent, in a certain position. Nobody is nobler than any other there, nobody has more rights, for the fighting sides have established connections between facts about which the fighters did not have the slightest idea. Even the dead arise and wonder why they have been buried like this, in separate graves, for they cannot possibly remember what that was supposed to mean. Jussi Toivola and the young officer are old acquaintances, for once somewhere on a clear night the officer shot Jussi. It must have happened quite casually, for he did not notice at all, then, what an important man Jussi really is. . . .

It is typical of several Finnish writers that solemn thoughts end ironically, if not humorously, although the material is not humorous. The French call this humor "black." The story makes clear that Juha Toivola is one of the least important people in the world. The first sentence states that he is a "disgusting-looking poor old man," and another character feels that "he is so old, so poor, and so definitively ignorant and stupid that the farmer is disgusted at his own feelings of hate toward him." It might be critical of the victorious side that some of them shot such a miserable character because he was a Red, but the book does not flatter the losers. Although the book does not deal primarily with the Civil War, its picture of the struggle is not impartial. It is slanted in favor of the Reds, but it does not deal with their essential problems. Kai Laitinen says that it is astonishing that *Hurskas kurjuus* could be published in 1919, but adds that the critics generally gave it fair treatment.[497] After a civil war manifestations of sympathy for the defeated are often viewed with suspicion by the winners, but in Finland the victorious side did not gain control of the country, and Sillanpää's book is double-edged. He and later writers who described individuals involved in the war seem to have accepted the idea that the Reds were wrong and have sought extenuating circumstances for their action. Their characters are usually bewildered and unaware of the meaning of the events and never commit criminal acts. In both Väinö Linna's *Täällä Pohjantähden alla* (3 vols., 1959-62) and *Hurskas kurjuus*, a member of the upper class is shot by a stranger who disappears, leaving others to suffer the consequences. Such things may have happened, but the Whites would hardly have found such stories convincing.

Hurskas kurjuus is mainly about the life of Juha Toivola before the Civil War and is one of the dreariest stories we have read. Contemporary literature is full of nauseating characters, but they are usually functions of violent protest or have a nightmarish, half-unreal intensity. Even Kianto's and Lehtonen's characters are cunning in spite of their laziness; they are gifted at making jokes and described with humor. In Sillanpää's book, however, the dull misery of Juha Toivola's life is unrelieved. After he is left a penniless orphan, he works for people who take advantage of him. He marries and leases a small piece of land, but everything goes wrong for him because he is unable to take care of himself. After drifting into the socialist movement he is shot at the end of the war because he was present when a man was killed. The only positive quality Sillanpää gave him is that he never commits a dishonest or cruel act.

Next Sillanpää published a collection of short stories, *Rakas isänmaani* ('My Beloved Country,' 1919), some of which also relate to the Civil War. Kalle Nieminen, a character in one, is to an extent the opposite of Juha Toivola, intelligent and alert within his limits, capable of analyzing and criticizing himself and his living conditions. He too takes part in the war; he is condemned to death, but pardoned. Consistent with his belief in the individual soul, Sillanpää finds the source of Nieminen's strength and courage not in a belief in social or political ideals, but in his love for his child. In other stories one notices that Sillanpää had reached a satisfactory attitude toward his original surroundings although he continued to pursue a literary career.

In the twenties he wrote several collections of short stories which Aarne Laurila considers among the best in Finnish literature.[498] Most important among them are *Hiltu ja Ragnar* (1923), *Enkelten suojatit* ('Under the Protection of the Angels,' 1923), *Maan tasalta* ('On Ground Level,' 1924), *Töllinmäki* ('The Hill with the Cabin,' 1925), *Rippi* ('The Confession,' 1928), and *Kiitos hetkistä, Herra . . .* ('I Thank You, Lord, for These Moments. . . ,' 1930). The story *Hiltu ja Ragnar* is about Juha Toivola's daughter Hiltu, who goes to the city as a servant, succumbs to the seduction of a young man of good family, Ragnar (a Swedish name), and drowns herself rather than be left alone with her shame. In *Enkelten suojatit* Sillanpää expresses his idea about the unity of body and soul, a conception opposed to his earlier belief in the essential man, the soul, who remained pure even when the body was defiled, and some of this contrast is reflected in *Hiltu ja Ragnar*. The obvious intent to describe a girl who remains pure amidst the brutality of life is tempered by the author's cool, objective realism.[499] Again in *Enkelten suojatit* Sillanpää is torn between pity for the suffering and ability to see them as ordinary people with all human failings. The half-sentimental title alludes to the guardian angels of the many children in the book, but the contents imply that any such angels have failed to do their duty. In some of the stories about crippled and retarded children Sillanpää seems tortured by honesty, a duty to admit that in the world meaningless, ugly suffering exists which he cannot explain away or find comfort against, but must describe, with alternating feelings of pity and repulsion. *Maan tasalta* is even more pessimistic, for Sillanpää describes people from the country, mainly small farmers, some of whom are even fairly successful, but he sees only their shortcomings. He calls them not petty bourgeois, but "dwarf bourgeois," "envious, scheming, proud of their small profits, and about as idealistic as young bullocks. . . ."[500] The negative aspects of this picture are relieved only by a few descriptions, such as one of a near-caricature of a miser and another of a good, honest man who dies young because he is obviously unsuited for the world.

Töllinmäki is somewhat brighter, as if the author had spent his bitterness in the previous collections. In the story *Talon tytär* Sillanpää introduces a person of higher social standing than that of his usual characters, the daughter of a well-to-do farmer. Differing in content from his other stories, it is an analysis of a woman unable to love or experience strong emotion, who therefore remains isolated although she is healthy, attractive, and well-off. The other collections of the period are weaker, for Sillanpää was facing a crisis: his creative powers seemed to be failing, but no career other than literature was open to him. His publisher entrusted him with editorship of a periodical, but, when he worked honestly to fulfill his obligations, his work left him mentally exhausted and unable to write anything personal.

In 1931, after this private trauma, he produced the novel awaited by the critics, his publisher, and himself throughout the twenties, *Nuorena nukkunut*, perhaps not his best book, but certainly the best known. Critics were enthusiastic, and the Dutch and Italian critics soon predicted a Nobel Prize for the author.[501] The book has nothing ugly or repulsive, and the author became as sentimental as he ever did in descriptions of young love and premature death. Still, the main character, Silja, and her father are somewhat similar to earlier Sillanpää characters, for they are unable to protect themselves, although they are above average intellectually and well developed emotionally.[502] In the short story, *Ohjelmaa* ('The Program' in *Maan tasalta*), a servant has such refined feelings and so much education that she occasionally writes poetry, but the tone of this earlier narrative is ironic. The weakness of Silja and her father is fatal, for their unwillingness to make others suffer even in defending themselves allows others to take advantage of them. They do no evil and forgive all their neighbors' sins, but they do little active good. By letting them die, Sillanpää is not compelled to describe their inevitable humiliations and sufferings in their prosaic surroundings. Annamari Sarajas points out that *Nuorena nukkunut* is a retrospective work; Sillanpää had already declared in the short story *Kevätrukous* ('A Prayer in Spring') that he was no longer interested in illness and decay, that he was turning away from them and looking toward the sun, toward a new, fresh humanity, "men and women who meet when the flowers are opening and possess each other when the fruits are ripening."[503] As do other characters from the novel, Silja appears previously in *Huhtikuinen tanssiaisyö* ('A Dance on an April Night' in *Töllinmäki*), where she is a servant working on a small farm. She is in love, half-engaged, to a young man, Iivari, but villagers begin to gossip about her in connection with another man, and, though she is innocent, Iivari breaks with her at the dance on an April night. The essential story is about two young people who are unable to communicate, to express their feelings or rebel against the public opinion that drives them apart. The atmosphere of sly meanness and envy in a small village is rendered with skill by the characters' incidental remarks just as Silja's character is described indirectly through her reactions to events around her. She is not exactly naive, but too innocent to understand fully the cruelty of the world and too passive to resist it. From the undramatic action we conclude that the heroine is too sensitive to be happy in her surroundings but powerless to change them or herself.

In *Nuorena nukkunut* Sillanpää describes Silja's childhood, her father, and the loss of his farm, which necessitated his daughter's working as a servant. The short story is only one of the episodes which illustrate that she is too refined to adjust to her environment, but nothing dramatic or unusual ever happens to her. Sillanpää's belief in the importance of instinct and biological life is apparent in her experience of love's fulfillment in a few romantic, dreamy encounters with a middle-class young man who then disappears as if he had never existed. Physical love is again discreetly symbolized by nature, the bright summer nights of the North, and flowers.[504] One feels that Silja's life can offer no further romance and that the author, wishing to maintain the novel's level throughout, had to give her an early death.[505] His heroine is somewhat reminiscent of Kivi's dreamy young girls, although Kivi's women often express religious or moral feelings with great strength; at the end of *Seven Brothers* the scene in which Eero's wife sings *Song of My Heart* to her child shares the atmosphere of Silja's death scene. Kivi wrote the song on a common folklore motif; the otherworldly spirit and yearning for death apparent in Eero's wife and Silja evidently had counterpart in reality.

Only two of the several works Sillanpää wrote after *Nuorena nukkunut* are considered on the level of his best compositions—*Miehen tie* ('The Way of a Man,' 1932) and *Ihmiset suviyössä* ('A Summer Night' or 'Destinies on a Summer Night,' 1934).[506] Part of *Miehen tie* was written simultaneously to *Nuorena nukkunut*. It expresses the ideas about life and man which Sillanpää felt that he held at the time and is the one work by him which justifies comparisons to D. H. Lawrence. Paavo Ahrola and Alma, the main characters, are predestined by nature, fate, or the deep forces of life for each other, but they are not united until the man learns, after many mistakes including an unlucky marriage, that she is the right woman for him. His mistakes are described in so much detail that some offended critics claimed that the book should have been called *The Way of a Bum*.[507] Sillanpää, however, stresses the connection between the rhythm of nature expressed in the seasons and the changes in the lives of his characters. In such passages the novel is not realistic; there is an epic breadth, perhaps not quite spontaneous or genuine, in the description of the work of the farmer, the succession of the seasons, and the actions of the man and woman destined to meet when their time is fulfilled. Again, the woman is conscious of their fate, whereas the man must struggle to reach the necessary maturity.

Ihmiset suviyössä is probably Sillanpää's most carefully composed and definitely his most complexly structured work.[508] It is about a group of persons, all of whom do not know each other and some of whom do not see each other, but whose lives are connected and fates are decided on a summer night. The author's biological conception of time has a part in the manner in which the events are described; the duration of the action is indicated, but the flow of duration is experienced differently by the characters. Helka and Arvid, the happy young lovers, live in timeless ecstasy; for an old woman time has also stopped: she lives in memories as real to her as the present and by the end of the novel dies peacefully; a young worker nicknamed Nokia, who has killed a man in a brawl, feels that each moment is an eternity; Jalmari Syrjämäki thinks that time is running too fast, for, despite his rushing about, he never arrives anywhere at the right moment and cannot find the midwife or physician his wife needs when she gives birth. The narration shifts from one character to another, stressing their relative importance and parallel destinies, and the events include all life's processes: birth, peaceful and violent death, young and mature love. An artist, representing Sillanpää more or less, arrives at a critical moment in his life and finds or thinks that he has found a solution for the crises. He is a man tortured by the gift of self-observation, who sees himself as an outsider even at the moment of strong emotional experience, and is similar to the poet in *Elämä ja aurinko*, which also describes the inebriating effect of summer and light and their power on destiny. The poet appears in the epilogue *Runoilijan syysmatka* ('The Journey of a Poet in Autumn'), coming to the place of the book's events after they have happened. He tries to capture their atmosphere but fails and feels ridiculous. Sillanpää seems to have hoped to be like his characters, to surrender to the forces of nature and be guided by intinct, but he never succeeded.

In the thirties he published two more collections of short stories, *Virran pohjalta* ('The Bottom of the River,' 1933) and *Viidestoista* ('The Fifteenth,' 1936), both unremarkable, and wrote the novel *Elokuu* ('August'), published in 1941. By that time he was the greatest writer in his country in the eyes of the public and many critics. Kilpi was too exclusive for a large audience, Lehtonen was dead, Kianto was no longer publishing anything of interest, Haanpää was ostracized because of alleged political views, and Pekkanen was considered a leftist or proletarian writer. Actually we find Lehtonen and Kilpi on a level equivalent to Sillanpää's. A brilliant young essayist and critic, T. Vaaskivi, published a biography *F. E. Sillanpää. Elämä ja teokset* (F. E. Sillanpää. Life and Works,' 1937), and Sillanpää received his Nobel Prize, but he was disillusioned and felt his powers failing. He once told Aarne Laurila that he was "tired of the phenomenon called life."[509] World events, too, disturbed him, for he was not interested in the mysteries of life and forces of nature alone, and, unlike Hamsun, whom he had admired in his youth, he was not attracted by the nationalist-socialist mysticism of the "blood and the ground." In 1938 he published a *Christmas Letter to the Dictators* in a social-democrat paper which expresses his faith in a better future.[510] However, the events of the following years were not encouraging to people who felt as he did. During the Winter War of 1939 and 1940 he wrote his only poem, *Marssilaulu* ('Marching Song'), for which an obscure composer wrote a tune which proved so catchy that after a few months no one could bear the sound of it. His private life was also difficult: his first wife died in 1939, his second marriage was short and unhappy, and in 1940 he went to a hospital, where he remained until 1943.

These problems are reflected in his late novels, especially *Elokuu*, which is about a man of modest origin who studied, tried to become a writer, but failed, and seeks comfort in daydreams and alcohol. The book is totally pessimistic and contains no hint that the inner man or soul remains untouched by the physical decay. *Ihmiselon ihanuus ja kurjuus* ('The Beauty and Misery of Human Life,' 1945) is about a successful poet who suffers from the feeling that his life has not been as he wished it and that his creativity is failing; although Sillanpää made the particulars of the poet's life differ from his own, autobiographical elements constantly appear.[511] Sections are romantic, such as the poet's visit to an old manor in his home region, where he meets a woman who, as the girl he loved but could not marry, has remained symbolic of an unattainable ideal.

Following this novel Sillanpää published three volumes of memoirs, *Poika eli elämäänsä* ('A Boy and His Life,' 1953), *Kerron ja kuvailen* ('Telling and Describing,' 1955), and *Päivä korkeimmillaan* ('The High Moment of the Day'). He grew a bushy beard, let himself be called Taata ('The Grandad'), gave talks, and read Christmas messages on the radio, expounding a homespun philosophy. He died peacefully, mourned by the nation, but he had not been elected to the Finnish Academy when it was founded in 1948.[512] Koskenniemi represented literature among its first members.

Pentti Haanpää (1905-55) was the last great writer in Finland to describe country people, but not as a continuation of Sillanpää's tradition. Even today such writers as Martti Merenmaa and Matti Hälli write of rural conditions, but they have concentrated on individual moral struggles, encompassing urban life as well, and have ignored nature, the changing seasons, the work of the farmer, and the influence of landscapes on man. Haanpää considered environment crucial; his characters, explicitly inhabitants of northern Finland, are formed by its conditions and their struggles with them. There are two common misconceptions about Haanpää: that he was a half-literate vagrant worker and lumberjack, who wrote as though he were telling stories to friends, and that he was a political writer with radical left-wing, even communistic ideas. In fact, his father was a well-to-do farmer active in local politics who lived for a while in the United States, wrote for newspapers, and composed short stories and a play; his grandfather sat in Parliament and published a few stories; even his uncle produced a novel. They all belonged to the category of folk writers represented by Päivärinta, Kauppis-Heikki, and Meriläinen.[513] Haanpää himself never had more formal education than elementary school or traveled much, though near the end of his life he journeyed to Communist China with a delegation of Finnish writers. However, he took correspondence courses in English and philosophy and read; his large library contained a number of English books in the original, and he played chess by correspondence in English. He closely followed current events and trends in literature. In the 1930s he wrote two short stories which were almost direct adaptations of stories from Joyce's *Dubliners*. At that time even literary specialists in Helsinki knew little about the Irish writer, and, since Haanpää did not reveal his joke, he died before it was discovered in 1962.[514]

Haanpää began to write early, had his short stories printed in periodicals, and in 1925 published a collection titled *Maantietä pitkin* ('Along the Road'). The same year he wrote *Rikas mies* ('The Wealthy Man'), a play which was neither printed nor performed, but he based a novel, *Kolmen Töräpään tarina* ('The Tale of the Three Töräpää,' 1927), on it. The least interesting of his early works, it is about three generations of the Töräpää family. The deliberate, often humorous exaggeration is occasionally reminiscent of a folktale or ballad. In 1927 another collection of short stories appeared, *Tuuli käy heidän ylitseen* (a modified quotation from Psalm 103:16, 'The Wind Passeth over Them'). These works were favorably received; some were translated into Swedish and printed in Helsinki. The young writer visited the capital which did not attract him, and he knew some of the members of *Tulenkantajat*, e.g., Olavi Paavolainen and Unto Seppänen, but was not a member himself, although he is sometimes described as one.[515] All features of Haanpää's art are apparent in these first works; of the nature of northern Finland he said:

> The man was born in the northern part of Finland, where the ground is full of folds and where one can see far and wide. There you have long hills covered with forests, bare mountaintops and moors and lakes to provide flat, open spaces. People in that country live by keeping reindeer and by catching the animals in the forests and the lakes. A tiny potato patch, a little field of barley were a mere scratch made by a nail in the midst of the boundless wilderness. A small haystack on the edge of the moor or on the shore of a creek seemed to be the work of mice.[516]

Among its people his favorites were the lumberjacks (Finn. *tukkijätkä, jätkä*), through whom he expressed his essential philosophy.[517] The settings and adventures—fights with wild animals, escapes from wilderness dangers—of Haanpää's books may remind us of Jack London, but Haanpää, a true realist, assigned his characters none of the superhuman qualities of London's heroes. They are strong and courageous, rely on their own resources, and fight until overcome by death, but they have no illusions about themselves and care about nothing. Life is a bad joke to them, but they prefer to laugh rather than cry, and they occasionally find a few moments of happiness. This happiness, of course, is of a simple nature—having an easy job, being posted on the river in spring, seeing the logs float by without jamming. Haanpää's only sentimentality is in the descriptions of nature, which is not always hostile, for it gives protection, peace, sunshine, and warmth, whereas relations between human beings are often frustating. At times his characters protest the feeling of life's futility, with senseless action, which at least interrupts the monotony of daily events. One form of protest is drinking, but the author has also imagined more original ways of rebellion. Närhi-Isko in *Jätkä ja jätkän onnea* decides, when he gets some money, to spend it on a vacation. He stays in a house and does nothing except swim, bask in the sun, and play cards. While people work in the fields on a hot day, he sits on the roof, "naked like a skinned eel," playing the accordion for them.

Haanpää also shows his readers how his characters die. Especially in his first collection, where this motif is frequent, certain macabre details of setting remind us of Toppila, but Haanpää lacks his supernatural elements, and, whereas the older writer is inclined toward pity and sentimentality, the younger is consistently hard. Death is even the pretext for a joke in *Viimeinen matka* ('The Last Journey' in *Lauma* 'The Herd,' 1937). A lumberjack falls sick in a forest camp, two friends try to carry him to the nearest physician, but the man dies on the road. Nevertheless the two carry the body to their destination, finally in a horse-drawn carriage where it is bound in a sitting position, and deliver it to the authorities. They have a few drinks to gather strength for their unpleasant mission, and the sheriff, who takes care of the body, does not receive them kindly.

In 1925 Haanpää was fulfilling the required military service. Before entering the army, he noted in his diary doubts about his ability to adjust to military life;[518] he was strong and healthy, but unable to accept an atmosphere of compulsory activities and restrictions. The Finnish army of 1925 was even less able than other armies to consider the individual feelings of its soldiers, for almost all officers had fought in the Civil War, were embittered by the fact that the leaders and policies of the victorious side were not the leaders and policies of the new republic, and knew that many of the recruits came from homes where everything White was hated and feared.[519] Haanpää was too individual to side with a party or organized group, and the protest in his collection *Kenttä ja kasarmi* ('The Barracks and the Field,' 1928) is an individual's protest against mental and physical brutality, stupidity, petty vexations, and bad living conditions. The last grievance was particularly well-founded because the Finnish military was being built from scratch. Because at that time any criticism of the army was generally considered synonymous with communism, none of the well-known publishers accepted the manuscript, which was eventually issued by a small, unknown company considered leftist, although respectable. The result was a general outcry of indignation against the author and book, but by chance the critic of the major conservative paper, *Uusi Suomi*, published the only favorable review.[520] Though not active in any party,[521] Haanpää was for seven years unable to have anything published by a known firm, but he continued to write, expressing no directly political opions in his books. The details of *Kenttä ja kasarmi* are humorous and sarcastic, bitter and tragic, not unlike those of other books of that type. He tried to understand the officers, but the one who is truly idealistic and honest resigns from the army.

Haanpää's next novel, *Hota-Leenan poika* ('Hota-Leena's Son,' 1929), could have rehabilitated him in the literary world, but it was hardly noticed. Set in the nineteenth century, it describes with warmth and understanding the life of an honest, hard-working man who gradually loses his small properties through his inability to defend himself. The author is satirical when he says that he is "one of those invisible props without which the whole wonderful thing would crumple up," but the satire is directed more against human nature than against specific social or political conditions. Haanpää was growing more bitter; he could not find publishers for the novels *Noitaympyrä* ('The Magic Circle,' written 1931) and *Vääpeli Sadon tapaus* ('The Case of Sergeant-Major Sato,' written 1935), both published posthumously in the *Collected Works*, or the short story collections *Väljän taivaan alla* ('Under a Wide Sky') and *Ilmeitä isänmaan kasvoilla* ('Expressions on the Face of Our Country'). Newspapers and periodicals refused his stories, and the printing of one in *Tulenkantajat* (openly leftist unlike the first by that name) resulted in Haanpää's prosecution and fine for contempt of the authorities. The only long work to be published was *Isännät ja isäntien varjot* ('The Masters and the Shadows of the Masters,' 1935), directly concerned with social problems, especially those caused by the great depression, which affected Finland as it did the rest of the world.

Noitaympyrä is about a man somewhat like Haanpää, a worker with some instruction. He becomes a foreman, but cannot accept the policies of his company in the depression. Dismissed, he joins the unemployed. Earlier in the book a romantic intermezzo reflects Haanpää's love for nature and dreams of a free life in the wilderness. He meets an educated man from Helsinki who wants to journey to Lapland and accompanies him. The romantic traveler represents one side of Haanpää's personality; significantly, for Haanpää knew that dreams of a free life in the wilderness were only dreams in modern times, the man kills himself, whereas the worker, the down-to-earth Haanpää, decides to go to the Soviet Union. One might guess that Haanpää considered drastic action at that time, but he worked these thoughts out in his books, remained in his home region, and stubbornly kept on writing. He is quoted: "One day I'll bounce back from the ground. Those literary gentlemen will still see that."[522] He took great pains in composing this novel and considered it his best, as did the critics,[523] but in general his short stories are better than his longer compositions.

Vääpeli Sadon tapaus, about military life, is a description of two individuals rather than the institution of the army. It is a bitter book, for the two men, a sergeant-major and a corporal, are hard, mean, and cunning; the one—the corporal—who has more of these qualities wins. Many years later he meets his former enemy, who has left the army and come down in the world, and thinks only that such is life. *Isännät ja isäntien varjot* is one of Haanpää's most aggressive books. In a description of the ruin of a farmer and his family, it underlines, perhaps somewhat heavily, the contrast between upper and lower classes. Government officials unaffected by the depression are shown arranging hunting parties, killing animals for sport, not necessity, celebrating a successful day with drinks and fine meals and giving the leftovers to the dogs. In 1930 Haanpää had published *Karavaani* ('The Caravan'), a collection of short stories dealing mainly with prohibition. The caravan consists of men carrying smuggled liquor on their backs inland from the coast. In *Elämän keinot* ('Means of Livelihood') two hoboes have found a way to get food and shelter from kind people: one feigns insanity, the other that he is taking his insane companion to a hospital.

In 1937 the curse of public opinion was removed. A well-known publisher released *Lauma* and a short novel, *Syntyykö uusi suku?* ('Shall a New Generation Be Born?');[524] the novel *Taivalvaaran näyttelijä* ('The Actor of Taivalvaara') appeared in 1938, and the collection *Ihmiselon karvas ihanuus* ('The Bitter Beauty of Human Life') in 1939. His familiar characters in their familiar situations fill the short stories, and the author sees their ignorance and brutality; in *Pimeyttä* ('Darkness,' in *Lauma*) the darkness is as much mental as physical. The main character of *Syntyykö uusi suku?* is unlike those in most of Haanpää's works: an elderly man who has made money in the United States spends his old days in the home country, where he hopes to found a new family. His dreams are frustrated, but the book is not quite convincing; Haanpää appears to fail in an attempt at something more literary and refined than usual. The subject of *Taivalvaaran näyttelijä* attracted him, and he treated it again in *Pojan paluu* ('The Return of the Son' in *Lauma*) and composed an unprinted, unperformed play on it. The common main character is a swindler, a con man who poses as an itinerant preacher, a man just back from America, or the son of a wealthy family returning after a long absence; he is always caught. Haanpää returned to this motif in the 1940s, and a Finnish essayist has examined its meaning for him as a self-portrait, a description of an artist, an urge to project his personality in new shapes through which he might define himself, and a feeling that these efforts, based on imagination, are ultimately meaningless.[525] The social aspect of Haanpää's authorship—his rebuff by Helsinki's literary circles—and his possible feeling of failure in his home region, because he was not a successful farmer, seem significant. Some of his characters are somewhat similar to Sillanpää's half-ironic poets and writers and Lehtonen's comic idealists.

Haanpää's collection of stories about the Winter War, *Korpisotaa* ('War in the Wilderness,' 1940), marked his conversion from communism to patriotism for those who had considered him communistic and unpatriotic. Those who knew that he had been neither saw that the book was not a conversion; he felt as did the characters of *Kenttä ja kasarmi*, who hated the peace army but considered the war different, a serious job which they did with remarkable efficiency and without heroics. The struggle of a small nation against overwhelming odds was desperate, and the army was composed of farmers, workers, and lumberjacks who had lived in the forests since birth. They called the war a lumbering job (*savotta*, a Russian loanword) in which they cut the enemies down and put them in piles (*motti*) like so many logs. When they lost, Väinö Linna says at the beginning of *The Unknown Soldier*, "they came back without any 'difficulties of adjustment.' First they got dead drunk like the Finns they were and then they went to work." Haanpää shows this attitude even better than Linna, who occasionally too obviously debunks patriotic propaganda; Haanpää writes as if unaware of its existence. He tells of a group of men, fighting, suffering, and sometimes dying without emphasizing death. The collection *Nykyaikaa* ('Present Times,' 1942) and the selection *Akkuna ja maantie* ('The Window and the Road,' published in the *Collected Works*, 1956-58) reflect a different mood, sometimes disillusioned and bitter; they include descriptions of deserters and are in places openly critical of the officers, though without the violent tone of his peacetime works. He wrote still another book on the war, *Yhdeksän miehen saappaat* ('The Boots of Nine Men,' 1945), a novel containing a series of episodes connected only by a pair of boots passing from man to man. The characters represent a variety of types, and the incidents are both comic and tragic. In one episode the men on an isolated base in the forest have nothing to do but play chess, which slowly drives them crazy; in another a gambler's life becomes meaningless when he can no longer indulge in his passion. A few of the characters return from the war, and one takes the boots, enjoying the thought that now, "for the first time [he can use them] for a real job, to work and get some food."

After the war Haanpää wrote three collections of short stories, the genre of which he was a master, which he called *juttu* 'story,' a funny story told in company of men: *Heta Rahko korkeassa iässä* ('Heta Rahko at a Good Old Age,' 1947), *Atomintutkija* ('The Atomic Physicist,' 1950), and *Iisakki vähäpuheinen* ('Iisakki, Not the Talking Kind,' 1955). He also published the novel *Jauhot* ('The Flour,' 1949) and descriptions from his journey to China, *Kiinalaiset jutut* ('The Chinese Stories,' 1954). Although the characters of the stories are similar to earlier characters, the stories themselves are not repetitious of previous ones. These last collections, especially *Heta Rahko* and *Atomintutkija* are among Haanpää's best. The subjects range from the serious and tragic, as in *Kaiken vanhen kohtalo*, to descriptions of sports, in which he was interested,[526] and humorous but admiring portraits of modest, energetic people. One such portrait is *Pussisen akka, kunnianarvoisa naishenkilö* ('Old Ma Pussinen, A Respectable Woman'), who teacher her children good manners and keeps them and her home clean in spite of difficulties, expressing her philosophy, "There'all always be more water than shit in this here world," now almost proverbial in Finland.[527]

Jauhot and *Noitaympyrä* are the best novels. The episodes in *Jauhot* form a coherent whole, not, as in some of his other long works, a loosely connected series of incidents. Its events take place during the great famine of 1867 and 1868. A high government official distributes flour instead of money as relief to the hungry, and people discover that flour can be used for business—some make a profit from it, some steal it, and others use it for making alcohol. Although the author sides, as always, with the poor and seems to approve their turning the well-meant, unpractical plans of the authorities to their own advantage, the tone is humorous rather than satirical. The recurring theme in Haanpää is that the poor, rebellious, or meek are never given a fair deal, so that it is just for them to strike back, no matter their means—force, cunning, or refusal to go along with the normal course of life. The theme coupled with his special humor makes some of his works seem bitter, cynical, and even coarse, but one feels that the author assumes this mask to conceal deeper feelings, which he sometimes expresses in pity for his characters. Even when they are successful, they are almost always overcome, at least by death.

By speaking of Haanpää in connection with older writers of his type, we have overstepped the chronological boundary of World War I, Finnish Independence, and the Civil War, a rather artificial boundary especially in literature. We return to the generation of Lehtonen, Kilpi, and Sillanpää to speak of two writers who began working before 1914 and published their best works between 1910 and 1930 approximately.[528] **Maria Jotuni** (pseudonym of **Maria Gustava Haggrén**, wife of V. Tarkiainen,[529] 1880-1943) belongs by birth and her characters to the social group of the writers we have discussed. The daughter of a small craftsman in Kuopio, she completed secondary school and studied at the University of Helsinki, where her future husband was then lecturer. She was a master of the concise short story, often made up of dialogue or monologue including letters, through which the speaker's personality is unveiled. She also wrote a few plays, some still performed, but her short stories are considered more interesting. The dialogue is not dramatic, but reflective; it allows the reader to piece together psychological problems and their background.

Her characters are usually of the lower middle class, country people, workers, small craftsmen, and shopkeepers, often described humorously but with an earnest if not bitter undertone. The motif of most of her stories is love, or the absence of it. The titles of collections such as *Rakkautta* ('Love,' 1907) and *Kun on tunteet* ('The Feelings One Has,' 1913) are satirical, for the author often shows that love and other tender feelings have little to do with human relations; her first collection is called *Suhteita* ('Relations,' 1905). She uses three methods: the characters constantly speak of love in sentimental terms but pursue material, selfish ends; they openly discuss these ends and how to achieve them, occasionally mentioning love for form's sake; or they describe their lives matter-of-factly while letting the reader glimpse their frustrations and the feelings they perhaps had behind the disillusioned words. She is extremely frank but not indecent in erotic matters—she tells the events but does not describe them. However, such a variety of illicit love, free relations between unmarried partners, adultery, incest, and sexual aberrations appears in her books that their publication by well-known firms (no undercover publishers exist in Finland) is surprising, for until very recent years books considered offensive to public morals were banned and destroyed and their authors fined. When read on the radio in 1969, Allen Ginsberg's

Howl produced an official protest in Parliament. Actually, a more liberal atmosphere prevailed then, demonstrated by publication of Eino Leino's and L. Onerva's sensuous poetry and prose, Kianto's works on free love, and Maila Talvio's novels about abnormal psychology. Maria Jotuni was respectable in private life; her husband's position, their happy relations, and two healthy children confirmed her good character. However, the main reason for the general acceptance of her works is that the public considered her a humorous author who wrote about funny people from the country. Her characters, socially below the reading public, express themselves with words and phrases from popular speech, and their declared intentions and feelings often contrast with their actions. Her most successful play, *Miehen kylkiluu* ('The Rib of Man,' 1914), is a comedy about funny people in the country and reinforces this inaccurate image.[530]

Her first collections of short stories, *Suhteita* and *Rakkautta*, deal mainly with serious subjects, although they contain a few exaggerated characters. She knew contemporary literature and was interested in the controversy over the position of women. Through her characters she often expressed her belief that women were still denied the right to an independent life. They speak with apparent cynicism of marriage as a business deal in which a woman must sell herself at the highest possible price; they also frequently express rebellion or resignation resulting from their former belief that they could suppress their true feelings.

In 1909 Maria Jotuni published *Arkielämää* ('Everyday Life'), a novel set in the country containing both humorous and serious sections.[531] It refers again and again to love, to the relations between the sexes, describing the variants at length; although it is like a collection of sociological and pyschological cases, it gives a natural impression.[532] Her attitude toward sex, like Sillanpää's, is ambivalent; she thinks that sex is a positive force often thwarted by society. Led in the wrong direction, it produces hate, fear, and pain. The characters of *Arkielämää* live in an almost Edenic state of innocence, following the call of nature and speaking of it frankly, almost casually. The author writes of these relations without the clumsy facetiousness or artificial solemnity common when writers try to depict "violent, naked passions" in a country setting where they can develop without restraint. However, the serpent of morals and controls has visited Jotuni's paradise, leaving unhappiness behind; only two of her characters are able to follow their inclinations to love and to have children. The girl is a farm servant, the boy a farmhand; they feel that they belong to each other and act accordingly. At the beginning of the book the girl meets on the road an acquaintance whom she has not seen for a long time, and he, noticing that she is pregnant, asks her whether or not she has received her engagement presents—the question is not facetious, but natural. The girl's mother has just died, and she must think of funerals before engagements or marriages;

Tuomas Anhava points out that the community has rules about social ceremonies, which must follow in proper order independent of biological facts in the lives of the individuals.[533] In this, as in others of Jotuni's works, the women are more active: they seek a man at any price although they let him believe he has made the choice; if they don't get the man they want, they take another, often causing unhappiness. Two girls besides the one who has the child are in love with the farmhand; one, a farmer's daughter, decides reasonably that she cannot marry a simple worker and fittingly decides to take a farmer's son instead; the other, a servant, must admit that she is the loser and accepts another suitor. At the end of the story she sits on the stairs of a building, "crying like a small child who does not know where his home is." Other characters are secondary and provide a background for the main events by introducing new variations in the relations between the sexes. One family shows the henpecked husband who is happy, another the unfaithful male. Somewhere in the backwoods a father has been having relations with his daughter for years; a shoemaker who has got religion tells that he considers all sex sin and, when he feels lust overcoming him, beats it out of his body with nettles. If Jotuni knew such words as *automasochism*, she was careful not to use them in an inappropriate context.

Kun on tunteet, which contains some of her best stories, presents further variations on love and marriage among simple people, whom she knew best. Her descriptions of middle-class characters were not always as successful: in the story *Martinin rikos* ('Martin's Crime,' 1914) the problem of guilt and responsibility is stated with force and simplicity and the action carried logically to inevitable conclusion, but the characters seem constructed for the story rather than observed in their natural surroundings. The main character is one of the disillusioned, bitter young men of the literature of that time. He commits a crime, but it is his father's crime of driving him to suicide that is indicated by the title. Unhappy love is used to explain the events: the mother admits that she never really loved the father and married him because she thought her fiancé had been unfaithful to her; her feelings have poisoned the atmosphere of the family.

Vanha koti ('The Old Home,' 1910), Maria Jotuni's first attempt at drama, is a somewhat Ibsenian tragedy in which skeletons are pulled from the cupboards of a respectable, middle-class family until, after a death, a suicide, and a nervous breakdown, only two unpractical dreamers who refuse to see life's ugliness are left. Eino Leino found similitudes with characters from Russian plays.[534] Her next dramatic work, *Miehen kylkiluu*, is somewhat reminiscent of *Arkielämää*: two women want to marry the same man, one secures him, and the other must take a less attractive one. One of them is an energetic widow, the other an old maid; the object of their love is a mild, dreamy, and philosophical man who has little to say about his own fate. Unnoticed by the public, the author's pessimism lurks in her presentation of the characters, for the marriages do not seem to have good futures. The following year, 1915, another of her comedies, *Savu-uhri* ('The Smoke Sacrifice'), was performed without the success of *Miehen kylkiluu.* Two people who have left the country and lived in the city return to show their superiority to those who have remained home, but this old plot is not enough to carry the play.

World War I brought a change in Jotuni's opinions, although it is not apparent in all her works. An admirer of Hamsun, she had published an essay on him in 1908, and he had some influence on her positive evaluation of the subconscious and instinctive forces of man. The conflict, however, showed her that instincts can be destructive, and she criticized sharply the shortsightedness of writers of her generation, including herself, in a letter rebuked Aho for his passivity apparent in *Rauhan erakko*, for example,[535] and wrote in various contexts about the necessity for the further moral development of mankind, which she predicted as a slow, difficult, painful process. We can now see better how prophetic her words were: "If our social self . . . would not control our . . . instinctive self . . . our world would be full of slavery, violence and disorder, and what would we not be able to do with our present efficient instruments of destruction."[536] The immediate result of these reflections was *Kultainen vasikka* ('The Golden Calf'), performed in autumn, 1918. It is a play about wartime profiteering and corruption, not a very original subject at that time, and, although she openly expresses bitterness and criticism, the end is conciliatory, offending no one. During the war she also published a children's book, *Musta Härkä* ('The Black Ox,' 1915), and in 1921 a collection of short stories *Jussi ja Lassi*, in which she expresses her ideas on many questions, especially religion and morals, sometimes through two children not even intended as natural or probable characters.

After the war she published two major works, *Tohvelisankarin rouva* ('The Wife of a Henpecked Husband,' 1924) and *Tyttö ruusutarhassa* ('The Maid in the Rosery,' 1927). The first is a comedy, but more bitter and satirical than *Miehen kylkiluu*. The satire, directed against an ambitious, scheming woman whose plans are foiled in the end, is less harmless than contempary audiences expected, and the play was not a success. *Tyttö ruusutarhassa* is a romantic title and fits only the title story, a description of the last moments of an old woman reflecting on problems which occupied the author at the time. The others are about characters similar to those in her earlier works, often women attempting to secure themselves husbands; they are superficially humorous, but the humor is frequently rather thinly spread. In *Onnellinen Heliina* ('Happy Heliina'; *onnellinen* 'happy,' or 'lucky') a country girl who comes to town as a maid manages to marry a young man with some money who is not too far above her in position. Later she tells her sister:

> After the wedding they seemed to think that they'd got a maid for nothing. In the morning, the old lady used to wait for me to get up and make the coffee. "Hey, daughter-in-law, won't you get up and make the coffee," she was saying. "Dunno, I'm so sleepy still," I said. So my husband got up and made the coffee. But the old lady was quite cranky all the day. Then I took a little girl to do the work so that the fighting would stop. But maybe the old lady didn't like that, either, because all of a sudden she died. It was perhaps a bad thing to do and if I'd known it, I need not have done it. But old people don't need much either before they get angry and pack up.

In *Ikkunanpesijät* ('The Window Washers') a woman tells her friend that she is only afraid that her husband might "start waiting for her to die"; the same expression appears in *Arkielämää*. It does not imply a plot against her life, but indicates that the two have only mutual hate in common and wish to see each other disappear.

Maria Jotuni wrote a number of works after these, but none are on the level of the previous ones. *Olen syyllinen* ('I Am Guilty,' 1929) is a play about Saul and David, biblical, but not Christian.[537] It opposes Saul's dark, violent, passionate character to David's almost childlike innocence and harmony, seemingly implying that their differences are due to ineluctable fate. Her last play, *Klaus, Louhikon herra* ('Klaus, Lord of Louhikko') was not published until 1946. The ballad about Elina's death, used by von Numers, inspired it, but she did not retain much of the original subject. The main character is a proud nobleman of the Renaissance, the kind of Nietzschean ideal so popular at the beginning of the century, who destroys himself. She also wrote three collections of aphorisms, one published posthumously, a comedy *Kurdin prinssi* ('The Prince of Kurd,' 1932), and a short novel (or long story) *Jouluyö korvessa* ('A Christmas Night in the Wilderness,' 1946). Her main work of the 1930s is now considered *Huojuva talo* ('The Tottering House'), a great novel not printed until 1963. The story is of an unhappy marriage, but, like Lehtonen's *Henkien taistelu*, the book is a more general protest against the violence and injustice in the world. Speaking often of man's primitive instincts, she sees them as dangerous, destructive forces; at that time she had little hope of their control, for the future seemed to be growing darker. Unevenly written, reflecting the anguish of the author, it is not a masterpiece, but the pictures of her reactions to contemporary events and the evolution of an entire generation of writers are interesting.

Aino Julia Maria Kallas (1878-1956) differs greatly from the writers we have discussed in this chapter; differs, in fact, from all Finnish writers in subjects and treatment. Part of her originality was due to a pose. Her father was the poet Suonio, i.e., the folklorist Julius Krohn; thus she belonged to a wealthy, cosmopolitan family with artistic and literary interests, and she married Oskar Kallas, an Estonian folklorist who entered the diplomatic service of independent Estonia and went as an envoy to Finland and London. She was attractive and had, she said, passionate love affairs with well-known artists, including Eino Leino, but there are doubts about the lengths to which she really went with them. She built an image of herself as a *femme fatale*, a *grande amoureuse* who regretted only that she had not met a truly great man, a king, to love.[538] The men in her life all proved disappointing. Parts of her diary were published even before her death, and she wrote several volumes of memoirs in which she stressed her role as a diplomat's wife who had been in the great world, but the envoy of an obscure republic and his wife must have been rather small fry in London. In 1920 she published *Katinka Rabe* (name), a novel describing her childhood, the Krohn family, and their estate at Kiiskilä.

However, she was not merely a lady of good family with literary pretensions, but a truly remarkable writer. She wrote mainly short stories in which she presented romantic but simple, stylized but realistic pictures from the past, when men and women had stronger passions than today and expressed them more directly. Her language embodies elements from old Bible versions and other archaic texts, and, although this dangerous device often parodies its intentions,[539] she used it well. Her prose has aged much better than the prose in which Aho, Eino Leino, and Linnankoski, for example, tried to create a style based on the *Kalevala* and old folk poetry. One reason is that she used original prose works as models; Eino Leino used the meter and motifs of the *Kalevala* successfully in his poems, but its nature makes it an unsuitable model for prose.

Aino Kallas's subjects are exotic in Finnish literature because they are from a romantic past in Estonia, her elected home country, for which she developed a strong attachment because she found it more attractive and interesting than Finland and there met and loved a man credited with considerable influence on her literary development.[540] Estonians and Finns have a common origin and speak similar languages, but the histories and social conditions of their countries are very different. Sweden ruled Finland benevolently, but the masters of the Estonians, German aristocrats, reduced them to serfdom and kept them in this state with ruthless cruelty. The period of Swedish domination, the seventeenth century and a few years before and after, was relatively happy, but the Russians then took the country and restored the old order. When serfdom was suppressed in the nineteenth century, a national Estonian civilization began to develop. In spite of her attitudes, Aino Kallas was intelligent, open-minded, and warm-hearted; immediately after coming to Estonia she became aware of the social conditions and evils in the country and described them from the point of view of the oppressed in her works.

Kai Laitinen indicates that in 1903 Aino Kallas planned to write a novel based on folktales told by her husband's uncle, but that she never carried the project through,[541] probably because she did not have the talent of a novelist, and published instead a collection of short stories, *Meren takaa* ('From beyond the Sea,' 2 vols., 1904/5). She had already written a collection of poems, *Lauluja ja ballaadeja* ('Songs and Ballads,' 1897), a volume of short stories, *Kuloa ja kevättä* ('Fire and Spring,' 1899), and a novel, *Kirsti* (name, 1902), but they are not very interesting. In the fragment of the novel which became *Meren takaa*, aristocrats appear, but in the short stories only men and women of the people, peasants, and serfs are present. Later she published other collections of similar stories, *Lähtevien laivojen kaupunki* ('The City of the Ships That Leave,' 1913), which received great praise, *Seitsemän* ('Seven,' 1914), and *Vieras veri* ('Foreign Blood,' 1921). In the same period she wrote *Ants Raudjalg* (name, 1907), a novel attempting to describe the evolution then taking place in Estonia, the biography of Lydia Koidula, an Estonian poetess, *Tähdenlento* ('The Shooting Star,' 1915), a series of biographies, *Nuori Viro* ('Young Estonia,' 1918), and a collection of poems, *Suljettu puutarha* ('The Closed Garden,' 1915). The short stories, best of the works, were also those noticed by the critics. Their action occurs on the great island of Saaremaa, off the western coast of Estonia, where she heard the old tales from which she took her subjects; the motifs are almost identical, although by individual characterization the author gives them variety. Some follow closely the pattern of the European short story tradition established by Boccaccio, and the brutal practical jokes Boccaccio liked appear in them, though they have none of his frivolity. In one story a peasant faithfully takes to the city a letter which contains an order to flog him. The erotic motifs are tragic, dealing mainly with the all-powerful master who forces a lower-class woman to be his bedfellow, e.g., *Häät* ('The Wedding'), which introduces the old belief in the *ius primae noctis*, and *Bathseba Saarenmaalla* ('Bathsheba of Saaremaa'), in which the lord has the troublesome husband of the woman he covets sent to the army. The author is best when describing strong individuals such as Bernhard Riives, in the story bearing his name as title, who prefers to be killed rather than submit to the humiliation of flogging, and Maltsvet, in *Lasnamäen valkea laiva* ('The White Ship of Lasnamäki'), the leader of a utopian revivalist movement, and a young woman attracted to the movement who eventually breaks away.

Some of the stories of *Vieras veri* herald her great works of the twenties. Neither short stories nor full-length novels, they were called "tales" by the author and "ballads" by some critics and scholars, who agree that they are the best part of her work, the fullest expression of her personality, and the first mature development of her style.[542] Actually we prefer her earlier stories and feel that, with their simplicity of motif and treatment, they are closer to contemporary standards than the later ones are, with their elaborate artistry and overdramatized descriptions. In the former, motifs are from daily life, although sometimes related to unusual events, and the language is just archaic enough to suggest the time and place, but in the latter, motifs are fantastic and supernatural or romantic and exceptional, and the language is completely designed to reproduce a centuries-old, solemn style with religious overtones. *Lähtevien laivojen kaupunki* contains a story, *Yksi kaikkien edestä* ('One for All'), about a fisherman contaminated with leprosy who is shunned from the village by his friends and neighbors. This action is decided upon at a meeting:

> Again the oldest of them said:
> ... Behold, our will is not that you shall perish, but we will give you food and drink until you die. But that you may not contaminate all of us, and your wife and children as well, we will keep you in Kaarel Reinu's old stable, and we believe that you shall willingly let this be done?
> And nobody said a word, neither the judges nor the man who was being tried, for this jury knew of no lawyer or defense, and the wind blew a cloud of quicksand that glittered in the sun into their eyes, and the seagulls, looking for remains of fish, flew over the enclosure with the nets where men were proclaiming the decision of God.

In *Sudenmorsian* ('The Wolf's Bride,' 1928; rewritten for the stage, 1937) Aalo, a young woman, becomes a werewolf, but the story is more an analysis of the conflicting forces within the soul than a mere tale of horror. Her definitive change is described:

> ... For this wolf was the *Diabolus sylvarum*, to wit, the Spirit of the Woods, although it was first now that he did reveal his true shape.
> Thus a bliss that hath no measure and is not contained within earthly boundaries came over Aalo, and into her soul was poured an exceeding happiness, for which there be no words in human language for reason of the marvelous and abounding joy it giveth to drink to the thirsting. For at that moment she was one with the Spirit of the Woods, the mighty Daimon which had chosen and overpowered her in the shape of a wolf, and all boundaries vanished between them so that they melted into each other, as two drops of dew are united, so that nobody may separate them from each other.
> And she was dispersed into the song of the spruces in the deep forests, she was pressed forth as a golden drop from the side of a red pine, and, disappearing, she became the green moisture of the moss, for she was the prey of the *Diabolus sylvarum* and of Satan.

In addition to *Sudenmorsian* Aino Kallas's main works in the twenties and thirties were the stories or tales *Barbara von Tisenhusen* (name, 1923), *Reigin pappi* ('The Priest of Reig,' 1926), and *Pyhän joen kosto* ('The Vengeance of the Holy River,' 1929), and the plays *Bathseba Saarenmaalla* (adapted from the short story, 1932), *Mare ja hänen poikansa* ('Mare and Her Son,' 1935), and *Talonpojan kunnia* ('The Honor of a Peasant,' 1936). *Bathseba*

Saarenmaalla, Mare ja hänen poikansa, and *Sudenmorsian* were adapted as libretti for operas by the Finnish composer Tauno Pylkkänen in 1940, 1945, and 1950 respectively.[543] Only the motifs of *Sudenmorsian* are fantastic; the others are mainly about exceptional individuals with violent passions involved in erotic conflicts or unusual, tragic situations. The characters are neither decadent nor morbid; their exuberant, healthy strength leads them to commit acts disapproved by society. Barbara von Tisenhusen is a young Estonian woman of noble birth who falls in love with a man socially below her in a period of Estonian history when such relations were impossible. In *Reigin pappi* the wife of a pastor is killed for committing adultery. *Mare ja hänen poikansa* describes a rebellion of Estonian peasants, and in *Pyhän joen kosto* the rational and irrational forces in man appear in the shapes of a German builder, who is erecting a dam, and the country people, who superstitiously fear the undertaking. The builder is eventually contaminated by this fear in the form of an erotic obsession typical of Aino Kallas; he imagines a mermaid in the river is irresistibly attracting him into it.

Aino Kallas published three more collections of short stories, *Seitsemän neitsyttä* ('The Seven Virgins,' 1948), *Virvatulia* ('Wills-o'-the-Wisp,' 1949), and *Rakkauden vangit* ('The Prisoners of Love,' 1951), a biography of her husband, and narrations about her travels in addition to the memoirs and parts of her diaries; but the most interesting of her late works are the poems, collected in *Kuoleman joutsen* ('The Swan of Death,' 1942; Pylkkänen wrote melodies for a selection from it), *Kuun silta* ('The Bridge of the Moon,'1943), and *Polttoroviolla* ('On the Stake,' 1945). They reflect her tragic experiences during World War II, when Estonia was occupied by the Soviet Union, Germany, and the Soviet Union again; she lost her children but escaped with her husband to Stockholm, where he died. She returned to Finland, which had remained free, and finished her life there. The poems do not tell of her individual fate but lament the sufferings of mankind in a simple but refined manner reminiscent of her early short stories. The war and devastation are not pictured directly, but represented symbolically, as in *Dies Irae, Dies Illa.* The author speaks of "the stars of destruction in the sky" and her "brothers and sisters who are sleeping their last sleep while the world is perishing." The poems are traditional in this respect,[544] but they represent the best of tradition, concluding her work worthily.

* * * * *

In the Scandinavian countries the development of a political workers' movement and trade unions in the late nineteenth and early twentieth centuries was surrounded by lively intellectual and artistic activity.[545] In Finland the folk writers had been noticed by the educated classes even by the end of the eighteenth century, so that a person of modest origin publishing literature was not unusual. Naturally, then, when a numerically important working class appeared with the development of modern industries after 1860,[546] its members began producing literary works of all descriptions, poetry and drama appearing more frequently than fiction, editing newspapers and periodicals, distributing political pamphlets and propaganda, and translating foreign literature. They organized societies— discussion groups interested in political and social questions, glee clubs, bands and orchestras, public libraries, and evening courses. The Finns' extraordinary passion for theater led to the birth of a number of amateur groups, soon organized in permanent repertory theaters, many of which are still active.

Due to the peculiar political and social situation before 1860, the theories of the utopian socialists, anarchists, and nihilists did not affect life in Finland, and eventually the workers' movement adopted Marxist socialism from Germany and the rest of Scandinavia. The enthusiasm spent in other countries in the revolutions, rebellions, and riots of the nineteenth century awakened in approximately 1900 in Finland. The leaders of the workers' movement and the workers themselves began to discuss theoretical questions, quoting Marx, Kautsky, Bebel, and others, following Belgium's social and political development, and referring to Jean Jaurès's opinions. They made passionate, inflammatory speeches against capitalism, hoping for the rising proletariat to sweep away the old, rotten world. Finland, a Protestant country, had a long tradition of Bible reading, so that imprecating against the wealthy and prophesying a better world to come might have taken biblical overtones, but the mood of the socialist movement was anticlerical and sometimes antireligious.[547] Kaarlo Halme, a well-known actor from the Finnish National Theater, who worked with Eino Leino in his ephemerous *Kalevala* theater, converted to socialism and worked in 1906 and 1907 to found the Helsinki Popular Stage (*Kansannäyttämö*); he declared a need for a theater to bring forth new ideas, reflect the spiritual aims of the proletariat, and "prevent us from leaving the road toward the source of socialism and true culture, show us the best and highest ideals of mankind."[548] Raoul Palmgren calls the approximate span from 1900 to 1918 the period of the old workers' movement in Finland and explains its spiritual and practical immaturity, coarse and plebeian character, and enthusiasm by its sudden development. Socialism gave its class-conscious members a feeling of higher ideals, morals, and human principles, and their lofty goals seemed to justify the merciless class struggle necessary for their achievement.[549] These attitudes were partially responsible for the events which led to the Civil War; afterwards some of the fire left the workers' movement, and peaceful reforms began under moderate leadership. Radicalism lived, however, fed by intolerance of the educated classes and rightist groups who did not distinguish between moderate socialist or labor union leaders and active communists; fascist movements erupted against socialists and liberals in the early 1930s. It was also nurtured by the underground Communist party and groups of leftist writers such as the second *Tulenkantajat* and *Kiila*. After World War II, however, many of the left-wing writers imprisoned during the war for opposition to Finland's pro-German policies were ejected from the communist-controlled Democratic League of the Finnish People for refusal to submit to Stalinist discipline; they have simply continued writing.

These events explain that after 1918 Finland could not have the kind of proletarian literature existing before; neither the Social-Democrat party with its cautious program of gradual reform nor the Communist party with its stern discipline could attract writers. Dr. Palmgren broadly analyzes this question and concludes that a true proletarian literature exists when the proletariat is already organized and class conscious but has not gained social influence; it disappears when the proletariat seizes power through revolution or class differences are attenuated through peaceful development and the mutual hostility disappears.[550] Although we would not use Dr. Palmgren's phrasing or specific terminology, we agree with his premise. He has gathered a vast amount of information, analyzed and presented it well, picturing a fascinating period of Finnish literature and history, but the theoretical portion of his work consists of little more than elaborate statements of the obvious.[551] More or less he says simply that, while the working class has to fight for a better social position, its writing members describe this fight in their works, but, when the struggle is over, they do not. We find more interesting the fact that so many workers, often living in appalling conditions and earning their living very young, acquired instruction and wrote works needing no allowances for their originating circumstances.

Much of the literature, however, was not of high quality, and almost until Dr. Palmgren studied it the majority of scholars, essayists, and critics have neglected it, partially because of political prejudice and partially because it was considered *a priori* to be pure *agitprop*. The socialist press noticed the proletarian or working-class writers,[552] but the nonsocialist critics noticed only the most prominent of them, e.g., Lehtimäki. Even in 1958, however, a scholar wrote that **Aku Rautala** (pseudonym of **Aukusti Ripatti**, 1896-1931) was the first modern worker to write and describe characters like himself in Finnish literature.[553] By 1930, when Rautala's two works appeared, Pekkanen had already published two collections of short stories. Lehtimäki was noticed during World War I, and 101 proletarian writers were active during the period of the old workers' movement. Of those, 46 published works not printed in newspapers or periodicals, and, although none of them was truly great, some were original and creative authors on the level of the best second-rate nonsocialist authors.[554]

The influence of the leading writers of the time is noticeable in the working-class literature. The formal patterns of Eino Leino were followed, especially his *Kalevala*-like poetry, the popular Finnish origin of which made it seem suitable for poems meant for the Finnish people.[555] Because of his poems about the Finnish peasants' rebellion against the Swedish aristocrats,

Kaarlo Kramsu was admired and quoted;[556] that side of his art was ignored when nonsocialists used him for patriotic and nationalistic purposes. Minna Canth, of course, was highly esteemed, especially by women, who have always been a large group within the Social-Democrat party.[557] Conspicuous among them early in the century was **Hilja Pärssinen** (or **Liinamaa-Pärssinen**, 1876-1935),[558] one of the few from the educated classes to join the party when it was dominated by genuine proletarians. She became a teacher and did temperance and welfare work, eventually collaborating with the workers in an effort to improve their lot. She was secretary and chairman of the Woman Workers' Union, long-time member of Parliament, and a party executive. She fled to the Soviet Union after the Civil War, returned a few years later, went to prison, but, freed, again became active in the Social-Democrat party and Parliament. She wrote newspaper articles, criticism, political pamphlets, and poems, translating several from Swedish and German. Her first collection of poetry, *Primuloita* ('Primroses,' 1899), is in Erkko's idealistic and sentimental manner—she was not yet a socialist—and the second, *Kyllikki ja Lemminkäinen* (characters from the *Kalevala*, 1902), describes the joys and sorrows of love and marriage. After 1901 she wrote for and about the working class. The poems are mediocre, some hastily written and poor in quality, and very typical of the writings of the workers' movement at that time, although personal taste and interest in specific problems, women's rights and religion, to which she was hostile, appear in them. Her first such collection, *Taistelon tuoksinassa* ('In the Thick of the Battle,' 1907), contains battle songs, which call the proletariat to fight for a better future and promise victory, and descriptions from the lives of workers, for example, *The Carpenter, The Poor Boy, The Song of the Factory Girl, The Seamstress*, et al. In 1911 she was involved in a polemic with bourgeois critics about socialism and the freedom of the writer, citing Gorki as a free socialist author to refute her opponents, who feared that political ideology would prove intolerant of views not in accordance with it. In 1913 the collection *Musta virta* ('The Black River') was printed by Finnish immigrants in Hancock, Michigan because of the Russian censure in Finland, but, after the March revolution in 1917, *Elämän harha* ('The Illusion of Life') was issued by one of Finland's major nonsocialist publishers. These poems are technically her best; they also express individiual problems, the disillusionment of middle age, and life's difficulties, though they accept them courageously. Although she published two more works in the twenties, her courage, energy, idealism, extraordinary working capacity and literary activities were typical of the early workers' movement, when every leader of labor was supposed to have written poetry.[559]

Two other female socialist writers were known more for their literary than political activities. They were noticed by the leading critics, but are almost forgotten now, partially because they took refuge in the Soviet Union at the end of the Civil War and remained there, severed from their native country, for the rest of their lives. **Elvira Willman** (1875-193?), from a lower middle-class family, lived with her mother in difficult conditions after her parents' divorce. She completed secondary school and studied at the university, however, but did not take a degree. Attracted by the theater, she soon wrote *Lyyli* (1903) with the help of Bergbom, who had it performed that year at the National Theater; the critics and public liked it, and it was printed. Somewhat in the manner of Minna Canth, whom the author admired, the play exposes the position of women. The plot is the old story of the virtuous, poor young girl seduced and abandoned by a wealthy young man. The author intended to have Lyyli kill herself, but, on Bergbom's recommendation, changed the end, showing her proudly rejecting the money offered by her seducer and declaring that she would take care of the expected child herself. The incisive description of the characters and their surroundings, a working-class home in Helsinki, lifts the play above the level of old-fashioned melodrama. When she wrote it, Elvira Willman had more idealistic and liberal than socialist ideas, but at the same time she began publishing short stories and articles in the socialist press. The subjects vary, but the motif of the seduced girl reappears. Many of her articles are about sexual morals and free love and express such extreme views that members of the workers' movement, e.g., Hilda Pärssinen, protested.[560] Her second play, *Rhodon valtias* ('The Ruler of Rhodes' 1904), was also performed at the National Theater, but without success, and was not printed. *Kellarikerroksessa* ('In the Basement,' 1907) is a chaotic description of the inhabitants of a Helsinki tenement in which prostitutes are prominent. The slight plot might better have been omitted, leaving a series of vivid sketches from the life of the small human community. Performed only by an amateur group, it was the last play she wrote until World War I, and the texts of many of the plays she had staged then by various small drama groups have disappeared. One, *Rakkauden orjuus* ('The Slavery of Love,' 1916), was noticed by socialist and nonsocialist critics; it is about a woman who refuses marriage as slavery, even when she bears an illegitimate child. In 1906 Elvira Willman had married a member of the Socialist party, and both eagerly took part in the revolutionary activities of 1917 and 1918. She wrote a pacifist play, *Veriuhrit* ('The Bloody Sacrifices'), and an autobiographic work, *Vallankumouksen vyöryssä* ('In the Turmoil of Revolution'), and with her husband escaped to the Soviet Union, where she came under the authorities' suspicion. Her husband was shot in the 1920s; she disappeared in the Stalinist purges of the thirties.

Hilda Tihlä (1870-1944)[561] had a similar life, although she fared better in the Soviet Union; she died a locally respected author in the Finno-Karelian SSR, now the Karelian ASSR. The daughter of a small farmer who lost his fortune, she never went to school but had her works printed by the main publishers in the country. She married a post office employee, settled in Helsinki, began writing for socialist publications, and joined the Social-Democrat party in 1905. Like Elvira Willman's, her radical views on women and sexual morals aroused protests. In 1907 a nonsocialist publisher issued her first novel, *Leeni*, a long description from the turn of the century in which the old customs of the countryside and modern life in Helsinki form the background for the biography of Leeni, a girl who comes to the great city, where she has a sad end. The incidents packed into her life are improbable in number but realistic in nature. Although this work was almost unnoticed, the next, *Metsäkyliltä* ('From the Backwoods Villages,' 1907), the first of several distributed by the country's major publisher, won the praise of bourgeois and socialist critics. Its longest story, *Kulkuri* ('The Tramp') is probably partly autobiographical; it is the story of a girl who grows up in miserable conditions in the country, comes to the city, where she finds some security and happiness, but finally becomes a homeless tramp again. Other stories describe mainly poor country people with sympathy and humor. Her second collection, *Kuopus* ('The Youngest Child,' 1910), is less interesting, but the third, *Jumalan lapsia* ('God's Children,' 1911) was another success. In it *Saarnaaja* ('The Preacher') tells of a poor, lonely girl who has ecstatic religious experiences and preaches in a trance, winning fame and disciples. As she begins to analyze herself, however, her preaching becomes more rational, and her supporters desert her. *Hilma, elämän satua* ('Hilma, a Tale from Life,' 1913), her next novel, is another story of a country girl who comes to the city. She resists attacks against her virtue. Eventually she is taken into the protection of the Salvation Army, but, unable to support its religious atmosphere, drowns herself. The last and longest novel she published in Finland, *Ihmisiä* ('Human Beings' or 'People,' 1916), is a confused narrative about a youth who rebels against his wealthy, tyrannical father, almost becomes a socialist, but takes over the family properties at the death of its head. He soon discovers that he is unable to manage them properly, and the book leaves unanswered the question of whether he is a disillusioned idealist or simply a man who cannot decide what to do with himself.

Hilda Tihlä's Finnish works are not specifically socialistic in spite of their sympathy for the poor and criticism of the wealthy. Later, in the Soviet Union, which she entered in 1918, she criticized the former, saying that she secretly admired the bourgeois and was a socialist for "sentimental reasons."[562] Both Elvira Willman and Hilda Tihlä were not unlike nineteenth-century female rebels, e.g., Georges Sand and George Eliot, whose political ideas were vague and even sentimental, but who considered the position of women important and expressed their protest in rebellion against society's sexual morals.

In accordance with traditional interests of the sexes, most works of the male socialist or proletarian writers do not deal with those questions, but appeal to unity in the fight against capitalism, promising a better future and describing the hardships of the working class, strikes, and other conflicts with employers, in which strike breakers often appear.[563] A persistent misconception among Finnish scholars is that the Great Strike of 1905 gave birth to the working-class poets, often called the "Poets of the Great Strike"; Kössi Kaatra, so called by Unto Kupiainen, published poetry from 1902, three collections appearing between 1903 and 1905, and less prominent writers began activity even earlier.[564] In 1905 the Finnish nation became united in its resistance to Russian oppression; the strike was actually a political demonstration which focused the attention of nonsocialists on the workers' movement and its writers, so that at that moment they were born in the consciousness of the bourgeois. Socialism and the workers' movement were fashionable among the educated classes, especially students,[565] although few of them remained in the Socialist party. Even Koskenniemi composed poetry expressing sympathy for the workers, and the greatest Swedish poet of Finland in that period, Arvid Mörne, was active among the Swedish-speaking socialists for several years.[566]

Kustaa Aadolf (Kössi) Kaatra (1882-1928) is the best of the poets of the early movement. He published his first works in Tampere, where he had spent his early life. Admired, they earned him the nickname of Tampere's Eino Leino, which reflects local patriotism and the fact that Leino was then the prototype of the poet, to whom all others were compared. Kaatra's poetry does show Leino's influence, and both had such facility for composing verse that not all of either's production is of high quality. Much of Kaatra's work, however, is quite good; his art distinctly develops from a loosely ornate, wordy style toward progressively more terse, chastised forms.[567]

Kaatra's father died when the future poet was quite young, and to maintain the children his mother worked in a factory, as did the boy after he had finished school at the age of twelve. Later he found a position as an office clerk and became a staff member of the socialist paper *Kansan Lehti*, a career similar to those of many other proletarian writers. Yrjö Mäkelin, chief editor of *Kansan Lehti*, deviated from official party policy and had to leave his post; Kaatra, whom he had protected, went with him to Oulu, where he was director of the local workers' theater. Then he settled in Teisko, near Tampere, opened a small shop, studied French and Russian, and translated poetry from Russian. In 1917 he reappeared in public, but, marooned in White territory during the Civil War, he escaped to Sweden, where he spent the rest of his life. The bitterness of exile, reflected in his later works, made him a communist. The autobiographical *Äiti ja poika* ('The Mother and the Son,' 1924) is less aggressive than *Punaiset ja valkoiset* ('The Reds and the Whites,' 1919), but in it he criticizes his earlier works and attitudes as too individual and sentimental. He claimed he had first attempted to describe "his own little individual *Weltschmerz*" from a "backyard perspective," but realized the futility of "caterwauling" about his own "difficulties and inner conflicts" and found, "instead of his former small god and goddess, instead of himself and his sweetheart, a new god and a new faith, a faith in work and the blessings of work, a faith in the strength of the working class and the justice of its cause, a faith in freedom and in a new life upon earth. . . ."[568] Religious overtones are not absent from Kaatra's language, but with that exception they were excellent propaganda for the orthodox communists. Even in 1962 a biography of Kaatra slanted in this direction was published by a communist critic, whose statements Dr. Palmgren protested.[569]

Especially at the beginning of his career Kaatra wrote poetry expressing the individual feelings that have inspired poets throughout the world: he loved, despised the false and debased world, doubted his own forces and convictions, passionately sought an ideal to follow, defied the powers which threatened to crush him, and asked justice from God. These concerns are typical of his first collection, *Kynnyksellä* ('On the Threshold,' 1903), and apparent in the second, *Elämästä* ('From Life,' 1904), although it contains more socially oriented poems. In some poems the author appeals to God for help; in others he expresses anticlerical, antireligious feelings, but contradiction is only superficial, for in Finland, as in other countries with a strong established church, people often felt that the church gave a distorted view of true religion, that the real teachings of God were quite different from the official dogma.[570] The second collection produced an argument between his admirers in Tampere and Edvard Valpas, also a writer, chief editor of the socialist paper *Työmies* in Helsinki, and a leader of the Socialist party. The praise of Kaatra in Tampere was exaggerated, but Valpas's criticism was malevolent. He attempted a definition of proletarian poetry and poets, using formal and literary as well as social criteria; according to him proletarian poetry had its own forms, and, if forms taken from nonproletarian poetry were used with proletarian motifs, the result was "hodgepodge" (*sekuli*), Kaatra being a typical "hodgepodge poet." Valpas always tried to write, speak, and behave in an exaggeratedly popular manner.[571] Kaatra's third collection does not differ greatly from the first two, but it is formally better, and the poems on social motifs are more aggressive and less vaguely sentimental than previous ones. His romantic spirit and probably Eino Leino's influence are still evident, however, in the poem *Murrosaikana* ('A Time of Great Changes'), he speaks of trumpets calling to war, the knights of the spirit preparing for battle, their shiny weapons, banners fluttering proudly, and white steeds waiting for the leader. The hope for a hero to lead the workers to a better future was frequently expressed at that time.

The events of 1905 and 1906 brought Kaatra to the fore as a poet and, for a while, a political personality. Elected to various committees, he wrote for the *Kansan Lehti* and published three collections of poetry during the latter year. Two, *'Suurlakkokuvia' ym. työväenlauluja* ('Scenes from the Great

Strike and Other Songs for the Workers') and *Murroksessa* ('The Great Change'), are exclusively political, but the third, *Kyttä* ('The Hunter'), deals with other subjects, mainly love. The first two reflect the moods of the workers' movement at the time, the enthusiasm for the Great Strike and its results, the revoking of the measures of Russification, parliamentary reform, and gradual disappointment when the nonsocialist parties remained firmly opposed to socialism and the imperial government withdrew in Russia and Finland most of the concessions it had been forced to make.

Between 1906 and 1917 Kaatra wrote little and published less, but from May 1917 to January 1918, while he worked for the newspaper *Kansan Tahto* in Oulu, he had a poem printed in it every week, sometimes almost every day. They follow the events of the time, revolution in Russia, and political changes in Finland. Initially optimistic, they become more aggressive and bitter as the hostility leading to the Civil War mounted. During his Swedish exile he published most of these compositions in a collection titled *Alhaisolauluja* ('Songs of the Mob,' 1922) as well as in *Äiti ja poika* and *Punaiset ja valkoiset*. Some of the poems from *Alhaisolauluja*, differing from his earlier florid style, attain a simplicity and strength of expression that Dr. Palmgren compares to Elmer Diktonius's compositions, written in defiance of traditional rules at the same time or slightly later.[572] Among proletarian poets who remained faithful to their class, Kaatra is the most remarkable. He is not a great poet but deserves mention in histories of Finnish literature which include Suonio, Jännes, Tuokko, Kasimir Leino, Kouta, and Juva; his omission in some of those was politically motivated.

Konrad Lehtimäki (1883-1937) has remained the best-known proletarian writer; he alone is featured in a collection of biographies of Finnish writers reprinted several times.[573] He was born near Turku, at Vahto, where his father leased a small farm which had to be relinquished when Konrad was nine. The boy worked as a shepherd, a farmhand, and, from the age of fourteen, a baker's apprentice, in Turku and then Helsinki. In spite of the long hours and unhealthy conditions of the profession, he finished elementary school at the same time and continued individual studies in Swedish, English, Russian, et al., read, and participated in wrestling, skiing, and bicycle racing, in which he won local championships. He worked as a stoker on a ship, going to London and returning to Finland via Hamburg, where he stayed awhile, and Sweden, through which he walked. At the beginning of the century he became involved in active resistance against Russification and had to hide from the police. Later he worked on the Finnish State Railroads, joined the Socialist party, and became a party executive and a member of Parliament from 1911 to 1917. Although there are romantic stories about his activities during the Civil War, he seems to have worked as a war correspondent. However, at the end of the war he was arrested and sentenced to death; through the intervention of Juhani Aho and other nonsocialist writers the sentence was not carried out and later reversed. Lehtimäki, granted a national pension for writers, spent the rest of his life peacefully although he suffered from tuberculosis contracted at an early age. No longer active in politics, he continued to write, but his later works did not have the popularity of the early ones.

He began his literary career by writing for socialist papers and published his first collection of short stories, *Rotkoista* ('From the Abysses), in 1910. The features of his later production are evident; for a man of his character and strength the discovery that he had a virtually incurable illness was a shock, and he dwelt in fantasies of death, suffering, accidental dismemberment, fighting, killing, suicide, and madness. In horror and gore no one in Finland surpasses him; even abroad it might be difficult to find his equal. Toppila's stories are relieved by expressions of pity for his characters' sufferings and by the fantastic or unreal nature of the action, but Lehtimäki gives a realistic though unlikely picture of all the suffering, misery, and cruelty in the world. He not only describes the horrible, gloomy, threatening, and terrifying, but also defines them as such:

> On a box, which was supposed to serve as a table, there was a short candle, which cast a dim, yellow light on the miserable room, so that the few broken pieces of furniture which were in it could barely be seen, and made it feel curiously cold, like a grave. . . . A mysterious twilight was lurking in the corners, and a terrifying, coal-black darkness stared into the room through the only window. . . . *(Jumalan äiti)*

A few details, such as the personification of darkness, are not entirely realistic; in this connection Dr. Palmgren speaks of symbolism, also mentioning the possible influence of Leonid Andreev, whom Lehtimäki probably met while living in Viipuri from 1907 to 1911.[574] Apart from Andreyev, there was a trend away from realism at the time apparent in, e.g., Eino Leino, L. Onerva, and Maila Talvio. This passage reproduces a literary archetype, the miserable and terrifying hovel; there are many examples in Dickens.[575]

Lehtimäki's works contain the inherent contradiction of socialist realism, i.e., the attempt to represent the facts of a dynamic world society by means of static art forms. Eminently a man of his time, he was aware of the expanding, changing nature of contemporary life and looked to the future, attempting predictions, but defining all that he saw and felt with traditional methods. A man as energetic and active as Lehtimäki could not stop to think of new literary forms, for his message was more important to him than his style.

Only one of his first short stories is socialistic; its subject is a lockout described in the conversations of a family of workers. All, however, are about workers, poor people, and revolutionaries and condemn the capitalist system as the cause of their sufferings. The issue may be, for example, the right to euthanasia or suicide. The most directly political deal with Russian revolutionaries; however, the macabre also predominates in them, e.g., in one about the execution of rebellious soldiers, which, because of the unwilling, frightened firing party's clumsiness, becomes a horrible butchery which drives the commanding officer insane. Another discusses the problem of individual terrorism. Although men like Lehtimäki tend to admire the lonely hero, one of the characters stresses the need for changing the entire social system, which can be accomplished only through the "unanimous efforts of the proletariat."[576]

His first work did not attract much attention, but the next, a tragedy in five acts with an epilogue, *Spartacus*, performed at the Tampere Workers' Theater in 1913 and printed the following year by a major publisher, was favorably reviewed by the leading critics, who also admired Linnankoski's *Ikuinen taistelu* and biblical plays. Lehtimäki undertook the task seriously, studying Roman history to verify the facts, but the result is less like an opera libretto (Dr. Palmgren's description) than a filmscript for a Hollywood historical extravaganza; some reviewers of his time criticized the superficial description of the characters. However, since the play is history, psychological problems of the characters are of secondary importance; it might be described as epic theater in the Brechtian sense. Lehtimäki's love for gory details is evident: after an attempted slave rebellion is put down at the end of act 2, act 3 opens with mutilated bodies lying around and wounded or tortured slaves groaning in fetters. In the epilogue Romans insult the defeated slaves crucified along the Via Appia; after they leave, vultures and wolves gather to feast on the corpses. In 1916 and 1917, when the author had to leave Finland, he lived in the United States, where he personally directed the production of the play in several Finnish theaters.[577]

During World War I Lehtimäki published two collections of short stories, *Kuolema* ('Death,' 1915) and *Syvyydestä* ('From the Depths,' 1915); a play, *Perintö* ('The Heritage,' performed at Tampere City Theater and the National Theater and printed, both in 1916); and a novel, *Ylös helvetistä* ('Up from Hell,' 1917). *Jäähyväiset* ('The Farewell') was published in the Finnish community in Fitchburg, Massachusetts, in 1917, and *Etuvartiotaistelu* ('The Outpost Battle') was first performed in the United States in more than thirty Finnish workers' theaters before it came out in Finland (1920).[578] In Finland his works were printed by important publishers, noticed by the critics, and usually favorably reviewed; *Ylös helvetistä* was a near sensation, quickly going through four editions and appearing in a Swedish and a Russian translation, for which Gorki wrote a preface.[579] The stories in *Kuolema* and *Syvyydestä* are built on the same themes of suffering, pain, and death that those in *Rotkoista* treated, only a few have a social message. *Kuolema* contains one about an old carpenter who dies on his job because, for fear of

252

losing it, he will not admit that he is ill, and another about a railway worker whose legs are crushed by a train, but the emphasis in both is more on the feelings produced by approaching death than on the causes of death. Many of the narratives seem to be horror for horror's sake, e.g., one about a woman, apparently dead but conscious, who follows the preparations for her own burial and the burial itself; the story does not end happily.[580] The motifs of *Syvyydestä* are from the war, which Lehtimäki did not experience directly, but which fascinated him with its opportunities for descriptions of death and destruction. Some of the stories are antimilitaristic and pacifistic, e.g., one about an old couple taking their son, leaving for the war, to the railroad station and one about two children surprised by the enemy, the girl raped and the boy killed after shooting one of the assailants. The motif of another is the well-known one of soldiers from the opposing armies who fraternize in no-man's land on Christmas Eve. Lehtimäki's stories are not in general a war protest; there is little pity in them, except in cases of mercy killing. In its morbid pleasure in suffering, his work seems more a protest against an external force (his illness) which prevented him from leading an energetic, daring life; his characters prefer annihilation to a limitation of their freedom.

In *Perintö* the author attempts to represent middle-class life. A young man in love with an actress is rivaled by a wealthy businessman, her lover. She falls in love with the young hero and declares that she will leave everything and marry him. Because he has been misled to believe that she is still carrying on her affair, he shoots her and her former lover, then poisons himself. The title refers to heredity. The hero has supposedly inherited a yearning for truth and honesty and a strong inclination to violence; his lawyer, who supplies him with the poison and makes the last statements, says that he was too honest to live in a world of conventions, lies, and hypocrisy.

Some critics thought that *Ylös helvetistä* had been inspired by the March Revolution in Russia and wondered how it had been written in such a short time.[581] Actually it was ready in the fall of 1916 and was not about Russia. The major motif is the overthrow of a military dictatorship by a heroic underground movement. The author predicts that World War I will not result in the establishment of democratic governments throughout the world and, further, that the growth of ruthless dictatorships—he does not say where—will result in a still more terrible conflict. His work is not science fiction in the sense of Wells's or Verne's books, but he predicts weapons of the future, not always accurately. Armored cars are used in street fights, warplanes are invisible in the dark, and tremendous bombs are used to destroy entire cities, but he is vague about their source of power. Foreseeing the consequences of modern warfare, the massive destruction of cities and aerial warfare, he describes the setting up of an international organization to prevent future wars, to help mankind to rise out of Hell. However, his pessimism was not deep enough to let him guess that, after a second world war, mankind would prepare for and rehearse a third. Dr. Palmgren thinks that Jack London may have influenced this work.[582] London was at that time considered a leading socialist and proletarian writer, and Lehtimäki could have read his books in the United States, where they were translated into Finnish earlier than in Finland. London's influence might explain the many situations and motifs from *Ylös helvetistä* which continue appearing in stories of that type, e.g., Robert A. Heinlein's *Revolt in 2100*. In one of the last scenes the creation of a better world and society is decided upon by a general meeting. Erwin Piscator thought of using a scene similar to one of Lehtimäki's in one of the plays he directed in Germany: a procession of horribly mutilated, half-human war invalids. But, although Lehtimäki could write it, he had to admit that an audience couldn't watch it.[583]

Like *Perintö, Etuvartiotaistelu* describes contemporary life without exceptionally violent or bloody incidents. Clearly Lehtimäki's most socialistic work, it is set in working-class surroundings and delivers a message at the end. Although it contains some melodrama, it is a realistic description of a strike ending in defeat for the workers. Afterwards one of them kills a representative of the employers, but he is told that individual violence is of no use and might even be harmful to the workers' interests. In the end he admits that they are right, reflecting the author's own ideas. Lehtimäki took a moderate stand in political questions in 1917 and 1918 and spoke against military action on the part of the Socialist party.

After the Civil War he published a romanticized autobiographical novel, *Taistelija* ('The Fighter,' part 1, 1922, rewritten and published with part 2, 1924), several short-story collections, and a play, *Gladiaattorin morsian* ('The Gladiator's Bride,' a revised version of *Spartacus*, which won a literary prize in 1935), but only portions of *Taistelija* are not inferior to his major works. No longer active in politics, he became in appearance adjusted to capitalist society and a target of violent attacks from the communists. Although he felt a part of the working class, only a small part of his works directly reflects its life and problems. His most interesting quality is his fight against and fascination with the brutality, violence, and destruction in the modern world.

Despite his views of the future, Lehtimäki was a man of the past in the 1920s and 1930s; it was not a time for romantic heroics or radicalism in literature. Although extremists expressed their views in writings, authors such as Sillanpää, Lehtonen, Kilpi, and Toppila dominated the period. **Toivo Pekkanen** (1902-1957) is more typical.[584] He was born in Kotka, a city founded on the Gulf of Finland, east of Helsinki, in 1879, which grew with the speed of an American mining town because of its good harbor, railroad, communications, and the proximity of the Kymi River. His father was a factory worker, and Pekkanen worked as a mechanic from the age of twelve until he became a freelance writer in 1932. He completed elementary and vocational school, read and studied foreign languages, especially English. Haanpää, a lively man with a sense of humor and gift for story telling, remained in his home region almost all his life, but Pekkanen, a serious, brooding character, was in contact with other people and made several long journeys to Europe. He died on a journey in Copenhagen; although eight years earlier a bad stroke had left him temporarily unable to speak, read or write, he had completely recovered, to the astonishment of the physicians, and published six more works before his death. In 1955 he was elected to the Finnish Academy.

The idea that Pekkanen was the first working-class representative to become a writer who lived by his pen and had his works read by all classes is still prevalent, but it is unfair to Kaatra and Lehtimäki, for example.[585] Lehtimäki was forgotten in the 1920s, whereas Pekkanen's fame continued to grow. We have mentioned Pekkanen's characters who do not live in the proper proletarian manner;[586] in the play *Sisarukset* ('Brother and Sister,' 1933) one of them says: "I do not have the thoughts, the desires and the hopes of a proletarian, but my position makes me one. Do you understand what that means?" In another context he writes: "For being a proletarian does not only mean that you have a low position in society, it is first of all a certain state of mind, a peculiar attitude toward life, burdened by the weight of the souls of the dead who were crushed and oppressed centuries ago."[587] Above all he was interested in moral problems, in discovering and describing impartially the causes of mankind's sufferings, although with a hope of helping his neighbors. In his memoirs, *Lapsuuteni* ('My Childhood,' 1953), he says: "He [the author] thought he would act as a reminder and try to write down facts that had really happened, what people around him had been thinking, hoping and doing, and what had been the consequences of that. And he also imagined that, should he find the true reason for the persistence of the misery and sorrow created by men, he would perhaps be able to spread light about it to others, even where darkness prevailed."

Unlike other Finnish writers who describe folk life, Pekkanen seldom attempts to reproduce popular forms of speech, and his narrative prose does not follow the free patterns of emotion and thought. His seriousness about his writing seems to have demanded a formal, correct form. Because writing was not an effortless task for him, his texts are often stiff and awkward; he has been compared to a blacksmith hammering slowly and painstakingly at hard iron to produce works which are solid and reliable rather than graceful and elegant.[588]

He began his literary career by writing short stories for magazines and published a first collection, *Rautaiset kädet* ('The Hands of Iron'), in 1927; *Satama ja meri* ('The Harbor and the Sea,' 1929) and *Kuolemattomat* ('The Immortals,' 1931) followed. All describe work—work in the factories, on buildings, and in the harbor—and attitudes toward work; at times it is pleasurable, an opportunity to show strength, skill, and energy, but usually it is burdensome. Written during the depression, these stories reveal that the author believes work an essential condition of organized society and workers its foundation, the true immortals; for kings, rulers, and empires may fall, but workers remain. Because of his social origin and subjects, Pekkanen was immediately classified a proletarian writer and realist, but his subjects include the middle class, and his works sometimes have a half-symbolic or unreal form. His plays, which are not as well known as others of his works, are the least realistic,[589] but indications appear even in his earliest stories. *Satama ja meri*, for example, refers to the well-known magic of the sea in opposition to everyday work in the harbor. His first works include *Tientekijät* ('The Road Builders,' 1930), an adventure novel from Lapland, viewed as a Finnish Klondyke, where an entire city springs up and disappears with equal speed. The book incorporates some of the history of Pekkanen's home town.

The novel *Tehtaan varjossa* ('In the Shadow of the Factory'), his first work to receive nationwide notice, appeared in 1932. Translated into French (1943), Swedish (1938), and Danish (1940), it is his best-known work. It tells about the life of a young worker, Samuel Oino, and is somewhat auto-biographical.[590] Oino matures, but his meditative mind and unwillingness to accept ready-made solutions to life's problems set him apart from his original surroundings without gaining him access to any other. He cannot accept an event without determining its causes, and he is criticized by his own class, especially by those members who want decisive action for the socialist cause, but he expresses no hostility toward them. No Finnish writer of low birth has ever insulted his original class to gain middle-class favor or turned against socialism, communism, or trade unions. Pekkanen chose and maintained the position of the dispassionate observer, accepting the consequences of suspicion from all social groups. He wrote most often sympathetically about the workers, most often critically about the middle class, and he wrote about himself, his attitude toward others, their attitude toward him, and the meaning of these things for him.

Samuel Oino's social and political problems are not the main issue of *Tehtaan varjossa*, however; just as important are his relations with his parents, friends, and girlfriends. Sex is treated frankly but without emphasis; sex without love and affection disappoints him, but love and affection without sex proves impossible—his love for a girl destroys his friendship with a man. Pekkanen does not romanticize his life and never represents the working class as stronger, less hypocritical, and more courageous than the bourgeois, but he insists that society is maintained by the toil of the working class.

His next novel, *Kauppiaiden lapset* ('Tradespeople and Their Children,' 1934), is about the middle-class life of individuals; a young woman out of pity marries a man to help him find a direction for his life, but, despite her good will and energy, is unable to give him the necessary confidence in himself. Pekkanen was successful in writing the book in a faultless manner, but he chose a situation and characters which he could not make meaningful.[591]

In a brief essay Pekkanen explains why and how he introduced the nonrealistic elements into his plays of the thirties,[592] *Sisarukset, Takaisin Austraaliaan* ('Back to Australia,' 1936), *Ukkosen tuomio* ('The Judgment of Thunder,' 1937), *Rakkaus ja raha* ('Money and Love,' 1937), and *Demoni* ('The Demon,' 1939); the latter two were printed posthumously in *Teokset* ('Collected Works,' 1958). He admits that he did not consider himself a good playwright and that he did not think play writing as serious a task as novel writing, but he says that drama gave him an opportunity to experiment and follow his inclinations. Here he alludes unconsciously to his dual personality: he felt obligated to do serious work, but wished to indulge in lighter activities. He came from difficult circumstances—his father soon died after the Civil War and he had to assume responsibilities for his relatives, thus missing most of the simple joys even a poor boy can have. He yearned, perhaps without consciousness, for a freer existence, but his basic earnestness made even the plays he wrote for relaxation deal with serious or tragic subjects.

He supplies another reason for the experimental nature of some of the plays: as a regular theatergoer, he wondered whether or not naturalistic plays could express "the innermost nature of contemporary man, or even describe factors on which he bases the life which he lives."[593] Always modest, he also says that seeing the defects of traditional plays is easy, but replacing them is not, adding that it was not his discovery, but an almost universal problem. In an article on the theater he calls for renewal of dramatic art, for "after all, we do not go to a theater in order to see a piece of reality reproduced as faithfully as possible, but to experience an illusion."[594] The wish to see the illusion created is directed to playwrights as well as to stage directors, actors, and set designers.

His first two plays are naturalistic in his own terms (he seems to use *naturalistic* as a synonym of *realistic*), although *Sisarukset* describes an unusual situation containing the sense of fatality of Greek tragedies.[595] The conflict is apparently social; a working-class girl accepts the courtship of a man with higher social status because she wants security. The presence of the depression is evident when she says: "There are twenty-five million unemployed in the world now, and everybody is fighting tooth and nail for a right to live. . . . The man I could have would perhaps not have a job the next day to make his family live." She also states some of Pekkanen's problems: "It is not good to be an intelligent and poor girl. It is hell. Poor and intelligent girls should never have books in their hands, they should never go to a theater or to movies. They all produce a longing which destroys them. They make them grow out of their own class but do not prepare them a place in the other." Elvira Willman's *Lyyli* contains similar thoughts. The girl's half-brother, who has always protected her, suspects the man of dishonorable intentions and kills him, then discovers that he has always been in love with her himself. The motif of fateful, illicit love is in contrast with the rest of the play. It creates problems in the production of the play and explains why Pekkanen's plays have not been very successful. They have been directed in a realistic manner which makes the nonrealistic elements seem out of place.[596]

Takaisin Australiaan is Pekkanen's only comedy, and it is provided with the epithet pessimistic.[597] It describes the relations of four persons, which slowly change during the play. A Finnish emigrant, Koponen, has come back from Australia with some money to open a shop, and a woman, Elli, returns from America with the same idea. Koponen is initially represented as a ruthless capitalist who thinks that poor people are bad, but his opinions are modified. Pekkanen seems to have been unable to describe a good capitalist; so Koponen marries Elli, and, because business is bad in Finland, they move back to Australia. Two secondary characters, Elli's sister Hulda, and Eero, an unemployed sailor, make comments which provoke thoughts and changes of attitude in the others. Like Chekhov's minor characters, they make penetrating remarks on numerous subjects, but we find it difficult to consider them quite seriously.

Rakkaus ja raha is mainly realistic. Juulia, the wife of a mechanic, Raittinen, proves a successful businesswoman. She begins with a small sweet stand; then, urged by Leppä, a real estate agent, she buys a cafe and eventually a hotel. By then her husband has left her, and she has become Leppä's mistress. Finally it is discovered that behind Leppä is a mysterious character, the Unknown, to whom she will be bound forever. By submitting to the power of money, she has acquired power and wealth at the cost of human relations. The figure of the Unknown is unnecessary for the play's message, but this heavy symbolism is typical of all Western literature since the 1930s. Still more of it appears in *Ukkosen tuomio*, where it is even more out of place. Two middle-age couples go on a picnic; one of the wives is much younger than her wealthy husband, and the other couple has a grown son, who seduces the young wife. A thunderstorm breaks out, and the young man asks the woman to choose between him and her husband; as she hesitates, he calls for the thunder to decide, and it strikes her husband dead. His dead body, the body of their love, will always separate the lovers.[598]

Demoni, Pekkanen's most ambitious play, contains his favorite dramatic character. He calls it a variation on the myth of Icarus, an attempt to show how Man is destroyed when he overreaches himself. It is also his strongest attempt to break from the "naturalist" theater, but he admitted that he never felt able to achieve his goal, although he rewrote the play many times.[599] He approved a critic's use of the word *cubist* in connection with the play; at that time French literary critics and scholars were speaking of cubist poetry. Pekkanen said that a cubist painter represents all sides of an object on the same canvas although in reality it can never be seen in that manner; the main characters of his play, a man and two women, are three sides of the man, so that he can be seen from more angles than in a traditional play. The play is about an actor, who represents the artist or the thinker; he feels that he can control the audience like God can, but his power is incomplete, for it lasts only as long as the performance. Eventually he feels that he has overcome this weakness, that his mastery over the minds of men is perfect, but this fact isolates him from mankind, and he becomes insane.

During World War II Pekkanen wrote a short patriotic play, *Raja merellä* ('The Border on the Sea,' 1942), and in 1951 a novel, *Täyttyneiden toiveiden maa* ('The Land of the Fulfilled Wishes'), from a play later performed in his native city. Although it is based on an interesting combination of fantasy and realism, it has attracted little attention. The characters, society's misfits and outcasts, are real, but the action is unreal. They have the opportunity to build the land of their wishes, a Utopia, which is destroyed by their inability to live together.

During the thirties Pekkanen also wrote several novels, the long *Isänmaan ranta* ('The Shores of My Country,' 1937) and *Ne menneet vuodet* ('Those Past Years,' 1940), rewritten and published in 1946 as *Jumalan myllyt* ('The Mills of God'), and the short *Ihmisten kevät* ('Human Spring,' 1935) and *Musta hurmio* ('Black Ecstasy,' 1939), as well as a collection of short stories, *Levottomuus* (1938). The author agreed with the many critics and scholars who considered *Isänmaan ranta* one of his best works[600] and indicated that Helminen, the main character, was his favorite among all he created.[601] It is a description of a strike which fails in a southern Finnish city much like Kotka. Helminen, at first its leader, eventually loses control over his fellow workers to Huttunen, who has more radical views. Helminen voices Pekkanen's opinion that the working class must acquire more instruction, material, and intellectual independence in order to become equal to the other classes, but Huttunen wants more power, not equality, for the working class. The factory owner, hostile to both the moderate and radical strike leaders, is a fairly accurate representation of employers. Helminen's son Yrjö is in some respects a self-portrait of Pekkanen: cut off from his working-class friends because he is studying in secondary school, he is not accepted by his middle-class schoolmates who have their parents' political opinions, although one of his friends is the son of the factory owner.

Ne menneet vuodet, a sequel to *Isänmaan ranta*, is less coherent; the author describes the lives of several characters from the first book, introduces new ones, treats some individual problems, and attempts a complete picture of social and political unrest in Finland in the 1930s. The book closes at the beginning of the Winter War, too recent for Pekkanen to see it objectively, but he renders the country's prewar atmosphere well.

Ihmisten kevät is a short, simple love story about two young, working-class people. Without comment, the author gives a very real view of the conflict between nature, which urges humans to love and to found families, and society, which prevents both by its inability to offer all people a means of livelihood.

Musta hurmio contains many motifs from Pekkanen's other works. It is set on an island, as is *Ukkosen tuomio*;[602] illicit love has death as its consequence, and the events are initiated by a temporarily predominant secondary character, the romantic tramp who comes from nowhere and disappears after disturbing the life of a small community. He works for the local shopkeeper, but proves stronger and more energetic than his employer; he has a love affair with the wife of the leader of the local amateur theater group (there are many of these in Finland), but she drowns herself. He is then forced to leave, but all who have been in contact with him are changed or have been compelled to see their shortcomings. The book was probably written under the influence of fashionable literary currents, e.g., D. H. Lawrence.[603]

Like most writers, Pekkanen did not do his best writing during the war. *Ajan kasvot* ('The Face of the Time,' 1942) is a collection of reflections on the problems of the period, *Tie Eedeniin* ('The Road to Eden,' 1942) comes partially from the sports world, and *Hämärtyvä horisontti* ('The Darkening Horizon,' 1944) deals with a man returning from the war. In a solution not typical of Pekkanen, the man reenlists in the army, where everything is ordered and defined in advance, because he cannot resolve his problems. The short-story collection *Elämän ja kuoleman pidot* (1945) and the novel *Nuorin veli* ('The Youngest Brother,' 1946) are on the level of his works of the 1930s. The collection contains several studies in individual psychology. *Voittaja* ('The Victor') is about the selfishness of a sick person, *Kaukainen saari* ('The Faraway Island') the destruction of a dream, and *Lankunpätkä* ('A Bit of Plank') a lifelong fixation. *Nuorin veli* is the only work in which Pekkanen describes country life. It is about a family whose farm is taken over by the most serious, hard-working brother; the more lively, sensitive younger one has to leave. Pekkanen describes country life here in an almost lyrical manner, but he criticizes the conservative ideas and ways of life of the rural areas.

In 1948 he published the first two parts of his epic on Kotka and its growth in the late nineteenth century, *Aamuhämärä* ('The Dawn') and *Toverukset* ('The Friends'; the title conveys the impression that the friends are men engaged in a common activity, such as work, war, or sports). After his illness he completed the third part, *Voittajat ja voitetut* ('The Victors and the Vanquished,' 1952); others were to follow, but he never finished the task. The three parts, however, form a well-balanced whole, and the book is generally valued highly in Finland.[604] It is faithful to the history of Kotka,[605] and most of the characters had real counterparts; the work is considered a well-written description of the somewhat wild, early period of the town's history. The most influential inhabitants, industrialists, business-men, government officials and others appear, but the narrative is fictional and includes fictional characters, describing at length the personal relations, love affairs, religious problems, and other difficulties of Pekka, a young worker. The skillful balance between historic description and the life stories of the individuals is one of the book's strengths; one result was the book covers only a short period and ends in 1875 with the bankrupcy of a large industrial company and its consequences for the community. A new period was to have begun in the next volume, which Pekkanen never had time to write. His own memoirs, *Lapsuuteni*, contain no fiction; his early life was not happy, and time did not embellish it. He said that he tried to suppress the hate which surged in his mind when he thought of that period and to write as impartially as possible.

Lähtö matkalle ('Starting on the Journey,' 1955) is an unremarkable collection of poems saved from mediocrity by that which is behind the words rather than in them.[606] The stories of *Mies ja punapartaiset herrat* ('A Man and the Gentlemen with the Red Beards,' 1950) include unreal elements. The title is fanciful, and, if it were not for the author's introduction, its connection with the stories would remain obscure. Pekkanen says that during one's life one meets gentlemen with beards of different colors and different things happen to one according to color. Since the worst is red, the book is about the worst things that can happen, but they are not very terrifying. Some of the stories are satires on human weaknesses. Pekkanen was planning to write these stories as early as the 1930s, and they are the only instance in which he tried to compose something not entirely serious. *Eversti Karhunkäpälä* ('Colonel Karhunkäpälä') is about wartime corruption, not criticizing or unveiling it, but describing the outwardly formal, correct manner in which all interested parties handle it. *Kuilun tuolta puolen* ('From the Other Side of the Abyss') is about a psychological problem: a man discovers suddenly that he cannot understand himself, his life, or his Russian-born wife, as mysterious as her homeland beyond the border. The time is 1939, but political events are only a background for his problems. *Painajainen* ('The Nightmare') is one of the most unreal stories; the action is not described as a dream in the narration itself. A series of disturbing, ridiculous, but only slightly frightening incidents occur in a restaurant, where the main character meets people he has once known who are now shabby and unpleasant. A child turns out to be the main character himself, and he is prevented from leaving, a probable statement that one cannot escape his past. In 1957 Pekkanen published a collection of aphorisms and notes made during his illness, *Totuuden ja kirkkauden tiellä* ('On the Road to Truth and Light'). Although the title is pompous, it expresses something essential about the author, a man who throughout his life sought the truth; it is to his credit that he never believed that he had definitively found it.

Frequently, the popular writers of a time are among the lesser writers, for they, unlike the great ones, are not critical or pessimistic, but represent a simple, conservative view of the world. In Finland they often choose historical or rural subjects, turning to the good old days in the country, where the people have not been corrupted by modern civilization. Since World War II no serious works of this type have appeared, but in the twenties and thirties a few writers produced such works, written without genius, but not without talent.

Artturi Järviluoma (1879-1942) is remembered solely for his play *Pohjalaisia* ('Ostrobotnians,' 1914), used as a libretto for an opera by L. Madetoja in 1924. Like Alkio's *Puukkojunkkarit*, it describes the people of southern Ostrobotnia. They are more idealized, however, and so it was admired as an expression of Finnish courage and fighting spirit during the Russian oppression. **Kyösti Wilkuna** (1879-1922) is best known as the author of sketches and short stories from Finnish history. The best are in two collections, *Aikakausien vaihteessa* ('A Turning Point in History,' 1910) and *Miekka ja sana* ('The Sword and the Word,' 2 vols., 1919); they are simple, showing a typical character in a situation illustrating some historical event. The author was active in the resistance movement against the Russians in World War I, was in a Russian prison, and fought in the Civil War, all activities which added value to his works in the eyes of patriotic readers. He was more complex than these books indicate, however, and *Suomen Kirjallisuus* devotes many pages to the analysis of his neuroses and the two short-story collections *Novelleja* ('Short Stories,' 1907) and *Yksin elämässä* ('Alone in Life,' 1908), in which he described decadent individuals full of *Weltschmerz*, much in the manner of Leino and other contemporary authors. Lehtonen, who saw only the outward Wilkuna, made fun of them, but the author was projecting his own tortures in his characters. Later he used patriotism to heal himself, but succeeded only in repressing his problems. His complexes eventually proved stronger than his rational self; if we have correctly interpreted the discreet wording of *Suomen Kirjallisuus*, he committed suicide.[607]

Wilkuna's first collection included a few stories on Lapland, but **Arvi Järventaus** (1883-1939) is credited with introducing that region to Finnish literature, which now has a tradition of Lapland writing with set characters, landscapes, situations, and a special vocabulary. Järventaus, a minister, spent his entire life in Lapland and northern Finland; his books were not written only for entertainment, although he had a sense of humor. The first, *Risti ja noitarumpu* ('The Cross and the Sorcerer's Drum,' 1916), is a historic novel on a familiar subject, the fight of a Christian priest against a medicine man; Aho had treated the same motif in *Panu*. The author's interest in folklore and anthropology is evident in several works to which old customs and beliefs give a fantastic and mysterious atmosphere, e.g., *Satu-Ruijan maa* ('The Fabled Land of Ruija,' 1920) and *Maan hiljaiset* ('The Meek of the Earth,' 1925). The novels *Synnin mitta* ('The Measure of Sin,' 1917) and *Hyljätty kylä* ('The Deserted Village,' 1934), and the short story collections *Tunturikertomuksia*

('Tales from the Mountains,' 1921) and *Tunturin tuolta puolen* ('Beyond the Mountain,' 1924)[608] in which even thieves and liars are viewed with forgiveness and humor, are more prosaic. In 1929 and 1930 Järventaus published a novel in four volumes on the war of 1808-09, when Russia conquered Finland, *Rummut* ('The Drums'). The war is seen mainly from the common soldier's point of view. He is honest, brave, patriotic, and God-fearing, although the author treats with tolerant humor his sins of drinking, swearing, and fighting with his fellow soldiers. Some of the book's Russians are portrayed sympathetically, an uncommon treatment in Finnish patriotic novels. The book also contains a young Finnish officer who believes that Finland must become completely Finnish and its inhabitants must speak the language of the majority. Parts of the work are similar to Tolstoy's descriptions of military life, including the fascinated horror at the maiming and killing on the battlefield.[609] His other novels include *Kirkonlämmittäjä* ('The Man Whose Job It Was to Heat the Church,' 1919), *Taivaallinen puuseppä* ('The Heavenly Cabinetmaker,' 1927), and *Tie selvä* ('The Road Is Clear,' 1928), which discard picturesque and exceptional elements to concentrate on individual problems.

Artturi Leinonen (1888-1963) worked as a teacher, participated in the resistance against the Russians in World War I, was caught and sent to Siberia, returned to fight in the Civil War, became a newspaper editor, was involved in many of the political troubles of the late twenties and early thirties, was twice elected to Parliament, and, according to him, wrote seventeen novels and approximately twenty plays, all of which are not included in his ten-volume *Teokset* (1959/60). His active mind was ever interested in new problems, about which he wrote books; *Profeetta* ('The Prophet,' 1926) is about religious ecstasy, *Kolmanteen ja neljänteen polveen* ('Unto the Third and Fourth Generation,' 1926) the effects of heredity, *Yrjänän emännän synti* ('The Sin of Yrjänä's Wife,' 1937) describes a childless couple, and *Perintötalo* ('The Family Estate,' 1946) a wartime marriage. Between 1932 and 1934 he published a three-volume historical novel, *Hakkapeliitat* (the title is the nickname for Finnish cavalry soldiers in the Thirty Years War), which he had prepared after careful research in archives and libraries. Here, too, the war is seen mainly from the common soldier's point of view. One of the characters, a young Finnish officer, wins fame on the battlefield but thinks of the honor and profits which go to Sweden, whereas his country is only called to send more men and money. The third volume describes the situation in Finland, the background of misery and privation for the war, which is described with attention to its ugliness and the fascinated horror at death and violence which appeared in Järventaus's novel.

Eino Railo (1884-1948), a friend of Wilkuna, wrote two biographical works on him. A lecturer in comparative literature at the University of Helsinki, he published a six-volume history of world literature (1933-37) and wrote a doctoral dissertation on the haunted castle (*Haamulinna*, 1925; tr. 'The Haunted Castle'), i.e., supernatural motifs in English romantic literature. Although they had readers, his other writings, including numerous novels, are not so enjoyable. He wrote criticism regularly for newspapers; as in other works, he expressed extremely narrow-minded, conservative ideas, which made him a favorite target for the liberal critics, e.g., T. Vaaskivi.

Viljo Kojo (1891-1966), born in Karelia, often describes Karelian country people, whom he knew best. In his works Kojo follows the principles expressed in literature by Lehtonen and in art by Sallinen and other artists he met in Helsinki, where he studied painting just before World War I. In his memoirs, *Taiteen tie on pitkä* ('The Road of Art Is Long,' 1960), he indirectly admits that, as a young man from the country, he found the intellectual discipline of avoiding preconceived ideas and describing reality spontaneously somewhat difficult to accept.[610] Active as a painter for a while, he soon began to write, first poetry, which will be discussed later, then prose, for which he is known. His first novels, *Velka* ('The Debt,' 1916) and *Autio talo* ('The Abandoned House,' 1917), are sentimental and melancholy, but the collection of stories *Aurinko, kuu ja valkoinen hevonen* ('The Sun, the Moon, and the White Horse,' 1919; the title alludes to a proverbial saying) shocked some contemporaries—he called them "Decamerone stories."[611] In two short novels, *Suruttomain seurakunta* ('The Congregation of the Careless,' 1921) and *Kiusauksesta kirkkauteen* ('From Temptation to Light,' 1922), his bohemian friends and their conservative opponents in the world of art appear under easily decipherable pseudonyms. The book does not choose sides as much as it presents a half-humorous picture of the life of young artists. Kojo was gifted at humor and satire and did not hesitate to attack the most respected authorities and values, although his radicalism was never political. *Piimärannan posti* ('The Piimäranta Post,' 1924) is a not entirely harmless satire of a small-town newspaper; according to the subtitle, it presents "facts out of the cultural life in rural areas" and follows the tradition of ridiculing great ideas by placing them in trivial context. In the 1920s and after he wrote many novels and short stories. A selection of the best of his short narratives—he is often called a master of them—appeared in 1947, *Tuulta ja tyyntä* ('Wind and Fair Weather'). His art had limitations, however. He liked well-constructed stories, often with unexpected endings, and he limited his character descriptions to one typical angle. He wrote serious as well as humorous pieces, and the rural ones are quite natural; the urban are more artificial. He was a born story writer, and his novels are inferior to the shorter works; in time he intruded more and more in his works, telling his readers that he intended to show the healthiness and honesty of country life compared to the artificiality of the cities. Such novels are, e.g., *Ihminen päättää* ('Man Decides,' 1931) and *Aika rientää* ('Time Passes,' 1932), both published as *Virta välkkyy* ('The Glittering Stream,' 1 vol., 1944), *Talo* *kalliolla* ('The House on the Rock,' 1937), and *Elomulta ja Asfaltti* ('The Life-Giving Earth and the Concrete,' 1953).

Lempi Jääskeläinen (1900-1964) knew her hometown Viipuri well and wrote novels about it throughout her life, producing close to forty volumes. She invented an eighteenth-century family of wealthy merchants whose life she followed through several generations. The first of these volumes, *Weckroothin perhe* ('The Weckrooth Family') appeared in 1930; under the same title several volumes of the family chronicle were issued together in 1944 and translated into French in 1946.⁶¹² Miss Jääskeläinen and her readers took her works very seriously, partially because they were about Viipuri and Karelia; the romantic attachment of the Finns for Karelia became even stronger when the city and province were lost in 1944. In 1952, with two other Karelians, Kersti Bergroth and Viljo Kojo, she published a book of memories, *Rakas kaupunki* ('The Beloved City'), thus joining hands over two centuries with another refugee, Frese.

By the time **Martti Santavuori** (b. 1901) retired from the army as a lieutenant-colonel in 1947, he had already written eight novels and short-story collections as well as a military history of the country (*Suomen sotahistoria,* 2 vols., 1941, 1943). Most of his novels are about past conflicts, e.g., *Hiiltynyt lehti* ('The Charred Leaf,' 1937), which describes the Civil War, and *Napue* (name of a battle, 1933), which deals with the war of 1700--21. *Petrus, kirjuri* ('Petrus, the Scrivener,' 3 vols., 1945-48) is set in the seventeenth century but reflects events contemporary to its publication. Many of his short stories are about the army, which he thought a wonderful place for fine men, where the only trouble available was of a humorous nature. His characters are often dashing cavalrymen; his last collection is titled *Kirkkaina kiiltävät säilät* ('The Swords Are Shining Bright,' 1963). One of the last firm royalists in Finland, he wrote *Suomen kuningas* ('The King of Finland,' 1965), a novel about the German prince who was elected monarch in 1918 without ever entering the country.

Juhani Konkka (1904-1970) came from Ingria, the Finnish-speaking region near St. Petersburg before the city was renamed Leningrad, to Finland after the revolution. He worked for newspapers and publishers and mixed in politics, meeting important personalities and crackpots, whom he put in his novels under transparent pseudonyms. His best works are about the vanished world of his youth, for example, *Kahden maailman rajalla* ('On the Borderline of Two Worlds,' 1939), rewritten as *Pietarin valot* ('The Lights of St. Petersburg,' 1958), *Kulkurin kesä* ('The Summer of a Tramp,' 1943), *Kulkurin kahleet* ('The Fetters of a Tramp,' 1945), and *Kulkurin koulut* ('The Schools of a Tramp,' 1946). He also translated much Russian literature into Finnish, including early nineteenth-century classics and contemporary works.

From the beginning of this century, many Finnish and Swedish newspapers have carried daily short humorous sketches by the same author. Traditionally, these sketches must be published under a pseudonym, most often an unusual first name, although the most famous of them, **Olli**, is not an unusual one. It was used by **Väinö Albert Nuorteva** (first Nyberg, 1889-1967), who began to write in 1917, became a regular contributor to *Uusi Suomi*, for which he continued writing for forty-two years. His sketches are estimated to number more than ten thousand; since 1921 he published at least fifteen collections of them and in 1956 two volumes of selected works, titled not *Valitut teokset* ('Selected Works'), but *Valitut tekoset* ('Selected Quirks'). Olli often uses slightly twisted language to give a slightly twisted image of reality, with devastating results. His subjects are not original; his characters are eternal types—husbands, wives, mothers-in-law, bosses, employees, snobs and bureaucrats—appearing in situations illustrating basic human weaknesses or criticizing minor social evils, such as bureaucratic inefficiency, high taxes, or complicated tax returns. Olli had a talent for ridicule in the guise of a serious message. Considered a classic humorist, he was even made honorary professor, but his most faithful readers are among older people; readers during and since World War II have different taste in humor.

The humorist of *Helsingin Sanomat* was **Ilmari Kivinen** (1883-1940), known as **Tiitus**. From 1914 until his death he regularly produced stories in ordinary language, less aggressive in humor than Olli's. In describing a businessman who has suddenly grown rich during World War I, Mr. Kenonen, who frequently appears in his stories, he is not satirical or critical, merely amused. He wrote humorous novels about funny country people and small-town originals in Savo, where he lived in his youth.

Ensio Rislakki (first Svanberg, b. 1896), or **Valentin**, is one of the very few Finnish writers who produced enjoyable literary parodies, which were published in a collection (1956). His sarcastic, wry style is reserved for small, everyday problems. Besides the traditional humorous sketches in newspapers and magazines, later published in collections, he wrote novels which sometimes verge on the serious, e.g., *Kuuden elämän saari* ('The Island of Six Lives,' 1944), adventure stories for boys, descriptions from his travels, and plays, some successful. Of the latter *Vihaan sinua, rakas* ('I Hate You, My Love,' 1944) is about the small difficulties of married life, *Rakas Wenander* ('Dear Wenander,' 1946) about humorous professors at the University of Turku in the seventeenth century, and *Ruma Elsa* ('Ugly Elsa,' 1949) about modern Helsinki students. *Musta Saara* ('Black Saara,' 1957) is quite serious, attempting to analyze the relations between Africans and Europeans, which the author viewed pessimistically; it is connected with *Tuolla puolen Limpopon* ('Beyond the Limpopo,' 1952), a book about his African journey.

Hjalmar Nordling (1860-1931), known as **Nortamo**, is foremost among the humorists who have written independent books and stories rather than newspaper sketches. Initially a physician who lived in Rauma and Pori on the west coast, he began to write humorous stories about small-town life for his friends' entertainment. The first collection, published in 1906, was so successful that the author was encouraged to continue his literary activities; in the 1920s he was known throughout the country. He, too, was honored with the title of professor, and a monument to him and one of his characters has been raised in Rauma,[613] one of the oldest towns in Finland—it has the ruins of a fourteenth-century church and a fifteenth-century abbey decorated with murals from the early sixteenth century. Although small, it had in the second half of the nineteenth century the largest sailing fleet in the country. The inhabitants speak a restricted dialect very unlike any other in Finnish; whether Nortamo's stories make the dialect funny or the dialect makes the stories funny is questionable. The stories picture ordinary life in a small town and on ships, and the characters have, in a limited way, their own personalities; the humor is the result of their reactions to events rather than the events themselves, and the stories are quite good.

Ernst Lampén (1865-1938), a friend of Juhani Aho and his brothers, was not really a humorist, but an open, curious man who traveled a great deal, discovering the amusing sides of people and places, which he describes in his books. Although he was a convinced atheist, an uncommon position in Finland, his attacks on church and religion, which he found generally ridiculous, were calm and casual, not bitter or sarcastic.

Yrjö Soini (b. 1896), Wilho Soini's son, known under the pseudonym **Agapetus**, has been Consul of Finland in Prague, worked for periodicals, taught in institutes for adult education, participated in organizations for tourism and travel, and written more than thirty novels and plays, most humorous, which were popular in the 1920s and 1930s, when the best of them were published. He has remained active in literature until recent years. His works are ordinary and harmless—the characters' only purpose is to become involved in misunderstandings and mishaps—presented with skill, and, in descriptions of young love, sentiment.

Uuno Hirvonen (1898-1971), better known as **Simo Penttilä**, worked all his life as a newspaperman and produced more than fifty adventure stories, plays, and boys' books. His immortal hero, T. J. A. Heikkilä, a young Finnish officer, ends up in Mexico, where he becomes a lieutenant-general and spends the rest of his life falling in love with beautiful señoritas and foiling the sinister plans of villains, traitors, bandits, and revolutionaries. The author bears no malice toward Mexico (his good Mexicans outnumber the bad) and probably chose that country for romance and color. Fortunately the stories are not to be taken seriously. Lassi Nummi, a contemporary poet, says that he enjoys reading them.[614] Hirvonen seems to have reconciled himself with the unrealistic desire to write old-fashioned romantic adventures like Anthony Hope's Ruritania novels—indeed, one of his earliest books, *Purppuravaippa ja baldakiini* ('The Cloak of Purple and the Canopy,' 1922), is about intrigue and conspiracy in a small German state—by producing half-nostalgic parodies of them.

Sakari Pälsi (1882-1965) was an archaeologist who traveled in Mongolia and northeast Siberia as well as other places, doing research and writing scientific and popular accounts of his journeys. The first, *Mongolian matkalta* ('From a Journey to Mongolia') was published in 1911. In 1931 he produced the first of a series of books on a small boy and his friends, *Ja sitten äitini antoi minulle tukkapöllyä* ('And Then Mother Pulled My Hair'), which was an immediate success and encouraged him to write the other nine; the last appeared in 1964. Part of their interest is the vividness of the picture of old-time life on a big farm—Pälsi has written some books for that purpose alone—but they are also masterful descriptions of the world through the eyes of a small boy. Devoid of attempts to educate children or satirize the adult world, they were written for the pleasure of telling stories. All are in the first person and reproduce without cuteness or elaborate humor the thinking and speaking of a boy. The ten vary in quality, but the best are unique.

Although they are not common, Finland has several female humorists. Elsa Soini (1893-1952), daughter of Wilho and sister of Yrjö, first published some well-written serious novels, of which *Jumalten ja ihmisten suosikit* ('The Favorites of Gods and Men,' 1926) is set mainly in the United States. Her chief interest in them is the position of women in society, which had changed since Minna Canth's time. Now that women had obtained their rights, they had to decide how to use them, especially if they were independent but fell in love. One of her characters says, "If you want to write something artistic, don't make it funny, and, if you write something funny, for God's sake don't pretend it's artistic." The author took the advice and, following *Rouva johtaja* (1932), which describes a woman estranged from her husband and children because of her successful career, wrote only humorous works, except a romanticized biography of Kivi, *Nuori Aleksis* (1947). She and another woman of talent, Seere Salminen (b. 1894; known under the pseudonym of Serp, author of more than five thousand humorous sketches in *Helsingin Sanomat* and several books) used the pseudonym Tuttu Paristo and composed a successful radio serial about a typical middle-class Finnish family, to whom only the nicest things happen.

Hilja Valtonen (b. 1897) enjoyed great success between the wars and produced a number of books in which the problems of the self-supporting woman are a pretext for light entertainment. Her heroines are pert, self-confident, and independent until they meet the right man. She follows the rule of all Finnish humorists, male and female: strictest chastity. Sex is not even hinted at. Young men and women may fall in love, hold hands in the moonlight, and perhaps kiss, but then they must hasten to marry.

Before and after World War II

AFTER 1918 YOUNG INTELLECTUALS AND ARTISTS proclaimed in Finland, as they did everywhere, that the world had radically changed. This feeling was so strong that even a man like Pekkanen, who did not often associate with the young writers of his time or indulge in outbursts of passion, caught the feeling of modernism which flamed all over Europe after 1918:

> ... We dreamt of a new world, of a new man who would be born out of our dreams. We wrote a poem about a young god who was sitting on a lotus leaf and bathing in the rays of the sun. We spoke about the common destiny of mankind and discussed ideologies, we enjoyed wealth and luxury and suffered when we saw unemployment and misery. In front and above us was the airy castle of our rosy ideals, and beneath us the volcano of discontent.
>
> And, one day, a new time began and a new man was born. But he was not a golden god, he was a grey soldier, and, on his steel helmet, the bloody dawn of a new era was reflected. [615]

A detail, the golden god on the lotus leaf, underlines the fact that much of the first Finnish modernism was not at all modern. The exoticism considered so daring by the poets was in a literary tradition dating to Leino, Onerva, European, mainly French,[616] symbolists and romanticists, and, when it wore off, it left purely traditional poetry about the problems of the individual. There are, of course, exceptions, but in general Finland did not discard literary traditions very quickly or decisively. Among the Swedish writers in Finland there were a number of poetic geniuses at that time: Edith Södergran and Elmer Diktonius, who had many contacts with the Finns, Rabbe Enckell, Gunnar Björling, and others, recognized as the pioneers of modern Swedish poetry. Finnish writers were not oblivious to current world events, but only the literature of the essayists reflects them. Finland and its capital were actually more provincial than they had been at the time of such cosmopolitans as Aho Järnefelt, and Leino.

When asked to name the greatest French poet, André Gide is supposed to have replied, "Victor Hugo, alas!"; in Finland similar words could describe **Veikko Antero Koskenniemi** (originally **Forsnäs**, 1885-1962), who began to publish at the age of eighteen and continued to produce poems, essays, biographies, travel descriptions, literary studies, speeches, and aphorisms for more than fifty years. He also wrote a calendar with a birthday verse for every day of the year and one novel. By 1918 he had published his collected works, and the selected followed in 1928. His nine-volume works came out between 1935 and 1944, another volume of poems in 1943, the twelve-volume collected works in 1955 and 1956, and another selection of poems in 1958. With the Bible and Runeberg's *Tales of Ensign Stål* they were a standard feature of Finnish middle-class homes.[617] The poet helped to set them up as models for the judgment of other poetry by writing criticism which, in a country of academic, scholarly, and conservative critical tradition,[618] commanded respect; from 1942 to 1954 he was chief editor of *Valvoja*.[619] For half a century all young Finnish poets and many prosaists were confronted with him. Satirical poems about him were written at thirty years' interval. In Aaro Hellaakoski's first collection (1916), *Maallinen onni* ('Earthly Luck') clearly refers to him without naming him:

> Who kept on dreaming all the night
> And let himself be frozen stiff
> Shall all his life be prisoner
> In dreamy fetters strong and tight
>
> He shall be caught by all at sight
> And sent to Finland right away
> To be a poet and to cry
> His sorrows at the moon by night.

Alluding to Koskenniemi's interest in Goethe,[620] Kullervo Rainio wrote in the late 1940s:

> One day all the Young Werthers in the world
> Met round Goethe's bust
> And when they saw each other's sorry faces
> They started laughing
> And danced the conga
> And last among them
> Came young Veikko Antero
> Kicking daintily about his elegiac legs.
>
> (Approximately)

Without pretense at depth this nonsense verse conveys Koskenniemi's basic flaw: his poetry leaves the impression that all its tragic, pessimistic feelings are attitudes which do not correspond to real emotions in the poet; moreover, he lacked humor and a sense of self-criticism. Unlike Eino Leino, who insisted that he was a healthy country boy, but had to fight throughout his life the demons of his mind and hostility of the world, Koskenniemi posed as a man suffering terrible pain and anguish in a bleak world, but was a very successful author, respected university professor and president, member of boards and committees, doctor *honoris causa* of the University of Helsinki, and member of the Finnish Academy.

Jouko Tyyri, a Finnish writer known as somewhat a radical, once said that Koskenniemi too was a radical to be appreciated because he made atheism and pessimism acceptable to his readers, who were basically religious and optimistic.[621] In an essay from the collection *Roomalaisia runoilijoita* ('Roman Poets,' 1919), Koskenniemi does describe Lucretius with understanding, and, in discussions of religious, moral, and metaphysical problems, he refers to Greek and Roman mythology, although he has written a few poems on Christian motifs.[622] That these attitudes never offended his readers is proof that, to them as well as to him, they were simply the noble, profound thoughts a poet should express, which had no relation to reality; Koskenniemi never attacked Christianity or the Lutheran church.

Koskenniemi's poetry and life were in close contact in one field only: politics. He was one of the few writers in Finland without qualms about the Civil War, which he viewed as a war of independence against Russians and misguided Finnish socialists, a view occasionally presented even today.[623] He wrote a short epic on an imaginary hero of the war, *Nuori Anssi* ('Young Anssi,' 1918) and continued to compose conservative, patriotic poems, which appeared in the collections *Uusia runoja* ('New Poems, 1924), *Kurkiaura* ('The Wedge of the Cranes,' 1930), and others. With many other educated Finns he decided that Finland should side with pre-1918 and post-1933 Germany in international questions. One of the poems in *Uusia runoja*, *Reinin vahti*, is a translation of the patriotic German *Die Wacht am Rhein*. In another one God and the devil cast dice over the world's fate; God wins first, and the world has peace; the devil wins next, and the peace is called Versailles. Koskenniemi considered himself a representative of the European humanist tradition, which he felt had found its most perfect embodiment in German civilization, but he saw no discrepancy between national-socialist Germany and European civilization. In March, 1942, he was elected deputy chairman of the European Writer's Guild in Germany, and in May, 1942, he won a German literary prize for foreign writers; Maila Talvio won the same prize, and forty-two other Finnish writers joined the Guild. To Koskenniemi and those similar to him the outcome of World War II was the destruction of civilization.[624]

His poetry can be grouped by subject. Patriotic poems become numerous after 1918, and the few Christian ones are from the same period.

He writes about man in the universe as a lonely, tragic, threatened figure in the face of fate or a merciless god, under cold stars in a lifeless space; to underline the proud loneliness of the aristocrat and warrior, he uses a character from antiquity, the Middle Ages, or modern times.[625] He celebrates love chastely, often through scenery contemplated by the lovers, and he portrays smiling landscapes expressive of life's simple joys—one cannot help wonder why he tried so hard to be a bad Byron when he would have made such a good Wordsworth. The following is one of his best-known love poems:

> Minä laulan sun iltasi tähtihin
> Ja sun yöhösi kuutamoita
> Minä laulan sun aamuhus armahin
> Kevätkiuruja purppuroita
>
> Minä laulan sun käteesi kukkasen
> Kun silmäsi surusta kastuu
> Teen ruusutarhaksi tienoon sen
> Missä jalkasi pienet astuu
>
> Minä laulan loitolle maailman
> Minä vien sinut kotihin uuteen
> Minä laulan sielusi valkean
> Yli aikojen ikuisuuteen.
>
> I sing thy evening full of stars
> And thy nights of moonlight bright
> I paint thy morning with golden bars
> And send a lark to his flight
>
> I sing a flower into thy hand
> When thy cheeks are wet with tears
> Into a rosery I make the land
> Where thy small foot thee bears
>
> I sing the world from us away
> Anew I build a home for thee
> I sing thy soul from earthly day
> To timeless spaces free.

Unfortunately Koskenniemi did not confine himself to writing these simple, lovely poems, but, as he would have liked to say, *de mortuis nihil nisi bene. Requiescat in pace.*

Other poets of the time wrote poetry from which Finland's modern verse has grown. **Otto Manninen** (1872-1950) is almost better known as a translator than as a poet,[626] but a few of his poems have become very popular, e.g., *Pellavan kitkijä* ('Picking the Flax') and *Joutsenlaulua* ('Swan Song'), both in *Säkeitä* ('Verses,' 1905). The first is somewhat like a folksong, whereas the second has a dual appeal. The common reader is attracted by the conventional image of swans gliding over misty water, driven by longing, to a faraway goal; the aesthete appreciates the deeper but unexpressed meaning of the image.[627] In this poem and others similar to it Manninen comes close to the modern type of poetic composition in which the image itself is the poem.

Säkeitä I and II (1910) were received badly, and, even after his works were accepted as art, Manninen was considered abstruse and learned and his works difficult. He came from a family of well-to-do farmers known from the sixteenth century, but his father sent him to school, where he was a brilliant student with highest marks in all subjects, and to the university, where he received an M. A. after studying Latin and philosophy as well as other subjects. In 1913 he became lecturer in Finnish at the University of Helsinki; later he received the title of professor and doctor *honoris causa* of both sciences and letters and theology (because of his participation in the new Finnish translation of the Bible). However, his poetry is not scholarly, but Finns were so accustomed to simple, straightforward verse that the merest deviation from the descriptive, idealistic tradition was branded intellectualism. Finland's literary traditions, based on nineteenth-century poetry, do not show influence of, e.g., the metaphysical and formally elaborate seventeenth-century European writers, although in that period something similar was attempted: poems were sometimes given the form of an object related to their contents.[628] Instead the traditions grew around the idealistic or realistic models of the nineteenth century, e.g., Runeberg, Tennyson, Longfellow, Hugo, Lamartine, Goethe, and Schiller. It is only since World War II that a reaction against this tradition has been observed.

Manninen's *Musa lapidaris* (in *Säkeitä* II) has been analyzed by five Finnish scholars and critics who have searched for deep meaning to the extent of giving it one of their own; supposedly his most difficult work, it is considered to describe creative poetic activity or the relation of poetry to life.[629] To us it seems clearly a description of woman's capricious, unwittingly cruel nature. Stanza by stanza its contents can be summarized as: a wish to play like an elf, an art to caress like a wave in spring / / a wave with enchanting whims, a golden foam over dark, treacherous depths (an image somewhat like Leino's vision of woman) / / woe to the wanderer who wants to play with you and be refreshed by caresses light as wind / / for the wave wants to have treasures to play with and to bury suns and stars in the blue depths (the image of the star's falling into watery depths appears in Leino's poems) / / but she prefers to play with hearts which burn and are put out like torches in the feast of the wave / / she laid her spell once on happy young hearts which sank heavy and tired into mud and algae / / but then the wave was sad because the play ended and fled to the open sea. / / Two other stanzas do not seem clearly related to the rest: the wave will eventually carve hearts out of stone, which will better resist her play. However, Pentti Lyly has discovered that the poem was written to a lady sculptor whom Manninen knew;[630] therefore, the end must be an *envoi* or dedication to her. The word *woman* does not appear in the poem, but the background clears up that difficulty. Manninen wrote the poem in Swedish although he grew up in a Finnish family from Kangasniemi, a Finnish-speaking region, and the Swedish version is simpler and more natural than the Finnish one he later produced, which reveals his major defects as a poet. In his great respect for meter and rhyme, he disregarded Finnish word formation and syntax, and he freely used words from varying dialects, including old literary Finnish and self-coined words. His style is still admired by some, but was criticized even in his lifetime.[631] No one has since followed the models he established.

Manninen published only two more collections, at long intervals: *Virrantyven* ('The Quiet Stream,' 1925) and *Matkamies* ('The Wayfarer,' 1938); two other collections were printed posthumously. He devoted his time to translations of world literature, including all of Runeberg's poetry. A controversy not yet resolved began over the respective merits of his and Cajander's translations. He also published Finnish versions of several of Molière's plays, many of Goethe's works, including *Faust* I and II, Hungarian poetry, Sophocles' *Oedipus*, Euripides' *Medea*, and numerous other texts. In translating the *Iliad* and the *Odyssey*, he closely followed the classical hexameter in the length of syllables; it is generally agreed that, of all the Finnish poets who used the Greek and Roman meters, he came closest to the original,[632] although he did have to deviate from standard Finnish usage. Koskenniemi, who wrote poetry in the elegiac meter on Greek and Roman subjects, seems justified in criticizing the occasionally artificial character of Manninen's texts. As a translator Manninen contributed greatly to Finnish culture by giving his countrymen some of the masterpieces of world literature in their own language. As a poet he had little direct influence,[633] but his allusive representation of his subjects, independent images, and concise metaphors are more related to contemporary poetry than to that of his own time.

Juhani Alarik Siljo (1888-1918), the son of a sailor who drowned when the boy was nine years old, was raised in difficult circumstances in Oulu, but was sent to secondary school and the University of Helsinki. He became an active translator of Goethe, Schiller, Lessing, Kleist, and others, and he wrote criticism and essays for newspapers and periodicals, e.g., *Valvoja*, on which he was a staff member during the last year of his life. He fought with the Whites in the Civil War, but he was shot in the legs near Tampere and taken prisoner by the Reds. Although he was freed when the Whites took the city, he died of his injuries a few days later.[634] After dropping his studies for literary activities, he had written violently antisocialist poetry which praised will and courage although it was not rhetorically heroic. He became a legendary young hero honored in numerous articles published after his death. He actually was a remarkable poet, and interest in his poems has not abated. His works were much admired in the late forties; in 1950 Lassi Heikkilä wrote that "his verse was as familiar to anyone interested in literature as Eino Leino's."[635] He is no longer appreciated to that extent, but he remains a respected name in literary history.

Siljo differed from the trend in poetry between the wars, a loose following of the traditions of Leino and Koskenniemi: ornate vocabulary, flowing rhetoric, formal rhyme and rhythm without strict treatment of language, loose metaphors, and predilection for solemn, deep attitudes. The poems of Siljo's first collection, *Runoja* ('Poems,' 1910) have been called "stiff and forbidding";[636] later he developed greater flexibility of expression, but his nature prevented his indulging in anything he considered word-play. He enjoyed exercise, once walking from Helsinki to Oulu, and wrote many poems expressing his love of nature, sunshine, and fresh air with philosophical implications or reflecting life's simple pleasures. His attitude toward love was ambiguous; he felt it weak and degrading, but he wrote love poems to women who attracted him. His emotional life seems to have remained on an idealistic, teen-age level.[637] Christian symbols and phrases appear in his work, but he was not a Christian poet; he respected an anonymous god, nature, and life, and he told himself "if believers think that you are a pagan and pagans that you are a believer, think yourself: *all right!*"[638] He was a moralist, even a puritan in his recognition of his own weaknesses and in his struggle to improve himself and the world. In his rejection of the sensuous and corrupt, he was an ascetic. There is something Platonic in *Elämän kemut* ('The Feast of Life' in *Maan puoleen* 'Toward the Earth,' 1914), where he rejects the "wine and dance" of life, for his soul will be inebriated on the "feast of its thoughts."[639] His quest for moral values was not optimistic; he believed the search more important than the result. His satirical poems about human weaknesses and his own weaknesses became anguished when he thought of his insufficiency and the emptiness of the bleak, threatening universe. *Paossa* ('Fleeing' in *Runoja*) ends: "He sees gloomy sights / he hears threatening sounds / they bring to his mind a strange fear / which words cannot catch." Siljo's insistence on moral integrity, emphasis on the need of building ethical values through choice, refusal to submit to fate, and despair at a hostile world, typical of existentialist writers, is so consistent that we must accept the idea that existentialism is not simply a literary fashion but a philosophy essentially concerned with the human mind.[640]

Between 1910 and 1920 several poets in Finland broke with the traditions of poetry, e.g., Lehtonen, who was a remarkable poet as well as prosaist.[641] In the three collections he published between 1912 and 1919, **Huugo Jalkanen** (b. 1888) attempted to introduce new forms to Finnish poetry, to do away with formal patterns by using free verse. In the first collection he wrote that he was putting "the poetry of life / into naked beautiful / natural verse / without the formal dress of patterns." He also composed in classical and regular modern meters;[642] later he was known as a playwright, translator, and critic.

Viljo Kojo, whose prose works we have mentioned, began his career as a poet; his first collection, *Aamutuuli* ('The Morning Breeze,' 1914), has been described as a "fresh gust of morning breeze coming directly from the woods and the lakes in the midst of the artistic sentimentality of the period from 1910 to 1920" and a "refreshing splash of color in the midst of the academic artistry (of the same period)."[643] He began publishing his poems and drawings in *Nuori Voima* ('Youth Power'), which from its foundation until the late twenties[644] introduced many young writers to the public. Many of his first poems, written in free verse, express a fresh, spontaneous feeling of nature, a keen sense for colors, and an untrammeled joy of life. Except the humorous descriptions of popular life written in Lehtonen's manner, his later collections are more consciously artistic and pessimistic; the best are included in *Kylä ja kaupunki* (1916) and *Sininen pilvi* ('The Blue Cloud,' 1920). In 1926 he wrote a mock epic, *Mainio kertomus suutarimestari Simeon Lestin syntymästä ja sankarillisesta elämästä* ('The Goodly Story of the Birth and Heroic Life of Shoemaker Simeon Lesti [Last]'). He also produced a serious epic in Leino's historic-mythological manner, *Ronko*, about the pagan past of the Karelians, a true anachronism in 1966, when it was published.

Siljo died young, Jalkanen and Kojo were not really important poets, and Lehtonen was better known for prose. Together they were unable to change the patterns of Finnish poetry, and even **Aaro Hellaakoski** (1893-1952) could not do that. The son of a geography teacher in Oulu, he published some works on geology and earned a Ph.D. in that subject, which he taught as a lecturer at the University of Helsinki and a secondary school. His literary career was marked by two distinct periods. In 1916 he published his first volume of poetry, which he continued writing, with essays and scientific works, until 1928. He then ceased publishing all but geological papers until 1943, when he issued a new collection of poems. After the war, his greatness was finally recognized because his work was in the spirit of the time. He continued writing poetry, and a few collections were printed posthumously.

In his youth Hellaakoski opposed the current trend of Finnish poetry, as is evident in *Maallinen onni*. He wished to replace learned, aesthetic expressions of melancholic dreams with simple, forceful, manly thoughts rendered appropriately. He was not an optimist, but he preferred fighting to lamenting, and he often used satire as his weapon. He knew well the painters of the November Group, analyzed Sallinen's works in 1921, married the sister of Finland's greatest sculptor, Väinö Aaltonen, did a few aquarelles himself,[645] and followed artistic events abroad. He was familiar with German expressionism, Apollinaire's formal experiments in poetry, which he tried,[646] futurism, cubism, and, later, surrealism, but he never followed one school.

Rilke and the Swedish poet Nils Ferlin also attracted him; of the older authors Shakespeare was his "absolute favorite" besides Kivi. He enjoyed the old Finnish hymnal and medieval German poetry, borrowing their simple, powerful, rough forms of expression with conscious defiance of his contemporaries' flowing constructions.[647]

His first books, differing greatly from the current standards and containing some immature work, were poorly received by the critics; surprisingly no one appreciated the broad humor or the powerful poems on nature.[648] His humor masked deeper truths; in the following the right of the individual to do that which pleases him is affirmed through the image of the topsy-turvy world, a folklore motif probably found in the old German poets: "It's no business of yours if a man / would be harnessed to your carriage and a horse given the reins / not if your brother would be jumping with his head on the ground / with bright daylight shining on the soles of his feet."[649] Hellaakoski's nature poems depict landscapes reminiscent of his native region, northern Ostrobotnia, without mentioning their symbolic value or the poet's emotions. This feature may have alienated the critics, who were not yet ready to accept an image which was nothing more or an unexplained symbol, as in the following:

> The same empty sky
> Over the rocky landscape
>
> No tree, no bush to be seen
> Only yellow dried-out grass
>
> No sign of life
> A lonely cloud goes
>
> Sailing across the sky
> Like a white ship
>
> Its shadow goes slowly
> From hill to hill
>
> And so the cloud fades away
> As if in a hurry to leave this place
>
> And then again there is nothing
> In the gloomy landscape. (in *Nimettömiä lauluja*)

The poet's presence is felt in the words "as if in a hurry" and "gloomy," but it is an unobtrusive part of the image.

His first collection, *Runoja* (1916), includes *Conceptio artis* in which he tells how he wants to present his ideal of beauty to the world:

Sinut tahdon alastonna
helmetönnä, maalitonna
vailla rihkamaa
muiden antamaa

Näytän muotos maailmalle
huudan joka kuulijalle
niinkuin *minä* näin
sinut edessäin.

Without paint or beads, but naked,
You shall be, with nothing faked
Trinkets shall you never bear
Nothing from another wear

I shall show your shape to all
Shout to people within call
How *I* saw you when you were
In my presence then and there.

Nimettömiä lauluja ('Nameless Songs,' 1918), *Me kaksi* ('We Two,' 1920), *Elegiasta oodiin* ('From Elegy to Ode,' 1921), and *Maininki ja vaahtopää* ('The Swell and the Breaker,' 1924) lead up to the best collection of Hellaakoski's first period, *Jääpeili* ('The Ice Mirror,' 1928), for which the conservatives, including Koskenniemi, showed more understanding than did the young generation who believed themselves ready to change Finnish literature.[650] It was not until twenty years later that a young generation found Hellaakoski's message congenial. The first four do not include such formal experimentals as *Jääpeili* does, and they are more pessimistic, whereas in *Jääpeili* the poet reaches a more balanced attitude toward life. In *Me kaksi* there is a poem on the Flying Dutchman in which the crew of the accursed vessel represents a Promethean rebellion against fate, which can send them to err without end on the seas but not crush their spirit, and *Syysilta* ('Autumn Night') ends with a vision of the earth, frozen, dead, and hopeless at the end of time. *Elegiasta oodiin* and *Maininki ja vaahtopää*, however, have sunny visions of Finnish nature, which inebriate the poet with happiness, giving him the impression of losing his identity and melting with the sun, breeze, waves, and trees; in one poem he says that "summer found my hand and walks on my side." A synthesis is reached in *Mysteerio* ('The Mystery'), where the end of the world is described positively as the suppression of all contrasts, the mutual annulment of good and evil:

There is no motion more. The circling
of the tired world is ended.
Beauty has spread its arms
As if it owned the universe.

> Hope and despair are united
> Dream and reality are confused.
> I am enrobed in gold and purple
> What I could not think of I receive as gift.

In *Maininki ja vaahtopää* Hellaakoski's first happy love poems express his own feelings and describe humorously the amorous adventures of country people. He married in the year that the collection was published.

While writing the poems of *Jääpeili* he intensively studied contemporary art, French modernists, cubists, and futurists, as well as ancient Egyptian and oriental sculpture.[651] The formal experiments in the collection are the most visible result. Some of the poems suggest by typographic arrangement the objects of their description, e.g., *Sade* ('Rain'). The pattern is interwoven with the contents, for the words present the continuous noise of falling rain as background for the aural and visual impressions, followed by *elämä häipyy* ('life is fading'), the core of the poem (see page 280).

Many other poems in the collection are now famous. *Keväinen junamatka* ('Traveling by Train in Spring') is futuristic. The rapid rhythm of the train is repeated in the poem. The flowers flashing past the windows are barely mentioned by name, and the verbs express rapid motion: the bright colors of the flowers hammer at the poet's eyes, the train runs, and trees covered with white flowers dance to his arms. Other poems express his mood with a nature image, a few words which only intimate slight change, recorded with the mixture of irony and melancholy so often present in Hellakoski's works. In *Ensimmäinen tähti* ('The First Star'):

> The painfully yellow
> Lilies of the water
> The silvery harp
> of the reeds
> The playful flight of the dragonfly
>
>   and the wings
>   of the gnat that swings
>
> Summer discreetly
> Left without taking farewell
> Right when the first feverish
> Star was lit.[652]

The original speaks of a *kantele* rather than a harp, and the last lines cannot be fully understood unless one realizes that in Finland, especially in Hellaakoski's northern home region, summer nights are so bright that stars cannot be seen.

Beyond the table

the white eye of the window

is dimming

```
d     d     d
  r     r     r
    o     o     o          sounds    SOUNDS
      p     p     p
        s     s     s            gushing
```

splashing

in the

narrow

gully

of the street

through the gushing

the echo of running steps

progresses

```
d     d     d     d     d
```
life   r   r   is fading

```
  o     o     o     o     o

    p     p     p     p     p

      s     s     s     s     s
```

the stony street

sounds   sounds   sounds

The well-known *Hauen laulu* ('The Song of the Pike') from this collection is built on one of his frequent motifs, the projection of his feelings to a powerful, fierce animal, e.g., a hawk (*Haukka* in *Elegiasta oodiin*), which might also be strange and clumsy, e.g., a cormorant (in *Nimettömiä lauluja*), a dinosaur (*Viimeinen dinosauri* ['The Last Dinosaur' in *Huojuvat keulat* 'The Swaying Prows,' 1946]), or a pike. The beginning of the poem is slightly similar to that of Baudelaire's *L'Albatros*, in which the majestic bird is lured onto a ship's deck, where, out of his element, he appears ridiculous, but

280

Hellaakoski's pike leaves his habitat voluntarily and appears more powerful than the creatures of his new surroundings. The poem opens:

> From his wet home
> the pike climbed into a tree to sing

then presents a glimpse of a summer morning on the lake and describes the pike, who has tasted the red cone of the spruce, seen, heard, or smelled the splendor of the morning:

> opening his bony mouth
> moving slowly his jawbones
> such a wild and heavy
> song he sang
> that the birds
> were quiet at once
> as if covered
> by the weight of waters
> and the cold embrace
> of loneliness.

The image of the powerful but uncouth individual who feels lonely in a world which cannot understand the depth of his thoughts is a self-reflection which appears in many of Hellaakoski's works, often with the humorous or ironical touch typical of many writers of the period. In *Viimeinen dinosauri*, told in the first person by the beast, the dinosaur is "lonely and highborn," the last of his race, in a world which goes out like a candle around him. The solemnity is alleviated in the last words, which say that when the dinosaurs ruled the world there was joy in being alone and everyone was free to carry about his neck. Earlier he mentions the proudly arching necks of the dinosaurs, but, in defining freedom as the right to carry about one's neck, the poet seems to warn himself against exaggerated attitudes. A possible meaning of these words is that the powerful are lonely and that this loneliness reduces their might to self-admiration.

His next collection, the unremarkable *Vartiossa* ('On Guard,' 1941), inspired by the Winter War, is indifferent but not typical patriotic poetry. Hellaakoski was not aggressively nationalistic and he felt his individualism as much a duty as a privilege, for the individual was bound to search his soul for growth toward greater and greater moral integrity. He was shocked by the Civil War and the treatment of Red prisoners; in *Rajasuutari* ('The Cobbler' in *Me kaksi*), which Kupiainen compares to Sillanpää's *Meek Heritage*, he identifies himself with those who were shot.[653] Like many other writers from the nineteenth and twentieth centuries, he followed the traditional view that Finnish history was an endless succession of war, catastrophe, calamity, suffering, and privation, expressed in *Normaaliajat* (perhaps 'Normal Conditions' in *Uusi runo* 'New Poetry,' 1943). He is ironical about people who complain of wartime inconveniences such as food rationing; he finds wartime conditions normal in Finland, considering exception to them "but the glitter of a fairytale."

The Finnish motif of *Yksinäisyys* ('Alone' in *Uusi runo*), which tells of a man who, tired of the "poisonous tongues" of his neighbors, wanders to the forests where he clears a field and builds a cabin, is a variation of Aho's *Onnela* and the seven brothers' house in the woods. Hellaakoski's critical attitude toward conventional romanticism appears when he tells how the cranes, flying high over the sky, see on his field the shape of a man who does not look at or raise a hand toward them. In Finland cranes are traditionally romantic, flying to faraway lands and trumpeting the coming of spring or fall,[654] but Hellaakoski concludes that in the desert:

> human sorrows are too small
> to be taken seriously here
>
> longing, unrest are vain
> as the desire for the pleasures of the eye and the ear
> the call of the cranes was a lie
> your impatient words were empty.

Hellaakoski's individualism was not the pride of an aristocrat who despises the mob, but the humility of a hermit who retires to meditate on his imperfections. His poetry is not specifically Christian, but *Uusi runo* contains poems on Christian subjects, e.g., *Pitkäperjantai* ('Good Friday'), *Itkevä Jumala* ('The Tears of God'), and *Vapautus* ('Freed'), in which he asks:

> Am I ripe for love
> not seeking its own, quiet
> can from me grow a humble strife
> sacrifice and daring?

In *Mefisto* he again warns himself against complacency; when he thinks his spirit freed from the power of evil, he soon feels "a small pull at my ear / behind my back / a short dry cough" (i.e., Mephistopheles').

In his life Hellaakoski was not a hermit; he enjoyed scientific pursuit and did some fieldwork. After World War II he was one of the country's foremost poets, who regularly published collections and served for a while as chief editor of the literary periodical *Näköala*.[655] In his late collections there are poems on love and family life, but most of his poetry is descriptive of his struggle to dominate the conflicting forces of his mind. Of his many meditations on death, *Kiitos* ('Thank You' in *Uusi runo*) presents the most harmonious conclusion:

282

> Man only can say:
> come, be here, extinction
> sink into the sea, sun—darken, dawn—
> be quiet, now, my happy soul.
> The scythe was raised and fell whistling
> Man only whispered: thank you.[656]

Huojuvat keulat contains many of the elements of *Uusi runo*. Some of the poems written during the war express the author's anguish when the country seemed on the verge of destruction, but even those on more human, individual subjects are pessimistic. The nature poems are the most harmonious, often hinting a message, e.g., *Viesti* ('The Message'), which serves as epilogue to the collection:

> The quiet waters
> Were broken, perhaps, by a splash!
>
> The unknown fish
> Was taken back by the depth.
> The message from the depths:
> A short ripple
> On the surface of the water
>
> I wish I knew that fish!

In *Ilta* ('The Evening') Hellaakoski reaches the conclusion that man can reach ultimate truths only through contemplation; efforts to uncover secrets are a futile "fathoming of the bottomless / a sifting of question marks"; only when one is empty and open will they come like clouds flying over the forest. *Hengen manaus* ('The Invocation of the Spirit'), although not dogmatic, is clearly Christian. The poet admits that he has denied God, who "is not fit to be a builder, not even a policeman," but has sought him everywhere. The man is then described as iron forged by God in the fire and on the anvil, bent into many shapes, growing smaller and poorer by the moment. Even if he is exhausted, God, who never tires, will eventually lift from his anvil a better-shaped work than the one now sparkling there.

The collection *Hiljaisuus* ('Silence,' 1949) is a transition between *Huojuvat keulat* and *Sarjoja* ('Suites,' 1952), the last which the poet had prepared for publication. *Huomenna seestyvää* ('Clearing Tomorrow'; the title is a standard weather-bulletin phrase, 1953), and a volume of aphorisms, *Lumipalloja* ('Snowballs'; the author chose the title, 1955), were issued posthumously. In these collections the poet reaches peace in a mystic, yet scientific communion with nature—the mystic and scientific are possible together through the teachings of modern science, which has discovered the relativity of all phenomena and the absence of sharp boundaries between aspects of reality. In *Piippulevolla* ('Pipe Rest' in *Sarjoja*; the title is a reference to a place near his summer house where he sat, meditated, and smoked his pipe),[657] Hellaakoski ridicules those who think that they can define the universe by deciphering one page of it because there may be many aspects, piled upon each other as the pages of a book are.[658] *Kevään kuuntelua* ('Listening to the Spring' in *Hiljaisuus*)[659] describes the coming of spring with a few allusive words, projecting the poet's expectancy into nature so that the reader is scarcely aware that he is there, listening. In *Satakieli* ('The Nightingale' in *Sarjoja*) the author's oneness with nature is so complete that he merely wonders in which part he is embodied: the glittering wave on the lake, a weightless wandering cloud, the shining pillars of the pines, the smell of wild rosemary on the marsh or the wing of a butterfly. The fusion of the elements is apparent in the first image: the wave is not described, only the sound and the glitter. The poet feels that "all those who are here now, at this moment, wish to die." *Huomenna seestyvää* contains many similar poems, e.g., *Paradiso*, in which the poet says that, when he is quiet and motionless, a wind seems to sigh at the bottom of his being, expressing that which was most tightly closed; the most joyful tune sounds through all dreamers when no one speaks. However, the collection also contains realistic descriptions of the world. In *Lokakuu* ('October') autumn is seen from a country home. *Hääruno* ('A Wedding Poem') is broadly humorous in expression though not superficial in thought.

At the time of his death, Hellaakoski was the greatest poet in Finland, especially appreciated by the younger generation of writers, whose view of the world parallelled his. Their forms differed, for Hellaakoski wrote rhymed verse, giving great variety and flexibility to his rhythmic patterns with apparent irregularities.[660] The work of a younger poet, Mustapää, shows Hellaakoski's influence in both rejection of the traditional formal patterns and refusal to adopt the fashions of the twenties. They also share humor, lack of sentimentality and forceful, simple treatment of subjects. Hellaakoski was a scientist and Mustapää a scholar; both, disappointed by the lack of understanding for their works in the 1920s, did not publish again until the war, when they became the foremost poets in the country.[661]

P. Mustapää (no one knows the meaning of the initial) is the pseudonym of **Martti Henrikki Haavio** (1899-1973), an internationally renowned folklorist, professor at the University of Helsinki, member of the Finnish Academy, chief editor of several periodicals and scholarly series, honorary member of the American Folklore Society, etc.[662] His first wife was also a well-known folklorist, and his second, Aale Tynni, is a well-known poet. His brother Jaakko Haavio, like their father a minister of the church, authored collections of religious poetry and other works. In spite of his fame in scholarship, Haavio is always called P. Mustapää as a poet.

His interest in folklore and mythology is apparent in his early poems, though they are not scholarly. In them elves, fairies, hobgoblins, witches, ghosts and characters from Greek mythology act, represented with slight irony or nostalgia which indicates that the poet does not really believe, but almost wishes to believe in them. His poems are not coherent fairytales or ballads and are certainly not nonsense for nonsense's sake. He resembles the Elizabethans, who wrote naturally about fairies, witches, and ghosts, probably without quite believing in them. He longs for the past, when Puck and Oberon (characters from his poems) walked among men, but his Finnish shyness and self-criticism does not allow him to reveal this longing directly. When such characters appear, they are introduced with slightly jarring humor, and, although they are not symbols, they ultimately present Mustapää's vision of the world.

In Finland he is generally considered the poet who contributed more than any other to the freeing of Finnish poetry from the regular patterns generally used until the 1940s.[663] Several of the poems in his first collection, *Laulu ihanista silmistä* ('The Song about the Wonderful Eyes,' 1925), but almost none in the next, *Laulu vaakalinnusta* ('The Song about the Bird Rukh,' 1927),[664] are in free verse, which was then fashionable among young poets. He did not return to the regular meters used by many poets; his verse is similar to modern Finnish folksongs, often with lines of fourteen to eighteen syllables in which apparent irregularities in rhythm emphasize certain features. Especially in some early poems he probably imitates the occasional clumsiness of folk poets, but most of his work is an attempt to create new forms for Finnish poetry or to evolve a meter in which stress and quantity are equally important.[665]

Mustapää tells his readers how he wants to write: he says, "what's the use of writing serious songs,"[666] and in *Selitys* ('Explanation' in *Koiruoho, ruusunkukka* 'Wormwood, Roseblossom,' 1947) he is more explicit:

> Sinä etsi, sanottiin,
> ei pinnalta, vaan alta,
> ja filosofialta
> ano viisaus laulus säkeisiin.

> En tehnyt niin.

> Minun laulussani on
> vain kuva kaivattuni
> ja kukka, leikki, uni.
> Puck. Oberon.

> You look for it, so was I told,
> not on the surface but below,
> and for your songs, it's best, you know,
> to ask philosophy her wisdom to unfold.

> That course I did not hold.

> Into my song, I, further on,
> my sweetheart's likeness shall lay,
> a dream, a flower, a children's play.
> Puck. Oberon.

The poet is not limiting himself, but stating that there are more things between heaven and earth than are dreamed of in any philosophy. In *Tasangot* ('The Plains' in *Jäähyväiset Arkadialle* 'A Farewell to Arcadia,' 1945) he appears in Chinese surroundings as a poet who, exiled from the plains, goes to the mountains and sings "a free song to the monkeys / a song of joy in the manner of the mountain people," but confides to the birds his secret longing to return to the plains. In *Sureva Orfeus* ('Orpheus Is Mourning,' same collection) he is more serious, as he often is during his second period:

> Oi Erämaa, oi äiti Erämaa.
> Orfeus soittelee.
> Hän soittaa harppuaan puun alla, tuskan alla,
> hän helkyttelee nyt:
> soi kuikan vaikerrus, soi metsäkanan itku,
> suloinen valittelu kyyhkyläisen,
> ja metsän huokaus.
> Sun poikas, Yksinäisyys, soittaa harppuaan
> ja poikas, Ikävyys.
>
> Ja Kaiku säestää.

> O Desert, mother Desert.
> Orpheus is playing
> He plays his harp beneath the tree, beneath the pain,
> His silver notes now sound:
> The loon gives forth his cry, the grouse his wailing,
> The dove his sweet lament,
> The forest his deep sigh.
> Loneliness, your son, his harp is playing
> And Sadness, your son.
>
> To Echo's accompaniment.

In this as well as many other poems we have the birds familiar to the unknown poets of old Finnish lyric verse, where Martti Haavio, the scholar, and other folklorists found them.[667] Mustapää regards animals as equals, his brothers, with whom he converses; the higher wisdom he finds in them is the full enjoyment of life without meaningless worry and sorrow, which he expresses in *Sammakon laulu sateen aikana* ('The Song of the Frog during the Rain,' same collection). The poem consists of the frog's words, telling his pleasure at hopping along a shady path through the forest toward a moist meadow with flowers and a pond.

In *Heedonee* (same collection; the title is Classical Greek for 'pleasure') he warns his brother to hide when he comes, for his heavy steps are breaking the landscape and his heavy thoughts, winged with sorrow, are filling the forest. He adds that, when he is gone, his brother will discover *heedonee* in a seed and sink into happiness and dreams again, he, the squirrel, a right good disciple of Aristippus. Mustapää's mixture of apparently childlike simplicity, hinted romanticism, realistic Finnish details, and half-humorous artistic allusions is clearly demonstrated in *Rannalla* ('On the Shore' in *Laulu ihanista silmistä*):

> Ihan pikkuisella kivellä,
> sormenmittaisella,
> asteli rantasipi minua kohden
> ja kertoi minulle monta salaisuutta.
>
> En nähnyt sen silmiä,
> sillä hämärä lauloi vakuvirttä.
> Näin sen keikailevan nokan,
> kun se aukaisi sen sanoakseen hyvän illan.
> Johon minä: Jumal'antakoon,
> liikutettuna,
> huovaten tervaista venettäni.
>
> Oi veljet,
> se ehtoo levisi hyvänä
> kuin mystillinen uhrilehto,
> jossa on tammia,
> jossa virvaliekit lämpöisinä tuohuksina palavat,
> jossa ilma on hiukan raskas
> horsman tuoksusta ja angervojen
> ja suurien mustien kukkien,
> joita ei ole kuin intialaisessa sadussa
> ja kumminkin on.
>
> Tsindalon, tsindalon.
> Varmaankin kyntörastas.
> Varmaankin se on sen posetiivarilta oppinut
> tai suoraan Arnon rannalta
> mustatukkaiselta, kaunisluomaiselta diivalta.
> Hieno, varjostettu melodia.
> Uskontunnustus.
>
> Nuottikodan takaa:
> Tsindalon.
>
> On a tiny little stone,
> no longer than my finger,
> a sandpiper stepped toward me
> and told me many secrets.

I did not see his eyes,
for dusk was singing a lullaby.
His pert little beak I saw,
when he opened it to say goodnight.
To which I: God bless you,
with feeling,
backing water in my tarred boat.

O my brothers,
that pleasant eve spread out
like a mystic grove of sacrifice,[667]
with growing oaks,
with burning *ignes fatui* like firebrands, and warm,
and the air a little heavy
with the scent of dropwort and the willow herb
and of great black flowers
only found in tales of India
and found nevertheless.

Tsindalon, tsindalon.
No doubt a thrush behind the plough.
No doubt he learned it from an organ-grinder
or directly on the Arno River
from a dark-haired diva with beauty spots so wonderful.
A fine, shaded melody.
A faith confessed.

Behind the net shed:
Tsindalon.

The poem contains west Finnish words which give it the slightly archaic flavor reminiscent of the old Bible; Mustapää's landscapes, like Larin-Kyösti's, are usually west Finnish with leafy groves, lush meadows, fields, brooks, and old churches, not the wild deserts of east Finland. That which is old in them dates to the Middle Ages or later, not to a mythical Finnish past; even the ghosts are medieval ghosts, not Finno-Ugric demons. In *Myllyn lakassa* ('On the Upper Floor of the Mill' in *Laulu ihanista silmistä*) the poet sits on the upper floor of a red mill and watches a perfect setting for a ghost tale: silent music sounds, a dead moon full of gall shines on the roof of the church, black jackdaws sit on the weathercock, and a barn owl hoots, but, when the poet adds, "And I am so afraid," his words produce an effect opposite to that seemingly intended. Ghosts then appear, the dead rise from their graves to dance to the tune of the pipe played by Death, who sits on a stone wall while the mill seems to grind shinbones, but the poet tunes his fiddle to Death's pipe and plays a country polka about three merry fellows and their shining knives.[668] *Dominus Krabbe* ('The Reverend Krabbe' in *Laulu Vaakalinnusta*) is a long ballad-like work on the ghost of a clergyman who appears to each of six people on a beautiful summer morning. The poet describes the people and their reactions to the apparition, who eventually delivers a sermon in the church. Reverend Krabbe, who had been little revered, was discharged by the bishop because he drank, sold liquor, and killed a man in a fight, but his ghost reminds the living that they, too, are sinners: "Every one of you is a Herodes, everyone a just / man has killed in his soul for the sake of an empty lust."

Many of Mustapää's works do not contain supernatural or fantastic elements. His love poems are happy and nostalgic, often set in familiar and romantic landscapes. He composed ballads openly in the manner of English poets, e.g., Kipling; one, *Miss Annabel* (in *Laulu vaakalinnusta*), tells about "two merry fellows, Thompson and Mustapää, who came sailing to the city of Tripolis," and others describe cities he has visited. Tinsmith Lindblad, a small craftsman, first appears in *Jäähyväiset Arkadialle* and develops fully in *Koiruoho, ruusunkukka*; half-humorous and mock-heroic, he becomes a serious central figure in many poems. Similar figures appear in Swedish poetry,[669] but Mustapää uses Lindblad as a very personal projection while keeping his distance by making Lindblad humorous and speaking about him or to him, for example, in *Muudan rikas mies* ('One Rich Man,' in *Koiruoho, ruusunkukka*):

> O, Lindbald, when angling
> yea, angling, you wonder
> about the mystery of life:
> the landscape may be black
> but the frames, you know, are red.[670]

By consistently writing in this manner, Mustapää gives himself an opportunity to comment on as well as describe his character's actions, which often deviate greatly from the experiences of a common tinsmith, calculated to produce the mock-heroic effect of speaking of the ordinary with ornate language and to emphasize that no one is so insignificant that his life is not worth our interest and his feelings not as deep as those of all others. In *Dolce far niente* (same collection):

> He is a philosopher, Lindblad
> who knows life
> its two opposite sides
> the harsh and the mild
> he knows the grey sorrows
> and knows the sweet joys
> yes, all this he knows.

In *Tuulimyllyfantasia* ('Windmill Fantasy,' same collection) his epithet is Musagetes. The image of Lindblad's being carried higher and higher on the mill's wing so that he can see a distant, blossoming grove and sinking to earth again is similar to Cervante's well-known episode, but there is no direct connection between the poem and *Don Quixote*. There are some similarities between *Tuulimyllyfantasia* and *Sweeney among the Nightingales*, the half-ironic treatment of standard romantic motifs, their mixture with prosaic details, learned allusions, and the basically serious purpose, but Lindblad Musagetes is not so deliberately outlandish as Sweeney Agonistes.

During the war Mustapää wrote patriotic poems which differed from conventional ones. *Satakieli Monrepoossa* ('The Nightingale at Monrepos' in *Jäähyväiset Arkadialle*) gives a complex picture of a romantic old manor near Viipuri lost in the war against the Soviet Union; past memories are presented in an elegantly nostalgic manner, but not without Mustapää's humor. The five characters are individuals, not types, and the poem concludes that:

> Riemu turha, murhe väärä,
> kunnia on matkan määrä,
> kunnia vain, kunnia vain, muista sotamies
>
> Joy is vain, sorrow wrong,
> Honor the end of your journey long,
> Honor only, honor only, soldier, remember that.

In the context this motif is but one among several. The motto of *Ruiskukkia* ('Cornflowers,' same collection) is contained in three lines typical of Mustapää:

> Me hentomieliset,
> soturit karkeat?
> Ei sitten milloinkaan!
>
> Sentimental,
> us, rough soldiers?
> Not likely!

However, these soldiers also tell that, crawling through a field,

> We picked flowers for our helmets
> yeah, flowers, cornflowers
> remembering the home country.
>
> In the petals of the cornflower
> there is the sky of the home village
> so blue
> and the black earth of the fields
> of the fields at home, at home.

The old motifs reappear in his last two collections, *Ei rantaa ole, oi Thetis* ('There Is No Shore, O Thetis' in *Kootut runot* 'Collected Poems,' 1948) and *Linnustaja* ('The Fowler,' 1952), but their form is more allusive than it was before. *Kummittelua Vanhankartanon puistossa* ('Ghosts in the Park of the Old Manor'), is not a coherent story, only a hinted impression. In meditations on death and the world beyond, two images from Finnish mythology, the soul of a deceased which flies as a bird[671] and the world of the dead which is like the image of the real world in a mirror, frequently appear. In other works in which the poet's fancy seems to roam to faraway lands, he is actually speaking of his own problems. He did write *Burjaattilainen rukous* ('A Buryat Prayer'),[672] but it is less about the horsemen of the Central Asian steppes, studied by Martti Haavio, than about the making of poetry:

> But the shapeless mist of memory
> dwells on your lips.
> Sleep has overcome your words. The land
> of once-upon-a-time is waiting.
> From beyond tomorrow, awake the bravest
> of your words, together
> with the battle-axe of wind and the blue steed of shining mirages
> to bring you hope.

Apollonin syntymä ('The Birth of Apollo, 1960)[673] has a similar theme, and the same material and immaterial images are juxtaposed:

> – he is a shadow
> a mist only,
> brightness he is, you do not see him
> he is a dream,
> his hairs are leaves.
> The white horse you are spurring
> will not catch him,
> a ripple he is
> a wind in the tree.

One poet who was admired by his own generation and accepted by the younger, **Einari Vuorela** (b. 1889), has led an uneventful life as a country elementary school teacher in his home region Keuruu. He spent a few years in the 1920s in Helsinki, where he was considered one of the *Tulenkantajat* although that which is typical of their poetry and of his work has little in common.[674] His first collection, *Huilunsoittaja* ('The Flute Player'), appeared in 1919, and he continued to write for almost forty years; his last collection *Tikan kannel* ('The Woodpecker's Kantele'), came out in 1958. The first collections, *Huilunsoittaja, Keväthartaus* ('Spring Devotions,' 1921), *Yön kasvot* ('The Face of Night,' 1923), *Varjoleikki* ('A Play of Shadows,' 1925), *Silkkikauppias* ('The Silk Merchant,' 1926), and *Täältä kaukana* ('Here, Far Away,' 1928), are agreed to be his best. In 1932, when *Kaukainen tuuli* ('A Faraway Wind') was issued, his poetry began to lose its spontaneity and to repeat itself, although all of his collections contain a few poems as good as his first ones.

Like Larin-Kyösti and Mustapää, he made use of the rhythms, patterns, and images of the modern Finnish folksong; he has been, perhaps, the most successful in adapting them to express the poet's feelings without appearing deliberately quaint. His poems do contain the traditional fairies, trolls, and other mythological creatures, and an old-fashioned Finnish village surrounded by fields, meadows, woods, lakes, or marshes is often the setting, but he speaks of them naturally, scarcely aware that he is speaking of old times. He describes, in fact, his own environment, central Finland, where life changed very slowly until recent years. He does not portray the past, but uses its elements to represent his feelings of joy, sorrow, love, friendship, and loneliness. His mythological creatures establish a mood with their actions; for example, "the Lady Dusk sows blue silk with a pine needle," "the Lady Mist wades over the marsh,"[675] and "Frost walks in felt boots." Although Vuorela has been called the "troubadour of the woods,"[676] the nickname is too refined and exotic; he is more simply a wandering folk singer, and the image of the happy wanderer is frequent in his poems. One is called *Onnellinen vaeltaja* ('The Happy Wanderer'):

> The sky is high, the cloud's way is long
> the earth alone is low.
> My mind is light as a white scarf waving
> at the window of the upper room
>
> . . . .
>
> The sky is high, the cloud's way is long[677]
> I am wandering through the world.
> My dreams are merry like the swallow nests
> under the eaves of my house in the clouds.

We have translated *tuulentupa* (lit. 'the wind's house') 'house in the clouds'; it is a common Finnish phrase for an impossible daydream,[678] and one of Vuorela's poems bears it for a title:

> I stepped under my hat
> and went out to the world
> to escape from misery.
> I made myself a cabin in the clouds, a house
> I was given sunlight as a present
> and moonlight for nothing.

The image shows, rather than tells, the unreal quality of the wanderer's luck; the poet uses the same technique to express his sadness and longing, reflected in a landscape, in the description of an abandoned house where

The oats of dusk are swaying on the fields
A magpie is laughing on the roof of the shed

The meadows disappear in the grass of darkness
Ghosts lean against the wall of the barn.

In some of Vuorela's poems, we find strange beings from his private mythology, such as Sadness, who "sighs often / and remains late standing at the window / in the blue nights of summer" and Waiting, who "is often found leaning his elbows / against the windowsill." The free use of images and rejection of more literary forms of poetry bring Vuorela close to contemporary poets of Finland, but he is a poet who looks to the past, the last of his line. Essentially he represents the transition from old to new in Finnish verse.[679]

The dates of the birth of modern poetry in Finland differ for the two linguistic groups. Edith Södergran, hailed as the Swedish-speaking pioneer, published her first collection in 1916, and the short-lived *Ultra*,[680] in which such young radicals as Elmer Diktonius and Hagar Olsson attacked traditional values, began in 1922. Nineteen twenty-four marks the appearance of the group of Finnish-speaking writers consciously opposed to the old, but they were less radical than their Swedish-speaking countrymen. In that year nine young poets published the anthology *Nuoret Runoilijat* ('Young Poets'), Katri Vala issued her first collection, and the brochure *Tulenkantajat* ('The Fire Bearers'), which eventually gave its name to the entire group, appeared.[681] In 1929 and 1930 the same group published a periodical with the same name, but they were not responsible for the *Tulenkantajat* of the 1930s, which represented radical left-wing ideas. The group concentrated on proclaiming that they would create something entirely new in literature more than on attacking the older generation[682] or expounding political or social ideas, so that it was not difficult for the public to accept them. They were disarmingly enthusiastic, optimistic, and publicized themselves in an almost childish and unashamed manner; the humorist Olli pretended to pity them because they had no one to fight. Kai Laitinen claims that there has probably never been a periodical "more playfully gaudy and charmingly self-assertive" than the first *Tulenkantajat*. Lauri Viljanen, who as a poet was once a member of the group, calls it "noisy," and Olavi Paavolainen, the leader of the young, says that in its first issue it "let out a bellow from its gigantic bullhorn."[683] The manifesto on the cover of that first issue begins:

Life is holy. We love life.
Art is holy. We serve it.

and ends:

Behold: How wonderfully young is our country, how full of strength!
Come, fear not: You have been designated to create something new and
   great.
Break the ring that is constricting your heart: Be yourself, avow life!

However, even by the time this declaration was released, it was nearly evident
that the writers who composed the group had little in common.[684] In the
manner of many such groups, youth and enthusiasm create common goals,
but later those who have real talent discover that they have individual views
which need not be placed under a common label. The group dissolved quietly;
one year everyone spoke about the *Tulenkantajat*, and the next year few
people remembered them even though the writers from the group continued to
publish and to see each other.[685] Paavolainen's satirical pamphlet about the
"big clean-up in the literary nursery," well written and funny, was received
with relative equanimity. Paavolainen recognized talent and was merciless
only to second-rate writers who offered nothing except the fads of the
period, but even some of the objects of his satire claimed that the work
entertained them. In the period that Paavolainen spoke of, the propaganda
for the young writers had so dazed the public and publishers that books
which would not have been considered seriously at another time were read
and reviewed with respect.[686]

Lauri Viljanen later said that "The first generation of poets in
independent Finland had had a close experience of wartime anguish, poverty,
and ugliness at a time of their development when their minds were most
impressionable. But, on the other hand, these young people had grown up in
a highly aesthetic atmosphere. They had been charmed by Leino's mirages of
beauty in his later period, they had listened to the crystal sounds of eternity
in Koskenniemi's elegies. ... In the atmosphere of new liberty, they were
overwhelmed by the idea that everything that was evil was behind and that
the building of the Athens of beauty, so to say, could earnestly begin."[687]
However, for a while they seemed to be building a Xanadu rather than an
Athens, with the wealth of palm trees, oases, pyramids, inebriating flower
scents, lotuses, tigers, and Indian gods appearing in the early works of Uuno
Kailas, who then developed in a different direction, and, half in jest, those of
P. Mustapää. Heikki Asunta satirized this exotism when he wrote "The lotus
and the orange seed, quite eagerly now sought / Into the fields of this bleak
land are brought / And the scent of myrrh for the fireplace of the pinewood
folk."[688] The fashion soon dated, Professor Viljanen thinks, precisely in the
spring of 1927,[689] and admiration of all that was modern replaced it. The
most typical product of the new fashion is *Valtatiet* ('The Main Roads,'
1928), published by Olavi Lauri (pseudonym of Paavolainen) and Mika
Waltari; neither author was a good poet, and the volume was soon forgotten
although Paavolainen's imagery influenced the works of the leftist poets of

the 1930s who wrote of a new technological world. The gay twenties were part of the fashion, and Helsinki, as in Eino Leino's time, was thought a great, sinful city where drinking was exciting (prohibition was in effect from 1919 to 1932).[690]

The most remarkable poet of the *Tulenkantajat* and one of the two best (Sarkia was the other) of the entire period between the wars was **Uuno Kailas** (first **Frans Uuno Salonen**, 1901-33). Superficial elements of his biography make him the prototype of the tragic poet in the public's eye: he had no money, his life was full of difficulty, his physical and mental health was poor, and he died young of tuberculosis.[691] In 1932 his physician reportedly promised him six years of life if he would take care of himself; his supposed reply was that he could not live regularly, it was impossible for him.[692] A tragic figure should be ignored by his contemporaries, but the *Tulenkantajat* were popular, Kailas had participated in a Finnish guerilla raid into Soviet territory in 1919,[693] and he wrote partiotic poetry calling for national unity in the face of the enemy. He emphasized the search for truth, attained through self-examination, self-denial, and struggle for self-improvement. He was, in fact, abnormally self-centered and has been called narcissistic; this trait became more dominant toward the end of his life. After 1928, when he had to have psychiatric treatment, his poetry progressively reflects more of his subconscious terrors, which attracted his readers' attention and produced baffled comments because the poetry could not easily be categorized.[694] His visions are not alien to general human experience; they are magnified, clearer expression of that which everyone has felt or dreamed; their simple, artless presentation makes them familiar and frightening. The poet's objectivity, his calm, distant observation, is unusual, but his schizophrenia partially explains it.[695]

Kailas published five collections of poetry, *Tuuli ja tähkä* ('The Wind and the Ear of Grain,' 1922), *Purjehtijat* ('The Seafarers,' 1925), *Silmästä silmään* ('From Eye to Eye,' 1926), *Paljain jaloin* ('Barefoot,' 1928), and *Uni ja kuolema* ('Sleep and Death,' 1931), and a selection of his works, *Runoja* ('Poems,' 1932). A posthumous collection, *Punajuova* ('The Red Streak'), was edited in 1933. Kailas did not write flowing verse, and his first collection is somewhat awkward. His images, too, give a constructed rather than spontaneous impression. An important motif is the poet's fate, a transmutation of his suffering to art without alleviating the pain; in *Midas-sydän* ('The Midas Heart') an image from the myth of King Midas expresses it:

> What avails it you although a tear
> you can make into bright gold?
> The burn of your longing
> will not be soothed by that.

The thought of death obsessed Kailas, but it becomes more apparent in later collections; in the first collection it appears in the traditional image of the poet who will die but whose work will live forever, rhetorically expressed in the title poem:

> I am frail and weak
> and you shall break me.
> But there is a will, victorious
> over yours:
>
> the holy will of creation
> the proudest and most eternal.
> You slew me, I shall die
> - sowing the seed of life.

and in *Finaali* ('Finale'):

> Proud is the lot of the singer:
> Blessing his song, his child
> to step, carrying high his head
> against oblivion.

Kailas's personal reasons for his feelings of guilt, inferiority, and anguish rarely appear in his works; there his transgression seems almost ontological, as though his existence has been a breach against a higher order. He uses Christian symbols, but he seldom speaks of the relation of man to divinity; for him the world was governed by blind fate.[696] His tragedy was his inability to believe in a merciful or wrathful God or to find comfort in philosophy or sensuous aestheticism. Although he tried to convince himself that his struggle for clarity had a positive value, the conviction sometimes wavered, and he became a dispassionate observer of his own disintegration. He tried to overcome the threat of death by equating it with sleep and dream or by imagining that he had reconquered the innocence of a child or a madman. He did not reach a final conclusion, but his last collection seems to express an occasional peaceful acceptance of death.

In his second collection, *Purjehtijat* ('The Seafarers'), Kailas comes closest to the style of the *Tulenkantajat* in the use of free verse and exotic imagery. A year earlier he had published an anthology of his translations of German poetry from Goethe to contemporary poets; his second collection also reflects the influence of German expressionism.[697] One poem in which he describes himself as a fish caught in a net is typical of him; the last line states that "Fate has slowly-killing nets."[698] *Syyllinen mies* ('The Guilty Man') shows his brief experience in the war while expressing the brotherhood of men and purification through suffering:

> He shall be shot. He is a guilty man.
> Without a word he looks at us and from us away.

He gives his eyes to me and orders: look!
And then I see who also is a guilty man.

All we wear the iron ring of guilt around our wrist.
All of us whom my eyes can see,
Debtors and slaves of guilt, fettered we are to him.
Surrounded by the host of what we feel in us.

But one of us the ring of death has broken.
His dirty clothes I see him shedding.
Into the light he steps from below the murky wings of guilt.

A new face I see: the thief he is, nailed to the cross,
He is my brother, the guilty man who shall be shot.

This poem is the most Christian of all his works; instead of turning inward, he reaches toward other humans in a feeling of shared fate. In the same collection a group of poems, *Lapsifantasioita* ('Child Fantasies'), reveals again the poet's fascination with death; in the concluding lines he attempts to deny it by identifying himself with a child to whom death is a word without meaning:

People have also empty words.
Words you cannot understand.
Like death and sin,
which do not mean anything.
But no matter what, you must be afraid of them.

Kailas's basic attitude was childish. The verbal magic he performs in his poem by denying reality in denying the meaning of a word relates to his work with words. He may have felt that their effect was also unreal.

Silmästä silmään made him known as a poet. It marks a transition in his art from free verse influenced by expressionism to a more traditional form characterized by regular rhythm and rhyme and shows his progressive turning inward. The collection includes four translations of Baudelaire, whose influence may be detected in some of Kailas's poems, in which he speaks of the sensuous pleasures of love in an open and perhaps intentionally provocative manner. Kailas occasionally wrote satirical poems expressing irritation at the narrow-mindedness and stuffiness of Finland,[699] e.g., *Pienessä maassa* ('In a Small Land' in *Silmästä silmään*):

Fences everywhere. And on the gates a sign:
"This is my property" and "Turn away from here!"
They deal out air by cubic inches to each other:
here, breathe this—and then stop breathing!

In this collection he titles one of his love poems *Pieni syntinen laulu* ('A Small Sinful Song'), as if pointing out for the reader its true nature:

297

My little delight, in my bed
you have been naked.
The memory of our sin in my song
I do not deny: it is beautiful.

The collection contains more such poems, e.g., *Trubaduuri* ('The Troubadour'), and a Christian periodical recommended that the poet be prosecuted.[700] They represent Kailas's dreams more than his experiences, however; he was mainly unhappy in his relations with the other sex.[701]

Other poems in the collection express Nietzschean pride in the poet's calling or project the author's personal terrors. *Yksinäinen ratsastaja* is the most typical of the former, but it seems only an exercise in ornate imagery. He attempts to idealize his loneliness by describing the proud rider, "of the breed of the lonely clouds of night, of the birds of prey and shying steeds," who scorns those who live and die in flocks, raising their arms and "calling the name of the Wraith of heaven"; the atheistic note is unusual for Kailas. The poem ends with an assertion, not sustained by the rest, that the rider has achieved immortality:

And over the shoulders of time and death
your horse is galloping toward the clouds,
and the hot flames of the Sun's eyes
glide over the gold of your coat of mail

Another composition of this type, *Pronssia* ('Bronze'), has an image confused between a bronze statue and a stone sphinx. The sphinx says that he was once a man of blood, bone, and flesh, with a heart feeding love and hate, until Fate touched him with his wand, making his face "eternal-stony"; a flaming heart still beats within him, but its suffering is mute. Although he is wordless, Fate speaks through him. Ibsen is often mentioned in connection with another poem, *Ihmisen määrä*; his definition of poetry, "To write poetry is to hold Doomsday over oneself,"[702] often quoted in Finland, becomes in Kailas's composition an exhortation not to leave "the human for the human," but to be a man in everything, to take one's steps from the morass to the mountains, and to reject the wrong, for the proudest lot of man is to fight in vain, knowing that the victory will be empty. In these poems Kailas's estrangement from the world takes a traditionally accepted form. A four-line poem often quoted proclaims the exalted character of truth: "Those who every day let their mouth swear in your name do not know you; you spread your wings on the wood of the cross and soar, eagle-like, in the skies."

The later poems which express the conflicts of Kailas's mind in simple images are not numerous in this collection. In *Ilta* ('The Evening') a sunset, a cloud, and the water near the shore reflect nameless terror felt by the poet, who concludes:

> The last flapping of the wind fails
> and it falls like a thought,
> frightened at its flight
> over a boundless, strange land.

Peitetyt kasvot ('The Hidden Face') contains the dream and the poet who observes himself as a stranger, two motifs which are typical of his later works:

> In my dreams I often see a man
> who hides his face —
> he does not say a word, with his hands
> he hides his face.
>
> What is he afraid of, what shies he from,
> why does he hide his face?
> Does he see a horrible sight
> and therefore hides his face
>
> or is he frightened of his own soul
> and hides his face — ?
> He is pale, he never says a word,
> but he hides his face.
>
> — He is my shadow, that pale man of night,
> who hides his face.
> Who is crushed by the yoke of guilty conscience,
> hides his true face.

A reversal of this motif appears in *Kuva* ('The Image' in *Paljain jaloin*) where the reflection in the water of the Narcissus myth is the impossible ideal which haunts the observer, for it remains beautiful no matter how repulsive he grows.

When Kailas wrote *Paljain jaloin*, he was already sensing the approaching mental collapse from which he later recovered. Some of its poems most directly express his private terrors, e.g., *Partaalla* ('On the Brink'), a nightmare of frightening intensity:

> I am afraid in my room.
> I am afraid of the window
> and of the human shadows, which
> it casts on the walls
> like lizards and reptiles.
>
> I am afraid of looking at the door.
> The door opens toward darkness—
> the handle might turn and those
> come for whom I have no names,
> those whom I see in my dreams. . . .

> And I am also afraid of the walls.
> All of a sudden I shudder and see:
> They will not resist anything,
> they will not stop anybody—
> they are but a dim net.

The poem concludes with a question: "Is there a God?—Nobody, nobody answers." *Autio maa* ('The Waste Land') is similar:

> The land of my soul
> is boundless like Asia,
> empty like the frozen sea.
> Grey sand,
> sand and grey rocks
> without any growth
>
> . . . .
> The last bird
> has covered his head with his wing.
> Nothing is alive.

Other poems are less negative. *Marttyyrit* ('The Martyrs') is mainly Christian in symbolism; the martyrs of all ages are

> The brazen serpent
> and the blood on the doorpost
> and the rainbow over the flood.
>
> The life of their death
> is endless.
> They are buried on the bosom of the whole world,
> in the lap of coming times.

Suffering and self-denial, however, are always present. In the title poem the image of the wanderer progressing barefoot with deep wounds in his heels has no expressed meaning, an ambiguity typical of Kailas. *Pyramiidilaulu* ('The Song of the Pyramids') is more explicit; the pyramids symbolize the poet's work and all human endeavor:

> Everyone of us according to his measure
> builds a pyramid.
> And in its heart
> We soon deeply slumber
>
> like the pharaohs, silent,
> like larvae under their crust.
> The pyramid remains and is seen.
> But the pharaoh is forgotten.

This image of death, burial, and continued existence appears in *Kun olin kuollut*, in which the poet imagines that, after he has been laid in his grave, he listens to a conversation between a woman he loved and another person. The remarks are intentionally ambiguous; they may express the poet's self-criticism or his bitterness at the contempt shown to him by a woman or by people of less bohemian habits. They are accurate about Kailas's private life: "He was poor. He wasn't quite right in the head. A fool, an original. He drank all night and killed himself slowly. It is true that he wrote songs, but they were what they were." The first three stanzas and the last are less prosaic; the poet describes life thereafter as a state in which he remains in the grave but can see "the space without any secrets" and turn his eyes "toward the sunrise and the East." *Poikani* ('My Son') has a more conventional image of immortality—the survival of the individual through his children. The small boy who looks at him and says "Father" disappears when he tries to take his hand, but, if his son would be there again when Death comes to take him away, he would not be afraid "to step into the circle of Nonbeing." Kailas never married or had children—the son may represent his work.

Uni ja kuolema repeats some of the motifs of *Paljain jaloin* in a more subdued manner. The poet's terrors survive, but he is better able to observe and describe them. The room and the door of *Partaalla* reappear in *Ovella* ('At the Door'), but the poet has decided to turn the door handle and step from the past toward the future, beyond the border of two worlds. Though not optimistic, the poem implies a conscious acceptance of death's necessity. A variation of the motif is in *Talo* ('The House'), which ends:

> There is no door
> for friends or visitors to come.
> But two doors have I,
> two: to dream and to death.[703]

Kailas uses the figure of the madman in *Viulu* ('The Fiddle') and *Ympyrä* ('The Circle'), in which asylum inmates have reached happiness in detachment from the world's sorrows. Both poems are simple and have no comment or symbolic interpretation by the author. Ernest Dowson's *To One in Bedlam* begins with an image similar to that in *Viulu*, but ends with the poet's address to the madman. Kailas's poem scarcely oversteps the boundaries of the dreamworld:

> All the day long he was a-sitting
> in the corner alone by himself.
> A leaf of grass he was holding
> and a birch twig in his hands.

And the dried-out leaf of grass
was the bow of a fiddle to him:
all the day long over the fiddle
—that twig—it did swing and swing.

What music that birch twig was making,
God Father only it knew:
the fiddle was a madman's fiddle,
and the man was a blissful man.

Ympyrä too describes a man in his cell; he walks continuously in a counterclockwise circle singing that, while he was in the world, he was sinning and turning in the other direction; by going the opposite way, he will now undo to skein of his sins, soon be a small child, and sleep in his cradle.

The longing for childhood is in other poems, e.g., *Uni* ('The Dream'), which describes a dream within a dream: the poet dreams that he is a child who has a bad dream. His mother comforts him, and he awakes to see that there is no mother, no child—both are dead. *Ajuri* ('The Cabdriver') gives the impression of a vivid nightmare although the poem contains no reference to dreams; like many of Kailas's works, it contains no commentary. The narrator drives in a cab with his grandmother, who died years ago, and arrives at the Park Hotel. An angel receives the woman at the door and says that she will wait there for him, but the cabdriver shouts brutally, "You won't see her again!" and whips his horse, "Hey, toward Hell!" The narrator jumps from the cab and finds himself in a strange town where he is left to err endlessly on the streets.

The feeling of estrangement is in a few lines of *Vieras mies* ('A Stranger'):

Everywhere I was a stranger,
they cast wondering looks at me,

. . . .

In the whole world
there was not a peaceful spot for me.
And a man who was a stranger to me
within myself dragged me.

Contemplation expresses his solitude in the most traditional manner; he concludes by saying that his heart is like a shell, making a pearl of its suffering, and like a seed, living by dying; it sleeps without sleeping, drawing strength from its slumber. *Syysaamu* ('An Autumn Morning') and *Ovella* are the last of his personal poems. In *Syysaamu* Kailas sees an old gardener walking in the park with a scythe on his shoulder and remembers, smiling, that he once prayed for the Gardener to come and cut. The end of the

302

volume also contains some indifferent ballads and patriotic poems, some of which, especially *Rajalla* ('On the Border'), were long popular.

Kai Laitinen points out that Kailas's fame unfortunately made illness and suffering the hallmarks of a poet for the public,[704] and the similar fates of Saima Harmaja, Kaarlo Sarkia, and Katri Vala, coupled with Koskenniemi's academically elegant and widely-read threnodies make Finnish poetry of the thirties and forties quite gloomy. The dejection of most of the poets was deep and personal, but one regrets that they began a fashion which probably discouraged more optimistic writers from publishing verse; that lack of understanding forced Hellaakoski and P. Mustapää into silence.

Kaarlo Sarkia (first **Sulin**, 1902-45), a contemporary of the *Tulenkantajat*, is not counted among them although his verse has many similarities to their art.[705] He and Kailas were, while Hellaakoski and P. Mustapää did not publish, the greatest Finnish poets of their time. The illegitimate son of a poor country girl in southwest Finland who died while he was young, he later wrote a moving, respectful poem, *Velka elämälle* ('The Debt to Life'), in her memory. With help he completed secondary school and studied at the University of Helsinki, then Turku, where he came under the influence of Koskenniemi and his literary circle. His first two collections, *Kahlittu* ('Fettered,' 1929) and *Velka elämälle* (1931), passed virtually unnoticed, but a translation of Rimbaud's *Le Bateau ivre* made him known.[706] He became a well-known poet, and his third collection, *Unen kaivo* ('The Well of Sleep,' 1936), received favorable attention, as did *Kohtalon vaaka* ('The Scales of Fate,' 1943), although it suffered somewhat from being published during the war. In 1944 he edited a general collection of his work, *Runot,*[707] and the following year tuberculosis ended his life.

Unlike Kailas, Sarkia became known for his formally faultless, melodious poetry. He had an extraordinary facility for rhyme, which he used so freely that even his admirers criticized him. His skillful use of varied rhythmic patterns drew admiration, and some critics claim that in his poems rhythm rather than words conveys the basic message.[708] His work is traditional in structure and syntax. Tuomas Anhava, who criticized Sarkia's translation of *Bateau ivre* and offered one he claimed was better, says that "In the history of our poetry, Sarkia occupies more or less the same position that Keats has in English poetry and Musset in French."[709]

Sarkia never had a regular job or permanent home, and he spent periods in sanatoriums, where the regulated life irked him. He was emotionally disturbed because his erotic feeling deviated from the normal—one of his biographers speaks of "quantitative and qualitative anomaly."[710] Nevertheless, it is evident from their poetry that Sarkia had a more balanced personality than Kailas had. He was able to give his personal problems less direct expression, and his work contains no nightmares or naked fright. Although he sometimes took refuge in beautiful dreams, he felt an urge for human contact. Kaarlo Marjanen considers this oscillation between extremes typical of his entire production.[711]

Sarkia's poetry is based on a few simple motifs, and especially in his first collections he is non- but not anti-intellectual. The simplicity is only apparent, for the whole is an elaborate structure of sound, rhythm, and meaning. His poems cannot be fully enjoyed unless read aloud by someone skilled in bringing out all their qualities. His motifs include childhood memories (in spite of the circumstances, his were happy), love, visions of landscapes or a dreamworld more beautiful than the real, and, in the last collections, exhortations to himself to leave his artificial paradise and share mankind's sufferings.

His dreams, beautiful and melancholy, rarely terrifying, are as auditory as visual.[712] He grouped most of the poems in which they appear under the heading *Varjorukki* ('The Spinning Wheel of Shadows') in *Unen kaivo*. In the simplest of them, *Huuto* ('The Shout'), the poet, while walking on a silent street, hears someone shouting his name, stops, terrified, but cannot discover who called him. When Kailas describes inner experiences, he concentrates on the experience, but Sarkia often adds comments or explanations, weakening the effect. After the initial stanzas of *Huuto*, he reflects that his own youth might be a betrayed ideal, or from her grave his mother might have called, thus converting the original image to little more than a conventional metaphor. *Rukkilaulu* ('The Song of the Spinning Wheel') combines childhood memories with a supernatural vision described in words and rhythms which suggest the motion and humming of the spinning wheel.[713] Watching his mother at the spinning wheel, a child happily falls asleep, dreaming of fairylands; at night he wakes, but his mother's hand against the dim window now seems a gigantic spider spinning "a thread of shadows". There is a break in tone when the poet adds that "the monstrous spinning wheel of shadows is whirring, the giant wheel of Fate is running." The title poem of *Unen kaivo* is typical of the ecstatically dreamy and ornate side of Sarkia's art, for which he is best known, perhaps without sufficient cause. It is a beautiful poem, often quoted, and to us it indicates that Sarkia might have become acquainted with the French surrealists with good results, for their outlook was similar to his and their style would have been congenial to him. The basis of the poem is an image of the poet, lying at the bottom of a well, or a pond or lake, who hears the flutes of the reeds purl and sigh, feels strange fish swim by, sees the algae sway, and perceives occasionally the distorted appearance of a person leaning over the water and reaching toward him.[714] The Shakespearean "Full fathom five thy father lies" is not unlike Sarkia's poem, where even the bells of the English poem peal:

> laine liikahtaa ja laulaa,
> hiljaa, unelias, velloin
> soittaa raakunkuorikelloin.

the wave moves and sings,
quiet, sleepy, rocking, rings
the sea-bells of the shells.

This motif of eternal sleep and dreams more beautiful than reality occurs in other poems of the same collection, e.g., *Endymion*,[715] which ends: "The youth of sleep is immortal," *Kuoleman hyväily* ('The Caress of Death'), in which the kiss of death is sweeter than any mortal lips, and *Uponneet puistot* ('The Sunken Gardens' in *Kohtalon vaaka*):

Sydämen syvyydessä puistot saartuu
niin ihmeelliset, ikivihannat.
Smaragdiketjut köynnöksien kaartuu
ja lehtokujat vilvaat, ihanat.

Ja sypresseissä satakielet valtaan
jää sävelten ja lämmin louna käy
ja loiske kaikuen soi kaivon altaan
kujilla, joilla kulkijaa ei näy

Uponnein puistoin, unelmain Atlantis,
maa onnen muistoin, rauhan rajaton,
sun kaivos virvoittaa, on altis antis,
hedelmäis kypsyntä on ajaton.

Into the heart these gardens have sunk deep
So wonderful and evergreen.
Like chains of emerald the vines there creep
And alleys stretch, which fresh boughs screen.

And nightingales in cypress trees
Their songs into the southern breeze let glide
And echoes, which the splashing fountain frees,
Roam in the streets where walkers do not stride.

Land of dreams, Atlantis, with gardens sunk into your rifts,
Of blissful memories, of peace unbound,
Your well is fresh, abundant are your gifts,
Your fruits are ripening whenever found.

Sarkia often describes luxuriant, colorful, though not necessarily exotic, flowers, as the poet's proud declaration that he will describe all the beauty he can, although it is doomed to destruction in autumn. They also symbolize the memory of love, e.g., in *Syyskuun kukkia* ('September Flowers'), *Syysyön fantasia* ('An Autumn Night Fantasy'), and *Daalia-uni* ('A Dream of Dahlias')[716] in *Unen kaivo*. The cactus flower of *Kukkiva kaktus* ('The Cactus in Bloom' in *Kahlittu*)[717] is the symbol of inner beauty erupting through a crust of ugliness. Sarkia experienced feelings of inferiority and guilt which he expresses in poems describing ugly, misshapen individuals who turn to the beautiful; such poems include *Kauniille veljille* ('To My Beautiful Brothers' in *Unen kaivo*) and *Kyttyräselkä puhuu* ('The Humpback Is Speaking' in *Kahlittu*), which states that those who do not have visible humps carry them in their souls or that, while the ugly, weak one was suffering, they despised him, so that, when he finds strength and frees himself, he should perhaps thank them.

Sarkia's happiest poems, which reveal his sense of humor, are those which he wrote on his visit to Italy in 1937 and 1938, grouped as *Intermezzo* in *Kohtalon vaaka*. Some are dreamy, ecstatic descriptions of natural beauty; others are playful images of ordinary life with verbal acrobatics, Italian phrases and words which rhyme with Finnish words, and humorously exaggerated renderings of the terrific din of Italian streets. Kaarlo Marjanen thinks that nothing else written in Finland so directly expresses simple, uninhibited joy of life.[718] Many of the compositions in *Kohtalon vaaka*, written before World War II began, present, consciously, a new side of his art. Two sequences in *Kohtalon vaaka*, *Runo rumuudesta* ('A Poem on Ugliness') and *Tuskan hukuttaminen* ('Drowning the Pain'), express it well. That which he called ugliness is actually that which others would call evil; in the sixth poem of the first sequence, he says: " . . . you, the enemy of life, / you, ugliness, death, whatever be your name." The fourth poem contains a reference to war; ugliness is equated to a

> cruel, unnatural monster without a human heart,
> which . . .
> defiling the laws of men, rejecting truth,
> drives nations with the whip of hate to be slaughtered like cattle,
> . . . drowns the whole country in the roar of an unheard-of madness.

Sarkia repeats this pessimism about the power of ugliness throughout the beginning of the sequence, but presents a broader, somewhat comforting vision in the last three poems. He states that ugliness and beauty, good and evil are so intertwined that it is impossible to separate them, then wonders how the soul conceived the yearning to extract from eternal unity something which is part of it, and concludes by affirming the soul's indestructible hope for a better world where unity will not be destroyed and truth will reign. This hope enables him to fight, live, and achieve more than human strength is able to. The longer, more heterogenous *Tuskan hukuttaminen* begins with the poet's exhortations that he should join the community of men, even if he might be bruised; the image is realistic and almost humorous. Other poems are directed against war, while still others describe life and human effort from both optimistic and pessimistic angles. The sequence ends on a *Credo* that all which is good and true in life will be united in great harmony under God's protection.[719]

Sarkia is the last representative of a period of Finnish poetry; although rhymed poetry has been written since, no one has tried to achieve such virtuosity of composition as he did, and no one has lifted beauty and dreams above reality in his manner. Even he eventually expressed other ideas.

Perhaps the most typical and most natural *Tulenkantajat* poet was **Katri Vala** (pseudonym of **Karin Alice Heikel**, *née* Wadenström, 1901-44). Her father was a official of the Forest Services whose family moved with him wherever he was stationed; she was born in Muonio, Lapland. He died when she was ten, and the family lived in straitened circumstances in Porvoo; she eventually became an elementary schoolteacher and worked in several out-of-the-way places in the country. The entire family had literary interests; her brother Erkki Vala became a leading figure of the *Tulenkantajat* and was conspicuous in the country's literary life of the 1920s and 1930s although he did not publish anything noteworthy. She began writing poetry at the age of eleven. Her first poems were published in *Nuori Voima*, and in 1922 she was attracted to the group editing the *Ultra*. At the same time she began to write free verse.[720] Olavi Paavolainen, then the center of a small literary group in Helsinki, became an enthusiastic, faithful admirer of her art. With his questionable literary taste, he introduced her to the moth-eaten exoticism of Loti and Countess de Noailles, but she was able to make something fresh and new from it. She was proud and independent; when critics wondered where she found her expressionism and modernism, she said that she must have "inhaled them from the air she was breathing."[721]

Her first collection, *Kaukainen puutarha* ('The Faraway Garden,' 1924), won the literary prize of the government, and the *Nuoret runoilijat* anthology included eight of her poems in the same year. She met young authors with similar ideas, and they published another anthology, *Hurmioituneet kasvot* ('The Rapturous Face,' 1925; the title is probably a translation of *Le visage émerveillé* by Countess de Noailles),[722] considered to capture the essence of the *Tulenkantajat* outlook. Her second collection, *Sininen ovi* ('The Blue Door'), appeared in 1926, and the third, *Maan laiturilla* ('On the Pier of Earth,' originally part of *Kolme* 'Three,' published with two other poets), which marks a transition in her art, came out in 1930. In 1928 she was found to have tuberculosis; she took care of herself and was able to work, write, marry, and bear a child, but the illness partly modified her philosophy and art. She lived in a part of Helsinki where she had direct experience with the suffering and humiliation caused by the depression, the brutal anticommunist policies of the government, and the fascist movement which developed in the country at that time. She openly sided with the workers' movement, pacifists, and internationalists for humanitarian rather than political reasons. She never accepted the Marxist ideology of many writers she met in the *Kiila* literary group and in connection with the second *Tulenkantajat*, founded by her brother. She expressed her ideas in *Paluu*

('The Return,' 1934), a collection which surprised and bewildered the public and critics, who had been unaware of the change in her opinions.[723] She continued to work as a columnist and essayist for *Tulenkantajat*, writing, for example, on the utopian socialists of the nineteenth century, who were closer to her than "scientific socialism."[724] A posthumous collection of her articles, *Henki ja aine* ('The Spirit and the Matter'), appeared in 1945. When her illness became worse, she went to Sweden for treatment and died there after publishing her last collection of poetry, *Pesäpuu palaa* ('The Tree with the Nest Is Burning,' 1942). In 1945 her ashes were brought to Finland and buried with honors by the government.

Her first two collections express passionate joy of life, an unquenchable thirst for all sensuous pleasures expressed in general terms and symbols, most often the sun, earth, a garden, or flowers. In *Kukkiva maa* ('Flowering Earth' in *Kaukainen puutarha*) she wants

> To live, to live, to live!
> To live furiously the high moment of life,
> with petals opening to the utmost,
> to live in wonderful blossom,
> raving with one's scent, with sun—
> fully, inebriatingly to live!

The impossibility of sustaining the *allegro furioso* is indicated by the end of the poem:

> No matter if the wonders with all their colors
> shall wither and be scattered on the ground.
> Once, there was a time of bloom!

Other poems express the quiet, even melancholy peace inspired by the contemplation of nature in autumn or winter. *Harmaa laulu* ('A Grey Song') creates the atmosphere of an old country house:

> I wanted to sing a song,
> which would be simple and frail
> and like soft, grey smoke.
>
> . . . .
>
> Such a song I wanted to sing
> that, when listening to it, you would think
> of a long winter dusk,
> when you feel so quiet and sleepy
> sitting in your house, sunken in the snow,
> next to the grey-red embers
> the hands sunken in your lap,
> your eyes drowsily watching
> quiet, sweet dreams.

308

> It has been humming long in my mind
> that song,
> like a sleepy spinning wheel
> on which you make grey yarn
> with soft tufts of wool which make you think of small clouds.

This first collection also has a series of poems reviving the world of fairytales and faraway lands, and for a long time both public and critics thought that she wrote mainly that type of verse.[725] The second collection too contains a group of fairytale poems, *Linnun satu* ('The Tale of the Bird'), which reveal a sense of humor which she later used with serious subjects. She peopled a world she seemed not to take seriously with animals, fairies, and goblins through whom she satirized human weaknesses. *Faunit* ('The Fauns') contains a classical scene of nymphs and fauns gamboling in the woods and around wells, but Katri Vala seems almost amused by her choice of such a subject. The second collection also includes love poems which are frank in expressing physical pleasure yet chaste in avoiding direct description. The happiness is blissful and quiet rather than frenetic, e.g., in *Riemu* ('Joy'):

> When you sing
> I see the sea of our love
> in which we are drifting,
> the reflections of the stars tremble on our limbs.
> Is it a thousand years we have been gliding like this
> or only the time for a star to go out?

Her style is not free from mannerism, and, although appreciative, critics were not as enthusiastic about her second collection as about her first.[726] Paavolainen, the exception, her ever-faithful defender, influenced her third collection; he insisted that the time of romanticism was past and that poets should turn to the modern world for motifs. Thus, poems in *Maan laiturilla* contain motor cars, trains, and airplanes, but Katri Vala was unsuccessful at incorporating them in verse, as are all poets, for mere technical devices do not adequately symbolize an age. The proximity of death, which she felt during her illness, appears for the first time in her poetry. She speaks of it as ecstatically as she previously spoke of life and sees it as a dissolution into the great river of the universe in *Onnellinen* ('Happy').

In *Paluu* Katri Vala abandons her old style and begins to write more concisely about the poor and the suffering, against injustice, oppression, and violence. In *Pajupilli* ('A Pipe of Willow') she says:

> I am not a banner-bearer
> not an eagle-hearted guide
> on your road toward the land of morning.
> I am a willow on the bank of the river
> through which the winds are blowing

> from which the rebellious spirit of the earth
> breaks a simple pipe
> to play a tune
> which has tempest, pain, love
> and some dawn in it.

Her poems are social, not political, but she received an indelible political label. She was consciously one-sided in her condemnation of the rich and powerful. In accordance with the traditions of proletarian poetry, she used Christian motifs, believing the Gospels to have a social as well as religious message; *Ihmisenpojan ruoska* ('The Whip of the Son of Man'), for example, threatens those who buy and sell in the temple. Her antiwar poetry reflects the fear of the mother for her children; in *Syntymättömälle* she says:

> Today is still peace.
> But when shall bursting death fall
> amidst the wondering players?
> O my children in the land of the unborn
> I am ashamed of the world into which I shall bring you.

However, war had not yet come, and she was still able to use humor and fantasy although they frequently expressed her new feelings. Her heroine is the fairy Si-Si-Dus and her enemies the little black men who decide not to tolerate happiness. In *Mustat miehet* ('The Black Men'),

> The little black men
> came threatening to see Si-Si-Dus
> — You do not bow to the sword,
> everybody comes to your ball,
> your country has no boundaries.
> We have decided
> to upset a bushel over you
> and to sit mightily down on it.

A similar spirit is evident in the series *Lapsen maailma* ('The World of the Child'), but fear of destruction also predominates and her joy sometimes seems forced. Her loathing of violence had made communism repulsive to her,[727] but she now concluded that violence must be met with force:

> Thoughts are circling the earth
> as birds a burning tree with the nests
> searching for the destroyers
> shouting a hard song of battle.

The last poem in the collection, admired by friendly critics,[728] centers on a Christian motif. She uses the images of the last book of the New Testament to portray the conflict from which a better world, one in which songs will again be heard, will grow:

Heaven and earth are full of the roar of battles
and fowls are eating the flesh of captains
when the Beast, the Serpent, is thrown into the bottomless pit.

The temple stands, silent,
filled with the smoke of transfiguration.
It is waiting for the return of the Son of Man
and for the great wind of songs.

Katri Vala was similar to a type of European intellectual common between the wars. She had enthusiastic faith in man and progress; she believed in instinct and emotion rather than intellect. International events, especially the war, bitterly disappointed her, but she hoped that it would be the beginning of a better world. After many misgivings, she decided that the Communist party embodied her ideals; she was naively idealistic, but her ideals were not at fault.

The first works of **Yrjö Jylhä** (1903-56) appeared in *Nuoria runoilijoita* and *Hurmioituneet kasvot*; thus he is considered a member of the *Tulenkantajat* although his work has little in common with that of Katri Vala, for example. The son of an unsuccessful businessman, Jylhä came from Tampere and studied at the University of Helsinki before becoming a poet. He did not publish much, but he did many remarkable translations including *Paradise Lost* (1931), a selection of La Fontaine's *Fables* (1935), stories by Cervantes (1936), *La chanson de Roland* (1936), Heine's *Buch der Lieder* (1937), many of Shakespeare's major plays (1955-56), and a selection of Wordsworth's poems (with Aale Tynni and Lauri Viljanen, 1949).

Jylhä's first two collections, *Ruoskanjäljet* ('The Weals,' 1926) and *Kurimus* ('The Whirlpool,' 1928), reveal his unusual conception of the world as a never-ending fight, which is not only spiritual but also physical. As his titles indicate, he liked brutal, bloody motifs: *Tiikerin häkissä* ('In the Cage of the Tiger'), *Tyrmästä tullut* ('Coming from Jail'), and *Kaleeriorja* ('The Galley Slave'). His love poems are more about hate than love; *Mustat helmet* ('The Black Beads') ends with the overcoming of an enemy and self-destruction, with a curious mixture of metaphor and direct description. Though he hates his former beloved, he is still ensnared by her string of black beads; he will break it or, if he fails, pull it tight around her neck and hang himself with it.

His next collections are more subdued; it is reported that his skill as a poet was improved by translating.[729] Elements of violence still appear, combined occasionally with meditations on nature. *Luodolla* ('On an Island' in *Toiviotiellä* 'The Pilgrimage,' 1938), for example, stresses the common origin of man and the world but changes to a mood of Promethean defiance against the elements and their ruler. After an acoustically and rhythmically skillful description of a tempest and thunderstorm, it ends with an admission of man's weakness. *Häätanhu* ('The Wedding Dance'), written in the manner of a Finnish folksong and constructed as an address to the poet's beloved, who is marrying another man, is a variation on the motif of how poets remain young forever through their works. He says that he is dying ("I've got my funeral, you've got your wedding"), but adds that she will grow old and find him young forever ("You've got your funeral, I've got my wedding"). This poem, too, contains Jylhä's nonlogical juxtaposition of metaphor and reality.

During the Winter War Jylhä commanded an infantry company involved in particularly heavy fighting; later he based *Kiirastuli* ('The Purgatory,' 1941), a collection of an almost unique type, on his experiences.[730] The violence and pathos of his earlier collections is apparent only in the first poems which deal with the time prior to the war; when the actual fighting begins, they disappear, as though actual violence made Jylhä aware of the artificiality of his imaginary violence. A frequent problem in the collection is the responsibility of the leader who sends his men to death, but it was not a personal problem to Jylhä, who fought with his men and believed that everyone did his duty like he, calmly and courageously, but without heroics, because it was necessary. *Kolme sanaa* ('Three Words') expresses the fighters' feelings with the phrase, "You get used to it" (Finn. *Siihen tottuu kyllä*, the three words). Jylhä's collection has, of course, been compared to *Ensign Stål*, and, although it is bad manners to criticize Runeberg in Finland, Jylhä's poems are considered for good reasons more realistic.[731] Jylhä deals with the war and his reactions, whereas Runeberg uses it as a background for the dramatic actions of individuals, and therefore Runeberg's *Tales* are more quotable and more popular. Jylhä lacks the humor of Väinö Linna, whose novel, *The Unknown Soldier*, became popular because it too tells about a group of well-defined individuals involved in the war. Like Runeberg, Jylhä has been treated as a patriotic war poet in biographies. Kauko Kare's *Yrjö Jylhä. Runoilijan- ja soturinkohtalo* ('The Fate of a Poet and a Warrior,' 1957) presents him as this ideal and neglects to mention an illness which troubled him for many years and eventually caused his death. Pekka Lounela, a Finnish critic, protested, and Kare, two officers who had known Jylhä and a publisher's representative wrote to the periodical to testify that Jylhä was indeed this ideal and that the critic was guilty of un-Finnish activities.[732] Jylhä was not, however, known as a patriotic poet before he published this collection, and he did have other interests.

Elina Vaara (pseudonym of **Kerttu Elin Vehmas**, née Sirén, b. 1903) is a more typical *Tulenkantajat* poet although her art has changed somewhat. She has published poetry and translations of poetry until recent years. Included in her translations are Aeschylus's *Oresteia*, Tasso's *Gierusalemme liberata*, the *Divine Comedy*, and Petrarch's *Sonnets*. Her first collection, *Kallio ja meri* ('The Rock and the Sea,' 1924), is romantic and exotic, with purple cloth and marble halls, nightingales, scents of myrrh and frankincense, but also horror. *Unen venhe* ('The Boat of Dreams') reveals her attitude by stating that the crew of this boat may never land and must continue gliding past the shores of life.[733] Although her poetry was modern according to the criteria then applied in Finland, it is actually rather traditional in both form and content. She wrote little free verse but showed great skill in the use of metric patterns; her romanticism is often reminiscent of Leino and Larin-Kyösti.[734]

In her first collections she speaks of love in an openly sensuous manner which is not as exuberant as Katri Vala's. *Hopeaviulu* ('The Silver Violin,' 1928) and subsequent collections contain the motif of the child to whom she speaks of life and the world. She reaches maturity in *Kohtalon viulu* ('The Violin of Fate,' 1933), discarding the romantic and ornate and declaring that beauty is also in the everyday. One poem in *Yön ja auringon kehät* ('The Circles of Night and Sun,' 1937) combines this subdued wisdom with simplicity of form:

> Child—one here is certain:
> the grey everyday
> is the only road,
> on which the sweet breath of love is felt
> and fresh peace.

Her love for Italy is apparent in *Loitsu* ('The Incantation,' 1942) and *Huone holvikaaren päällä* ('The Room over the Vault,' 1943), which utilize descriptive elements to materialize her faith in the strength and lasting character of beauty, her veneration for sacred youth, and awareness of death's tragic presence. *Sadunkertoja* ('The Teller of Fairytales,' 1954), the result of a long stay in Sicily, includes Arabic elements abundant on the island. Her motifs have not changed, but the style is less traditional than that of earlier collections. In *Mimerkki* (name, 1963) she turns to old Finnish mythology to build an allegory on good and evil supported by belief in the ultimate victory of the former. She fits the traditional image of the poet who writes noble, beautiful, strange and perhaps tragic compositions in a noble and beautiful language. However, her work is without affectation; it describes her own reactions to the world.

Lauri Viljanen (b. 1900), another of the *Tulenkantajat*, was Elina Vaara's husband for a few years when they were young; they soon divorced. He is now best known as a scholar and an essayist, but he was a poet and critic until the age of forty-seven, when he took his M.A.; two years later, after receiving a Ph.D., he became professor of Finnish literature at the Finnish University of Turku and moved to the same post in Helsinki in 1954. He has translated numerous poems from several languages. One of his essay collections, *Taisteleva humanismi* (1936), introduced the phrase "fighting humanism" to Finnish, but there is little of actual fighting spirit in the book.

There is a second edition (1950) of these literary studies, although second editions of such works are no more common in Finland than they are elsewhere. The volume is an intelligent, dispassionate, and impartial discussion of matters of general interest backed by solid, well-informed scholarly research which expresses clearly, without teaching or preaching, the author's opinions. The immediate subject is literature, but, inasmuch as literature reflects the human mind, the mind and its freedom, which were threatened in Finland at that time, are also prominent. Mika Waltari, ever alert to changes in public opinion, felt that, after the gay, international twenties, the thirties were to be serious and patriotic and quickly produced, after having belonged to *Tulenkantajat*, a series of novels in that vein; he publicly denounced Viljanen and another leading critic, Kaarlo Marjanen, for "intellectual infiltration work," i.e., insidious spreading of communism.[735] Critics, newspapers, politicians, church, and the authorities became involved in the ensuing argument. Any word on political or social issues in Viljanen's book is there incidentally, but he speaks freely on Gide and Lawrence; in the Finland of the 1930s, such subjects were to be discussed with care. Later essay collections, *Hansikas* ('The Glove,' 1955) and *Lyyrillinen minä* ('The "I" in Poetry,' 1959), failed to arouse controversy.

In keeping with his character, Viljanen's poetry is outwardly moderate. Although his emotional and intellectual involvement with his message is deep, it is expressed in structural elaboration rather than in direct outburst of feeling.[736] He contributed to *Hurmioituneet kasvot* and published a first collection, *Auringon purjeet* ('The Sails of the Sun,' 1924), which contains little exoticism or free verse, both fashionable at the time. In this respect *Tähtikeinu* ('The Swing of the Stars,' 1926) conforms more to the ideals of the *Tulenkantajat*.[737] Partially because of the strength of expression of the erotic, it has been called his "most expressionistic" collection.[738] In subsequent poetry he becomes more conscious of form and structure, through which he attempts to express the unity of life's many manifestations with highly synthetic language, in which disconnected concepts are brought together; Valéry may have been an influence in this respect. Thus, the poem is an autonomous creation shaped by its own laws, but Viljanen also wrote simple compositions in which, e.g., his love for western Finland, his native region, is expressed. Both sides of his art are found in *Musta runotar* ('The Black Muse,' 1932) and *Näköala vuorelta* ('The Sight from the Mountain,' 1938), which many consider his masterpiece. The complex, carefully composed quality of his poetry is frequently called "orchestral."[739] *Atlantis* (1940), written before the war, reveals his anguish and concern about the fate of humanity, affecting the form of the poem, which borders in places upon prose. *Tuuli ja ihminen* ('The Wind and Man,' 1945) reflects war events, in *Revontulet* ('The Aurora Borealis') e.g., which grew from the atmosphere of the Winter War, but the title poem uses the tragic events of the time to express the poet's personal philosophy. The poems are actually more serene than anguished. *Seitsemän elegiaa* ('Seven Elegies,' 1957) is more troubled, indicating that life is meaningless, and dwells on visions of its fading beauties, although it does convey the poet's belief in the harmony of the universe, especially in the poem *Empedokles.*

The poetry and prose which **Arvi Kivimaa** (originally Rinne, b. 1904) wrote while a young newspaperman in Helsinki is of poor quality, but the level of his works has improved in proportion to his growth in age, respectability, and importance. He is now the director-general of the Finnish National Theater, member of numerous boards and committees, and participant in international organizations. He is by nature moderately conservative, humane, and tolerant; writing in the manner of the *Tulenkantajat* in the 1920s and early 1930s was a forced effort. From the 1940s, when he published the collections *Omenapuu lumessa* ('The Apple Tree in the Snow,' 1944), *Puolipäivä* ('Noon,' 1946), and *Vaskikäärme* ('The Brazen Serpent,' 1948), he has expressed interest in the fate of mankind and civilization, concern about the brutality of present times, and belief in a better future. These largely intellectual motifs contrast to his intimate pictures of everyday happiness, loving relations between parents and children and his native region in central Finland.[740] He has also written descriptions of his extensive travels including *Manhattan, Amerikassa* ('Manhattan, in America,' 1958), and directed many plays, especially those of Anouilh, who was extremely popular in Finland in the late forties and early fifties.

Ilmari Pimiä (b. 1897) and **Antero Kajanto** (1895-1968) also belonged to *Tulenkantajat.* Pimiä wrote two volumes of dreamy, melancholy meditations inspired by Finnish landscapes, *Näkinkenkä* ('The Seashell,' 1926) and *Taivaan polku* ('The Path of Heaven,' 1929), a collection of religious poetry, *Viimeinen porras* ('The Last Step,' 1936), and one dedicated to his lost home region of Karelia, *Unen maa* ('The Land of Dream,' 1942). Kajanto, a more effusive poet, has published a number of poems, short stories, and children's books. His verse flows but is not very original. In some of his last collections, e.g., *Maa laulaa* ('The Earth is Singing,' 1945), he has attempted an expression of deeper, more personal feelings, stressing especially the need for love, tolerance, and understanding.

Heikki Asunta (1904-59), who was ironic about the exoticism of the *Tulenkantajat,* wished to differ from the others. The title poem of *Sudenmarja* ('The Wolfsbane,' 1950),[741] his last collection, expresses his lonely bitterness by describing that plant; the berry "oozing with poison / remains coal black and, without words, / whispers: stay away and beware!" He was a good painter who exhibited regularly and lived in Paris for a while. In the 1930s he adhered to an extreme rightist political movement and wrote aggressively patriotic verse, such as that in *Leirinuotio* ('The Campfire,' 1934). He also composed meditative, resigned poems in which ruined buildings and ships symbolize the ephemerous nature of man and his creations, and ballads on bloody, terrifying subjects or on characters such as Franz Hals, Filippo Lippi, and François Villon, into whom he projected himself.

Yrjö Kaijärvi (originally Törnqvist, 1896-1971) did not publish his first collection, *Multa laulaa* ('The Song of the Soil'), until 1934; the next, *Maan viini* ('The Wine of the Earth') appeared in 1937. Admired in their time, they are good, if not great, poems.[742] Especially appreciated was his refined sensibility and delicately shaded language; he is much in Sarkia's vein without Sarkia's inner conflicts. Although he wrote some poems similar to folksongs on Finnish country life, collected as *Kotikylä* ('The Home Village,' 1953), which some critics now consider his best, others have said that there is something not quite Finnish in his artistry.[743] Originally an elementary teacher, he later traveled in France, Italy, and India, writing about the countries he visited and translating mainly from French and Italian. His last collections—*Vuoret ovat* ('The Mountains Are') appeared in 1963—bear the mark of his meditations on Indian philosophy and speak of attempts to be united with the harmony of the universe.

Toivo Lyy (first Mähönen, b. 1898) has published poetry which can be praised for strict traditional regularity of form and little else. His translations, however, are remarkable and include the *Nibelungenlied*, Omar Khayaam's *Rubaiyyat* (not from the original), several of Schiller's plays, and the *Canterbury Tales.*

Lauri Pohjanpää (originally Nordquist, 1889-1962), a minister, published between 1910 and 1960 more than fifty volumes of inspirational works, hymns, biographies, essays, novels, short stories, plays; and poems; only the poetic fables have lasting value, but they are unique in Finland. Freely mixing humor and seriousness, they occasionally point out a moral, but they often simply tell a small story in which animals function as humans, developing the mood of a situation with mildly humorous intensity. *Hautajaiset* ('The Burial') treats death in this manner:

> Although the sun is already rising
> heaven and earth are sad
> the bluebells are softly chiming
> the crickets are playing a funeral march.

The works of two dialect poets, **Nortamo** (Nordling), whose prose has been discussed, and **Kalle Väänänen** (1888-1960), are known throughout the country. Many of Nortamo's poems, similar to his stories, survive as songs, and one of Väänänen's pieces on Lake Kallavesi in eastern Finland has equal fame. The poet, a high school teacher from Savo, wrote most of his poems and prose in the Savo dialect, and, although they are mainly humorous, he intended that some should be received seriously.[744] It is the fate of most dialect poets not to be taken seriously, and Väänänen remains known as a humorist.

After the heyday of the *Tulenkantajat*, no other assault on poetic traditions in Finland was so concerted until the 1950s, when the entire structure of poetry was altered. The politically-oriented writers of the *Kiila* were more interested in a poem's message than its form, although, under the influence of Katri Vala, as well as Whitman and Sandburg, they generally considered free verse the best vehicle for political and social poetry. They endured the hostility of public opinion, the malevolent stupidity of conservative, influential critics, and physical harassment from the authorities.[745] They reacted by becoming even more leftist, but, during the Winter War, they were as patriotic as their countrymen. Arvo Turtiainen fought against the Soviet army, and some, for example Viljo Kajava and Olavi Siippainen, changed their minds completely. When, beginning in 1941, Finland fought the Soviet Union, all that was German was admired even more than before;[746] however, some of these writers, including Arvo Turtiainen, protested and went to prison on dubious charges of treason. After the war, they regained freedom, but they used it only to publish works which would previously have been forbidden. Jarno Pennanen said that "We of the *Kiila* are not out after the scalps of other writers."[747] Eventually the Stalinist regime in particular caused their break with the extreme left, but they retained their ideals, and none of them has tried to court their former critics by exposing the left. As political fires have cooled, their works have been appraised for artistic value.[748]

Viljo Kajava (b. 1909) from Tampere, Finland's most important industrial city, began to write about the "problems of proletarian poetry" before the formation of the *Kiila* in 1936.[749] He considered early proletarian poetry too general and rhetorical and, with reference to Sandburg, (who, with Whitman, was often read in left-wing circles in Finland), called for the description of graphically presented individual cases. His first collections, *Rakentajat* ('The Builders,' 1935) and *Murrosvuodet* ('The Years of the Crisis,' 1937), the most radical and social in his production, show more of an attraction to nature than to cities and factories. He did write about Tampere, but even in *Hyvästi muuttolintu* ('Farewell to the Birds That Fly Away,' 1938) he praises nature and a natural life in a refined, subdued manner. A peculiarity of his style is the choice of small, seemingly insignificant details from which he builds images. During the war he broke with the *Kiila* and wrote poetry inspired by the events of the time. From 1945 to 1948 he lived in Sweden, where he became acquainted with contemporary Swedish poetry and published two collections in Swedish. When he returned to Finland, he published *Siivitetyt kädet* ('The Winged Hands,' 1949) and *Hyvä on meri* ('Good Is the Sea,' 1950), both of which had considerable influence on the new poetry then developing.[750]

His verse is now devoid of rhetoric and the ornate imagery of the *Tulenkantajat;* it consists of sequences of seemingly disconnected images with subtly changing moods and thoughts reminiscent of Chinese poetry. Recently he has redeveloped an interest in social and political motifs; *Kymmenen ilmansuuntaa* ('The Ten Points of the Compass,' 1961) takes up contemporary African problems more, it is said, in the spirit of a United Nations observer than in that of a revolutionary socialist.[751] *Tampereen runot* ('Poems of Tampere,' 1966) is a panorama of his hometown's growth with emphasis on the Civil War, during which Tampere suffered considerably. One of his last collections, *Käsityöläisenunet* ('The Dreams of a Craftsman,' 1968), is a kind of epitome of his production, with love poems, meditations on nature, reflections on workers' conditions, and invocations of peace. One section is dedicated to Lorca.

He has also written some prose: the partly autobiographical novel *Muistatko vielä Paulin?* ('Do You Still Remember Paul?,' 1943) and *Yksinäisiä naisia* ('Lonely Women,' 1950); *Vihreä kartta* ('The Green Map,' 1951); and *Lintukauppias* ('The Man Who Sells Birds,' 1957), collections of short stories which do not directly discuss political or social problems. The author is primarily interested in the psychology of his characters, but he provides only a few allusive details of their relations to other individuals and leaves much to the reader's imagination.

Arvo Turtiainen (b. 1904) has remained faithful to the ideals of the *Kiila* even while in prison. In 1946 he published his diary from that period, *Ihminen N:o 503/42* ('Individual No. 503/42'), which reveals that difficult conditions did not impair his mental alertness. It is more impartial than are the poems published immediately after the war, *Palasin kotiin* ('I Came Back Home,' 1944), *Laulu kiven ja raudan ympyrässä* ('The Song in a Circle of Stone and Iron,' 1945), and *Laulu puolueelle* ('A Song to the Party,' 1946), which express bitterness, aggressiveness, and a wish to have the old order changed.

He has contributed literary criticism and essays for left-wing periodicals and newspapers, and, in a review of Sarkia's *Unen kaivo*, defines his poetic theories. He says that he does not want to be a poet if it means rejecting one's flesh and attempting to conquer a Beauty not of this world; he wishes to be a leader and teacher and to proclaim new ideas to mankind. He admits that all poets do not share his particular ambitions, but adds that they must not then take offense if people turn their backs to them and listen instead to politicians, in whom "there often is not, unfortunately, an ounce of poetry."[752] *Saliini* in *Tie pilven alta* ('Under the Cloud and Away,' 1939), which has become very well known, is humorous and resigned. The collection, perhaps partially inspired by *Spoon River Anthology*, which Turtiainen translated in 1947, contains epitaphs to workers and simple people who suffered or died prematurely in the Civil War, with whom Turtiainen identified perhaps more strongly than did any other proletarian poet in Finland:

You work eight hours out of twenty-four,
you sleep thirteen hours. Three hours you use to eat
and to tell stories about women, sitting on the edge of your bed.

When somebody says to you: My friend,
why don't you read something,
your life is completely wasted,
you answer:
When you live like this
you get everything for yourself.

Saliini, Saliini,
is it for you the world should be changed?[753]

This poem, like others, has strength in the simple and the familiar, and what rhetoric and pathos were in his earlier poems completely disappear in *Minä rakastan* ('I Love,' 1955) and subsequent collections. *Kuokkija ja vaakalintu* ('The Ditchdigger and the Bird Rukh,' 1950) contains some poems in the Brechtian manner (*A Horrible Song about War and Soldiers, A Song about Tiny Little People,* etc.). Later, having come "down from the rostrum to street level,"[754] he published *Minä paljasjalkainen* ('Me, Barefoot,' 1962; the title refers to the Finnish saying "to have come barefoot to a place,' i.e., to be born there), a book which describes Helsinki and its modest inhabitants in city slang which has amused readers without obscuring the fact that the book is more than a mere joke.

Besides *Spoon River Anthology* Turtiainen has translated *Leaves of Grass*, Mayakovski's *A Cloud in the Trousers*, Pasternak's poems from *Doctor Zhivago* (with Helvi Juvonen), and other works.

Although **Jarno Pennanen** (1906-69) was the most active member of *Kiila* in practical politics, he wrote the least political poetry. He worked as a newspaperman for most of his life, for a conservative paper in his youth, until he adopted the left-wing ideas which sent him to prison during the war and earned him important positions on communist papers afterwards. He broke with them, too, and maintained his own periodical, *Tilanne*, for five years, a difficult task. Alert to international questions, he traveled before 1939 in Europe and became one of the first in Finland to notice Africa's growing importance; the influence of African and other primitive poetry is noticeable in his works. He translated works by Lorca and Neruda and published his first collection, *Rivit* ('The Lines'), in 1937; the others have appeared since 1944. They comment on contemporary events and present his personal feelings and reactions, which the reader may be unable to share, especially when they are described in a very personal style, sometimes reminiscent of the Bible, sometimes of surrealism.

Olavi Siippainen and **Elvi Sinervo**, both known as prosaists, have also published verse. Siippainen collaborated with his wife, Laura Latvala, on

319

some volumes. His verse is unimportant in both quality and quantity, but Sinervo's deserves some attention. Although her prose is usually socially and politically oriented, her poetry is personal. Before the war her poems appeared in periodicals and the anthology *Vaella nuoruus* ('Wander, Youth,' 1938); her first collection, *Pilvet* ('The Clouds') did not appear until 1944. She proclaims a sensuous love for life's simple, everyday manifestations in *Yö kanavalla* ('A Night on the Canal,' 1936),[755] for example. She too was in prison during the war, but the poems recalling these experiences are not directly political or social; they often attempt to deny reality and turn to a somewhat mystic inner world. A later collection, *Neidonkaivo* ('The Well of the Virgin,' 1956), re-examines this attitude, which she views as a rejection of the world, but expresses in almost biblical terms the hope that love will prevail. In the late forties one of her poems, the half-ironic, half-sentimental *Pieni Liisa parka* ('Poor Little Liisa'), became a popular song.

With the *Kiila* we have reached a generation of writers who first published in the 1930s, approximately ten years after the *Tulenkantajat*. Besides the members of *Kiila*, only two wrote poetry, and one, **Saima Harmaja** (1913-37), had a brief career. A precocious genius, she wrote four volumes of poetry, one issued posthumously, and a diary first printed in 1939; by 1948 eight editions had been published. Schoolgirls have so enjoyed her work that she has been called "the schoolgirls' poet," an unjust label.[756] Her verse reveals a mature personality, innocent but not ignorant, and capable of sensuous love.[757] Her first collection, *Huhtikuu* ('April,' 1932), shows the influence of the *Tulenkantajat* in free verse, which she discarded in her other works and a few exotic motifs, but reveals her as an already remarkably independent artist. It expresses the inescapable dualism of life and death in human destiny in a manner both intense and subdued; the author seems to feel that the intensity of her emotions make rhetoric unnecessary, and every reader should agree. She felt that her duty as a poet was to discover beauty in the world and to communicate her vision to others. She found it in awakening nature, e.g., *Kevät* ('Spring' in *Huhtikuu*), but thought at the same moment of the frailty of her own life,[758] somewhat in the manner of Frese.

Aale Tynni (b. 1913, wife of Martti Haavio [P. Mustapää]) came from Ingria, the Finnish-speaking province around Leningrad, but has spent most of her life in Finland. She has published numerous collections of poetry and translations, including the old sagas of Snorri Sturlusson, Shakespeare's *Sonnets*, poems by Wordsworth and Yeats (with Yrjö Jylhä and Lauri Viljanen), Ibsen's *Brand*, an anthology of one thousand years of Western poetry, and another of ten modern French poets. Her poems, simple in structure and unambiguous in feeling, were traditional in form until the 1950s. They impress the reader as the spontaneous expression of a strong personality dominated by one elemental emotion at a time. Her first three collections, *Kynttilänsydän* ('The Wick of the Candle,' 1938; in Finnish the word for 'heart' is also used for 'wick'), *Vesilintu* ('The Waterfowl,' 1940), and *Lähde ja matkamies* ('The Well and the Traveler,' 1943), form the "early spring" of her production.[759] They are not weak or sentimental; she speaks of love as a force of nature in powerful terms and reveals her acceptance of life by seeing love as the condition for the continuity of life. She has written many poems about motherhood, comparing its pains to the struggles of artistic work, and about children. These collections reflect the war and the situation in the world and Finland in poems expressing her anguish or in symbolic ballads, e.g., *Kuolemantanssi* ('The Dance of Death'), but they are balanced by optimistic compositions.

With the collections *Lehtimaja* ('The Arbor,' 1946), *Soiva metsä* ('The Sounding Forest,' 1947), and *Ylitse vuoren lasisen* ('Over the Glass Mountain,' 1949),[760] the poet reaches maturity. They are again full of optimism and joy in life, calm in a feeling of fulfillment. Sensuous love, the major theme in almost all her collections, appears in general though clear symbols. In *Marskimaa* ('The Land behind the Dam') the land, protected from the sea by dams, fears the sea yet hopes that one day he (the male principle) will break them and overflow her (the female principle). Love is not an end but a means to create new life. Poems in *Lehtimaja* reflect the difficult period during which they were written; the poet says that her songs are an arbor for her children but that she is afraid it is a poor shelter against the harsh winds of the time. The poems are, however, basically optimistic, including those which relate directly to contemporary events. The motifs of *Ylitse vuoren lasisen,* as the title suggests, are mainly from folktales, but the poems are not intended for children. They illustrate the definition of her poetry as "seemingly soft and melodious, but, at closer scrutiny, purposeful and energetic."[761]

In the 1950s her philosophy profoundly changed, and she began to use free verse. *Tuntematon puu* ('The Unknown Tree,' 1952) expresses sorrow, despair, and hate, and *Torni virrassa* ('The Tower in the River,' 1954) is hardly brighter although folk motifs introduce a little gaiety. *Yhdeksän kaupunkia* ('The Nine Cities,' 1958) and *Maailmanteatteri* ('The World Theater,' 1961) show new interests, using old Egypt and the Middle Ages as background. The play *Muuttohaukat* ('The Peregrine Falcons,' performed 1965) is set in classical times. In her two most recent collections, the poet has regained faith in life. There are refined love poems, poems praising simple, joyful acceptance of life, and some satirizing pretentious pessimism.[762]

Helvi Hämäläinen (b. 1907) has divided her activities equally between prose and verse. She is slightly better known as a novelist, but much of her latest prose is more lyrical than narrative. Her first poems, from the 1930s, are ethereal and melancholy, quite different from those for which she is now known. *Voikukkapyhimykset* ('The Dandelion Saints,' 1947) was considered a bold work opposing poetic traditions when it was published; before its publication sections were translated, printed, and discussed in a leading Swedish periodical.[763] A few years later young poets began to publish works now considered to have introduced new types of poetic vision and form to Finnish literature, and her poetry slipped to the background. Her difference from these younger writers is not mere fashion; she has remained faithful to a philosophy not consonant with today's world. Many of her later works are set in a countryside untouched by modern times, where elemental instincts are free and the forces of nature and life are represented by the supernatural. Her world is romantic, colorful, exuberant, and ecstatic, and she spares no words in describing it.[764] Her men are strong, her women beautiful, healthy, and fertile; her sun is brighter, moon lighter, grass greener, and water cleaner than any others. Death's servant, often mentioned in *Pilvipuku* ('A Dress of Clouds,' 1950), is a friendly hobgoblin with mud on his boots and bees in his hair, whom no one should fear. *Surmayöt* ('The Nights of Death,' 1957), *Punainen surupuku* ('The Red Mourning Dress,' 1958), and *Pilveen sidottu* ('Bound to a Cloud,' 1961) vary the same themes, but *Poltetut enkelit* ('The Burnt Angels,' 1965) dwells on cruelty, torture, violence, and death.

Oiva Paloheimo (first **Pietilä**, b. 1910) is a prosaist who writes some poetry having the same defect as his fiction: it is well written in traditional form, but wavers between nonsense and pathos. The children, originals and misfits he loves, criticize the clever and strong and express deep truths about the world, life, and religion, which strongly attracts him although he is not a religious writer. His fantasy is charming, and many of his poems on children, especially in the first collection, *Vaeltava laulaja* ('The Wandering Singer,' 1935), gently and humorously criticize the adult world in a very convincing manner. *Elopeltojen yli* ('Over the Fields of Grain,' 1943) contains similar poems, but other, religious ones are quite serious. He did not write completely childish, playful poetry seemingly because he feared his message would be lost, and he did not compose totally earnest work apparently because his public image was that of a poet who can tell deep truths while laughing. His vacillations make his childishness appear affected and his metaphysics shallow.[765] Many of the poems in *Pan kuuntelee virttä* ('Pan Is Listening to a Psalm,' 1947) are about the childhood of Jesus and his apocryphal miracles, which figure in popular legends in all Christian countries. *Palaa ne linnut vielä* ('The Birds Will Return One Day,' 1963) is directed against modern poetry, which he finds "heartless."[766]

The numerous religious poems of **Jaakko Haavio** (b. 1904, younger brother of Martti Haavio),[767] a minister and author of inspirational works, are probably the best of their type in Finland, written by a true poet with a need to communicate his religious experience, not a clergyman with an urge to compose verse. Between 1933 and 1956 he published five collections; *Runot* ('Poems') appeared in 1964.

Unto Kupiainen (1909-61), a scholar often quoted here, produced approximately forty volumes of literary studies, poetry, humorous sketches, and novels (the latter under pseudonyms). His earliest verse (1935-42) is simple and patriotic, but he later acquired depth and power in the expression of feelings. He had a scholarly interest in humor, and some of his humorous poems are among the best in Finland, e.g., those in *Rakastunut koppakuoriainen* ('A Beetle in Love,' 1950) and *Peeveli ja peipponen* ('The Buster and the Bullfinch,' 1958). Although he witnessed the change in poetry, his last collections are as traditional in form as his first.

Matti Kuusi (b. 1914), a well-known folklorist, discards in his scholarly works the often wild speculations on Finnish folklore made by his predecessors, but seriously voices extravagant opinions on social and political questions.[768] He has published two collections (1935, 1947) which include romantic, aggressively patriotic poems describing dreams of Finno-Ugric greatness in the manner of Ahlqvist and Genetz. His satirical compositions on contemporary matters are of a type uncommon in Finland.

Although most of the *Tulenkantajat* were poets, a few prosaists are generally discussed with them.[769] In the twenties and thirties it was fashionable to be a man of the world, blasé, traveled, and involved in risqué experiences described in books which the authors considered sinful. Because of public opinion and lack of true experience, these sinful books are rather harmless and, as a consequence, amusing; it was not difficult for Paavolainen to ridicule them in his famous pamphlet.[770]

Mika Waltari (b. 1908) is the prosaist who perhaps was most representative of the ideals and theories of the *Tulenkantajat* in his early works. A child prodigy,[771] he registered at the University of Helsinki at the age of eighteen and took an M.A. at twenty-one; he published a volume of poetry, *Jumalaa paossa* ('The Flight before God'), at seventeen and produced one or more books per year until 1949. His production has now slowed, but not stopped. His best works are the early ones, the novels *Suuri illusioni* ('The Great Illusion,' 1928) and *Appelsiininsiemen* ('The Orange Seed,' 1931), the short stories *Jättiläiset ovat kuolleet* ('The Giants Are Dead,' 1930), and the description of his journey to southeast Europe, *Yksinäisen miehen juna* ('The Train of a Lonely Man,' 1929; Waltari has both described his European travels and used them in fiction). In them is an image of Helsinki and the young people living there in a time which has now acquired the charm of a period piece, for the twenties were as gay in Finland as in the rest of the Western world. Two things are noticeable in these early books: the innocence of the characters and the innocence of the author. If a girl from a good family drinks too much at a party and a man gets fresh with her, she runs home, disgusted. In books written in the first person, the narrator is an educated young man with high moral principles who is horrified and attracted by the sinful actions around him. He is sorry for himself because he does not have the courage to join the naughtiness. Waltari poses in these books as an old though inexperienced person who watches the young enjoy life and feels depressed because he cannot do so himself. The story of a young man too timid to find a girlfriend has endless variations in Waltari's works. His contemporaries consider him a great writer and have bought his books in large numbers, but younger people find him uninteresting.

Ever sensitive to changing public taste, Waltari became serious and consciously moral in the 1930s, denouncing immoral writers and producing serious, moral books—a trilogy on a family who settles in Helsinki and witnesses the growth of the city, *Mies ja haave* ('A Man and a Dream,' 1933), *Sielu ja liekki* ('The Soul and the Flame,' 1934), and *Palava nuoruus* ('Burning Youth,' 1935), published in one volume, *Isästä poikaan* ('From Father to Son,' 1942); a novel on Helsinki in the 1930s, *Surun ja ilon kaupunki* ('The City of Sorrow and Joy,' 1936); and one on violent passions in a rural setting, *Vieras mies tuli taloon* (1937; tr. Naomi Walford, *A Stranger Came to the Farm*, 1952); and a complementary volume, *Jälkinäytös* ('The Epilogue,' 1938). Under his name and pseudonyms he wrote comedies, e.g., *Kuriton sukupolvi* ('The Wild Generation,' 1937); detective stories, e.g., *Kuka murhasi rouva Skrofin?* ('Who Murdered Mrs. Skrof?', 1939); light novels, e.g., *Ihmeellinen Joosef eli elämä on seikkailu* ('The Wonderful Joosef, or Life Is an Adventure,' 1938); and film scripts.

During the war, when he worked for the Government Information Service, he wrote a book on how to plan production, accounts of Soviet activities in the Baltic countries and Finland, and historical and wartime novels, *Antero ei enää palaa* ('Antero Will Not Come Back,' 1940) and *Rakkaus vainoaikaan* ('Love in Wartime,' 1943). After the war he discovered the colorful, romantic, thrilling historical novel and has written five, which have made him the best-known, wealthiest Finnish author of all times, elected to succeed Pekkanen in the Academy. They have been translated into most major languages, some more than once, and *Sinuhe the Egyptian* has been filmed in Hollywood. They accurately reflect the mood of the Finnish middle class after the war.[772] Its members had seen in imperial and national-socialist Germany the embodiment and champion of European civilization and had gone to war as its ally in 1941. They saw themselves as the heroic defenders of a higher order of life which was about to be destroyed by barbarians. Waltari's historical novels describe periods of war and violence, the conflict between the Egyptian and Hittite empires, the destruction of the Byzantine Empire by the Turks, the sixteenth-century wars in Italy and the Balkans, the fighting between the Etruscans and the Romans, with the conclusion that democratic, peace-loving countries are always destroyed by ruthless, violent neighbors unless they become ruthless and violent themselves under the leadership of a military dictator. (The film of *Sinuhe*, however, conveys the impression that peace and freedom will rise again.) The undecided, melancholy young man of Waltari's books on the twenties appears in all of these faraway places and times, cheated, fooled, and beaten, still sighing after a girl he never finds.

Waltari has also written short novels and short stories which, like his first works, give the impression that the author wrote them to please himself rather than the public. The novel *Fine van Brooklyn* (name), written in 1938, appeared in 1941; *Ei koskaan huomispäivää* ('No More Tomorrows'), composed in 1937, in 1942; *Kultakutri* (tr. Naomi Walford, *Goldilocks* in *Moonscape and Other Stories*, 1954) in 1948; *Neljä päivänlaskua* (tr. Alan Beesley, *A Nail Merchant at Nightfall*, 1954) in 1949;*Feeliks Onnellinen* (tr. Alan Blair, *The Tongue of Fire*, 1959) in 1958; *Valtakunnan salaisuus* (tr. Naomi Walford, *The Secret of the Kingdom*, 1960) in 1959; and *Ihmiskunnan viholliset* ('The Enemies of Mankind') in 1964. The collections of short stories *Kuun maisema* (properly called 'Moonscape') and *Koiranheisipuu* ('The Woodbine') were published in 1953 and 1961 respectively. *Fine van Brooklyn* and *Ei koskaan huomispäivää*, striving for refinement and melancholy, are sometimes artificial. In the former a Finnish archeologist, another of Waltari's fools who cannot learn to make love, investigates prehistoric monuments in Brittany where he thinks of the fragility of civilizations and falls in love with an American girl. In *Ei koskaan huomispäivää* a middle-aged playboy runs over a child with his car and remembers him "stretched in the forest among white anemones" while he kisses his employer's wife. *Kultakutri* shocked Waltari's faithful readers, for the main character is a prostitute who destroys three men. *Feliks Onnellinen* is an unconvincing book about the religious conversion of a man who becomes a happy, active member of society through his experience, and *Valtakunnan salaisuus* and *Ihmiskunnan viholliset* return to the grand historical style and describe early Christians.

Waltari has proved himself a hard-working, skillful literary craftsman, and a few of his works indicate that he might have developed artistically if he had tried. He had no reason to try, however, for he achieved everything a writer could wish for without doing more.

Unto Seppänen (1905-55) was originally considered a prosaist of the *Tulenkantajat* school, mainly because of his first work, a collection of short stories, *Taakankantajat* ('Those Who Carry the Burdens,' 1927).[773] The style is described as expressionist, with short, abrupt sentences and sudden shifts in motif; the characters, living in urban surroundings, are often mentally or physically abnormal. Seppänen, who was of Karelian origin although he was born and died in Helsinki and spent many years as a newspaperman in Kouvola, soon changed his manner and described Karelia and Karelians in most of his later works. He wrote not of the romantic Karelia on the eastern border of Finland but of the southwestern part of the province, the Isthmus of Karelia between the Gulf of Finland and Lake Ladoga. The people were in close contact with Viipuri and the capital of the empire, St. Petersburg.

Wealthy Russians who spent summers there gave the region an exotic atmosphere and the local population an opportunity for earnings as horse-cab drivers and teamsters, for example, whom Seppänen often describes. He pictures three periods: the good old times before 1917; his own time, when Finland's independence changed conditions in the area; and the time after 1944, when the Soviet Union annexed the region and its inhabitants moved to Finland, retaining romantic memories of their home region.[774] His second novel, *Iloisten ukkojen kylä* ('The Village of the Merry Men,' 1927), begins before 1917 and ends with the changes brought about by independence. Seppänen describes the Karelians traditionally: they are gay and hospitable, fond of singing, eating, and storytelling; but a few of his books are more serious, and violence or cruelty sometimes appears even in funny stories. *Tinuriin suostunut* ('The Tinker's Sweetheart', in *Myllytuvan tarinoita* 'Tales of the Mill,' 1945) begins as a humorous description of a fat, busy housewife baking cakes and pies for a party while her lazy husband sleeps. He wakes up and pilfers a pie, but she surprises and beats him, and he swallows a hot morsel which burns his insides badly, so that he pines away while she refuses to take care of him and invites a wandering tinker to live with her.

Seppänen wrote two novels which describe Russians in an unusually friendly manner. *Juhla meren rannalla* ('The Feast on the Shore of the Sea,' 1928) and *He janosivat elämää* ('They Thirsted for Life,' 1929; the title is typical of the *Tulenkantajat*) are about the Russian aristocracy, which Seppänen knew little about. The first is unconvincing, but the second, dealing with a later time, when the aristocrats had become refugees in Finland, is better. In it one of the Russians comes to an understanding with a Finn, a development which would not have occurred in a later Seppänen novel. Another novel written in that period, *Pyörivä seurakunta* ('The Whirling Parish,' 1930) differs from his later works; the action, like that of a medieval allegory or morality play, is unreal. Prisoner and Merry (*Vanki* and *Iloinen*), the main characters, travel from village to village throughout the world with a horse and a tame magpie. The inhabitants of each place symbolize a human defect such as vice or greed, and the two wanderers play practical jokes, some typically medieval in cruelty, to teach them a lesson.

Early in the 1930s Seppänen wrote a trilogy about a Karelian family: *Myrsky ja aurinko* (1931; tr. Kenneth Kaufman, *Sun and Storm,* 1939), *Ilohuoneet* ('The Houses of Joy,' 1932), and *Voittoon* ('Toward Victory,' 1934), which he condensed and published as *Markku ja hänen sukunsa* (tr. Kenneth Kaufman, *The House of Markku*, 1940) in 1940. Many translations were made abroad even though the book is unremarkable.[775] The author's descriptions of characters and situations congenial to him are not bad, but his attempts to be earnest, moral, patriotic, and instructive are superficial. The book was probably translated because the characters, who grow prosperous and happy during the narrative and fight the communists and Russians, were exotic to West European readers. In the spirit of the thirties, Seppänen forgot his understanding of the Russians.

The best of his serious books, *Synnin miilu* ('The Crime of the Charcoal Pit,' 1941), is set in old, Russian-dominated Karelia, where a group of peasants kill a hated foreman and burn his body in a charcoal pit. They are eventually discovered and made to atone; the author, who sides with them, considers their action more a sin than a crime. The nightmarish atmosphere and cruel descriptions of brutality are well written, sustained with consistent concentration on the main subject.

The works for which Seppänen is known are his best: stories from the Isthmus of Karelia published in the collections *Myllytuvan tarinoita* and *Myllykylän juhlaa* ('Feasting at Myllykylä,' 1946) and novels such as *Huoleton on hevoseton poika* ('No Horse and No Worries,' 1947), *Vieraan kylän tyttö* ('The Girl from the Other Village,' 1949), and *Evakko* ('The Refugees,' 1954), which is a serious narrative on the Karelians' leaving their home country in 1944. The others, about old-time country life, describe the half-humorous situations which might occur in a small village. The books become repetitious, and some are only slightly modified folktales which Seppänen collected, but his lively fancy and talent for storytelling keep them entertaining. He did not write them in the local dialect, but his style shows its influence and appears, in the eastern part of the country, as far from standard Finnish as Kilpi's in the western section.[776] He intended his later works, in a sense, as a monument to his lost home and its inhabitants, but the best of them have independent artistic value.

Waltari and Seppänen are the only prosaists who even partially fulfilled the ideals of the *Tulenkantajat*, but it was for a long time fashionable to classify all writers of the late twenties and early thirties under the almost meaningless heading. **Martti Heikki Merenmaa** (originally Karjala, b. 1896) spent his childhood and youth in Raahe, a small town not far from his birthplace, Oulu. During World War I he studied painting in St. Petersburg, returned to Finland, and began a literary career. In the early thirties he wrote several novels on fashionable life in Helsinki which made him, in the public's vision, a member of the *Tulenkantajat*; it was, however, a subject he was not equipped to deal with.

The first of his more than thirty novels takes place in a small town not unlike Raahe which he humorously calls Kissapotti. All rather similar, they have been compared to aquarels, thin and immaterial.[777] An impractical young man in love with a girl he loses to a more energetic rival often appears in these stories of Kissapotti, whose wooden houses and shady streets are viewed as in a dream. These novels, now generally forgotten, receive deprecating treatment in discussions of Merenmaa's works, but a frail charm is suggested by the titles, *Sininen lasipiippu* ('The Blue Glass Pipe,' 1923),

Sieluja maan tomussa ('Souls in Earthy Dust,' 1924), and *Kevätilta Kissapotissa* ('Spring Evening at Kissapotti,' 1927).

In 1941 he published the first of the books which have made him one of the foremost novelists of his generation in Finland. The fashion for novels has greatly changed since the war, and his works, even recent ones, are no longer in keeping with the contemporary spirit, but they are of recognized artistic and human value. Most of them are set in the country although they do not center on country life or people. The most important ones are *Jaakob painii enkelin kanssa* ('Jacob Wrestles the Angel,' 1941), *Mustan kukon laulu* ('The Song of the Black Rooster,' 1944), *Penjami, vaeltaja* ('Penjami, the Wanderer,' 1949), and *Pyörä* ('The Wheel,' 1955). Some, especially *Mustan kukon laulu*, contain folklore elements used as symbols of the characters' feelings; in Merenmaa's world the supernatural no longer has a place. The interest of the books is on a psychological or spiritual level. The author creates the same character again and again—an outwardly weak, even ridiculous man or woman who, though basically good, is unable to resist the schemes of more ruthless individuals but manages to follow through his will at the price of much suffering. These novels take up the themes of his first works, now developing them fully and giving them depth by linking them to moral problems. His love for nature too reappears, now set in Savo, where he had moved. The best descriptions are in *Vettä kalliosta* ('Water from the Rock,' 1946) and *Lintuja taivaalla* ('Birds on the Sky,' 1961), where the landscapes symbolize purity and give his characters the strength to fight the world's evils spiritually.

Olavi Paavolainen (1903-64) directly told the reading public the nature of modern times while his contemporaries expressed their ideas in poetry and prose. He came from the Isthmus of Karelia, where his father was a well-to-do civil servant, and he became acquainted with art and literature at home. Some of it must have been decadent and *fin-de-siècle*, for that type of art interested him, especially in his early works,[778] and, although he made fun of himself, he remained something of a snob throughout his life, intent upon finding something no one else had yet discovered and upon shocking the Finnish middle-class morality. Katri Vala's faithful champion and the purveyor of young writers in modern fashions and ideas, he was a leading critic among the *Tulenkantajat*. He began writing articles for newspapers and periodicals, often receiving due credit for the illustrations and layout; his eye for pictorial effects is evident in his many descriptions of landscapes and cities. Although his prose is ornate and rhetorical, it is tasteful and consistent.[779] He collected these articles in a volume titled *Nykyaikaa etsimässä* ('Looking for Modern Times,' 1929), perhaps more appropriately than he thought, for his search for the new was more important to him than the findings. He wrote at length about the futurists and dadaists, admitting that few if any of their works had lasting value, but adding that they expressed the spirit of the time because they wanted to destroy all that was old. However, he never mentioned the film or the experiments being made in theater. One chapter discusses the three great Russian poets of the time: Blok, Esenin, and Mayakovski; the others deal with the sensational subjects of jazz, nudism, women's fashions, growing interest in sports and outdoor life, and the beauties of the modern technical civilization. The picture of the time is interesting though superficial, and the writing is good and witty although he sometimes breathlessly piles adjective upon adjective in his praises.

In 1932 Paavolainen published *Suursiivous eli kirjallisessa lastenkamarissa*, which attacked the weaknesses of the no-longer-extant *Tulenkantajat*. In the thirties he also wrote descriptions of his travels in Europe, mainly Germany, and South America, *Kolmannen valtakunnan vieraana* ('Invited by the Third Reich,' 1936), *Lähtö ja loitsu* ('The Spell and the Separation,' 1937), and *Risti ja hakaristi* ('The Cross and the Swastika,' 1938), and he included an account of his journey to the Soviet Union, during which his plans to return via the Balkans were altered when war broke out in 1939, in an introduction to his wartime diary, *Synkkä yksinpuhelu* ('Gloomy Monologue,' 1946). Especially his books on Germany are more than mere recountings of the places and people he saw. He does not treat political, economic, or social questions deeply, but does give a vivid portrait of the national-socialist state and society. The stagecraft of the parades and meetings fascinated him, but he described national socialism with an impartiality that is more frightening than criticism would have been. Although unable to check his tendency toward rhetorical generalizations, he clearly saw national socialism as an aggressive ideology seeking military conquest and domination, a fact many people in Finland and throughout Europe did not want to believe. During the war against the Soviet Union, he was drafted as a reserve officer; he did not protest openly but worked for the Army Information Service (i.e., news and propaganda, not intelligence), keeping the diary which records his opposition to Finland siding with Germany, its admiration for national socialism, and the indifference about occupied countries in Europe. He hoped for victory but feared its consequences for Finland.

He was sentimentally attached to Karelia, his birthplace, and he was assigned to the territories occupied by the Finnish army beyond the Finno-Soviet border in the ASSR of Karelia (then a Soviet Republic). The old customs and folk civilization had almost completely disappeared by that time, but some of their atmosphere lingered, and Paavolainen described the melancholy beauty of their decline, enhancing his feelings with his artistry and providing the book with excellent photographs.

Reaction to the publication of his diary was violent. *Synkkä yksinpuhelu* candidly mentions people by name, and many took offense at the criticism leveled at them. Their defense was to accuse Paavolainen of treachery and opportunism, if not communism. His earlier books, of which the diary is a logical sequence, illustrate the falseness of the charges, and ten leading critics eventually protested publicly against the attacks,[780] but they had already broken Paavolainen's spirit. He did not appear in public or write again.

Tatu Vaaskivi (first Vahlsten, 1912-42), a well-known critic, essayist, and novelist, shows Paavolainen's influence in his heavy, ornate, rhetorical style and attempts to synthesize the period.[781] *Vaistojen kapina. Modernin ihmisen kriisi* ('The Rebellion of the Instincts. The Crisis of Modern Man,' 1937) deals with psychoanalysis, and *Huomispäivän varjo. Länsimaiden tragedia* ('The Shadow of Tomorrow. The Tragedy of the West,' 1938) purports to picture the entire modern world, the new psychology, art, science, religion, and other aspects. Although intelligent and alert, Vaaskivi was self-educated and too ambitious; his information and his books are chaotic and superficial, but the brilliance of his style gives them a coherent appearance. In 1937 he issued *F. E. Sillanpää. Elämä ja teokset* ('Life and Works'), in which he explained Sillanpää's works with the help of psychoanalysis, but he was insufficiently equipped for the task. He is best in his reviews, which contain verbal fireworks but have a definite, more limited purpose. He desired more intellectual sharpness and psychological depth in Finnish literature,[782] and he attacked conservative critics who were very influential in Finnish literary life at that time.[783]

His first novel, *Loistava Armfelt* ('The Magnificent Armfelt,' 1938), was followed by a description of his journey to Rome, *Rooman tie* ('The Way to Rome,' 1940), and another novel, *Yksinvaltias* ('The Absolute Ruler,' 2 vols., 1941, 1942). After his death a fragment of his novel on the life of Christ, *Pyhä kevät* ('The Holy Spring,' 1943), a collection of his letters (1945), and another description of a journey abroad, *Kurjet etelään . . .* ('The Cranes Fly South . . . ,' 1946), appeared. Like his essays, the novels are heavy and ornate, full of sometimes inaccurate scholarship,[784] insistence on the characters' instincts and subconscious, and attempts at period panoramas. Specific foreign influences have been pointed out, needlessly, for the books are in a style prevalent in the 1930s.[785] *Loistava Armfelt* relates the life of a real character, a Finnish nobleman of the late eighteenth century who rose to high positions in Sweden and in Russia, and *Yksinvaltias* is about Emperor Tiberius. Both indulge in long, elaborate descriptions of surroundings and attempt to load every word with fateful meaning, a stylistic device which becomes self-defeating. However, they have a remarkable unity of composition, and Vaakivi wrote them—both have hundreds of pages—in an incredibly short length of time, which his probable knowledge of whatever disease he died from may account for. His necessary haste requires allowances for their defects.

Matti Kurjensaari (first Salonen, b. 1907) shares the basic views of Paavolainen and Vaaskivi, but he is less literary and more political. He has worked for several newspapers and periodicals, and most of his articles from the 1930s are in *30-luvun vihainen nuori mies* ('An Angry Young Man from the Thirties,' 1961/62). In them he attacks intolerance and aggressive nationalism, opposing liberal and democratic ideals to them. In the book *Taistelu huomispäivästä. Isänmaan opissa 1918-1948* ('The Fight for Tomorrow. Taking Lessons from One's Country 1918-48,' 1948) he surveys the first thirty years of independence, reviewing the consequences of the Civil War and the ideologies which divided the country in a wider perspective. In *Suuntana suomalainen* ('Direction: Finland,' 1955) and *Suomalainen päiväkirja* ('A Finnish Diary,' 1956) he analyzes the country's postwar development and looks for the most typical positive characteristics on which to build its future. Kurjensaari, who has often called his countrymen too self-centered and unaware of international events, tries to understand but remains suspicious of the young writers who were indifferent to national values, in *Jäähyväiset 50-luvulle* ('A Farewell to the Fifties,' 1960), for example.

Yrjö Kivimies (originally Uuno Mattila, b. 1899) is a writer of a type more often found in larger countries with older literary traditions. He has translated numerous works from English and collected through reading a store of information on many subjects, mainly history, literature, and philology, which he has used to write half-humorous essays and short prose pieces in which he talks to his readers about whatever he is thinking of at the moment. They have been collected in *Tyhmyydestä sakotetaan* ('Fined for Stupidity,' 1937), *Kantaäidin kylkiluu* ('The Rib of the First Woman,' 1953), and others.

Alex Matson (b. 1888) spent his youth in England, where he studied painting; when he returned to Finland he taught at an art school. In the twenties and thirties he published a few novels and with his wife, Kersti Bergroth, whom he later divorced, edited *Sininen Kirja* ('The Blue Book,' 1927-30), a periodical expressing moderate, sensible views on literature in contrast to the exuberant outbursts of the *Tulenkantajat* and other groups.[786] He translated into English *Seven Brothers* and works by Aino Kallas and Sillanpää, and into Finnish works by Faulkner, Joyce (not *Ulysses*), Steinbeck, and others. In 1947 he published *Romaanitaide* ('Art of the Novel'), which was widely accepted, followed by more works on literature, *Kaksi mestaria* ('Two Masters,' 1950), *Muistiinpanoja* ('Notes,' 1959), and *Mielikuvituksen todellisuus* ('The Truth in Fantasy,' 1969).

Kersti Bergroth (b. 1886) began writing in Swedish but changed to Finnish. She has written numerous novels and books for girls which were popular in the 1920s, but she is best known for essays, reviews of foreign literature, and short sketches, published under pseudonyms (Tet, Asser), which criticize with humor and gentle satire human foibles. They are collected in, for example, *Suurin hulluus auringon alla* ('The Greatest Madness under the Sun,' 1928), *Suloisia aikaihmisiä* ('Those Charming

Adults,' 1936), *Hymyile kanssani* ('Smile with Me,' 1943), *Esseitä* ('Essays,' 1950), and *Katseita maailmaan* ('Looking at the World,' 1950). Born in Viipuri, she expresses her attachment for Karelia in two successful, somewhat sentimental comedies about Karelian country people, *Anu ja Mikko* ('Anne and Michael,' 1932) and *Kuparsaare Antti* (name, 1956). With Lempi Jääskeläinen and Viljo Kojo she edited a book on Viipuri.

Of the minor prosaists related to the *Tulenkantajat*, **Onni Halla** (b. 1899) is appreciated for the psychological depth and stylistic refinement in his novels, *Mustat loimet* ('The Black Warp,' 1925), *Pentti Harjun nuoruus* ('Pentti Harju's Youth,' 1946), and *Oudot virrat* ('Strange Rivers,' 1949). His only other works are a few poems included in *Nuoret runoilijat*.

Riku Sarkola (b. 1910) wrote several books, but his first three novels, *Tanssiaisten jälkeen* ('After the Ball,' 1931), *Mies, joka rakasti elämää* ('The Man Who Loved Life,' 1937), and *Mitään ei voi salata* ('Nothing Can Be Hidden,' 1938), are his best. The situations are exceptional—the second deals with the last period in the life of a dying man, the third with a slowly planned and enacted revenge—and the style is unusual, characterized by short, quick, nervous sentences.

The extraordinary interest of the Finns for theater has resulted in the establishment and maintenance of repertory theaters in remote towns through the use of government and local funds, but the acting, directing, and writing of most plays has been mere honest craftsmanship. Aleksis Kivi, Minna Canth, and Hella Wuolijoki remain Finland's best playwrights. Lauri Haarla occupies a conspicuous position in Finnish literary history, but he earned it more through his thundering manifestos than through artistic merit.

Hella Wuolijoki (*née* Murrik, 1886-1954), of Estonian origin, came to the University of Helsinki in 1904 and remained in Finland. She married but later divorced the Social-Democrat politician Sulo Wuolijoki. She read French, German, Russian, and Scandinavian literature and met many people, conservative Finnish professors, socialists, and Russian revolutionaries. She soon began writing for socialist papers and had *Talon lapset* ('The Children in the House') performed at the Finnish National Theater in 1914.[787] She then went into business, at which she was successful for many years until, in 1936, she began to write plays again under the masculine pseudonym Juhani Tervapää. These plays were successful. She also wrote many radio dramas and a number of interesting memoirs. During World War II she housed Bertolt Brecht at her country estate, and together they wrote *Herr Puntila und sein Knecht Matti* ('Mr. Puntila and His Farmhand Matti'),[788] but neither the Finnish nor the German version has had much success. During the Winter War her old friendship with a former Russian revolutionary, then the ambassador of the Soviet Union to Sweden, Alexandra Kollontay, was useful in re-establishing contacts between the two governments for peace negotions,[789] but during the war of 1941-44 she was involved in an obscure spying incident and sentenced to prison. When she was released with other left-wing writers and politicians at the end of the war, she was elected for one term to Parliament and appointed to the post of director-general of the Finnish Broadcasting Corporation, which she held from 1945 to 1949.

Except her last play, *Entäs nyt Niskavuori?* ('What Now, Niskavuori?,' 1953), her drama says little about the events she witnessed in her life;[790] its structure is traditional, and neither her characters nor her plots are very original. Critics and others who write about theater praise them, for there is not much else in contemporary Finnish drama to praise. She did understand the necessities of the stage, and her characters and situations, although conventional, are plausible.[791] The plays are serious in purpose and have attracted, with the author's political opinions and daring subjects (adultery, divorce), people with liberal or radical ideas.

In *Niskavuoren naiset* ('The Women of Niskavuori,' 1936), she introduced a large country estate (Niskavuori) in western Finland and the people living there. Because the public and critics liked them, she produced more plays about Niskavuori and its people, moving back in time to describe the youth of a character who was old in an earlier play, taking a secondary character from one to give him the major role in another, or inventing previously unmentioned illegitimate children to create new complications. *Niskavuoren naiset, Niskavuoren leipä* ('The Bread of Niskavuori,' 1939), *Niskavuoren nuori emäntä* ('The Young Mistress of Niskavuori,' 1940), *Niskavuoren Heta* ('Heta of Niskavuori,' 1953), and *Entäs nyt, Niskavuori?* unfortunately resemble a television soap opera or the family chronicle so popular in second-rate literature, but it is impolite in Finland not to admire them (the renewed popularity of Galsworthy's *Forsyte Saga* is an appropriate comparison). The problems in these plays are serious, e.g., the conflict between generations, the clash of a traditional way of life and new ideas, the contrast between city and country, but her treatment is superficial; following age-old theatrical traditions, the author allows the problems to dissolve into love stories. Mrs. Wuolijoki opposed the antidemocratic tendencies which appeared in Finland during her lifetime, and she considered herself a socialist, although her idea of a socialist, much like Minna Canth's, was vague. She was also an energetic, successful businesswoman and the owner of a large country estate, accustomed to see her orders carried through. These contrasting facets of her personality work in her plays. She was not unlike the earlier socialist female writers in Finland, e.g., Elvira Willman and Hilda Tihlä; well-meaning and aware of the world's evils, they were unable to probe deeply these problems, and, instead, they felt that allowing people to love freely would erase social prejudice and class barriers.

The relatives of **Lauri Haarla** (first Harberg, 1890-1944) control several paper industries, but he was a secondary school teacher also active in the field of adult education. He made flamboyant declarations and felt himself called to lead others toward lofty, undefined goals. He claimed that two or three strong men could dominate literary life in Finland, but he never explained what they would do then.[792] He published the periodical *Ultra*, which attracted interesting people but did not last long, and organized the May Group, which was forgotten when the *Tulenkantajat* invaded the literary stage.[793] His literary aim was to make dramatic art noble again, in conformity to the German expressionism which he preached in articles, proclamations, and essays collected in *Teatterikirja* ('A Book on Theater,' 1928). Accordingly, he took the subjects of his plays from history and mythology and wrote in a rhetorical, convulsive, and artificially forceful language.

These plays are analyzed by Irmeli Niemi, but almost all receive negative comments: *Sophonisbe* (1916) is "artistically immature and confused," *Lemmin poika* ('The Son of Lemmi,' 1922) is "stylistically incoherent and has an artificial atmosphere," *Synti* ('The Sin,' 1923) "does not come alive as a dramatic whole," *Uskottomuus* ('A Breach of Faith,' 1924) shows that "his literary talent was not adapted to the treatment of social problems," *Kaksiteräinen miekka* ('The Two-Edged Sword,' 1932) has "artificial passages," and *Velisurmaajat* ('The Fratricides,' 1927) "breaks up into a series of disconnected conflicts." Only *Juudas* (1927) received favorable treatment.[794]

An interesting feature of Haarla's plays is the recurring situation in which an individual, convinced that he is right, meets the disapproval and rejection of the people he comes in contact with. The action of his first plays, *Sophonisbe* and *Onni Maallinen* ('Earthly Luck,' 1921), takes place in Greek and Roman times, but the setting is Carthago and Palmyra, two states hostile to Greece and Rome. In *Lemmin poika*, on a subject from the *Kalevala*, the hero fails in his mystic struggle to help good overcome evil; in *Synti*, which takes place during the seventeenth-century witch-hunts in Finland, a priest falls short of his duty. *Uskottomuus* begins as a contemporary family tragedy, but eventually underlines the truth that an individual must, if necessary, sacrifice himself by breaking traditional rules. *Kaksiteräinen miekka* attempts to describe the Civil War impartially. *Velisurmaajat* is about a war between two brothers in a distant Finnish past. Haarla's subjects expose basic human problems, but his preconceptions of the theater prevented him from giving them adequate treatment. *Juudas* shows him at his best. The action centers around a real event in the late eighteenth century: a conspiracy of Finnish officers want to make Finland an autonomous country under Russian protection but fail because they have no support.[795] *Kunnian mies* ('A Man of Honor,' 1941) is based on an incident in modern history, the assassination of Governor General Bobrikov, the organizer of the Russian oppression, by E. Schaumann, a young Finnish patriot. Schaumann, who acted alone, did it from idealistic and patriotic motives and, considering himself to have violated divine and human laws by taking justice into his own hands, shot himself immediately afterwards. Haarla's play attempts to show how Schaumann became convinced of the necessity to act.

Haarla wrote several other plays and novels, some on a half-mythical Finnish past, e.g., *Kurkien taru* ('The Kurki Saga,' 3 vols., 1938-40), which deals with a powerful Finnish family. Others, sometimes lighter in mood, are on contemporary subjects.

Between the prewar and postwar generations there is a gap in Finnish literature.[796] Of the writers who first published in the 1920s, Haanpää, Paavolainen, Pekkanen, and Jylhä died relatively early, leaving only Waltari and Merenmaa as prosaists, and many who first published in the thirties and forties have also disappeared or are no longer active. The gap is fortuitous; although many writers took part in the war, only one of importance, Eino Hosia, was killed in action. Finnish prose literature is now dominated by authors who first published in the early 1950s, and there is almost no living elderly or middle-aged novelist. The exception is the *Kiila*, whose members are active even now.

Helvi Hämäläinen has published a number of prose works as well as poems. One of the first, *Katuojan vettä* ('Water in the Gutters,' 1935), is a realistic description of working-class life in Helsinki during the depression, but love and relations between the sexes are as important as economic or political problems, if not more. Her later books differ from this one, but a few features typical of her appear. She now emphasizes more than she did in the past instincts, feelings, and strong passions at the expense of intellect, but she sees their destructive sides as well as their romance and does not embellish the sufferings love can cause. The action of *Säädyllinen murhenäytelmä* ('A Well-Mannered Tragedy,' 1941) takes place in the upper middle class in Helsinki, but this novel, too, deals with the conflict between instincts and the limits placed upon them by society. She describes, with some humor, the life of a well-to-do, intellectual family which is disrupted by the husband's sudden love affair with a neighbor's maid. A tragedy is averted by good manners, and all is smoothed over. A similar atmosphere is in *Hansikas* ('The Glove,' 1943) and *Sarvelaiset* ('The Sarvelainen Family,' 1947); the former describes a middle-aged teacher who falls in love with a small farmer but refuses to marry him because of their differing social backgrounds; the latter follows a wealthy middle-class family from 1879 to 1939, concentrating on conflicts of erotic feelings with morals or propriety in the family.

In 1938 the author published the first of four short novels about a village in Finland, *Kylä palaa* ('The Village Is Burning'). It, like the others, *Kylä vaeltaa* ('The Village Is Wandering,' 1944), *Pouta* ('The Drought,' 1946), and *Tuhopolttaja* ('The Arsonist,' 1949), deals with a crisis symbolized by fire and heat in the small community. Although described realistically, these elements funtion as symbols of sudden violence which unleashes repressed forces and instincts. No thing or person in the books is unreal, but descriptions are stylized; the women are archtypes of motherhood and sex, placed in situations which reveal their basic urges.

The atmosphere of *Ketunkivi* ('The Foxstone,' 1948) is more subdued. The author describes at length the lives of two odd, humorous characters in the country without coming to any conclusion, except, perhaps, that country life is better than city life. *Kolme eloonherätettyä* ('The Three Resuscitated,' 1953) and *Suden kunnia* ('The Wolf's Pride,' 1962) are historical; the former deals with the three individuals resuscitated by Christ, the latter with the life of a Roman soldier. *Karkuri* ('The Deserter,' 1961), shows boldness in the impartial treatment of the subject, a man who refuses to go to war.

Iris Uurto (pseudonym of **Lyyli Ester Mielonen**, b. 1905, wife of Aku Rautala [August Ripatti]) shares Helvi Hämäläinen's conviction that man will find happiness by following his instincts, but they differ as writers. One of her first novels is titled *Ruumiin ikävä* ('The Longing of the Body,' 1930), which she later wanted changed to *Villit henget* ('The Savage Spirits') because she thought the title had been misinterpreted (*ikävä* 'yearning' has a secondary meaning of a 'sad' or 'unpleasant' fact, which she claimed to have intended).[797] The book, however, is so outspoken in matters of sex that it shocked a number of Finnish readers. The author proclaims the importance of sex for a happy married life, describing young members of the middle class and their extramarital adventures based on lust, not love. She insists that these affairs do not bring happiness, which can be found only in a marriage based on a harmony of senses, but, although she is serious, her characters' earnestness mildly amuses her. This kind of irony and lightness has never been common in Finnish literature, and, especially uncommon in the solemn works of Mrs. Uurto's contemporaries, it makes a refreshing impression.

A later novel, *Ruumiin viisaus* ('The Wisdom of the Body,' 1942), is not connected with *Ruumiin ikävä* though the titles are similar. It tells of a young couple who find perfect happiness in a marriage based on harmonious, sensuous love, from which all else derives. The author never states that sensuous love alone is enough, and some characters are unhappy because for them love is only a pleasure of the senses. Boldly for that time in Finland, homosexuality is mentioned. It is a more serious book than *Ruumiin ikävä*; one scholar calls it "slow and grinding,"[798] but humor enlivens it, especially at the beginning. *Kypsyminen* ('The Ripening,' 1935) and *Rakkaus ja pelko* ('Love and Fear,' 1936) are similar in style, but true happiness is achieved in neither of them. In *Kypsyminen* a woman has to sacrifice herself for an invalid, and in *Rakkaus ja pelko* a husband forces his wife to have an abortion. The action of both novels is on an inner level; the couples analyze their relations and feelings, struggle for understanding, and torture each other.

Joonas ei välittänyt ('Joonas Did Not Care,' 1950) and *Kapteenin naiset* ('The Captain's Women,' 1952) have both humor and satire. They present individuals dominated by a single idea which they follow throughout their lives despite the consequences. In *Joonas* the main character, a writer, becomes, almost by accident, the manager of a theater. He preserves his goodness and honesty in the midst of the cabals and intrigues of his new surroundings, making his decisions according to his conscience. The main characters of *Kapteenin naiset* are the women who surround the captain, especially one, who is obsessed with the idea of revenge on the male sex because her husband has betrayed her. Although the captain has a wife and children, she attempts to conquer him; her attentions bewilder him, and the author pushes her demonstration that "Hell hath no fury" to extremes—the woman declares as her purpose the unveiling of the hypocrisy of society.

Iris Uurto has also written poetry, short stories, and four plays published under the common title *Suomalainen kohtalonäytelmä* ('A Finnish Play on Destiny,' 1945). The title play treats the Civil War critically, and one called *Satu sankarista* ('A Tale about a Hero') attacks the brutalization brought about by military conflicts. Perhaps because they deal with subjects unpopular during wartime (the time of their writing), they were unsuccessful on the stage. Mrs. Uurto's most recent published work, the novel *Puut juuriltaan* ('The Uprooted Trees,' written 1957, published 1968), is also concerned with moral problems in wartime.

Irja Salla (pseudonym of **Taju Birgitta Tiara Rantalainen**, *née* Sallinen, 1912-66), published the memoirs *Isä ja minä* ('Father and I,' 1957) about her father, the well-known painter Tyko Sallinen, a friend of Kojo, Lehtonen, and Hellaakoski. She also wrote a few novels. The most interesting, *Lisa-Beata* (1940), *Kohtalon päivä* ('A Fateful Day,' 1942; both published in 1952 as *Lisa-Beatan tarina* 'The Story of Lisa-Beata'), and *Unissakävijä* ('The Sleepwalker,' 1942) have a peculiar atmosphere. They describe the marriage of a young woman and the life of her daughter in a simple, subdued manner which avoids conflicts. If it were not for the main characters' constant, silent struggle against the conventions of life, their efforts at self-analysis, their relations to others, and their attempts to retain mental freedom and integrity, the books would be old-fashioned stories about family life in a small town and in the country. The latent tension never climaxes, but never disappears. The author does not entirely avoid monotony, but her novels offer penetrating psychological analysis.

Elvi Sinervo (b. 1912, wife of Mauri Ryömä), whose poetry we have mentioned in connection with the *Kiila*, titled her first book *Runo Söörnäisistä* ('A Poem about Söörnäinen,' 1937) although it is a volume of short stories about working-class life in Helsinki. Her characters are honest workers rather than slum dwellers and are not necessarily class conscious. (Her own father was a small craftsman.) Their main concern is providing for their families; when they occasionally steal, they do so, for example, to obtain coal for the winter. In the novel *Palavan kylän seppä* ('The Smith of the Village of Palava,' 1939), a man who comes from the city to the country after the Civil War tries to begin a new life in the midst of class hatred and suspicion, but the author focuses on the individual rather than on the group and describes his relations to his wife and children vividly. Most young people in the book are energetic and optimistic, striving for individual, better futures.

Works she published after the war and her release from prison are marked by her experiences. The short stories of *Vuorelle nousu* ('Climbing the Mountain,' 1948) describe those experiences and the unimportant underground movement led by communists against the Finnish government. Her motives are so idealistic that even readers who do not approve of her actions can enjoy her stories.[799] Some reflect her difficulties in engaging in left-wing organizations. Although of modest origin, she had studied and become a writer, but in Finland leftist political organizations, which are well organized and powerful, have been dominated by grassroots politicians and workers, among whom intellectuals sometimes feel uncomfortable.[800] The novel *Toveri, älä petä* ('Comrade, Don't Betray Us,' 1947) centers on the conflicts in the family and in the mind of a woman who, through her husband and his friends, becomes involved in political activities whose scope she is initially unable to grasp. *Viljami Vaihdokas* ('Viljami, the Changeling,' 1946) is about a boy, born of well-to-do parents, who is exchanged in the maternity hospital with a child of a poor family. Although the book is basically realistic, passages have an atmosphere of dream or fantasy in keeping with this opening. The author may have intended the novel to prove the Marxist theory that people are molded by environment, but the hero is an exceptional character in the poor surroundings in which he lives although he never suspects that by birth he does not belong there. When coming of age, he takes part in the pro-Soviet resistance against the Finnish government.

Elvi Sinervo has also written books for children, a few plays, and has done numerous translations of, e.g., Howard Fast, Henry Miller, Anna Seghers, and Ivo Andrić; some of her works have been published in several foreign languages.[801]

Eino Hosia (1905-41), the writer killed in the war, was born in the region between Rauma and Hämeenlinna in southwestern Finland, where he lived as a farmer for the greatest part of his life. He studied at the School of Social Sciences in Helsinki and made a few trips to Estonia. He published novels including *Tulipunaiset ratsastajat* ('The Scarlet Riders,' 1938), *Musta aurinko* ('The Black Sun,' 1941), and *Tuliholvin alla* ('Under the Fiery Vault,' 1940), which describes his experiences in the Winter War, and the long story *Kypsynyttä viljaa* ('Ripe Grain,' 1937); *Kukkivia hautoja* ('Flowering Graves'), a collection of short stories, was printed in 1945. *Tulipunaiset ratsastajat* is a description of an ecstatic revivalist movement written with a predilection for neurotic individuals and scenes of dark, frenzied atmosphere; it is not unlike some of Toppila's works, but has less of the supernatural and macabre. Its major flaw is the trite romantic vocabulary which shows that Hosia had not yet mastered a style. In *Musta aurinko* a small boy loses his parents in the Civil War and, after many adventures, ends up in an orphanage. Although it contains many romantic details, it is more realistic than the first novel, and some war descriptions are quite simple. The author animates his seriousness with irony at some points. He ignores the social aspects of the war and treats it as a vast cataclysm, a struggle between good and evil, as he does in *Tuliholvin alla*, where the war is a gigantic natural catastrophe, both terrifying and fascinating. His short stories often deal with more prosaic subjects, reflecting ordinary social problems such as unemployment or intolerance.

Oiva Paloheimo, more a prose writer than a poet, as which we first discussed him, published his best novel, *Levoton lapsuus* ('A Restless Childhood,' 1942), first. It views through the eyes of a small boy in Tampere a period of approximately four months before, during, and after the Civil War. The children live under almost normal conditions at home and in school, and only occasional remarks by adults allude to the country's situation. Actual fighting is treated briefly, but its tragic impact is clearly stated. The features typical of Paloheimo's art are already apparent in this book. He often describes the world from the viewpoint of children or harmless originals. Criticism of society and the world is sometimes implied, often through distorted, nonsensical, and humorous pictures of them. In *Levoton lapsuus* his method is a strength, consistent with the choice of a child for the main character, but in some works it is a weakness, for he appears to waver between mere funniness and the conveyance of a serious message. He also explains too much, e.g., this passage from *Levoton lapsuus* begins with a small boy's thoughts on the war:

> Lauri thought that . . . neither the Reds nor the Whites had anything to do with the war itself. Why, they had gone to the war. That meant that the war had been somewhere, if you could go to it. It was like a factory, to which you went and from which you came out. The war, like the factory, was something permanent and fateful; both were a necessary part of life. . . .[802]

The thoughts become Paloheimo's, rendered with words a nine-year-old boy would not use, but such shifts in tone do not occur often enough to mar this book. Most of his books contain children.[803] In the novel *Punainen lintu* ('The Red Bird,' 1945), a child brings about a total change in the lives of the main characters. In 1953 he wrote a book entirely for children, *Tirlittan*, named for the main character, a little girl.

In the period between the end of the war and the early 1950s, it was fashionable in Finnish literature to examine seriously metaphysical, religious, moral, artistic, and other deep problems in a symbolic manner, but the results were meager.[804] Paloheimo was a leading writer of this trend. In the novel *Peili* ('The Mirror,' 1946) an idealist and a swindler sell mirrors to people to teach them to know themselves and, ultimately, God. In *Lepakko* ('The Bat,' 1949) a boy grows up believing an angel to be at his side, then identifies the angel with his unfaithful beloved, whom he shoots. In *Ratsastus Eedeniin* ('Riding to Eden,' 1952) a wounded lieutenant wanders with his double between life and death, meeting characters from his earlier life. All three contain witty remarks and demonstrate the author's serious interest in religion and morals,[805] but they are not convincing, and his continual intrusion mars them. Many of his short stories are better than his long works. When the length of narration is limited, he keeps a unity of style and writes good prose. The best are perhaps in the collections *Tuonen virran tällä puolen* ('This Side of the River of Death,' 1948) and *Salonki* ('The Salon,' 1961).

Olavi Siippainen (1915-63), who has also been mentioned as a poet, was born in Kuopio. He worked from 1924 as an errand boy, a printer, a cabinetmaker, and a mailman, and studied in institutions for adult education. In a wartime poem partially addressed to Walt Whitman (in *Ylistän rakkautta* 'I Praise Love,' 1943), he tells why he left the *Kiila*: "Our forests do not know your peace, Whitman, / your message to brothers, comrades, lovers. . . ." His first works, the short-story collections *Nuoruus sumussa* ('Youth in the Fog,' 1940) and *Loppuun saakka* ('To the End,' 1942), clearly and concisely describe the immediate reality he experienced in war and peace. His largely autobiographical novels *Suuntana läntinen* ('Course West,' 1943) and *Maata näkyvissä* ('Land in Sight,' 1946) tell of the life of a poor boy who grows up in difficult circumstances and slowly develops an interest in intellectual activities. A third novel forms a conclusion; he rewrote it many times until it was published in 1959 with *Suuntana läntinen* and *Maata näkyvissä* as the trilogy *Nuoruuden trilogia* ('The Trilogy of Youth').

Siippainen wrote two more novels, *Ikuisilla niityillä* ('On the Meadows of Eternity,' 1951) and *Pyörättömän piiri* ('The Circle of Pyörätön,' 1958). Three men, dead when the action begins, discuss in the first, a symbolic narrative in the manner of the time, various problems, but the book does not go beyond stating these problems in the inconclusive discussion. The second novel quietly tells of a remote village to which modern times are coming. Although the characters are well drawn, the book is loosely composed. Siippainen's short stories are much better; the collections *Sinimekkoinen tyttö* ('The Girl with the Blue Dress,' 1946), *Tarinaniskijä* ('The Storyteller,' 1951), and *Herätys* ('The Waking Up,' 1955) are carefully constructed. In *Pakolainen* ('The Refugee' in *Tarinaniskijä*), a homeless wanderer given shelter for a night tells his host three different stories about himself, leaving the listener to decide which, if any, is true. It is reminiscent of Haanpää's *Taivalvaaran näyttelijä*, but Siippainen was reflecting upon the problem of creative literary work and the loss of identity experienced by the writer who is diluted in his characters.

Matti Hälli (first Swed. Häll, b. 1913), from Oulu, is a good humorist, but he has written a series of remarkable novels which have placed him, with Merenmaa, among the best contemporary writers of the traditional school in Finland. He wrote before the war, but it was *Suopursu kukkii* ('The Wild Rosemary Is Blooming,' 1943) which made him known. *Valmista sydämesi unohtamaan* ('Prepare Your Heart to Forget,' 1945), which tells about a dying man and his son, followed; both are serious works. Meanwhile he was publishing humorous short prose, which could be called essays, sketches, or stories, and this work became very popular.[806] Many collections, such as *Ystävämme Andersson* ('Our Friend Andersson,' 1945), *Vanha mukava Andersson* ('Good Old Andersson,' 1946), *Aurinkoisia tarinoita* ('Sunny Stories,' 1951), and *Mies ja neliapila* ('A Man and a Four-Leaf Clover,' 1960), have been issued; two selections, *Matti Hällin huumoria* ('Humor by Matti Hälli,' 2 vols.), appeared in 1962. Many of them describe the adventures, mishaps, and meetings of penniless young students, writers, and newspapermen in Helsinki. *Viheltäjä* ('The Whistler,' 1969) is a slightly romanticized autobiography. The stories do not differ greatly from other such stories, but Hälli never uses unusual, complicated, or boisterous incidents for humor, and his characters have individual personalities. He often ends his stories with a surprise twist. *Varas* ('The Thief' in *Mies ja neliapila*), reminiscent of O. Henry's *The Cop and the Anthem*, tells of a successful thief who decides to spend his vacations on a quiet island, where there are still good old times; people trust each other and leave their houses open during the day. He enters one, finds money and valuables in open drawers, but cannot bring himself to take them. Feeling himself a better man, he leaves, but is immediately arrested.

In some serious novels Hälli follows to some extent the symbolic trend of Paloheimo and Siippainen. He examines moral and religious problems, which he exemplifies, occasionally too pointedly, with symbolic characters and situations, although all his stories are well written and coherent. *Noutajat* ('They Come to Take You Away,' 1955) is about political dictature; *Valkea kaupunki* ('The White City,' 1957), *Lassinkallio* (name, 1959), and *Kosken kuuluvissa* ('Listening to the Waterfall,' 1967), which are set in Oulu, describe everyday life, but the symbolism bares the struggle between good and evil; the author makes it clear that he wishes his readers to think of Dr. Faustus. *Isä Jumalan Ilveilijä* ('The Jester of God Father,' 1961), *Ruottinojan aurinko* ('The Sun of Ruottinoja,' 1963), and *Meri-Heikin perintö* ('Meri-Heikki's

341

Inheritance,' 1965) take place on Hailuoto, a large island not far from Oulu. Supernatural elements, folktales, and folk beliefs appear, usually treated with humor. Hälli is best in these books in which he is less serious.

Reino Rauanheimo (first Järnefelt, 1901-53) combined in his novels traditional motifs and ideas with a search for new structures of narrative. The results set him apart from the average writers. Rauanheimo's interest was in the essential problems of today; he saw the greatest danger to man's spiritual integrity in the spread of materialism and mediocrity and examines these questions in *Aamusta iltaan* ('From Morning to Night,' 1930) and *Kultavasikka* ('The Golden Calf,' 1935). In *Taikapiiri* ('The Magic Circle,' 1945) two people set out to discover the fates of their old schoolmates and find that, no matter how life has treated them, they are basically the same. *Hangas* (1944), more conventional though well written, describes the construction of a big power plant and industries around Hangas. The novel is broad and detailed, but one wishes that the author had not emphasized so heavily the importance of the manly virtues, e.g., courage, strength, and honesty. Rauanheimo had been an officer in the Finnish army before he turned to literature and became an executive in a publishing company.

Simo Puupponen (1915-67), known under his pseudonym **Aapeli**, was a humorist who, like Hälli, wrote a few serious books. He lived in Kuopio, Savo, the land of jokers, and worked for seventeen years as a journalist, publishing humorous sketches in papers which employed him. His characters are unmistakably from Savo, and words from the local dialect appear in his stories, but he did not rely on local oddities for humorous effect. *Meidän Herramme muurahaisia* ('The Ants of Our Lord,' 1954) has been described as one of the sharpest satires on small-town life after the war in Finland.[807] *Pikku Pietarin piha* ('Little Pietari's Backyard,' 1958) is narrated by a boy. It is also set in a small town, but the author's intent is not satirical. Serious motifs not often treated by humorists, such as sex, religion, and death, appear throughout Aapeli's stories, which have been collected in, e.g., *Onnen pipanoita* ('Bits of Luck,' 1947), *Mutahäntä ja muita* ('Mudtail and Others,' 1953), *Sipuleita* ('Onions,' 1956), and *Timonen ja muita tuttavia* ('Timonen and Other Friends,' 1963).

Postwar Modernism

AFTER THE WAR POETRY SUSTAINED another change. Since 1950 little has been written in the traditional style in Finland. The poets did not form groups, but the discussion, criticism, attacks, and defense that accompanied the change gave them the appearance of a group. They wrote in very individual styles, which make a collective definition of them impossible; it is easier to list characteristics they did not have.[808] Except Tuomas Anhava, they did not write articles to defend themselves or essays to expound their theories, but a number of young critics, essayists, and scholars rallied to them; eventually their art was analyzed more extensively and intensively than any other, and the 1950s have been called "the ten years of criticism."[809] Before we can examine them, however, we must say a few words about their predecessors.

The generation gap in Finnish literature is not as apparent among poets as among prosaists. Although Koskenniemi was still active and influential after the war, his poetry belonged to the past. The young appreciated but did not imitate Hellaakoski or P. Mustapää, who had both begun to write again. Although his art had not remained static, Lauri Viljanen did not give impulses to new poetry. Elina Vaara and Yrjö Kaijärvi represent the ornate, elegant traditional poetry against which the young rebelled, and the *Kiila*, reconstituted, formed a group of its own. In the 1940s, however, a few female poets who link the older and younger generations appeared. The form of their poetry is mainly traditional, and its contents fluctuate between the old and new. Having turned their backs on the past, they groped toward the future, and some eventually expressed themselves in new forms.

Eila Kivikk'aho (pseudonym of **Eila Sylvia Sammalkorpi**, *née* Lamberg, b. 1921) published her first volume, *Sinikallio* ('The Blue Rock') in 1942. It contains a contrast found in her later collections between lively contents and succinct form. Although not placing restraints upon herself, she did not allow her talent for writing melodious verse to degenerate into wordiness. She has stated that the poet she most admires is Otto Manninen.[810] Later her inclination toward concise, allusive form led her to reproduce the Japanese *tanka* meter in Finnish.[811] With *Niityltä pois* ('Away from the Meadow,' 1951) she adopted free verse, though not exclusively. The title is somewhat symbolic; from descriptions of nature, which often included her lost home region, Karelia, she has turned to more introspective poetry. Her familiarity with Japanese poetry may have influenced her in the direction of the simple and meditative. One poem in the collection, *Venelaulu* ('The Boatsong,' 1952), illustrates her attitude:

> No longer do I
> lean on shards.
> Happiness I found, unbroken.
> What shall I hide in its cup?
> – The bits of the old crock.

Sirkka Selja (pseudonym of **Sirkka Liisa Tulonen**, b. 1920) also published her first collection, *Vielä minä elän* ('I Am Still Alive'), in 1942. Unlike Eila Kivikk'aho, whose reticence prevented her from revealing her innermost feelings, Sirkka Selja speaks above all of her instincts and emotions as a woman, passive but creative, to whom love is foremost. In a poem from the first collection, she identifies herself with the earth and her beloved with the sun. Water replaces earth in the second collection, *Vedenneito* ('The Mermaid,' 1944), but the attachment to nature remains. This view of life is fully developed in *Taman lauluja* ('Songs of Tama,' 1945), in which Tama, a mythical creature of the author's creation, symbolizes the feminine element in the world. The same ideas reappear in her later collections, *Linnut* ('The Birds,' 1948), *Niinkuin ovi* ('As a Door,' 1953), and *Enkelin pelto* ('The Field of the Angel,' 1957), which, though sometimes monotonous, sincerely and well express the author's feeling.

Anja Vammelvuo (b. 1921, wife of Jarno Pennanen), whose poetry especially resembles that of Katri Vala in form and content, has written that she admires Vala and Edith Södergran. Her first collections, *Auringon tytär* ('The Daughter of the Sun,' 1943) and *Muottiin tuntemattomaan* ('Unto an Unknown Mold,' 1946), show an interest in her own problems and feelings, some erotic, which she expresses with joy or deep dejection. She later published a novel, a short-story collection, and a play, in which her growing awareness of the problems of other individuals and society is evident. It is also reflected in her next poems, *Kukkia sylissäni* ('Flowers in My Lap,' 1954). She never speaks directly of social or political questions, but defends the rights of life and freedom. She does not forsake her earlier motifs in later collections; love and the destiny of women are still prominent. The form and mood of later work, e.g., *Kuuma, kylmä* ('Hot, Cold,' 1960) and *Integer*

Vitae (1964), are more subdued than those of her first collections, in which images often crowd each other.

Poetry by young women and girls became fashionable in the 1940s. The first edition of *Ruiskukkaehtoo* ('The Night of the Cornflowers,' 1947), and the first collection of **Anna-Maija Raittila** (maiden name of **Anna-Maija Nieminen**, b. 1928), sold out within a few weeks; two more appeared in the same year. Written by an emotionally developed but inexperienced young girl, it expresses in simple, fresh lines the happiness felt at the sight of nature. The religious poems in the volume are more subdued, although she expresses God's might and majesty in powerful words. One of the few modern poets to express directly religious feelings, she has a degree in divinity and has taught religion.[812] Her faith is simple and joyful, based on a trusting love for God, the humble admission of her imperfections, and her effort to overcome them. *Päivänvarjopuu* ('The Sunshade Tree,' 1955), *Aurinko on jäljellä* ('The Sun Remains,' 1957), and *Lähteet* ('The Springs,' 1961) are broadened by the introduction of love, affection, and understanding between two people, which indirectly reflect her marriage.

Laura Latvala (b. 1921, wife of Olavi Siippainen), a practicing physician, published as her first volume poetry about a happy childhood and its landscapes, *Yökkömökki* ('Bat Cabin,' 1945). Although the collection is optimistic, it contains some poems such as *Epäuskontunnustus* ('A Profession of Unbelief'), which is a bitter complaint about God's way of ruling the world, addressed to Him. *Yökkömökki* is not very original, but critics received it well because of the poet's skillful and individual use of poetic forms. She next published one volume with her husband and more collections of her own, *Aamusignaali* ('The Morning Signal,' 1953) and *Keulaneitsyt* ('The Virgin at the Bow,' 1958), in which the spontaneous happiness of her first collection gives way to more serious meditations, still basically optimistic. *Toisillemme* ('To Each Other,' 1965), one of her last works, was a joint effort with her husband which was not published until after his death.

The many collections printed to satisfy the immense demand for poetry which followed the war were not of uniformly good quality. Critics, who were becoming concerned, were happy to read *Muuttolintu* ('The Migratory Bird,' 1946), the first collection of **Helka Hiisku** (1912-62). She had become thoroughly familiar with poetry before its publication, and it was formally faultless though conventional in content. She translated from Italian, but published only one more volume of verse, *Karannut tuli* ('The Runaway Fire,' 1948), which set her apart from other contemporary Finnish poets. Most of the poems are ballads reminiscent of such compositions by Eino Leino, Larin-Kyösti, and Mustapää, with no loss of individuality. Based on recent folk beliefs and tales, they often point out a general truth. In one a greedy farmer who has used false measures in the sale of grain sits after his death at the graveyard gate, endlessly filling two sacks. In *Pitkäpieksu* ('Longboots'),

345

modeled on an Ostrobotnian ghost story, a tailor known as a quick runner tries to catch Death. He is sent back having been advised to turn his curiosity to life, in the manner of Leino's *Kouta*.

Anja Samooja (maiden name of Anja Gersov, 1919-66), who lived for a long time in Denmark, her husband's homeland, translated many works from Danish to Finnish, but wrote only three volumes of poetry: *Luode ja vuoksi* ('The Ebb and the Flood,' 1947), *Sydänjuuret* ('The Roots of the Heart,' 1948), and *Uralin ja Atlantin väliltä* ('Between the Urals and the Atlantic,' 1964). The first two, somewhat above average technically, do not differ from most poetry of the period, but her last, much more original, promised future development which her death prevented.

Only three of the poets who first published in the late 1940s tower above the others; Aila Meriluoto, Lauri Viita: and Helvi Juvonen shared a new outlook and an artistic quality which places them among the best contemporary lyricists. Although Aila Meriluoto and Lauri Viita were married from 1948 to 1956, their art does not show cross-influence. Both Helvi Juvonen and Lauri Viita died at a relatively early age.

Aila Meriluoto (b. 1924) was twenty-two when she published her first independent collection, *Lasimaalaus* ('The Stained Glass Picture,' 1946). Besides Linna's *Tuntematon sotilas*, it is probably the most sensational work ever published in Finland. Young critics and conservative scholars such as Tarkiainen and Koskenniemi praised it, and in a short time twenty-five thousand copies were sold.[813] The poetry itself is not sensational, i.e., erotic, social, or political. Its success is due to a hunger for art and literature when no other luxury was to be had and to the work's merit. Although Aila Meriluoto was a so-called nice girl from a good family, her feelings and expression are mature and strong. Her subjects are chaste love and moral and religious problems. *Kivinen Jumala* ('The Stone God'), much quoted at the time, is a protest against the god who permits the horror and suffering of war, but neither the poet nor most of her generation pitied themselves or rebelled. She states that man, rising from the ruins, will, like his lord, be of stone. The collection is formally traditional with regular rhythms and rhymes, but the artistry is neither elaborate nor conscious; Viljo Tarkiainen has pointed out her apparent attempt to make the rhymes inconspicuous.[814] The poetry is more complex than it seems; ordinary words are combined in a manner which reveals new relations between facts. She admitted the influence of Rainer Maria Rilke, who was then rather unknown in Finland,[815] translated some of his poems, wrote an essay on him,[816] and composed a poem on his grave in Valais.

The author reportedly said that the appreciation won by *Lasimaalaus* was enough to free her from worries about the reception of her future works.[817] Her subsequent collections have been well received; they have confirmed her place among the country's best poets, but have not attracted special attention. The modernist offensive of the 1950s has left her somewhat neglected because her art is not as aggressively new or controversial as that of her younger contemporaries. In *Sairas tyttö tanssii* ('The Dance of the Sick Girl,' 1952) and *Pahat unet* ('Bad Dreams,' 1958), she retreats more and more to her individual problems, and critics feared that she had depleted her inspiration.[818] She did not write directly of herself; although most of *Sairas tyttö tanssii* is in the first person, the poems are told by a legendary or an impersonal "I," the typical woman who expresses the feminine viewpoint. The collection tells of woman's difficulty in adjusting to a man's world, an adjustment which she sometimes refuses to make. It may also represent the arduous transition from maidenhood to womanhood. In *Puhkeavat oksat* ('The Budding Branches') women are dry branches which burst into leaves (*puhkeava* lit. 'bursting') when rain falls over them, then slowly forget this pain and bitterness. The poem concludes: "This we are: smile and silence." It is evident from the context that the "smile and silence" are not happy. Among the translations of Rilke at the end of the volume is *Orpheus. Eurydice. Hermes.* Eurydice almost wishes to return to Hades rather than follow her husband because, as a virgin again, she feels estranged from him. To Meriluoto's women men are not only brutal but also ridiculous. Aloof, the women watch the men; they "smile," (the author often uses this word), faintly amused but also contemptuous.

In *Pahat unet* she transposes personal problems which she could not make general and relevant, and the form of the poems is sometimes uneven. *Portaat* ('The Stairs,' 1961) is more serene; it contains descriptions of landscapes which expand to cosmic visions and express the unity of man and the universe. Her dreams of peace and happiness, however, are not so complex; she declares that we should strive for the simplicity of children. The motif of seeking communion between man and nature is extended in *Asumattomiin* ('Into the Uninhabited,' 1963) and *Tuoddaris* (name, 1965), which reflect the vast, empty landscapes of northern Sweden, where she had been living. The love poems of these collections are peaceful and somewhat melancholy, but the poet is not resigned to an entirely contemplative attitude; she declares that she will not accept the mediocrity of the masses.

Lauri Viita (1916-65), the son of a worker at Pispala, a working-class suburb of Tampere, was victimized by a misconception similar to that about Pentti Haanpää. He earned his living as a carpenter and construction worker for a while and became known as a poet with little formal education but much strength and vitality. After his reputation had been established, a number of young writers, some with similar backgrounds, who appeared in Tampere formed a discussion club which met at the city library. Alex Matson provided the theoretical information for the conversations.[819] Early in his career, Viita enjoyed playing a rough, strong man who criticized learned and refined poetry, artificial and ornate language, educated people, and almost

347

everything else, although his own work was well received by critics.[820] He was not uneducated himself: after he had completed more than half of secondary school, where Latin was taught, he left, charged with a prank which he considered "too childish for him to commit."[821] He continued reading, for example, popular works on modern science throughout his life. He mainly published poetry, in which he practiced successfully his principles of natural simplicity although he did not discard regular rhythm and rhyme. He did brilliantly what so many learned poets had vainly attempted: to write traditional, rhymed verse without artificially shortening or lengthening words or using unnatural word order. Hellaakoski and Lehtonen had achieved similar success.

His novel, *Moreeni* (1950),[822] is a realistic, well-written, energetic story about daily life in Pispala at the end of the nineteenth and beginning of the twentieth centuries. Although the period of the Civil War is covered and his characters involved, political and social questions are not important. The description of the conflict is impartial, but he sees the Reds as good-natured, honest workers who went to the war because they were told to go, but who never understood what they fought for, a view not unlike that in *Meek Heritage* or even in Linna's *Täällä Pohjantähden alla*.

His first volume of poetry, *Betonimylläri* ('A Miller of Concrete,' 1947), contains many half-real, half-imaginary poems. The one which gives the collection its title describes the bad dreams of a concrete worker sleeping during his lunch break. Partially using the language the worker might use, it goes beyond his everyday problems and hints at deep philosophical questions. In places it is aggressive and satirical, but in other poems in the collection Viita's attitude is more balanced, especially in his expressions of faith in the human spirit, which he believes can free itself from and dominate the material world.

Viita's next volume, *Kukunor* (1949), bewildered critics and readers. It is presented as a tale about a fairy and a troll in love with each other, who find an atlas and choose the nicest names in it for themselves; he is Kukunor, a lake in Central Asia, and she is Kalahari, a desert in South Africa. Whether it is purely nonsensical or deeply symbolic has been debated;[823] the poet did not indicate the correct interpretation. Some passages, e.g., that in which he meditates on the desert of humanity and the possibility of its becoming fertile again, reminiscent of T. S. Eliot's *Waste Land,* are serious; but many seem to be a play of his imagination. *Käppyräinen* ('Crinkly,' 1954) differs less from poetic standards in spite of its whimsical title. In it Viita's satire becomes less aggressive, more tolerant, and broadly humorous.

Finnish critics and scholars generally deny any connection between the odd features of Viita's art and the psychosis for which he was treated from 1954 to 1961, but certainly both reflect his personality, as does his successful struggle against his illness. He had returned to normal life when he died in an

FRANS EEMIL SILLANPÄÄ,
painting by Erkki Kulovesi
Werner Söderström Oy. Publishers

JUHANI SILJO,
painting by Pekka Halonen
Werner Söderström Oy. Publishers

ELMER DIKTONIUS,
painting by Georges von Hueck
Werner Söderström Oy. Publishers

MARTTI HAAVIO/P. MUSTAPÄÄ,
aquarel by Ina Behrsen-Colliander
Werner Söderström Oy. Publishers

HAGAR OLSSON
Holger Schildts Förlags Ab. Publishers

EDITH SÖDERGRAN
Holger Schildts Förlags Ab. Publishers

AARO HELLAAKOSKI
Press Bureau,
Ministry for Foreign Affairs of Finland

OLAVI PAAVOLAINEN
Otava Oy. Publishers

KATRI VALA, painting by Väinö Kunnas
Werner Söderström Oy. Publishers

UUNO KAILAS, painting by Väinö Kunnas
Werner Söderström Oy. Publishers

TITO COLLIANDER
Söderström & Co. Förlags Ab. Publishers

TOIVO PEKKANEN,
painting by Väinö Kunnas
Werner Söderström Oy. Publishers

MIKA WALTARI
Pressfoto Inc. and the Press Bureau,
Ministry for Foreign Affairs of Finland

ARVO TURTIAINEN
Tammi Oy. Publishers

PENTTI HAANPÄÄ (right) with his father
Press Bureau, Ministry for Foreign Affairs of Finland

ELVI SINERVO
Tammi Oy. Publishers

EVA WICHMAN
Söderström & Co. Förlags Ab. Publishers

LAURI VIITA
Werner Söderström Oy. Publishers

MIRJAM TUOMINEN
Söderström & Co. Förlags Ab. Publishers

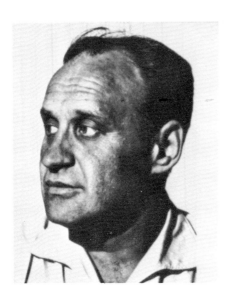

VÄINÖ LINNA
Lehtikuva Oy. and the Press Bureau,
Ministry for Foreign Affairs of Finland

EEVA-LIISA MANNER
Tammi Oy. Publishers

MARJA-LIISA VARTIO
Press Bureau,
Ministry for Foreign Affairs of Finland

AILA MERILUOTO
Lehtikuva Oy. and the Press Bureau,
Ministry for Foreign Affairs of Finland

TUOMAS ANHAVA
Otava Oy. Publishers

CHRISTER KIHLMAN
Söderström & Co. Förlags Ab. Publishers

VEIJO MERI
Lehtikuva Oy. and the Press Bureau,
Ministry for Foreign Affairs of Finland

PAAVO RINTALA
Lehtikuva Oy. and the Press Bureau,
Ministry for Foreign Affairs of Finland

KARI ARONPURO
Kirjayhtymä Oy. Publishers

PENTTI SAARIKOSKI
Otava Oy. Publishers

PAAVO HAAVIKKO
Lehtikuva Oy. and the Press Bureau, Ministry for Foreign Affairs of Finland

automobile accident. His last collection, *Suutarikin suuri viisas* ('A Shoemaker Is a Wise Man Too,' 1961) continues the direction of *Käppyräinen* and
contains some love poems, which he had previously avoided as though he had
distaste for an open display of his feelings. His use of traditional rhymed
verse, the old Finnish meter, modern Finnish folksong patterns, and free verse
is masterful. His essential attitude, a bitter but optimistic struggle against the
world's evils, especially the moral ones, is as clear in this volume as in earlier
books.

Like Meriluoto and Viita, **Helvi Juvonen** (1919-59) is a poet of the
transition between traditional and modern verse, but her work does not reveal
an awareness of her position. She used a form suitable to her, sometimes
writing, like Viita, in the old Finnish meter. Her poetry reflects suffering
from illness and loneliness, but she overcame depression with humor and with
her odd philosophy in which a religious state of mind is important, although
she did not follow a particular dogma.[824] She wrote an essay on Emily
Dickinson, whose shy solitude was akin to her own, and translated some of
Miss Dickinson's poetry, which may have influenced her own.[825] Her poems
are brief and terse in the manner of the works of Hellaakoski, Kailas, Siljo,
and Manninen, but hers are even more allusive than theirs. Her poetry departs
from tradition in its use of free images which convey in condensed form a
vision of the world, as in *Pikarijäkälä* ('The Cup of the Moss'):

> Jäkälä nosti pikarinsa hauraan
> ja sade täytti sen, ja pisarassa
> kimalsi taivas tuulta pidättäen.
>
> Jäkälä nosti pikarinsa hauraan:
> Nyt malja elämämme rikkaudelle.
>
> The moss raised its frail cup
> and the rain filled it, and in the drop
> the sky glittered, holding back the winds.
>
> The moss raised its frail cup:
> This is to the fullness of our life.

She has added a reference to St. Luke 17:21, which she did not intend as an
explanation: "Neither shall they say, Lo Here! or Lo there! for, behold, the
kingdom of God is within you." Seeing a reflection of the great in the small is
typical of Juvonen. In her first collection, *Kääpiöpuu* ('The Dwarf Tree,'
1949), as well as in later works, we find small plants and animals which suffer
because they are strange and ugly or express an innocent joy in life through
humor.

Pain, suffering, anguish, and lack of communication are recurring
themes in her work. Occasionally they produce only passive bitterness, but

more often a religious experience converts the bitterness into something positive. Clearly differing from the Christian religion, Helvi Juvonen does not view suffering as an atonement of man's sins or as an unquestionable punishment wreaked by God. She describes it and draws conclusions one might call desperately optimistic. In many poems, after enumerating pains and trials, she makes a positive statement that good exists on the side of evil or even because of it. The motif of the poem *Kivikide* ('The Stone Crystal') seems to be from Andersen's tale about the Snow Queen and a small boy into whose eye and heart a splinter of her mirror falls, making him cold and insensible to human feelings. When the splinter is removed, the boy feels joy and pain again, but in Juvonen's poem the crystal remains in the eye, even when "in the dusk of the evening the moon weaves / nets of dreams, of frail sentiments" and continues asking questions, hard and stiff-mouthed. It is a protest against the dreamy sentimental poetry in favor and an assertion of belief in the value of an unsentimental attitude toward life. The poems *Siemen* ('The Seed') and *Annan* ('I Am Giving') are similar. The seed never grows to be a tree, and a narrator tells that she gives to her companion or beloved "half of the wealth" of her life, years and years without sleep, a contempt which words cannot express, dry grass, stones, wrinkles on the cheeks, and yet he stands there. She concludes: "Why is the uphill road now beautiful?"[826]

Kuningas Kultatakki ('King Goldcoat,' 1950) is her most romantic and experimental collection. She tries a variety of mainly traditional forms. The religious poems show the influence of the Bible, especially the prophets and psalms, and Finnish hymns. She uses the animals which appear in all her collections, including humorous compositions on animals which represent a small, safe world where sorrows and pains are unknown. The ideas of her most mature collection, *Pohjajäätä* ('Deep Ice,' 1952), which is intensive and laconic in form and thought, are no different: the hate and lack of trust between humans, the importance of religious experience, and the value of the inconspicuous and modest, but they are now crystallized, stripped of all that is unessential.

Päivästä päivään ('From Day to Day,' 1954) is also simple, occasionally folksonglike. In it life is often conceived as a journey through the seasons, materialized in images of a house or a road or feelings of cold, weariness, or hunger. *Kalliopohja* ('Bedrock,' 1956) returns to the majestic poems influenced by the Bible or Leino's *Helkavirsiä* found in *Kuningas Kultatakki* and deals with pain, suffering, and death in impressive settings. At her death she left poems which indicate that she may have been taking a new direction, more soft and melodious, but Tuomas Anhava correctly says that it is impossible to evaluate her art definitively, for, although it contains masterpieces, it is incomplete.[827]

The precise time assigned to the modernization of Finnish poetry is between 1949 and 1956;[828] the former date marks the publication of first collections by Lasse Heikkilä and Lassi Nummi and a translation of Eliot's *The Waste Land* by Anhava and Laitinen, the latter the success of Eeva-Liisa Manner's *Tämä matka* ('This Journey'), the first volume of entirely modern verse to be praised by traditional and new critics and read by a substantial public. A fifth revised edition was issued in 1964. In 1957 *Uuden runon kauneimmat* ('The Most Beautiful New Poems'), an anthology edited by Osmo Hormia, was quickly sold out, and a new, enlarged edition was published in 1968. After the obstacle of the new form had been overcome, readers seemed receptive to the message of the new generation. Even older readers were not hostile. Many of the young poets were not unlike T. S. Eliot, who was influential in Finland at that time. They rejected feelings proclaimed in traditional forms, which they wished to replace with more complex and refined ones. They were extreme individualists,[829] and only recently have they voiced political, social, moral, or religious opinions in their poetry. It is difficult to understand why the traditionalists, headed by Koskenniemi, attacked them; even the well-behaved, conservative Eliot gained the reputation of a dangerous rabble-rouser. In his youth Eliot was intensely disliked by conservative critics to a great extent for the same reasons for which his later Finnish followers were disliked.[830] These critics were antagonized by the avoidance of lofty, poetic language, the combining of the noble and the trivial, the rejection of traditional forms, and the independent, freely connected or seemingly disconnected images. Leftist writers charged them with lack of idealism because they did not engage in the political, social struggle,[831] but, when the younger generation treated political subjects, they did it in a maner which irritated the older generation. They have never been charged with obscenity, for love, spiritual or physical, is secondary in their poetry; however, the generation of the 1960s is different in this respect.

Lasse Heikkilä (1925-61) wrote six collections of poetry, a play, *Medeia*, and a story, *Matkalla* ('Traveling'). The first collection, *Miekkalintu* ('The Sword Bird') shows the influence of Swedish poets from the 1940s and includes translations of some of their work. The title of his second volume, *Paatos ja lyyra* ('The Pathos and the Lyre,' 1950), indicates the characteristics of his work. The other poets of his generation wrote carefully composed poetry with elaborate, refined structure, but his works are at times uneven, as if torn apart by his eagerness to express all his thoughts. He is more often rhetorical and pathetic than his contemporaries, but he can suddenly shift to a more contemplative mood. His collections develop: from aggressive intellectualism he passes to religious meditations influenced by catholicism, which occasionally lean toward mysticism; his last collection is entitled *Terra Mariana* (1959). *Sinä* ('You,' 1951) pleased the older critics more than it did the younger.[832] It is full of youthful optimism and eagerness uncommon among the new poets. Its theme is love, raised to a universal level by his frequent rhetorical generalizations.

Unet ja Medeia ('The Dreams and Medea,' 1953), poetry and a play published in one volume, is one of his major works, containing the characteristics of his earlier pieces. Here, however, the subdued verse is opposed by irony and broad, farcical humor rather than rhetoric. One such poem, *Olen ihminen* ('I Am Human'), dedicated to T. S. Eliot, shows that his Finnish disciple studied him; Heikkilä sees in him a man of humor as well as a learned composer of subtle and complex meditations. The change in Heikkilä's art is first apparent in *Carmen* (1956), in which he gives motifs from earlier collections, especially *Paatos ja lyyra*, new treatment, and is complete in his last collection. As one of the first Finnish poets to write in an entirely new manner, he is recognized as a pioneer, but most contemporary poets have followed other directions.

That the publication of first collections by Heikkilä and Lassi Nummi is considered the beginning of modern poetry in Finland is evidence that the new poets did not form a homogeneous group, for Nummi differs greatly from Heikkilä. Their poetry was modern in form because the new form was natural to them,[833] but **Lassi** (Lauri Juhani) **Nummi** (b. 1928) has been called the most tradition-conscious poet of the new generation; he said himself, "You can always save on bread, clothes, baby carriages, but how could a poet save on jewels, daggers, orchids?"[834] He sometimes also wrote rhymed verse or what he called his new hexameter, an experiment he soon dropped,[835] and he insisted on the "ceremonial" (traditional) elements in poetry rather than the "improvisatory" (new) ones. Chinese poetry and philosophy attracted many poets from his generation, but he appreciated them perhaps more than the others did because of their form and ritual.[836] His first collection, *Intohimo olemassaoloon* ('A Passion for Existence,' 1949), is, perhaps intentionally, not very original, showing the influence of many earlier Finnish poets. One of the best sections, the "pastoral suite" *Vuoripaimen* ('The Shepherd of the Mountains'), is located in China. When he published it as a separate collection in the same year he added new elements. His early poetry contains much that is typical of his art: descriptions of nature, especially rivers and the sea, and a melancholy attitude toward life and its ephemerality.

His next collection, *Tahdon sinun kuulevan* ('I Want You to Hear,' 1954), also differs from his contemporaries' work in the use of many visual and ornate adjectives. It is divided into *The Book of Glass, The Black Book, The Book of Silver,* and *The Book of Brass,* in which we find "tinkling springs between the hills," "a rosy shine like flames and stars on the mountains," "the snowy neck of a swan reflected in the black river," "a pearl-colored sounding night," and similar images which, although well-known, seem fresh in their new context. Waves and the sea, rivers and springs, shores, and bridges represent the freedom and joy of life as well as its passing nature, which is especially felt in poems with love as a motif, e.g., *Valossa männyt* ('The Pines in the Light') and *Jano* ('Thirst'). His art has a material-immaterial, realistic-dreamlike quality, illustrated by *Varjojen syvetessä* and *Elegia* respectively:

When the shadows are deepening
a spring calm and clear and dark

the light and the ripple have fled
have played on the river, have disappeared

higher up, on the slope
between the leaves a shudder, a light
flees, catches up, flees, laughter, play, joy

all is but flight between the leaves
the wind sweeps lightly over them
there is no shadow

The wind sweeps away the footsteps from the shore.
The bright laughter has sounded. The white brightness
is emptiness, lingers on the sand, fades away. The white shores
mirror for the last time their height in the deep water.
The white shores and the white footsteps and the white foam of the waves,
no more.
    The bright, white salt of the waves remains on the sand.

Although uneven in places, *Taivaan ja maan merkit* ('The Signs of Heaven and Earth,' 1956) contains his masterpiece, *Chaconne*, the long section in which his irony and earnestness, playfulness and melancholy, ornate, musical rhythm and proselike simplicity are successfully blended. *Kuusimittaa* ('Hexameter,' 1963) is the only collection written almost entirely in his new meter. *Keskipäivä, delta* ('Noon, Delta,' 1967) introduces new aspects to his poetry; the dreamer who composes exquisite elegies now realistically describes the journey of a tourist group along the Danube to its delta in Rumania. The narrator feels guilty for enjoying his journey while "somewhere death is reality on a morning like this," later mentioning Vietnam, and reflects that he does not belong "to this generation or to that. I am of the middle generation, a tourist in the audience of a cruel arena." He even refers to himself as a "fattish member of the middle class." The old Nummi returns in *Aamiainen ruohikolla* ('Lunch on the Grass'), where he thinks of Manet's painting. When speaking of sensuous feminine beauty, he refers to Rembrandt, and his eyes select Chinese details in the landscape, reeds, a lone man fishing in a boat, and pelicans flying. The last image is elaborated at the end of the collection, where it has a further, undefined meaning; perhaps it renders the flight of the human spirit toward ultimately unknown goals:

> and the flock does not know where it is headed to, it does not know
> if somewhere a great nesting area is waiting, a wonderful blossoming
> without cries of pain and soiled feathers
> it does not know and nevertheless it must fly
> . . . .
> all together each one alone, consciousness is expanding and consciousness
>   is contracting
> like an eye, like a heart

Tuomas Anhava (b. 1927), the poet who has most explicitly defined modern poetry (or that which modern poetry should be) and its reasons for the public, has argued with persons opposed to modern poetry in general and to himself in particular, using satire and humor as weapons. A philosophical humor is a major element of his poetry, and a lighter turn of mind results in half-nonsensical verse without deep meaning. The third poem in the series, *Lokakuu* ('October'),[837] begins:

> This year October began on the thirtieth of August,
> when yesterday it was still summer and the family left for the city.

and continues:

> I went to the porch with my head drawn between my shoulders.
> . . . and then, I took a step,
> the bush in front of the porch blew up.
> The migratory birds.
> Twenty thousand warbling thrushes.
> Then it was really quiet.

The fourth poem is autobiographical:

> I was born in a loud voice,
> fell on my nose and was then silent for
> five years. Those were my parents' happiest years
> those happy years.
> At the age of six I started wondering where I had come from
> Then I did not wonder anymore,
> I wondered where everything has come from.
> Now I am a man of a certain age and I wonder
> when everything is not gone, when everything has not gone
> when there is life
> when there is hope
> And I am writing I am writing.

Anhava, too, is interested in oriental poetry, which he has translated
(not from the originals), and Chinese philosophy. In *Yleiset opit* VIII ('The
General Theories')[838] he says:

"All visible is form," and the virtue of form is emptiness,
the virtue of an earthenware vessel is not the earth but the vessel,
the virtue of a door and of a window is not the wood or the glass but the
    opening.

a Taoist statement. His *General Theories* give an extensive account of his
philosophy, which justifies the charges of lack of idealism and sense of social
responsibility. Not unlike T. S. Eliot, whom he has translated, Anhava, a
highly intellectual man, attacks in these poems and others intellect and
learning, praising the sage who retires from the world and eschews social
activity, another Taoist attitude. These *Theories* are addressed to his son, who
is told to avoid cabinet members, company presidents, newspapermen,
general managers, pacifists, militarists, ideologists, orators, sociologists,
psychologists, and female welfare workers. He is also told not to raise the
banner of ideal, which would be wrapped around his coffin, and is instructed
about the nature of truth:

my son, What is Truth?
it is what the thing now seems to be to me,
    but Knowledge says it as follows:
    "Truth is a Certain position of a certain Thing in a certain System
    if is is and not not so so,"
and knowledge is a net,
    with small meshes for sardines
    but big meshes are needed for tunafishes,
    and then the sardines swim through
    to make bubbles glitter on the surface of the water,
    and no matter what kind of meshes the net has, deep down
    improbable fishes
    twist it into terrible knots
    and each of them contains a mackerel:
concentrate then on the tails of the mackerels, cook them in butter on the
    shore[839]

Although in his early collections he insisted that the world was evil and
wise men did best to retire, he declared again and again his opinions of world
events. In his later poems, however, he seems to have accepted, perhaps with
sarcastic resignation, that one must take the world as it is. In a poem from
Kuudes kirja ('The Sixth Book,' 1966) he says:

Educated eyes, a cultivated voice.
Spends pleasant evenings.
In the company of good friends.

> Drinks a glass of wine.
> Knows that there is everything in this world
> the small the middle-size and the big.[840]

His sarcasm is apparent in the one which follows it:

> No living being
> has ever seen him except
> before or after a meeting.

Many of the poems in this collection, however, are impressionistic small images from nature reminiscent of Japanese poetry:

> No wind. Water
> in which one sees bud by bud
> the trees more clearly than the tree itself.

and:

> Sunday, grey silent streets,
> the face of that child, and the sky
> and a useless autumn between them.

In Anhava's works there are other simple, subdued allusions to children and love poems, composed as though the poet has done his best to avoid mentioning the emotions, which do reveal that ordinary human feelings are not foreign to him.

Paavo Haavikko (b. 1931) is the poet of his generation most difficult to describe or follow; we do not use the word *understand*, which, by its intellectual nature, is an anathema to the new poets.[841] Although "imagims," "decadent surrealism," and "romanticism" have been suggested as classifications for his art, many critics have stressed its originality and the fact that little has been written about it.[842] Nummi said that a poet cannot do without daggers, jewels, and orchids, but Haavikko finds even flowers materialistic in *Synnyinmaa* ('The Native Country,' 1955). He opposes the "peasants" to the "poet" and says of the former:

> but, they will, say then: I told you so,
> I know that they will plant rows of chrysanthemums into the landscape,
> for, they say, I am a lie,
> . . . .
> for, they say, I am a lie, my chrysanthemum is but smell,
> the chrysanthemums of the peasants are true, they are planted and they
> blossom.

Especially in his first collection, *Tiet etäisyyksiin* ('The Roads That Lead Far Away,' 1951), Haavikko uses subjects familiar to readers of traditional poetry: kings riding at the head of their hosts, palaces, gardens, cities, villages, hills, valleys, and roads with rolling carriages. With a few simple, solemn words he suggests times and places long past and dwells on the ephemerality of human creations. In spite of the ambiguity caused by his allusive style, and the structure of his images, which often interlock, the following should convey the same message to all readers:

> Each house is built by many and never finished
> and history and the mythical times are retold.
> Contradictory corridors lead to an awareness of the error
> and to memories of the only distant past
> which the rooms are echoing all through to the end.
>
> Once flowers will be grown on the deserted stairs.
> The great aqueduct will burst and rust will close the gates and the silvery
>   pond will spread out.
> Somebody will wonder at the individuality of the machineries and look for
>   tools
> laugh at a timetable and live in the period of morning.

The image of the growth of a new civilization on the ruins of the old is familiar, with biblical overtones. The third line is an example of the interlocking images: the "corridors" that "lead" somewhere refer to the house, whereas "contradictory" and "awareness of the error" relate to the mental sphere to which history, myths, and memories belong. Both images are part of a whole which represents the collective memory of history and myth wherein the partially conflicting individual memories are included.

Haavikko's sense of humor is sometimes manifested in an odd manner. In a poem from *Tuuliöinä* ('On Windy Nights,' 1953), we find:

> Orpheus, dressed in the despised garb of one who has been to Hades
> went up to the husbandman and asked a question,
> then the husbandman took the shape of fertility
> and answered the inescapable words of origin and opening,
> from which the echo fled:
>
> Take it easy. The way is long.

This last line, in English in the original, is incongruous in the solemn, mythical context; beyond the joke, the poet may have meant that age-old myths have importance today.

Haavikko's interest in the past extends beyond the imaginary to real history. His early collections allude superficially to historical facts out of context. A poem in *Juhlat* ('The Festivity')[843] begins with a regiment which rides to battle and ends with an umbrella needed in 1938. The few lines, mainly about the Munich crisis, between beginning and end fail, we feel, to establish a connection, logical or poetic. Another poem in *Juhlat* relates the progress of a character driving through a country, and ends with a statement that the king could not do more and the journey ended at Varennes; the king, therefore, is Louis XVI. In another, an old king playing the flute at Hubertsburg Hunting Lodge appears—he is Frederic II of Prussia. The historical hints lead the reader astray more than they help him, for there is a relation between these characters and the poems, but it is more that each is part of the whole rather than that one provides a key to the other. His later collections include poems about well-defined historical events, e.g. *Suomalainen sarja* ('A Finnish Suite' in *Lehdet lehtiä* 'Leaves the Leaves,' 1958) about Russia's annexation of Finland in 1809. Although it took place peacefully, Haavikko stresses the lack of true communication between the countries. One line has become a popular saying, an unusual fate for a work by a contemporary poet: "Finnish is not a language, it is a way of sitting at the end of the bench with your fur cap pulled over your ears." The next section in the collection pretends to be the memoirs of the Finnish Secretary of War during the Winter War;[844] the aim of the satire is quite obvious. Haavikko describes a politician more interested in justifying his own actions than in the fate of the country. The irony is not very subtle, and the unfortunate secretary had already become a public scapegoat. *Puut, kaikki heidän vihreytensä* ('The Trees, All Their Greenness,' 1966)[845] contains sections on similar subjects: *Selvä johdatus myöhempään historiaan* ('A Clear Introduction to Later History'), *Faabeleita vuodelta 1965* ('Fables from the Year 1965'), and *Niin katosi voitto maailmasta* ('So Profit Disappeared from the World'). The last title is the first line of a poem which continues: "Now it is called a risk when you talk about it / an excess of returns in accounting."[846] The first section is a criticism of A. F. Upton's *Finland in Crisis 1940-1941*, a recent British work of which Haavikko does not approve. However, Haavikko, instead of reviewing the author's views, makes derogatory remarks about England, suggesting that the country did nothing in the last war, hardly an accurate accusation. With rather poor taste, we think, he includes Poland:

> How did Poland make it
> with the help of her five great allies.
> She literally moved
> quite a bit toward the West.
> She is wandering
> toward the West.

Although Haavikko is usually described as a poet interested in the problems of the individual or the poet,[847] we have stressed the political and social motifs in his works, for he has used them to such an extent that to ignore them would give an inaccurate picture of his art. *Talvipalatsi* ('The

Winter Palace,' 1959), however, is, according to him, "a journey through the known language," a poem about poetry.

Eeva-Liisa Manner (b. 1921) published two traditional collections which attracted little attention, then achieved fame with *Tämä matka* ('This Journey,' 1956), which used the new style. A novel written in 1951, *Tyttö taivaan laiturilla* ('The Girl on the Pier of Heaven'), describes her art: "The child drops like a cone from a spruce tree into the world, where logical disorder prevails instead of magical order";[848] the poem *Kromaattiset tasot eli johdatus vangitun muodon murtamiseen* ('The Chromatic Levels or An Introduction to the Breaking of the Captive Form' in *Fahrenheit 121*, 1968) says: "The Devil poured small wheels of logic into the ear of the world / and said: now it can hear well." Like Anhava, Miss Manner is an intellectual who professes anti-intellectual views; in this poem she criticizes a statement by Wittgenstein and mentions Leibnitz's monads, Heidegger, Heraclitus, and the Taoist truth that "the hollow in the pot makes the pot." Her ideal poet is probably not unlike the early Greek philosophers—learned, but transcending learning through knowledge of deeper truths.[849] She seems strongly to disapprove of Plato, however; in *Looginen kertomus* ('A Logical Story' in the same collection) a man demonstrates that Plato is wrong by asking for a fruit in a grocery and refusing the figs, plums, apples, et al. offered to him, concluding, "This was a lesson in pure realism. As you can see, there is not such a thing as a fruit, and I am not crazy." Nevertheless, in *Kromaattiset tasot* a few lines may be a criticism of pure realism, perhaps an invention of Satan:

> Everything is what one wants it to be.
> Everything is logical within my logical system.
> Strict solipsism coincides with "pure realism."
> The whole West is sleeping in the tight shell of solipsism
> and speculating in the pure language of science,
> and meanwhile the East comes and hollows out the flesh of the West
> unless it has not been entirely changed into language before
>   into a linguistic game.

Five editions, modified by the author, of *Tämä matka*, one of the best-known collections of modern poetry in Finland, had been printed by 1964; the last is considered definitive. This work also criticizes man's intellectual faculties. It opens with a description of a state of isolation and alienation from all natural, the fate of Western man, who "has lost everything but reason." The poet goes back to the most remote times, the Cambrian period in geology, and retells the history of life and the anguish of the alienated mind. The method is reminiscent of the reciting of a magic formula believed capable of destroying evil by describing it. Near the end of the collection the newly won union, communion with a "fourth dimension" especially represented for the poet by music, is described.[850] The language is no longer spontaneously mystic, but ceremonious in *Orfiset laulut* ('The Orphic Songs,' 1960), and the vocabulary proves the author's wide interests. Sources include the Book of Revelations, troubadour poetry, mysticism, and astrology. Her attention is not limited to truth and wisdom; *Strontium* is a prophetic warning against nuclear weapons. In the next collection, *Niin vaihtuivat vuoden ajat* ('So the Seasons Changed,' 1963),[851] she reverts to a simple style reflecting meditations in landscapes in a manner reminiscent of traditional Chinese poetry.

The motifs of the early collections reappear in the later *Kirjoitettu kivi* ('The Written Stone,' 1966), *Fahrenheit 121*, and *Jos suru savuaisi* ('If Smoke Would Rise out of Sorrow,' 1968), but many attest to her interest in contemporary events without centering around them. *Fahrenheit 121* mentions the war in Vietnam and the Arab-Israeli conflict but deals with quite different subjects. *Jos suru savuaisi* is dedicated "to my friend and colleague Václav Havel," who was brutalized by the secret police during the Russian invasion of Czechoslovakia.

Of Miss Manner's several plays, the first, *Eros ja Psykhe* ('Eros and Psyche,' 1959), is in verse. Others, such as *Uuden vuoden yö* ('New Year's Night,' 1965) and *Poltettu oranssi* ('Burnt Orange,' 1968), are more realistic, but not in the traditional manner.

After the modernists had established the poet's right to differ from tradition, those who followed were free to apply their methods.[852] The first collection, *Vedessä palaa* ('Fire in the Water,' 1954), of **Mirkka Rekola** (b. 1931) is in traditional, rhymed verse; its form and contents have been compared to those of Helvi Juvonen. However, the young critics liked Rekola's work.[853] In *Vedessä palaa* and *Tunnit* ('The Hours,' 1957) she uses hard, precise, and very personal images to express the struggles of an ego attempting to adjust to the world or reject it because of its flaws. The dualism disappears in later collections, *Syksy muuttaa linnut* ('Autumn Migrates the Birds,' 1960)[854] and *Ilo ja epäsymmetria* ('Joy and Asymmetry,' 1965), but the concentrated form still contains paradoxical combinations.

The first collection, *Klassilliset tunteet* ('Classical Feelings,' 1957), of **Maila Pylkkönen** (b. 1931) shows the influence of Haavikko and Manner but is quite personal. She has an open attitude toward nature reflected in lively, finely shaded poems. Later her poetic monologues received notice. They are a very personal form, in which characters give images of themselves with their seemingly trivial comments on ordinary matters. Such collections are *Arvo* ('The Value,' 1959), *Ilmaa / Kaikuu* ('Air / Echoes,' 1960), and *Valta* ('The Power,' 1962). Her collection of short stories, *Virheitä* ('Errors,' 1965), is closer to poetry than to traditional narrative.

Pertti Nieminen (b. 1929), an elementary school teacher, who learned Chinese through self-study (no institution in Finland offers studies in that language), has edited anthologies of Chinese literature, translated Chinese poetry, and written scholarly articles on the language, so that the public sometimes forgets that he is a good Finnish poet.[855] He often uses Chinese materials to build poems—in *Uurnat* ('The Urns,' 1958) poems have such titles as *Chinin herttua teetti maljan* ('The Duke of Chin Had a Bowl Made') and *Pan-shanin haudat* ('The Tombs of Pan-shan')—but they express his individual thoughts and feelings. Many are quiet meditations on nature sometimes expanded to melancholy thoughts about life and the world, e.g., in *Kivikausi* ('The Stone Age,' 1956) and *Päivät kuin nuolet* ('Days like Arrows,' 1961). His style changes in the collections *Silmissä maailman maisemat* ('The Landscapes of the World in the Eyes,' 1964) and *Rautaportista tulevat etelätuuli ja pohjoistuuli ja vihassa kaikki tuulet* ('From the Iron Gate Come the South Wind and the North Wind and in Their Wrath All the Winds,' 1968). They are composed of prose poems which present a surrealistic, absurd picture of a world which is somewhat frightening.

A number of the younger generation authors have written prose and poetry, for example, **Juha Mannerkorpi** (b. 1915), who first published three volumes of verse, *Lyhtypolku* (The Path of the Lanterns,' 1946), *Ehtoollinen lasikellossa* ('The Supper under the Bell Jar,' 1947),[856] and *Kylväjä lähti kylvämään* ('The Sower Went Forth to Sow,' 1954); *Runot 1945-1954* ('Poems 1945-1954') appeared in 1962. He is often described as a poet on the limit between traditional and new poetry; he has written rhymed verse, and he expresses his feelings in older forms. Critics have said that he most resembles Siljo, Sarkia, and Hellaakoski,[857] but we feel that he is more like Kailas than like Sarkia. He presents his dark, disconsolate, almost nightmarish vision of the world in concentrated images; his longest poem is the title poem of *Kylväjä lähti kylvämään*, which is built on the parable of the sower who went forth to sow (Matt. 13:4-8), but develops, quite apart from the Bible, into a protest by a seed which fell upon stony places or by the wayside, thus denied the possibility to grow. Most of his poems are not so explicit, for he seldom indicates the source of his anguished outlook.

Interested in existentialism, he wrote an introduction to his translation of Sartre's *La nausée*[858] that criticizied Sartre's theories, but he has expressed the existential torment that man is made so that he cannot be happy or that the world is made so that man cannot be happy in it. The only poems which express happiness are about love, e.g., the title poem from *Ehtoollinen lasikellossa*, which is among his most hermetic; the accompanying poems rather than its own text indicate that its subject is love. The motif of *Kirje* ('The Letter' in *Lyhtypolku*) reappears in Mannerkorpi's novel, *Matkalippuja kaikkiin juniin* ('Tickets to All Trains,' 1967): a letter a man has to take to a woman, who accepts it although he feared she would not. Seldom in his works do people communicate with each other; in his novels the problems of mistrust and loneliness are especially prominent.

Pentti Holappa (b. 1927) also published poetry first, then switched to prose. His first collection of poems, *Narri peilisalissa* ('The Jester in the Hall of Mirrors,' 1950), has a solemn, somewhat overwrought style, introducing literary figures such as Hamlet, Othello, Mephistopheles, a troubadour, and a jester with the effect of an attempt to show the vastness and importance of the matters.[859] *Maan poika* ('The Son of the Earth,' 1953) is equally majestic in style, but the concern is for the poet's personal problems; *Lähellä* ('Close By,' 1957) follows this line, stressing the importance of instincts, the subconscious, and the senses, but expresses fear and anguish as well as joy. *Katsokaa silmiänne* ('Look at Your Eyes,' 1959) is similar but subdued, hinting that Holappa has achieved, on an everyday level, a balance between his mental conflicts.

Tyyne Saastamoinen (maiden name of Tyyne Schimmerling, b. 1924) published three short-story collections, *Ikoni ja omena* ('The Icon and the Apple,' 1954), *Tulikukka* ('The Flower of Fire,' 1957), and *Vanha portti* ('The Old Gate,' 1959), before turning to poetry, but the prose of *Vanha portti* might be called prose poetry. Even stories following ordinary patterns of narration seem unusual, with much between the lines. She is the Finnish poet whose works are most surrealistic.[860] Her disconnected images convey fresh, unfettered impressions, but sometimes become mere mannerisms, e.g., in the poetry collections *Yön sarvet* ('The Horns of Night,' 1960), *Jääkausi* ('The Ice Age,' 1962), *Jokainen vuodenaika* ('Each Season,' 1963), *Olen lähtenyt kauas* ('I Am Going Far Away,' 1965), and *Vieras maa* ('A Strange Country,' 1969).

Pekka Lounela (b. 1932) has served as editorial secretary of *Parnasso*, written criticism, worked as stage director for a Helsinki theater and the drama department of the Finnish Broadcasting Corporation, published short humorous and satirical sketches in magazines (under the pseudonym Kala), described his European travels, and commented on social and political issues. He has also published three volumes of poetry: *Epätieto* ('Doubt,' 1954; the word is synthetic),[861] *Jos kielin voisi kertoa* ('If a Tongue They Had to Tell,' a quotation from an old, well-known poem, 1960), and *Asiaa* ('Facts,' 1964). The poems range from serious meditations on Lounela's own problems to satirical comments on contemporary events. One poem, notorious before it was published, could not be printed for a while because of alleged obscenity.[862]

Anselm Hollo (b. 1934), son of Juho A. Hollo, a professor of education at the University of Helsinki and chancellor of the School of Social Sciences, who was one of the foremost translators of work and fiction in Finland, inherited his father's interest in foreign languages. He has published English translations of works by Anhava, Haavikko, Hyry; and Saarikoski; Finnish translations of English, Spanish, and Russian works (sometimes with others); English translations of German and Russian works; and German translations of English and Russian works. He has also published original poetry, *Sateiden välillä* ('Between the Rains,' 1956) and *Trobar: löytää* ('Trobar: To Find,' 1964), which is Finnish post-1960 in nature. He speaks gayly about the everyday world and occasionally indulges in abstract, intellectual humor.

Kirsi Kunnas (maiden name of Kirsi Syrjä, b. 1924) has edited a series of children's books, *Aarteiden kirja* ('The Book of Treasures,' 1956-60), translated English nursery rhymes, Czech folk poems, and other works, and written *Tiitiäisen satupuu* ('Tiitiäinen's Story Tree,' 1956) and *Tiitiäisen tarinoita* ('Stories by Tiitiäinen,' 1957), stories and poems for children. She has also published serious poetry which has earned her the description of a moderate modernist, one of the few postwar poets whose art is reminiscent of the *Tulenkantajat* and Edith Södergran.[863] In *Uivat saaret* ('The Swimming Islands,' 1950) there is a contemplative attitude toward life and nature which changes into a more active search for human contact in *Tuuli nousee* ('The Wind Is Rising,' 1953) and *Vaeltanut* ('Wandered,' 1956).

After the new generation of poets had consolidated their positions in the 1950s, a different group appeared. The distant, refined, individual, metaphysical poetry of Anhava, Manner, and Nummi is no longer an ideal; Kai Laitinen says that poets no longer follow the lines of Anhava's *General Theories*, and they no longer avoid pacifists, orators, and female welfare workers.[864] At a meeting in Turku in 1962, Osmo Hormia, Arvo Salo, and others predicted the nature of the poetry of the 1960s; they believed or hoped it would be more communicative, if possible topical, and suited to conversion into songs. Poetry and art did develop along these lines; protest songs were written, set to music, and recorded, and happenings were organized even earlier than in other European countries.[865] Salo wrote a Brechtian opera, *Lapualaisooppera* ('The Lapua Opera') on a fascistlike movement in Finland in the 1930s.[866] However, not all of the new poetry is social and political, and certainly not all of it is for the masses. The poets are disrespectful and disruptive toward everything, including language, throwing on paper disconnected images, reflections, remarks, and extraneous materials, e.g., advertising slogans, newspaper headlines (collage technique). Enjoying new liberties of press, they sometimes write that which used to be considered obscene, and their work occasionally has the appearance of surrealism, dadaism, or American beat and postbeat verse.[867] In contrast to American rebels, however, they never express radicalism through personal appearance, drugs, or oriental religions. In Finland it was the respectable generation of modernists which had an interest in Chinese poetry and philosophy.

Pentti Saarikoski (b. 1937) is one of the most controversial poets, but his poetry, although free in form and disrespectful of traditional values, is not especially aggressive or shocking. His extremely bohemian public behavior has antagonized the older generation. Väinö Kirstinä, a young poet, has satirized the middle class who have transferred their dislike of Saarikoski to his poetry:

"If you read Saarikoski ten minutes your breath begins already to smell of liquor,"[868] and Kai Laitinen says that his name is like a "red rag" to many, alluding probably to Saarikoski's declaration of communism.[869]

His carefree first collections, *Runoja* (1958), *Toisia runoja* ('Other Poems,' 1958), and *Runot ja Hipponaksin runot* ('Poems and Poems by Hipponax,' 1959), deliberately irritated conservative critics with their style. Even when overbearing, Saarikoski is ironical about himself and melancholy about life. He says: "life has been given to man / so that he may carefully consider / in which position he wants to be dead." However, as Pekka Virtanen says, he could not endure "his permanent autumn, his endless death,"[870] and he shifted his attention to the world in *Maailmasta* ('About the World,' 1961) and *Mitä tapahtuu todella?* ('What Is Really Happening?,' 1962). The latter collection especially comments directly on contemporary political events; of its composition Saarikoski says: "I gathered various sentences from newspapers, from what people had said, from books—anywhere and built then new units from them and my own sentences; I described my way of writing as 'democratic' or 'dialectic,' since different opinions were free to fight each other in the work."[871] His compositions were still far from traditional political poems, and he did not feel at ease as a political poet. *Mitä tapahtuu todella?* has received both admiration and criticism, not only from conservative critics. Although he admits that Saarikoski is the leader of the most recent Finnish poetry, Pekka Virtanen declares that the collection lacks true life and fire and describes the present and even the past without turning to the future as true political verse should do.[872]

Saarikoski's change, however, was neither total nor permanent. *Kuljen missä kuljen* ('I Walk Where I Walk,' 1965) is more like his early work, and *Laulu laululta pois* ('Away Song by Song,' 1966) and *En soisi sen päättyvän* ('I Wish It Would Not End,' 1967) are about love, happy and unhappy, which has an important place in his last novels as well.

The first two collections, *Lakeus* ('The Plain,' 1961) and *Hitaat auringot* ('The Slow Suns,' 1963), of **Väinö Kirstinä** (b. 1936) are in the manner of the 1950s, but *Puhetta* ('Talk,' 1963) is different. Kirstinä also wrote two essays on children's nonsense rhymes, *Loruista lettrismiin* and *Näkyvien runojen koulukunta, lettrismi*, baroque poems shaped as objects, futurist, dadaist, lettrist, and concrete poetry,[873] thus indicating his ideas about the genre. His new poems were impure; he used words generally considered dirty, words associated for reasons of similarity, and possible and impossible quotations; one poem, a page from the Helsinki telephone directory, may be pop art.

His next collections, *Luonnollinen tanssi* ('A Natural Dance,' 1965) and *Pitkän tähtäyksen LSD-suunnitelma* ('Long-range LSD Planning,' 1967), less whimsical although free in form and thought, are more oriented toward daily reality. *LSD* is divided into sections numbered by the public library system; 0, subsection 01, *Reading Exercises* (for children) begins: "A was an Ashtray. – B was a Banana. – C was Cassius Clay who ate the Banana. . . . X was a Xenophobe who ate the Xylophone." There are remarks on more serious subjects, e.g., 6, *Economy and Technology*, and 67, *Agriculture and Connected Activities:*

> A Message to the Consumer. Buy a sausage.
> your money back
> if you are not happy at once.
>
> Who do you think you are anyway,
> be happy
> it is the duty of every citizen.
>
> Or else the inflation will come.

Superficially he protests a type of advertising, but in his manner he also protests a society which treats everyone like a child. He plays the role of a child who states truths without knowing how devastating they are. *Atomipompotusta* ('Atomic Bang-Bang'), a section of prose poems in *Luonnollinen tanssi*, is not a traditional protest against the atom bomb but a criticism of the atomic age, of a self-destructive, violent and commercial civilization, which is relevant on several levels. The poet describes a world he cannot regard seriously, a world so absurd that everyone has lost his sanity, or a world so horrible that, to preserve one's sanity, one must laugh.

Kirstinä is interested in French poetry; he has translated Baudelaire's *Le spleen de Paris,* and some of his poems are reminiscent in form and content of Jacques Prévert's work. Apollinaire's *Calligrammes* have inspired others, and one pretends to be a translation of a nonexistent poem by Villon. Jarry's *machine à décerveler* appears in one under a Finnish name. However, they all bear the mark of Kirstinä's individual, refreshing personality.

Matti Rossi (b. 1934) first studied in Helsinki but took his M.A. at the University of Pennsylvania. He worked in Great Britain and traveled as far as Latin America. He has translated Latin American poetry into Finnish and published essays and translations of Finnish poetry in Argentina and Mexico.[874] He has political ideas of protest rather than definite ideologies; in *Näytelmän henkilöt* ('The Characters in the Play,' 1965) a section called *From the European Zoo* presents critical portraits of Nikita Krushchev, Charles de Gaulle, the pope, and others, and another, *The Dang Pong Tree*, protests the war in Vietnam. His antipathies are directed against all violence and oppression. The last section of *Tilaisuus* ('The Occasion,' 1967) gives a series of images from the world today, including one of Red China, where the Red Guards are mistreating Revisionist Dog Mrs. Peng Tsen; the disapproving poet implies that, although "anything might happen, nothing happens." The collection includes sections on Finnish politics and Hannu Salama, a Finnish author prosecuted for allegedly blasphemous passages in one of his books. They are not rhymed newspaper articles but poems of freely associated images often calculated to produce an absurd effect. His last collection, *Käännekohta* ('The Turning Point,' 1968), deals with events of 1968 in Czechoslovakia, which produced immediate strong reaction in Finland.

Besides politics and morals, Rossi's major interest is love. *Leikkejä kahdelle* ('Games for Two,' 1966) may mark the beginning of the era in Finnish literary life during which writers are no longer prosecuted for obscenity. For an open-minded reader the book is a frank picture of an aspect of life which interests the author, which he finds beautiful, and which we find beautiful.

Jyrki Pellinen (b. 1940) also represents the poetry of the 1960s. His first collection, *Näistä asioista* ('About These Things,' 1962), shows Haavikko's influence but also reveals that he has a very personal vision of the world and an individual manner of describing it. Even friendly critics have said that the structure of his poems can be confusing, the significant elements almost nonexistent, and the poems themselves verbal performances. Haavikko called his poem *Talvipalatsi* a "journey through the known language," and critics have said that Pellinen's works are "journeys in the world of language" and his sentences the "image of a metaphor."[875] Pellinen has probably pushed the dislocation of language further than has any other young poet; he sometimes builds images from sentences which do not follow basic rules of grammar, e.g., in *Kuuskajaskari* (name, 1964) "black ivy adorns the wall, because of her skirt this woman has loved anybody." A review of *Niin päinvastoin kuin kukaan* ('So on the Contrary than Nobody,' 1965) stated that the poet is more interested in the verbal forms that he can give facts than in the facts themselves.[876] *Toisin sanoen kuuntelet* ('In Other Words, You Are Listening,' 1969) is closer to ordinary verbal expression and meditative in tone.

Easier to appreciate are the poems which take the form of humorous essays, such as *Kirjallisuuden muodosta* ('On the Form of Literature') and *Mitä moderni arkkitehtuuri ansaitsee* ('What Modern Architecture Deserves') in *Kuuskajaskari*, although they are no more logically constructed than the others. Some of the short poems in *Tässä yhteiskunnassa on paha nukkua* ('You Cannot Sleep Well in This Society,' 1966), though free in composition, have a somewhat traditional lyrical atmosphere. Some lightly drawn images from nature combine with slightly melancholy thoughts in impressionistic flashes which seem to fade before read. Pellinen's novel, *Nuoruuteni ilmastot* ('The Climates of My Youth,' 1965), is scarcely less unconventional than his poems.

Kari Aronpuro (b. 1940) falls between Pellinen's subjectivity and Rossi's and Kirstinä's political attitudes. He and Arvo Ahlroos made his first collection, *Peltiset enkelit* ('The Tin Angels,' 1964), into a television movie titled *Pohjoinen Guernica* ('The Northern Guernica') produced in 1966. It contains lengthy enumerations of facts strung together without comment but in a manner suggestive of the author's critical attitude toward the contemporary world. A reviewer said that he collected his facts "from the dumps created by the modern way of living."[877] This stylistic device is apparent in his novel *Aperitiff—avoin kaupunki* ('Aperitiff—An Open City,' 1965), whereas *Terveydeksi* ('Your Health,' 1966) is openly satirical of a number of social and political situations in Finland and elsewhere. Writers who take themselves too seriously are included; one poem, *Kirjailija tässä maailmassa* ('The Writer in This World'), is presented as a public lecture by an author.

Poetry has remained extremely popular in Finland, and many young poets have recently published interesting collections, but the only thing one can say is that they follow individual directions and do not submit to schools or ideologies.

In postwar prose there has been no clear trend, no sudden break with the past, no great discussion of new theories and methods, and no opposition between generations; of course, many older writers have ceased writing. Controversial books have been traditional in form, with content the focus of the argument. In 1960 Pentti Holappa stated that at that time it was impossible "to speak of a new prose and to mean by that some kind of a dominating, leading trend."[878] It is now evident, however, that the best contemporary writers view and describe the world in a manner unlike that of older writers, and some of the youngest have discarded the traditional form of the narrative. Contemporary prosaists share an objective, matter-of-fact method of description. They have dissociated themselves from their books by withholding their comments and opinions from the reader, and they do not present social, moral, or political messages. Their common characteristics are rather general, for they do not describe the same world. Hyry and Haavikko present seemingly meaningless everyday life, Mannerkorpi chooses the workings of suffering, distorted minds, and Meri presents absurd sequences of events. There seems to be more attention to the craft of fiction than was given before; the dislocation of the traditional form of narrative, e.g., in Korpela's and Holappa's works, seems to be imposed by the subject rather than dictated by the author's individual fantasies.

The most famed postwar prosaist is **Väinö Linna** (b. 1920), whose war novel, *Tuntematon sotilas* ('The Unknown Soldier,' 1954), an immediate sensation, produced violent polemics in the press and sold in unprecedented numbers. Translated into several languages, it was successful only in the

Scandinavian countries, primarily Sweden. It has been made into a movie, a play, and an opera.[879] Its readers, who are slightly fewer than the Finns who fought in the war, have in many cases read it as a collection of good stories from the front, some funny, some serious, sustained as a novel by the device of centering all events around a single platoon, a group of men drafted shortly before the war.[880]

Linna, the son of a butcher, worked as a factory mechanic before he began to write, and his novel is among the few serious war novels written by a private from a private's point of view; most books in which simple soldiers appear in the foreground are written by educated people.[881] The work is full of yarns, jokes, colorful language, humorous situations, and strange characters, but the author's seriousness of purpose, criticizing the Finnish war of 1941-44 in particular, and war in general, involves the descriptions of men's reactions in conflict conditions and the explosion of some national myths.

Linna has read and expressed his views on many subjects. He especially approves Tolstoy's philosophy of history, one of his favorite writers, but his works do not contain Tolstoy's ideological preaching. Linna often presents the text of a rhetorical, idealistic speech or proclamation, then contrasts it to a description of the brutal or unrefined reality to which it refers, one of his mannerisms which has made him controversial. Opposed to the policies which led to the war, and the aim of the Finnish government in that war, he was attacked by all who found the conflict a simple struggle for survival in which everyone had a patriotic duty to participate. Actually, because of the nature of the characters, *The Unknown Soldier* rarely rises to such a general level, and the patriotism of his men is unquestionable, for all, even one who voices communistic ideas, fight bravely. But they never do anything without griping, as one of them says, annoying Linna's critics, who charged him with undermining the morale and discipline of the army, distorting the picture of the Finnish fighting men, and debasing patriotic ideals. The controversy was resolved when it was decided that Linna had written a great patriotic novel.[882] The strength of the book is its weakness: it renders in vivid, faithful manner the characters and situations. It never goes beyond this traditional realistic manner, and its interest is in the events rather than in a personal vision of them.

Resentment and *aggression* are words often used in discussions of Linna.[883] After finishing *The Unknown Soldier*, he attempted to show why he and his characters were so critical in the trilogy *Täällä Pohjantähden alla* (1959-62),[884] which covers three generations from 1884 to the present. The purpose is to explain the causes of the Civil War, which ends at the closing of the second volume. The narrative then disintegrates into a series of disconnected scenes from daily life. The effect may be calculated to illustrate

Linna's Tolstoyan philosophy that great changes occur slowly, almost unnoticeably, in spite of man's intentions.[885]

Täällä Pohjantähden alla is presented from the point of view of the poorest people in a small west Finnish village. The central character is occasionally the pastor or a wealthy landowner, but more often a member of a family of agricultural tenants. The problem of the lease of farmland is demonstrated again, now in light of subsequent events and without idealization. As in *The Unknown Soldier,* Linna shows that the patriotic ideals of the upper classes are remote to those whose main concern is the finding of daily bread, and that these ideals are sometimes used to obscure selfish interests. To protect themselves against high rents and the landowners' right to evict them at will, tenants in many parts of the country organized strikes and demonstrations often blocked by the police. The tenants replied to the charge of betraying national unity before the Russian oppression that national unity was not synonomous with the financial interests of landowners. These events prior to the Civil War, the war, and the building of a new Finnish republic appear in Linna's book. Although the author sides with the poor, he does not romanticize them; Civil War questions, however, remain controversial in Finland, and his treatment of them produced another polemic, which also brought this book great success.[886] Like *The Unknown Soldier*, it derives strength from the description of simple characters, groups engaged in common action, violence, and suffering. The events are related in chronological order in a simple, straightforward style, so that the interest is in the facts and the author's opinions, not in the method of narration.

Before his successful books Linna published *Päämäärä* ('The Goal,' 1947) and *Musta rakkaus* ('Dark Love,' 1948), two novels which deal with individual problems. After he became engrossed in social and political matters, he transcribed all his thoughts on them, then seemed exhausted.[887] He has, in a sense, made himself a national monument, isolating himself from the mainstream of contemporary Finnish literature, which he has often criticized for "its empty formalism and lack of interest in serious subjects."[888] It seems that his public image has paralyzed his creative power and that he ought to change it in order to be able to write again.

None of the many other war novels and short stories has achieved the fame of *The Unknown Soldier* except, perhaps, *Ystäviä ja vihollisia* (1954; tr. *Friends and Enemies*, 1957) by **Jussi Talvi** (pseudonym of **Yrjö Johannes Talvio**, b. 1920). It deals as much with the moral problems of war as with fighting and examines the relations between the Finns and the Germans, which were not as consistently good as they were officially stated to be. A previous novel, *Kivikasvoinen jumala* ('The Stone-Faced God,' 1947; the title is similar to that of Aila Meriluoto's poem *Kivinen Jumala*), discusses how God can allow war to happen. Talvi has since published several novels on serious subjects which are average in quality.

Martti Larni (b. 1909), who has worked for newspapers and publishers, lived a few years after World War II in Wisconsin. He wrote a satire on contemporary life, especially in the United States, *Neljäs nikama* ('The Fourth Vertebra,' 1957), which, although unremarkable, was noticed by the Russians, who translated it and adapted it for the stage. It was a huge success in the Soviet Union, which the author did not expect.[889] Like Talvi, Larni has written a number of uninteresting works.

Paavo Rintala (b. 1930) belongs to the generation who did not participate in the war, but, like Linna, he has an interest in war and violence, takes his subjects from recent history, and tends to insert moral and religious comments in his books.[890] One, a romanticized biography in three parts of Field Marshal Mannerheim, *Mummoni ja Mannerheim* ('My Granny and Mannerheim,' 1960), *Mummoni ja marsalkka* ('My Granny and the Field Marshal,' 1961), and *Mummon ja marskin tarinat* ('The Tales of My Granny and the Field Marshal,' 1962), aroused controversy by its imagination of the thoughts of this famed character which did not correspond to the public image of the national hero. The "granny" is probably a fictitious character who has nothing to do with the field marshal. The author shows the great events of the time reflected in the lives of an aristocrat and officer and a simple woman. He probably wished to show that this woman and Mannerheim had much in common, for he stresses Mannerheim's understanding of ordinary soldiers. Obviously Rintala admires Mannerheim, but he endows him with human weaknesses and an insensibility toward suffering and death which a soldier must possess, emphasizing the latter rather heavily in a description of his attitude toward the Reds.

Sissiluutnantti ('Lieutenant of the Commandos,' 1963) also produced argument. The main character is much like the tough heroes of modern spy and adventure stories, and he has a number of realistically described affairs with members of the Women's Auxiliary Corps. Former members of the corps angrily testified that none of them (in 1943 they numbered approximately 150,000) had ever had improper relations with a man, and a history of the corps soon appeared to prove it.[891] The book is set at the front of the last war, and the theme is the glorification of the perfect killer and superman who is permitted everything and feels contempt toward the men in his own army who belong to the common crowd; but this aspect of the book went by unnoticed in spite of the great number of people who read it.

Rintala's aristocratic attitude is apparent in many books. *Palvelijat hevosten selässä* ('The Servants upon Horses,' 1964; the title is from Ecclesiastes 10:7), which describes the defeat of an honest man in the tough, modern world, demonstrates that people who are born servants should not reach leading positions.[892] In *Pikkuvirkamiehen kuolema* ('The Death of a Small Official,' 1959), which continues the lives of the boys living in Oulu during the war, who are described in *Pojat* ('The Boys,' 1958), the main character remarks, "The wish to succeed in life killed everything in us and made us into good members of a democracy, the slaves of modern times: the contact with God, religious feeling, was completely suppressed. . . ." Rintala identifies democracy with the hectic struggle for a higher standard of living typical of the contemporary world; he would prefer a world in which men with true aristocratic spirit would be freed from the necessity to work so that they could engage in lovemaking, hunting, war, art, and philosophical meditation. Nostalgic dreams about good old times when gentlemen were gentlemen and servants servants are common in countries older than Finland; their being dreamed there may be a sign of a "ripe" society.[893]

Rintala has written a number of other books and some plays. His latest works are meditations which he calls "reports" on God, nature, love, music, and similar subjects collected in *Sukeltaja* ('The Diver,' 1965) and *Keskusteluja lasten kanssa* ('Conversations with Children,' 1965).

Leo Kalervo (pseudonym of **Leo Kalervo Eklin**, b. 1924) writes heavy, meditative prose, sometimes like that of Pekkanen, which is concerned with the fate of the individual in the modern world. In one of his novels, *Pelivara* ('The Limit,' 1961), the main character reflects that, although people no longer need to fear hunger, they are afraid about how they will make it in life. *Pyörille rakennettu* ('Built on Wheels,' 1958) is about the owner of a trucking company who gives up the murderous competition which would ruin him as well as his family.

Marko Tapio (pseudonym of **Marko Vihtori Tapper**, b. 1924) has written on many subjects. *Aapo Heiskasen viikatetanssi* ('Aapo Heiskanen's Dance with the Scythe,' 1956) is considered his most interesting novel. Heiskanen contemplates suicide, but "life eventually outwits him."[894] The brooding style with repetition and symbolic motifs is not easy to read but is meaningful and effective. *Korttipelisatu* ('A Tale of Playing Cards,' 1958) is light and witty, whereas *Terassi* ('The Terrace,' 1962) is an ambitious description of the problems of a writer who is planning to divorce; parts of the novel he is working on are interspersed with the narration.

The first of his planned tetralogy, *Arktinen hysteria* ('Arctic Hysteria,' a phrase sometimes used to describe the mood induced by the long, dark, cold fall and winter),[895] appeared in 1967 as *Vuoden 1939 ensilumi* ('The First Snow of 1939'). The second, *Sano todella rakastatko minua* ('Tell the Truth: Do You Love Me?'), was published in 1968. Tapio shows the Finnish character, picturing Finnish society from the end of the nineteenth century to the present. Although the project was enormous, critics agree that it is interesting. Some readers, however, have protested Tapio's antitraditional views.

Veikko Huovinen (b. 1927) is considered a humorist because of his popular novel *Havukka-ahon ajattelija* ('The Thinker of Havukka-aho'). The main character, a homemade philosopher, has been living in the backwoods but has been thinking about the world. When two scientists come to survey his home region, he voices his opinions, a mixture of horse sense and nonsense. The theme is not new even in Finland, but the book is well written; it was eventually adapted as a play.

Huovinen's later books are somewhat humorous, but satire predominates, and some contain sections which express pessimism. *Rauhanpiippu* ('The Peace Pipe,' 1956), a satire on war, may be Finland's only successful pacifist book; it is similar to a folktale with specific reference to neither country nor time. The main character, a typical folk hero, pretends to be stupid although he is sly and saves his life in a future conflict by playing the fool and tricking people in high positions. *Hamsterit* ('The Hamsters,' 1957) is a humorous description of winter life in the North, but *Talvituristi* ('The Winter Tourist,' 1965) is pessimistic about man. Some parts are symbolistic, as are sections of *Lemmikkieläin* ('The Pet,' 1966), in which the pet is a human.

Lauri Leskinen (b. 1918) began writing modest descriptions of ordinary life in the country. He became known through *Läpikäytävä* ('The Corridor,' 1962) and *Kunniakuja* ('The Guard of Honor,' 1966), traditional realistic plays with attractive seriousness and honesty. There are still few playwrights in Finland, and their works are unassuming realistic descriptions of daily life with interest in the message rather than in the form; Paavo Haavikko and Eeva-Liisa Manner are not properly playwrights, and their few dramatic works, despite literary merit, have not been successful on the stage. **Reino Lahtinen** (b. 1918) indicates the modesty of his plays in their titles; his major plays are *Vain ihmisiä* ('Only People,' 1958) and *Arvottomat* ('The Worthless,' 1959). The drama of **Lauri Kokkonen** (b. 1918) is no more pretentious; *Hopeinen kynttilänjalka* ('The Silver Candlestick,' 1958) and *Laahus* ('The Train of the Dress,' 1958) deal with contemporary events, and *Viimeiset kiusaukset* ('The Last Temptations,' 1960) treats the life of Paavo Ruotsalainen, the revivalist leader of Runeberg's time in whom Aho was interested.

Although prose did not suddenly break with tradition after the war, a new manner of writing was slowly developing. Two very general trends are evident: the introduction of the unreal in the narrative which gives it an incoherent, broken form—the implication is that the world is viewed by a disintegrating personality—and total realism without comment from the author. In the latter the message seems to be that life is largely meaningless, that all its events are equally important or unimportant so that the authors are indifferent to what they describe. This quality, however, typical of the Finns, does not seem to produce depression, anguish, or pessimism in them. Their general attitude is one of cheerful resignation, similar to the mood at the end of *Täällä Pohjantähden alla*.

One of the first writers to deviate from traditional patterns was **Jorma Korpela** (1910-64), a deeply religious man whose father, Simo, was a well-known religious poet. He participated in the war, which made a permanent impression on him. All of his four novels do not deal with the war, but the conflict and its consequences appear in them. War revealed for Korpela the opposing forces in the soul of man and forced him to face moral problems. *Martinmaa, mieshenkilö* ('A Man Called Martinmaa,' 1948) is about an idealist who tries to help people but makes things worse; Korpela shows his self-analysis and the recognition that we usually do not know the ultimate motives for our actions. *Tohtori Finckelman* ('Doctor Finckelman,' 1952) is his most decisive break with literary tradition. A psychiatrist in a provincial city describes himself. On one level the book satirizes life in such a town, but the doctor derives from his profession the feeling of a Doctor Faustus who knows the town's secrets and can control the inhabitants' lives. The more he is convinced of his power, the more his relations to other people and the world deteriorate, and he loses contact with reality. The narrative becomes more and more unreal; in fact, "the novel itself is the world which breaks up."[896] *Tunnustus* ('The Confession,' 1960) is more conventional, for the characters are more normal, but the situation is not ordinary. Here, as in *Kenttävartio* ('The Outpost,' published posthumously in 1964), the author examines the moral problems created by war from the point of view of the individual who feels responsibility for his actions. An officer tormented by the knowledge that he has sent a subordinate to death during the war, although he is not held responsible, tries in peacetime to make amends to the dead man's family. The nondramatic solution, typical of Korpela, is not the outcome the officer expected.

Juha Mannerkorpi, discussed above as a poet, has translated, in addition to Sartre, Malraux, Camus, and Beckett. His characters seldom try to relate their actions to religious or other moral criteria, and they do not illustrate metaphysical or philosophical problems. Mannerkorpi rejects existentialism mainly on artistic grounds, but metaphysics is implicit in his books. His characters wonder about their relations to others, the consequences of their actions, and the meaning or lack of it in the problems they create for themselves.

His first prose works were *Avain* ('The Key,' 1955; defined as a monologue in the subtitle), the short-story collection *Sirkkeli* ('The Circular Saw,' 1956), and the novel *Jyrsijät* ('The Rodents,' 1958), which tells the undramatic story of an unhappy marriage from the point of view of the husband, who eventually wonders whether or not he is indirectly guilty of his child's death by subconsciously wishing for it. The book does not answer his questions, but concentrates upon the opposing personality types, those of the man and wife. Unlike *Jyrsijät, Vene lähdössä* ('The Boat Is Leaving,' 1961)

373

describes only the actions and conversations of the characters in a manner somewhat reminiscent of Hyry's novels. A family is leaving in a motorboat, but they cannot immediately start the engine. Bystanders comment, and the boat eventually leaves. The function of the narration is the description of the differing reactions to the same trivial situation.

Jälkikuva ('The Lingering Image,' 1965), written after the author had suffered a personal loss, shows a person in his situation who overcomes his sorrow. His moods and actions are often presented through his surroundings rather than through direct description. *Matkalippuja kaikkiin juniin* reverts to Mannerkorpi's early style. A first-person narrator relates memories from his childhood and youth and his present actions. His past is made up of traumatic sexual experiences, and the unreal present is taken up by the writing of a letter which is finally received with understanding by a woman. The novel is a description of a neurotic personality and, perhaps, an analysis of literary work.

Although **Veijo Meri** (b. 1928) is known as an author of the new generation, his style and language are traditional. His contents rather than his form are new. The son of a noncommissioned officer in the Civil War and subsequent conflicts who rose to lieutenant in World War II, Meri spent his childhood in garrison towns and belonged to the generation which had been taught "to die for the country on land, on sea, and in the air,"[897] although he was too young to fight himself. Most of his works are about individuals in the war and army, but are not traditional war fiction or political protests against war. He often contrasts war's irrationality with the superficially regimented character of military life, but he does write stories about civilian life with the same characteristics, contrasts which reflect his general view of the world. In his preface to *Manillaköysi* he says: "I had to . . . map my past and the past of the community to which I belonged, and, as it was directly and indirectly connected with the war, I had to write about the war. It has of course been my intention . . . to show how war, with all its dramatic qualities, is also haphazard, repetitious, easily forgotten, and small. . . . War is made by man, and it reveals in him many characteristics and possibilities which also, of course, appear in peacetime, but which can first be seen in wartime in such a general shape and so clearly that they cannot be forgotten and explained."[898]

Two peculiarities in Meri's works stand out: long stories told by the characters often interrupt the narration, and characters sometimes wander off, later returning and noticing that everything is going on as it did before. One of his most recent works, *Yhden yön tarinat* ('The Stories of One Night,' 1967), consists mainly of stories told by characters. In *Sujut* ('Quits,' 1961) a noncommissioned officer who has fought bravely during a disorderly retreat is left on the enemy's side when a bridge is blown up. He does get back to his side but is nearly shot by his own men in doing so, decides in disgust that he is quits with the army, and goes home. He does not resist when the authorities arrest him and send him back to the front, where an officer toying with a pistol tells him to dig a grave. He does so, but the officer then says that he (the officer) has no right to shoot him and sends him back to his unit for court-martial. Although details in Meri's works are improbable, the improbable is quite realistic, especially in war. He describes absurd behavior and situations, but his narratives do not have the unreal quality of the works of Ionesco and Beckett; they have more affinity to those of Pinter, Grass, and Gogol.[899] His main characters are often energetic, intelligent, courageous men who try to remain cool in the midst of disorder and to set things straight, but discover that their efforts are useless. At this point they walk away; their return occurs when they see that the rest of the world is also crazy.

There is humor in Meri's works,[900] but its context is so far from funny that it could be called by the common term *black*. He has called some of the greatest writers humorists (Boccaccio, Gogol, Kafka, Rabelais, Swift, and Kivi) and has said that "humor is a serious thing. Dictators know it, when they reward the best jokes with death." He also says that "it is a bad mistake to think that an imperfect tragedy is humor. A hundred percent tragedy is humor. When a man [Chaplin] is timid and weak and cannot run very well and, in spite of that, is beaten and chased, that is humor."[901]

Meri is a prolific writer. Many of the short stories in *Ettei maa viheriöisi* ('So That the Earth Might Not Be Green,' 1954), the novels *Manillaköysi* (1957; tr. *The Rope*, 1964), *Vuoden 1918 tapahtumat* ('The Events of the Year 1918,' 1960), *Tukikohta* ('The Base,' 1964), and the play *Sotamies Jokisen vihkiloma* ('Private Jokinen on Leave to Get Married,' 1965) deal with war, whereas military life in peacetime appears in the novels *Irralliset* ('The Rootless,' 1959), *Everstin autonkuljettaja* ('The Colonel's Cardriver,' 1966), and *Yhden yön tarinat*. The short-story collection *Tilanteita* ('Situations,' 1962) and the novels *Peiliin piirretty nainen* ('A Woman Drawn on a Mirror,' 1962), *Suku* ('The Family,' 1968), and *Sata metriä korkeat kirjaimet* ('Letters Hundred Meters High,' 1969), which he describes as "dialogue short stories," have subjects from civilian life.

Antti Hyry (b. 1931) may be the most original of Finnish writers, but his originality comes from his commonplace manner of describing ordinary situations. Pentti Holappa says that Hyry's works are close to poetry because his images are without commentary: "I think that he observes the world and limits himself in many respects to an enumeration of facts, but the sum of the facts then runs as by itself into the mold of images."[902] They have been compared to Alain Robbe-Grillet's objective registration of facts, but similarity between the two authors is slight. Hyry received a degree in electronic engineering from the Helsinki Institute of Technology. Both his technical studies and literary style seem due to a practical mind, and many of his works include descriptions of work or physical activity. The work is always manual and simple so that results are immediate. Born in the country, Hyry has retained a close relation to nature and natural activities. He has preserved faith in man's abilities, but he protests indirectly the complex world created by modern technology.[903]

Kaivonteko ('Digging the Well' in Junamatkan kuvaus ja neljä muuta novellia, 1962) does no more than describe the successful digging of a well by two men unskilled at such work. The novel Maailman laita ('The Edge of the World,' 1967) is about a fishing trip in which a boat drifts away but is recovered in good condition the next day. Neither the story nor the novel is interrupted with improbable incidents or is used to show frustration; Hyry seems to feel that the success of careful work is as important. He presents the characters' thoughts, which are not always superficial, so casually that they are hardly noticeable. Maailman laita begins: "The seashore is like the edge of the world, he thought. The hard and relatively warm crust of the earth ends there and the water begins, with no trees or houses on it. He wondered why this was giving him a kind of unpleasant feeling." Later there is a long, confused though basically correct passage about nuclear reactions in the sun which ends with the main character's reflection that it is strange to think that, while these tremendous processes are going on, human life depends on very small things. Other passages in this and other books reveal that Hyry is not indifferent to religion.[904] The same character also misquotes the Bible: "The foxes have holes and the birds of the air have nests, but man maketh shacks"; the words are intended as serious criticism of human activities.

Hyry describes children in some books. The main character of Kevättä ja syksyä ('Spring and Fall,' 1958) is a small boy in northern Finland; Kotona ('At Home,' 1960) and Alakoulu ('The Lower Grades,' 1965) are autobiographical novels. In other books characters think nostalgically of their childhoods. Here Hyry expresses most directly his opinions of life; he sees childhood and youth as the period of full, direct experience of the world, the capacity for which man later loses.[905] Hyry feels that those things which are really important are generally considered too trivial to mention.

Paavo Haavikko, whose poetry has been mentioned, also has written prose. Critics and the public received his plays, Münchhausen (1960) and Nuket ('The Puppets,' 1960), which are similar to his poetry, with bewilderment. In Nuket Gogol's characters come to life and discuss matters with their creator. Münchhausen takes its title from a German nobleman of the eighteenth century known for his fantastic lies and tall tales, which are still read in Germany and Scandinavia, but has little in common with this character. Audun ja jääkarhu ('Audun and the Polar Bear,' 1967)[906] tells of a man who is lucky because he always tells the truth. It reproduces the atmosphere and style of an old Icelandic saga in simple language; one of its morals is that truthfulness is so rare that a consistently honest man is lucky because people assume that the simple truths he states have hidden meaning.

The style of Haavikko's fiction is similar to that of Hyry's, but the point of view is different. His novels and stories describe unimportant individuals and meaningless actions in a dry, colorless manner, conveying a pessimistic view of a world in which such individuals exist and such actions happen. *Yksityisiä asioita* (1960) is about a man who regards the political events of 1918 as an occasion for business deals. *Toinen taivas ja maa* ('Another Heaven and Earth,' 1961) is about the break-up of a marriage. *Vuodet* ('The Years,' 1962) is about a derelict on the lowest level of society. The author seems to observe these people as a scientist observes small animals which are part of his world.

Lasi Claudius Civiliksen salaliittolaisten pöydällä ('The Glass on the Table of Claudius Civilis's Conspirers,' 1964), a short-story collection, is concerned with more directly meaningful social situations. The cryptic title refers to a Rembrandt painting; a character says that some facts are "like a detail in a painting, of which we do not know the size. Let us say the glass on the table. . . ." Many of the stories do not give more than a few such details. Although *Lumeton aika* ('The Snowless Time') is about a political struggle in an imaginary communist-dominated Finland, we are not told what the struggle is about. *Arkkitehti* ('The Architect') is about a man who is successful although he criticizes the contemporary world; the author approves of his criticism but disapproves of the ease with which the architect adjusts to existing social conditions. In Haavikko's prose, as in his poetry, individual motifs become social, but social questions receive personal treatment.

Pentti Holappa, another poet, has published in recent years only prose, including a volume of essays on modern French literature, *Tuntosarvilla* ('Using One's Feelers,' 1963). With another poet, Olli-Matti Ronimus, he has translated Jarry, Robbe-Grillet, Sarraute, and Simon. He spent a long time as the Paris correspondent of the largest Finnish newspaper, on which he has become a noted political columnist. His first prose, the short-story collection *Peikkokuninkaat* ('The Kings of the Trolls,' 1952) and the novel *Yksinäiset* ('Alone,' 1954), describes individuals who, because of difficulties in communicating, make intense efforts to emerge from isolation. The style is traditional, but successive works have more unreal elements. Holappa has probably experimented more deliberately than other writers of his time with new forms of prose, but he has few followers.

The short stories of *Muodonmuutoksia* ('Metamorphoses,' 1959) are based on fantastic motifs: a dog learns to speak and fly, a man goes to the land of the centaurs; most of the metamorphoses have tragic ends. In the novels *Tinaa* ('Tin,' 1961) and *Perillisen ominaisuudet* ('The Qualities of an Heir,' 1963), his "sabotage of reality" is accomplished through other means.

377

Both begin on a real level and become more and more unreal.[907] The respectable middle-class family of *Tinaa* slowly breaks up, but the treatment of this traditional motif emphasizes the lack of meaningful quality in middle-class life and the destructive factors in the minds of the family, which are expressed in concrete but incoherent and absurd actions much in the manner of the theater of the absurd. The conflict between generations, a major motif in *Tinaa*, appears in other works, e.g., the play *Matti ja Maija* (1967), for which Holappa received the prize of the Helsinki City Theater. It is part of the pattern in *Perillisen ominaisuudet*, in which a young worker, chosen to be educated as director of his company, develops the necessary qualities for an heir to a large company but uses them against the establishment.

Of **Lassi Nummi**'s few prose works, the novel *Maisema* (The Landscape,' 1949) is known as the most interesting. In it a man is parachuted into an unknown land where he experiences everything he sees as new and strange, although it may not be unusual. The stories in *Ristikot* ('The Iron Bars,' 1952) resemble prose poems; the author calls some of them "etchings." *Runoilijan kalenteri* ('A Poet's Calendar,' 1968) is a collection of thoughts on questions from everyday incidents to literature, art, and music. A second volume followed in 1969.

Marja-Leena Mikkola, a Finnish writer, once complained of the unfair treatment given her sex by critics who speak of men as "writers" and women as "women writers."[908] Actually a number of woman writers in Finland have been criticized for their ideas, not for their sex, but traditional roles for the sexes are still accepted in Finland, as they are elsewhere; these were the target of Mrs. Mikkola's attack. Of course, the differences between the sexes produce different behavioral patterns best described by those to whom they are natural; therefore, a woman who describes women should not be considered less important than a man who describes men. In Finland there are a number of female writers whose works share only this trait of centering around women.

Eila Pennanen (maiden name of Eila Jaskari, b. 1916), one of the few writers of her generation to change with the times, began to write during the war and altered her style later. She is one of the foremost contemporary prosaists, for her change was natural, the result of her intellectual awareness rather than an effort to be fashionable. One of the best contemporary translators in Finland, she has published more than thirty translations, some with her former husband Juhani, mainly from English (Austen, Murdoch, Forster, Capote, Nabokov, et al.) and Swedish.

Her first novels, *Ennen sotaa oli nuoruus* ('Before the War There Was Youth,' 1942), *Kaadetut pihlajat* ('The Felled Rowan Trees,' 1944), *Proomu lähtee yöllä* ('The Barge Is Leaving at Night,' 1945), and *Leda ja joutsen* ('Leda and the Swan,' 1948), are characterized by contrast between realistic elements and refined artistic symbolism.[909] Two historic novels, *Pyhä Birgitta* ('Saint Bridget,' 1954) and *Valon lapset* ('The Children of Light,' 1958), form a transition between these and her later works. Unlike traditional historical novels, they center around individuals rather than adventure or setting. These individuals have both strong practical or worldly interests and deep religious feelings. Saint Bridget, widow of a Swedish nobleman and mother of eight, is engaged in religious activities, e.g., an attempt to persuade the pope to return to Rome from Avignon and the organization of a religious order, which eventually led to her canonization. The main character of *Valon lapset,* a member of the Society of Friends in seventeenth-century England, becomes a successful businessman.[910] Although the author treats him with mild satire and humor, the end is edifying.

She retains this mildly critical but understanding attitude toward her characters in the short stories of *Tornitalo* ('The High-rise Building,' 1952), *Pasianssi* ('The Solitaire,' 1957), and *Kaksin* ('Twosome,' 1961), and the novels *Mutta* ('But,' 1963), *Mongolit* ('The Mongols,' 1966), and *Tilapää* (a nonexistent word derived from a real one, e.g., 'Temporar' from Eng. *temporary,* 1968). These ordinary contemporary characters are often insecure, bewildered, and unaware of their real motivations, which are revealed during the narratives. Like many other Finnish writers today, Eila Pennanen uses the art of understatement, describing seemingly uneventful circumstances. She keeps that part of her early traditional manner which skillfully brings out a psychological trait in a character.

Eeva Joenpelto (maiden name of Eeva Helleman, b. 1921) has published novels written in a concise, matter-of-fact style which avoids author's intrusions, emotional overtones, and psychological analysis of the characters. Nevertheless it is easy to see which characters and actions she approves. In many respects close to traditional narratives about popular life, *Kaakerholman kaupunki* ('The Town of Kaakerholma,' 1950), which describes working-class surroundings, embodies these characteristics.[911] Many of her books are set in the country, but they are not specifically about country life. *Johannes vain* ('Only Johannes,' 1952), which made her known, is about a modest owner of a country store who leaves his business and wife to live close to nature, in protest against soulless modern life, an attitude common among Finnish writers in the 1950s. The somewhat similar *Kivi palaa* ('The Stone Is Burning,' 1953) is about a worker and his family.

Her next novel, *Neito kulkee vetten päällä* ('The Maid Is Walking on the Waters,' 1955; the title is from a folksong in the book), introduces new motifs. Neither romantic nor sentimental, it tells the story of a young woman of modest origin who, in becoming part of a large family, is received reluctantly. She accepts many disappointments, but through energy and common sense gains a place in the home and becomes its head when the old mother dies. This novel and its sequel, *Kipinöivät vuodet* ('The Sparkling

379

Years,' 1961), present women as sustaining forces, energetic and practical though good-hearted and capable of love. Relations between mother and daughter, between successive generations, prominent in these books, reappear in *Viisaat istuvat varjossa* ('The Wise Sit in the Shadow,' 1964), which is her first novel set in Helsinki. *Ritari metsien pimennosta* ('The Knight from the Dark Forests,' 1966) deals with relations between Finland and Russia mainly in this century. The main character is a public official; other characters are seen through their relations with him in which the conflict between generations is again a factor.

Marja-Liisa Vartio (*née* Sairanen, wife of Paavo Haavikko, 1924-66) produced two volumes of poetry, *Häät* ('The Wedding,' 1952) and *Seppele* ('The Wreath,' 1953), which were favorably received but are now forgotten; she is remembered for her prose. Her fancy and humor are more lively than those of Eila Pennanen and Eeva Joenpelto, but she shares their avoidance of personal comment and explanations in her texts. The short stories in *Maan ja veden välillä* ('Between Land and Water,' 1955) have poetic qualities, but the novels which followed, with the exception of her last, posthumous one, *Hänen olivat linnut* ('His Were the Birds,' 1967), are quite realistic.

Se on sitten kevät ('So It's Spring,' 1957) begins as a description of two lovers; but the woman dies, and the second half of the book shows the modification her memory causes in the life and mind of the man. *Mies kuin mies, tyttö kuin tyttö* ('A Man like Another, a Girl like Another,' 1958), intended as an ordinary story about ordinary people, is the least imaginative of her books—it has been called "dry".[912] The girl decides to keep and educate her illegitimate child. *Kaikki naiset näkevät unia* ('All Women Have Dreams,' 1960) is a satirical but understanding portrait of a middle-class housewife, her family, and their daily difficulties with payments for a new home and similar matters. The author does not suggest that the small problems of middle-class life are ridiculous, but she does not idealize or pity her characters, leaving the reader to draw his own conclusions, in an impartial manner typical of the literary style of postwar Finland.

Her humor is most apparent in *Tunteet* ('Feelings,' 1962), which is the story of the difficulties a boy and girl meet on the road to marriage; it is evident that they are exaggerating the importance of their sentimental problems, but the author feels that they are typical young people who must find out about life by trial and error and mutual adjustment. In *Hänen olivat linnut* the humor is carried to the point of nonsense. A widow who has been left a collection of stuffed birds by her husband's uncle imagines them to be almost real. As in all Marja-Leena Vartio's books, the superficial structure hides a serious purpose; this story is about the tragedy of human isolation.

Iris Kähäri (*née* Ijäs, b. 1914), from Viipuri, displays the traditional qualities of the Karelians—lively fancy and colorful colloquial language—making her books pleasant even when they are loose and disconnected.

Although they are about her home region, they present problems of general interest. *Pantti* ('The Pledge,' 1956) is about a woman who does not know whether her husband has been killed or taken prisoner in the war; *Viipurilainen iltapäivä* ('An Afternoon in Viipuri,' 1964) describes in the form of a monologue an old woman's memories and her unhappiness in new surroundings; *Elämän koko kuva* ('The Whole Image of Life,' 1960; the title is a modified quotation from Kivi) portrays the life of Karelian refugees. She has also written interesting short stories collected in *Armon ja kunnian portti* ('The Gate of Mercy and Honor,' 1956) and *Kymmenes* ('The Tenth,' 1962).

Tuuli Reijonen (b. 1907) is known for her good, classical short stories, which are contained in *Kasvoja* ('Faces,' 1948) and *Yksisiipinen enkeli* ('The One-Winged Angel,' 1952); *Makuusäkki* ('The Sleeping Bag' in *Yksisiipinen enkeli*) won an international prize.[913] *Kannaksen mosaiikkimaailma* ('The Mosaic World of the Isthmus,' 1968) is about an artists' and writers' community on the Isthmus of Karelia in the 1930s whose members included Paavolainen, Kianto, Seppänen, Pekkanen, Colliander, Diktonius, and Russian emigrees.

Helvi Erjakka (Helvi Erjakka-Rania, first Eriksson, b. 1909) published her first books in the 1930s. They were insignificant, but her style changed after the war. Her most interesting books are *Minä itse sen tein* ('I Did It Myself,' 1961), a swindler's portrait of himself, and *Ensimmäinen näytös* ('The First Act,' 1963), a novel set in the world of the theater which she knows well, for her father was an actor and she has done stage work herself.

Anja Vammelvuo, whose poetry we have mentioned, has written some prose; the short stories in *Rakkauskertomus* ('A Love Story,' 1953) and *Valkoinen varis* ('The White Crow,' 1962), her most interesting work, deal mainly with the many aspects and unexpected variations of love.

The newest prose in Finland, like the most recent poetry, completely discards traditions, even those developed in the 1950s. Some authors reject the traditional linguistic form of the narrative, and most use common motifs which leave the interest in the style. **Pentti Saarikoski** is one of the first writers of such prose as well as of the new poetry. His first novel, *Ovat muistojemme lehdet kuolleet* ('Dead Are the Leaves of Our Memories,' 1964), is a series of images and conversations from contemporary Helsinki and a character's reminiscences from the Civil War and afterwards. This juxta-position seems to indicate that these memories, with their hollow patriotic rhetoric, refer to events as meaningless as those happening at present. His other novels, *Aika Prahassa* ('The Time in Prague,' 1967) and *Kirje vaimolleni* ('A Letter to My Wife,' 1968), are similar to each other. Both are interior monologues which describe brief intervals of time spent in Prague and Dublin by a writer much like Saarikoski. The author violates rules of decency, but his transgressions are not the focus of the books, which are somewhat disappointing in their lack of meaning. The narrator declares that he is not interested in seeing the cities or meeting people; he simply enumerates trivial incidents and memories of his wife and other women. The books may be considered interesting because of their effort at spontaneous expression,[914] but they are not very original.

Pekka Kejonen (b. 1941), one of the most modern writers in Finland,[915] writes in a manner similar to Saarikoski's, but he describes a more energetic, colorful, though not always happy, world. His characters form a distinct group within his own generation. Most are nightclub musicians who drift aimlessly around the world, have casual affairs with women they meet, and maintain interest only in jazz—not the kind of music they play for a living—which they view as a kind of spiritual bond between people throughout the world; his first novel is titled *Jamit* ('The Jam Session,' 1963). Kejonen writes mainly in the first person, but third-person characters also tell about themselves without pretenses, e.g., in *Napoleonin epätoivo* ('Napoleon's Despair,' 1964), *Käyttögrafiikkaa* ('Practical Design,' 1965), and *Uskomattomat* ('The Unbelievables,' 1966).

Markku Lahtela (b. 1936) has gone furthest in eliminating traditional rules of language. His novel *Jumala pullossa* ('God in a Bottle,' 1964) criticizes religion and militarism.[916] His next, *Se* ('It,' 1966), is about young people in the modern world, but his attempt to write "meaningless prose" is by nature self-defeating,[917] even though he is a talented writer.

Timo M. Mukka (b. 1944), a romanticist who believes love is the power which unites all humans and influences their actions, writes slightly stylized novels which tell of life in northern Finland, *Maa on syntinen laulu* ('The Earth Is a Sinful Song,' 1964), *Tabu* ('The Taboo,' 1965), *Täältä jostakin* ('Hereabouts,' 1965), and *Laulu Sipirjan lapsista* ('A Song about the Children of Siberia,' 1966; Siberia is intentionally misspelled).

Other contemporary writers do not go so far in attempting new forms of expression, and some do not attempt at all. Traditional novels on the life of agricultural and industrial workers are regularly published, often by authors from the working class, e.g., Eero Hietala, Kaarlo Isotalo, Martti Joenpolvi, and Kalle Päätalo. Other authors describe historical and social situations. Eino Säisä's *Yöstä tullut* ('Coming from the Night,' 1964) looks at the last war through the civilian population; Erkki Ahonen's *Kyyditys* ('Taken for a Ride,' 1962) deals with the political violence of the early thirties.

Hannu Salama (b. 1936) gained notoriety for nonliterary reasons. Although his first works, the novel *Se tavallinen tarina* ('The Usual Story,' 1961) and the short stories *Lomapäivä* ('The Day Off,' 1962), attracted little attention, *Juhannustanssit* ('The Midsummernight Dance,' 1964) incited conservatives, especially church representatives, who disliked the entire book but could have it prosecuted only for three allegedly blasphemous passages. The author and the publisher were sentenced under a near-obsolete section in the law, but the president pardoned them against the advice of a majority in the Supreme Court, which is a stronghold of conservatism in Finland. The liberal outcry obscured the book's lack of merit, and many critics believe it is a great novel. Some sections are poorly written, and the author displays no awareness of his characters' stupidity, nastiness, and brutality. Few critics have noticed the book's real defects; even those who disliked it criticized superficial details such as the obscenities.[918]

Salama has continued publishing, and the critics who defended his freedom of speech continue to admire him. His volume of short stories, *Kenttäläinen käy talossa* ('Kenttäläinen Comes to a Visit,' 1967), and his novels *Minä, Olli ja Orvokki* ('I, Olli and Orvokki,' 1967), *Joulukuun kuudes* ('The Sixth of December,' 1968), and *Kesäleski* ('When the Wife Is Away,' 1969) are similar. No one should object simply because an author describes life as an endless gray hell enlivened by a few moments of violent nastiness, but Salama seems to think that this is what life should be.[918]

More interesting though less famous young authors are publishing books written in the traditional manner but personal in style; most of them are about young people. **Marja-Leena Mikkola** (b. 1939) has written short stories collected in *Naisia* ('Women,' 1962), two novels, *Tyttö kuin kitara* ('A Girl like a Guitar,' 1964) and *Etsikko* ('The Front,' 1967), protest songs, texts for variety shows, and filmscripts. Her avowed intention in her work is to avoid superficial romanticism.[920] When she discovers that she has not been told the entire truth about her grandmother, a young girl in *Legendantekijät* ('The Legend Makers' in *Naisia*) decides that she will not "forge legends," but that she will "tell about people as they lived." The author admits that there are hidden balladlike motifs in *Tyttö kuin kitara*, which is the story of the unhappy love between a young female nightclub singer and the pianist and leader of her musical group. The book ends with her death, for which he is and is not responsible since he took advantage of her love without knowing whether or not he loved her. In *Etsikko* love mingles with politics.

Arvo Salo (b. 1932), whose political opera, *Lapualaisooppera*, has been mentioned, has also written protest songs and organized demonstrations against the war in Vietnam. He is not a hippie—hippie ideas and tactics have not caught on in Europe—but he has held posts in the Social-Democrat party, Parliament, on the Helsinki City Council and a socialist newspaper, and he is a lieutenant of the reserve. He optimistically believes that one can work through organization to destroy the world's evils, and his works often call for such action and warn against individual anarchy in writing. One of his essays, *Joku järjestys* ('Some Kind of Order),[921] protests the rejection of traditional prose forms by some of the young authors. *Valitut huulet* ('Selected Lip,' 1966) is a collection of prose on topical subjects.

Political and social radicalism, however, are not common among young prosaists, who are more interested in individual problems, e.g., Hannu Mäkelä, whose two-part novel *Matkoilla kaiken aikaa* ('Away All the Time,' 1965) and *Kylliksi! tai liikaa* ('Enough! or Too Much,' 1965) is poetic in style, Aulikki Oksanen, who has published *Hevosen kuolema* ('The Death of a Horse,' 1967), which contains her poems, prose sketches and drawings, and a novel, *Tykkimiehen syli* ('In the Arms of the Artillerist,' 1968), and Tytti Parras, who has written the novel *Jojo* ('The Yo-Yo,' 1968). Even those interested in social and political problems describe specific situations rather than propose theories or sketch panoramas. Jalo Heikkinen's novel *Kolhoosi* ('The Kolkhoze,' 1968) shows an imaginary attempt to found a kolkhoze in Finland, Seppo Urpela's partly autobiographical *Kommunisti karvarinta* ('A Hairy-Chested Communist,' 1967) retells Pekkanen's and Siippainen's story of a working-class young man's difficulties in rising, and Jorma Kurvinen's *Velkakirja* ('The Promissory Note,' 1968) relates the struggle for position in the business world. Jorma Ojaharju's *Kakku* ('The Cake,' 1966) presents life in prison, whereas *Koiravahti* ('The Dog Watch,' 1966) and *Harvoin mekin ansaitsemme* (an intended misquotation from an old song, 'We Have Not Often Earned,' 1967) describe the life of sailors and longshoremen. In all these works a main character experiences these problems on an individual level.[922]

Linna and Rintala seem to have been the last representatives of the great novel dealing with great problems. The books mentioned in the last pages are short but intense, and they offer no conclusions for the reader. Although it is clear that panoramic novels are no longer in fashion, it is useless to predict future directions for Finnish literature. Nevertheless, it is apparent that the literature will be interesting and will find a large readership.[923]

Swedish Literature in Finland
at the End of the Nineteenth and
the Beginning of the Twentieth Centuries

FINNISH AND SWEDISH LITERATURE in Finland have progressed in the
same direction since the end of the nineteenth century without influencing
each other. This is a general pattern in bi- and plurilingual European
countries. The Swedish writers of Finland (hereafter referred to simply as
"Swedish writers") look to Stockholm for literary life although they remain
attached to Finland; few have moved to Sweden. Runeberg and Topelius
wrote in Swedish, but their works were almost immediately translated into
Finnish and are still used as readers in both Finnish and Swedish elementary
schools. It is ironical that they thus awakened the nationalistic feelings which
resulted in the successful effort to make Finnish the predominant language of
Finland. This outcome was inevitable, because more than 80 percent of the
population was always Finnish-speaking. It was a Swedish-speaking statesman,
Leo Mechelin, who in 1905 opened the sessions of the Senate in Finnish and
introduced the resolution to keep its minutes in Finnish. In the Socialist
party and in the labor movement, linguistic quarrels were disapproved and
formally forbidden at a party congress; this prohibition was respected.[924]
Abroad, the Civil War has sometimes been mistakenly viewed as a struggle of a
Finnish proletariat against a Swedish aristocracy, but, in fact, the Swedish
group also comprises workers, farmers, and craftsmen, most of whom lived in
Red territory, whereas the majority of the White rank and file were
Finnish-speaking.

Although Runeberg and Topelius were admired in Finland and Sweden,
those after them who wrote specifically for the Swedish-speaking group
received less notice in the old mother country. Thomas Warburton says that

the Swedish literature of Finland is doubly provincial, in relation to Sweden and Finland, where it is written for a small group, not even for the entire Swedish-speaking population.[925] Most Swedish writers belong to middle-class families, and they reflect urban middle-class views more often than Finnish writers do. A few writers of modest origin in Swedish Finland, comparable to Päivärinta and Kauppis-Heikki, produced works of some literary value: **Anders Allardt** (1855-1942), **Oscar Behm** (1867-1933), **Josefina Bengts** (1875-1925), and **Anders Nygrén** (1869-1902). Like Päivärinta and Kauppis-Heikki, some of them achieved middle-class status. Allardt took a Ph.D. at the University of Helsinki and worked in the schools as a teacher, principal, and inspector. Swedish writers who directed their words to the masses, e.g., Arvid Mörne, did so because they supported democratic or socialistic ideals or felt that the small Swedish group must unite to resist Finnish nationalism.[926] It was perhaps more a sense of duty than natural inclination that made them express feelings of community with the people. Elmer Diktonius, who wrote in Swedish and Finnish, is a notable exception. In terms of the audience, the group has a disproportionate number of writers; there have been several great Swedish poets in Finland, some of whom totally changed Swedish poetry in both Finland and Sweden. It is perhaps only due to chance that there is no great prosaist among them.

The Swedish reaction against Runeberg's and Topelius's idealism, in part produced by the influence of the French, Norwegian, and Swedish realists and naturalists, was not as strong as the Finnish reaction was. The first writer of the new trend was **Karl August Tavaststjerna** (1860-98),[927] and in a sense he was the only one. He completely dominated the Swedish literature of Finland in his lifetime; Yrjö Hirn, a Finnish scholar, rode in his funeral procession with Mikael Lybeck, the only writer comparable to Tavaststjerna, who was just beginning to publish, and remarked, "Here I am riding with the entire Swedish literature of Finland."[928] Twenty-five years after his death Elmer Diktonius correctly wrote that he was the first modern Swedish poet in Finland,[929] but one can find traditional elements in his works. His poetry is better in quality than his prose. He never took a definite stand in controversial matters. Although he belonged to the Swedish group, he sometimes commented ironically on the linguistic quarrel in his works. He knew Minna Canth, spent some time in Kuopio, and wrote a play in Finnish. He criticized the upper classes for indifference to the suffering of the poor, but he also described unpleasant common characters. He made no ideological claims in his works, but conservative critics, then a majority, wrote unfavorably about them even though his talent was recognized. He had friends among the artists in Helsinki, which the Swedish writers of Finland call Helsingfors, but he was alone in literature, and he became bitter and estranged. His private life, too, was unhappy; he had to work as a newspaperman in provincial towns, which he disliked intensely. His death was the result of a stupid accident in the hospital where he was being treated for pneumonia.[930]

He first took a degree in architecture at the Institute of Technology of Helsinki, but soon became a journalist and freelance writer, which he remained his entire life. His first poems, *För morgonbris* ('With the Morning Breeze,' 1883), contain material typical to young poets: love, nature, especially descriptions of the Finnish coasts, which the Swedish writers have always loved, and sketches from daily life, which were common at that time. Today these sketches would be in prose, but Tavaststjerna skillfully used verse. It is for such poems that he was called a realist, and, although his immediate prodecessors, e.g., Topelius, also had them in their works, he produced more of them.[931] His second collection, *Nya vers* ('New Verse,' 1885), contains a series which is the partially autobiographical account of a boy, *Lille Karl* ('Little Karl'). In a description of a traditional Christmas celebration, the poet implied that overeating was the most important part of the festivity for the majority of those present and thus offended some critics.

Dikter i väntan ('Poems While Waiting,' 1890) also contains many satirical and humorous verses, e.g., *Hemåt* ('Bound for Home'), which realistically details a ship journey, describing the ship, its captain, the passengers, and a waitress. On another level the poet wonders why he feels patriotic abroad but loses these feelings at home. The last lines reveal his routine life at home: he meets people, eats in good restaurants, pays his bills, keeps his mouth shut, and does not bother anyone. At this time relations between Finland and Russia were beginning to deteriorate, and Tavaststjerna expressed his patriotism in the poem *På svensk botten* ('On Swedish Ground'), which shows him forgetting the literary and philosophic questions he has been discussing with friends in Sweden when a letter and newspaper bring alarming news from Finland.

His best poems are in his last collections, *Dikter* ('Poems,' 1896) and *Laureatus* ('The Laureate,' 1897). They are expressive, forceful, and lively, although they follow strict metric patterns—his skill in inventing rhymes never became artificial.[932] *Dikter* is both melancholy and aggressive. There is another homecoming by boat, and in another poem he voices the wish to sail, in spite of rules and warnings, to the open sea. Other poems, less realistic, express yearning for a peaceful death. *Skuggornas ö* ('The Isle of the Shadows') presents a romantic, imaginary landscape where the poet and his beloved might "die smiling, before the sands of the desert cover us up." Some, written in the simple, melodious manner of folksong, are reminiscent of Leino's and Larin-Kyösti's works. This style was much favored by Swedish writers of the period.[933] *Laureatus* contains a series of sonnets composed in strict accordance with the rules of the art. It has been suggested that his extraordinary concern for form in his last collections borders on the neurotic.[934] The title poem of *Laureatus* is avowedly autobiographical. He declares his intention to describe the life of a typical Finnish poet, which, he believed, could only end in misery. Aggressive parts affirm that he will not accept defeat, and in fantastic allegorical passages oriental images mingle with allusions to Goethe's *Faust*. Although the poem is not entirely coherent, he does complete his plan. In the short poems the erotic images in the sonnets on Diana and the dreamy love poems with memories of Swedish landscapes stand out especially.

Tavaststjerna wrote much prose, but it does not rise to the level of his poetry. He wrote hastily, and the form of his prose suffers, but it reflects his strength and sensitivity. A critic once warned him that, since he had almost no competition in Finland, he could afford to write carelessly, but that more should be expected from him.[935] His first novel, *Barndomsvänner* ('Childhood Friends,' 1886), brought him recognition, although it received some disapproval. Some of his disappointed friends had expected him to attack old ideas and institutions, but he dealt mainly with individual problems, anticipating his own life in the narration about a young man of good family who wants to become an artist, studies music abroad, but never achieves success in art or love, and finishes his life as a small-town stationmaster. The final scene reflects Tavaststjerna's romantic indulgence: the man plays a composition by Rubinstein while a shooting star flies across the cold winter sky.[936]

En inföding ('A Native,' 1887) also blends romanticism and realism. Two friends become rivals over a cabaret singer; the cynic loses, and the good one marries her. His two story collections, *I förbindelser* ('Liabilities,' 1888) and *Marin och genre* ('Marine and Genre,' 1890), contain less romantic narratives. The title story of *I förbindelser* is about a man who mismanages his affairs, becomes indebted, and flees to America. In another story a guard accidentally kills a prisoner. The "marines" of *Marine och genre* are descriptions of the sea, and the "genre" are pictures from everyday life, often critical of prevailing social conditions.

His best novel, *Hårda tider* ('Hard Times,' 1891), attracted attention although it was received negatively. It sharply criticizes the indifference and hypocrisy of the upper classes toward the sufferings of the poor in the great famine of 1867 and 1868, although the author is basically objective. The main figures in a complicated criminal plot interwoven with the rest of the events are from the common people. The conservatives disliked the book's attacks of the authorities and the upper classes. With the help of Juhani Aho, Tavaststjerna adapted this novel in Finnish for the stage under the title *Uramon torppa* ('Uramo Farm,' 1892).

His next novel, *I förbund med döden* ('The Alliance with Death,' 1893), reflects his interest in the mystic speculations then fashionable in Europe.[937] A man from Helsinki meets, while traveling abroad, a mysterious lady with whom he has long discussions about spiritualism, hypnotism, and similar subjects. He eventually returns to his family, but he can never be happy again. His next collections of short stories, *Unga år* ('Young Years,' 1892) and *Kapten Tärnberg* ('Captain Tärnberg,' 1894), leave these fantastic concerns and center around everyday life, often satirically. *Kvinnoregemente* ('The Rule of Women,' 1894) is an open satire somewhat similar to Joel Lehtonen's descriptions of half-educated, energetic, successful people and unpractical idealists; the motif was common in Finland at that time.

Tavaststjerna's last novel, *En patriot utan fosterland* ('A Patriot without a Country,' 1896), again reflects his estrangement in Finland as a Swede, not, however, hostile toward the Finns. The improbable main character is a Russian officer with a Finnish father and a Tatar mother. He feels sympathy for the Finns when stationed in Finland, but he cannot win their confidence, and his superiors are suspicious of him. He retires in Italy and writes a diary, the novel.

For a while the only Swedish author besides Tavaststjerna of any importance in Finland was **Mikael Lybeck** (1864-1925). His life was typical for the upper middle class; his father was a wealthy businessman from a small town in Ostrobotnia who left his son an estate which freed Lybeck to dedicate himself to literature. Lybeck received a master's degree from the University of Helsinki and led a quiet life, regularly producing novels, short stories, plays, and poems.

His first poetry collections, *Dikter* I, II, and III ('Poems,' 1890, 1895, and 1903), the long poem *Gengångaren* ('The Ghost,' 1899), and the collection *Dödsfången* ('In the Death Cell,' 1918) follow the patterns of Swedish poetry at the time, with realistic descriptions from ordinary life, expressions of a skeptical attitude toward the world, a few chaste love poems, and patriotic poems inspired by contemporary events. *Dödsfången*, influenced by World War I and the Finnish Civil War, rejects the horrors of war with a frankness not typical to Lybeck, who refrained from revealing his feelings. Such ideas were not then fashionable in Finland.[938] The poetry is unremarkable and did not attract attention, and he turned almost exlusively to prose.

His first short stories also attracted little attention, but his personality is fully developed in them. Besides skepticism and rationalism, they reflect reluctance toward love, especially in *Unge Hemming* ('Young Hemming,' 1891), *Ett mosaikarbete* ('A Piece of Mosaic Work,' 1892), and *Allas vår Margit* ('Our Common Friend Margit,' 1893). A story in the collection *Dagar och nätter* ('Days and Nights,' 1896) anticipates his later inclination toward the mysterious. A wealthy factory owner, happily married and apparently in perfect health, is tortured by secret terrors which he cannot confess to anyone and by sudden urges to act against reason which drive him to suicide.

Lybeck's major works are his novels and plays. The main character of his first long narrative, *Den starkare* ('The Stronger One,' 1900),[939] is a portrait of the author as he wished to see himself, and, in many respects, as he was—a refined man who feels himself weaker than the strong and vulgar. But the book is not an autobiography. It attacks certain forms of religion personified by a revivalist preacher who converts the main character's fiancée and her mother from rational agnosticism to ecstatic faith. The preacher is so dishonest and repulsive that he is not quite convincing.

Tomas Indal (1911) is considered Lybeck's best novel. Like the story in *Dagar och nätter,* it analyzes the breakdown of a man who has slowly become unable to maintain human contact because of his growing feeling that all human effort and perhaps life itself are worthless. *Breven till Cecilia* ('Letters to Cecilia,' 1920), admired for its elegant language, is a series of letters written by an art historian, an aesthete like Lybeck, to the woman he loves, whose unfaithfulness drives him to suicide. The story *Hennerson* (1915) combines motifs from *Den starkare* and *Breven till Cecilia.* Hennerson, a man of simple origin, drowns himself when driven half mad by religious meditations and by his love for a woman who is his social superior.

Although his short stories contain humor, Lybeck's last work, the novel *Samtal med Lackau* ('Conversations with Lackau,' 1925), a mild parody on Boswell's *Life of Johnson* and Eckermann's book on Goethe, (which Lybeck knew better), is his only humorous work. Both the narrator and the person he describes, Baron Lackau, are fictitious; Lackau is a secondary character in *Hennerson,* a wealthy, well-meaning eccentric who has done nothing except study history and his family's genealogy. He provides comic relief by making seemingly deep but actually nonsensical remarks about life. In *Samtal med Lackau* a friend attempts to portray him more fully.

Lybeck's plays, his most romantic works, show the influence of European symbolism. In *Ödlan* ('The Lizard,' 1908) the lizard symbolizes evil; its appearance in some situations is artificial, but it is basically consonant with the unreal atmosphere of the drama.[940] Alban, a young man, loves two women, a pure girl and a temptress, also called "the lizard." She seems to win, but is killed in the end by Alban, who has consistently tried to resist her. In its simplicity *Bror och syster* ('Brother and Sister,' 1915) is a contrast to this romantic work. The brother is an impractical dreamer taken care of by his sister, who falls in love with an unworthy man, commits a crime to help him, and takes poison when her act is discovered. The brother tries in vain to assume the guilt himself.

Schopenhauer (1922) represents the German philosopher in his youth, when he first conceived his pessimism. As a young rebel he is violently critical of the world, but in the last act his seventy-year-old self appears to teach him moderation and to give him courage. *Domprosten Bomander* ('Canon Bomander,' 1923) voices much of Lybeck's antireligious tendency. A dignitary of the church leaves his post because he has lost his faith. He lives in the company of artists, and in the melodramatic ending his mistress kills him for suspected unfaithfulness. His other two plays, *Dynastin Peterberg* ('The Peterberg Dynasty,' 1913) and *Den röde André* ('Red André,' 1917), are on topical subjects, the Russian oppression in Finland and the revolution. They and all his works have traits which became typical among his successors, especially his interest in exceptional, refined individuals who cannot adjust to the world.

After the turn of the century an atmosphere of despondency pervaded the works of most Swedish writers of Finland. The mood was the result of the symbolist fashion in Europe, the weakening position of the Swedes in society, and the Russian oppression in Finland. The Finns were less dangerous than the Swedes believed,[941] but the Russians were overwhelmingly powerful, and Finland seemed doomed to loose its national identity. Thus, a similar despondency was present in the works of Eino Leino and Maila Talvio, for example. Writers reacted in different ways to this situation, but very early in the century it was fashionable to take refuge in a distant, romantic past, preferably a sumptuous, decadent Orient such as that in Wilde's *Salomé*, to compose exquisite works of art for a select few, and to despise the masses and their morals, religion, and sense of duty. The pursuit of pleasure was proclaimed the only worthwhile aim. Some authors practiced these attitudes in life as well as in literature.[942] Another popular view was that the Swedes were conquerors who had introduced civilization to Finland and were now about to fall and die nobly on their isolated outposts, submerged by a rising wave of barbarism.[943] This idea became more common and took the form of aggressive nationalism, especially at the time of the Civil War. A few authors proclaimed socialist ideas in their works but experienced disappointment when trying to establish permanent contact with the working class.

Bertel Gripenberg (1878-1947) was one of the most representative poets of his time. He was proud to be a baron in the Finnish nobility,[944] and he despised the common people, socialists, communists, liberals, democrats, and the Finns. His view on the latter mellowed after the Civil War, and he admired Finns who had the right ideas. Koskenniemi was his friend, and he translated Linnankoski's *Song of the Blood-Red Flower* into Swedish. In his works he praises youth, energy, courage, and strength, but he expected his heroes to have ennobling tragic ends. Some of his erotic poems, about Salomé, Empress Theodora, and others, although innocent enough, scandalized the middle-class society of his time in Helsinki. He exaggerates these attitudes to the point of doubtful sincerity.

Gripenberg failed in all activities he most admired: the proud warrior left the officers' school because he could not stand the discipline, the irresistible lover had only a few, unsatisfactory relationships with women, and the country gentleman who loved horses and hunting suffered bad eyesight and rheumatism. He served in the quartermaster corps during the Civil War, and, to compensate for his feeling of inferiority, he furiously wrote patriotic poems filled with paranoic hate for the enemy. He had already published two prose descriptions of imaginary rebellions, *En dröm om folkviljan* ('A Dream about the Will of the People,' 1908) and *Det brinnande landet* ('The Burning Country,' 1910), unlike anything ever written. In the former, Finnish nationalist rebels loot, burn, and destroy. In the latter, the rebels are the local peasants of the Baltic countries, who had indeed revolted against the rule the local German aristocracy and the tsarist regime. Aino Kallas describes their point of view, but Gripenberg pictures the brutal slaughtering of these peasants with approval. An aristocratic girl is raped by Russian officers, but she pardons them because they mistook her for a peasant. She marries one of them, and the couple take an oath to hate the mob forever. Although these works were criticized by Swedish liberals, e.g., Arvid Mörne, Gripenberg never regretted them, and he had *En dröm om folkviljan* reprinted with a jubilant preface in 1918, after the Civil War had broken out.

Ideologies aside, one must admit that Gripenberg's poems are masterpieces of traditional lyric form and language, and they were much admired among the Swedish middle and upper classes until approximately the last war. Since he was a pessimist, (although he admired energy), his best poems are those in which he stresses the necessity of noble submission to inevitable fate and laments the ephemerous nature of all that is beautiful. Even when he speaks of the lonely Swedes defending civilization in the desert, his manner is subdued. In the following lines from the collection *Skuggspel* ('A Play of Shadows,' 1912), there is much of Kipling:

> The outposts are thinning in Eastern land,
> of silent men a scattered band
> is falling proud with sword in hand.
> Once shall the singers perhaps tell
> how in the East the outposts fell.[945]

One poem in the collection, *Gallergrinden* ('The Iron Gate,' 1905), expresses his feeling of estrangement from the world, represented by a garden seen through a gate which will always be closed to the wanderer. Written in the form of a sonnet, it purports to be a description of the sonnet as a form of poetry, the closed gate between Beauty and the spectator, but it also clearly reveals Gripenberg's philosophy.

Most of his best poems are in the collections *Drivsnö* ('Loose Snow,' 1909), *Aftnar i Tavastland* ('Evenings in Tavastland,' 1911), *Skuggspel* ('A Play of Shadows,' 1912), and *Spillror* ('Broken Bits,' 1917), published when he was living in Häme or Tavastland. Although this Finnish area was the threatening desert of his poetry, he loved it, more than any other Swedish writer did, as a wild country where man could feel free and strong and as a mysterious, secluded place for meditation.[946] His ponderings appear more frequently in his last collections, *Skymmande land,* ('The Land That Sinks into Darkness,' 1925), *Vid gränsen* ('On the Border,' 1930), *Livets eko* ('The Echo of Life,' 1933), *Sista ronden* ('The Last Round,' 1941), and the posthumous *Vid gallergrinden* ('At the Iron Gate,' 1947). The meditations often center on death, that of friends and defenders of his ideas as well as his own. In *Sista ronden* the ultimate fate of humanity is pictured as skulls lying on the steppe, emptied of thoughts, questions, and answers, for, when Death blows his trumpet, even honor flutters away like a cobweb in the wind. Although Gripenberg never lost his fascination with dramatic effects, he shows their emptiness in his last works.

Hjalmar Procopé (1868-1927) is even more typical of his time than is Gripenberg. Although Procopé's father occupied the highest posts in the Finnish administration, Procopé wished only to be a newspaperman and poet, and his works were among the most popular of his time. Far more sociable than Gripenberg, he had many friends and appeared often in clubs and restaurants, and his poetry reflects his congeniality although it is serious in nature.[947] Its greatest flaw is that it is not always carefully composed.

His first collection, *Dikter* ('Poems,' 1900), has little significance. His play, *Belsazars gästabud* ('Belshazzar's Feast,' written in 1905), for which Sibelius wrote the incidental music, made him known when it was first performed in 1906. It is the well-known story from the Book of Daniel, written in skillful biblical style and influenced by *Salomé.*[948] He also used the biblical style effectively in the poems of *Mot öknen* ('Toward the Deserts,' 1905), although they are not on biblical subjects. The collection *Röda skyar* ('Red Skies,' 1907) is the first to show clearly his artistic personality, characterized by great skill in the use of a variety of styles; he could write classical, romantic, and folklike poems with equal ease. The personal stamp is his ironic, even flippant superiority over stupidity and narrow-mindedness, which scarcely hides his concern for serious problems. He is not unlike Heine, whom he admired and translated. His pity and understanding for the poor is even more apparent in *Vers och visa* ('Verse and Song,' 1909), which reflects the bitterness an unhappy love affair had left in him.

After the publication of the collection *Oväder* ('The Tempest,' 1910), his verse became more serious. He was among the first Swedes to write patriotic poetry inspired by the Russian oppression, and his poems, less pathetic than Gripenberg's, are so topical that it is surprising that they were openly published.[949] *Under stjärnorna* ('Under the Stars,' 1913) and *I sanden* ('In the Sand,' 1915) are his best collections. The first contrasts the will to accept life and community with others, in spite of the disappointments they offer, with melancholy meditations about man's basic solitude. His images are built from ordinary details which reflect great truths, somewhat reminiscent of Runeberg's method.[950] He uses the same details in lively sketches of the Helsinki of his time, the atmosphere of which is graphically preserved in *I sanden*. His three later collections are less interesting; *Osamse strängar* ('Discordant Strings,' 1920) contains several patriotic poems as unpleasantly violent as Gripenberg's.

In Finland **Arvid Mörne** (1876-1946) stands alone among the Swedish writers of his time. Although he belonged to the middle class, he worked to improve the conditions of the Swedish-speaking proletariat, who had been neglected by the upper and middle classes of their linguistic group. At times the Swedes found the Finnish country people more romantic.[951] Mörne was also active in adult education from 1899 to 1911. He announced approval of socialism at the beginning of the century, and his political activities culminated during the Great Strike of 1905, when he spoke to a large group of demonstrating workers and headed the delegation which requested the resignation of the governor-general and the Senate. When peaceful constitutional reform resulted, Mörne was disapproved by the moderates. To the socialists he remained too much a gentleman and proud individualist. His resignation from his post in adult education was forced by the harassment and intrigue which followed. Mörne admired courageous men who stood against injustice, but he had none of Gripenberg's inclination for self-glorification, and the injustice against which he stood was very real. He saw this virtue in the entire Swedish population of Finland, which he often described in images from the rugged coasts of his country better than did any other writer. Such description is found even in his first collection, *Rytm och rim* ('Rhythm and Rhyme,' 1899), though neither it nor his second, *Nya sånger* ('New Songs,' 1901), which contains many descriptions of the south Finnish countryside, are very interesting. In *Ny tid* ('A New Time,' 1903) he first appears as a political poet, virtually the only one at that time in Swedish Finland, calling the workers to fight for a better future. This attitude is reflected even in his nonpolitical poems. After his disappointment in the Great Strike, he expressed pessimism about the future,[952] but in his everyday life he was active and energetic. He obtained a doctorate from the University of Helsinki, where he taught as a lecturer; he worked as a newspaperman, and he helped prepare the active resistance to the Russian oppression. He also wrote a number of scholarly works, many on Swedish literature and nineteenth-century Finnish newspapers, some on Kivi and Kramsu, and published Swedish translations of Finnish poetry.

Mörne's best works from the period 1910 to 1926 are the poems in the collections *Döda år* ('The Dead Years,' 1910), *Skärgårdens vår* ('Spring among the Islands,' 1913), *Sommarnatten* ('The Summer Night,' 1916), *Offer och segrar* ('Sacrifices and Victories,' 1918), *Höstlig dikt* ('Autumn Verse,' 1919), and *Vandringen och vägen* ('The Journey and the Road,' 1924), although they are not on the level of his great lyrical compositions from his later years. *Döda år*, full of pessimism with many symbols of death, marks a transition in his work to more personal poetry. He did not lose interest in world events and continued to express his views, but he wrote much less topical verse. *Skärgårdens vår* has many colorful, fresh descriptions of the Finnish coast which form the background for a series of subdued poems on unhappy love. *Sommarnatten* is depressed; he says that he is not living, only brooding. Even *Offer och segrar*, written under the impression of the events of 1917 and 1918, does not rejoice over his country's independence, although it does contain some patriotic poems.

In spite of his socialist sympathies, Mörne could not accept the violence committed by the Reds during the Civil War, and he experienced confusion although some poems express hope for a better future. In a few of his poems he expresses belief in the superiority of the Swedes in a manner similar to Gripenberg's, but he is not contemptuous. He speaks of Viipuri as the "farthest outpost of the Germanic peoples" and describes Agricola's work as "an unselfish sacrifice for the profit of strangers."[953] The play *Den helige Henricus* ('Saint Henricus,' 1914; Mörne's taste for erudite archaisms is evident in the Latin form) is directed against the "slavish spirit" of the Finns.[954] He lacked dramatic talent, and his plays, with the exception of *Solens återkomst* ('The Return of the Sun,' 1920), attracted little attention. There are two others, *Fädernearvet* ('The Heritage of Our Fathers,' 1918) and *De sex orden* ('The Six Words,' 1914); the latter had a social message and appeared in a socialist publication.

After 1926 Mörne published volumes of excellent poems which form two distinct groups. The first includes *Mörkret och lågan* ('The Darkness and the Flame,' 1926), *Morgonstjärnan* ('The Morning Star,' 1928), *Den förborgade källan* ('The Hidden Well,' 1930), *Det ringer kväll* ('The Bell Tolls the Evening,' 1931), and *Under Vintergatan* ('Under the Milky Way,' 1934). Almost all pessimistic, they are built with a few forceful words on images of the stormy, grey sea of autumn; they express joy only in the fact that the poet can still give form to his feelings. He does not pity himself, but he describes his sorrow in contemplating a cold, lonely, dying world. A few poems reveal that Mörne still possessed a will to live, with their descriptions of the beautiful sea, islands in spring and summer, sunshine, fresh winds, and sparkling waves; their style is often the folklike one he used from the first. One of his early poems, *Båklandets vackra Maja* ('Bonnie Mary of Båkland'), translated into Finnish, is still sung by many people who believe it is a genuine folksong.

The second group comprises *Hjärtat och svärdet* ('The Heart and the Sword,' 1935), *Atlantisk bränning* ('The Swell of the Atlantic,' 1937), *Över havet brann Mars* ('Mars Was Burning over the Sea,' 1939), *Sånger i världskymning* ('Songs in the Twilight of the World,' 1941), and *Sfinxen och Pyramiden* ('The Sphinx and the Pyramid,' 1944). The pessimism of the earlier collections remains, but these poems have a new vigor, rekindled when he saw his democratic ideals threatened in Germany, Italy, and even Finland. In the following poem from 1936, he alludes to Heine's satirical composition on the Germany of his time, *Deutschland. Ein Wintermärchen* ('Germany. A Winter Tale'):

> Now should he live—all would him curse, pursue—
> to be the poor man's friend, the mighty to chastise,
> a serpent in a stolid middle-class paradise,
> the scourge of his own time, truly the Great Jew.
>
> . . . .
>
> Now should he live! When poets cry and pale
> So like the swan who in the ice of winter dies,
> He should have written, proud and sharp and wise,
> His Germany's, nay, all Europe's Winter Tale.

Mörne was thinking of Mallarmé, as well as all the other dreamy poets who found the image of the swan in icy winter congenial,[955] but he actually foreshadowed a poem by Gripenberg published in *Sista ronden* in 1941 in which the artistocrat meditates on his proud solitude, using the image of a swan flying over a lake soon to be frozen and covered with snow. As the world grew darker, however, Mörne lost faith in a better future and dreamed of a universal catastrophe which would leave only the sphinx and the pyramid to "speak to the times to come in riddles without answers." He was lamenting the fate of mankind, and his feeling of solidarity with all men remained typical of him from the beginning to the end of his life.[956]

Mörne's prose has some literary value. His collections of short sketches, *Lotsarnas kamp* ('The Fight of the Pilots,' 1917) and *Från fjärdarna* ('Among the Islands,' 1917), are little more than reports on actual conditions in Finland, such as his diary, *Den röda våren* ('The Red Spring,' 1917); all describe contemporary events and people from the coastal regions. His novel *Den svenska jorden* ('The Swedish Ground,' 1915), which is not much more fictitious, was widely attacked. An impatient idealist, Mörne grew frustrated when reforms he advocated were not immediately carried through or failed to produce the expected results, and in this book he criticizes the selfishness of wealthy Swedish landowners and their lack of solidarity with small farmers, tenants, and agricultural workers.

Two of his novels, *Inför havets anlete* ('Facing the Sea,' 1921) and *Kristina Bjur* (1922), have no message. The first, a well-written, realistic description of life on the Finnish islands in the early nineteenth century, has an overdramatic plot in which a student who spends his summer in the country unveils old crimes. *Kristina Bjur* tells the domestic tragedy of an unhappily married couple during the war of 1700 to 1721 in an effective though sometimes artificially archaic language; this style had been in favor in Scandinavia for quite a while, and it appears in the works of Aino Kallas.[957]

The title story of the collection *Klas-Kristians julnatt* ('Klas-Kristian's Christmas Night,' 1923) and the novel *Ett liv* ('A Life,' 1925) contain many autobiographic elements. Both describe bitter, isolated men who cannot live according to their ideals. In the story the main character takes his own life; in the novel he writes that he no longer feels longing for his youth, or pain, because a soul which feels no longing is dead. In the collection *Någon går förbi på vägen* ('Somebody Passes on the Road,' 1928), he admits that Christian belief is impossible for him, but Christian motifs appear in his poetry both then and later. He wrote one more volume of prose, *Det förlorade landet* ('The Lost Country,' 1945), which expresses his complete loss of faith in humanity after World War II.

Mörne's children also wrote. His son **Håkan** (1900-1963) traveled and published books about the countries he visited. They emphasize the real, daily lives of the people he saw and purposely neglect the tourist attractions.[958] His daughter **Barbro** (b. 1903) has produced several volumes of poetry in which a feeling of communion with nature is combined with quiet images of happiness.

Jacob Tegengren (1875-1956) is virtually the only Swedish poet of the period to have his poetry read by people outside a select group among the Swedish-speaking Finns.[959] He was born in Vaasa and spent his entire life in the same region, Swedish Ostrobotnia. Initially active in adult education, he worked as a bank manager. He published a large number of poems and a few essays, biographical works, and translations of Finnish poetry. Simple and undramatic, his verse is not at all clumsy or artificial. After a few hesitant collections, *Dikter* ('Poems,' 1900), *Skuggor och dagrar* ('Shadows and Light,' 1901), *Nya dikter* ('New Poems,' 1903), and *Dikter* IV ('Poems IV,' 1906), he matures in *Ny vår* ('A New Spring,' 1913). A few poems on patriotic motifs lament the sufferings of the country and submissively hope for a better future. Little interest in the events of the time appears in his poetry. Instead he describes the landscapes of his home region, which reflect his moods, some joyful, and uses religious motifs more and more frequently in his later works. In Tegengren religiosity is humble submission to God's will and suppression of one's individuality; however, his God, the almighty ruler of nature and the universe, is not primarily interested in human destinies,[960] and he says in *Dikter* VII ('Poems VII,' 1916) that His "starry mouth" speaks words "never to be solved."

Sånger och hymner ('Songs and Hymns,' 1919), *Pärlfiskaren* ('The Pearlfisher,' 1923), *I väntan och vaka* ('While Waiting and Waking,' 1925), *Den svåra vägen* ('The Hard Road,' 1929), and *Beredelse* ('While Preparing,' 1931) are his best collections. In them his thoughts become more introspective, not so as to give himself more importance, but to suppress all selfishness in his soul and excessive interest in worldly matters. He often speaks of suffering as the necessary mean to achieve this goal, but he is not explicit about its nature. He felt satisfied to have won God's grace and did not think it essential to emphasize his former sins.[961] Quietly he meditates his problems; he does not attempt to convert others. His last collections, *Mot skuggorna* ('Toward the Shadows,' 1930) and *Sista milstolpen* ('The Last Milestone,' 1946), are not really different, but they do contain some new images from nature. The images are from his home region, but he almost never describes folk life there; he cannot, therefore, be considered the poet of that region.

Joel Rundt (1879-1971), too, was born in Ostrobotnia, where he worked as an elementary school teacher and a newspaperman, but he also lived in Helsinki. He was a church organist and a member of the committee appointed to write the Swedish hymnal for the Church of Finland. His poetry contains less conflict and tragedy than does Tegengren's—and still less formal elegance. His many collections, ranging from *Ödemark* ('The Desert,' 1912) to *Bara i denna frid* ('Only in This Peace,' 1964), give a monotonous impression, but his best poems have an appealing simplicity, freshness, and intimacy with nature. Rundt also published translations of Finnish poetry.

The most typical expressions of the period's atmosphere were produced by the prosaists. Lybeck is really the only important Swedish prose writer from the years immediately after 1900. Many who began literary careers near 1910 published few works, but only one of them, Runar Schildt, became a great author. This is the *dagdrivare* or *flanörer* generation, the "men-about-town," and the first to voice their feelings was **Gustav Alm** (pseudonym of **Richard Malmberg**, 1877-1944), who was somewhat older than the rest of the group. Of his three books, the first two are elegantly satirical, and they contain some bitter caricatures of Finland and current problems. Although these issues were passionately discussed at the time, he considers them from a distance which reveals their undignified sides. His irony is often directed against the Finns, especially in the first volume, *Höstdagar* ('Fall Days,' 1907). His third book, *Fångstmän* ('Hunters and Fishers,' 1924), is a collection of short stories which seriously describes individuals who cannot bear the limitations society imposes and reveals the author's bitter disillusionment.

Many of these writers displayed the cynicism of their works in their own lives. After a few bitter books, they stopped publishing, and three of them committed suicide. Others forgot their elegant detachment in 1918 and became violently patriotic. Two, disgusted with Finland, moved to Sweden.

Torsten Helsingius (1888-1967) was responsible for their being called "men-about-town" by naming his first novel *Dagdrivare* (1914); its alternate title is *Överklassbarn* ('Children of the Upper Class').[962] It is the story of young men who have the means to live without doing serious work. One admits that he is living on borrowed money, contracts a venereal disease,[963] but returns, healed, in the author's next book, *Utveckling* ('Development,' 1915), to work as a bank executive in a small town. In the end his faith in life is restored by true love. Helsingius's only other works are a collection of short stories published in 1917 and a volume of memoirs, *Det var* ('It Was,' 1947).

Henrik Hildén (1884-1932) produced more works on a wider variety of subjects. His romanticism is apparent in his contrasts of sophisticated cities and healthy countryside and his occasional fairytale style. His first work, *Indiansommar* ('Indian Summer,' 1910), is the diary of a well-known, world-weary painter who has returned to his childhood home among the Finnish islands to re-establish contact with simple people and with nature, but fails. Hildén's most pretentious book, *Drottning Liv* ('Queen Life,' 1913), describes a man of the world who lives in a luxurious villa on the French Riviera. In his enthusiasm for the information on high life in fashionable places, which he was acquainted with through living abroad, the author almost forgets his intended message about the corrupting influence of civilization. The strength of *Storön* (name, 'The Main Island,' 1914), considered his best novel, is in the description of life in the past on one of the Finnish islands; the modern love story contrasted to it is weaker.

The title story of *Den röda frun* ('The Red Lady,' 1915) is invaded by a ghost, the Red Lady, who influences the course of a love affair. *Christoffer eller lyckans underbara pärlor* ('Christoffer, or the Marvelous Pearls of Good Luck,' 1916) is called a fairytale of adults,[964] but only its artifically sophisticated language is adult. A boy, with the help of a friendly ghost, finds seven lost pearls which are supposed to bring good luck to their owner.

Hildén also wrote three plays: one history, *Hertigen av Finland* ('The Duke of Finland,' 1919); one light comedy which also contains a war satire, *Kvinnan och segraren* ('The Woman and the Winner,' 1922); and *Barnet* ('The Child,' performed 1919, printed 1920). The latter attempts to analyze seriously a situation in which a man loved by three women has to choose, but it flounders on the improbabilities of character and plot in spite of being well-written.

His last book, *Folket på Krogen* ('People at Krogen,' 1921), is a historical novel about the tragic destinies of simple people in the Finnish coastal region during the war of 1700 to 1721. The story is simple and forceful, but the language, elaborately reconstructed eighteenth-century Swedish, makes a somewhat artificial impression. After this book he wrote only his last play and a few short stories, which were published after his suicide.

In Finland the family of **Henning Söderhjelm** (1888-1967) has distinguished itself in many fields. His father was a well-known linguist and scholar. He studied abroad himself and took a doctorate in psychology, but worked as a journalist and author in Finland and in Sweden, where he settled in 1923. He has written essays, criticism, biographies, and adventure stories under pseudonyms. Three novels make up his literary work: *Gränsmarksluft* ('Borderland Atmosphere,' written 1914, prohibited by the censure, printed 1917), *Lärospån* ('The First Experience,' 1915), and *Familjen Magnus* ('The Magnus Family,' 1917). In the first, a criticism of the lack of idealism among the middle class, a young man who is disgusted with his meaningless life accepts a post in the administration so that he will be arrested when he protests Russianization. The second is an account of young love and disillusionment, and the third is another description of corruption and selfishness in middle-class surroundings.

Erik Grotenfelt (1891-1919) has been called the only man of action among the *dagdrivare*.[965] He first published two volumes of poetry, *Dikter* ('Poems,' 1914) and *Det röda vinets barn* ('Children of the Red Wine,' 1915), which contain much of Gripenberg's proud attitude as well as an ironical self-criticism typical of the new generation. Of his friends and himself he says:

> We think we can break all fetters, all dams
> with one proud word, with one *beau geste.*
> We love fair women and companies merrily carousing.
> We love the dreams of fights and dangers and deeds arousing.
> But ourselves we however love best.

The main character of Grotenfelt's novel *Bengt Walter's lycka* ('Bengt Walter's Luck,' 1916) is the most typical man-about-town in the literature of the period, a young man who inherits a large country estate which he prefers to sell than to maintain. He states happily, "It is wonderful to be able to sit here with decent people without having to think of tomorrow." Grotenfelt's ideas, however, changed at that time, and he secretly went to Germany with other young Finns to receive military training for a future fight against Russia. He soon returned because of poor health, and, as a newspaperman, he began to propagandize his ideals in articles published posthumously in *En pennas strid* ('The Fight of a Pen,' 1919). He also wrote the novel *Det nya fosterlandet* ('Our New Country,' 1917), which briefly summarizes the feelings of the Swedish upper class of Finland at that time. His political writings are full of hatred. After the White victory in the Civil War, he took part in a search for fugitive Reds. In letters to his wife he boasted that the prisoners were terrified of him and that he shot several of them.[966] In 1919 he shot one more person: himself.

Ture Janson (1886-1954), like Mörne, was sympathetic to the socialist and workers' movement at the beginning of the century. He soon became estranged from it, however, and in 1917 and 1918 wrote newspaper articles against it and for a Finnish monarchy with a German ruler; these articles are as violent and vulgar as anything in the socialist papers.[967] From his student days he worked as a journalist, developing a facile, elegant, and ironic style which aged quickly, as do all fashionable jargons.[968] His partially autobiographical first book, *Inga medmänniskor* ('No Neighbors,' 1911), tells of a young, idealistic man who comes to Helsinki and discovers no one who shares his good intentions. The poems in *Mitt Helsingfors...* ('My Helsinki...,' 1913) the short stories in *Knock me down* (1914; text in Swedish), and *Journalisten Bergman* ('Mr. Bergman, Journalist,' 1915) contain colorful, ironic sketches from contemporary Helsinki. Janson's skepticism goes beyond the humorous in *Journalisten Bergman*, in which he expresses doubts about the meaning of life.

The title of the novel *De ensamma svenskarna* ('The Lonely Swedes,' 1916), an appeal to solidarity among the Swedes, caught on as a phrase, but in it Janson also expresses fear that this solidarity will not be achieved. Mörne himself is a character in the book, but the person who listens to his stirring speech feels that its effect will soon dissipate in the midst of daily life. Janson soon lost the enthusiasm he wrote with in 1917 and 1918, and the novel *Från far till son* ('From Father to Son,' 1922) summarizes his disillusionment with the direction of events. His irony returns to the collection of prose sketches *Jorden går under och andra bagateller* ('The Earth Is Breaking Up and Other Trifles,' 1923), in which he seems to describe himself in stating that the writings of a "newspaperman in disguise" can sometimes be amusing; he goes about the world in the dress of various characters and reports what he observes.[969] *Verkligheten* ('Reality,' 1923), *Maskinmänniskan* ('The Mechanic Man,' 1924), and *Vänskapsbyn* ('The Friendship Village,' 1925) attempt to analyze the impact of modern science and technology on man. Janson generally regards the impact negatively, but he demonstrates that one can counteract it through selfless action. He dropped this serious line in the books he published in Sweden after moving there in 1929, but readopted it in his last novel, *Lugn, min herrar* ('Please, Gentlemen, Quiet,' 1948), wherein two men who thought they had lost everything find new meaning for their lives. However, because Janson did not renew himself after the 1920s, his last books were anachronistic in style even when they were published.

The best writer of the period, who did not belong to a specific group, was **Runar Schildt** (1888-1925). He too belonged to the middle class and first wrote a few works in the *dagdrivare* style, but he soon developed in another direction. Although he had a lonely childhood and was shy in his youth, upon his arrival at the University of Helsinki he was drawn into the gay life he describes in his first works, the short-story collection *Den segrande Eros* ('Eros the Victorious,' 1912) and the story *Asmodeus och de tretton själarna* ('Asmodeus and the Thirteen Souls,' 1913). Schildt could write with a light style better than almost anyone writing at that time in Finland,[970] but the short stories have a touch of sentimentality in the description of characters who, more refined and sensitive than their surroundings, suffer from the vulgarity of ordinary pleasure-seeking. The sentimentality is in fact thinly veiled self-pity, his worst literary flaw. His father had a severe neurosis which Schildt discovered after his father's death, when he was already grown. Schildt himself had fits of depression and finally committed suicide.[971] *Asmodeus och de tretton själarna*, Schildt's lightest story, was criticized for its lack of substance, and he was later embarrassed for having written it. It is the old story, set in contemporary Helsinki, of people ready to sell their souls to the Devil for worldly goods and is an amusing satire of the time.

Schildt had just married and accepted a job in a publishing company, and he felt that he should become a serious citizen and writer. Many of his next works are set in the Swedish area of southern Finland in a fictitious Räfsbacka, which resembles a village near the town of Loviisa (Swed. *Lovisa*), where Schildt spent his childhood; in this respect he is unlike most of the Swedish writers of Finland, who were city-oriented.[972] *Regnbågen* ('The Rainbow,' 1916) is a series of sketches from life in the countryside in the middle of the nineteenth century. One of the characters, Mr. Carstenius, an educated, sensitive, shy, impractical man, is a portrait of the author. In the stories *Rönnbruden* ('The Bride of the Rowan Tree,' 1917) and *Prövningens dag* ('The Day of the Trial,' 1917), there is a leaning toward mysticism which reappears in *Galgmannen*, but both stories can be understood to mean that the supernatural exists only in our belief in it. In *Rönnbruden* a gypsy boy makes a country girl believe that he has bound her fate to that of a rowan tree, that she will die when the tree is felled; her belief causes her to die when the tree falls. The main point is the opposition between the good but weak girl and the evil but strong boy, a contrast which also reappears in later works. The incidents of *Prövningens dag* are simpler: a miserly farmer of means who is frightened by an old, legless beggar (because there is something mysterious about the beggar) is soon convinced that imagination is playing tricks on him.

Schildt's next works show the influence of World War I and the Civil War, during which he lived in Helsinki. He did not take part in the events, and he did not suffer personal molestation. He was neither sympathetic nor bitter toward the Reds, who were then occupying Helsinki, and his works on the events of the time show more interest in characters than in the events themselves. Some show characters involved in the incidents simply through bad luck, a portrayal similar to that in Sillanpää's *Meek Heritage. Den svagare* ('The Weaker' in the collection *Perdita* [name, 1918]) is another variation on the theme that the ruthless and strong succeed when the good and weak are destroyed. Only the fact that the ruthless man is a black market dealer and speculator makes the story timely. Two stories in *Hemkomsten* ('Coming Home,' 1919) relate to the war. *Aapo* tells the story of a country boy, Aapo, who is ridiculed at the estate where he works; in the war he takes revenge. In

Hemkomsten a man comes home from the war to hide; the story is mainly about the anxieties of his mother, who helps him until he is discovered.

The long story *Armas Fager* (1920) describes a supernumerary in a theater who spends his free time dreaming about the great things he might have done. He reappears in the play *Den stora rollen* ('The Big Part,' 1923), set during the Civil War, which, he thinks, has given him the opportunity to become a great artist and director. Nothing comes of his ambitions, however, and he is shot by a fellow Red because he is ready to betray the Reds to save his life. The title story of the collection *Häxskogen* ('Witchwood,' 1920) deals with an artist of a different sort, a writer, who experiences the problems many artists, including Schildt, have to face.[973] The writer feels that he is losing his inspiration and cannot write again, until he has been disillusioned by an unhappy love affair. His problem is complicated by his temperament, for he is one of Schildt's shy characters, ill at ease and unable to relate to others.

The magic of the play *Galgmannen* ('The Man of the Gallows,' 1922),[974] less important than it seems, is a male figure made from the wood of the gallows, a talisman which brings luck to its owner but eventually destroys him. The motif appears in many mystery stories; Balzac's *La Peau de chagrin* is another serious treatment of it. The play does not begin, however, until the owner, a retired colonel, is about to die, bitter and lonely on his country estate. He finds final comfort in a young woman who appears ready to sacrifice herself to save him. The play has only one act and these two characters, whose opposite personalities are analyzed briefly but with great penetration. Schildt's last work, *Lyckoriddaren* ('The Adventurer,' 1923), is also a play. It is long and has an improbable, melodramatic plot about a diplomat with a dark secret. When his colleagues discover it and suggest that he resign, he proudly rejects the offer and the love of a woman who would have stood by him and kills himself.

Thomas Warburton points out that Schildt's unhappy life and tragic death give his works a romance which made objective appreciation difficult.[975] Although the romantic inventions of some of his works are things of the past, his best writing provides convincing analyses of people, and his professional skill is above question.

Schildt's son, **Göran** (b. 1917), a former art historian who published a doctoral dissertation on Cézanne, has written several books on the Mediterranean countries, which he has visited in his yacht. He treats his subjects with more depth than does the ordinary tourist, and the books are available in several languages, including English.[976]

Jarl Hemmer (1893-1944) and Tegengren are the only poets of their time in Swedish Finland to have their works widely read in all circles of their linguistic group.[977] Hemmer, who began writing verse in secondary school, showed some to Tegengren, who liked them. His first collection, *Rösterna* ('The Voices,' 1914), seemed to begin a new era of open, strong emotion and self-confidence contrasting with the irony, cynicism, and doubt of the *dagdrivare*, whom he criticized in many works. The division between the good, bright and pure, and the bad, dark and impure, which is typical of Hemmer's later works, first appears here. Love is spiritual; he describes sex and instincts as base. This polarity, though initially accepted as natural, produced increasing tension, reflected in his works, especially in the story *Fantaster* ('Idle Dreamers,' 1915), which reproduces discussions between Hemmer and his friends on life, love, and art. The majority of the readers of the Swedish literature in Finland did not find the cynicism of the *dagdrivare* congenial; Hemmer's naive idealism was more to their liking, and he gave them more of it in the collection *Pelaren* ('The Pillar,' 1916), in which he states that even a kiss is beauty's downfall, for that which one adores most becomes dust. The pillar of the title poem is made "of the fire of a thousand souls," of dreams from hearts which have the strength to "rise a-yearning over the low shores of earth," and it burns against a background of darkness.

After the Civil War Hemmer published a few violently antisocialist poems, *Ett land i kamp* ('A Fighting Country,' 1918), a short-story collection, *Förvandlingar* ('Changes,' 1918), and the long poem *Prins Louis Ferdinand* (1919), but none are very important. Soon he viewed the war from a different perspective, and he appears as a mature artist for the first time in the poems *Över dunklet* ('Over the Darkness,' 1919), through which he expresses his agony over the violence and brutality of the time. He wonders at it, but predicts a better future, which is sometimes only a dream. The island of the poem *Drömmen om ön* ('The Dream about an Island') is the Isle of Blessed, beyond the sorrow and strife of the world.

Although in his initial works Hemmer rejects ugliness, he becomes fascinated by pain and suffering in his later works and concludes that they are a necessary purification, a penance. In 1920 he published the novel *Onni Kokko*, in which the main character retains his real name. Onni Kokko was a fourteen-year-old boy who joined the White army in the Civil War, was killed in action, and became a hero to his side. Although the novel begins as the usual narrative about a hero's deeds, it becomes a description of the boy's growing doubts about the glorious patriotic nature of the war. He finds his own uncle, an honest, peace-loving worker, among the Red prisoners, and a somewhat improbably disillusioned White officer comments in his presence on the meaningless cruelty of the conflict.[978] Two stories in the collection *De skymda ljusen* ('The Shaded Lights,' 1921) are as extreme as the attitudes of his early poems. Both consider the motif of guilt and atonement. In one a man convinced that he has accidentally shot a child while hunting still feels guilty after he is proved innocent because he knows that he could have done it. In the unimportant collections *Skärseld* ('Purgatory,' 1925) and *Helg* ('Holy Time,' 1929) Hemmer balances guilt and ecstasy, but he does not explain the nature or origin of the guilt.

The long narrative poem *Rågens rike* (1922; trans. *The Realm of the Rye*, 1938), however, is a robust, happy tale about a wealthy farmer and a poor young man in love with the same girl. It is the only such poem after Runeberg worthy of interest.[979] Its happy atmosphere is retained in the poetry collection *Väntan* ('Waiting,' 1922), which contains an almost ecstatic worship of beauty and harmony. The images are well-known—a butterfly who flies perilously far from land and a lark who sings in the sunshine. The butterfly, however, symbol of beauty, is frail and in danger, and the lark, symbol of the poet, sings until he is "tired to death." Although Hemmer was praised by the traditional and influential critics,[980] *Väntan* was attacked by young radicals. One of the most conspicuous, Elmer Diktonius, spoke of him with such phrases as "spiritual lace-making" and "manicure for the souls."[981]

His verse drama *Med ödet ombord* ('With Fate on Board,' 1924) has a romantic plot. The main motif first appears in Alfred de Vigny's *Servitude et grandeur militaires*. A man sentenced to exile boards a ship with his wife; the captain discovers from sealed instructions when they are at sea that he is to have the man shot. Instead he throws himself into the sea when he finds out that the wife loves her husband.

In *Fattiggubbens brud* ('The Bride of the Poor Man,' 1926) Hemmer combines mysticism and folk life, as did Schildt. A wooden figure of a man was often set near the doors of churches in old Finland; he was the "poor man," and the faithful could put alms for the poor in a slot on his breast. A country girl has a strong religious experience when her fiancé dies after committing what she considers sacrilege by making fun of the "poor man." The story follows her life in the village, where her pious activities attract followers and opposition. Her friends and enemies finally fight, and she is killed trying to separate them, but her memory is revered in the village. In spite of the ethnographic paraphernalia, the novel convincingly portrays her religious experiences and life in the village.

Hemmer's last two important works are the short-story volume *Budskap* ('Messages,' 1928) and the novel *En man och hans samvete* (1931; trans. *A Fool of Faith*, 1936). The title story of *Budskap* again deals with the Civil War: a young White futilely tries to establish contact with a Red prisoner. The prisoner escapes and badly wounds him, but he still believes that love and understanding is possible between men. However, since he is half-delirious, the ending may mean that love and understanding between men is only a dream. *En man och hans samvete* returns to the theme of guilt, which is here clearly motivated. A young divinity student loses his position because he publicly denies Christ's divine nature, and he lives in poverty, trying to save sinners. He is involved in a sordid incident with a prostitute and sentenced to prison. He becomes a prison chaplain and is sent to a prison camp after the Civil War, where he has himself shot in the place of a man sentenced to death.

Hemmer's resemblance to the great Russian writers, especially Dostoyevski and Tolstoy, has often been mentioned.[982] He visited Russia before the revolution, learned the language, and published translations of Russian poetry, e.g., half the poems in *Lyriska översättningar* ('Lyrical Translations,' 1922) and drama (Chekhov), and essays. Although Hemmer's best works are on a high level, he is not as great a writer as the Russian masters. In his optimistic works he is brighter and more energetic. His duality, at first a strength, eventually destoyed his creativity. After *En man och hans samvete* he published a novel, three poetry collections, and *Brev till vänner* ('Letters to Friends,' 1937), which includes the Russian essays; but even friendly critics could find little positive to say about them. He committed suicide on December 6, 1944, probably choosing the date because on that Independence Day the very existence of his country seemed to be threatened.

Gustaf Mattsson (1873-1914) is the only true humorist among the melancholy Swedish writers we have discussed. His early death was due to tuberculosis, and the disease seems to have given him an urge to make the most of his life. He took a chemistry degree from Helsinki Institute of Technology, where he taught, and wrote newspaper articles on popular science He helped found the periodical *Argus*, forbidden by the censure and continued as *Nya Argus*. He was also a regular journalist, an author, member of Parliament, and a good amateur pianist. He is most remembered for the more than nine hundred sketches he published under the pseudonym Ung-Hans in the daily papers. They contain humorous and satirical reflections on events in Helsinki, Finland, and the world, and reflect the author's intelligence and wit as well as his tolerance and humanity. Selections of them are still printed and read, e.g., *I dag* ('Today,' 1950-56; Finn. *Tänään*, 1961) and *Kreatur och professorer* ('Creatures and Professors,' 1953).

Modernism in literature appeared earlier in the Swedish verse of Finland than in either Finnish verse or the Swedish verse of Sweden.[983] These new poets were more radical than their Finnish counterparts, the *Tulenkantajat*, and provoked their opponents to more violent resistance. They were not all political, but some, especially Diktonius, proclaimed their faith in a new society and their contempt for the old with flamboyant vehemence, and others, especially Gunnar Björling, purposely irritated traditional critics with disruptive and occasionally nonsensical experiments in poetic and linguistic form. Internationally aware, they boasted of following everything new happening abroad (they especially favored German expressionism),[984] but their information was fragmentary, and their famous periodical *Ultra* now makes a very uneven impression. They did not seek objectivity; Diktonius published an article which warned readers against looking for beauty or truth in their works. He stated that philosophy, in life or art, belonged to quiet periods of history and that his contemporaries could be honest only when furiously charging forward.[985] They sought total freedom of expression, and they stressed instinct and the unconscious. Their modernism was not intellectual, and many of them, including Diktonius, later reverted to admiration of simple life and direct contact with nature.[986] Although initially united by common interests and friendship, they never formed a literary group such as the *Tulenkantajat*, and they soon went different ways.[987]

Although her poetry found defenders in Finland, **Edith Södergran** (1892-1923) was almost a stranger in her own country. Her parents belonged to the Swedish population of Finland, but she was born in St. Petersburg, where she went to a German school, read German poets, and wrote her first lyrical compositions in German.[988] She contracted tuberculosis when she was sixteen, and her parents lost their fortune in the revolution; she spent her last years in a Finnish village on the Isthmus of Karelia, so poor that her death was partially a result of malnutrition.[989]

If it were not for the form of her poetry, Edith Södergran might be called a romantic poet. Her works contain typical romantic images and details, lyres of silver and ivory, vines, and red veils. She speaks of St. Petersburg as a fairytale town with violets strewn over "the golden sidewalks of dreams." She expressly wished to exclude from her verse all that would "profane the temple of art."[990] Because of her youth, interests, and studies, she was estranged from her own country and often experienced disappointment in trying to establish contact with the literary circles, and Thomas Warburton considers it very possible that the originality of her verse is due to the influence of the German language and her initial unfamiliarity with Swedish literature.[991] Strongly influenced by Nietzsche, she describes the poet as the creator of beauty on earth, a beauty for the few which must be protected from sordid reality. Nevertheless she insists that energy and courage are essential attributes of the poet. She approved of all that was fresh and alive and felt united with nature. Most critics did not look beyond the form of her poetry and were hostile to it.[992] Gripenberg and Grotenfelt defended it, and so did Mörne and Schildt, for her ideas were aesthetic; she did not express contempt for those who could not be admitted to her world of beauty. Only when considering that it was not for the weak did she express superiority, along with a yearning for harmony and rest.

Illness had not yet weakened her before the publication of her first collection, *Dikter* ('Poems,' 1916), and it expresses a gay, sensuous acceptance of the world and an almost arrogant attitude of carefree spiritual freedom. It also expresses shyness, her difficulties in establishing human contacts, and her resulting tendency to retire into her private dreamworld. Her conflicting feelings result in a rejection of ordinary happiness and acceptance of suffering as the highest spiritual element. In the last poem she says:

Do you know pain? She is strong and clenches secretly her fists.
Do you know pain? She has a smile full of hope and traces of tears in her
    eyes.
Pain gives us all we need
. . . .
she gives us all the highest winnings of life:
love, solitude and the face of death.

Her second collection, *Septemberlyran* ('The Lyre of September,' 1918), was published when she had experienced the Russian revolution, a disappointing visit to Helsinki, and the Civil War, but her poetry does not reflect worldly events. The turbulence of the time and her suffering turned her away from the world, and the critics' lack of understanding for her art probably intensified her retreat into the world of her fantasies.[993] Her appreciation of Nietzsche matured, and she became convinced that she should take pride in the fact that she was not meant for ordinary happiness, but to contemplate a world of beauty hidden from common mortals and to grasp the universe in her mind. There is something disarming in the exaggeration of her intellectual and artistic pride. In the collection's introduction she says calmly: "I am so sure of myself because I have discovered my dimensions. It behooves me not to make myself smaller than I am." She had severed herself completely from the sordid reality in which she lived and saw herself as a spirit in communion with the universe. Her romanticism is apparent in her dualistic conception of mind and matter on totally different levels. She was convinced, too, that she wrote for a few select, "for the few who are closest to the border of the future."

The reviews of her second collection were so unfavorable that Thomas Warburton says they overstepped the limits of decency, but another young female writer, Hagar Olsson, defended her, became her friend, and had a long correspondence with her. Her next collection, *Rosenaltaret* ('The Altar of Roses,' 1919), though similar, has more subdued, small poems. In *Framtidens skugga* ('The Shadow of the Future,' 1920), generally considered her best volume, she gradually discards her pride and conviction that she is a prophet of higher truths. She had had a deep religious experience and, rejecting Nietzsche, had adopted the Christian faith in a very personal form. In a few passages of this collection we feel her beginning to doubt the truths she had until then accepted. One poem, *Den stora trädgården* ('The Great Garden'), combines her pride and her newfound community with other humans. She speaks of the poets as homeless wanderers in rags, superior to princes because they take from the air treasures which cannot be measured with the weight of gold. She says that they have nothing to do with the rest of creation "except to give it our souls." She dreams of building an iron fence around a great garden to which she would like to invite all brothers and sisters (she does not call them poets) so that no sound from the world will reach them, but adds:

"From our silent garden we shall give the world a new life." She felt the triumphant strength she had derived from aesthetic contemplation failing, and she took comfort in religion although she could not submit to it unconditionally. Many of her doubts and inner struggles are reflected in the collection of aphorisms *Brokiga iakttagelser* ('Mixed Observations,' 1919).

The spiritual conflict probably sapped some of her creative power during her last years, when her illness was becoming much worse.[994] More young Swedish poets were appearing in Finland, and they admired her and recognized that she had marked their road. She could have joined them, but it was too late. Her last poems have a new harmony, an acceptance of death and submission to fate. Hagar Olsson published them with other papers as *Landet som icke är* ('The Land That Is Not,' 1925). After her death she was idolized by the young and recognized by the old. Possibly no Swedish poet of Finland after Runeberg has had greater influence on succeeding generations.[995]

Hagar Olsson (b. 1893) made her initial reputation as a critic and essayist. She found in the writing of literary essays and reviews an opportunity to present worthy new ideas and to change literature and art for the better. The daughter of a minister, she grew up in Karelia and Viipuri, then moved to Helsinki, where she worked as a journalist and writer. Of her generation she was perhaps the best informed about world events in the 1920s, and her cosmopolitan attitude helped her to objectivity toward the linguistic quarrels which agitated Finland at that time. She was one of the main contributors to *Ultra* in 1922, in which she published several articles which introduced contemporary European literature to Finland. Her aim was to convert, and she sought literature which put the individual in contact with the great forces of the world. Partially reacting against the tired cynicism of the *dagdrivare*, she sincerely believed that modern man's major flaw was his lack of ideals and apathy. She was unaware that her anti-intellectualism and cult of action foreshadowed the totalitarian movements which threatened to destroy civilization in the 1930s and 1940s. In an essay from *Arbetare in natten* ('Workers in the Night,' 1935), there is an enthusiastic address to the new youth in Russia, Germany, and Italy "which does not criticize and which does not care about looking for the truth—it marches with enthusiasm and *élan*!" She did not foresee where the action and change she admired would lead. She wrote that she approved of Walt Whitman's "passionate will to follow a direction without thinking of the goal, to move, to go forward without knowing the aim."[996] Her ideas conformed to the spirit of the time; we find the same attitude in the proclamations of the *Tulenkantajat* and Haarla.

Her first works are a direct protest of the literary fashion in Finland at that time, but they offer no clear answer to literary or moral questions and contain a vague mysticism in which death and awareness of death figure importantly. This theme develops from her first book, the novel *Lars*

Thorman och döden ('Lars Thorman and Death,' 1916), to its end in *Kvinnan och nåden* ('A Woman and Grace,' 1919) with the affirmation of the Christian belief that death is the ultimate step to grace. Subsequently she was in contact with a group of radical young writers and began writing for *Ultra*; a collection of her essays was published as *Ny generation* ('The New Generation,' 1925). Her further attempts to deal with problems of the contemporary world are not entirely satisfactory; her irrational conception of the world prevented her from thoroughly analyzing her subjects. Some of her works from this period are plays, which were performed. The first, *Hjärtats pantomim* ('The Pantomime of the Heart'), was produced in 1927 and has not been printed. *S.O.S.* (1928) deals with the conversion of a specialist in poison gas into a pacifist with the help of a loving woman; but the characters are not convincing, and the play does not seem real. *Det blå undret* ('The Blue Miracle,' 1932) is less vague. A brother belongs to a fascist organization; his sister is a socialist. After a street riot in which she is arrested (a daring scene at that time), they learn to understand each other.

She continued to write. *Mr. Jeremias söker en illusion* ('Mr. Jeremias Looks for an Illusion,' 1926), a description of a person searching for higher truth, is in her earlier style, but *På Kanaanexpressen* ('On the Canaan Express,' 1929) attempts as modern as possible a form to tell the story of a group of young people who come to a deeper view of life through a love tragedy which happens among them. *Det blåser upp till storm* ('A Storm Is Rising,' 1930) is about the rebellion of the younger generation, told by a working-class girl who is about to finish secondary school with middle-class young people. She falls in love with one of them, and they begin propagating radical ideas among their schoolmates. When she becomes pregnant, they attempt to live together, but the boy's parents bring him home, and he shoots himself.

Hagar Olsson's modernism was always somewhat forced, and after *Det blå undret* she returned to her mysticism, now less vague and esoteric, expressed in realistic descriptions. The novel *Chitambo* (1933; the symbolic title refers to an incident in David Livingstone's life) is partially autobiographical, the description of the development of a young girl into a young woman. The book is serious, but it has touches of humor and many images from a happy childhood in the countryside before World War I, a period already romantic when the book was published. Her obsession with death reappears, and she again gives it a positive value. The book ends as the young woman finds spiritual balance. *Träsnidaren och döden* ('The Woodcarver and Death,' 1940) is a near legend set in Karelia, the land of legends. Formally it relates contemporary events. An artist who feels that his inspiration is failing him and that he has lost contact with other humans comes to a Karelian village, where he witnesses the peaceful and happy death of a sick girl under the image of a miracle-working icon to which she has made a pilgrimage. He settles in the village and meets a girl who has run away from home. The style is intentionally romantic, and the book is well-written, but not for men of little faith.[997]

The play *Rövaren och jungfrun* ('The Robber and the Maiden,' 1944) presents a poor man who takes the law into his own hands during the famine of 1868 and distributes the grain of a wealthy farmer to the hungry. He kills the farmer, then submits to the law and goes to prison. The girl he loves, who had been forced to accept the proposal of the dead man, remains alone and dedicates her life to charitable work.

In 1948 she published a long essay, *Jag lever* ('I Am Living'; traditionally Aleksis Kivi's last words, Finn. *Minä elän*), which describes poetically man's communion with the collective spirit, a primitive Christian idea, according to her, corrupted by Western individualism. *Kinesisk utflykt* ('A Chinese Excursion,' 1949) is a fantasy about the events of her own life. A collection of short stories, *Hemkomst* ('Coming Home') appeared in 1961 and a volume of memoirs, *Möte med kära gestalter* ('Meeting Those Whom I Have Loved') in 1963. In 1969 she was awarded an honorary doctorate by the University of Helsinki.

Elmer Diktonius (1896-1961) was the most controversial of the new literary figures. He was aggressive and intentionally brutal, inventing picturesque insults which he delivered to his opponents with great gusto. Born in Helsinki, the son of a printer, he was apart from the upper middle-class Swedish writers of Finland, and he attended a Finnish secondary school. Later he wrote in both languages and translated poems by Eino Leino and *Seven Brothers* into Swedish. He studied music at the Helsinki conservatory, and he later sometimes earned his living as a café musician. He met a young literary scholar with socialist ideas, Otto Ville Kuusinen, who escaped to the Soviet Union after the Civil War and reached the highest positions any Finn has occupied abroad. Kuusinen's influence on Diktonius was beneficial. He recommended the use of pregnant, realistic images and the avoidance of generalities as well as adoption of socialist ideals. He did not, however, appreciate Diktonius's gifts for nonpolitical poetry and his love for nature.[998] Diktonius never became an orthodox socialist or communist poet, and, with age, he turned away from topical questions toward the elemental forces of life, as did many other writers of his generation.

In 1920 Diktonius lived in Paris and London, at times in dire poverty; his descriptions of the suffering of the poor are partially based on this experience. In 1921 he published his first work, *Min Dikt* ('My Poetry'), printed by a small company in Sweden after rejection in Finland.[999] It is a collection of aphorisms almost exclusively about art and artistic creation. They are more a search for truth than a proclamation of it, but the author is certain about the unity of art and life. He does not believe in art for art's sake or in beauty higher than any other worldly thing, and he attacks aesthetic theories based on this premise. He says, "In order to live, a work of art does not need beauty; not ugliness either. It must have life."[1000] His view was in opposition to Edith Södergran's, but he admired her art, just as he later admired that of Volter Kilpi, also his opposite in many respects. He was not bound by theories.

His next collection, *Hårda sånger* ('Hard Songs,' 1922), was published in Finland by L. A. Salava (1894-1955), who did much for the young poets at that time and printed *Ultra* (Salava also wrote some poetry and prose). It is full of violent images, fantasies about storms, earthquakes, and volcanoes which will shake the old order to bits:

> I want to have life that pulls the roots up,
> howling air, roaring waves
> floods earthquakes volcanoes erupting.
> More red on the sky, more ragged black clouds!
> There are still a few tall trees standing unbent against the wind.
> Break down with them!
> – and I shall sing my triumphal song
> about the holy fear of strength.

Jaguaren ('The Jaguar'), a famous poem from this collection, is impressionistic in technique: the beast is never described; only the most striking details are mentioned briefly. Although there are other symbols of lasting, quiet power, the book's breathless intensity makes an uneven impression.

In 1922 Diktonius met Edith Södergran and Hagar Olsson and wrote for *Ultra* and *Arbetarbladet*, the Swedish socialist paper whose chief editor encouraged him and helped him find a more positive direction for his radicalism.[1001] The aphorisms of his next collection, *Brödet och elden* ('The Bread and the Fire,' 1923), are quieter in tone, but more aggressive in their precise formulation. Some of the poems in *Taggiga lågor* ('Thorny Flames,' 1924) were written as early as 1918 and 1919, and they show the calm atmosphere which reappears in his last works. They have revolutionary fantasies, but they also have images from the daily life of the working class. He includes in this volume poetic portraits of authors and composers he liked, Strindberg, Dostoyevski, Edgar Lee Masters, Mahler, Schönberg, and others.

In 1923 Diktonius married and lived at Jyväskylä, a small town which he later describes in *Ringar i stubben* (1954):

> A winter night in a small town: a dog, a police officer, a dog (perhaps the same), still another dog. But all are so far from each other, without any external communication, without any internal sympathy. Streetlights like red eyes. Thy sky like the brain of a neurasthenic. The walls bulge under the snores of the middle class. Not a soul to whom one could go. The silence is laying its cuckoo's eggs into my soul.

However, the contact with nature he found there was a revelation to him, and he described it in *Onnela* in prose interspersed with poetry. Juhani Aho had written of an Onnela, the imaginary land of happiness, but Diktonius's, although free of political and social overtones, is completely different. He was drunk with sunshine, the smell of the forests, grass, earth, dirt, and dung. He wished to omit nothing from his picture of the countryside, and he ridiculed the "monks of civilization" who were unable to enjoy it.

His happiness was short-lived. He returned to Paris in 1925 with his wife, but the trip was unsuccessful, and they eventually divorced. The experience was difficult for him, but afterwards he produced some of his best poems in *Stenkol* ('Hard Coal,' 1927) and *Stark men mörk* ('Strong but Dark,' 1930). In *Stenkol* there remain revolutionary songs, less violent but more penetrating than earlier ones. Although Diktonius has a simplified view of social problems, always siding with the poor and oppressed, he realizes that revolutionary dreams can be dangerous:

> Beware of the red fog
> which appears before sunrise!
> It makes everything confused
> and lets the crazy seeds of fanaticism
> drop into your hearts, all too ready to catch
> fire.

In *Stark men mörk* and thereafter he turns more and more to nature, which gives him peace:

> So I have again a foot on the earth[1002]
> and the earth is my friend
> . . . .
> there is sun living in the earth
> I am living in the earth—
> everything I love is living in the earth
> and is a bit of earth.

The collection also includes poems on social motifs, e.g., *Maskinsång* ('The Song of the Machine') and *Röd-Eemeli* ('Red Eemeli'), some gentle compositions on poor children which reappear in *Mull och moln* ('Clods and Clouds,' 1934), a collection which includes more prose than verse.

In 1928 Diktonius published a collection of short stories, *Ingenting* ('Nothing'), which does not have the strength and originality of his poetry. One of the best, *Bilderbok från Nurmijärvi* ('A Book of Pictures from Nurmijärvi'), describes Aleksis Kivi's home region, which he loved and used in later works. He seemingly wrote his first prose works carelessly; the first story which he took pains with the composition and form of was *Janne Kubik* (1932), which he called "a woodcut in words." It was especially noticed and discussed for its personal style. When he rewrote and published it in Finnish (*Janne Kuutio*, 1946) it was discovered that it had been "thought in Finnish" from the beginning—the original, Swedish version was almost a translation.[1003] It describes with broad, harsh lines (similar to those of a woodcut) the life of a simple man who witnesses and participates in the violence which occurred in Finland from the Civil War through the early 1930s, a man who is not always on the side Diktonius considered right. It was the author's intent to show that, once one has accepted violence, one cannot tell where it will ultimately take him. The collection of stories *Medborgare i republiken Finland* ('Citizens of the Republic Finland,' 1935) is a successful blend of his satire, violence, and understanding for the sufferings of all humans. *Gossen och grimman* is about an orphan boy raised in a brutal, miserly family. *Älgkulan* ('Buckshot') tells of an old man who views the destruction of his life's work when his farm is auctioned. *Medborgare* II (1940) is much weaker than the first collection; the best section contains his memories from childhood.

His last collections of poetry, *Jordisk ömhet* ('Earthly Gentleness,' 1938), *Varsel* ('Forebodings,' 1942), and *Annorlunda* ('Otherwise,' 1948), speak of nature and the earth as elemental forces which forever remain to protect and comfort against hostile forces, but the poet is not fleeing the world. He is merely leaning on the reliable in the face of adversity. The same atmosphere prevails in the prose *Höstlig bastu* ('Autumn Sauna,' 1943), which contains descriptions from Nurmijärvi, essays on Aleksis Kivi, and a eulogy to the sauna, which the Finns take as seriously as the French do their cuisine and wines.

A collection of his poetry written or translated into Finnish was published as *Kirjaimia ja kirjavia* ('Colors and Characters,' 1956). In 1957 a collection of essays, *Meningar* ('Opinions'), was published in Swedish; it includes a series of articles on music originally printed in 1933 and suggests the importance of music in his poetry.

Although Diktonius was consciously narrow-minded, he appreciated works very different from his own, and he was informed about world events. The authors and composers who caught his interest are among the most significant of our time, unlike those who were studied and translated by more respected Finnish authors and scholars contemporary to him.

Gunnar Björling (1887-1960) studied more extensively than any other modernist poet of his time, and he was attracted by the relativism of the Finnish sociologist Edward Westermarck. Basic to Björling's philosophy is the idea that nothing is complete, that everything constantly develops and changes. His intellectual scrutiny resulted in an effort to break down old ideals and reach an attitude of spontaneity opposed to all conventions in his first book, *Vilande dag* ('The Resting Day,' 1922), though the work is somewhat conventional and betrays the influence of romantic nineteenth-century idealism. It and *Korset och löften* ('The Cross and the Promises,' 1925) consist mainly of prose reflections and aphorisms largely on ethical questions and art, two aspects of the same problem to Björling.

Subsequent works seldom present his convictions directly; they are anti-intellectual in form although built on intellectual foundations. Even *Korset och löften* is somewhat violent and sarcastic in its attacks on sentimentality and convention in life and art (even on his own sentimentality in his first book). These characteristics also appear in the reflections and aphorisms he wrote for the short-lived but now famous literary periodical *Quosego*. Some are logical: "We cannot give the truth to those who wish to decide what it must be like;" others are whimsical: "Life is the banana the monkeys do not reach." Poems and short prose passages in *Korset och löften* contain statements such as, "God smote me, I socked it back to him," and strings of meaningless syllables.[1004] They are still more numerous in *Kiri-ra!* (1930). The title poem begins "harakiri-ka! ki, ka / hara-ra!" and continues in a similar vein. The collection also contains poems describing scenes in the impressionistic manner to be found in some compositions by Diktonius, e.g.:

> This morning. Peace
> and seagull screech.
> A boat and flower
> are land and water.
> The boat of the flower is the day,
> its air under the horizon.

After publishing *Solgrönt* ('Sungreen,' 1933), Björling becomes less aggressive and fully develops his art, in which scenes from nature have an important place. They represent a reaction against his intellectualism, an attempt to refind direct contact with the simplest form of life, to be one with the world, and to draw new forces from it. The poems are built with a unique splintered language in which all unnecessary words are deleted and the others combined in a new way. The connections established by the poet between worn-out elements of speech are unusual and fresh, e.g., in *O finns en dag* ('Oh Is There a Day'):

> My day my evening my night
> take spruce and pine and the roses
> and rowan-tree, the lilacs
> and tree and the grass
> take sand and stone and the brokensplinter of the earth
> take this hour, and take me
> me and beloved were dead, and killed
> all of man heart limb and the movements
> on the earth been.

The collections which immediately follow *Solgrönt* retain much of the ethical meditation of his early books, this time in scattered observations, metaphors, and insights rather than in systematic reflections, especially in the first two, *Fågel badar snart i vattnen* ('The Bird Bathes Soon in the Waters,'

1934) and *Men blåser violer på havet* ('But Blowing Violets on the Sea,' 1936). (Like his poems, Björling's titles are both simple and baffling.) In the latter collection and in the next, *Att syndens blåa nagel* ('But That the Blue Claw of Sin,' 1936), his reflections begin to take the form of concentrated, pregnant declarations and maxims. The search for a human ideal in *Att syndens blåa nagel* takes the poet far from reality, so far that it hints of mysticism, although too many efforts have been made to find mysticism in everything he wrote.[1005]

It is not possible to recount here all of Björling's poetry because he was among the most productive poets in Finland. Between 1938 and 1959 he published fifteen collections with titles such as *Där jag vet att du* ('Where I Know That You,' 1938), *Ord och att eannat* ('Words and That Nothing Else,' 1945), and *Vårt kattliv timmar* ('Our Catlife Hours,' 1949). They are monotonous in the same manner that the sky and sea are monotonous for those who do not have the patience to study them. Patience is needed to read Björling's works; he implicitly admitted that they were fragments of a whole which could never be completed. His poetry has not been popular, and he was hardly known even in literary circles until the 1940s, when poets and critics of the "difficult school" in Sweden discovered him and aroused interest in his works, which has sometimes taken what Dr. Lindström calls "badly panegyric forms."[1006]

Rabbe Enckell (b. 1903) began writing for *Ultra* at the age of nineteen and soon developed into a remarkable poet and sharp theoretician of the modern school. His poetry differs from that of Södergran, Diktonius, and Björling. His art is not visionary, prophetic, or violent; it frequently consists of delicate analysis of his feelings. In his later work classical myths are treated importantly, in a very personal manner. He shared with the writers of the 1920s the wish to write in a style different from previous styles, and he formulated an artistic program for himself in an article published in *Quosego*.[1007] Although not revolutionary, it is a clear rejection of traditional forms of art. Enckell, a somewhat paradoxical figure, arrives at something not unlike art for art's sake, although he criticizes that old theory. He defines the goals of art as follows: "The power which drives art to the highest achievements can not be anything but the interest in art," and "art, in its efforts to reach the highest goals ... may forget all human interests, all ethical claims." However, he finishes the sentence: "knowing that it serves human interests in the best and purest manner and fulfills ethical claims when it attempts to find the highest forms for itself: the infinite and the perfect."[1008]

His first two collections, *Dikter* ('Poems,' 1923) and *Flöjtblåsarlycka* ('Flute-Player happiness,' 1925), contain delicate poems on nature and, especially in the latter, on love. They reveal a balanced personality with a natural bias for the exquisite and a gift for catching subtle shades in landscapes and feelings. These feelings, although not strongly expressed, are strongly experienced, and this genuine quality is what makes his art more than formal exercises and elegant trifles.[1009] As one might expect, his poetry did not immediately attract a large audience, and he was for many years better known as an essayist and critic.[1010] His early essays, collected in *Tillblivelse* ('The Becoming,' 1929), *Ljusdunkel* (1930; the title reveals Enckell's interest in painting–it is the Swedish word for the Italian *chiaroscuro*), and *Ett porträtt* ('A Portrait,' 1931), are mainly self-analysis and justification of his art. Initially he advocates extreme subjectivity; he concludes that "we [poets and artists] are constantly driven toward the ultimate goal: a self-portrait."[1011] But, he also says, "We identify ourselves with parts of our surroundings. . . . Our personality consists of a quantity of vague sensations, of communications with a world which is both outside and inside us. It is formed of places, people, inflections of voices, sensory perceptions, impulses, and, finally, of–the creative trend in life." Laitinen says that Enckell does not find in nature symbols of man and his activities or feelings,[1012] but he does not view it with complete objectivity. He has achieved a peaceful identification of man and nature.[1013] His capacity for objective description of himself and nature does appear in the volume of peotry and prose *Landskapet med den dubbla skuggan* ('The Landscape with the Double Shadow,' 1933). *Vårens cistern* ('The Well of Spring,' 1931) and *Tonbrädet* ('The Soundboard,' 1935) further prove his mastery at drawing delicate pictures from nature.

Tonbrädet reflects the awareness of passion and sorrow, which grew from events in the poet's life. The short stories in *Herrar till natt och dag* ('Lords of Night and Day,' 1937) openly criticize his earlier attitudes, and the poems in *Valvet* ('The Vault,' 1937) meditate on a threatening world, often combining these thoughts with the poet's self-criticism. This collection reveals the full development of Enckell's later style, which uses myths and images from classical antiquity. Here again we see his refusal to unveil totally his personal feelings. He has said that he loves the "deeply human qualities of the myths" and wants to "combine personal experience with their objective form and deep truth" and that he does not see them as a "costume" but as a "manner of living."[1014] Pursuing this direction, he has written verse dramas characterized by the discretion in expressing personal feeling that is so apparent in his poems. Warburton says that "Sophocles is more his master than Euripides or Aeschylus," but we suspect that the influence of French classical tragedies is detectable in his drama.[1015] The first two, *Orfeus och Eurydike* (1938) and *Iokasta* ('Iocaste,' 1939), deal with the problems of the individual, whereas *Agamemnon* (1948), *Hekuba* (1952), *Mordet på Kiron* ('The Murder of Khiron,' 1954), and *Alkman* (1959) reflect antiquity and the great problems of our times, e.g., war, although they are not allegories.

In spite of his distant attitude toward reality, the great events of his time have not left Enckell indifferent. The poetry of *Lutad över brunnen* ('Leaning over the Well,' 1942) is filled with deep despair about the fate of man. Hope appears in *Andedräkt av koppar* ('A Breath of Brass,' 1947), but it is based on seemingly insignificant details. In *O spång av mellanord* ('O Steps of Words Between'), a long poem about language, life itself is represented by the "words between," which bind together and serve, and which are "transparent of / what the spirit has in common with all and everything."

Andedräkt av koppar made the author known, even in Sweden, and he has since published many other collections, e.g., *Sett och återbördat* ('Things Seen and Gathered,' 1950), *Skuggors lysen* ('Lights of Shadows,' 1953), *Kärnor av ögonblick* ('Hearts of Instants,' 1959), and *Det är dags* ('The Day Is Here,' 1965), in which small refined poems appear with more meditative ones, such as the title poem of *Det är dags*. He has also published more collections of essays, *Relation i det personliga* ('Relation in the Personal,' 1950), *Essay om livets framfart* ('Essay on the Progress of Life,' 1961),[1016] and *Och sanning?* ('And Truth?,' 1966), for which he has been called one of the foremost Swedish essayists of our time.[1017] In them, however, he shows that he lacks understanding for types of poetic modernism more recent than his own.

After the modernists had won the right, grudgingly granted by traditionalists, to call themselves poets and serious writers, the next generation followed their footsteps, although no author of the stature of the great pioneers emerged. One of the most exotic and provoking (for the time) modernists was **Henry Parland** (1908-1930), whose two brothers are well-known writers. He was born in Viipuri to a family who spoke Russian, German, and Swedish. He lived with his parents in St. Petersburg and Kiev and attended school in Finland. He died in the capital of Lithuania. Of all the writers in his country, he caught most naturally and elegantly the spirit of the 1920s; Warburton says that he would have fit into the American colony of writers then in Paris, with their lack of respect for the old and their underlying uncertainty and melancholy.[1018] He wrote for *Quosego* and published one volume of poetry, *Idealrealisation* ('A Sale on Ideals,' 1929), in which he speaks of a universal hangover, when "the stars have the hiccups / and archangels drink soda water," though he is ironic about himself also. He had a curious idea, taken up by later poets, that material things might rebel at man's indifference and that it was necessary to establish a new form of contact with them. In his posthumous book, *Återsken* ('Reflected Light,' 1932), he speaks of a victory over the "great indifference which separates men from life."

His brother, **Ralf Parland** (b. 1914), published two collections of short stories, *Dush* ('Shower,' 1934) and *Ebonit* ('Ebonite,' 1937), in which he attempts to picture the world from the point of view of a sophisticated young man. They are somewhat affected, but the affectation was intended. *Avstånd* ('Distance,' 1938) revealed him to be an interesting poet, and the quality of his poetry was sustained in his subsequent collections, *Abel y Aifars sånger* ('The Songs of Abel y Aifar,' 1941), *Mot fullbordan* ('Toward Achievement,' 1944), *Oavslutad människa* ('Unfinished Man,' 1946), *Eolita* (1956), and others. The first are clearly influenced by Björling and Diktonius, but the style of the later work is personal. He shared with Diktonius an active interest in music, and his poems have a rhythmic and thematic structure. He has shown an attraction for oriental poetry and religious mysticism. He has expressed pessimistic views of the modern world in poetry written during the war and in short stories included in *Eros och elektronerna* ('Eros and the Electrons,' 1953) and *En apa for till himmelen* ('A Monkey Went to Heaven,' 1961), which present satiric visions of the future. They are among the few science fiction stories in Finland.

Some poets who were attracted by the modernists in the 1920s soon went their own way. Diktonius and Björling repelled many with their violence and extreme linguistic experiments.[1019] Among them was **R. Eklund** (1894-1946), whose first collection of prose poems, *Jordaltaret* ('The Altar of Earth,' 1919), was strongly influenced by Hagar Olsson, at that time Eklund's fiancée. Their engagement was soon broken, and Eklund found his own style. He had a personal message for his readers, but he was unable to give it convincing form.[1020] It was a struggle for him to express his feelings; few writers have described a state of psychic isolation as complete as that which is reflected in *Grått och gyllne* ('Grey and Golden,' 1926), a volume of aphorisms. To communicate with his surroundings (nature as often as people), he often identifies with a child, who experiences more directly and immediately than does an adult, e.g., in the poems in *Det unga ögat* ('The Young Eye,' 1927), or describes his own childhood, for example, in the prose of *Liten drömmarpilt* ('A Little Dreamer,' 1943) and *Ny dag börjar* ('A New Day Begins,' 1944). In his poetry there is clear development toward a more open attitude in the face of life and people. *Värld från veranda* ('The World from the Porch,' 1934) still consists of an artificial philosophic and poetic discussion among three people who represent the poet, but the aphorisms in *Rymd och människa* ('Space and Man,' 1938) show the poet's experience of simple happiness, expressed through the image of walking barefoot over the grass of his native region, Ostrobotnia, which appears many times in his works, e.g., in the novel *Himmelstimran* ('The Building of Heaven,' 1937). This new contact with the world is fully shown in *Du stallbror med Gud* ('You, God's Old Friend,' 1940) and *Gissel och möjor* ('The Scourge and the Caress,' 1942), which contains some narrative poetry written in hexameters. His last works are prose, even the aphorisms and sketches of his last book, *Loggbok på landsbacken* ('A Logbook on Dry Land,' 1945). A posthumous collection, also titled *Rymd och människa* (1950), contains aphorisms and poetry.

Erik Therman (1906-1948) protested in an article in 1929 the style of Diktonius and Björling, although much later he declared his approval of the principles of modernism in literature.[1021] He wrote free verse exclusively, but he differed from his contemporaries in content. He leaned toward an undefined mysticism (he spoke of life as a metaphysical entity), and he wrote about dreams, love, art, and the struggle for life in a form which avoids definite formulations and constructions. The result in the collections *Glidande bilder* ('Gliding Images,' 1928), *Förvandling* ('Modification,' 1932), *Ljus ur mullen* ('Light out of the Earth,' 1935), *Inför Dionysos' anlete* ('Facing Dionysos,' 1938), *Hjärtats seger* ('The Victory of the Heart,' 1941), and *Kanske ett leende* ('Perhaps a Smile,' 1946) is often confused, although all his works contain passages of half-magic beauty. He wrote some prose, for which his style was less suited than for verse; the novels *Människan är mot människan upprorisk* ('Man Is Rebellious Against Man,' 1931), *Mannen som förlorade* ('The Man Who Lost,' 1943), and *Mannen som segrade* ('The Man Who Won,' 1943) describe life in Helsinki and suggest the deeper meaning of reality. The latter two attempt to establish parallels between the inner life of a contemporary person and the legends of Parsifal and Tannhäuser. His last work, *Under Graals förbannelse* ('Under the Curse of the Grail,' 1948), is a direct transposition of the legend of the Holy Grail. At one time he discovered Lapland and expressed his love for it in a few interesting books. His novel *Renhandlarna* ('The Reindeer Dealers,' 1945) is set there. Simple in style, it is considered his best prose work. Two others, *Kettil Rödes saga* ('The Saga of Kettil the Red,' 1936) and *Bergtagen* ('Under a Spell,' 1937), are also set in the extreme north of Scandinavia.

Kerstin Söderholm (1897-1943), a very lonely person, suffered from a severe disease and eventually took her own life. Her diary, *Endast med mig själv* ('Only with Myself,' 1947-48), published after her death, reveals her constant struggle, from the age of sixteen, to understand herself and her problems. It is pervaded by melancholy and helplessness, but not self-pity. The theme of her poetry is the discrepancy between expectations and reality. In her first collections, *Röster ur tingen* ('Voices Coming out of Things,' 1923) and *Mot ljuset på bergen* ('Toward the Light on the Mountains,' 1926), she expresses the impossibility of establishing satisfactory human contact and seeks a mystic union with nature, in which her own identity would be dissolved. Her only prose, a short-story collection with the typical title *Det var icke verklighet* ('It Was Not Reality,' 1930), describes individuals standing apart from life. The first poems of *Ord i natten* ('Words in the Night,' 1933) are her one expression of joy in life, a feeling which love had brought out in her, but she transposes them into bright, almost unreal pictures of nature. *Mörkret och människan* (Darkness and Man,' 1941) reveals that the suffering she saw in the war brought her a new feeling of solidarity with humanity, which she expressed in simple language. Her best verse is in these two collections and *Porten* ('The Gate,' 1937).

One of two poets who remained faithful to tradition, **Ragnar Ekelund** (1892-1960), translated into Swedish many important Finnish literary works. He was also a well-known painter.[1022] His first three collections, *Sånger i sol och skymning* ('Songs in the Sun and in the Twilight,' 1914), *Gatans dikter* ('Poems of the Street,' 1915), and *Intermezzo* (1916), are typical painter's poems, descriptions of landscapes and streets in spring and autumn, at twilight or night. Although he followed a tradition for such poetry, he did not fully master the traditional form. *Disticha* ('Distichs,' 1918), *Visioner* ('Visions,' 1918), and *Vägarna* ('The Roads,' 1919) follow this line but contain a more personal message. In them Ekelund overcomes his hesitation to use poetic forms. A recurring motif in his poetry from this period is the contrast between light and darkness, expressed in images of bright landscapes viewed against the dark background of forests or marshes and the clear, fresh water of springs or fountains flowing out of the shadows. These visions symbolize something high, but the poet never defines it. In these poems his traditional form is well adapted for the solemnly festive tone of his verse. When he speaks more simply and examines the world from the viewpoint of a moralist or satirist, e.g., in the collections *Improvisationer* ('Improvisations,' 1922) and *Strofer i grått* ('Stanzas in Grey,' 1926), he becomes monotonous in form and content. His last volume, *Ljust i mörkt* ('Bright in the Darkness,' 1941), is his best. In it a series of love poems express strong personal feeling without egocentrism, the trap of that type of verse. The collection also contains some patriotic poetry inspired by the war of 1939-40, conventional, but no more so than most patriotic work.

Ekelund was a tradionalist because tradition was natural to him, but **Örnulf Tigerstedt** (1900-1962) was consciously and aggressively conservative and aristocratic, a true heir to Bertel Gripenberg. His first poetry collection, *Vågor* ('Waves,' 1918), was followed by two prose works, *Noveller* ('Short Stories,' 1923) and *Exercitia* ('Exercises' Lat., 1924). Conspicuous in them is his love for imitation and adoption of styles and mannerisms from the past. He was fascinated by an aristocratic and violent past in which fateful things happened, great lords fought wars, and dynasties rose and fell. In *Exercitia* he outlines his philosophy, a contrast between beautiful but wild nature and man, who must establish order. In the poems of *Vid gränsen* ('At the Border,' 1928), he further illustrates this philosophy. The central figure is Caesar, an ideal ruler not fully materialized on earth although the Roman emperors, the pope, Mussolini, the dictatorship of the proletariat, and the state embody something of him.[1023] Tigerstedt also expresses the desire to become strong and without fault, but his inner uncertainty is apparent. Although he revealed his admiration for the totalitarian states of his time in *Vi reser söderut* ('We

Travel Southward,' 1930), *Skott i överkant* ('Aiming Too High,' 1934), and *Utan örnar* ('Without Eagles,' 1935), he did not adhere to a fascistlike organization or propose political programs. He yearned for peaceful contact with nature, though it is not yet evident in the poetry of *Block och öde* ('Block and Fate,' 1931). It does appear in *De heliga vägarna* ('The Holy Roads,' 1933), in which he describes himself as the "scarecrow of the gods," which is no longer able to frighten nature with its tales of terror. He is ironical about himself again in *Den lycklige Joker* ('The Happy Joker,' 1945; published in Sweden, where he settled in 1944). The war did not stir in him admiration for the deeds of the new Caesars. Even in *Sista etappen* ('The Last Stage,' 1940) he saw the destruction of his hopes in the war; later he saw the destruction of the new political order he had praised. The few volumes of poetry he published in Sweden, *Floden rinner förbi* ('The River Flows By,' 1948) and *Fälld vindbrygga* ('The Drawbridge Is Down,' 1950), and the novel *Katedralen* ('The Cathedral,' 1946) again describe the creative work of civilization, but without his former enthusiasm and brilliance.

The 1920s were a period of poetry in the Swedish literature of Finland, whereas the 1930s were a period of prose. Of these new prosaists, **Tito Colliander** (b. 1904) is considered foremost.[1024] The son of a Finnish officer serving in the Russian army in St. Petersburg, he came with his parents to Finland after the revolution. He retained knowledge of the Russian language and an interest in czarist Russia which is apparent in his works. He often describes Russian émigrés living in Finland. Eventually he converted to the Eastern Orthodox faith and wrote several inspirational books, e.g., *Samtal med smärtan. Anteckningar 1953-56* ('Conversations with Suffering. Notes 1953-56,' 1956), and also taught religion in schools. His first works, the short stories and sketches in *En vandrare* ('A Wanderer,' 1930) and *Småstad,* (1931) and the novels *Huset där det dracks* ('The House Where They Were Drinking,' 1932) and *Taina* (1935), are not distinguished. The latter two tells of Russian émigrés living on the Isthmus of Karelia.[1025]

In his next books, the short-story volumes *Bojorna* ('The Fetters,' 1933) and *Ljuset* ('The Light,' 1936) and the novel *Korståget* ('The Procession,' 1937), his personal style and motifs are fully developed. Because of his religious interests and his characters, Colliander has been compared to great Russian authors, especially Dostoyevski,[1026] but he lacks the Russian master's furious commitment to his ideas, and, instead of portraying individuals, he often constructs situations to prove the same point again and again: that the poor are good, humble, and generous and the rich arrogant, selfish, and ridiculous. His irony is frequently heavy, for example, in the short story *Den gamle banktjänstemannen* ('The Old Bank Clerk' in *Ljuset*). A Finnish businessman offers to give an old Russian émigré a nominal job in his company, but the émigré refuses because he cannot accept pay for work he will not do. He feels "that the other was so funny and childish, not quite mature somehow, and he thought of a shiny dummy he had seen in a shop window." The title story of *Ljuset* is intended to be symbolistic and realistic, but neither aspect is convincing. A physicist who has been writing a treatise on the nature of light all his life (the story is set in the twentieth century) has such poor eyesight that he must stay in a darkened room. When the work is finished, he goes out to see the light he has written about, and the bright sunlight blinds him.

Colliander's novels concentrate less on moral points, and the characters, although exceptional, are convincing enough that the improbability and melodrama of the action is insignificant. The main character of *Korståget*, considered one of his best novels,[1027] is a young man who has fled Russia to Finland after the revolution. He is tortured by the thought that he has unwillingly caused the death of his best friend. He goes to a place in Estonia where things remain as they were in Russia and takes part in a religious procession. The image of Christ carried in the ceremony appears to have the face of his dead friend, who pardons him so that he can live in peace after experiencing a religious conversion.

Förbarma dig ('Have Mercy,' 1939) is the most interesting of Colliander's other novels. It is narrated by a boy who describes his father, an impractical, optimistic, generous dreamer (Colliander's favorite type of character) whose life is destroyed by a woman. *Grottan* ('The Cave,' 1942) also has a child as a central figure. The theme is the conflict experienced between an eight-year-old girl, her mother, and her mother's second husband. Colliander's interest in children is evident in many of the short stories in the collections *Två timmar* ('Two Hours,' 1944) and *I åratal* ('For Years,' 1949).

The novels *Bliv till* ('Come into Being!,' 1945) and *Vi som är kvar* ('We Who Are Left,' 1959) are weaker than the others. They examine sin and guilt in human relations. In the long essay *Träsnittet* ('The Woodcut,' 1946), the author examines very personally the problems created by the last war. He speaks of spiritual freedom—he has little interest in political freedom. Among his last works is a childhood memoir, *Gripen* ('The Griffin' or 'Fascinated,' 1965). He has also published two volumes of poetry, *Dagen är* ('The Day Is,' 1940) and *Glädjes möte* ('The Meeting with Joy,' 1957), and biographies of the Russian painter Repin (1942) and of Tyko Sallinen (1948); Colliander is known as a painter and has taught art.

Göran Stenius (b. 1909), a Roman Catholic convert, has described his spiritual experiences in the novel *Klockorna i Rom* ('The Bells of Rome,' 1955), which has been called the best religious novel written in Finland after the war.[1028] Like many Swedish writers of his generation, Stenius has felt an attraction to Karelia, where his father was a magistrate before the war.[1029] He found an intensity of religious feeling there which he did not sense in other parts of the country, and he pictures it in his first novel, *Det okända helgonets kloster* ('The Monastery of the Unknown Saint,' 1934). His major work is the novel *Hungergropen* ('The Hunger Pit,' 1944), which describes life in a wild region during the war of 1808-09. Others, such as *Fästningen* ('The Fortress,' 1945) and *Brödet och stenarna* ('The Bread and the Stones,' 1959), are set in or near Viipuri at a later date. He also published a collection of poems, *Fiskens tecken* ('The Sign of the Fish,' 1940).

Olof Enckell (b. 1900), brother of Rabbe, displayed a similar interest in Karelia and the orthodox faith in the novels he wrote in the 1930s. In *Ett klosteräventyr* ('An Adventure in a Monastery,' 1930) he describes a traveler who comes to the orthodox monastery of Valamo (then in Finnish territory), where he is fascinated but not converted. *Vårt hjärta* ('Our heart,' 1933) and *Guldkedjan* ('The Golden Chain,' 1934) are about a man who arrives in the half-Russian village Kyyrölä oppressed by memory of a crime, but finds peace of mind and a girl whom he marries. Enckell's close observation of the Finnish part of Finland is apparent in the long story *Halmstacken* ('A Stack of Hay,' 1931), which borrows its title from a place where the main character, who is wandering around Häme, or Tavastland in order to become acquainted intimately with the inhabitants, spends a night. Later Enckell described his own travels through Finnish Karelia in *Vakt i öster* ('Sentinel in the East,' 1939), *Krigaren och bonden* ('The Warrior and the Peasant,' 1940), and *Rapport från ödemarken* ('A Report from the Wilderness,' 1942). He also published a satire on postwar conditions in Finland, *Solnedgång* ('The Sunset,' 1945). He was professor of literature at the University of Helsinki and produced scholarly works on, e.g., Diktonius and Edith Södergran.

Solveig von Schoultz (b. 1907) has written remarkable poetry and prose. She followed a girls' book (1932) with the novel *December* (1937), which details the development of a teenager in a small town. Her interest in children and young people is evident in her short stories, collected in *De sju dagarna* ('The Seven Days,' 1942), *Närmare någon* ('Closer to Somebody,' 1951), and *Ansa och samvetet* ('Ansa and the Conscience,' 1954). She has also treated women in the volumes *Ingenting ovanligt* ('Nothing Unusual,' 1947), *Den blomstertid* ('The Time of Flowers,' 1958), and *Även dina kameler* ('For Thy Camels Also,' 1965). She uses her nontraditional style, influenced by the writers of the 1920s, to analyze sensitive children and young people who must adjust to the adult world while living in a world of their own and to portray the conscious and unconscious aspects of women's minds. She does not, however, illustrate psychological theories. She finds important that which remains unsaid and often hidden, though it influences relationships and creates mysterious tensions or affinities between people.

She published her first poetry in 1940, *Min timme* ('My Hour'). *Den bortvända glädjen* ('The Joy Turned Away,' 1943), *Eko av ett rop* ('The Echo of a Call,' 1945), *Nattlig äng* ('The Nightly Meadow,' 1949), *Nätet* ('The Net,' 1956), and *Sänk ditt ljus* ('Dim Your Light,' 1963) are built of a wealth of symbols and images which seem to take shape slowly from the poet's fantasy.

Their weakness is also their strength: quantity. Most of the images are from nature, and they express the joy of life and sensitivity for all shades of being. The poet intertwines these images from nature and from man in a way which stresses the unity of the world in its complexity.

Eva Wichman (b. 1908) began a career as a designer of wooden toys, for which she won a gold medal at the Triennale of Milan in 1933 and the Paris World Fair in 1937. Her books contain something of the toys' capricious fantasy and of the child's disrespectful attitude toward the adult world, but they are not childish or funny. The little animals which sometimes appear in them may illustrate, as they do in the story *Gallret* ('The Iron Bars' in *Molnet såg mig* 'The Cloud Saw Me,' 1942), the meaningless suffering the world inflicts on living things. The freedom and inventiveness of her first book of short stories, *Mania* (name, 1937), attracted the attention of the critics.[1030] The main character works in a toy mill, and the author describes the employees as frighteningly like the dolls they are producing.[1031] The concern for the difficulties a person with artistic temperament has in adapting to the everyday world is apparent in her second collection, *Här är allt som förut* ('Here Everything Is As Before,' 1938).

Molnet såg mig contains stories which might be called prose poems. In it Nature expresses feelings which are, though human, simpler and more forceful than human feelings. Some stories are satires, mainly of middle-class pettiness, which border on fables. The novel *Ohörbart vattenfall* ('The Waterfall That Cannot Be Heard,' 1944) is in a similar style, but the artistry in the presentation of complex reality is perhaps pushed too far. A distinct change occurs in the two stories of *Där vi går*–('Where We Go–,' 1949). Her satirical attitude becomes more definite and is directed toward specific social questions, especially in the story which describes both critically and poetically a working-class neighborhood in Helsinki.

Her poetry underwent a similar evolution, and her increased interest in the social and the political is even more apparent in it. Since the war she has worked for a leftist newspaper. Her first volumes, *Ormöga* ('Snake-Eye,' 1946) and *Den andra tonen* ('The Other Tune,' 1948), express with great strength her struggle for truth and her efforts to simplify and purify poetry. *Dikt i dag* ('Poetry Today,' 1951) and *De levande* ('Those Who Live,' 1954), however, present aggressively communist ideas.[1032] In her more recent collections, such as *Dikter 1960* and *Det sker med ens* ('It Happens Suddenly,' 1964), the monotonous party ideology has given way to a return to personal style.

Mirjam Irene Tuominen (1913-67) first published two collections of short stories, *Tidig tvekan* ('Early Doubt,' 1938) and *Murar* ('Walls,' 1939), which have all the characteristics of her later books. Her interest is in humble, poor individuals who, possibly despised by society, feel acutely the wrongs of the world. In this respect she is similar to Tito Colliander, whose interest in religion she shared without following an established creed. Some of her later works meditate on very personal spiritual experiences akin to those of the great mystics. Many of her stories, collected in *Visshet* ('Certitude,' 1942), *Mörka gudar* ('Dark Gods,' 1944), *Kris* ('Crisis,' 1946), and *Bliva ingen* ('To Become Nobody,' 1949), are about children, who represent an unconscious refusal to adjust to society's patterns. Actually her characters often accept suffering, not willingly, but with bewilderment. Sometimes their search for reasons is to no end; other times they conclude that suffering is necessary, that some individuals, "sacrificed men,"[1033] are born to suffer for others. Suffering is produced by guilt or by the consciousness of illness, pain, and death, and her works are all variations on these themes and, therefore, repetitious. They are not all on the same level, but the best show intense feeling in their relentless analysis of the soul.

She has also written essays on these problems. *Besk brygd* ('A Bitter Brew,' 1947) refers to World War II and in a sense comes to the conclusion that torturer and victim are bound by a common fate. *Stadier* ('Stages,' 1949) includes essays on writers for whom she feels an affinity; one is the German poet Hölderlin, on whom she wrote a book (1960). Another is Rilke, whom she translated. *Gud är närvarande* ('God Is Present,' 1961) is on her religious experiences. In 1954 she published a collection of poetry, *Under jorden sjönk* ('Sank into the Ground'). She produced several more collections, including *Monokord* ('Monochord,' 1954), *Dikter* III (1956), and *I tunga hängen mognar bären* ('Berries Are Ripening in Heavy Clusters,' 1959), all in the spirit of her prose but without its intensity.

Good playwrights are as rare among the Swedish Finns as among the Finns.[1034] One of them is **Walentin Chorell** (b. 1912), whose plays and radio and television dramas are known throughout Finnish-speaking Finland, and in Sweden and other countries.[1035] He began writing novels, e.g., *Calibans dag* ('Caliban's Day,' 1948), *Blindtrappan* ('The Secret Stairs,' 1949), and *Intim journal* ('A Personal Diary,' 1951), which describe individuals too weak to resist life in society. Religion is absent in Chorell's works,[1036] but they portray human relationships more fully than do the works of Colliander and Tuominen. *Intim journal* is presented as a neurotic's record of his thoughts, and it also reveals how his neurosis develops as he is being brought up by his elder sister. He is bound to her by a relationship of hate and love, and he cannot view it rationally. *Miriam* (1954), *Främlingen* ('The Stranger,' 1956), and *Kvinnan* ('The Woman,' 1958) are more optimistic. Their shared character, Miriam, never loses courage, faith, or strength in spite of many difficulties.

Chorell has a natural talent for playwriting and has produced over fifty dramas.[1037] He makes his characters' thoughts and emotions appear naturally in their words and actions, without comment.[1038] He describes sordid surroundings and abnormal individuals without focusing on sordidness and abnormality, but because he finds them human and interesting.[1039] Normal people in unusual situations also appear, e.g., in *Madame* (1952), whose main character is an aging, once famous actress, and in *Fabian öppnar portarna* ('Fabian Opens the Gates,' 1949), which deals with the attempt of a middle-aged foreman to escape old age through adventure. Chorell has written so many plays that not all are on the same level, and some repeat themes. A motif which recurs is the dream of happiness contrasted to the realization that it is forever lost; it appears in *Min älskade är en fiskare* ('My Lover Is a Fisherman,' 1960) and *Tomflaskan* ('The Empty Bottle,' 1949).

Chorell's interest in feminine psychology made the sister in *Intim journal* as important as the neurotic. *Miriam, Främlingen,* and *Kvinnan* are about the same woman. *Systrarna* ('The Sisters,' 1955) presents women who share a dream. *Kattorna* ('The Cats,' 1961) deals with a group of women who work in a factory. Chorell never treats women as characters better or worse than men, however. Characteristic of his work is a combination of deep commitment and objectivity. The intensity with which he describes his characters reveals his involvement with their problems, and he does not use them to prove a point.

The third **Parland** brother, **Oscar** (b. 1912), is a psychiatrist who has published three remarkably original and well-written novels. *Förvandlingar* ('Transformations,' 1945) follows the development of a neurosis in a middle-aged women, but it is not a fictionalized case history from the author's professional experience. It becomes an epic description of a family in which relations between generations figure importantly. *Den förtrollade vägen* ('The Enchanted Road,' 1953) and *Tjurens år* ('The Years of the Bull,' 1962) describe the author's childhood up to 1918. War-caused tragedies are juxtaposed with everyday events often described with warm humor. The half-magic way in which a child experiences reality is rendered masterfully. A third volume of these memories is planned but has not yet appeared; the first two have been translated into Finnish.

Marianne Alopaeus (b. 1918) was awarded a literary prize in Sweden for her first novel, *Uppbrott* ('Preparing to Leave,' 1945). It was somewhat conventional, but her later books show greater originality, especially in dealing with the problems of women, e.g., *Avsked i augusti* ('Farewell in August,' 1959) and *Mörkrets kärna* ('The Heart of Darkness,' 1965). The Finnish translation of the latter has been very successful among the public.

Tove Jansson (b. 1914) studied painting in Helsinki, Stockholm, and Paris before the war. She has traveled abroad and exhibited her works, and she has painted murals for public buildings. Her father, Viktor Jansson, was a well-known sculptor, and her mother, Signe Hammarsten-Jansson, was an active artist. In 1945 she began writing and illustrating books on the Moomins.[1040] The Moomins are human in their reactions and slightly animal- or troll-like in appearance. They live in their own world and have their own worries, joys, and adventures. They think and speak in their unique manner, a slightly nonsensical logic, not unlike the speech of the creatures Alice met in her adventures. The author's intent was not to satirize human nature and society, but the Moomins reflect such things, and over time they have taken on new dimensions. The first Moomin books are for children (the author has also written and directed children's plays and designed their sets), but the last ones are for a larger audience, e.g., *Pappan och havet* ('Daddy and the Sea,' 1965). Her books are very popular in Scandinavia and England.

Lorenz von Numers (b. 1913) writes old-fashioned historical novels; he contends that they can be as realistic as a modern novel, for he believes that most of what we know about our time is as vague as that which we know about history.[1041] He has translated many works into Swedish, mainly from French, including Froissart's and Commynes's old chronicles as well as Gide and Robbe-Grillet. He has studied quantities of old documents on bizarre characters and strange events as the basis for his books. *Snäckans bröder* ('The Brotherhood of the Shell,' 1946) is about François Villon and his adventures with robbers and thieves. *Spel med fyra knektar* ('A Game with Four Knights,' 1948) is about thirteenth-century Palestine, and *Drottningens handelsmän* ('The Queen's Merchants,' 1964) is set in seventeenth-century Moscow. They are well written, colorful, and entertaining, and they have a serious note of reflection. He also published poetry early in his career and has written satiric sketches on modern life, but the irony sometimes misses its mark.

Sally Salminen (maiden name of **Sally Dührkop**, b. 1906) merits inclusion in this volume only because of her best-selling first novel, *Katrina* (1936). It is a competently written, honest, unassuming book which does not contain the usual elements of a best seller—glamor, adventure, sex, violence, or a happy ending. A country girl, seduced by promises of a wonderful life, marries a sailor and discovers that his promises were lies. The book is a down-to-earth description of her struggles to maintain her family, and in the end she has a quiet old age. The author has continued publishing novels, but she has produced nothing exceptional.

Her sister, **Aili Nordgren** (*née* **Salminen**, b. 1908), has written several books on the poor people of their home region, the Aland Islands. The best, *Visa en väg* ('Show a Road,' 1948) and *Brinn eld* ('Burn, Fire,' 1951), are autobiographical. In them she describes the psychology of the characters as well as the circumstances of their lives. *Innan dagen börjar* ('Before the Day Begins,' 1946) describes New York in the 1930s, when the author lived and worked there. *Väljer du stormen* ('Should You Choose the Tempest,' 1955) is about the Finnish Civil War. In it the author's political convictions (she belongs to the Finnish Communist party) intrude on the narrative to the point of detracting from its artistic balance.

Anna Bondestam (*née* **Elfving**, b. 1907) is the daughter of a small craftsman from Jakobstad (Finn. *Pietarsaari*) in Ostrobotnia. In her books she has described people living in modest conditions in a small town or in Helsinki. Her sympathy for her characters is evident, and her lack of social and political concerns furthers her concentration on the psychology of her characters, especially women, e.g., in the short-story collections *Bergtagen* ('Spellbound,' 1941) and *Enskilt område* ('Private Ground,' 1952). She is a realist in the traditional sense: her purpose is to describe ordinary people and their everyday problems. She avoids the exceptional. Her style is in keeping with her subject matter, but her books avoid the pitfall of monotony through her sense of humor and her ability to describe simple joy.

Her first novel, *Panik i Rölleby* ('Panic in Rölleby,' 1936), is a historical description of some humorous events in a small town, with a trace of social satire. This book is not outstanding, but it contains most of the material the author uses in her best books, *Lågt i tak* ('Humble Homes,' 1943) and *Klyftan* ('The Rift,' 1946). The former is about her hometown in the 1920s and 1930s. Her sympathies are with young people from the working class who try to find a way of life amidst the political and social troubles of the time, but she avoids sentimentality or bias. The latter presents autobiographically the reactions of a ten- or eleven-year-old girl to the events of 1918, which had not yet been extensively treated in Finnish literature. A major theme is the contrast between the lively fantasy world of the girl and brutal reality; another is the rift between Reds and Whites. Mrs. Bondestam has begun a several-part novel, two sections of which have been published, *Vägen till staden* ('The Road to the City,' 1957) and *Stadens bröd* ('The Bread of the City,' 1960). They describe Finnish and Swedish workers of Finland who have difficulties in adjusting when they migrate from the country to town in search of work at the end of the last century. The second book carries the action to the first years of this century, and the author presents some interesting observations on the different reactions of the Swedish and Finnish populations to the events of that time. Mrs. Bondestam is not a working-class writer, but she is probably foremost among the few Swedish writers of Finland who have treated the life of the working class. She has also translated many Finnish works into Swedish.

The Swedish literature of Finland has not undergone the extreme change since World War II that the Finnish literature has endured. The new generation of modern poets won their battle in the 1920s,[1042] and modernism also came early in prose although there is no specific school or trend.

Bo Carpelan (b. 1926) is the foremost among postwar poets. His first collection, *Som en dunkel värme* ('Like a Dark Warmth,' 1946), received unanimous praise by the critics. Subsequent volumes, *Du mörka överlevande*

('You Dark Survivor,' 1947) and *Variationer* ('Variations,' 1950), are of equally high quality and secured him the leading position among his generation. The influence of older authors can be detected in his poetry, especially that of Björling and the Swedish poets of the 1940s,[1043] but his major characteristics are his own. In his first volumes he appears elegiac, refined, and melancholy, formulating his feelings in a few allusive words. The technique is Björling's, but, whereas Björling speaks of sunshine, Carpelan turns to darkness.[1044] In the first collection there is an optimistic yearning underneath the pessimistic words, but it disappears in the next two. The prose poems of *Minus sju* ('Minus Seven,' 1952) best express his total loss of hope; they are a series of caricatures of the world with a thin veil of humor over his pessimism.

Objekt för ord ('An Object for Words,' 1954) clearly marks a change in Carpelan's attitude. The style is unchanged, but he begins to express, with initial hesitation, more openness and confidence especially evident in the delicate love poems included. The evolution continues in his next books, *Landskapets förvandlingar* ('The Transformations of the Landscape,' 1957). Earlier landscapes were spiritual, but now they are real. The next collection, *Den svala dagen* ('The Cool Day,' 1961), confirms his growing confidence. In it he expresses joy over small realities, the presence of his child or wife, sunshine on a lake. Rabbe Enckell has called his change a transition from "mysticism of words" to "mysticism of reality."[1045]

Peter Sandelin (b. 1930) also shows the distinct influence of Björling. His poems are often light, evanescent impressions from nature in which he has attempted to "cast eternity into the immediate."[1046] He published his first collection, *Ur svalans loggbok* ('From the Logbook of a Swallow'), in 1951. His second, *De lysande och de döda* ('The Bright and the Dead,' 1953), shows a mystic inclination toward death but is not convincing. *Stunder av ljus* ('Instants of Light,' 1960) and *Hemma i universum* ('At Home in the Universe,' 1962) express a love of life characteristic of Sandelin.

Carolus Rein (b. 1935) began writing poetry influenced by Rimbaud and the French surrealists. He has a lively imagination and finds pleasure in making unexpected combinations of words and images, though they are not always meaningful, e.g., in *Färd genom verkligheter* ('A Journey through Realities,' 1954) and *Vårsvart* ('Springblack,' 1958). Interest in religious problems is apparent even in his first poems, and in 1957 he became a Roman Catholic. His conversion is reflected in *Seende* ('Seeing,' 1960) and *Världen är endast du* ('The World Is Only You,' 1963), which emphasize the mystic's ecstatic vision of divinity.

Per-Håkon Påwals (b. 1928) published a first collection, *Glas emellan* ('Between Glasses,' 1956), which contains elegant and funny satirical sketches on unimportant subjects. The short stories in *Snuviga gatlyktor* ('Streetlights with a Cold,' 1960) are often attacks on middle-class values, but the author is careful not to formulate them too seriously. A similar mixture of protest and humor is found in the poems in *Minnet av en vinge* ('The Memory of a Wing,' 1960).

Evert Huldén (b. 1895), a farmer active in local politics, has traveled abroad and founded the Society for the Literature of Swedish Ostrobotnia.[1047] His first volume of poetry, *Jorden och drömmar* ('The Earth and the Dreams,' 1951), was followed by ten collections of poems and short stories. His style is straightforward, and his subjects are familiar to him. Tradition and modernism are well combined in his works, and reviewers in Helsinki have received them favorably.

His son **Lars Huldén** (b. 1926), professor of Scandinavian languages at the University of Helsinki, has published scholarship on the eighteenth-century Swedish poet Bellman, among others, and a few volumes of verse, *Dräpa näcken* ('To Kill the Water-Sprite,' 1958), *Speletuss* ('The Music Box,' 1961), and *Spöfågel* ('The Whip-Bird,' 1964), for which he has been called the most promising poet after Carpelan.[1048] His verse is in original form and full of humor. In reminiscences of his home region, he sometimes resorts to local dialect and folklore.

In 1965 the Swedish newspapers of Finland published a polemic about contemporary poetry, which its critics found too artistic and refined. Their ideal was a poetry open to social and political realities. A similar argument happened earlier among the Finnish Finns, with the appearance of Kirstinä, Rossi, Saaritsa, Salo, and their contemporaries. The protesters are called the FBT Group after the periodical they publish in,[1049] and one of their leading poets is **Claes Andersson** (b. 1937), who combines radical proclamations and fanciful wordplay. Others are **Mauritz Nylund** (b. 1925), called a "mild ironist,"[1050] who published his first works in the early 1950s but did not develop a personal form of expression until later, and **Tom Sandell** (b. 1937), who is close to the group but not an actual member. He began by imitating, sometimes unsuccessfully, the surrealists, but later developed as a sharp critic of our time.

The strength of postwar Swedish literature is in poetry, although there are a few good prosaists. **Christer Kihlman** (b. 1930), generally considered the most interesting, began his career by publishing some well-written though unoriginal poetry, *Rummen vid havet* ('The Rooms near the Sea,' 1951) and *Munkmonolog* ('The Monk Monologue,' 1953), which shows the influence of Rabbe Enckell. He printed literary reviews and his sharp criticism of the Swedish society in Finland produced violent arguments in the press. His novels are to a great extent attacks on the surroundings in which he grew up, but he gave them artistic form and voiced his protest only indirectly. The first, *Se upp, salige* ('Watch Out, Ye Blessed,' 1960), is a satiric description of a small town and its self-centered Swedish middle class. The second, *Den blå modern* ('The Blue Mother,' 1962), follows two brothers through childhood, revealing that which may be hidden behind middle-class respectability. The author is very intense, and he sometimes resorts to complex, heavy imagery. The characters' psychological problems are mainly erotic, and Kihlman's frankness in treating them has shocked some. His third novel, *Madeleine* (1965), is about a writer and his relations with his family during a depressed, unproductive period. All of Kihlman's novels have been translated into Finnish.

Anders Cleve (b. 1937) has written fiction with Kihlman's intensity and attempt to make language reflect the world, and his works sometimes have a chaotic heaviness. They possess a strength and vitality, however, which Kihlman's books do not have. Cleve is an extrovert who floods his pages with the world's smells, sounds, and colors. His characters act, rather than brood. Cleve also has an earthy sense of humor. He first published two volumes of poetry, *Dagen* ('The Day,' 1955) and *Det bara ansiktet* ('The Bare Face,' 1956), and a book of short stories, *Gatstenar* ('The Pavement,' 1959), about Helsinki, which he often views as an organism with a life in common with its inhabitants. He says that the houses in a working-class neighborhood look like wrestlers with broad shoulders (for readers of American literature, he need not have added that the inhabitants called it Chicago). He describes characters of modest position, reproducing their colloquial language, which in Helsinki is full of Finnish words and phrases. He brings out their shortcomings, but he believes in the basic goodness of every human being. Kalle in *Gårdskarln* ('The Janitor') is strong and short-tempered. He drinks and fights, but finds time to play with a little boy and to save a bird's nest. As he is dying of cancer in the end, his softer qualities become more evident, and his wife, who has suffered from his angry outbursts, worries that he should not think so much. Cleve's novels, *Vit eld* ('White Fire,' 1962) and *Påskägget* ('The Easter Egg,' 1966), are in the style of his short stories. *Vit eld* especially has been criticized for chaotic language and lack of form, but both books have engaging qualities.

Jörn Donner (b. 1933) began the literary and political periodical *Arena*, which he edited for three years, at age eighteen. He has since worked for Swedish and Finnish newspapers, written books on his travels (*Rapport från Berlin* ['Report from Berlin,' 1958] and *Rapport från Donau*, ['Report from the Danube,' 1962]), directed films, some with Ingmar Bergman, on whom he wrote in 1962 *Djävulens ansikte* (tr. *The Personal Vision of Ingmar Bergman*, 1964), and won a position on the Helsinki City Council on a leftwing ticket (in 1970 he severed his party connections). He is better at reporting than at creating fiction. His early works, the short stories in *Välsignade liv!* ('Blessed Life!,' 1951) and the novel *Bordet* ('The Table,' 1957), are unconvincing protests against middle-class values. *På ett sjukhus* ('At a Hospital,' 1960), which tells of his work as a conscientious objector in a hospital, is more to the point because he directly discusses a problem which interests him. *Den nya boken om vårt land* ('The New Book about Our Country,' 1967) is very different from Topelius's *Boken om vårt land*. It contains descriptions and interviews and is very interesting, although the reader must be careful to distinguish Donner's opinions from fact. Some of his predictions about the future of Finland and its institutions are somewhat hasty, but Donner is a refreshingly intelligent and alert person with great openness about his wide interests. Many of his books have been translated into Finnish, and his criticism of the Swedish middle class is aggressive. For example, he has said that its days are over and its last representatives should be exhibited in monkey cages at the Helsinki Zoo.

Leo Ågren (b. 1928) lived in Ostrobotnia until 1960, when he moved to Stockholm. He took part in the literary group to which Evert Huldén belonged. He first published the autobiographic *Hunger i skördetid* ('Hunger in the Time of the Harvest,' 1954), depicting with humor and self-criticism his difficult childhood in a small village. His next novel, *Motsols* ('Counter-Clockwise,'1955), shows him as a mature artist with an individual style. His subject is again a family of small farmers, not often treated in the Swedish literature of Finland, especially not by one with direct experience of such a life. He next began a vast trilogy tracing the fate of a family of agricultural workers from the eighteenth century to the present, *Kungsådern* ('The Mainstream,' 1957), *När gudarna dör* ('When the Gods Die,' 1959), and *Fädrens blod* ('The Blood of the Fathers,' 1961), but he admits in the preface to the last volume that he was unable to make an epic whole from it. It is more a series of sketches than a continuous narrative, but it is interesting, especially the second book. His next work, *Ballad* ('A Ballad,' 1962), is about religious freedom; its style is symbolic and it approaches being a prose poem.

His brother **Gösta Ågren** (b. 1936) is known as a poet whose leftist sympathies are apparent sometimes to the disadvantage of artistic balance. His collections are *Folkvargarna* ('The Wolves among the People,' 1958) and *Ett brev från Helsingfors* ('A Letter from Helsinki,' 1956). He too has written an autobiographic novel about the rural proletariat, *Jordlös bonde* ('A Farmer without Land,' 1956), and a book of essays and sketches, *Din makt är alltför stor* ('Your Power Is Too Great,' 1962).

In 1859 Professor Törnegren of Helsinki predicted that the grand-children of his generation would no longer know Swedish,[1051] and Jörn Donner has expressed his pessimism about the future of the Swedish population in Finland. Nevertheless, the Swedish writers of Finland continue to publish poetry, drama, and prose, and their audience is no longer limited to Helsinki. It is also encouraging to note that writers of both linguistic groups now take more notice of each other than they have in the past.

Notes

Abbreviations

Antologia—Suomen Kirjallisuuden Antologia (companion volumes to *Kirjallisuus*).
Kirjallisuus—Suomen Kirjallisuus, 8 vols., Matti Kuusi and Simo Konsala, gen. eds. (Helsinki-Keuruu, 1963-70). Volume editors: I, Matti Kuusi; II, Martti Rapola; III, Lauri Viljanen; IV, Rafael Koskimies (also author); V, Annamari Sarajas; VI, no. ed.; VII, Matti Kuusi; VIII, Pekka Tarkka.
KTSVK—Kirjallisuudentutkijain seuran vuosikirja.
SKST—Suomalaisen Kirjallisuuden Seuran toimituksia.
Skr SLSF—Skrifter utgivna av Svenska Litteratursällskapet i Finland.

CHAPTER I

1. See John H. Wuorinen, *Nationalism in Modern Finland* (New York, 1931); Roberta Gifford Selleck, "The Language Issue in Finnish Political Discussion 1809-1863" (Ph.D. diss., Radcliff College, 1961); Yrjö Nurmio, "Talonpoikaiskirjailija Antti Mannisen anomus suomen kielen aseman parantamiseksi vuodelta 1854," *Historiallinen aikakauskirja* (1940): 149 et seq.; idem, "Vuoden 1850 kielisäännöksen yleispoliittista taustaa" in *Historiallinen* (1942), pp. 1 et seq.; idem, *Taistelu suomen Kielen asemasta 1800-luvun puolivälissä* (Porvoo-Helsinki, 1947), esp. pp. 11-14 and no. 3, where an official letter from St. Peterburg to Helsinki is given (in Swedish): "His Majesty the Emperor . . . considering that the persons, who possess only a knowledge of the Finnish language belong exclusively to the working or agricultural classes of the nation, deigns to find that in certain cases books, which are harmless for the educated citizen, can be wrongly understood by the uneducated reader from the common people and also that in general useless reading diverts the working and agricultural classes of the nation from more useful pursuits. . . ."

2. See V. Salminen and G. Landtman, "The Folk-Lore of Finland and How It Was Collected," *Folk-Lore* 41 (December, 1930): 359-69; E. Mäkelä-Henriksson, "Recent Folklore Research in Finland," *Midwest Folklore* 2, no. 3 (1952): 151-58.

3. Domenico Comparetti, *The Traditional Poetry of the Finns,* intr. A. Lang, trans. I. M. Anderton (London, New York, and Bombay, 1898); cf. C. M. Gayley and B. P. Kurtz, *Methods and Materials of Literary Criticism, Lyric, Epic, and Allied Forms of Poetry* (University of California semicentennial publication, Boston, 1920), p. 352 (lyric poetry of the Lapps and the Finns), pp. 773-74 (the Finnish epic).

4. See Martti Haavio, *Väinämöinen Eternal Sage,* trans. H. Goldthwait-Väänänen (Porvoo-Helsinki, 1952).

5. See Matti Kuusi, "Sydänkalevalainen lyriikka ja epiikka" in *Kirjallisuus* I, p. 226. Professor Kuusi's method of typological analysis is presented by Jouko Hautala, *Suomalaisen kansanrunouden tutkimus*, SKST 244 (Helsinki, 1954), p. 394 et seq. Cf. U. Holmberg, *The Mythology of All Races* IV, *Finno-Ugric, Siberian* (Boston, 1927); U. Harva (U. Holmberg), *Sammon ryöstö* (1943).

6. See Felix Oinas, *The Mutual Influence between Slavic and Balto-Finnish Epic Songs* (Paper read at the Second International Congress of Finno-Ugrists, Helsinki[?], 1965), Finnish summary in *Suomenkieliset Tietosanomat* 3 (Helsinki, 1966); idem, "An Ingrian-Finnish Ballad and Its Slavic Background" in *Commentationes Fenno-Ugricae*, Suomalais-Ugrilaisen Seuran Toimituksia 125 (1962); idem, "Vesitiellä viipyneen neidon runo itämerensuomalaisilla ja slaaveilla," *Virittäjä*, 1963, pp. 17-30 (English summary p. 31); *Studies in Finnic-Slavic Folklore Relations*, FF Communications 205 (Helsinki, 1969).

7. According to Martti Haavio and Kaarle Krohn. According to Väinö Salminen, "Väärin tulkittu runo. Hirtettävä ylkä ja lohikäärmeen kitaan tuomittu neito," *Virittäjä*, 1945, pp. 16-33 (French summary p. 121), it is not connected with the legend.

8. See Matti Hako, "Riimilliset kansanlaulut" in *Kirjallisuus* I, p. 418 et seq., esp. p. 423. Cf. Lauri Viljanen, "Antiikin puhkeaminen Italian renesanssikirjallisuudessa" in *Juhlakirja Rafael Koskimiehen täyttäessä 60 vuotta* (Helsinki, 1958), pp. 294-95 (French summary p. 313).

9. Kuusi, "Sydänkalevalainen epiikka ja lyriikka," pp. 265-68.

10. This poem, like the next, is presented in the form given in *Antologia* I, pp. 74, 76. These poems, although very old, were generally not transcribed until the nineteenth and twentieth centuries (interest in them had begun in the eighteenth), in the local dialect, which is usually respected or only slightly altered in publications for the general public rather than specialists. The metric form in which the poems are presented (not the meter proper, but the number of lines, their grouping, etc.) is the result of long, careful reconstruction made by comparing all the found variants. See Pentti Leino, *Strukturaalinen alkusointu suomessa* (Helsinki: SKST 298, 1970).

11. See Eino Leino, *Poems* (Prologue, Tuuri, Carmen Saeculare, Väinämöinen's Song, Kouta), trans. C. E. Tallqvist, in *Life and Letters* 52 (1947), pp. 21-36.

12. The novel was published in 1870. The action is set thirty or forty years earlier.

13. At the beginning of this century writing on subjects from the Finnish past was fashionable. Lehtonen himself wrote in 1904 a wildly romantic poem, *Perm*, situated in mythic prehistory.

14. On Lönnrot's method of composing the *Kalevala* (and other cycles), see *Kirjallisuus* III, pp. 138-50; Hautala, *Suomalaisen*

NOTES

kansanrunouden, pp. 116-22; Väinö Kaukonen, *Vanhan Kalevalan kokoonpano* I-II, SKST 213 (Helsinki, 1939-45); idem, *Elias Lönnrotin Kalevalan toinen painos*, SKST 247 (Helsinki, 1956).

15. Hautala, *Suomalaisen kansanrunouden*, pp. 167-73.

CHAPTER II

16. Uno Harva's *Suomalaisten muinaisusko* ('The Old Religion of the Finns,' Helsinki, 1948) is, to a great extent, a commentary on Agricola's list, as is Martti Haavio's *Karjalan jumalat* ('The Gods of Karelia,' Helsinki, 1959). A facsimile of the list appears in Hautala, *Suomalaisen kansanrunouden*, pp. 28-29, and Annamari Sarajas, *Suomen kansanrunouden tuntemus 1500-1700-lukujen kirjallisuudessa* (Helsinki-Porvoo, 1956), pp. 10-11.

17. F. Burlington Fawcett, *Broadside Ballads of the Restoration Period from the Jersey Collection, Known as the Osterley Park Ballads* (London: John Lane the Bodley Head Ltd., 1930), Intr. p. vi.

18. See Tobias Norlind, *Latinska skolsånger i Sverige och Finland*, Lunds Universitets Årsskrift N. F. Afd. 1. Bd. 5 Nr. 2, (1909). There is an English edition by G. R. Woodward, *Piae Cantiones. A Collection of Church and School Songs* . . . (London, 1910).

19. Porthan was greatly influenced by the German philosopher Christian Wolff, who often indicated in the titles of his works that they contained "rational thoughts" (see *Kirjallisuus* II, pp. 515-17). Later Porthan also studied Locke, whom he admired.

20. Scotland has something similar in the anonymous ballad *Quhy sowld nocht Allane honorit be?* (Allan-a-Maut=John Barleycorn) preserved in an anthology of the sixteenth century. In "Ruotsin vallan loppukauden suomenkielinen runous" (*Kirjallisuus* II, p. 320), Vilho Suomi says that the poem is by Achrenius. In *Antologia* I (p. 394) it is given as anonymous. The poem, signed *Anonym*, was published in 1777 in Vaasa on the same broadsheet with another signed H. A., generally presumed Henrik Achrenius. This circumstance has led Professor Suomi to consider that Achrenius was also the author of the other composition, but other scholars disagree with that conclusion. See Vihtori Laurila, "Kustaa III:n ajan suomalaisia runoja," 1. "Viinasta valitus-virsi" in *Laulu ja raipat* (Oulu, 1968), pp. 195-99.

CHAPTER III

21. One of the first popular English prose books was John Trevisa's translation of *De Proprietatibus Rerum* by Bartholomeus Anglicus (1398).

22. The dance of death was so popular that in England, for example, there are broadsheet poems on the subject. Such is *The Shaking of the Sheets and the Dance and Song of Death* (sixteenth century). John Gower (1325-1408) wrote in French *Mirour de l'Omme* ('The Mirror of Man') on a similar subject.

23. The English poem, *The Vox and the Wolf*, dates from the thirteenth century.

24. Not Archbishop J. Tengström, but his nephew. Quoted in *Kirjallisuus* II, p. 383 (original in Swedish).

25. Franzén, in *Den gamle knekten*, wrote of Charles XII: "Greatness in victory and defeat he shared / Greatest perhaps he was when he disappeared." He was not the first to express such sentiments.

26. For example, James Shirley's poem *The Levelling Dust:* "Sceptre and crown / Must tumble down / And in the dust be equal made / With the poor scythe and spade."

27. The family, still represented in Finland, is one of the oldest in the country and originated in Sarvilahti, Pernaja (Agricola's birthplace), where its first known member lived in 1450.

28. Rousseau is expressly mentioned by Olof Enckell, "Suomen ruotsinkielinen kirjallisuus" in *Kirjallisuus* II, p. 444, but we wonder how much he really influenced Creutz, whose poems were published between 1754 and approximately 1761, while Rousseau's major works were written during virtually the same period (1757-62).

29. See Sarajas, *Suomen kansanrunouden*, pp. 230-34, no. 23, p. 351. Kellgren became later renowned as a poet in Sweden.

30. However, these exact words do not seem to be in Milton's text.

31. What is given in *Antologia* I, pp. 490-93, seems to be one of the later versions, whereas the description in *Kirjallisuus* II, pp. 563-4, applies to the first one.

32. See Sarajas, *Suomen kansanrunouden*, pp. 112-14. In the theories he evolved between 1697 and 1708, Leibnitz placed the Finnish and Scythian languages in the same group. Porthan and P. A. Gadd, who were among the Aurora Society founders, published in the first issue of *Åbo Tidningar* a poem in which the Finns are addressed as "Thou Folk of Scythic Stock and oldest line in North." In the article on Finns in the *Encyclopedia Americana*, (1938) we still find that "The Finns may properly be identified with the Scythians." In 1712 Pope placed the Scyths next to the Scandinavians in *The Temple of Fame:* "There sat Zamolxis with erected eyes, / And Odin there in mimic trances dies. / There on rude iron columns, smear'd with blood, / The horrid forms of Scythian heroes stood, / Druids and bards, their once loud harps unstrung." Pope was probably thinking of the Russians, but Leibnitz, following the theory of Marcus Z. Boxhorn, a Dutch scholar of the seventeenth century, placed both Finnish and Russian in the Scythian family, though in different subgroups. Boxhorn postulated a common language, which he called Scythian, as the mother of Greek, Latin, German, and Persian. He never published his work, but through his friend George Horn his ideas became known in Europe in the latter half of the seventeenth century. See G. Bonfante, "Ideas on the Kinship of European Languages from 1200 to 1800," *Journal of World History* I: 679-99.

NOTES

33. He chose for his coat of arms the motto *Yxitotinen*, a Finnish word meaning 'constant' or 'faithful.'

CHAPTER IV

34. Kivi's characters, for example, often speak of *Ruotsin riksit* 'Swedish rixdales.'

35. During the war against Russia (1788-89), some Finnish and Swedish officers who belonged to the nobility and disapproved of the king's reforms (to curtail the power of the ruling aristocracy, Gustavus III had increased his own power and abolished the privileges of the nobility) plotted at Anjala (Finland) to force him to make peace with the enemy. Among the Finns there were even plans to make Finland independent of Sweden under Russian protection, but they came to nothing, and the conspirators were condemned by all outside their own circle, i.e., mainly by persons who, twenty years later, took an oath of allegiance to the emperor of Russia while he was at war with their lawful ruler.

36. These words express Arwidsson's ideas and are always attributed to him, although Snellman actually wrote them.

37. Even in Longfellow's lifetime the origin of the meter used in *Hiawatha* was often discussed, but this source seems to be definitive. See Erich Kunze, "Freiligrathin ja Longfellowin 'suomalainen trokeemitta' " in *Juhlakirja Lauri Viljasen täyttäessä 60 vuotta* (Helsinki-Porvoo, 1960), p. 106 (French summary p. 371); James Taft Hatfield, *The Longfellow-Freiligrath Correspondence*, PMLA 48 (1933), p. 1244; Väinö Nyland, "Kalevala as a Reputed Source of Longfellow's Song of Hiawatha," *American Literature* XX (1950): 1-20; Ernest J. Moyne and Tauno Mustanoja, "Longfellow's *Song of Hiawatha* and the *Kalevala*," *American Literature* XXV, no. 1 (1953).

38. Cf. Nurmio, "Talonpoikaiskirjailija Antti Mannisen," p. 1 no. 1.

39. Few, if any, of the founders (not even Snellman) ever learned to speak or write Finnish correctly.

40. Joel Lehtonen's novel *Putkinotko* (1st ed., 1919-20) expressly mentions *Saarijärven Paavo* (p. 512, 5th ed., Helsinki, 1947).

41. Like the English, the Germans and Swedes have believed into this century that they could reproduce classical meters in their languages, but, as the quantity of syllables is much less prominent in their language than in the antique models, the result has usually been an arrangement of stressed and unstressed syllables, called hexameter when it follows the pattern of stressed-unstressed-unstressed-stressed, etc. See, e.g., George Sampson, *The Concise Cambridge History of English Literature* (Cambridge, 1945), pp. 747-49.

42. These peddlers, who were familiar figures in nineteenth- and early twentieth-century Finland, came from east Karelia, which has always been under Russian rule. As their homes were in Russia and they carried their merchandise—ribbons, pins and needles, small mirrors, and such—in bags, they

were called *laukkuryssät* 'bag-Russians' (*ryssä*, although derived from the proper name of the nation, is derogatory in Finnish; the correct name is *venäläinen*). The *Encyclopedia Fennica (Otavan Iso Tietosanakirja)* contains an article on them, s.v. "laukkuryssä."

43. Strindberg, *Complete Works* XVIII, part I (Stockholm, 1920), pp. 175, 177. Topelius, always an idealist, replied indirectly by writing in a personal letter that he would not "defile his hands" by reading a Strindberg book; he also called an Ibsen play a "theatrical monster" and its female lead an "octopus" (quoted in *Kirjallisuus* III, pp. 319-20). Initial reactions to Ibsen were similar everywhere; in England one of the gentler terms applied to him was "a muck-ferreting dog" (Sampson, *History of English Literature*, p. 758).

44. Quoted in *Kirjallisuus* III, p. 210.

45. Now celebrated on May 1, the *Vappu* of the Finns.

46. See *Kirjallisuus* III, p. 339. On the facing page is a caricature drawn on the occasion by August Mannerheim (of the family of Field Marshal C. G. E. Mannerheim), who was present.

47. Another statement from the same period reads: "These are the men, an inheritance left by the best of our realists, among which a future Runeberg will find his Sven Tuuva" (character in *Ensign Stål*; Kalle Salo in *Ilta-Sanomat*, 7 January 1955).

48. Work of this nature appears even in a recent book, O. Nousiainen, *Vänrikki Stoolin maailma* (Helsinki-Keuruu, 1961), pp. 285, 303-4, for example. Eirik Hornborg has shown the futility of this kind of work in *Fänrik Ståls Sägner och verkligheten* (Helsingfors, 1954). See Gunnar Castrén, "Runebergs väg till Fänrik Ståls sägner" in *Humanister och humaniora*, Skr. SLSF 368 (Helsingfers, 1958), pp. 119-35; idem., "Fänrik Ståls sägner och verkligheten" (a comment on Hornborg's work), same volume, pp. 136-42.

49. From the English translation by Charles Wharton Stork, Clement Burbank Shaw, and C. D. Broad (Helsinki, 1952).

50. Quoted (in Finnish) in *Kirjallisuus* III, p. 239.

51. Finns and Swedes are traditionally fond of honorary titles, which their governments generously bestow. No fewer than sixty-eight titles are now in use in Finland; a wealthy and influential pharmacist becomes Councillor of Pharmacy, a person active in education Councillor of Education, a successful gardener Councillor of Gardening, a famous stage director Councillor of Theater, and so forth. (See *Encyclopedia Fennica*, s. v. "arvonimi.")

52. See *Kirjallisuus* III, p. 320. *The Nation* (New York) carried his obituary March 31, 1898. Others appeared in the *Athenaeum* (March 19, 1898) and *The Dial* (April 16, 1898).

53. In *Books in English on Finland* (Hilkka Aaltonen, Publications of Turku University Library 8 [Turku, 1964], p. 185), no fewer than nineteen

entries appear under Topelius's name. *Canute Whistlewink and Other Stories* first printed in London, 1927, has been reprinted in 1928, 1942, 1955, and 1959. Finnish authors who write in Swedish risk confusion with Swedes, and so Topelius's *The Pitch Burner Who Always Got to the Top* (trans. C. W. Stork, London, 1928) was included in *Sweden's Best Stories. An Introduction to Swedish Fiction.*

54. Quoted (in Finnish) in *Kirjallisuus* III, p. 315.

55. On Topelius's political poems, see Gunnar Castrén, "Topelius's politiska diktring" in *Humanister*, pp. 171-87.

56. He belonged to the Finnish branch of that well-known Scots family, a member of which settled in Sweden (later in Finland) in 1577. For these facts see, e.g., Heikki Nurmio and R. W. Palmroth, "Suomen sotalaitos viiden vuosisadan aikana" in *Suomen puolustusvoimat*, ed. Felix Johansson, 2nd ed. (Porvoo, 1931), p. 34; Johannes Salminen, *Levande och död tradition* (Porvoo, 1963), pp. 16-26. Many young Finnish noblemen served in the Russian army, which provided broader opportunity than did the modest Finnish defence forces.

57. See n. 35.

58. See n. 43.

59. A contemporary point of view is presented in Pentti Renvall, "Suomalaisten historia," *Suomalainen Suomi*, 1963, pp. 204-9.

60. *A History of Western Philosophy*, 2nd imp. (London, 1947), p. 757.

61. *Kirjallisuus* III, p. 268.

62. Ibid., p. 281 (in Finnish).

63. The representative of the emperor in Finland, Governor General Prince Menshikov, said that Snellman was a communist, and the most influential member of the Finnish cabinet, Baron L. G. von Haartman, described Finnish as *la langue de Perkelä* [*sic*], "the Devil's tongue." (*Kirjallisuus* III, p. 282.)

64. He published it in the literary magazine of the *Saima* (*Literaturblad till Saima* and *Kallavesi*), later in Helsinki in *Finlands Allmänna Tidning, Morgonbladet,* and *Literaturblad för Allmän Medborgerlig Bildning*, which he again edited between 1855 and 1863. Gunnar Castrén, "J. V. Snellmans kritik och Aleksis Kivi" in *Humanister*, pp. 156-60, thinks that Snellman's wish to see a great novel by a Finnish author, formulated in his articles, may have encouraged Kivi to write *Seven Brothers.*

65. Béranger was very popular in France because of the patriotic and democratic message of his works; some of his influence is detectable in *Ensign Stål*. Many quotations from *Richard II*, for example, attest to the national and patriotic character of Shakespeare's plays, for example, the equality felt

among all men fighting for their country expressed in *Henry V* (III, i. 25), "... and you, good yeomen, / Whose limbs were made in England, show us here / The mettle of your pasture; let us swear / That you are worth your breeding; which I doubt not; / For there is none of you so mean and base / That hath not noble lustre in your eyes"; this one is much like two episodes in *Döbeln vid Jutas* and *N:o 15 Stolt* from *Ensign Stål*. Love for one's native language is expressed, e.g., in *Richard II* (I, iii, 160 et seq.): "My native English now I must forego / ... / I am too old to fawn upon a nurse, / Too far in years to be a pupil now: / What is thy sentence then but speechless death, / Which robs my tongue from breathing native breath."

66. *Kirjallisuus* III, p. 270.

67. Quoted from the English translation by Stork, Shaw, and Broad.

68. See note 46. In *Kirjallisuus* III are three other caricatures of him (p. 329) and a reproduction of Ekman's drawing (p. 324).

69. Founded under the Swedish rule (1779) at Haapaniemi (between Savonlinna and Varkaus in southeast Finland), moved to Hamina (on the Gulf of Finland, less than one hundred miles east of Helsinki) in 1819, closed by the Russian government in 1903. Today the Reserve Officers' School is housed in the old buildings.

70. *Kirjallisuus* III, p. 332.

71. *Kirjallisuus* III states (p. 341) that "their relationship was perhaps confirmed by a civil wedding of sorts," but, as civil marriage was not introduced in Finland before 1917, a civil ceremony seems unlikely.

72. *Kirjallisuus* III, p. 348.

73. See, for example, Bunyan's *Grace Abounding to the Chief of Sinners* (1666).

74. *Kirjallisuus* III, pp. 353-54.

75. Johannes Salminen, *Levande och död tradition*, pp. 10-15.

76. Ibid., p. 14.

77. See "Cajander, Jännes ja muita albumirunoilijoita" in *Kirjallisuus* III, p. 410. Both Cajander and Jännes, placed among "other album poets," were well-known writers in their time. On von Qvanten's political activity, see Michael Futtrell, *Northern Underground* (London, 1963), pp. 25-28 and 30-32.

CHAPTER V

78. One of its characteristics is very short word forms, e.g., *tytre* 'daughters' (corresponding to modern literary Finn. *tyttäret;* the English and Finnish words are etymologically the same). The forms *me weisam, puhum ia iloitzem (iloidzem)* appear in Agricola's work and the 1642 Bible, whereas the

NOTES

modern forms are *me veisaamme, puhumme, iloitsemme* 'we sing, speak, rejoice.' See *Kirjallisuus* II, pp. 146-47, 153-59; Martti Rapola, *Vanha kirjasuomi* (Helsinki: Suomalaisen Kirjallisuuden Seura, 1945).

79. Quoted in *Kirjallisuus* II, p. 229.

80. See *Kirjallisuus* II, p. 215-16. A reproduction of the 1747 title page is included.

81. See Martti Rapola, "Suomenkielisen proosan huomattavimmat isonvihan jälkeen" in *Kirjallisuus* II, p. 240.

82. Ibid., pp. 240-43.

83. The short biographic notice on Poppius in *Kirjallisuus* III (p. 623) states that he was one of the Finns who helped the German scholar H. R. Schröter publish his collection of Finnish poetry (cf. p. 36 and n. 37 this volume), but elsewhere the book states (p. 23) that Schröter worked with Gottlund, Aminoff, and Pippingsköld. Vihtori Laurila has recently published a study of Poppius, "Varhaisin lyyrinen romantikkomme" in *Laulu ja raipat* (Oulu, 1968), pp. 106-22. He says (p. 111) that he collaborated on Schröter's collection and that he probably procured an appendix with music for it. Cf. Viljo Tarkiainen, "Abr. Poppiuksen osuus H. R. Schröterin julkaisuun 'Finnische Runen, finnisch und deutsch'," *Virittäjä*, 1915, pp. 27-28.

84. See pp. 2-3. The situation remains similar in Finland; in 1964 a book by Hannu Salama displeased the church representatives, who continued public condemnation until the author and editor were indicted, sentenced to prison and fined, and the book censored. (See, for example, Lars Hamberg, "Translations of Drama into Minor Languages," *Babel, International Journal of Translation*, 1965, p. 105.) Soon afterwards the administration introduced in Parliament a bill intended to abolish the old law permitting such action and to institute a more liberal one, but an influential minority within the legislature was able to postpone its enactment until April, 1967, when further action was deferred until 1970, election year. On March 19, 1968, the Supreme Court, after a split vote, upheld lower court decisions after which two Finnish writers, Pentti Saarikoski and Jorma Ojaharju, sent a public protest to the Minister of Justice and Saarikoski announced that he would start a public collection for the payment of the fines. On March 29 the Finnish Writers' Guild sent a protest to the President of the Republic, pointing out that the section in the criminal law under which the decision had been made had not been enforced for thirty years. On August 9, 1968, the president pardoned Salama and the publisher. See pp. 3 and 382-83 this volume.

85. Quoted in Hautala, *Suomalaisen kansanrunouden*, pp. 96-97. We maintain that ours is not a faulty translation and that the text is not an expression of something too deep for understanding, but nonsense.

86. Ibid., p. 117. Lönnrot's part in the *Kalevala* amounts to approximately five percent.

87. Quoted ibid., p. 191.

88. Lönnrot used two Finnish words in the title, *laulu* and *virsi*. By *laulu* he meant purely lyrical poetry, by *virsi* short epic compositions, ballads, legends, etc. (Now *virsi* indicates a hymn). See *Kirjallisuus* III, p. 151.

89. For the *Kanteletar* in general, see *Kirjallisuus* III, pp. 150-55.

90. He boasted that, with Hannikainen, he could provide the Finnish theater with one hundred plays in less than ten years. Quoted in V. Tarkiainen-Eino Kauppinen, *Suomalaisen kirjallisuuden historia,* 3rd ed. (Helsinki, 1962), p. 154.

91. Much has been written on Kivi in Finland. On his genius, see, for example, Lauri Viljanen, "Aleksis Kivi" in *Kirjallisuus* III, pp. 469-73.

92. In a letter written at the end of 1868 to Kaarlo Bergbom. Quoted, with partial reproduction, ibid., pp. 464-66.

93. Few Americans realize that their educational system is rather different from the European. No European country seems to have anything comparable to an American college. In Europe secondary school includes the American high school and college work. At the university, at age eighteen or nineteen, European students begin what is called graduate work in the United States. If they study humanities, they receive the M. A. in four or five years.

94. Called *osakunta* in Finnish, *nation* in Swedish. They continue the traditions of the so-called nations in the medieval universities and membership in them was compulsory until 1937. Political, social, and other similar subjects were often discussed at meetings, and they were officially forbidden between 1852 and 1868.

95. Letters are quoted in *Kirjallisuus* III, pp. 569 (to Rein), 570 (to Bergbom).

96. See Viljanen, "Aleksis Kivi," p. 522. On Kivi's plays, see Aarne Kinnunen, *Aleksis Kiven näytelmät* (Helsinki, 1967).

97. No reason that she is not his daughter is given, and one surmises that Kivi was thinking of either an incestuous relation between them or, more simply, the young wife of an elderly man with a young lover, but felt both of these subjects too *risqué* for the Finland of his time. Cf. n. 105.

98. No sexual motif is introduced. The monster is represented as a kind of vampire which sucks blood from his victim. She remains half-alive as a kind of wraith, the "Pale Maid" (*Kalvea Impi*) for whom the story is named.

99. Also Anjanpelto, in old times a well-known marketplace near Vääksy, north of Lahti. (Cf. the song in *Seven Brothers*, Chap. 6.)

100. Young people in a Finnish village often built a swing (a permanent wooden structure), around which they met to talk, sing, and play.

101. See pp. 4-5.

102. At Whitsuntide it was customary for Finns to make bonfires around which the young men and girls would gather to sing and dance; this same custom is still observed thoughout the country, even in cities, at Midsummer Day's Eve.

103. The poem may be only a moving story of human misery, but it may also reflect Kivi's religious doubts and be understood as a warning not to ask God for help or gifts, which might be other than the kind we wished, as in the story of Cleobis and Bito, told by Herodotus, *History* 1:31, or in Heine's poem *Die Wallfahrt nach Kevlaar* (from *Heimkehr* in *Buch der Lieder*, 3rd ed. [Paris, 1839]).

104. See *Kirjallisuus* I, pp. 364-65. In some west Finnish variants, the country of death takes to some degree the aspect of a fairyland, with a little house built of strange materials, etc.

105. See Viljanen, "Aleksis Kivi," p. 512. He adds to these Byron's *Parisina*; we fail to understand why. The story of the two young lovers killed by the girl's stepfather (p. 77 and n. 79 this volume) is not unlike Byron's poem.

106. ". . . amoena uirecta / fortunatorum nemorum sedesque beatas." (*Aeneid* 6.638-39.)

107. It is said that the island is the "heaven and the earth of the waiting children," i.e., the abode of the unborn souls, but this idea is dropped in the following lines.

108. "Sembianza avean nè trista nè lieta." (*Inferno* 4. 84.)

109. "pedibus plaudunt choreas et carmina dicunt" (ibid., 644).

110. The name of the poem is not related to Aristophanes' satirical Νεφελοκκυγία.

111. See Harva, *Suomalaisten muinaisusko*, pp. 58-63, 66-68; cf. Y. H. Toivonen, "Taivaanääreläinen" in *Kalevalaseuran vuosikirja* 15 (1935), pp. 235-47.

112. Cf. n. 104. *Linnunlaulupuu*, known in popular poetry, lit. 'the tree on which the birds sing' (*puu* means both 'tree' and 'wood').

113. Quoted in *Kirjallisuus* III, p. 542. Esko Ervasti, " 'Ikävyyden' Aleksis Kivi," *Parnasso*, 1965, pp. 262-67, contends that Kivi had lost faith in the traditional Christian (Platonic and idealistic) conception of the world when writing this letter. His arguments, mainly based on an analysis of the poem *Ikävyys*, are rather convincing.

114. Swedish and Estonian are often the languages into which Finnish works are first translated. *Seven Brothers* first appeared in Swedish, (trans. Per Åke Laurén) in 1919; of the several later translations, Elmer Diktonius's

1948 version is considered a masterpiece. A German one was done by Gustav Schmidt in 1921, and three later translations have been made, the last in 1961, now through eight editions. An Estonian was done by Friedebert Tuglas in 1924, a French by Jean-Louis Perret in 1926, a Latvian by Elīnā Zālīte in 1926, an English by Alex Matson in 1929. Danish, Polish, Serbian and Croatian, Rumanian, Russian, and Japanese versions appeared later. On Swedish and Scandinavian translation of Finnish literature, see Lars Hamberg, "Strötankar om Finlands litterära kontakter med Norden" in *Nordisk Tidskrift*, Ny serie (Stockholm, 1960), pp. 395-404; idem, "Finsk litteratur i översättning" in *Finsk Tidskrift* 165-6 (1959), pp. 142-46. Cf. Thomas Warburton, "Finsk diktning i svensk dräkt" in *Finland i dag* (Stockholm-Örebro, 1960).

115. Reproduced (in Finnish) in *Antologia* II, pp. 254 et seq.

116. A. Kivi, *Valitut teokset*, 3rd ed. (Helsinki, 1946), pp. x-xiv (original italics).

117. *Ilosteleva kertomus*; Kivi translated *ilosteleva* as *humoristisk* in Swedish, but we feel that 'merry' is a better English translation than 'humorous.' A general analysis of the work is given by Aarne Kinnunen, *Tuli, aurinko ja seitsemän veljestä* (Helsinki, 1973).

118. Kivi abhorred violence. It is said that he was upset even by news from the American Civil War (see *Kirjallisuus* III, p. 533).

119. The scene, with the slain animals on the ground and opponents exchanging threats over them, is probably inspired by the similar incident in *Chevy Chace*, which Runeberg translated into Swedish and Kivi could have read, although it is not certain that he did. See F. J. Child, *English and Scottish Popular Ballads* (n.d.), 162 A, sts. 7-17.

120. Kivi's free use of adjectives is typical of Finnish writers. Here "a heartbreaking distance" is a distance so vast that the realization of it makes one's heart feel as if it were about to break.

121. We know of no such motif in Finnish folklore; the story seems to be a creation entirely of Kivi's fancy.

122. See the illustrations reproduced in *Kirjallisuus* III, p. 563. The episode on the Devil's Stone is represented by A. Gallen-Kallela.

123. These words are always mentioned in connection with Kivi's poems. For example, they are quoted in *Kirjallisuus* III, p. 510; Lehtonen, Preface to *Valitut teokset*, p. vi; Tarkiainen-Kauppinen, *Suomalaisen kirjallisuuden historia*, p. 190. (The two latter sources give the form *kultarakeita* 'nuggets of gold,' whereas *Kirjallisuus* III has only *kultaa* 'gold.') The original text, reproduced in *Antologia* II, p. 260, says that "Finnish beginners . . . offer gold that has not been minted into coins at all. Kivi's lyrical poems are such nuggets of gold." Lauri Viljanen first brought about a decisive change in the evaluation of Kivi's poems in his work *Aleksis Kiven runomaailma* (Helsinki, 1953). See his introduction to *A. Kivi. Kootut runot* (Helsinki, 1954).

NOTES

124. Runeberg, Kivi, and some others are called "national writers" (*kansalliskirjailija*) in Finland. This epithet, now rather meaningless, merely indicating a generally admired author, was probably taken from Germany (and Italy), where, due to the peculiar historical development of the country, there was one nation divided into various political units. A national writer (Goethe or Dante) was a writer whom the whole nation recognized as its own. In nineteenth-century Finland, the phrase could also mean that such an author was proving with his work that Finland was a nation capable of self-expression in the Hegelian meaning of the term. (*Kalevala* is called a "national epic.") On Snellman's theories about national literature, see, e.g., *Kirjallisuus* IV, pp. 7-8.

CHAPTER VI

125. The famous Finnish minutes of Lizelius's parish council did not deal only with religious matters. See p. 64.

126. We mentioned that Runeberg had to take the orders to become a teacher. See p. 44. The teaching of the Lutheran faith has remained compulsory in all public and private schools. Parents of other denominations must apply for special authorization to exempt their children.

127. Finn. *kansankirjailijat* in *Kirjallisuus* IV, p. 204. Vihtori Laurila, *Suomen rahvaan runoniekat* SKST 249 (Helsinki, 1956), calls them *rahvaan runoniekat* and explains (pp. 7-13) his reasons for choosing this name.

128. Property, profession, or birth were the bases of franchise in the elections to the old Parliament or Diet of the Four Estates. However, since one of the Estates (Nobility, Clergy, Burgesses— i.e., city dwellers— and Farmers or Yeomen) represented the agricultural population, its most influential members also had a voice in the government. See *Kirjallisuus* III, pp. 89-92.

129. One of the earliest known poems of this type was printed in 1829 in Oulu. Written in 1677 by Anders Mikkelinpoika Kexi (Keksi or Kieksi), it is about the break-up of ice in the Tornionjoki River.

130. See Laurila, *Suomen rahvaan runoniekat*, pp. 192-97.

131. See p. 38 this volume. Cf. n. 1.

132. Laurila, *Suomen rahvaan runoniekat*, p. 162.

133. Ibid., pp. 180-81, n. 1 ("matoja juoksi kallossaan ulos ja sisälle / Mi kauhistuksen kauhean tuotti hääväelle," sung to a "melancholy waltz tune."

134. Ibid., p. 180, n. 2.

135. Byron's Epitaph for *Joseph Blackett, Late Poet and Shoemaker* (1811) contains mainly disrespectful puns: "Stranger! behold, interr'd together / The *souls* of learning and of leather. . . ." See also Sampson,

History of English Literature, pp. 648-49; William F. Thrall and Addison Hibbard, "Primitivism" in *A Handbook to Literature* (New York, 1936); Robert Southey, *Lives of Uneducated Poets* (London, 1836), pp. 12, 113; Louis James, *Fiction for the Working Man 1830-1850* (London, 1963), pp. 1, 3-11, and Appendix I, "Working Class Poets and Poetry," p. 171; Michel Ragon, *Histoire de la littérature ouvrière* (Paris, 1953), pp. 62-74, 91; Raoul Palmgren, *Työläiskirjallisuus* (Helsinki, 1965).

136. See *Kirjallisuus* III, p. 86, where Runeberg's words to Kymäläinen are quoted (in Finnish).

137. Russia reduced the country population in the conquered provinces to serfdom, but did not otherwise persecute it. After 1861 vigorous spiritual development took place among it. Finnish schools were founded and various societies formed (in 1917 Finnish-speaking inhabitants numbered approximately 200,000). In St. Petersburg a Finnish-speaking group under the empire numbered more than 22,000 before 1917; they had their own churches from 1743, a school active between 1820 and 1918, newspapers, and various cultural activities. The separation of the Finnish and Swedish parishes in the first half of the eighteenth century resulted in the Finnish-speaking population's growing up in Finnish-speaking families and attending Finnish schools. This was impossible in Finland before the second half of the nineteenth century. When Kaarlo Gustaf Samuel Suomalainen (see pp. 140-41 this volume) began writing in Finland in 1876, he was the only author of the time who had grown up in a Finnish-speaking family and attended a Finnish school. He became one of the foremost translators of his time and published in Finnish works by Pushkin, Tolstoy, Gorki, Anatole France, Jules Verne, Oliver Goldsmith, Swift, H. G. Wells, and others.

138. The poem is reproduced in *Antologia* II, pp. 412-14.

139. See Sulo Haltsonen, *Suomalaista kaunokirjallisuutta vierailla kielillä* (Helsinki: Suomalaisen Kirjallisuuden Seura, 1961). Dr. Haltsonen does not mention editions later than 1930, but *Kirjallisuus* III, p. 438, states that "gigantic" issues of his short stories were still published in the U.S.S.R. after 1950.

140. In "Kauppis-Heikki ja Santeri Alkio" in *Kirjallisuus* IV, p. 195.

141. Ibid., p. 186.

142. In 1863 Snellman obtained from the emperor a decree providing that Finnish would have a position equivalent to that of Swedish within twenty years.

143. He first changed his Swedish names to Finnish ones. Later, when the emperor made him a knight, then a baron in the Finnish nobility, he combined his first and last names in a title.

144. The title's imprecise terms present translation difficulties: *Suomen suku*, used to indicate all peoples speaking Finno-Ugric languages, implies racial unity (*suku* lit. 'family, stock,') an idea not founded in fact.

Muinaisuus 'distant past' does not necessarily refer only to prehistory. The general impression is literary and romantic rather than scholarly and means approximately "The Finnish Family of Old."

145. A new edition was published in Helsinki in 1965.

146. For information about Ahlqvist-Oksanen's literary theories, see, e.g., Ilmari Kohtamäki, "Suomalaisen kirjallisuuden elpyminen" in *Kirjallisuus* III, pp. 381-93; idem, *Ankara puutarhuri. August Ahlqvist suomen kielen ja kirjallisuuden arvostelijana,* SKST 248 (Helsinki, 1956). Cf. V. A. Koskenniemi, "Suomalainen heksametri" in *Juhlakirja Lauri Viljasen,* pp. 77-78 (French summary p. 369).

147. See, e.g., Kai Laitinen, "Mikä uudessa lyriikassamme on uutta?" in *Puolitiessä* (Helsinki, 1958), pp. 203-56. Although not mentioned, Ahlqvist is obviously thought of.

148. Composing Finnish poems in bad popular meter is so easy that there are quantities of doggerel which have depreciated its value.

149. See n. 41.

150. Such words as *tuli* 'fire,' *tuuli* 'wind,' and *tulli* 'custom duty' or *taka* 'back' (as in "backyard"), *takaa* 'from behind,' *takka* 'fireplace,' and *taakka* 'burden' are distinguished only by length of vowels and consonants.

151. A syllable ending in a short vowel is short (e.g., both in *ko-ti*); any other is long whether it ends in a long vowel (*kaa-taa*), a dipthong (*lau-loi*; only dipthongs ending in *-i* are found after the first syllable); or a consonant (*lap-set*). According to rules of classical prosody, the latter syllable is long Θέσει 'by position,' not φύσει 'by nature.'

152. Kohtamäki, *Ankara puutarhuri,* p. 391. Formulated rather curiously, it gives a good example of the personification of language typical for some of the Finnish writers which we have mentioned. The literal translation is: "In the future, the Finnish language would build its meter only upon stress."

153. *Isosti erehtyvät.* Quoted in Koskenniemi, "Suomalainen heksametri," p. 77-78. Note again the personification of poetry in the original: "Our poetry builds its meter upon...."

154. See p. 11.

155. *Murrelmasäe.* The name is perhaps not well chosen, for the line is not defective. See Matti Kuusi, "Varhaiskalevalainen runous" in *Kirjallisuus* I, pp. 129 et seq. (esp. 132-33); Paavo Ravila, "Vanhan runomitan probleema" in *Virittäjä* 1935; Matti Sadeniemi, *Die Metrik des Kalevala-Verses,* FF Communications 139 (1951); idem, "Kalevalan mitta" in *Perinteen parissa* (1957); idem, *Metriikkamme perusteet ja sovellutusta moderneihin ja antiikin mittoihin* (Helsinki, 1949); László Gáldi, "Contributions à une typologie de la versification finno-ougrienne," *Ural-Altaische Jahrbücher* 36, nos. 1-2 (1964): 1-30.

156. In Finnish the first syllable of a word has the main stress; the third or fourth and every second one following have a secondary one.

157. Both lines are given by Kuusi, "Varhaiskalevalainen runous," p. 133. On p. 134 he says that the broken line was necessary to allow the use of three-syllable words in a basically trochaic meter. Several subtypes of broken lines are apparent. We would divide *selviä sinä ikänä* 3-2-3 with the two middle syllables unstressed ($\stackrel{\prime}{-} \smile \smile/\smile \smile/\smile \smile$), but Kuusi mentions other types. Cf. Sampson, *History of English Literature*, pp. 743-44, where the principle of substitution (of three syllable feet for two syllable ones) in old English ballads is discussed. Kuusi also says that in the poems found in Karelia and Ingria the proportion of dipodic to broken lines is one to one, in northeast Estonia two to one, in Inner Estonia three to one, and near the Latvian border seven to one.

158. There are doubts that poetry was read in this manner in Greece and Rome. However, the classical texts on prosody and the reading of poetry are contradictory and unclear; therefore, *adhuc sub iudice lis est.* See, for example, Dag Nordberg, "La récitation du vers latin," *Bulletin of the Modern Language Society* (of Helsinki) LXVI, no. 4 (1965): 496-508.

159. The quotations are from Ahlqvist's *Syksytoiveita* ('Hopes of Autumn') and Cajander's *Aamulla* ('In the Morning'), both in *Antologia* II, pp. 202-203, 365-66. For Kallio's poem see *Antologia* II, pp. 47-48. In Viljo Kojo's novel, *Suruttomain seurakunta* ('The Congregation of the Careless,' Helsinki, 1921), depicting the life of young artists in Helsinki, a character ridicules the second of the two Ahlqvist lines quoted here as a good example of the artificial character of old-fashioned poetry. Cajander's second line is as bad as Ahlqvist's. Read according to traditional rules, it is *túollaki méltäen séisovi* . . . since Finnish ears always hear the stressed syllable in a word as first. Kallio's poem contains an ictus on the last syllable of *kitelkööt*, which has a secondary stress however. A syllable containing a short vowel and ending with a consonant can be either long or short (*siellä mŭn huolĕni ŏn*); occasionally even long syllables appear in falls (*kauniimpĭ, kalliimpĭ*).

160. Koskenniemi, "Suomalainen heksametri," pp. 80-82. He also mentions Otto Manninen's hexameter used in the Finnish translations of the *Iliad* and the *Odyssey* (see p. 274 this volume). He calls these translations, in terms of prosody, "the closest to the classical model," but adds that, to follow this model, the poet had to "shorten a great number of words, arrange them in an unnatural order, use artificial and dialectal forms for the words and all kinds of additional rhetorical ornaments, which are alien to the original." Manninen's translations are, however, widely read and greatly admired; see Aarne Heino, *Otto Mannisen Homeros-suomennosten kuvakielestä*, SKST 296 (Helsinki, 1970).

161. A contemporary poet, Lassi Nummi, claims to have developed a new Finnish "hexameter" (*kuusimitta*), but it has failed to arouse noticeable interest. For a few poems and a theoretical discussion, see Lassi Nummi, "Kuusimittaa," *Parnasso*, 1960, pp. 249-51. For information on the evolution

of free verse in Finland, see Unto Kupiainen, *Suomalainen lyriikka Juhani Siljosta Kaarlo Sarkiaan* (Porvoo-Helsinki, 1948), pp. 9-10, 550, and Laitinen, "Mikä uudessa lyriikassamme on uutta?," pp. 207-10. J. V. Lehtonen applied the term *kuusimitta* to a meter used by Kivi. See Lauri Viljanen's introduction to *A. Kivi. Kootut runot,* pp. 45-46.

162. As early as the eighteenth century some of these practices were criticized. In a Latin manuscript written between 1745 and 1757, the anonymous author says that "some drop the last syllables when composing verse, but such lines are considered less genuine by purer Finns" (*puriores Fenni,* opposed to those of the coastal districts). The author could be Carl Rein; see Sarajas, *Suomen kansanrunouden,* pp. 136-39, which contains a facsimile of part of the manuscript.

163. Both poems are quoted by Laitinen, "Mikä uudessa lyriikassamme on uutta?," pp. 203, 219, and the question discussed pp. 219-22. See also the opinion of one of the foremost contemporary Finnish poets, Tuomas Anhava, " 'Runokieli' ja loppuheittoisuus," *Parnasso,* 1955, pp. 354-59, which answers an article by Aarni Penttilä, "Runokieli ja loppuheittoisuus," *Virittäjä,* 1955. Two further arguments by the same authors were published in *Parnasso,* 1956, pp. 187-91.

164. Published in Helsinki 1847-66. *Uusi Suometar* ('New' *Suometar,* 1869-1918) is considered to have carried on its tradition. In 1918 *Uusi Suometar* was changed to *Uusi Suomi,* as which it is still published by the Conservative party (*Kansallinen Kokoomuspuolue*).

165. See *Kirjallisuus* III, pp. 396-97.

166. Because "ethnography" (or "cultural anthropology") has a Finnish equivalent, *kansatiede,* the English words make a more scholarly impression than the original *kansatieteellinen unelma.* See *Kirjallisuus* III, p. 384.

167. Or 'The Savolainen's Song,' i.e., an inhabitant of the province of Savo. The old provinces have never been self-governing, but their inhabitants form distinct subgroups within the Finnish nation. They speak their own dialects and have common customs and traditions. They are also supposed to possess common character traits; the people of Savo and Karelia, for example, are said to be merry and fond of tales, jokes, and songs, whereas the people of Häme are reported dour, earnest, and slow. The country is now divided into administrative districts called *lääni.* They have some of the same names as the old provinces had, which can be confusing.

168. Ahlqvist's intentions in this poem are a matter of controversy. After Finland had become independent, it was often sung with the words *vieras valta* 'foreign power, domination,' instead of *väkivalta* 'violence.' In the third and fourth lines of the first stanza, *punainen on Pohjan kulma,* / *vertä* [*sic*], *tulta ennustaa* ('the northern corner [of the sky] is red / it forebodes blood and fire'), "the northern corner," which does not make sense, was changed to "the southeast corner" (*kaakon kulma*), where Russia lies.

169. At the end of the fifteenth century, when Finland was attacked by the Russians, Sten Sture the Elder, virtual ruler of Sweden, hesitated so much to send help that a contemporary chronicle says: "The Lord Lieutenant, Knight Sten / Does everything a bit late." Quoted in Einar W. Juva-Mikko Juva, *Suomen kansan historia* I (Helsinki, 1964), p. 241.

170. The Russians call this river Northern Dvina (*Severnaya Dvina*) to distinguish it from Southern Dvina, Latv. Daugava, which flows through Latvia.

171. One of the most active was the AKS (*Akateeminen Karjalaseura* or the Academic Karelia Society), most of whose members were students. In Finland, as in Germany, the academic world was usually conservative or extremely right-wing, unlike that of France, Great Britain, or the United States.

172. The eastern Karelians called the inhabitants of Finland "Swedes," and the Finns called them "Russians" when their relations were strained. See Kustaa Vilkuna, *Kainuu-Kvenland. Mikä ja missä?* (Helsinki, 1957), p. 59, et pass., and Erkki Kuujo, *Raja-Karjala Ruotsin vallan aikana* (Helsinki, 1963), pp. 195-96.

173. Literally *koskenlaskija* refers to a man, skilled in shooting the rapids (*koski*) of a river, who was often appointed and sworn in by the authorities to take boats with passengers or valuable cargo through dangerous spots. Shooting the rapids has long been a memory but is retained in a few places as a tourist attraction. See the picture in *Kirjallisuus* IV, p. 155.

174. Kivi's letters reveal that he was very painstaking in his work and rewrote the entire text of *Seven Brothers* (600 pp.) at least twice. See *Kirjallisuus* III, pp. 544-47.

175. The name is not related to *Suomi*, the Finnish name for Finland.

176. Here is a better formulation of Topelius's idea from *A Summer Day at Kangasala*. See p. 50.

177. This pessimism extended to surprising areas. In 1896 a society founded by Finnish businessmen to promote the country's foreign trade published a *Catalogue of Finnish Exports* intended as Finland's introduction to prospective English-speaking customers. However, it described the country as a poor, backward area with few products of quality to offer to the Western market (Juhani Paasivirta, *Plans for Commercial Agents and Consuls of Autonomous Finland*, Turun Yliopiston julkaisuja B89 [Turku, 1963], p. 30).

178. See, for example, Kauko E. Joustela, *Suomen Venäjän-kauppa autonomian ajan alkupuoliskolla vv. 1809-1865* (Helsinki, 1963), pp. 121-23, 139-40.

179. The Finns ascribe their success against enemies and in other difficulties to *sisu*, a quality mentioned by almost all visitors who write about the country. Reportedly untranslatable, the word could, we think, be aptly rendered by the American expression "guts."

180. *Semmoinen lallallaa.* Quoted in *Kirjallisuus* III, p. 406.

181. In Finland skiing is a popular means of locomotion, not a sport for the wealthy. Krohn's poem is a sign of awakening interest in physical exercises among the middle classes, who had until then considered them too aristocratic or too common.

182. The magazine with this title now published is not a direct continuation of Krohn's magazine.

183. The title page of the forty-ninth school edition (Helsinki, 1961) says "Finnish translation by Paavo Cajander." See *Kirjallisuus* III, p. 410. The *Encyclopedia Fennica* says that "the so-called Cajander's translation was published in 1889."

184. *Kaunokirjailijaliitto,* now *(Suomen) Kirjailijaliitto,* founded 1897. *Finlands Svenska Författareförening,* the corresponding organization for Swedish authors in Finland, was founded in 1919.

185. See *Kirjallisuus* III, p. 412. The statement that it was to be sung to the tune of *Integer vitae* refers to Horace's *Odes (Carmina)* 1.20, a humorous love poem. However, because its first and second stanzas can also be read as a praise to a virtuous man, they were taken out of context in late eighteenth-century Germany and a mournful tune was written for them by a little-known composer, F. F. Flemming.

186. *Isänmaa* is the emotionally-loaded Finnish word for one's own country, corresponding to Lat. *patria,* Fr. *patrie,* Ger. *Vaterland,* Russ. *ochestvo,* etc.

187. *Theatre in Finland* (special issue of *World Theatre,* published by the International Theatre Institute with the assistance of Unesco, Bruxelles s.a.), pp. 36-37, published statistics showing that between 1948 and 1958 Shakespeare was more often presented than any other foreign playwright.

188. See *Kirjallisuus* III, p. 413, or Tarkiainen-Kauppinen, *Suomalaisen kirjallisuuden historia,* p. 209.

189. See Hamberg, "Translations of Drama," p. 106.

190. *Heimoushenki.* In anthropological use *heimo* 'clan, tribe' is a human group with a common language, common traditions, and a supposedly common racial origin, but the word is used with emotional connotations in literary texts.

191. See pp. 60-61, (J. J. Wecksell), 60 (Fredrik Cygnacus, Gabriel Lagus, K. R. Malmstrom), 73 (Pietari Hannikainen), 94 (Y. S. Yrjö-Koskinen). The War of the Maces was seen as a popular uprising against aristocratic oppressors or as a Finnish rebellion against Swedish domination, but its events do not conform to this popular conception (see *Kirjallisuus* IV, p. 173). The rebels were not serfs, but independent farmers who protested the billeting of soldiers in their homes and sided with a Swedish pretender to

the throne against the reigning king. After their side won, the new king upheld the privileges of the aristocracy and increased taxes.

192. When the rebels, led by Ilkka and Yrjö Kontsas, met the king's troops at Nokia December 31, 1596, they stopped to parley, then fled. They were followed, their leaders taken as prisoners and executed. A few battles all ended in defeat of the rebels.

193. *Tappelu* 'battle' (old), now *taistelu; tappelu* 'fight, brawl.'

194. A nobleman of Baltic German origin. The German nobility of the Baltic countries (now Estonia, Latvia) was known for its ruthless brutality toward the conquered people. Many served in the Swedish army and administration, acquired estates by the king's grant, and brought their own methods of government to their new homeland.

195. See p. 134 this volume and *Kirjallisuus* IV, p. 172.

196. *L'Etranger* in *Le Spleen de Paris* (1869).

197. For a comparison of Siljo and Kramsu, see Kupiainen, *Suomalainen lyriikka*, p. 22.

198. See p. 61 and n. 77. Their poems were mainly "society verse" which made "drawing-room songs," but great musicians occasionally gave an appropriate musical form to the words of good poets, for example, Sibelius's music for Wecksell and Cajander.

199. Before trade unions were organized in Finland, workers already had musical societies. The first successful strike on record was organized by the Helsinki Printers' Glee Club in 1872. See Hannu Soikkanen, *Sosialismin tulo Suomeen* (Helsinki-Porvoo, 1961), p. 43.

200. *Kirjallisuus* III, p. 418. Later writers who suffered this fate include Konrad Lehtimäki, Uuno Kailas, Saima Harmaja, Edith Södergran, Kaarlo Sarkia, Katri Vala, and many others, less famous.

201. In Ahlqvist it was a literary pose (see pp. 98-99), for, besides an authoritarian character, he had a high opinion of himself, which his quarrels with Yrjö-Koskinen reveal.

202. Most Finnish scholars and critics do not share our opinion of Kramsu's greatness. Professor Koskimies, *Kirjallisuus* IV, pp. 166-74, praises his patriotic poems but places him below Eino Leino and other poets traditionally considered the greatest. The younger generation ignores Kramsu.

203. Thomas Moore is of course an Irish poet. As soon as a literature in Finnish developed, world literature was translated into Finnish by almost all writers mentioned in this chapter—Hannikainen, Ahlqvist, Krohn, Genetz, Cajander, Rahkonen, von Schrowe, Törneroos, Suomalainen, and others. Very soon a number of literary works were available to Finnish readers. See Eila Pennanen, "Finnish Translators," *Babel, International Journal of Translation,* 1965, pp. 60-61.

204. The poem was originally called *Helsingin Työväenyhdistyksen marssi* ('March of the Helsinki Workers' Society') and written for the tenth anniversary of that organization (not a trade union) in 1894. In 1893 J. H. Erkko had published *Työkansan marssi* ('The Working People's March'; see p. 143); the two compositions are sometimes confused, but Tuokko's is the one which remained popular.

205. There was often great discrepancy between originals and translations. At that time Finland, as part of the Russian Empire, did not recognize international copyrights, and both translators and publishers were sometimes quite free in their handling of foreign works. Older works were not respected any more than new ones; see Kasimir Leino's opinion (1890) on Tuokko's translation of Calderón's *La Vida Es Un Sueño* in Tyyni Tuulio, "Calderónin 'Elämä on unta' Maila Talvion innoittajana" in *Juhlakirja Lauri Viljasen*, p. 356 (French summary p. 383). Finland joined the international agreement on copyrights (Bern Convention) in 1928.

206. Marxists ideas were prevalent in the political workers' movement, however. See Soikkanen, *Sosialismin tulo*, p. 82 et seq.

207. One exception seems to be Julius Krohn (Suonio), who evolved for his folklore research the "historical and geographical method," which is reportedly based on the theory of evolution (see Hautala, *Suomalaisen kansanrunouden*, pp. 190-95). However, some of Krohn's terminology was borrowed not from Darwin, but from the fashionable Darwinistic jargon of the time. His theory was a practical method for the study of folklore based on his own observations and is still used in a modified form. Krohn was too intelligent to pretend that there was an observable similarity between the evolution of poems and that of living organisms.

208. Quoted by E. H. Carr, *What Is History?* (London, 1962), p. 52.

209. Quoted in Tarkiainen-Kauppinen, *Suomalaisen kirjallisuuden historia*, p. 218.

210. The government of autonomous Finland, in which Yrjö-Koskinen was Secretary of Education from 1885. His efforts were greatly responsible for the satisfactory relations between Finland and Russia for more than ten years after his appointment.

211. *Née* Johnson, Johansson, or Johnsson. *Kirjallisuus* IV, pp. 29, 585; *Encyclopedia Fennica*, s.v. "Minna Canth."

212. *Suomalainen Teat / t / eri.* See picture in *Kirjallisuus* IV, p. 46. It received the name of Finnish National Theater (*Kansallisteatteri*) in 1902.

213. *Kirjallisuus* IV, p. 32.

214. Each is usually called *kansannäytelmä* 'popular play,' a term used to describe plays written for the enjoyment of simple people supposedly unable to understand real literature. Their authors seldom declare that they are intended for mentally deficient persons. An interesting short study of this

type of novel was published by Walter Nutz, *Der Trivialroman*, Schriften zur Kunstsoziologie und Massenkommunikation 4 (Cologne and Opladen, 1962).

215. Quoted in *Kirjallisuus* IV, p. 32.

216. In 1958 (?) there were, in addition to the National Theater and the National Opera, thirty-three regular repertory theaters and approximately eight thousand amateur groups, each staging at least one play per year. All were subsidized in some form by the government, which has been granting regular financial support to dramatic art since 1907, and by local authorities. (*Theatre in Finland*, pp. 28-31.)

217. Quoted in *Kirjallisuus* IV, pp. 35-36.

218. Soikkanen, *Sosialismin tulo*, quotes both letters on pp. 13-14. Minna Canth's letters from 1860 to 1897 were published in Helsinki, 1944.

219. The entire debate on sexual morals is recorded in Armas Nieminen, *Taistelu sukupuolimoraalista* (Helsinki-Porvoo, 1951) (English summary, pp. 399-410, translates the title as 'The Battle over Sexual Morality,' approximately 1860-1920). Minna Canth's opinions are presented pp. 128-29, 133-52, 170-71.

220. Similar arguments were presented in Italy after World War II, when the Merlin Act, prohibiting prostitution, was discussed in Parliament. See Nieminen, *Taistelu sukupuolimoraalista*, pp. 90-91.

221. Tolstoy did not shrink from the extreme conclusion that overcoming sexual desire was the ultimate goal of mankind (which would bring about its extinction) (*Confession* [1894] quoted by Nieminen, *Taistelu sukupuolimoraalista*, pp. 162-63). The practice of sexual intercourse only for the procreation of children has had wide support throughout Christian times. Swift mentions it as an ideal reached by the Houyhnhnms, and C. S. Lewis imagines the same situation prevailing among the inhabitants of Mars in his novel *Out of the Silent Planet*. Nieminen also quotes several works in which sexual desire was treated as a disease and cures for it were given (pp. 46, 250-51).

222. This view was expressed by Milton in *Paradise Lost*: Adam and Eve had intercourse without feeling of sin or shame.

223. Quoted by Nieminen, *Taistelu sukupuolimoraalista*, p. 133. We are not given her husband's view.

224. Ibid., p. 134 (original italics).

225. Ibid., pp. 139-44.

226. Ibid., pp. 142-43; cf. *Kirjallisuus* IV, p. 60. Aho was seventeen years younger than Minna Canth.

227. See *Kirjallisuus* IV, pp. 34-35, 42.

228. Ibid., p. 44.

229. A good example of Minna Canth's *naïveté,* the name is a (now somewhat outdated) noun meaning 'a slattern.'

230. See Nieminen, *Taistelu sukupuolimoraalista,* p. 133. Genetz-Jännes wrote *Inhuuden ihastelijalle* ('Lauding the Loathsome'), a poem (printed in *Antologia* II, p. 445) directed at her.

231. *Kirjallisuus* IV, p. 44.

232. Ibid., pp. 44-47; Nieminen, *Taistelu sukupuolimoraalista,* p. 137. The Board of Trustees represented the persons and organizations giving support to the noncommercial Finnish theaters (cf. *Theatre in Finland,* p. 28). Bergbom's opinion of Minna Canth's play was irrelevant in the face of the Board of Trustees; the National Theater has a history of such control, especially between 1930 and 1945, when anything believed communistic was forbidden. Marc Connolly's *Green Pastures,* which presents biblical scenes imagined by Negroes, was called blasphemous by the church and not performed. See *Kirjallisuus* V, pp. 360-62.

233. *Kirjallisuus* IV, p. 47.

234. Soikkanen, *Sosialismin tulo,* pp. 14-15. He believes that Minna Canth was the Finnish author most appreciated in the workers' movement (p. 138).

235. The inhabitants of Denmark, Finland, Iceland, Norway, and Sweden now refer, officially as well as unofficially, to their homelands as the "Nordic" countries. *Scandinavia* traditionally refers to Denmark, Norway, and Sweden only. This use of the adjective *Nordic* is not approved in Great Britain. See *The Incorporated Linguist* (Journal of the Institute of Linguists, London) 5, no. 3 (1966): 91; 5, no. 4 (1966): 115; 6, no. 1 (1967): 21.

236. Two works on proletarian literature have been published by Raoul Palmgren, *Työläiskirjallisuus* (*Proletaarikirjallisuus*) (Helsinki, 1965) (English summary pp. 279-87); *Joukkosydän,* 2 vols. (Helsinki, 1966). Cf. Soikkanen, *Sosialismin tulo,* pp. 13-15, 137-40, 174-78, 221-23, 331-35; Annamari Sarajas, "Työväenkirjailijat" in *Kirjallisuus* V, pp. 128 et seq.; Tarkiainen-Kauppinen, *Suomalaisen kirjallisuuden historia,* p. 349.

237. *Theatre in Finland,* pp. 26-27, 29-30.

238. See the letter quoted in *Kirjallisuus* IV, p. 44-45, and p. 112 and n. 218 this volume.

239. *Kirjallisuus* IV, p. 47.

240. Soikkanen, *Sosialismin tulo,* p. 14.

241. The director was Mikko Majanlahti of the Tampere City Theater, the performance in 1965. Majanlahti later received an appointment at the Tampere Workers' Theater.

242. See Soikkanen, *Sosialismin tulo*, p. 39.

243. *Kirjallisuus* IV, p. 61.

244. Partially quoted in *Kirjallisuus* IV, p. 64. For Minna Canth's "second conversion," see Raoul Palmgren, "Minna Canthin 'toinen kääntymys,'" *Parnasso*, 1954, pp. 289-305. See also Väinö Kaukonen, " 'Papin perhe' taitekohtana Minna Canthin kirjailijantiellä," *Virittäjä*, 1962, pp. 424-31 (French summary p. 432).

245. *Kirjallisuus* IV, p. 63.

246. Tarkiainen-Kauppinen, *Suomalaisen kirjallisuuden historia*, pp. 230-31; Viljo Tarkiainen, *Minna Canth* (Helsinki, 1921).

247. *Kirjallisuus* IV, pp. 66-67. Tudeer's article is also mentioned.

248. See *Kirjallisuus* IV, p. 67.

249. Finland has virtually one church, the Lutheran, as do the other Scandinavian countries, and a small Orthodox one. In spite of freedom of religion, few people leave it; approximately 92 percent of the population belong to it, slightly more than 1 percent are Orthodox, the rest are other Protestant, Catholic, Jewish, Mohammedan, or agnostic. Although this 92 percent belong to the established church despite thier freedom to leave it, they seldom attend the services.

250. See Soikkanen, *Sosialismin tulo*, pp. 7-10; cf. Nils Westermarck, *Finnish Agriculture*, 2nd ed. (Helsinki, 1957), pp. 24-26.

251. The first proposal to regulate working hours was presented in Parliament in 1877, but rejected by all estates of the Diet. The first act for the protection of industrial workers was passed in 1899. See Soikkanen, *Sosialismin tulo*, p. 114; Heikki Waris, *Suomalaisen yhteiskunnan sosiaalipolitiikka* (Helsinki, 1961), pp. 8-9; Iisakki Laati, *Social Legislation and Work in Finland*, 3rd ed. rev. (Helsinki, 1953).

252. *Kirjallisuus* IV, p. 48.

253. Ibid., p. 55.

254. Ibid., p. 54.

255. Ibid., p. 70.

256. Ibid., pp. 71-72.

257. Ibid., pp. 74-76.

258. John I. Kolehmainen, "Homeros from the Other Side of the Arctic Circle" (address to Heidelberg College, Ohio, published in Finnish in *Suomalainen Suomi*, 1963, pp. 212-16). He said that Väinämöinen is described as a musician "greater than Orpheus." Lönnrot held the traditional

idea that magic formulas represent the oldest form of folk poetry and introduced a number of them in the *Kalevala*, which did not conform to the original spirit of epic songs (see Hautala, *Suomalaisen kansanrunouden*, pp. 117-18, 128). Although there are "shamanistic epic poems" (see Matti Kuusi, "Šamaaniepiikka" in *Kirjallisuus* I, pp. 251-60), in which fighting is accomplished mainly through singing, i.e., reciting magic formulas, Juhani Aho and his friends could not know at that time their origin. Although many Finnish folklorists protested, this theory is now generally accepted. On the "shamanistic epic poems" and the *Sampo*, see pp. 3-4 this volume.

259. *Metsämiehen muistelma* ('A Hunt,' *Lastuja*, second collection). It reminds us of the story Chekhov told: he and his friend Levitan went to shoot birds, wounded one, then argued over killing it because neither had the heart to do it (Constance Garnett, trans., *Letters of Anton Chekhov to His Family and Friends* [New York, 1920], pp. 304-5).

260. See *Kirjallisuus* IV, pp. 77-78, 107. A very interesting and frank biography of Aho was published by his son, Antti J. Aho, *Juhani Aho. Elämä ja teokset*, 2 vols. (Helsinki-Porvoo, 1951).

261. In *Squire Hellman and Other Stories*, trans. R. W. Bain (London, 1893), and *Stories by Foreign Authors. Scandinavian* (New York, 1901), pp. 19-38.

262. See *Kirjallisuus* IV, pp. 79, 83-86. In a way Professor Koskimies agrees with our opinion in saying that Matti and Liisa, the main characters in *Rautatie*, "do not possess Kivi's Homeric greatness, Runeberg's robust strength, or the exuberance and lustiness of Nortamo's townspeople. . . . Matti and Liisa are small, their animals, the horse and the cow, are small, and so are their cabin and their household. . . . The neighbors, up to the vicarage itself, are also somewhat like taken from a toybox; and the railroad itself is a kind of toy."

263. In *Kirjallisuus* IV, pp. 80-81, 583, the year of publication is listed as both 1884 and 1885. Statements on p. 81 indicate that the second date is correct.

264. See *Kirjallisuus* IV, pp. 80-82. Professor Koskimies there states that, in his father's biography, Antti Aho gives almost too conclusive a demonstration of the correspondence between the story and Aho's life, which could not be hidden. Minna Canth and Kaarlo Bergbom, for example, seem to have noticed.

265. See p. 87 et seq.

266. Also in *Squire Hellman and Other Stories*.

267. Quoted in *Kirjallisuus* IV, p. 94.

268. See photograph of the editors of *Päivälehti* in *Kirjallisuus* IV, p. 293.

269. For a while there was interest in Finland's cause in Europe, and some of Aho's patriotic sketches were published in English in *Finland. An English Journal Devoted to the Cause of the Finnish People.* Of course, they were not read for their literary value.

270. The repeated *ka-* sound makes the phrase more catchy in Finland, where everyone is familiar with the alliteration of the old folk poetry. See p. 5.

271. See pp. 102-03.

272. A monument to the pioneers of the region was actually erected at Ilmajoki (approximately forty miles southeast of Vaasa) in 1954.

273. Especially abroad the agricultural problem in Finland has been oversimplified and represented as a struggle between Swedish-speaking aristocrats and Finnish-speaking tenants. However, not all Swedish-speaking persons belonged to the upper and middle classes. There was also a significant Swedish-speaking rural population that included tenants and laborers and a number of wealthy Finnish-speaking landowners and farmers who, though not considered part of the educated class, also had large estates and tenants. Of the approximately 350,000 Swedish-speaking inhabitants of Finland in 1957, 3 percent were employers, 18.5 percent self-employed (including farmers not using hired labor), 1.4 percent executives with no share in their companies, 24.6 percent clerical workers, 34.1 percent manual workers, 18.4 percent working members of households; 31.9 percent worked in agriculture and forestry, 27.7 percent in industry, 10.5 percent in commerce, 9 percent in transportation, and 10.9 percent in various services. See Nils-Börje Stormbom, "Suomenruotsalainen perinne," *Parnasso*, 1957, pp. 123-28.

274. Almost all Finnish works encompassing the political and social history of the period mention this affair. *Encyclopedia Fennica* contains an article s. v. "Laukon lakko" ('The Strike at Laukko'; cf. "Laukko"). See also Soikkanen, *Sosialismin tulo*, pp. 378-79. Tenant strikes were possible because, in many parts of the country, the tenants paid at least part of their rent by working a fixed number of days for the landlord, an archaic system which produced bickering between the parties.

275. See *Kirjallisuus* IV, p. 113. The publication of such a picture during the Russian rule is another indication of the peaceful nature of the struggle between Finland and Russia. In 1906 and 1907 there was also temporary improvement in their relations.

276. See *Kirjallisuus* IV, pp. 101-2.

277. Chekhov included dreams in nature in longer stories, e.g., *The Lady with the Small Dog, His Holiness,* and *The Steppe.* Reportedly he often went to a river in pretense of angling when he wanted to sit alone and dream. We note many similarities between the characters and outlooks of Chekhov and Aho, but there seems to have been no influence of Chekhov on Aho. Finnish scholars, critics, and biographers mention instead the Norwegians and the French; *Lumoissa* contains two direct allusions to Ibsen's *Peer Gynt.*

NOTES

278. Finland did have a frontier, beyond which a man could go if he was unhappy in society, but, like that of the United States, it disappeared, and only the myth remained.

279. See p. 43. Cf. Martti Ruuth, "Juhani Aho herännäisyyden kuvailijana," *Valvoja*, 1911, pp. 432-37.

280. Aho saw that many of the Finnish people were not interested in old poetry whose spirit and even language they could not understand. Cf. pp. 8-9 and n. 315. In *Kevät ja takatalvi* two enthusiastic students unsuccessfully try to convince a farmer of the *Kalevala's* beauties. Aho does not see the scene in a humorous light although he might have. The farmer rejects the epic not because he is apathetic toward art, but because, as a religious man, he cannot accept pagan poetry. (I, pp. 10-28, 1st ed.)

281. *Kirjallisuus* IV, pp. 122-23.

282. Instead of a peddler, the man should have been called a trader or an adventurer. Cf. p. 41, n. 42 this volume. Some Russian Karelians were offended by Aho's description and protested that none of them would behave as his character behaves. See *Kirjallisuus* IV, pp. 124-25; Rafael Engelberg, "Juhani Ahon uusi teos ja Karjalan olot," *Helsingin Sanomat* 90 (1911); Iivo Härkönen, " 'Juha' ja Wienan Karjala," *Uusi Suometar* 110 (1911); idem, "Juhani Ahon uusi romaani ja vienankarjalaiset," *Uusi Suometar* 100 (1911).

283. Pp. 18-22 (1st ed.).

284. See pp. 64-65 this volume. *Kirjallisuus* IV is probably in error in saying "the rector of Sotkamo, Juhana Frosterus, who died in 1763 and has his place in the history of Finnish literature, was ... his great-great-grandfather" (p. 139). *Kirjallisuus* II gives as the years of Frosterus's birth and death 1720 and 1809 and states that he was appointed rector of Sotkamo in 1763. Unlike many of his compatriots, the later Frosterus did not have to invent a Finnish name. The family came from Pakkala farm at Lohja (approximately twenty-five miles west of Helsinki); Frosterus was a fanciful translation of that name. Pakkala is from Finn. *pakkanen* 'frost,' which corresponds to Swed. *frost* 'frost.' The *-erus* is a pseudo-Latin ending. Another well-known family, Gummerus (see p. 140 this volume), derives its name from Pihkala (Finn. *pihka* 'gum, resin,' Lat. *gummi*).

285. Finland's slums, like those of most other European countries, were situated in the suburbs. In books by Aho and other contemporary writers, "to go to the suburbs" (*laitakaupunki*) is a euphemism for "to go to the prostitutes." See *Kirjallisuus* IV, p. 90.

286. Quoted in *Kirjallisuus* IV, p. 142.

287. *Kirjallisuus* IV contains photographs of the part of Oulu in which Pakkala lived and of a tar-loaded riverboat shooting the rapids (p. 155).

288. *Kansannäytelmä* 'popular play.' See p. 111 and n. 214.

289. See a photograph of such a performance in Tampere in *Kirjallisuus* IV, p. 150.

290. Its actual name was *Kakaravaara* (lit. 'Childhill' or 'Kid-' or 'Brathill'; *kakara* is a colloquial, if not vulgar, word for a child, an allusion to the inhabitants' numerous offspring). Later, in honor of the author, it was renamed *Pakkalan vaara.*

291. Quoted in *Kirjallisuus* IV, pp. 144-45.

292. *Kirjallisuus* IV, pp. 183-206; cf. pp. 87 et seq. this volume.

293. Cf. pp. 91-92. This education and the dramatic, literary, musical, and other activities connected with it were thought primarily to benefit young people. Interested organizations were usually called *Nuorisoseurat* 'Young People's Societies.' If the education were given at a formally organized school, the school was called *Kansanopisto* 'Popular Institute.' See Heikki Leskinen, *The Provincial Folk School in Finland,* Indiana University Monograph Series in Adult Education 3 (Bloomington: Bureau of Studies in Adult Education, 1968).

294. See p. 43. Ostrobotnia was not a poor, backward area, but a region of vast fertile plains from which grain was exported to Sweden (see p. 102). Its inhabitants, known for their proud and violent spirit "waxed fat and kicked" like Jeshurun. George North, *Description of Swedland, Gotland, and Finland* (London, 1561; facsimile ed., intr. M. W. S. Swan, New York, 1946), says "Finlande is called a fayre countrye, because it is more pleasanter than Swecia. . . . This countrye doth excell Swecia, in corn and grain, both for plenty and goodness, because it is for the most part playne, and not so fenny nor hylly as Swecia is." (Quoted by Göran Stenius, Introduction to Mario de Biasi's volume of photographs, *Finlandia. Profile of a Country* [Helsinki, 1967], p. 6.) This description, although misleading about Finland as a whole, is a good picture of southern Ostrobotnia.

295. See the texts in *Antologia* II, pp. 367-71, and the pictures in *Kirjallisuus* IV, p. 198.

296. *Kirjallisuus* IV, p. 207.

297. See p. 4 this volume. Finnish scholars have been unable to determine whether or not the poem's events are accurate history. See also Tarkiainen-Kauppinen, *Suomalaisen kirjallisuuden historia,* p. 47.

298. The main character, a proud, violent nobleman, confesses many crimes, murder, manslaughter, arson, robbery, etc. (a list unbelievable even for the late Middle Ages), and the priest tells him that he may atone for them by paying five, ten, fifteen, or more gold ducats to the Church. Smirking contentedly (in the production we saw at *Tampereen Työväen Teatteri*), the priest scoops up the coins with an audible clink. Finally the sinner admits having eaten meat on Friday when no other food was to be found, whereat the priest, horrified, declares that at least fifty ducats must be paid for such a heinous offense. There were few Roman Catholics in Finland at the time von

Numers wrote his play, and their numbers are still limited, but echoes of the great struggle between the Church and its opponents in the nineteenth century were heard in Scandinavia. The Finns were proud of their participation in Gustavus Adolphus's campaigns in the Thirty Years' War, and Catholics were traditionally the archvillains of history, ignorant, superstitious, backward and full of devilish cunning and cruelty. This view, expressed in Topelius's novels, was especially applied to the Jesuits.

299. See pp. 112-13.

300. *Kirjallisuus* III, p. 451.

301. Unto Kupiainen considered the period from 1870 to 1880 characterized by these small humorists and called it "the ten years of small humor." See *Kirjallisuus* III, p. 439; Unto Kupiainen, *"Pienoishuumorin" vuosikymmen suomalaisessa kirjallisuudessa* (Tampere, 1939); idem, *Huumori suomalaisessa kirjallisuudessa* I. *Aleksis Kivi ja 1880-luvun realistit* (Tampere, 1939; also SKST 215).

302. *Kirjallisuus* IV contains a chapter entitled "Realismin taite lyriikassa" ('Breakthrough of Realism in Poetry,' pp. 157-82), in which Kramsu is treated, but we do not think this an apt classification for him.

303. See p. 111. *Päivälehti*, later *Helsingin Sanomat*, was eventually taken over by the Erkko family, in whose hands it remains, now the largest daily paper in the country. Another Erkko was Minister for Foreign Affairs of Finland in 1939, when the Winter War broke out. Cf. Pirkko Alhoniemi, "Realistien ihanteista," *Sananjalka* 14 (1972): 191-99 (German summary pp. 199-200), mainly on Aho and Kasimir Leino.

304. *Antologia* II, p. 425.

305. See n. 204.

306. See *Kirjallisuus* IV, pp. 217-18. A reproduction of the playbill is included.

307. See *Kirjallisuus* I, p. 358; cf. p. 363. Finnish scholars point out that such names in folk poetry often designate creations of the poet's fancy, not mythological beings in which his community believed.

308. *Kirjallisuus* IV, p. 175.

309. Cf. pp. 97-98.

310. *Kirjallisuus* IV, p. 179.

CHAPTER VII

311. In that year Emperor Nicholas II signed the famous February Manifesto in which he declared, in essence, that henceforth all laws affecting Finland and the empire would be made by the Russian legislators alone and

that Russian authorities would decide which laws belonged to this category. Thus, both in theory and practice, the legislative powers of the Finnish Parliament could be reduced to nothing, in open contradiction to the constitutional position of Finland defined in the declarations of Alexander I and his successors. The Manifesto was given without consultation with Finnish authorities.

312. See R. Koskimies, "Suomalainen uusromantiikka" in *Kirjallisuus* IV, pp. 292-308.

313. Quoted in Tarkiainen-Kauppinen, *Suomalaisen kirjallisuuden historia*, pp. 273-74; cf. *Kirjallisuus* IV, p. 331.

314. Pohjola Insurance Company (Aleksanterinkatu 44), designed in 1901 by H. Gesellius, A. Lindgren, and Eliel Saarinen, father of Eero Saarinen. A survey of the artistic movement of that period is given by N. -E. Wickberg, *Finnish Architecture*, 2nd ed. (Helsinki, 1962), pp. 80-85, illus. pp. 92-114. The period corresponds to the *Jugendstil* and *Art Nouveau* in other European countries and has similarities in architecture to Henry Hobson Richardson's romanesque revival in the United States. It was in architecture that the period proved most fruitful. Although by 1905 architects were moving toward a more sober style, national romanticism was the first step toward a new, nonclassical conception of their art.

315. "What would our present-day Finnish civilization have to offer us if it had not been built on the foundations of the *Kalevala?* Let us assume that the relief by Sjöstrand would be removed from the hall of our University . . . and also the painting by Ekman and the mural by Gallen-Kallela from the auditorium of the Students' Union Building. . . . Let us think that Helsinki would be deprived of its most charming statue, representing Elias Lönnrot . . . and the museums of art in our capital of all the paintings and sculptures on subjects from the *Kalevala*. . . . Let us still suppress in our minds . . . the numerous compositions by Sibelius on subjects and words taken from the *Kalevala*. Let us erase from our literature Aleksis Kivi's first work, *Kullervo*, Erkko's *Aino*, *Kullervo*, and *Pohjolan häät*, Juhani Aho's *Panu*, Eino Leino's *Helkavirsiä* . . . and we shall understand the importance of this one poem for our national civilization." From Kaarle Krohn's article on the *Kalevala* in *Oma Maa* I, 2nd ed. (Porvoo, 1920), pp. 1045-57. Krohn was a remarkable folklore scholar, but he had little taste for music and art and judged works from these fields in light of their connection (or lack of it) to the *Kalevala*, selecting the most mediocre sculptor, Sjöstrand, and painter, Ekman, of nineteenth-century Finland. See this volume for Kivi's works, Erkko's *Aino*, *Kullervo*, and *Pohjolan häät*, Aho's *Panu*, and Leino's *Helkavirsiä* (neither of the latter two are on subjects from the *Kalevala*).

316. Yrjö Oinonen speaks of poetry "in Eino Leino's time" (*Vesiluonto Eino Leinon ajan runoudessa* [Kouvola, 1945]), but Unto Kupiainen objects (*Suomalainen lyriikka*, p. 1). See also Mauno Niinistö, *Uuno Kailas* (Helsinki, 1956), p. 14 and n. 4.

317. *Kirjallisuus* IV, pp. 326-428, mentions approximately fifty major works. The biographical notice, pp. 593-94, lists eighty-two titles and thirteen translations, including all of Dante's *Divina Commedia*.

NOTES

318. *Matti Meikäläinen*, February 17, 1899, *à propos* his activity as a theater critic. Reprinted in *Kirjallisuus* IV, p. 341.

319. The classification was established by Aarre M. Peltonen, "Keskeisiä ongelmanasetteluja Eino Leinon runoudessa" in *Juhlakirja Lauri Viljasen*, pp. 267-76 (French summary p. 379). Eino Leino has been studied with great interest in Finland. At least 160 books and articles on him have been published since his death; see the catalogues on Finnish literary research, Sulo Haltsonen, ed., *Luettelo suomalaisista kirjallisuudentutkimuksista* several vols. (Helsinki: Suomalaisen Kirjallisuuden Seura, 1936—) (tables of contents in French).

320. See p. 4.

321. Cf. p. 131.

322. See *Kirjallisuus* IV, p. 338-9.

323. Viljo Tarkiainen, who wrote numerous books and articles on Leino, in part published by Eino Kauppinen and Aarre M. Peltonen, eds., *Eino Leinon runoudesta. Tutkielmia* (Helsinki, 1954), divides the *Helkavirsiä* poems into ballads (on nonreligious subjects) and legends (on religious ones); see Tarkiainen, "Eino Leinon Kristus-legendat" in KTSVK 9 (1947), pp. 128-46; idem, "Neitsyt Maria-aihe Eino Leinon tuotannossa" in *Kalevalaseuran vuosikirja* 22 (1942), pp. 131-48.

324. Cf. p. 7 and n. 10. *Helkavirsi* is an old word used in modern times only by Leino, and its meaning is obscure to most Finnish readers of his works. *Helka* is etymologically the same word as Eng. *holy*, Ger. *heilig*, Swed. *helig, helg*; the old festival at Ritvala described by Gottlund (see p. 69) was called *Ritvalan helka*. *Virsi* presently has only the meaning 'hymn,' not 'song' in general, as it did earlier.

325. See Pentti Lyly, "Otto Manninen Eino Leinon kriitikkona" in *Juhlakirja Rafael Koskimiehen*, p. 160 (French summary pp. 305-6); cf. Pekka Lappalainen, "Realistisen aatevirtauksen kontinuitiivisuus [sic] vuosisadanvaihteen suomalaisessa kaunokirjallisuudessa" in *Juhlakirja Lauri Viljasen*, p. 166 (French summary pp. 373-74). The latter article has been expanded and published as *Realistisen valtavirtauksen aatteet ja niiden kontinuatiivisuus [sic] Suomen kirjallisuudessa vuosisadan alkuun saakka* (Helsinki, 1967).

326. On Leino and Manninen, see Lyly, "Otto Manninen Eino Leinon kriitikkona."

327. Unto Kupiainen, *Suomalainen lyriikka*, p. 2 and p. 3 n. 1, says, as only 229 copies were sold the first year, that Leino's contemporaries did not give due attention to *Helkavirsiä* I. That this figure is considered small is an indication of the popularity of literature in Finland. In "Kirjailija pienessä maassa" ('A Writer in a Small Country'), Veijo Meri says that he obtained information about literary life in the United States by a representative of the Library of Congress, who said that "in the United States two or three poets

465

are living by their royalties. A collection of poetry is printed in about three to five thousand copies. A novel might be sold in ten or fifteen thousand. A publisher may require an author to make a considerable deposit before embarking upon anything as hazardous as publishing the text of an unknown author. . . ." (originally published in *Parnasso*, 1966, pp. 313-15; reprinted in *Kaksitoista artikkelia* [Helsinki, 1968], pp. 89-94).

328. Begun in 1881, still published in Helsinki (between 1923 and 1943 the title was *Valvoja-Aika*). It introduced literary realism to Finland, and for a while both Leino and Manninen wrote for it. However, its editors have always belonged to the academic world, and it tends to be conservative in outlook. In addition to criticism and literary essays, it carries articles on theater, art, sciences, politics, social questions, etc. It merged in 1968 with *Suomalainen Suomi.*

329. See Lyly, "Otto Manninen Eino Leinon kriitikkona," pp. 165-66; cf. L. Onerva's words, quoted in *Kirjallisuus* IV, p. 350.

330. Leino took his subject from the *Kalevala*, not directly from folk poetry. Lönnrot had composed the Lemminkäinen episode from one lyric and three epic poems; the first was *Päivölän virsi* ('The Song of Päivölä,' published by Z. Topelius the elder). It had nothing in common with the second but the name of the main character; the second was *Hiidestä kosinta* ('The Wooing of the Maid of Hiisi') which Lönnrot published himself and combined with another, *Lemminkäisen surma* ('Lemminkäinen's Death'). He added to it an episode, the killing of the Swan of Tuonela, from a lyric poem in which Lemminkäinen does not appear (see Väinö Kaukonen, "Elias Lönnrot" in *Kirjallisuus* III, p. 140; Kuusi, "Varhaiskalevalainen runous," p. 156; idem, "Sydänkalevalainen lyriikka ja epiikka," pp. 253-55; Annamari Sarajas, "Eino Leinon joutsenet" in *Juhlakirja Lauri Viljasen*, pp. 301-13 [French summary p. 381]). Although Leino first conceived the work as the libretto of an opera, it was not performed until November 18, 1966, at the Helsinki Students' Theater (*Helsingin Ylioppilasteatteri*), under the direction of Kaisa Korhonen, to music written by a young contemporary composer, Kaj Chydenius.

331. December 22, 1896; see Rafael Koskimies, "Eino Leinon Tuonelan joutsen" in *Kalevalaseuran vuosikirja* 40 (1960), pp. 18-25.

332. For example, *Hän kulkevi kuin yli kukkien* ('She Walks As If on Flowers'), *Oi muistatko vielä sen virren* ('Oh, Do You Still Remember That Hymn?'), and *Jo lapset laivoja veistää* ('The Children Are Already Making Boats') in *Yökehrääjä.*

333. Kaukonen, "Elias Lönnrot", p. 146. The motif, called *Päivän päästö* ('The Liberated Sun') by folklorists, is briefly mentioned in *Kirjallisuus* I by Matti Kuusi, pp. 70-71, 252.

334. Perma (Swed. *Biarmia, Bjarmia, Biarmaland*) was a half-mythical country perhaps on the White Sea, inhabited by a people speaking a Finno-Ugric language (see Martti Haavio, *Bjarmian vallan kukoistus ja tuho,* Porvoo-Helsinki, 1965). It has excited the fancy of Finnish historians and

writers with its mysterious character and the information about it in old Anglo-Saxon chronicles and Scandinavian sagas; we hear of Vikings sailing there in the ninth and eleventh centuries, trading with the inhabitants, and finding in the temple of Jomali (cf. Finn. *Jumala* 'God'), which they plundered, a great wealth of gold and silver.

335. See pp. 4-5 this volume.

336. Imatra, a great waterfall in southeast Finland, is often used by writers to symbolize indomitable power.

337. Leino became a legendary character in his lifetime (see *Kirjallisuus* IV, pp. 394-95). Even today highly priapic and probably spurious poems attributed to him are recited in men's circles.

338. *Kirjallisuus* IV, p. 364.

339. Quoted ibid., p. 368.

340. His brother Kasimir also had a sad end; he died insane, wrapped in dreams about a glorious Finno-Ugric past. See *Kirjallisuus* IV, p. 180.

341. The Don Juan who invited the statue of the man he had killed to dinner and was dragged to Hell with it, not the Don Juan of amorous adventures.

342. Leino seldom used the name of the Christian Hell, *Helvetti*, in his works, choosing instead old Finnish words such as *Mana* (*la*), *Tuoni, Tuonela,* etc.

343. Leino's words are referred to in *Kirjallisuus* IV, p. 352.

344. See *Kirjallisuus* IV, pp. 352-53.

345. The idea that the gods' gifts might be dangerous to men is reminiscent of Kivi's poem *Äiti ja lapsi*, mentioned on p. 78. The simplicity of the last scene also reminds us of Kivi.

346. *Turilas* 'beetle' is not a common Finnish insult and makes a humorous impression on a contemporary reader; we thought it best rendered by the colloquial English 'varmint.' *Räähkä*, an east Finnish word, means 'illness, sickness, sin.'

347. This stylistic device is often mentioned but never fully discussed in *Kirjallisuus* I, e.g., pp. 278, 294, 299, 320, 339, 343, 352.

348. See *Kirjallisuus* I, pp. 313, 352-53, where *Ihmemaa* is partially quoted.

349. See p. 4.

350. The Orthodox church was more tolerant toward old customs; partially for this reason they were preserved in Ingria and Russian Karelia

while they disappeared in Finland. One Ingrian said to a Finnish folklorist who visited the region in 1858: "Our new (Lutheran) pastor won't allow us to cry (lament or keen) at the grave or on our way to it, although the Russian (Orthodox) priest doesn't mind it at all." (*Kirjallisuus* I, p. 127). From its foundation the Lutheran church of Finland (and Sweden) took a negative attitude toward all folk traditions; see, e.g., Sarajas, *Suomen kansanrunouden*, pp. 10, 16-17, 41-42.

351. He wrote original poems in the old folk manner and used the old folk meter in his own way. He followed its rules rather closely, but all his lines do not have the required eight syllables, and he used rhyme, which was unknown to the old poets. See *Kirjallisuus* IV, pp. 335, 337-38 and 358-61.

352. Annamari Sarajas, "Eino Leinon joutsenet" ("Jäinen joutsen" ['The Icy Swan'], pp. 310 et seq.

353. See p. 42 this volume. Note the common water symbolism, though differently treated, and the dejected mood of both poems.

354. In a letter to L. Onerva, with whom he was in love at that time, quoted in *Kirjallisuus* IV, p. 367.

355. As he did in *Karavaanikuoro*, Leino used *kuoro* 'choir' to indicate the sound of voices singing together; the best English translation might be 'The Voices of Midnight.'

356. *Tarha* lit. 'enclosure,' used in compound words such as *hedelmätarha* 'orchard' or *puutarha* 'garden,' suggests a purposeful, pleasant arrangement of features; so *tähtitarha* implies the sky as a garden in which the stars are flowers or something similar. *Taivaan tähtitarhat* is a common literary phrase in Finnish.

357. *Eino Leino. Runoilija ja ihminen*, 2 vols. (Helsinki, 1932).

358. Finn. *sähkö* 'electricity' keeps the phrase from sounding as pedantic in the original as in English, but the introduction of a modern word in a mythical context (used by Leino in still other poems) is not an entirely happy innovation.

359. *Metamorphoses* 2.49-102. Another similar description appears in Lucan, *Pharsalia* 1.45 et seq., where deified Nero drives the chariot of Sun and threatens to tilt the axis of Heaven under his godlike weight. Even in classical antiquity Lucan was considered part of the Silver (no longer Golden) Age of Roman poetry.

360. See *Kirjallisuus* IV, p. 405; Tarkiainen-Kauppinen, *Suomalaisen kirjallisuuden historia*, p. 283.

361. See *Kirjallisuus* IV, pp. 373-75.

362. Ibid., pp. 381-83.

NOTES

363. Like many other contemporary writers, Leino sometimes described Helsinki as a sinful Babylon, sometimes as a stuffy, small town from which he wanted to escape to Rome or another great metropolis.

364. See *Kirjallisuus* IV, p. 412.

365. Published in his *Runoja* (Helsinki-Porvoo, 1932). V. A. Koskenniemi, Leino's rival and complete opposite, also composed a poem on his death, which, in its clumsy imitation of Leino's style and total lack of sentiment, is little short of an insult.

366. There are no grizzlies in Finland, but the word used in the original, *kontio*, suggests a fiercer, more powerful and majestic animal than the ordinary *karhu* 'bear.'

367. It has been conclusively demonstrated that there were Christians in Finland before the first Swedish expedition in 1155 approximately. Centuries earlier the Finns maintained trade relations with Scandinavia, North Germany, and the East.

368. See a reproduction of the cover in *Kirjallisuus* IV, p. 430.

369. A few works by Larin-Kyösti have been published in English; *Ad Astra* appeared in Finland in 1933 subtitled *A Night-Painter's Dream in Six Tableaux*. The description of *Ad Astra* should indicate how dangerous translations can be—one who reads the *Ad Astra* translation would certainly receive a false impression of Larin-Kyösti. Other translations were a collection of short stories, *Northern Lights* (1937; in Finland), a short story and poem translated by C. D. Lockock and Friidi Hedman (Webster Groves, Mo., 1932), and a collection of poems called *Kantele* (E. Howard Harris and Aulis Nopsanen, trans., London, 1941), an inappropriate title.

370. Tarkiainen-Kauppinen, *Suomalaisen kirjallisuuden historia,* p. 289.

371. Analyzed by J. J. Meyer, "Modern Finnish Cain (J. Linnankoski's Eternal Struggle)," *Modern Philology* 7 (1909-10): 221-34. When Linnankoski first conceived this play in 1891, he knew only Finnish, but in 1898 he was able to read Byron's *Cain* in a German translation (*Kirjallisuus* IV, pp. 497-98). In Finland and other European countries, English was not at that time the first foreign language studied.

372. See *Kirjallisuus* IV, pp. 499-500. A Hungarian work on a similar subject, well known and often translated in Europe, Imre Madách's *Az ember tragédiá* ('The Tragedy of Man,' 1860), is not mentioned; it would be interesting to know whether or not Linnankoski knew it.

373. Produced by Maurice Stiller in 1919 (see picture in *Kirjallisuus* IV, p. 504). On this occasion a four-page illustrated pamphlet in English was printed in Stockholm, *Swedish Biograph Stockholm. Sweden Presents The Song of the Blood-Red Flower, from a Novel by the Finnish Author Johannes Linnankoski. Scandinavia's Greatest Photo-Play.*

374. In addition to English, the book has been translated into Czech, Slovak, Danish, Dutch, Estonian (3 versions), French (3 eds. 1934-47), German (2 versions), Hungarian, Icelandic, Italian, Latvian, Norwegian, Polish, and Swedish (Bertel Gripenberg, a well-known Swedish poet of Finland, made the Swedish translation, which had been issued in 16 eds. by 1956).

375. See *Kirjallisuus* IV, p. 509. Tuomas Anhava presented a structural analysis of the work, "Pakolaiset," *Parnasso*, 1956, pp. 147-51.

376. In 1900 49.3 percent of Helsinki's inhabitants spoke Swedish; by 1960 the figure dropped to 14.5 percent. Swedish-speaking percentages for the entire country were: 12.89 in 1900, 8.64 in 1950, and 7.4 in 1965. Maila Talvio was justified in her action because Finnish had been proclaimed one of the official languages of the country more than forty years earlier. Some of the cartoonists' works are reproduced in *Kirjallisuus* IV, p. 487.

377. Reproduced in *Kirjallisuus* IV, p. 479; on p. 478 there is a picture taken at a meeting of the Students' Literary Club.

378. *Kurjet* (1925), *Kirkonkello* (1927), *Huhtikuun Manta* (1937), *Itämeren tytär* (1939), *Yölintu* (1941), *Kihlasormus* (1942), *Pimeänpirtin hävitys* (1943). Two others were published after the war.

379. P. 491. No comments are offered, either in the caption or the text. Cf. "To many people in the West it appeared that Germany was a bulwark of Europe against the Communist East. . . . It was the best possible line for the Nazis to follow to make it appear that their terror was directed against the Communists; with terror against the Communists in the foreground—and Jews were often labelled Communists—brutality against Social Democrats, liberals, pacifists, and others might well be overlooked." T. L. Jarman, *The Rise and Fall of Nazi Germany* (London, 1955), p. 186.

380. *Pimeäpirtti* means 'the dark cabin,' but there is no particular symbolism in the name.

381. Lit. 'nightbird,' but it is only the name, without special meaning, of a manor in the novel. Maila Talvio had a taste for such phony titles.

382. See Rafael Koskimies, "Maila Talvio" in *Kirjallisuus* IV, pp. 481, 484.

383. See Tuulio, "Calderónin 'Elämä on unta' Maila Talvion innoittajana," pp. 354 et seq.

384. Nevertheless, between 1951 and 1960, many works on him were published in Finland. Some of his works were published abroad, two in France, two in Germany, two in the Netherlands, five in Russia (two after 1917), and two in Sweden, in addition to the ten which were translated into Swedish in Finland.

385. The periodical *Sunnuntai* carried a notice on this event under a title formulated to allude to one of his plays (*Kuolema*), "Arvid Järnefelt ja

hänen kirkkokohtauksensa" (no. 19, 1917). Forty years later an illustrated paper took up the incident again (*Uusi Kuvalehti* 20, 1957).

386. The Eastern Orthodox church, the Jewish and other small religious communities have their own cemeteries, but all others in Finland are under the administration of the Lutheran church. (Now deceased not belonging to the latter church may be buried in them.)

387. There were other unconventional politicians, thinkers, and writers in Finland at that time, e.g., the theosophists with whom Eino Leino came in contact. The most notorious theosophist was probably Matti Kurikka (1863-1915), who combined his religious beliefs with socialism, edited the socialist newspaper *Työmies* for a while, wrote some literature, and tried to found a utopian community on Malcolm Island, renamed *Malkosaari* in Finnish, near Vancouver in British Columbia. Not possessing Järnefelt's social background, he was ridiculed, attacked, threatened, and personally assaulted. Directly active in politics, he was more conspicuous and aggressive than Järnefelt. See Soikkanen, *Sosialismin tulo*, p. 67, 158-60; Palmgren, Joukkosydän I, pp. 67-76; cf. John I. Kolehmainen, "Harmony Island: a Finnish Venture in British Columbia," *The British Columbia Historical Quarterly*, 1941, pp. 111-24.

388. See Rafael Koskimies, "Arvid Järnefelt" in *Kirjallisuus* IV, p. 226. On Tolstoy and Järnefelt, see John I. Kolehmainen, "When Finland's Tolstoy Met His Russian Master," *The American Slavic and East European Review* 16, no. 4 (1957): 534-41.

389. Tolstoy's teachings were never popular in Finland. We wonder if the success of the play, produced during the Russian oppression, might have been at least partially due to the (erroneous) idea that, in the person of Titus, the author was criticizing the Russian emperor.

390. There is an anecdote which tells that Sibelius, after the success of *Valse Triste*, could not go to a better restaurant in Helsinki without the orchestra's striking up the tune. He immediately left and went to a place without music, where a friendly drunk told him how much he liked that composition.

391. See *Kirjallisuus* IV, pp. 232-33; cf. Soikkanen, *Sosialismin tulo*, pp. 243-48.

392. Although the Swedish-speaking population of Finland includes a fairly large rural and industrial percentage, Swedish literature in Finland is often urban in character. Järnefelt's description of country life in a Swedish region is unusual. See Thomas Warburton, *Femtio år finlandssvensk literatur* (Helsinki, 1951), pp. 11-15.

393. Now Serdovol', since 1944 in Soviet territory.

394. Palmgren, *Työläiskirjallisuus*, pp. 117-19, 123-24; cf. Joukkosydän II, pp. 249 et seq. Palmgren has also analyzed Untola's first novels ("Irmari Rantamalan Harhama-romaanit," *40-luku*, 1947, pp. 392-408).

395. See *Kirjallisuus* V, pp. 115-17, and reproductions of the book covers on p. 118. On p. 647 it is mentioned not only that Akseli Gallen-Kallela is suspected of having participated in composing those covers, which are in his style, but also that he probably did not want to have his name appear in that connection.

396. Quoted by Annamari Sarajas, "Maiju Lassila" in *Kirjallisuus* V, p. 120.

397. Elsa Erho, *Maiju Lassila*, Turun Yliopiston julkaisuja B 63 (Turku, 1956); see also idem, "Maiju Lassila aikansa ilmiönä," *Valvoja*, 1958, pp. 256-61, and "Maiju Lassilan tyylistä," *Sananjalka* 1 (1959): 135-47.

398. Tuomas Anhava in a series of five essays, "Romaanityyppejä" ('Types of Novels'), *Parnasso* (on *Tulitikkuja lainaamassa* in 1956, pp. 51-57).

399. Aatos Ojala, "Irmari Rantamalasta Maiju Lassilaksi," *Parnasso*, 1959, pp. 198-204, and "Mekaaninen kosija," *Parnasso*, 1962, pp. 71-80.

400. Anhava, "Romaanityyppejä"; see also idem, "Arkielämää," *Parnasso*, 1957, pp. 66-71. Similarities between Untola's and Gogol's humor are pointed out by Sarajas, "Maiju Lassila," p. 126.

401. Perhaps Untola was thinking of Kasimir Leino's fate (n. 340).

402. See Ojala, "Mekaaninen kosija," pp. 71, 73.

CHAPTER VIII

403. Quoted in *Kirjallisuus* V, p. 141.

404. They did not, however, write directly in dialect. On Kianto's use of the Kainuu dialects, see Alpo Räisänen, "Kainuun murteiden piirteistä Ilmari Kiannon 'Ryysyrannan Joosepissa,'" *Virittäjä*, 1965, pp. 30-46 (German summary p. 47).

405. Dorrit Cohn, "Narrated Monologue: Definition of a Fictional Style," *Comparative Literature* XIII, no. 2 (1966): 97-112. Professor Cohn remarks that Anglo-American criticism has virtually neglected it, considering it "irrelevant to literary judgment" (Wayne C. Booth, *Essays in Criticism* XI [1961]), but adds that scholars in the United States have discussed it under different names. She cites, as examples of the feature, Lawrence, Joyce, Faulkner, Woolf, James, Kafka, Dorothy Richardson, Mann, Broch, Musil, and Sartre.

406. Staffan Björck, *Romanens formvärld* (Stockholm, 1953), pp. 120-27, 159-65, analyzes the narrated monologue, calling it *erlebte Rede*. He finds a number of examples in Swedish literature and never says that its use is unusual or daring. However, we have found only two scholarly works devoted to this problem in Finland; it apparently is not a problem of particular interest in that country. Liisa Dahl, "The Attributive Sentence Structures in the Stream-of-Consciousness Technique," *Bulletin of the*

Modern Language Society of Helsinki LXVIII, no. 4 (1967): 440-54, does not make clear what she means by "stream-of-consciousness technique" or how it should be distinguished from similar stylistic devices, e.g., first-person interior monologue, direct rendering of a character's thoughts by the author, and narrated monologue. Maila Valkeakari's "Eläytymisesityksen tulo suomalaiseen kirjallisuuteen," *Sananjalka* 11 (1969), is entirely devoted to the narrated monologue (*eläytymisesitys*).

407. "Conversation et sous-conversation" in *L'ère du soupçon* (Paris, 1956), pp. 81-124; *sous-conversation* means approximately the narrated monologue or *erlebte Rede*. Cf. R. -M. Albérès, *Métamorphoses du roman* (Paris, 1966), pp. 177 et seq. An interesting comparison might be made between Finnish authors and Albérès's opinion of American and European authors: "There is nothing common between the inspiration of the Europeans (e.g., Proust and Virginia Woolf), which represents a somewhat decadent aesthetic research, and the inspiration of the Americans (e.g., Faulkner and Dos Passos), which is an affirmation of realism; as the thoughts of twentieth-century man are confused, the novel shall be made of confused thoughts" (p. 212).

408. See *Kirjallisuus* II, pp. 299-303.

409. *Helsingin Sanomat*, 9 May 1970.

410. See Vihtori Laurila, *Ilmari Kianto. Kirjailijakuvan piirteitä* (Helsinki, 1944).

411. A more radical protest on the matter was staged at the same time in Finland by a Swedish-speaking philosopher and writer, Rolf Lagerborg, who discovered an old provision, then formally still in force, that a man who promised to marry a woman, made her pregnant, and refused to fulfill his promise, could, at the request of the betrayed, be declared her husband by a court. He acted in accordance with the provision and was declared his fiancée's husband by the city court of Viipuri in 1903 (Nieminen, *Taistelu sukupuolimoraalista*, pp. 181-82). It was referred to as "Lagerborg's method" for a while.

412. See Nieminen, *Taistelu sukupuolimoraalista*, pp. 279-82; cf. Laurila, *Ilmari Kianto*, pp. 69, 100.

413. Illegal liquor is called *korpikuusen kyyneleet* 'tears of the backwoods pine,' as well as other names, in Finnish.

414. On Kianto's humor see U. Kupiainen, *Kiannon "Punainen viiva" ja "Ryysyrannan Jooseppi" humoristisina teoksina*, KTSVK 8 (Helsinki, 1945), pp. 196-211.

415. Seventy percent of Finland's land is covered with forests. Before the introduction of modern wood and paper industry, people took all the wood they needed, but now, since forests are valuable, productive capital, they are protected. The country people did not understand, and allusions to this matter reappear in books written early in this century, e.g., *Putkinotko*.

In Kianto's novel the main character is further irritated because the high officials speak Swedish. See Liisi Huhtala, "Ison isännän torpparit," *Sananjalka* 14(1972): 201-10 (English summary pp. 211-12).

416. Matti Kassila made a film of the novel in 1959 (see picture in *Kirjallisuus* IV, p. 465, which shows a socialist speaker at an electoral meeting). L. A. Puntila, *Suomen poliittinen historia 1809-1955* (Helsinki, 1964), p. 79, provides the figure of 10 percent; Raoul Palmgren, *Joukkosydän* I (Helsinki, 1966), p. 13, fixes it at 30 percent of all adult *males*.

417. Russia's relaxed rule happened following the defeat of the Russians in the war against Japan in 1904-05 and the threat of a revolution in Russia. After 1908, when measures of Russification were resumed against Finland, the Parliament was not suppressed, but ignored.

418. See Unto Kupiainen, "Tuomiopäivä-aihe humoristisessa kirjallisuudessamme," *Virittäjä*, 1938, pp. 83-99.

419. *Kirjallisuus* V, p. 45.

420. The name has a meaning not immediately apparent, explained in the book. *Putki* is a kind of weed, *notko* a small valley, and the caretaker allows weeds to grow everywhere. Magnus Björkenheim, *Joel Lehtosen Putkinotko*, K T S V K 14 (Helsinki, 1955), and " 'Putkinotkon' todellisuuspohja," *Valvoja*, 1954, pp. 78-87, describes the locality. See photograph in *Kirjallisuus* V, p. 54.

421. Cf. p. 8.

422. Quoted in *Kirjallisuus* V, pp. 42-43.

423. This was actually the name of a house of ill fame in Helsinki (Nieminen, *Taistelu sukupuolimoraalista*, p. 94).

424. See *Kirjallisuus* V, pp. 48-49; cf. Leo Tiainen, *"Orjantappura ja kruunu"-novellin eräs toisinto*, KTSVK 12 (1952), pp. 238-46.

425. *Kirjallisuus* V, p. 49, quotes this passage, claiming it refers to Boccaccio, Rabelais, and Cervantes, but *Putkinotko* itself mentions Cervantes, Rabelais, and Tolstoy, in that order (5th ed. [Helsinki, 1947], p. 510).

426. Kupiainen, *Suomalainen lyriikka*, p. 58, speaks of Lehtonen's direct influence on Kojo and mentions, p. 10, that Lehtonen wrote a few unnoticed poems in free verse. He often, pp. 11, 196, 290, calls Lehtonen's poetry "expressionistic and realistic." Cf. Annamari Sarajas, "Joel Lehtonen" in *Kirjallisuus* V, pp. 60-62. See also Kaarlo Marjanen, "Joel Lehtonen" in *Kirjallisuus* VI, pp. 72-81; Unto Kupiainen, *Joel Lehtonen runoilijana* (Helsinki, 1956).

427. Sarajas, "Joel Lehtonen," p. 49.

428. Pekka Tarkka, "Kainin sukua. Tyyppihahmoista Joel Lehtosen tuotannossa," *Parnasso*, 1963, pp. 15-22, studies the symbolic functions of

Lehtonen's human types, placing them in two categories: the dark, wild, and proud and the meek and pacific. Tarkka feels that Lehtonen's entire production reflects his mental conflicts, represented by these archetypes. He points out that one of the dark characters in the serial *Atla* (1903) exlaims, "Cain, Cain, I am of the race of Cain." In *Putkinotko* Aapeli Muttinen's first name (Abel) must then be symbolic, and his seemingly meaningless remark at the end (5th ed., p. 523), "I want to be . . . Aapeli," acquires a new meaning.

429. His specific target was Yrjö Blomstedt, professor at the Teachers' College of Jyväskylä, known for his passion for the *Kalevala* and Karelian folk culture (*Kirjallisuus* V, p. 105).

430. When Finland was not yet an independent country, the truly remarkable feats of Finnish athletes in international competitions aroused extraordinary enthusiasm in the country. Sports writers and others without literary talent wrote patriotic dithyrambs about the nation's new heroes, but it's still not always safe to mention their lack of quality in Finland.

431. Vilho Suomi, "Lapsuuden merkitys luonnonkuvaajalle" in *Juhlakirja Rafael Koskimiehen*, pp. 241-51 (French summary p. 311).

432. See Lauri Viljanen's essay on Joel Lehtonen in *Lyyrillinen minä ja muita kirjallisuustutkielmia* (Forssa-Helsinki, 1959).

433. Eila Järnfors, "Putkinotko—ikuisen kesän tyyssija," *Suomen Kuvalehti* 43 (1955), calls the place "Putkinotko—the Home of the Eternal Summer."

434. The English translation, *Remembrance of Things Past*, of Proust's work is inaccurate because *recherche* indicates an active search, not a mere remembrance.

435. Tarkka, "Kainin sukua," p. 18, says that it was the probable consequence of a cheap amorous adventure Lehtonen described in a poem from *Munkkikammio* and in a letter to Aho.

436. *Kirjallisuus* V, p. 29. See an illustration from *Lintukoto* on p. 61; cf. picture in *Encyclopedia Fennica*, s.v. "Suomen kirjallisuus."

437. *Kirjallisuus* V, p. 60.

438. Pointed out by Aaro Hellaakoski, "Sakris Kukkelmanin asema Joel Lehtosen tuotannossa" in *Kuuntelua* (Porvoo-Helsinki, 1950).

439. Sarajas, "Joel Lehtonen," p. 62.

440. Lehtonen said that it followed the "vast swell" of Goncharov and Dostoyevski (*Kirjallisuus* V, p. 63).

441. The term of abuse currently applied to them is *gulašši* 'goulash,' which came from Germany, where all such individuals were supposed to be Eastern Jews with a liking for this dish.

442. See Kai Laitinen, *Suomen kirjallisuus 1917-1967* (Helsinki, 1967), p. 29.

443. *Kirjallisuus* V, p. 66.

444. Founded in 1925 by Lauri Haarla, it included the novelist Martti Merenmaa, the poet Uuno Kailas, and L. Onerva. Supposedly young and radical, it was soon outdone by *Tulenkantajat* and forgotten, whereas the latter secured a permanent place in Finnish literary history. See *Kirjallisuus* V, p. 367; cf. p. 334 and n. 793 this volume, and Mauno Niinistö, *Uuno Kailas* (Helsinki, 1956), p. 122, n. 4.

445. A selection of similar folktales, Lauri Simonsuuri, *Myytillisiä tarinoita*, SKST 229 (Helsinki, 1947), includes motifs used by Toppila.

446. Reproduced in *Encyclopedia Fennica*, s.v. "Sallinen."

447. See Simonsuuri, *Myytillisiä tarinoita*, pp. 110-14. One story on p. 113 is from Ylikiiminki in northern Ostrobotnia, where Toppila lived.

448. Cf. Simonsuuri, *Myytillisiä tarinoita*, pp. 38, 149-53.

449. French translation in Roger Caillois, ed., *Anthologie du fantastique* (Paris, 1958), pp. 511-20.

450. The Imperial Russian Administration was reluctant to carry out death sentences. In 1826 a law was passed in Finland commuting them to Siberian exile. Independent Finland has had capital punishment only in times of war.

451. See Stith Thompson, *Motif Index of Folklore Literature* (Bloomington, Ind., 1955-58), E 411.0.4 (sinner wanders between earth and heaven, with reference to Danish folklore).

452. Toppila's graphic fantasy called for illustrations, which were supplied by Aukusti Tuhka (*Päästä meitä pahasta*), Veikko Vionoja (*Auringon nousun maahan*), and other Finnish artists.

453. Not much later than 1859. This penalty had already been limited, was soon obsolete, and was formally abolished in 1889.

454. Viljo Kojo, "Tosikertomuksen parodiako?," *Karjala*, 1941, p. 282, thought the book might be a parody; *tosikertomus* 'a true story' designates the trashy, sentimental narrative from cheap magazines, one of which was titled *Tosikertomuksia* ('True Stories').

455. See the picture of his ship *Weljekset* in *Kirjallisuus* V, p. 504.

456. See *Kirjallisuus* IV, p. 313, and Vilho Suomi, *Nuori Volter Kilpi. Vuosisadan vaihteen romantiikka* (Helsinki, 1952). Kilpi seemed, however, to imitate Nietzsche in appearance; see photographs of him with a Nietzschean moustache *Kirjallisuus* IV, pp. 320, 323. Later, when he modified his ideals, he changed his appearance; see *Kirjallisuus* V, pp. 498, 508.

NOTES

457. In "Taiteesta ja siveydestä," *Valvoja*, 1901, pp. 265-72, 646-56. Cf. Eila Pennanen, "Nuoruus ja kauneus. Kaksi Volter Kilven henkilöhahmoa," *Parnasso*, 1959, pp. 293-97, reprinted in *Tunnustelua* (Helsinki, 1965).

458. See Pennanen, "Nuoruus ja kauneus," p. 294.

459. See *Kirjallisuus* V, p. 497; Sampo Haahtela, "Volter Kilpi ja hänen huonokuuloisuutensa," *Kuulovikainen*, 1940, pp. 80-83.

460. As does Chrestien de Troyes, but Eschenbach calls it a large precious stone. See M. Delbouille, "A propos de 'L'oiste qui el Graal vient,' " *Revue de Linguistique Romane* XXXI, nos. 123-24 (July-December, 1967): 300-307; cf. Eino Krohn, "Graal-taru suomalaisessa kirjallisuudessa," *Sananjalka* 2 (1960): 167-74.

461. See *Kirjallisuus* IV, pp. 315-16.

462. Called hypallage in classical rhetoric; one famous example is in the *Aeneid* (6.268): *ibant obscuri sola sub nocte per umbram* 'dark they went under the lonely shadow of the night.'

463. Quoted in *Kirjallisuus* IV, pp. 315, 317.

464. The use of the instructive case, which transforms *kaipaussilmä* to *kaipaavin silmin* and *sinikirkkoinen* to *sinisin kirkoin*. In 1957 and 1958 several scholars had an argument on this point; see Pekka Piirto, "Lyriikan instruktiivit," *Parnasso*, 1961, pp. 334-40.

465. *Kirjallisuus* IV, p. 590.

466. Ibid., pp. 319-21.

467. Quoted ibid., p. 324. The original, more elegant than our translation, seems to convey more meaning, but we feel that it does not.

468. The unicameral Parliament established in 1907 was so generally accepted that talk of bicameralism was branded reactionary, although even today most democracies have bicameral legislative bodies.

469. In a letter to Vilho Suomi, quoted in *Kirjallisuus* V, p. 496.

470. Even when *Antinous* appeared, critics noticed the west Finnish flavor of Kilpi's language and received the book poorly. In *Valvoja* he was advised to study "East Finnish dialects." See Pennanen, "Nuoruus ja kauneus," p. 293; intending to prove its unpopularity, Pennanen says that slightly over two hundred copies of *Antinous* were sold in the year of its publication but, considering the size and rural character of Finland's population, we think the figure high (cf. nn. 327, 923).

471. In "Volter Kilven myöhäistuotanto" in *Kirjallisuus* V, p. 515.

472. Ibid., pp. 498-99.

473. Ibid., pp. 504-5.

474. In "Vaasan Villen fregatti," *Parnasso*, 1957, pp. 59-65, reprinted in *Tunnustelua.*

475. In *Romaanitaide* (Helsinki, 1947), quoted in *Kirjallisuus* V, p. 499.

476. Quoted in *Kirjallisuus* V, p. 506. Even the titles are parallel: *Alastalo* 'lower farm,' *Ylistalo* 'upper farm'; *salissa* '(formal) livingroom,' *tuvassa* '(ordinary) room (in a farm building).'

477. Pennanen, "Nuoruus ja kauneus," p. 296.

478. Laitinen, "Volter Kilven myöhäistuotanto," p. 511.

479. *Kirjallisuus* V, p. 513

480. Ibid., p. 512.

481. Ibid., p. 502; cf. p. 514. Diktonius was actually a Swedish author of Finland who also wrote in Finnish.

482. In *Kuuntelua.*

483. One edition appeared titled *Fallen Asleep While Young*, a literal translation of the Finnish, which is not grammatically perfect itself. 'The Short Dream of a Young Life' or 'Young Dawn and Early Dusk' might convey the spirit of the original.

484. Besides Swedish and English, *Nuorena nukkunut* appeared in Norwegian (1932), German (1932), Danish (1933), Hebrew (1934), Italian (1934), Dutch (1936), Czech (1937), Hungarian (1939), French (1940), Japanese (1940), Oorya (Cuttack, India, 1959), as well as other languages; *Hurskas kurjuus* appeared in Swedish (1920), Estonian (1923), Danish (1924), French (1928), Spanish (1930), Italian (1933), Dutch (1939), and other languages. See Saara Sihvola, "F. E. Sillanpään teosten käännökset," *Bibliophilos*, 1956, pp. 59-64.

485. Lauri Viljanen writes that "*Hurskas kurjuus* is a historical and social novel, in which the events are seen from neither a historical nor a social point of view—insofar that all the main questions are concerned." (Quoted in *Kirjallisuus* V, p. 147).

486. "Alkoholista—siitäkin kerran," *Elanto*, 6 September 1935. Quoted in Aarne Laurila, "Voitot ja väsymys," *Parnasso*, 1958, p. 201. Included in modified form in A. Laurila, ed., *F. E. Sillanpää vuosina 1888-1958* (Helsinki-Keuruu, 1958). In 1927 Sillanpää wrote, following the suicide of Runar Schildt, a well-known Swedish writer of Finland, that, approximately two years earlier, he had also been "on the brink of the same abyss." (Quoted in *Kirjallisuus* V, p. 158.)

NOTES

487. See Annamari Sarajas, "F. E. Sillanpää" in *Kirjallisuus* V, p. 144; cf. Laitinen, *Suomen kirjallisuus*, p. 36.

488. Quoted in A. Laurila, "Voitot ja väsymys," pp. 199-200. Basically Laurila agrees with Anhava.

489. *Tylsä* 'dull' seems to have strong emotional implications for Sillanpää. He uses it in the simile of souls viewed as caves in a mountain and in a description of himself in which he is ironical about his own sentimentality. He brought two old millstones as childhood memories to his country home, where they were only two "dull-looking cakes of stone." In a short story from *Maan tasalta*, he speaks of the "dullness" which lingers around a familiar landscape (quoted in *Kirjallisuus* V, p. 154).

490. Lauri Viljanen, "F. E. Sillanpää, Satakunnan D. H. Lawrence" in *Taisteleva humanismi*, 2nd ed. (Hämeenlinna, 1950), pp. 425-26, speaks of Sillanpää's "whimsical (and) bizarre fancies," calling them an attempt to avoid ready-made literary phrases, but we feel that, especially in *Elämä ja aurinko*, Sillanpää was suffering from much badly-digested literature; some of his later works have much less such writing.

491. See Lauri Viljanen, "Sillanpään ajanelämyksestä," *Parnasso*, 1954, pp. 338-42; cf. Kai Laitinen, "Ihmiset suviyössä," *Parnasso*, 1958, pp. 221-22.

492. Cf. Viljanen, "Sillanpää, Satakunnan Lawrence," p. 426.

493. In "Ihmiset suviyössä," p. 217.

494. In "Lapsuuden merkitys," p. 248.

495. "Sillanpää, Satakunnan Lawrence," pp. 424-48.

496. See Sarajas, "F. E. Sillanpää," pp. 148-50, 154; cf. Viljanen, "Sillanpää, Satakunnan Lawrence," pp. 427-28. Sillanpää took these ideas from Arvid Järnefelt, the Finnish author who, according to Sillanpää, influenced him most. His ideas are not completely clear, and they changed with time. The quotations given by Sarajas, p. 149, seem to indicate a belief in metempsychosis, but in *Omistani ja omilleni* ('About My Own and To My Own' in the collection *Enkelten suojatit* 'Under the Protection of the Angels,' 1923) he says that "I am *at this moment* of the opinion that the duality apparently represented by the 'body' and the 'soul' is really only apparent." Cf. Viljanen, "Sillanpää, Satakunnan Lawrence," pp. 427-28.

497. *Suomen kirjallisuus*, p. 36. On his publisher's advice Sillanpää suppressed a few passages which might have been particularly offensive. See Aarne Laurila, " 'Hurskaan kurjuuden' alkuvaiheita," *Parnasso*, 1961, pp. 126-29; F. E. Sillanpää, "Poisjäänyttä. 'Hurskaan kurjuuden' syntyhistoriaa," *Parnasso*, 1961, pp. 130-33.

498. "Voitot ja väsymys," p. 195.

499. Sarajas, "F. E. Sillanpää," p. 154.

500. Quoted ibid., p. 155.

501. A. Laurila, "Voitot ja väsymys," p. 195-96.

502. Rafael Koskimies (*Elävä kansalliskirjallisuus*, 3 vols. [Helsinki, 1944, 1946, 1949]), V. A. Koskenniemi (in a review), and Alex Matson (*Romaanitaide*) criticize *Nuorena nukkunut* for lack of unity; in it they find two main characters, Silja and her father. Aatos Ojala (*Kohtalon toteuttaminen* [Hämeenlinna, 1959]) disagrees with them; see Timo Kukkola, "Nuorena nukkuneen kaksiaiheisuus," *Tilanne* 6 (April, 1964): 203-9.

503. See Sarajas, "F. E. Sillanpää," pp. 160-61.

504. On the meaning of flowers and the influence of E. A. Karlfeldt, a Swedish poet awarded a posthumous Nobel Prize in 1931, in Sillanpää's work, see Elsa Erho, "F. E. Sillanpää ja lehdokki" in *Juhlakirja Lauri Viljasen*, pp. 23-32 (French summary pp. 366-67).

505. Although D. H. Lawrence is usually mentioned in connection with Sillanpää, the importance of the erotic problem and discretion with which it is treated, frequent descriptions of nature, understanding for people of modest condition, motif of the young woman who remains pure in spite of humiliation, and figure of the well-meaning, impractical father are features in *Nuorena nukkunut* which remind us of *Tess of the d'Urbervilles*. The forced solution of an early death for the heroine is more plausible in Sillanpää's book than in Hardy's.

506. See Sarajas, "F. E. Sillanpää," pp. 163-65.

507. *Rentun tie*, quoted by Viljanen, "Sillanpää, Satakunnan Lawrence," p. 446.

508. Laitinen, "Ihmiset suviyössä," p. 218, quotes Rafael Koskimies who considered the book one of the "most refined written in Finland." Sillanpää called it an "epic suite" (Viljanen, "Sillanpää, Satakunnan Lawrence," p. 448).

509. Quoted in "Voitot ja väsymys," p. 202.

510. Included in the collection *Päivä korkeimmillaan* ('High Noon,' 1956).

511. See A. Laurila, "Voitot ja väsymys," pp. 200-201.

512. The law governing the appointment of academicians provided that the first ones could be sixty years of age or older. The usefulness of the Academy was often questioned. A sculptor elected to it refused the post and wished the funds appropriated for his salary to be given as scholarships and grants to young artists. In 1969 the institution was abolished, but funds are

appropriated as grants and scholarships to artists, scholars, and scientists (called Academy professors).

513. Haanpää's grandfather, who knew Päivärinta, was a founder of the Finnish Writer's Guild; see Eino Kauppinen, "Piirteitä Pentti Haanpään kirjailijankehityksestä" in *Juhlakirja Rafael Koskimiehen*, pp. 96-97 (French summary p. 302). Cf. E. J. Ellilä, *Haanpään kirjallinen sukupuu*, KTSVK 12 (1952), pp. 15-32.

514. See Kai Laitinen, "Pentti Haanpää" in *Kirjallisuus* V. pp. 387, 398-99.

515. See Tarkiainen-Kauppinen, *Suomalaisen kirjallisuuden historia*, pp. 346-47.

516. Quoted in Laitinen, "Pentti Haanpää," p. 385.

517. A story in *Tuuli käy heidän ylitseen* is titled *Jätkä ja jätkän onni* ('To Be a Lumberjack and To Be Happy'). *Jätkä* is also used for an itinerant worker who accepts those jobs he can find (not a vagrant or beggar).

518. Quoted by Eino Kauppinen in his foreword to Haanpää's collected works (10 vols., Helsinki, 1956-58). Cf. idem, "Piirteitä Pentti Haanpään," p. 99; Laitinen, "Pentti Haanpää," p. 390.

519. In 1939-40 and 1941-44, the entire Finnish nation fought the Soviet Union with conviction, but in 1945 23.5 percent of the voters cast ballots for the Democratic League of the Finnish People (SKDL), an organization under communist control.

520. By Huugo Jalkanen, a poet and playwright himself (see *Kirjallisuus* V, p. 390).

521. He was in contact with the radical left-wing writers who wrote for *Kirjallisuuslehti* and *Tulenkantajat* (the second) and in 1936 formed the *Kiila* ('Wedge' group). See Palmgren, *Työläiskirjallisuus*, pp. 86-87.

522. Quoted in *Kirjallisuus* V, p. 395. Haanpää is suspected to have committed suicide, for his boat was found floating empty on a calm lake and his body, when recovered, showed no signs of violence or illness.

523. See Laitinen, "Pentti Haanpää," p. 396.

524. The company founded by K. J. Gummerus.

525. Laitinen, "Pentti Haanpää," pp. 399-400.

526. As an amateur participant; there are few professional athletes in all Scandinavia.

527. Quoted in two recent publications: Laitinen, *Suomen kirjallisuus*, p. 96 (spelling out the four-letter word); Pauli Anttila, "Pentti Haanpää

oppikoulun kirjallisuuden opetuksessa," *Parnasso*, 1966, p. 298 (substituting hyphens for the word).

528. On the feeling of spiritual estrangement many of these writers, e.g., Järnefelt, Kilpi, and Lehtonen, experienced in 1918, see Annamari Sarajas, "Murrosten aika" in *Kirjallisuus* V, pp. 35-36; Laitinen, *Suomen kirjallisuus*, p. 22.

529. Her husband, one of the foremost literary scholars in Finland in his time, somewhat exaggerated her importance in his works. In Tarkiainen-Kauppinen, *Suomalaisen kirjallisuuden historia,* she receives seven pages, whereas Sillanpää gets five and Lehtonen four. When her second collection appeared, Tarkiainen greeted it with immoderate praise and drew ironical remarks from Eino Leino, who found her short stories characterized by "tasteless cynicism" (quoted in *Kirjallisuus* V, p. 71).

530. Although he does not pretend that Jotuni is a humorist only, Unto Kupiainen, *Huumorin sukupolvi 1900-luvun suomalaisessa kirjallisuudessa* (Helsinki-Porvoo, 1954), places her among humorists.

531. Analyzed by Anhava, "Arkielämää," pp. 66-71.

532. Joel Lehtonen expressed his approval of her ability to write "without the slightest bias, without trying to serve an 'ideal' or . . . to express a great idea." (Quoted in *Kirjallisuus* V, p. 72.)

533. Anhava, "Arkielämää," p. 69.

534. *Kirjallisuus* V, p. 80.

535. Ibid., p. 84.

536. Quoted ibid., p. 85.

537. Annamari Sarajas, "Maria Jotuni" in *Kirjallisuus* V, p. 90.

538. *Kirjallisuus* IV, p. 540.

539. Rafael Koskimies, "Aino Kallas" in *Kirjallisuus* IV, pp. 530-31.

540. Not her husband; see *Kirjallisuus* IV, pp. 524-25. On her vacillation between realism and romanticism early in her career, see Lauri Viljanen, "Aino Kallaksen Eeden-myytti," *Parnasso*, 1961, pp. 10-19, passim.

541. In "Valtiaat ja vallanalaiset" in *Juhlakirja Lauri Viljasen*, pp. 139-47 (French summary, pp. 372-73).

542. See Koskimies, "Aino Kallas," pp. 531-32. They were probably first called "ballads" by Viljanen, "Aino Kallaksen Eeden-myytti," p. 15. While the author lived in London, several were translated (most by Alex Matson) and published there: *The White Ship* (1924), *Barbara von Tisenhusen* (1925), *Eros the Slayer* (1927), *The Wolf's Bride* (1930), and *Bath-Sheba*

(sic) of Saaremaa (1934). Some were also published in Italy and the Netherlands. She never wrote in Estonian and all nineteen editions of her works available in that language are translations. Her selected works were published in Tallinn in 1957.

543. *Sudenmorsian* was sent to an international competition for operas composed for the radio in Italy, where it won a prize. A revised version of *Bathseba Saarenmaalla* by the composer appeared in 1958.

544. Some are in free verse, which Koskimies, "Aino Kallas," points out is "what was considered free verse in Finland before the modernism of the forties and fifties"; they are not at all similar to contemporary poems.

545. See pp. 115-16 and n. 199 this volume; cf. Palmgren, *Joukkosydän* I, pp. 10-12, 44-56; idem, *Työläiskirjallisuus,* pp. 56-61, 85-94; Annamari Sarajas, "Pekkanen−Siippainen−Viita−Linna: näkökulman asettelua," *Parnasso,* 1955, pp. 193-203; idem, "Työväenkirjailijat," pp. 128-30; Soikkanen, *Sosialismin tulo,* pp. 137-40, 177, 334-35; Rauno Velling, "Proletaarirunoilijoita ja vasemmistoradikaaleja" in *Kirjallisuus* VI, pp. 434-57; Leo Vuotila, *Kirjailija ja omatunto* (Helsinki, 1967), pp. 9-16, 24-42.

546. Factories equipped with the modern machinery of the time had been built in Finland from approximately 1820, but their number remained small.

547. See Palmgren *Joukkosydän* I, pp. 43-44; cf. ibid. II, pp. 420-24; Soikkanen, *Sosialismin tulo,* pp. 140-58.

548. Quoted Palmgren, *Joukkosydän* I, pp. 47, 387.

549. Ibid. I, pp. 40-41.

550. In *Työläiskirjallisuus,* pp. 223-28; cf. Vuotila, *Kirjailija,* pp. 10-11.

551. Dr. Palmgren, however, had to follow academic tradition, which demanded this sort of theory, to have his work published; he was not accepted in academic circles because of his political opinions (see the postface to *Työläiskirjallisuus,* pp. 309-10). He has since been appointed professor at the University of Oulu.

552. E.g., Kössi Kaatra and Matti Turkia, over whose merits the primary figures in the Social-Democrat party, Yrjö Mäkelin, Yrjö Sirola, and Edvard Valpas-Hänninen, clashed. Sirola referred to Diderot's authority in giving Kaatra friendly advice for improving his poetry; see Palmgren, *Työläiskirjallisuus,* pp. 57-58; idem, *Joukkosydän* I, pp. 131, 318-19.

553. E. J. Ellilä, "Aku Rautala−Aukusti Ripatti" in *Juhlakirja Rafael Koskimiehen,* pp. 25-44 (French summary pp. 298-99).

554. See Palmgren *Joukkosydän* I, p. 342, II, pp. 353-54; cf. idem, "Kaatra Äikiän pakkopaidassa," *Tilanne* 3 (May 1963): 148-53. Kaatra is rated on the level of Kianto and Kouta, perhaps even that of Larin-Kyösti and

Onerva, but not that of Eino Leino or Manninen. There is an anthology of working-class poetry titled *Käy eespäin* (Helsinki, 1957).

555. The old folk meter was also used directly, rather than through Leino, and some early working-class poets who published their poems as broadsheet ballads were very similar to the folk poets discussed earlier in this volume. See Velling, "Proletaarirunoilijoita ja vasemmistoradikaaleja," p. 435. Cf. Matti Hako, "Riimilliset kansanlaulut" in *Kirjallisuus* I, p. 445 (illustration); V. Laurila, *Suomen rahvaan runoniekat*, pp. 165-66; Palmgren, *Joukkosydän* I, pp. 89-112; idem, *Joukkosydän* II, pp. 345-49.

556. E.g., by Yrjö Mäkelin in Parliament, July 10, 1917, when on behalf of the Socialist party he urged the legislature to take the executive powers of the emperor in its hands. He referred to Kramsu as "our poet" and to the popular leaders in the War of the Maces as "our dead" ("our" includes the members of the Agrarian and Socialist parties). See Palmgren, *Joukkosydän* I, p. 42.

557. Nine of the eighty Social-Democrats elected to the first modern Parliament in 1907 were women.

558. *Née* Lindgren; she later took the Finnish name Liinamaa and in 1899 married Jaakko Pärssinen, also a teacher. Her biography is in Palmgren, *Joukkosydän* I, pp. 197 et seq.

559. "(All) with the exception of Väinö Tanner"—an obvious quip at the long-time moderate leader of the party after 1920, disliked by the radicals and communists (Palmgren, *Joukkosydän* I, p. 44).

560. See Nieminen, *Taistelu sukupuolimoraalista*, pp. 232-33, 252-54; cf. Vuotila, *Kirjailija*, pp. 36-37.

561. Hilda Tihlä is her literary pseudonym, but she kept her early life secret, probably because of some unpleasant experiences, and no one is sure of her real name. See Palmgren, *Joukkosydän* I, pp. 227-29 and n. 216.

562. Ibid., p. 230.

563. As early as 1896 A. B. Mäkelä had *Ruukin jaloissa* ('Trampled by the Mill') performed at the Finnish Theater. In the end the employer and the workers begin to understand each other.

564. "It is during the Great Strike that a true proletarian poetry is born in Finland, the most remarkable representative of which is Kössi Kaatra." ". . . The fighting socialist poet of the Great Strike, Kössi Kaatra. . . ." (Kupiainen, *Suomalainen lyriikka*, pp. 332, 565.) Cf. idem, "Suurlakon kirjailija," *Yhteiskunta* 2 (1950): 99-120. Velling, "Proletaarirunoilijoita ja vasemmistoradikaaleja," p. 438, is more accurate in his account, but he too calls Kaatra "the first among the poets of the Great Strike."

565. Antti Thulé (later Tulenheimo), a student who was to become one of the leaders of the Conservative party, prime minister, secretary of

education, mayor of Helsinki, etc., in independent Finland, suggested as early as 1901 that students should join the Helsinki Workers' Society "as disciples, not as teachers." See Soikkanen, *Sosialismin tulo*, pp. 207 et seq., 231, 239.

566. Some critics and scholars consider Bertel Gripenberg better; we prefer Mörne's works, opinions, and personality.

567. Palmgren, *Joukkosydän* I, pp. 316, 327, says that Kaatra's poetry became more like Kramsu's, less like Leino's, that from a romanticist he became a realist.

568. Quoted in Palmgren, *Työläiskirjallisuus*, pp. 60-61.

569. Armas Äikiä, *Laulaja tulivuoren juurella* (Helsinki, 1962). Palmgren's answer is in "Kaatra Äikiän pakkopaidassa," where he also protests Kupiainen's views of Kaatra (p. 148).

570. See Soikkanen, *Sosialismin tulo*, pp. 140 et seq., 158 et seq., who explains the favor theosophy briefly enjoyed in the workers' movement (see pp. 159-60 and 165 and n. 387 this volume). Finland conforms to the European socio-religious pattern: although there is opposition to the established church, 92 percent of the population belongs to it. Other protestant denominations are unimportant; individuals with strong religious convictions belong to the "Low" church, i.e., the pietist movement (see p. 43; n. 249 this volume). Over 40 percent of the electorate voted socialist and 20 percent procommunist in the last elections; therefore, many of those who voted for either party must belong at least nominally to the established church.

571. See Palmgren, *Joukkosydän* I, pp. 135 et seq.; cf. idem, *Työläiskirjallisuus*, p. 120.

572. Palmgren, *Joukkosydän* I, p. 335. Elmer Diktonius, "Tre svalor och en kråka," *Arbetarbladet*, 20 December 1922, reviewed Kaatra's poems. Although he appreciated them, he criticized their form, which he found too traditional. See also Palmgren, *Työläiskirjallisuus*, pp. 210-11.

573. Martti Haavio and Veli Mikkonen, eds., *Juhani Ahosta Saima Harmajaan* (Porvoo, 1938); Albin Ahonen, Martti Haavio, and V. I. Mikkonen, eds., *Aleksis Kivestä Saima Harmajaan* (Porvoo, 1943); Albin Ahonen, Martti Haavio, and V. I. Mikkonen, eds., *Aleksis Kivestä Martti Merenmaahan* (Porvoo, 1954).

574. In *Joukkosydän* II, pp. 184-86 and n. 296. In Viipuri Lehtimäki also met many Russian revolutionaries, e.g., Gorki and Lenin, who took refuge in Finland, where they were safer than in Russia. In the Finnish Parliament Lehtimäki could criticize the Finnish authorities because they had arrested Russian revolutionaries and turned them over to the imperial police (ibid. n. 299; cf. Michael Futtrell, *Northern Underground*, London 1963, pp. 54-56). Slavic influence also appears in the title of the short story *Jumalan äiti* ('The Mother of God'), which has Eastern Orthodox or possibly Roman Catholic connotations in Finland.

575. All the set characters and situations of the sentimental, melodramatic nineteenth-century novels (the poor, persecuted orphan, the poor, honest girl whose virtue is threatened, and the honest man swindled by a heartless villain) appear in the works of the early proletarian writers— Willman, Tihlä, et al.—at the beginning of the century.

576. Quoted in Palmgren, *Joukkosydän* II, p. 185.

577. Ibid., pp. 188-92 and nn. 306, 307.

578. Ibid., p. 194 and n. 340. *Syvyydestä* is mistakenly called a novel in *Kirjallisuus* VI, p. 662. Frederika Blankner, ed. and trans., *The History of the Scandinavian Literatures* (Port Washington, N. Y. 1966), contains a chapter on Finnish literature in the U.S. by George Sjöblom (pp. 311-18).

579. Palmgren, *Joukkosydän* II, p. 204, n. 332. The Russian title translates 'Away with the Arms'; when Lehtimäki was no longer in communist favor in the 1920s, the book disappeared from the Soviet market.

580. Ibid., p. 197.

581. Ibid., p. 203. It came out late in the spring of 1917.

582. Especially the novels *The Iron Heel* and *The Jacket* (ibid., pp. 209-10, n. 336).

583. Erwin Piscator, *Das Politische Theater* (Berlin, 1929); Fr. ed. *Le théâtre politique* (Paris, 1962), p. 202. Piscator was referring only to a type of scene; he had probably never heard of Lehtimäki.

584. See Palmgren, *Työläiskirjallisuus*, p. 151.

585. Kai Laitinen, "Toivo Pekkanen" in *Kirjallisuus* V, p. 410. Sarajas, "Pekkanen—Siippainen—Viita—Linna," pp. 193-203, expresses the same view.

586. P. 183.

587. Toivo Pekkanen, *Teokset* II (Porvoo-Helsinki, 1957), p. 256, quoted in Vuotila, *Kirjailija*, p. 54.

588. See Laitinen, "Toivo Pekkanen," p. 413. Eila Pennanen called him "the stonecutter at his work" ("Kivenhakkaaja työssään," *Parnasso*, 1952, pp. 190-93). Cf. Aarne Laurila, "Toivo Pekkasen näytelmät," *Parnasso*, 1959, p. 73. Pekkanen's style resembles the official administrative usage in use of participial constructions. See Keijo Ahti, "Lausevastikkeiden yleisyydestä Toivo Pekkasen kielessä," *Sananjalka* 2 (1960): 103-11. Vuotila speaks of the somewhat naive enthusiasm with which young writers and critics of the 1920s received Pekkanen, "a true blacksmith" and a writer (*Kirjailija*, pp. 75-76).

589. A. Laurila, "Toivo Pekkasen näytelmät," p. 70; cf. Kaarlo Marjanen, "Pekkanen fantastina," *Näköala*, 1950, p. 391, and Vuotila, *Kirjailija*, p. 63.

590. Kauko Kare, *Toivo Pekkanen. Kirjailijakuvan piirteitä* (Helsinki-Porvoo, 1952), pp. 6-8, believes that true proletarian literature exists only in Scandinavia and that the urge to write "at least one" autobiographical work is typical of a proletarian writer. Palmgren, *Työläiskirjallisuus* p. 92 contests this geographic limitation of proletarian literature (ibid. p. 165).

591. It is a situation which Chekhov would have better handled. See Lauri Olkinuora, "Tšehov ja Pekkanen," *Parnasso*, 1956, pp. 312-17. Cf. Vuotila, *Kirjailija*, 82.

592. *Rakkain näytelmähenkilöni* ('The Character I Like Best in My Plays'), read on the radio in 1948, published with another under the common title "Rakkaimmat henkilöhahmoni" ('The Characters I Like Best in My Works'), *Parnasso*, 1957, pp. 291-95.

593. In "Rakkaimmat henkilöhahmoni," p. 294.

594. "Teatterista" in his collected works (vol. VII); cf. A. Laurila, "Toivo Pekkasen näytelmät," p. 71.

595. A. Laurila, "Toivo Pekkasen näytelmät," p. 70.

596. Ibid., p. 67.

597. Ibid.

598. The play is not included in Pekkanen's collected works.

599. Pekkanen, "Rakkaimmat henkilöhahmoni," p. 294-95.

600. See Laitinen, "Toivo Pekkanen," p. 417.

601. Pekkanen, "Rakkaimmat henkilöhahmoni," passim. See also Vuotila, *Kirjailija*, pp. 84-89.

602. Annamari Sarajas, "Onnellisten saari. Teema ja muunnelmia Toivo Pekkasen teoksista," *Parnasso*, 1954, pp. 196-203, points out the importance of the island as a symbol in Pekkanen's works. Cf. Toivo Pekkanen, *Katoava saari* ('The Vanishing Island,' a short story first published in the 1930s), reprinted in *Parnasso*, 1958, pp. 252-55.

603. Laitinen, "Toivo Pekkanen," p. 422.

604. See Laitinen, "Toivo Pekkanen," pp. 425-27.

605. Tuomas Anhava, "Kotkan eepos," *Parnasso*, 1957, pp. 149-57, describes it as a "chronicle," though still a novel.

606. Laitinen, "Toivo Pekkanen," p. 430.

607. "Torturing self-examination, tension, and unrest put an end to his journey before he was forty-four years old." See Annamari Sarajas, "Kyösti Wilkuna" in *Kirjallisuus* V, pp. 95-104.

A HISTORY OF FINNISH LITERATURE

608. *Tunturi* is a word always used in Lapland stories; in English translations it is sometimes represented by the Dano-Norwegian *fjeld*.

609. Including the fact that the upper classes speak French (and Swedish) so that translations must be provided in footnotes.

610. See Annamari Sarajas, "Kirjailijoita ennen maailmansotaa," in *Kirjallisuus* V, pp. 132-33. Kojo cannot be easily classified; perhaps for that reason Sarajas includes him in an article about pre-World War I writers. He published his first work in 1914 and the bulk of his production after 1918. He is included under the subhead "Karjalan kuvaajia" ('Descriptions of Karelia'), but he described people, not places, and many of his works are not about people in Karelia.

611. Ibid., p. 133.

612. The only other translation is Swedish (1957).

613. Photographs in *Encyclopedia Fennica*, s.v. "Rauma."

614. In *Runoilijan kalenteri* (Helsinki, 1968), p. 8.

CHAPTER IX

615. From *Mies ja punapartaiset herrat*, quoted in *Kirjallisuus* V, pp. 358-59.

616. Lauri Viljanen, "Tulenkantajat—Ultrasta Kiilaan" in *Kirjallisuus* VI, p. 302. Although he was a prosaist, Loti influenced Finnish poetry, and Countess de Noailles' prose work *Le visage émerveillé* (Finn. tr. 1909) had a similar impact.

617. Even between 1910 and 1920, when publishers were complaining of poetry's lagging sales, Koskenniemi's work was a "brilliant exception" (Kupiainen, *Suomalainen lyriikka*, p. 2).

618. Although the situation has changed since World War II, young writers still occasionally complain, as Tuomas Anhava did in a public address printed as "Suomi ja maailmankirjallisuus" in *Kulttuuripoliittiset neuvottelupäivät 20.-27.1.1962 Helsingissä*, ed. Erkki Salonen and Matti Ilmanen (Helsinki: Suomen Kulttuurirahasto, 1962), pp. 45-46.

619. From 1912 to 1921 he was chief editor of *Aika*, which merged with *Valvoja* and became *Valvoja-Aika*. In 1944 the name was changed back to *Valvoja*.

620. Koskenniemi published three biographical works on Goethe.

621. See *Runoseminaari*, ed. Turun Kirjailijat (Turku, 1963), pp. 40-41; Jouko Tyyri, "Erään minuuden muisto," *Parnasso*, 1966, pp. 7-17. A more academic approach to Koskenniemi's pessimism is in Rafael Koskimies, "V. A. Koskenniemi ja pessimismin ongelma" in *Suomalaisia kirjailijoita XX*

vuosisadan alussa (Helsinki-Rauma, 1927); cf. Pekka Mattila, "Prometheus-symbolin asema V. A. Koskenniemen runoudessa," *Valvoja*, 1951, pp. 272-85. In his memoirs Sillanpää said that Koskenniemi was to him "like a public building symbolizing generally respected values, near and around which I move with feelings of deep veneration, but into which, for various reasons, I'm not very likely ever to step." Sillanpää added that, compared to the ornate, melodious poetry overflowing with sentiment of the beginning of the century, Koskenniemi's verse was "terse and to the point" (quoted by Laitinen, *Suomen kirjallisuus*, p. 48).

622. Lauri Viljanen, "V. A. Koskenniemi" in *Kirjallisuus* VI, pp. 58, 60-62. Viljanen points out that Koskenniemi's attitude toward the Christian God was never grim and tense as it was toward the supreme God of antiquity or Fate. Cf. Leevi Valkama, "Raamatun aihepiiri V. A. Koskenniemen tuotannossa," *Valvoja-Aika*, 1942, pp. 63-76.

623. The Conservative party candidate in the presidential elections said in a speech given December 3, 1967: "A misled part of the Finnish nation began to fight on the side of these troops belonging to a foreign power" (i.e., the Soviet Union). Actually the Russian troops stationed in Finland in 1918 showed no interest in fighting with the Reds, and the Red leaders who escaped to the Soviet Union at the end of the war charged them with betraying the cause of the Finnish revolution. See Juhani Paasivirta, *Suomi vuonna 1918* (Helsinki, 1957), pp. 123-28.

624. Lewis Mumford, "Reflections. European Diary," *The New Yorker*, 6 July 1968, p. 38, said that "More than once I have been shocked, since the Second World War, to discover that some of the most internationally minded Europeans I know—human, deeply cultivated men, not shameless barbarians—had stultified themselves by their sympathetic attitude toward Hitler and nazism."

625. In this respect Koskenniemi resembles some Swedish poets of Finland, e.g., Bertel Gripenberg, his friend (Viljanen, "V. A. Koskenniemi," pp. 54-55).

626. In 1911 the Finnish government awarded to him a scholarship to go to Greece and Italy in preparing his translation of Homer (Pentti Lyly, "Otto Manninen" in *Kirjallisuus* VI, p. 30).

627. The poem is similar in feeling to Yeats's *The Wild Swans at Coole*, but Yeats explains the meaning of the swans at length.

628. E.g., a cross, a chalice, an orb; in England George Herbert followed this fashion, which was known everywhere at that time. See *Kirjallisuus* II, pp. 269, 458 (illus.); Toini Melander, *Suomen kirjapainotaitoa barokin vuosisadalla* (Helsinki, 1960).

629. See Pentti Lyly, "Otto Mannisen 'Musa lapidaria' ja sen kaksi muusaa" in *Juhlakirja Lauri Viljasen*, pp. 191-207 (French summary pp. 375-76). Cf. idem, "Otto Manninen," p. 32. Manninen's original in *Valvoja* 1906, p. 519, has the correct *lapidaris*.

630. Lyly, "Otto Mannisen 'Musa lapidaria,' " pp. 196 et seq.

631. Lyly, "Otto Manninen," p. 46; see n. 160 this volume.

632. Lyly, "Otto Manninen," pp. 36-37.

633. Ibid., p. 47; Lauri Viita is reportedly similar to him in some respects.

634. See Kupiainen, *Suomalainen lyriikka*, pp. 13-16.

635. Quoted by Matti Suurpää, "Juhani Siljo" in *Kirjallisuus*, VI, p. 82.

636. Kupiainen, *Suomalainen lyriikka*, p. 39; cf. Suurpää, "Juhani Siljo," p. 83.

637. Ain'Elisabet Pennanen, also a poet, wrote an autobiographical novel based on Siljo's love for her, *Kaksi raukkaa* ('Two Wretches,' 1968). It was edited by her son, Jarno Pennanen, who also wrote the postface, and published posthumously.

638. Quoted in Kupiainen, *Suomalainen lyriikka*, pp. 17-18 ("all right" in English).

639. Kupiainen, *Suomalainen lyriikka*, p. 26, speaks of the influence of the poetry of antiquity in connection with his works, but seems to refer mainly to the meter.

640. See Kalle Sorainen, "Siljo ja eksistentialismi," *Valvoja*, 1958, pp. 99-103; Jouko Tyyri, "Logiikka, filosofia ja kieli," *Parnasso*, 1958, p. 184; Suurpää, "Juhani Siljo," pp. 83, 85; Kupiainen, *Suomalainen lyriikka*, p. 22. Cf. Claude Mauriac, *L'alittérature contemporaine* (Paris, 1958).

641. On his poetry see Kaarlo Marjanen, "Joel Lehtonen" in *Kirjallisuus* VI, pp. 72-81. It is remarkable because it is bound to rhythm and rhyme patterns but contains few shortened or lengthened word forms. He anticipated the poets of the 1950s with his interest in Chinese poetry which he considered free of "the ephemerous stuff of idelogies" and "almost free of thoughts: it is only through images that thoughts are expressed in it—not even through metaphors!" (*kuva* 'image' and *vertauskuva* 'metaphor' are markedly opposed in Finnish).

642. Whether Jalkanen's use of the elegiac meter inspired Koskenniemi to use it or vice versa is a matter of controversy. Probably both used it spontaneously because of their attraction to antiquity. See Kupiainen, *Suomalainen lyriikka*, pp. 53-54; Pekka Piirto, "Maisteri- ja maakuntarunoilijoita" in *Kirjallisuus* VI, pp. 105-6.

643. Kupiainen, *Suomalainen lyriikka*, p. 57; Piirto, "Maisteri- ja maakuntarunoilijoita," p. 104.

NOTES

644. *Encyclopedia Fennica*, s.v. "Nuoren Voiman Liitto," gives the date 1908; s.v. "Jäämaa, I." 1914. Kupiainen, *Suomalainen lyriikka*, pp. 200-201, gives 1906.

645. See his self-portrait in *Kirjallisuus* VI, p. 117; the eye patch is merely decorative.

646. See poems in Kupiainen, *Suomalainen lyriikka*, pp. 114, 116, 118.

647. Kaarlo Marjanen, "Aaro Hellaakoski" in *Kirjallisuus* VI, p. 112.

648. Ibid., p. 115.

649. See *Kirjallisuus* I, p. 415 (illus.); cf. Martti Haavio, "Nurinkäännetty maailma," Suomalainen Suomi, 1957, pp. 83-90; Antti Aarne, *The Types of the Folktale*, trans. Stith Thompson, FF Communications 184, 2nd ed. (Helsinki, 1961), types 1930, 1935. The motif is also found in Finnish folklore.

650. Descriptions of the critics' reception of *Jääpeili* vary. Marjanen, "Aaro Hellaakoski," p. 118, says that the *Tulenkantajat* were reticent and Paavolainen negative, but that others appreciated it. Viljanen, "Tulenkantajat—Ultrasta Kiilaan," pp. 295-97 et seq., says that the young generation of the 1920s was shy in its relations with Hellaakoski but did not underestimate his work and that one *Tulenkantaja* reviewed it respectfully. Kupiainen, *Suomalainen lyriikka*, p. 551, says that it was "executed by the critics with Indian warwhoops."

651. See Marjanen, "Aaro Hellaakoski," p. 116.

652. Kupiainen, *Suomalainen lyriikka*, p. 160, points out that the change of seasons is indicated by a change of rhythm.

653. Kupiainen, *Suomalainen lyriikka*, p. 85.

654. The motif is known in literatures throughout northern Europe, appearing, e.g., in Kalatozov's film *The Cranes Are Flying*. See Kupiainen, *Suomalainen lyriikka*, pp. 508-9, with reference to Sarkia and Vuorela; Rafael Koskimies, *Heikki Toppila. Kertojan kehityshistoriaa* (Porvoo-Helsinki, 1938), p. 27.

655. Founded 1949, amalgamated 1951 with *Ajan Kirja* to form *Parnasso*.

656. The third line may be reminiscent of Kallio's *Pois meni merehen päivä* (see p. 67), showing Hellaakoski's liking for early Finnish poetry.

657. See photograph in Marjanen, "Aaro Hellaakoski," p. 131.

658. See Marjanen, "Aaro Hellaakoski," p. 130. On Hellaakoski's philosophy of life, see Kaisa Kantola, *Olen, enkä ole* (Helsinki, 1972).

659. See Unto Kupiainen, "Aaro Hellaakosken runo 'Kevään kuuntelua'" in *Juhlakirja Lauri Viljasen*, pp. 118-27 (French summary p. 372).

660. See Marjanen, "Aaro Hellaakoski," p. 133; cf. Kupiainen, *Suomalainen lyriikka*, pp. 157-60.

661. Mustapää himself said that he had stopped writing poetry because "One cannot serve two masters at the same time" (with reference to his scholarly activities) in Septima (pseudonym), "Ei voi palvella kahta herraa, totesi dos. Martti Haavio ja hylkäsi Pegasonsa," *Aseveli* 28 (1944). Under the name Martti Haavio he has edited two volumes of old Finnish folk poetry, *Kirjokansi* and *Laulupuu* (Helsinki, 1952).

662. Lauri Hakulinen published an account of his official activities ("Martti Haavio kulttuuripolitiikkona," *Suomalainen Suomi*, 1949, pp. 7-8). His official and scholary image became somewhat separated from the literary one. Yrjö Kivimies, "Tuntematon Martti Haavio," *Suomalainen Suomi*, 1949, pp. 12-13, wrote of "the unknown Martti Haavio," the poet P. Mustapää.

663. See Annamari Sarajas, "P. Mustapää" in *Kirjallisuus* VI, pp. 356-57; Kupiainen, *Suomalainen lyriikka*, pp. 380-82, 390-92; Laitinen, "Mikä uudessa lyriikassamme on uutta?" pp. 211-13; idem, *Suomen kirjallisuus*, pp. 92, 94.

664. *Vaakalintu*, the name of a mythical bird, appears in the Finnish translation of the *Arabian Nights*; the English has "the bird Rukh." However, Mustapää, who had visited Estonia, was thinking of the bird *Siur* from Estonian mythology; its song was a fateful portent to lovers. A literary group in Estonia took its name (*Kirjallisuus* VI, pp. 300, 351, 359; both *siur* and *siuru* are used).

665. Laitinen, "Mikä uudessa lyriikassamme on uutta?," p. 213.

666. Quoted in Laitinen, *Suomen kirjallisuus*, p. 93.

667. Years later Haavio wrote a scholarly work on holy groves in different religions (*Kuolemattonten lehdot* [Helsinki, 1961]).

668. *Puukko*, e.g., those carried by Alkio's *puukkojunkkarit*.

669. See Kupiainen, *Suomalainen lyriikka*, p. 402. Cf. Laitinen, *Suomen kirjallisuus*, p. 92; Viljanen, "Tulenkantajat–Ultrasta Kiilaan," p. 298.

670. The English should have *thou* and *thee*, but the tone of the poem does not call for such archaic usage; addressing a man by his last name is sufficiently familiar to give the correct impression.

671. Haavio published an article on this subject, "Sielulintu" in *Kalevalaseuran vuosikirja* 30 (1950); also in *Essais folkloriques* (Helsinki, 1959), in honor of his sixtieth birthday.

NOTES

672. Quoted in Laitinen, *Suomen kirjallisuus*, p. 95.

673. Quoted in Sarajas, "P. Mustapää," pp. 368-69.

674. See Kupiainen, *Suomalainen lyriikka*, p. 169; cf. Elsa Erho, "Einari Vuorela" in *Kirjallisuus* VI, pp. 138, 140.

675. Erkko created similar female beings. See p. 144 and n. 307 this volume.

676. Kupiainen, *Suomalainen lyriikka*, p. 163.

677. The repetition at the beginning of each stanza of a line containing an image from nature apparently unconnected with the rest of the poem is borrowed from the modern Finnish folksong of the *rekilaulu* type (lit. 'sleigh-song'). For the origin of the name see Mikko Saarenheimo, "Sananen suomalaisen rekivirren alkuperästä" in *Juhlakirja Rafael Koskimiehen*, pp. 220-24 (French summary p. 310). See also Vihtori Laurila, *Suomen rahvaan runoniekat*, pp. 59 et seq.; Matti Hako, "Riimilliset kansanlaulut (Rekilaulu)" in *Kirjallisuus* I, pp. 418-33.

678. The *château en Espagne* 'castle in Spain' of the French.

679. Lauri Viljanen, "Kirjallinen elämä" in *Itsenäinen isänmaa* (Helsinki, 1942), pp. 321-22; cf. Kupiainen, *Suomalainen lyriikka*, p. 169.

680. Published in Finnish and Swedish and edited by the Finnish-speaking Lauri Haarla, though known for its Swedish-speaking collaborators (Huugo Jalkanen, Viljo Kojo, Uuno Kailas, and Katri Vala also wrote for it). See Thomas Warburton, "Moderni proosataide ja dramatiikka" in *Kirjallisuus* V, pp. 242-43; Kai Laitinen, "Suursotien välillä" in *Kirjallisuus* V. p. 352; Kupiainen, *Suomalainen lyriikka*, pp. 197-99. Cf. Laitinen, *Suomen kirjallisuus*, p. 72.

681. Formally published by the literary club of *Nuoren Voiman Liitto*, which had been founded by the supporters of the periodical *Nuori Voima*. Kupiainen, *Suomalainen lyriikka*, p. 426, credits Elina Vaara, then eighteen, with its founding; cf. Mauno Niinistö, *Uuno Kailas* (Helsinki, 1956), pp. 91-92 and n. 644 this volume. The periodical and organization were (and are) intended to help secondary school students to pursue hobbies and develop talents. Competitions are organized and badges awarded. However, immediately before and after 1920 many talented young artists used them as outlets for their early activities; consequently caricatures from the period sometimes picture them as naughty children. After publishing the first *Tulenkantajat*, these writers left the organization. For additional information on the group, see Kerttu Saarenheimo, *Tulenkantajat. Ryhmän vaiheita ja kirjallisia teemoja 1920-luvulla* (Helsinki, 1966).

682. Kupiainen, *Suomalainen lyriikka*, pp. 203-4.

683. Laitinen, "Suursotien välillä," p. 355; Viljanen, "Tulenkantajat—Ultrasta Kiilaan," p. 296; Olavi Paavolainen, "Suursiivous eli kirjallisessa

lastenkamarissa" in *Valitut Teokset* I, 3rd ed. (Helsinki, 1961), pp. 434-41. Paavolainen's phrase is a good example of the over-emphatic *Tulenkantajat* prose; he wrote the book (1st ed. 1932) after he had grown critical of his friends.

684. Laitinen, *Suomen kirjallisuus*, p. 73.

685. Viljanen, "Tulenkantajat–Ultrasta Kiilaan," p. 304.

686. Paavolainen, "Suursiivous," pp. 433-34, 444. It was Unto Karri whom he "simply could not take seriously." Karri, a very mediocre writer, tried to hide his deficiencies behind coarse, artificially forceful denunciations of what he considered the corruption of the time, but had twenty books published between 1928 and 1948. (See *Kirjallisuus* V, p. 461.)

687. In "Kirjallinen elämä" in *Itsenäinen isänmaa* (Helsinki, 1942), p. 320. Cf. Kupiainen, *Suomalainen lyriikka*, p. 200.

688. Quoted in Laitinen, *Suomen kirjallisuus*, p. 73.

689. In "Tulenkantajat–Ultrasta Kiilaan," p. 303. Kupiainen, *Suomalainen lyriikka*, p. 437, says that even in 1925 Paavolainen had suggested that it was time to discard "romantic beauty" and describe a new time characterized by "speed, mechanization, internationalism, collectivism, and a common European spirit"; in 1926 he published a poem called *Auto*, later renamed *The Red Fiat*. Waltari combined the exotic and modern. In *Dshinnistanin prinssi* ('The Prince of Dshinnistan,' 1929) oriental stories contain supernatural beauty and terror, but another tale is a sports car's narration of its life, describing its masters, the lands it has visited, and the girls who have traveled in it.

690. Juhani Konkka has written some amusing *romans à clé* on the Helsinki of his youth; one, *Tuhlattu aarre* ('The Wasted Treasure,' 1947), deals with this side of bohemian life there. Viljo Kojo too describes it in *Suruttomain seurakunta* and *Kiusauksesta kirkkauteen*.

691. Cf. Laitinen, *Suomen kirjallisuus*, p. 77.

692. Kupiainen, *Suomalainen lyriikka*, p. 207.

693. His patriotism was not traditionally right-wing. In the poem *Kylmän kevään maa* ('The Land of the Cold Spring') he declared strong opposition to a fascistlike movement (Kupiainen, *Suomalainen lyriikka*, p. 60). While still at school in 1918, he wanted Finland to be a republic rather than a monarchy, contrary to the opinion of his teachers and friends. Although he sided with the Whites, he spoke for understanding toward the Reds. In a letter to his relatives from 1927, he says that he had always been "somewhat a leftist." (Niinistö, *Uuno Kailas*, pp. 82-83, n. 79, 141-42).

694. Kupiainen, *Suomalainen lyriikka*, p. 213, with quotations from T. Vahlsten (Vaaskivi), "Uuno Kailas," a psychoanalytic description of Kailas's poetry; cf. p. 245. Laitinen, *Suomen kirjallisuus*, pp. 80, 82.

NOTES

695. Mauno Niinistö, "Uuno Kailas" in *Kirjallisuus* VI, p. 307; cf. Kupiainen, *Suomalainen lyriikka*, p. 214.

696. Kaarlo Marjanen wrote that Kailas is separated from Christian dogma of redemption by a short interval: a chasm (quoted by Niinistö, "Uuno Kailas," p. 318). Cf. Armo Nokkala, "Uuno Kailaan runous ja uskonto," *Vartija*, 1942, pp. 177-84.

697. Only a few expressionist poems are contained in the anthology, but Kailas's interest in expressionism was obvious. See Kupiainen, *Suomalainen lyriikka*, pp. 221-22; Laitinen, *Suomen kirjallisuus*, p. 77; Niinistö, *Uuno Kailas*, pp. 217-26, 260-64.

698. Kailas liked to coin such compound words, e.g., *ylpeän-turha* 'proudly-vain' (in *Purjehtijat*), *nälän-kuoloon* 'hunger-death' (in *Tuuli jatähkä*), *liekin-kirkkaus* 'flame-brightness' (in *Tuuli jatähkä*), and *janon-sairain* 'thirst-sick' (in *Silmästä silmään*).

699. See Kupiainen, *Suomalainen lyriikka*, pp. 229, 235.

700. *Kotimaa* (founded 1906), then edited by Martti Ruuth, professor of theology at the University of Helsinki (Niinistö, "Uuno Kailas," p. 309).

701. Ibid., pp. 306-7, 309-10; Kupiainen, *Suomalainen lyriikka*, p. 232. Niinistö speaks of "pathological sexual factors" and the "qualitative anomaly of his emotional life."

702. Laitinen, *Suomen kirjallisuus*, p. 78; Niinistö, "Uuno Kailas," p. 310. An Ibsenian image at the end of *Eräs in memoriam* ('One in memoriam') would be understood by few outside Scandinavia: "Your soul passed into the crucible of the button-founder." Ibsen compared the souls of men to metal buttons, melted after death and cast into new ones by the Button Founder (God, Fate); this image has become familiar in Scandinavia.

703. *Uni* 'sleep' or 'dream' is ambiguous in the original; the poet gave no indication of which meaning he intended.

704. In *Suomen kirjallisuus*, p. 81.

705. Although most scholars treat the *Tulenkantajat* and Kailas together and Sarkia separately (e.g., Kupiainen) Laitinen correctly, we think, devotes a common chapter to them (and Yrjö Jylhä) (*Suomen kirjallisuus*, pp. 81-86).

706. Kupiainen, *Suomalainen lyriikka*, pp. 449-50.

707. Not in 1945, the date Kupiainen gives (ibid., p. 450).

708. See Kupiainen, *Suomalainen lyriikka*, pp. 537, 541-42; cf. Kaarlo Marjanen, "Kaarlo Sarkian runouden kehitysviivoja" in Kaarlo Sarkia, *Runot* (Helsinki-Porvoo, 1944), pp. xxxvii-xxxix. Of rhythm, Marjanen says: "At times, it happens that rhythm and melody add something so essential and so

495

decisive to the poem that the words lose their dominant position and become almost an accompaniment." (p. xxxviii.) Marjanen's readings of Sarkia's poems emphasize this fact. Eeva-Liisa Manner has written a parody of *Viulu* ('The Violin' in *Unen kaivo*), in which Sarkia rhymed *kiulu* 'pail, bucket' with *viulu*, a rather unfortunate combination though the only possible rhyme. The parody is quoted in Laitinen. "Mikä uudessa lyriikassamme on uutta?," p. 215; cf. Mirjan Polkunen, "Lyriikan modernismi" in *Kirjallisuus* VI, pp. 588-89.

709. In " 'Humaltunut venhe,' 'Juopunut pursi,' " *Parnasso*, 1958, p. 363. See Jaakko Ahokas, "Kieli ja runous," *Parnasso*, 1957, pp. 316-20, where Sarkia's explanations are contrasted to the unelaborated images of Gunnar Björling, a pioneer of modern Swedish poetry in Finland. Sarkia's traditional taste in poetry is evident in his choice of authors for translation (though they may have been suggested to him by Koskenniemi): Leconte de Lisle, Sully-Prudhomme, Hérédia, Moréas, Countess de Noailles. A few have more contemporary appeal: Villon, Leopardi (one poem), Baudelaire and Rimbaud. See Aune Hiisku, *Kaarlo Sarkia uneksija ja kilvoittelija,* (Helsinki-Porvoo, 1972).

710. Magnus Björkenheim, *Kaarlo Sarkia*, trans. Maija Lehtonen (Helsinki-Porvoo, 1952); quoted in Eino Krohn, "Kaarlo Sarkia" in *Kirjallisuus* VI, pp. 394-95.

711. Marjanen, "Kaarlo Sarkian runouden kehitysviivoja," pp. xv, xvii, xx; cf. Kupiainen, *Suomalainen lyriikka*, pp. 451-52; Krohn, "Kaarlo Sarkia," pp. 396-97.

712. Although Sarkia was better balanced than Kailas, Sarkia went through one period of severe depression in which he experienced auditory hallucinations. See Kupiainen, *Suomalainen lyriikka*, pp. 490-91.

713. The poem is much admired in Finland (ibid., pp. 489-90; Marjanen, "Kaarlo Sarkian runouden kehitysviivoja," p. xxii). In it Sarkia's formal skill blends with the contents without becoming a technical *tour de force.*

714. *Le temps entretenu*, a painting by Yves Tanguy (1939), suggests with its title the same suspension of time and shows a fantastic sea bottom. Kupiainen, *Suomalainen lyriikka*, pp. 494-502, analyzes *Unen kaivo* at length, referring to Aarne Anttila, "Kaarlo Sarkian runo 'Unen kaivo' " in *Juhlajulkaisu suomalaisen kirjan merkkivuotena 1942* KTSVK6 (Helsinki-Forssa, 1942), pp. 5-18.

715. The original is ambiguous, again because of the dual meaning of *uni* (n. 703). Endymion is described sleeping, but *sinut saartaa untesi vuori* must mean 'you are surrounded by the mountain of your dreams' because of the plural form.

716. Sarkia had a predilection for this flower; the *georgiini* in his poems is another name for it.

717. In his collected poems Sarkia combined his first two collections.

718. In "Kaarlo Sarkian runouden kehitysviivoja," p. xxix. He also says (p. xxviii) that the poet "had taken a vacation from himself."

719. At the end of this poem Sarkia makes his most unusual rhymes, by dividing a word between lines so that the first syllable(s) make the rhyme (Taivaallisen harmonian / jatkuvaisuudessa ian- / kaikkisen ja lian). At the same time in France, Louis Aragon, a poet with whom Sarkia was probably unfamiliar, was protesting the war and using similar devices, formulating a theory to defend them (in the preface to *Les yeux d'Elsa*, Les cahiers du Rhône, série blanche III (Neuchâtel, 1942). Sarkia did not have such a theory.

720. Kupiainen, *Suomalainen lyriikka*, p. 285, gives an exact date, April 17, 1922, and says, p. 201, that "she raised the banner of modernism." She was not inspired to write free verse by Edith Södergran, her contemporary and the first great modernist poet in Finland and Sweden. Maija Savutie, "Katri Vala" in *Kirjallisuus* VI, p. 342, mentions an early collection, *Apilaan kukka*, written in the traditional manner.

721. Kupiainen, *Suomalainen lyriikka*, p. 285. Cf. Savutie, "Katri Vala," pp. 342-43. There is some confusion about Countess de Noailles in most Finnish works which speak of her and Loti's exotism (Kupiainen; Viljanen, "Tulenkantajat—Ultrasta Kiilaan," p. 302). Louis Perche, *Anna de Noailles*, Poètes d'aujourd'hui 116 (Paris, 1964), includes five poems with exotic (oriental) elements in a selection of sixty-three. *Choix de poésies*, a selection of her poems, has approximately the same proportion. In *Eblouissements* (1907), where her taste for the Orient is most conspicuous, no more than thirty-two of one hundred seventy poems have oriental elements. In France the sensuousness of her poetry is stressed as her most typical characteristic; this quality Katri Vala shares.

722. See n. 616. The Finnish translation was inappropriately titled *Kummastuneet kasvot* ('The Astonished Face,' 1909). Although it is a novel, Katri Vala found the title attractive.

723. Kupiainen, *Suomalainen lyriikka*, p. 287.

724. Raoul Palmgren, "Katri Vala—tulipatsas" in *Katri Vala—tulipatsas*, ed. Olavi Paavolainen (Porvoo-Helsinki, 1946), p. 174. See Kupiainen, *Suomalainen lyriikka*, p. 288.

725. Kupiainen, *Suomalainen lyriikka*, pp. 297-98.

726. Ibid., pp. 307-8.

727. Ibid., p. 329. The "black men" in the poem about Si-si-dus were inspired by Italian fascists and German SS troopers, who wore black shirts.

728. E.g., Raoul Palmgren and Jarno Pennanen. See Paavolainen, *Katri Vala—tulipatsas*, pp. 176, 201-2; Kupiainen, *Suomalainen lyriikka*, p. 330.

729. Urho Johansson, "Yrjö Jylhä" in *Kirjallisuus* VI, p. 374; Kupiainen, *Suomalainen lyriikka*, p. 343.

730. Good war poems were written in, e.g., England during World War I by Wilfrid Owen, Herbert Read, and Siegfried Sassoon, but Jylhä's picture of the war is fuller and less prejudiced than most war poetry. Jylhä also describes the indirect changes it caused in his own attitudes. In the Soviet army, in the sector opposed to Jylhä's, the Russian poet Evgeni Dolmatovski fought. One of his poems, *Taipaleenjoki,* is titled for the river which Jylhä writes of in *Laulu joesta* ('A Song about the River'). See Laitinen, *Suomen kirjallisuus,* p. 86.

731. Kupiainen, *Suomalainen lyriikka,* pp. 358-61.

732. Pekka Lounela, "Ihanteen tarpeet," *Parnasso,* 1958, pp. 90-92. The letters appeared in *Parnasso,* 1958, pp. 188-91.

733. Elsa Erho, "Elina Vaara" in *Kirjallisuus* VI, pp. 331-32.

734. Kupiainen, *Suomalainen lyriikka,* pp. 426-27.

735. Kai Laitinen, "Suursotien välillä" in *Kirjallisuus* V, pp. 348-49. See Eino Krohn, "Lauri Viljanen esseistinä" in *Juhlakirja Lauri Viljasen,* pp. 93-106 (French summary pp. 370-71).

736. Kupiainen, *Suomalainen lyriikka,* p. 282, says that he is not a poet of "ideologies" but of "ideas."

737. A Finnish humorist felt that Viljanen's title was typical of the *Tulenkantajat* and, thinking of their infatuation with Paris, imagined that a Bar Tähtikeinu had been opened there.

738. Sakari Vapaasalo, "Lauri Viljanen" in *Kirjallisuus* VI, p. 323.

739. Ibid., p. 325. See Kaarlo Marjanen, "Lauri Viljasen lyriikan keinoja ja ratkaisuja" in *Juhlakirja Lauri Viljasen,* pp. 208-20 (French summary pp. 376-77).

740. See Eino Krohn, "Arvi Kivimaan kaksi maisemaa," *Suomalainen Suomi,* 1959, pp. 432-35.

741. The plant mentioned by Asunta is called herb Paris or truelove in English; the Finnish name possesses greater emotional overtones.

742. Kupiainen, *Suomalainen lyriikka,* p. 555, says that he "rose to the first rank of the youngest generation of poets."

743. Pekka Piirto, "Yrjö Kaijärvi" in *Kirjallisuus* VI, p. 428; Laitinen, *Suomen kirjallisuus,* p. 87.

744. Kupiainen, *Suomalainen lyriikka,* p. 443, declares that some have "lasting artistic value." Cf. Pekka Piirto, "Maisteri- ja maakuntarunoilijoita" in *Kirjallisuus* VI, pp. 108-9.

745. Velling, "Proletaarirunoilijoita ja vasemmistoradikaaleja," p. 442.

NOTES

746. See C. Leonard Lundin, *Finland and World War II* (Bloomington, Ind., 1957); A. F. Upton, *Finland in Crisis 1940-1941* (London, 1964); Olavi Paavolainen, *Synkkä yksinpuhelu*, 2 vols. (Helsinki, 1946), also included in *Valitut teokset* IV.

747. "Kirjailijaryhmä Kiila 'ei kulje puukko hampaissa tavoittamassa porvarillisten ammattiveljiensä päitä,' " *Taiteen Maailma* 4(1945).

748. Their political commitment is consequently omitted at times. Tarkiainen-Kauppinen, *Suomalaisen kirjallisuuden historia*, says that Katri Vala's "poetry took a somewhat political character" (p. 340; nothing of her relations to the *Kiila* is said), that Viljo Kajava belonged to the *Kiila* (p. 366), and that "the appearance of the *Kiila* gave its own color to postwar years. Its foremost representatives are Arvo Turtiainen and Elvi Sinervo" (p. 375). No more is said although the most recent edition is dated 1962. *Kirjallisuus* VI, however, contains an entire chapter on "proletarian writers and left-wing radicals," Velling, "Proletaarirunoilijoita ja vasemmistoradikaaleja." Cf. Laitinen, *Suomen kirjallisuus*, pp. 113-21.

749. Velling, "Proletaarirunoilijoita ja vasemmistoradikaaleja," pp. 442-43.

750. Ibid., p. 447; cf. Laitinen, *Suomen kirjallisuus*, p. 116. Kai Laitinen, "Lokki ja ruiskukka" in *Puolitiessä* (Helsinki-Keuruu, 1958), pp. 179-202, gives a very positive evaluation of Kajava's art. He does not speak of direct influence, but says that Kajava was nevertheless a "pioneer" (*tienavaaja*) and that "a whole new generation of poets and critics has given its support to the type of poetry he represented."

751. Velling, "Proletaarirunoilijoita ja vasemmistoradikaaleja," p. 447.

752. Ibid., p. 448. It reminds one of Palmgren's remark about the early period of the workers' movement, when all its leaders (except one) wrote poetry (*Joukkosydän* I, p. 44); n. 559 this volume.

753. Quoted ibid., p. 450; Laitinen, *Suomen kirjallisuus*, p. 117. The name is Swedish but is written as it would be pronounced by a Finn. It refers to Helsinki (Helsingfors), until recently largely Swedish, where Swedish names were common even among the Finnish-speaking citizens.

754. Velling, "Proletaarirunoilijoita ja vasemmistoradikaaleja," p. 451.

755. Quoted ibid., p. 455.

756. Laitinen, *Suomen kirjallisuus*, p. 85. The published diary was given the misleading title *Elämän auetessa. Koulutytön päiväkirja* ('When Life Is Opening. The Diary of a Schoolgirl'). The author had finished secondary school several years before her death. Cf. Maija Lehtonen, "Saima Harmaja—nuoruuden runoilija," *Parnasso*, 1959, pp. 4-5.

757. See the poems *Ruusu* ('The Rose') and *Auran alla* ('Under the Plough'), quoted in Lehtonen, "Saima Harmaja," pp. 9-10. Both have a bold erotic symbolism somewhat hidden in conventional linguistic form.

758. Lehtonen, "Saima Harmaja," pp. 6-8.

759. Kai Laitinen's phrase, quoted in Pirkko Alhoniemi, "Aale Tynni" in *Kirjallisuus* VI, pp. 417-18.

760. The title refers to a widespread folktale motif. See Antti Aarne, *The Types of the Folktale,* type 530.

761. Laitinen, *Suomen kirjallisuus,* p. 129. The description is very applicable to her personal appearance as well. See photograph *Kirjallisuus* VI, p. 418. In 1948 she won a gold medal for literary and artistic works at the London Olympic Games; her poem, *Hellaan laakeri* ('The Laurel of Hellas') is what one would expect such a composition to be.

762. E.g., *Le Douanier* (on Henri Rousseau). Her interest in France is shown by another poem, *Reimsiin* ('To Reims'), published in *Parnasso,* 1959, p. 3, obviously inspired by Charles de Gaulle's *coup d'état* the previous year. Joan of Arc comments indirectly upon present-day France: "Is the one a king who is crowned? / Soldiers, answer:—or shall the one be crowned / who is a king?"

763. Ragna Ljungdell, "Helvi Hämäläinen," *Bonniers Litterära Magasin,* 1946, pp. 834-35; Pirkko Alhoniemi, "Helvi Hämäläinen" in *Kirjallisuus* VI, pp. 410-11.

764. In his review of *Punainen surupuku, Parnasso,* 1959, p. 87, Pekka Lounela says that he could not help thinking "how much fine raw material was wasted here" although he appreciated several poems in the collection. He quotes an opinion, which he does not share, that 1958 was the year of the breakthrough of modernism in Finland because of the new collections of Helvi Hämäläinen, Aila Meriluoto and Aale Tynni. By now everyone agrees that this opinion was far from accurate.

765. Yrjö J. E. Alanen, "Kaipuu idylliin," *Parnasso,* 1952, pp. 33-37, expresses aptly Paloheimo's never-fulfilled longing for a final solution to his problems in its title ('The Yearning for an Idyll'). His internal strife seems to have defeated his efforts at self-expression.

766. Pekka Piirto, "Oiva Paloheimo" in *Kirjallisuus* VI, p. 424.

767. Not older, although so designated in Pekka Piirto, "Jaakko Haavio" in *Kirjallisuus* VI, p. 426. The biographical notices at the end of the volume (pp. 639, 669) give the correct birthdates.

768. Cf. Kai Laitinen, "Miten opin kirjoittamaan paremmin," *Parnasso,* 1959, pp. 35-36 (on one of his practical works); Hannu Taanila, "Pohjoiset reservit," *Parnasso,* 1965, pp. 375-76 (on one of his extravagant ideas). See the editorial "Pohjoinen myytti," *Parnasso,* 1958, p. 98. Cf. this volume p. 4, n. 5.

769. See Kai Laitinen, "Tulenkantajien proosaa" in *Kirjallisuus* V, pp. 458 et seq.

NOTES

770. See p. 294 and n. 686 this volume.

771. Alex Matson titled an article on him "Kirjallinen ihmelapsi".

772. Matti Kurjensaari, *Suuntana suomalainen* (Helsinki, 1955), pp. 153-60. Cf. Laitinen, *Suomen kirjallisuus*, p. 107; Aarne Laurila, "Mika Waltari" in *Kirjallisuus* V, pp. 454-55.

773. Kai Laitinen's chapter "Unto Seppänen" in *Kirjallisuus* V, pp. 438 et seq., is subtitled "Itäinen tulenkantaja" ('A *Tulenkantaja* from the East').

774. The best known of the many Karelians who wrote about their home region are Kersti Bergroth, Lempi Jääskeläinen, Viljo Kojo, Iris Kähäri, and Olavi Paavolainen.

775. The Finnish edition of *Markku ja hänen sukunsa* is dated 1940, but Seppänen must have submitted the manuscript to foreign publishers before the Finnish publication; the German edition appeared in 1938, and the Dutch and French versions came out in 1939. Sulo Haltsonen, *Suomalaista kaunokirjallisuutta vierailla kielillä*, Tietolipas 24 (Helsinki: Suomalaisen Kirjallisuuden Seura, 1961), pp. 22-23, 41, 74.

776. Laitinen, "Unto Seppänen," p. 443. An article on his vocabulary has been written by a Finnish linguist, Veikko Ruoppila, "Unto Seppäsen tyylistä. Sanastollinen tutkimus," *Suomi* 108, no. 1 (1958). On Seppänen's descriptions of his native region, see Erkki Paavolainen, "Unto Seppänen kotiseutunsa kuvaajana" in Paavo Montonen (ed.), *Kanneljärvi* (Lohja, 1957), pp. 295-308.

777. Kai Laitinen, "1920-luvunkertojia" in *Kirjallisuus* V, p. 376.

778. See Kai Laitinen, "Olavi Paavolainen" in *Kirjallisuus* V, p. 431.

779. See Kai Laitinen's foreword to O. Paavolainen, *Valitut teokset* I, pp. viii-ix. This volume includes *Nykyaikaa etsimässä* and *Suursiivous eli kirjallisessa lastenkamarissa*.

780. Laitinen, foreword to O. Paavolainen, *Valitut teokset* I, p. xxii. On October 24, 1944, when Finland had had a cease-fire with the Soviet Union for more than a month and the country's policies were undergoing radical change, Paavolainen wrote in his diary: "No, I cannot take part yet in the new enthusiasm. There is something wrong with the whole new style. Is there a real change behind it? Isn't there a slight taste of *opportunism and taking advantage of the situation* in all this?" (our italics) (*Synkkä yksinpuhelu* in *Valitut teokset* IV, p. 586).

781. Kai Laitinen, "T. Vaaskivi" in *Kirjallisuus* V, pp. 552, 554.

782. Ibid., p. 554.

783. See p. 264 this volume.

784. In a text about ancient Rome quoted in *Kirjallisuus* V, p. 555, he mentions "Aristophanes' ivy, the holy *efeu* of the wine god." *Efeu*, intended to add exotic flavor to the text, is neither Latin nor Greek but modern German.

785. E.g., Stefan Zweig and Lion Feuchtwanger, especially in connection with *Loistava Armfelt* (Laitinen, "T. Vaaskivi," p. 554).

786. See *Kirjallisuus* V, p. 358; cf. O. Paavolainen, "Suursiivous" in *Valitut teokset* I, p. 436.

787. For her early life and works see Palmgren, *Joukkosydän* II, pp. 18-28. *Talon lapset* was forbidden after one performance.

788. The names are different in Mrs. Wuolijoki's Finnish version, *Iso-Heikkilän isäntä ja hänen renkinsä Kalle* (1946). Neither author indicated that the theme of the play, unless general folklore, is from Chaplin's *City Lights*.

789. Mrs. Kollontay, born in Finland, spent some time there in 1899 and wrote several articles on Finnish social questions for foreign periodicals. See Soikkanen, *Sosialismin tulo*, p. 35 and Michael Futtrell, *Northern Underground*, pp. 92-3. A Finnish diplomat says of their discussions: "Their way of conducting business was, by the standards of professional diplomats, horrifyingly unconventional and haphazard." (Max Jakobson, *The Diplomacy of the Winter War* [Cambridge, Mass., 1961], p. 209).

790. Jakobson, *Diplomacy*, p. 209, approaches the truth in saying that Hella Wuolijoki "was taking part in real life in a plot more exciting and complex than any she had devised for her plays." She speaks of these events in her memoirs *Luottamukselliset neuvottelut Suomen ja Neuvostoliiton välillä 1938-39-40-41* (Helsinki, 1945).

791. Lauri Viljanen credits her first play with "dramatic qualities, strength, and life seldom seen in our country," and Olavi Paavolainen shared his view (*Kirjallisuus* V, p. 481). The former stage director and general manager of the Tampere Workers' Theater, Eero Salmelainen, was reported by members of the theater to have helped her give definitive form to her plays. See Vihtori Laurila, "Hella Wuolijoki näytelmäkirjailijana" in *Suomen Kirjallisuuden Vuosikirja 1947* (Porvoo-Helsinki, 1947), pp. 179-87.

792. Kupiainen, *Suomalainen lyriikka*, p. 200 and n. 1.

793. Ibid. They did so by disrupting under Paavolainen's leadership a public discussion organized by the group.

794. Irmeli Niemi, "Lauri Haarla" in *Kirjallisuus* V, pp. 471-77.

795. Topelius wrote of the same incident in *The King's Glove*. Although living under Russian rule, he took the simple moral position that the conspiracy was a heinous crime because it was directed against the lawful ruler of the country in time of war. See n. 35 this volume.

796. Laitinen, *Suomen kirjallisuus*, p. 145, says that "literature was made by grandfathers and grandsons; the generation of fathers was almost silent." Cf. Mirjam Polkunen, "Lyriikan modernismi" in *Kirjallisuus* VI, p. 547.

797. Aarne Laurila, "Iris Uurto" in *Kirjallisuus* V, p. 537. The sensuous cover illustration reproduced there shows that the artist and publisher had definite ideas about its contents.

798. Ibid., p. 539, in connection with two other books by Uurto. Cf. p. 540.

799. Aarne Laurila, "Elvi Sinervo" in *Kirjallisuus* V, p. 563.

800. In a speech following a crisis in the Finnish Communist party in 1969, its leader, Aarne Saarinen, criticized some members for, e.g., their "prejudiced attitude toward all persons with higher education" (*Kansan Uutiset*, 18 April 1969).

801. Chinese, Czech, German, Latvian, Swedish, Polish, and Russian. Some of her poems were published in a French anthology, Henry Gröndahl, ed. and trans., *Poètes finnois* (Paris, 1951). The anthology has been criticized in Finland; at least two of the authors included, Siippainen and Uurto, are not very representative poets.

802. Quoted in Kai Laitinen, "1940- ja 50-luvun kirjailijoita" in *Kirjallisuus* V, p. 592.

803. See Eino S. Repo's review of Paloheimo's novel *Ei puu yksin pala*, *Parnasso*, 1958, pp. 373-74.

804. See Kai Laitinen, "Sodasta rauhanvuosiin" in *Kirjallisuus* V, pp. 575-76; cf. idem, *Suomen kirjallisuus*, p. 128.

805. On the religious aspects of Paloheimo's works, see Eino Krohn, "Vangittu Jumala ja itkevä Saatana" in *Kaksi lukittua lipasta* (Helsinki, 1961).

806. Kai Laitinen, "Novellisteja ja humoristeja" in *Kirjallisuus* V, p. 591.

807. Ibid., pp. 591-92. However, Jouko Tyyri, "Aapelin rooli ja maailma," *Parnasso*, 1959, pp. 102-6, criticized the author for not daring to become a serious writer: "at his most serious Aapeli can also be at his best."

CHAPTER X

808. Laitinen, *Suomen kirjallisuus*, pp. 149-50.

809. Polkunen, "Lyriikan modernismi," p. 545.

810. Kerttu Saarenheimo, "1940-luvun naislyyrikoita" in *Kirjallisuus* VI, pp. 460-61.

811. Poems of this type were first written in Finland by Ain'Elisabet Pennanen (1881-1945). See n. 637.

812. It has been possible for women to receive degrees in divinity and to teach religion for a long time, but the Lutheran church of Finland still refuses to ordain them.

813. By 1966 the figure was 32,000 (Tuomas Anhava, "Miksi puhe ei tehoa," *Parnasso* 1966, p. 97).

814. Viljo Tarkiainen, "Aila Meriluoto" in *Suomen Kirjallisuuden Vuosikirja* 1947, pp. 279-90. Cf. Laitinen, "Mikä uudessa lyriikassamme on uutta?," p. 217. She did so by means of "backward rhyming"; the second of a rhyme pair is placed in a sentence beginning after that in which the first appears. S. Deligiorgis, "Structuralism and the Study of Poetry," *Bulletin of the Modern Language Society of Helsinki* LXX, no. 2 (1969): 299, speaks of "open" couplets, where rhyme does not coincide with syntactical completion, and of "closed" ones, where it does coincide. In the poem *Kuolema*, quoted by Laitinen, a third sentence is intercalated between the two with consecutive rhymes; the poem's rhyme scheme is *a b a b c d c d.* . . . *Enjambement* is frequently used, and the rhymes are followed by stops neither in the formal sentence structure nor in the logical sequence of thoughts and are, thus, inconspicuous. The same device appears in Franzén's ode to Creutz (see pp. 30-31 this volume); he probably made a conscious effort to give an Old Norse flavor to his poem in opposition to the rhymed verse of his time.

815. Laitinen, *Suomen kirjallisuus*, pp. 146-47.

816. "Rainer Maria Rilke" in *Suomen Kirjallisuuden Vuosikirja 1947*, pp. 164-71.

817. Pirkko Alhoniemi, "Aila Meriluoto" in *Kirjallisuus* VI, p. 479.

818. E.g., Osmo Hormia in a review of *Pahat unet, Parnasso*, 1958, pp. 374-76.

819. See Laitinen, *Suomen kirjallisuus*, pp. 177-78; cf. Kaarlo Marjanen, "Lauri Viita" in *Kirjallisuus* VI, pp. 484-85. Väinö Linna, although of similar background, did not join the group.

820. See Jouko Tyyri, "Tampereen futuristi," *Parnasso*, 1966, pp. 144-46.

821. Quoted in Marjanen, "Lauri Viita," p. 484.

822. The title *Moreeni* is typical of Viita. A scientific word unfamiliar to the average reader, it refers simply to the sandy ridge (moraine) on which Pispala is located. He wrote one other novel, *Entäs sitten, Leevi* ('What Then, Leevi'), which was issued the year of his death. It was intended as the first volume of a trilogy.

823. See Unto Kupiainen, "Kukunor," *Näköala*, 1949, pp. 314-21.

NOTES

824. Laitinen, *Suomen kirjallisuus*, p. 150, says that she had a "religious, almost Christian" conception of the world.

825. See Laitinen, *Suomen kirjallisuus*, pp. 152-53. Cf. Mirjam Polkunen, "Helvi Juvonen" in *Kirjallisuus* VI, p. 559; Mikko Kilpi, "Helvi Juvosen runouden peruspiirteitä," *Valvoja*, 1959, pp. 270-77. The essay and translations appeared in *Parnasso*, 1958, pp. 243-49.

826. It is not clear whether a man or woman tells the poem, for it is not so personal that we must assume that the "I" refers to the poet.

827. "Helvi Juvonen, kehityksen piirteitä," in *Helvi Juvonen: Sanantuoja* (Helsinki, 1959).

828. See Polkunen, "Lyriikan modernismi," pp. 544-45, 589. Cf. Laitinen, *Suomen kirjallisuus*, p. 148. The best introduction to modern Finnish poetry is idem, "Mikä uudessa lyriikassamme on uutta?"; see the bibliography in *Puolitiessä*, pp. 263-64. See also idem, "Lokki ja ruiskukka" in *Puolitiessä*, pp. 179-202; Annamari Sarajas, "Contemporary Finnish Writing," *Books Abroad*, Spring 1955, pp. 149-54.

829. Pekka Lounela, "Runoilijan viesti," *Parnasso*, 1957, pp. 109-13, says: "The poet does not attempt to communicate with the reader, but tries to put his art at a proper aesthetic distance. The words are addressed to eternity, in the best case to an ideal humanity." Osmo Hormia, "Talonpoikien krysanteemit," *Parnasso*, 1957, pp. 101-5 (the title is a quotation from Haavikko), says: "Poets understand that human beings are strangers to each other and that misunderstandings may arise. They understand that every expression of one's personality, every poem, is an unpredictable attempt at addressing another person; they are not surprised if they receive an unexpected answer."

830. Laitinen, *Suomen kirjallisuus*, p. 148. The Finnish-speaking Finns lagged thirty or forty years behind in their discovery of modern poetry, a fact which they admit. Before the breakthrough of modernism, Lauri Viljanen, "Suomalainen lyriikka v. 1946" in *Suomen Kirjallisuuden Vuosikirja* 1947, p. 368, stated: "It is possible that the language of our poetry is a kind of archaic tongue, once spoken as a living language among people who lived before World War I." Cf. Laitinen, pp. 125, 128. See also Aatos Ojala, "Runollinen ilmaisu," *Parnasso*, 1957, pp. 99-100, which criticizes modern poetry; Vihtori Laurila, "Modernistisia kosketuksia" in *Laulu ja raipat* (Oulu, 1968), pp. 70 et seq., which concludes with a violent and inaccurately based rejection of contemporary Finnish fiction and poetry; V. A. Koskenniemi, review of *Puolitiessä, Uusi Suomi*, 7 May 1958.

831. Raoul Palmgren, "Nuoren kirjallisuuden petos," *Päivän Sanomat*, 19, 21, 23 October 1958, in light of "the general ideological trend of our whole national literature," calls moderism "a surrender, a treason." (Quoted in Laitinen, *Suomen kirjallisuus*, p. 170.)

832. Lassi Nummi, "Lasse Heikkilä" in *Kirjallisuus* VI, p. 563.

833. See Laitinen, "Mikä uudessa lyriikassamme on uutta?," pp. 217-19.

834. Polkunen, "Lyriikan modernismi," pp. 571-72.

835. See n. 161. Since the classical hexameter is called *heksametri*, an English equivalent of Nummi's Finnish tern might be 'six-beat.'

836. He was born and has lived in Finland, but his father was a missionary in China.

837. In *Runot 1951-1966* (Helsinki, 1967), pp. 222-33.

838. Ibid., pp. 59-61.

839. Wherever necessary we have substituted commonly known European fish (of approximately the same size) for Anhava's Finnish ones.

840. Since there is no grammatical distinction between *he* and *she* in Finnish, the educated eyes could belong to a woman, but, considering Anhava's feelings about female welfare workers, we find it unlikely.

841. See n. 829 Joukotyyri, "Vaikeatajuinen demokraatti," *Parnasso*, 1958, pp. 368-70, has a "cleric" declare that persons claiming not to understand modern poetry are acting out of ignorance or arrogance, but admits that a guide to modern poetry is needed and that poets and readers of poetry are dealing with a wider and more complex world than does the average citizen. See also Ahokas, "Kieli ja runous," pp. 316-20, which expresses no surprise that poets have expressed their new feelings about the new world in a new language.

842. Vilho Viksten, "Analogian ja relaation mestari," *Parnasso*, 1965, pp. 244-55.

843. Not listed as a separate collection in Haavikko's biographies, but printed as such in *Runot 1951-1961*, pp. 63-76.

844. Secretary Juho Niukkanen, a controversial figure, published his memoirs in 1951 but died (1954) before Haavikko's collection appeared.

845. The title is as strange in Finnish as it is in English. It is the first line of the initial poem, which continues: "I wanted to give you the lawn, / on my hand, / as it was spring. / I did not have the time."

846. A pun is most likely intended. *Voitto* means both 'profit' and 'victory.' The last poem in the same section begins: "Now the helplessness of the great powers is so great / that their only threat is a double suicide."

847. Mirkka Rekola, review of *Puut, kaikki heidän vihreytensä*, *Parnasso*, 1966, pp. 417-19, barely mentions Haavikko's political poems. Kari Tarkiainen, "Lumiukon vaatteet eli historialliset kuvat Paavo Haavikon lyriikassa," *Parnasso*, 1961, pp. 186-91, attempts to explain the function of

historical motifs in Haavikko's poetry, but comes to no clear conclusions. Tarkiainen also states that two years passed before anyone understood the contents of the poem on the Secretary of War. See also Kai Laitinen, "How Things Are: Paavo Haavikko and His Poetry," *Books Abroad,* Winter 1969 and Jaakko Ahokas, "Two Poets of Finland; Paavo Haavikko and Bo Carpelan," *Books Abroad* (Winter 1972). Laitinen points out the elapse of time before people noticed the contents of the short story *Lumeton aika* (see p. 377 this volume). The story has been published as *Before History Begins* in the anthology *The Story Today* (New York, 1967).

848. Laitinen, *Suomen kirjallisuus*, p. 154.

849. In her essay "Moderni runous," *Parnasso,* 1957, pp. 117-19, Eeva-Liisa Manner says that "for a long time, poetry has been too much understood as a matter of feeling, although it ought to be a matter of the whole personality" and adds that "modern forms of expression have first of all meant to me the discarding of self-centered lyrical feeling and the finding of new points of view." See Jaakko Ahokas, "Eeva Liisa Manner: Dropping from Reality into Life," *Books Abroad* (Winter 1973).

850. In "Moderni runous" Miss Manner says: "But everything in fact began with Bach; when I learned to understand Bach, everything else came to me as a present. . . . I believe that this is due to Bach's precision; that is just why he is so difficult. You cannot mix precision and your own feelings." See Polkunen, "Lyriikan modernismi," pp. 590-91, for her other interests.

851. The ambiguity in the title is intended. *Vuodenajat* means 'the seasons,' *vuoden ajat* 'the periods of the year.'

852. Polkunen, "Lyriikan modernismi," p. 592.

853. Ibid., p. 594.

854. *Muuttaa* means 'to migrate' and 'to change, to modify.'

855. See Laitinen, *Suomen kirjallisuus*, p. 169.

856. The title is no less strange in Finnish although *ehtoollinen* refers to the Holy Supper.

857. See Polkunen, "Lyriikan modernismi," pp. 570-71; Laitinen, *Suomen kirjallisuus*, p. 144.

858. He has also translated Beckett's *Comment c'est . . .* , Camus's *La peste,* and Malraux's *La condition humaine.* The myth of Sisyphus, used by Camus, appears in two of Mannerkorpi's poems, *Pieni poika ja lumipallo* and *Voittamaton.*

859. Osmo Hormia, quoted in Polkunen, "Lyriikan modernismi."

860. Ibid., p. 597. It is more likely a case of similar outlooks and temperaments than one of direct influence although the author knows French and has lived a long time in Paris.

861. 'Noledge' rather than 'knowledge' would produce a similar effect in English.

862. Written on the occasion of the death of Marilyn Monroe, it crudely but forcefully criticized the publicity which destroyed her by using her as a sex symbol. *Ylioppilaslehti*, the student paper at the University of Helsinki, had accepted it for publication, but the printing press manager refused to print it because the printer is also responsible for obscene or criminal matter published in Finland. It eventually appeared in *Tilanne* 9 (September 1962): 329-31, with comments by the editor. No action was taken by the authorities.

863. Laitinen, *Suomen kirjallisuus*, p. 164.

864. See p. 359 this volume. See also Kai Laitinen, *Suomen kirjallisuus*, p. 198.

865. See *Runoseminaari*, pp. 12-16, 22-24, 51-65; Max Rand, "Happeningin uhka, vaara ja mahdollisuudet," *Parnasso*, 1964, pp. 177-79. Hormia published his views as "60-luvun lyriikka—mitä se on oleva," *Parnasso*, 1962, 293-98, and Salo published his as "60-luvun runous, mitä sen tulisi olla," *Parnasso*, 1962, 299-303.

866. Music by Kaj Chydenius, first performed at the Helsinki Students' Theater March 21, 1966, printed in Helsinki 1967. Not all radicals approved of *Lapualaisooppera*. Kaisa Korhonen admitted that she should not write about it because she "actively and passively took part in creating it," but explained in *Parnasso*, 1966, pp. 142-43, why she liked it. Max Rand, "Lapuan valhe," *Parnasso*, 1966, pp. 198-99, however, said that the performance was, at best, "agitprop" and the ideological basis of the play weak. Kari Rydman expressed appreciation of the music in the same issue, pp. 143-44, saying that it was "a pure, agitating, simple, and clear popular opera." Chydenius has also written music for four protest songs by Salo from *Tilauksia*, recorded under the title *Protestilauluja*. Music and lyrics of such songs are hard to find because they are usually not published, but Salo's *Toivomuslista* ('A Letter to Santa Claus') is printed with Chydenius's music in *Parnasso*, 1965, p. 363.

867. The notorious *Fanny Hill* was translated and published by a reputable company in Helsinki (1969). The section on contemporary poetry in Laitinen, *Suomen kirjallisuus*, pp. 200 et seq., is titled "Impure Poetry," after Pentti Saaritsa, "60-luvun epäpuhtaasta runoudesta," *Kiila* 30 (1966); the phrase goes back to Pablo Neruda (Robert Penn Warren's essay "Pure and Impure Poetry" in not mentioned). On the collage technique, see Laitinen, p. 202; cf. what is called William Burrough's "cut-up technique," the sticking together of unrelated sentences from newspapers, "Cutting Up Rough," *The Times Literary Supplement* 3514 (3 July 1969), p. 721.

868. In *Puhetta* ('Talk,' 1963); see Laitinen, *Suomen kirjallisuus.* p. 204, where the "red rag" is mentioned.

869. In "Maailmankatsomuksen rakentumisesta" in *Jäädytetyt saatavat*, ed. Arvo Ahlroos (Jyväskylä, 1965), pp. 84-91. Pekka Virtanen, "How to Make It New; Pentti Saarikoski," *Parnasso*, 1965, p. 166, says that he is "unsatisfied with the products of Saarikoski's individual communism" (article in Finnish).

870. Quoted in Polkunen, "Lyriikan modernismi," p. 599; Virtanen, "How to Make It New," pp. 166-67.

871. Quoted in Laitinen, *Suomen kirjallisuus*, p. 205, originally published in the Soviet-Estonian *Looming* 11 (1963): 1736. Although Saarikoski considers his method "dialectic" and "democratic," it does not conform to socialist realism; it is therefore interesting that the article was printed in the Soviet Union.

872. Virtanen, "How to Make It New," p. 166.

873. "Loruista lettrismiin," *Parnasso*, 1963, pp. 357-65; "Näkyvien runojen koulukunta, lettrismi," *Parnasso*, 1964, pp. 119-25; cf. n. 628 this volume.

874. In *el corno emplumado / the plumed horn*, April 1965 (Mexico City).

875. Laitinen, *Suomen kirjallisuus*, p. 207; Vilho Viksten, "Kuvien kuulija," *Parnasso*, 1964, pp. 325-26.

876. Juhani Koskinen, "Tyyliä toisaalta", *Parnasso*, 1966, p. 88.

877. Pentti Holappa, "Runoilija maailman kaatopaikoilla," *Parnasso*, 1965, p. 81.

878. In "Kertojan nykyiset kasvot," pt. 1, *Uusi Suomi*, 14 August 1960; pt. 2, *Uusi Suomi*, 21 August 1960.

879. It sold 50,000 copies in its first three months and approximately 350,000 by 1966 (Tuomas Anhava, "Miksi puhe ei tehoa," p. 97). In July, 1968, however, the publisher announced that 345,000 copies had been printed. Nils-Börje Stormbom published a Swedish translation in 1955 and translated others of Linna's works as well as writing articles and a book, *Väinö Linna—kirjailijan tie* (Helsinki, 1963). On the reception of Linna's books in Sweden, see Harry Järv, "Mottagandet av Linna's böcker i Sverige," *Horisont* XVI, no. 2 (1969): 28-40. Other translations include German, Danish, Dutch, Norwegian, Italian, French, English, Spanish, Croatian, Slovak, Estonian, and Latvian. The play had been performed for five years and seen by 300,000 people by 1965 (Max Rand, "Teatteria," *Parnasso*, 1965, p. 234). Rand says: "The performance does not have much in common with theater, unless any performance by professional actors should be called theater." The performance was at an open-air theater in Tampere where real trucks, tanks, and an airplane were used.

880. Cf. Laitinen, "1940- ja 50-luvun kirjailijoita," p. 608.

881. *Les croix de bois* by Roland Dorgelès from World War I is similar, but Dorgelès was a journalist who mixed with artists and writers in Paris before 1914. Kléber Haedens, a French critic who liked Linna's book, said in *France-Dimanche*, 12-18 April 1956, that "the book, which should make us feel surprised and bewildered, reminds us, on the contrary, of the tales told by our fathers" (i.e., the French war novels of 1914 through 1918). Finns were one war late; they did not undergo heavy fighting in World War I, and their operations in World War II were mainly trench warfare. They also felt that their war was with Russia, their old enemy, rather than on a worldwide ideological level.

882. Well-known figures who sided with Linna included Martti Haavio and Arvi Korhonen, a military historian and teacher at the Finnish Command and General Staff School. *Nya Pressen*, a Swedish newspaper in Helsinki, published their opinions on January 14 and 15, 1955. Jouko Tyyri, "Sissipäällikkö," *Parnasso*, 1962, pp. 367-68, said that "it is the nationalistic conservatives who have given the highest praise to *Tuntematon sotilas.*"

883. By Toini Havu in *Helsingin Sanomat* ("not freed himself yet of wartime aggressions"), Kalle Salo in *Ilta-Sanomat* ("The volcanic bitterness ... of *Tuntematon sotilas*"), Timo Tiusanen in *Helsingin Sanomat* ("resentment is Linna himself," "Linna is the writer of aggression"), Matti Kuusi in *Parnasso* ("a more than usually tense attitude of hostility"). Not all these critics made such statements in unfavorable reviews; Kuusi's and Salo's are very favorable, and Tiusanen's critical but understanding.

884. See pp. 70, 223 this volume.

885. Kai Laitinen, "Seitsemän vuosikymmentä," *Parnasso*, 1962, p. 274.

886. By 1962 170,000 copies were sold. It was also quite successful in Sweden. Part of it was dramatized and first performed at the Tampere Workers' Theater.

887. Linna told Tore Borglund, a Swedish journalist, said that work on the trilogy "almost killed him" and that he wrote it "to the point of exhaustion" (quoted in *Finnish Features* 10 [1968]).

888. E.g., in "Hailuotolaiset," *Parnasso*, 1962, pp. 304-9.

889. *Kuka kukin on* 1966 (the Finnish *Who's Who*) says that his works have been translated into seventeen languages but does not enumerate. Haltsonen, *Suomalaista kaunokirjallisuutta vierailla kielillä*, mentions Bulgarian, Estonian, Greek, and Russian translations.

890. Pekka Tarkka titled a book *Paavo Rintalan saarna ja seurakunta* ('Paavo Rintala's Sermon and Congregation') (Helsinki, 1966). On May 4, 1969, Rintala was elected chairman of the Finnish Society of the Defenders of Peace, a communist-dominated and Soviet-oriented organization which has

condemned Israel's policies in occupied territories and the war in Vietnam but did not criticize the Soviet occupation of Czechoslovakia. Rintala has extended his admiration for military virtue to the Russians. Soviet authorities allowed him to visit Leningrad and interview its inhabitants to write a book on the siege of the city from 1941 through 1944, *Leningradin kohtalosinfonia* ('The Symphony on the Destiny of Leningrad,' 1968; the title alludes to Beethoven's *Schicksalsymphonie*). The military qualities of Soviet citizens are supposed to be pacific qualities in keeping with Soviet thought, according to which Russian soldiers showed great courage and love of peace in the occupation of Czechoslovakia (see, e.g., *Pravda*, 25 August 1968).

891. Airi and Rafael Koskimies, *Suomen lotta* (Helsinki, 1964), reviewed in Eila Pennanen, "Naisjärjestön työstä," *Parnasso*, 1964, pp. 186-87. Conservative critics attacked and radical critics praised *Sissiluutnantti*; no one noticed that its message is conservative in the extreme.

892. Eila Pennanen, "Asia ei ole niin yksinkertainen," *Parnasso*, 1964, p. 325, calls the main character of *Palvelijat hevosten selässä* "an aristocratic hero" and adds that the theme of the book is "a criticism of the weakness of our democratic society: the servants are the men who reach leading positions . . . the princes who go on foot are the men who think." It is not clear whether the last remark refers to Rintala's opinions or the reviewer's.

893. Among the Finnish-speaking people. They were fashionable among the Swedish-speaking inhabitants at the turn of the century and are now virtually forgotten.

894. Laitinen, "1940- ja 50-luvun kirjailijoita," p. 614.

895. The phrase is also used in connection with the beliefs and magic of primitive tribes in northern Russia and Siberia. See Matti Kuusi, "Esisuomalainen runous" in *Kirjallisuus* I, pp. 31-33, 39-40. Laitinen, "1920-luvun kirjailijoita," p. 368, uses it when speaking of Toppila.

896. Laitinen, *Suomen kirjallisuus*, p. 142. Laitinen also suggests that adverse reviews of the book shocked Korpela into writing his next work in a more conventional manner. Cf. idem, "1940- ja 50-luvun kirjailijoita," p. 601.

897. Veijo Meri, preface to *Manillaköysi*, printed separately in *Kaksitoista artikkelia* (Helsinki, 1967). Meri's last book, *Leiri* ('The Camp,' 1972), mixes civilian and military motifs. The partly autobiographical *Kersantin poika* ('The Son of a Sergeant,' 1971) was awarded the Literary Prize of the Nordic Council (see n. 235 this volume) on 18 Feb. 1973.

898. Cf. Kai Laitinen, "Two Aspects of War: Väinö Linna and Veijo Meri," *Books Abroad*, Winter 1962.

899. His admiration for Gogol is evident in *Kaksitoista artikkelia*, pp. 12-17. (There has been much interest in Gogol in Finland recently.) Pekka Lounela, "Puimakoneita," *Parnasso*, 1962, pp. 33-34, calls Meri's books "well-built and well-oiled mechanisms which work efficiently for no purpose

whatsoever." In a recent analysis of Meri's works, *Se oli se kultamaa* (Helsinki, 1969), Kalevi Haikara minimizes their absurdity by omitting some patently absurd features in them, such as the motif of aimless wandering.

900. See Laitinen, "1940- ja 50-luvun kirjailijoita," pp. 619-20, 622, where the words *cruel humor* are used.

901. Veijo Meri, "Huumorista ja humoristeista" in *Kaksitoista artikkelia*, pp. 9, 11.

902. In "Kertojan nykyiset kasvot," pt. 2, p. 14. Maila Pylkkönen, "Neljä runodebyyttiä," *Parnasso*, 1964, pp. 181-84, echoes Holappa: "From the point of view of poetry, the most noteworthy person in our country still is, according to me, Antti Hyry, the engineer who has learned to write."

903. Laitinen, *Suomen kirjallisuus*, pp. 190-91.

904. Ibid., p. 190.

905. Hyry has also stated so directly, quoted in Laitinen, "1940- ja 50-luvun kirjailijoita," p. 626.

906. First performed on German radio, 1967, in Finland the same year, and in Iceland, Norway, and Poland in 1968; printed in Jyrki Mäntylä, ed., *Kahden vuoden äänet* (Helsinki, 1969).

907. Laitinen, *Suomen kirjallisuus*, p. 186.

908. In "Naiskirjailija," *Parnasso*, 1965, pp. 353-58.

909. Kauko Kare, "Satakieli ja proomu. Eila Pennasen kirjailijan-kehityksestä," *Näköala*, 1950, pp. 166-73, described this contrast with the words *nightingale* and *barge*.

910. Actually a member of a group within the society led by James Nayler; the beginning of the book is based on historical events.

911. Laitinen, "1940- ja 50-luvun kirjailijoita," p. 611, calls it her first novel, but the biographical notice in *Kirjallisuus* VI, p. 648, indicates that it is her second and that *Johannes vain* is her fifth. Laitinen, *Suomen kirjallisuus*, p. 176, says that *Johannes vain* is her third.

912. Laitinen, "1940- ja 50-luvun kirjailijoita," p. 624.

913. Translated into English by D. Barrett and published in *World Prize Stories* (London, 1952), pp. 86-93.

914. Laitinen, *Suomen kirjallisuus*, p. 211, says that Henry Miller has set an example followed by such writers as Saarikoski (who translated *The Tropic of Cancer, The Colossus of Maroussi* and *The Air-Conditioned Nightmare*) and Kejonen, but Saarikoski's pessimistic view of the world is the opposite of Miller's attitude.

915. Pekka Lounela, "Naiset näkevät yhä unia," *Parnasso*, 1965, p. 33, observes that on an international level he is a "post-beatnik."

916. Väinö Kirstinä, review of *Jumala pullossa, Parnasso,* 1965, p. 182, wishes that Lahtela "would stop chopping up his sentences." *Se* indicates that Lahtela disregarded Kirstinä's friendly advice.

917. Laitinen, *Suomen kirjallisuus*, p. 212.

918. A summary of both views is presented ibid., p. 215. Laitinen has a favorable opinion of the book. Salama's publisher issued a collection of articles written about it, *Arvosteluja ja mielipiteitä Hannu Salaman romaanista 'Juhannustanssit' 7.10.1964–14.1.1965 väliseltä ajalta* (Helsinki, 1965). See n. 84 this volume. Pentti Saarikoski, "Sääli ihmisiä," *Parnasso,* 1962, pp. 275-76, says that Salama's attitude toward others is pity, but a particular kind of pity: he cannot bear people who do not accept his pity. (In one of his stories, a character wants to hit another because he looks happy.)

919. Salama's view of the world is almost psychotic, but it makes a less unpleasant impression when expressed in verse, i.e., through images rather than characters' actions. Some images in his poetry collection, *Puu balladin haudalla* ('The Tree on the Grave of a Ballad,' 1963), e.g., "the stalks on the potato field stiffen like the hair of a madman," have the intensity of van Gogh's late paintings. See Pekka Lounela, "Neljä runodebyyttiä," *Parnasso,* 1964, pp. 183-84.

920. See Marja-Leena Mikkola, "Balladi, kansanlaulu, iskelmä," *Parnasso*, 1966, pp. 216-20.

921. Published in *Parnasso*, 1965, pp. 350-52.

922. In 1966 Christer Kihlman, a Swedish writer of Finland, complained in *Uusi Suomi* that Finnish radicals were too interested in individual cases of oppression and injustice to give attention to more general problems, but Finnish writers criticize social problems in many contexts. Parts of *Kylliksi! tai liikaa* protest the treatment given a deserter from the army. Ojaharju's *Kakku* is primarily a criticism of prison conditions. Hannu Taanila, review of *Kakku, Parnasso,* 1966, pp. 248-49, says that Ojaharju was in prison himself and charges that he sacrificed "art" to "bias."

923. Laitinen, *Suomen kirjallisuus*, p. 216, says: "TV has not killed literature, it has not even reduced the demand for it, for not a few books are still sold in numbers of twenty thousand copies in one autumn, and many reach the figure of ten thousand" (in a country of 4.7 million inhabitants). Veijo Meri, "Kirjailija pienessä maassa," takes a more pessimistic view and states that it is exceptional for ten to twenty thousand copies of a book to be sold (see n. 327, 470).

CHAPTER XI

924. See Wuorinen, *Nationalism*; Soikkanen, *Sosialismin tulo*, pp. 291-95; n. 376 this volume. When Finns had definitively become dominant,

the Finnish sign *Posti* was placed on the new Helsinki post office building. The Swedish Finns wanted a Swedish sign (*Post*), and Helsinki newspapers gravely debated the *i*. Both signs are there now. The linguistic quarrels seem now forgotten; at any rate, a book about them, Pekka Hämäläinen, *Kielitaistelu Suomessa 1917-1939* (Helsinki, 1968); also in English, *The Nationality Struggle Between the Finns and the Swedish-speaking Minority in Finland, 1917-1939* (doctoral dissertation, unpub., Indiana University, Bloomington, Indiana, 1966), has had no success, according to what was told us in the summer of 1969 by an executive of the publishing company.

925. In *Femtio år finlandssvensk litteratur*, pp. 9 et seq. Topelius is reported to have been the last Swedish writer in Finland who felt that he was writing for the entire nation. See Johannes Salminen, "Suomenruotsalaisen lyriikan renesanssi" in *Kirjallisuus* VI, p. 147. Cf. Nils-Börje Stormbom, "Twentieth-Century Swedish Literature in Finland" in *Scandinavia Past and Present*, 3 vols. (Odense, 1960).

926. In 1906 the Swedish People's party (*Svenska Folkpartiet*) was organized to represent the interests of the Swedish-speaking population, which has supported it with unaminity. In the 1962 elections the party won fourteen seats in Parliament (7 percent); at that time 7.4 percent of the total population were Swedish-speaking; both figures have since dropped.

927. The name consists of two parts (pronounced Tavast-sherna) and belongs to one of the oldest noble families in the country, which includes many well-known personalities.

928. Quoted in *Kirjallisuus* V, p. 167.

929. Quoted in J. Salminen, *Levande och död tradition*, p. 30.

930. See I. Havu, "Miten K. A. Tavaststjerna kuoli?" in *Juhlakirja Lauri Viljasen*, pp. 38-41 (French summary p. 367).

931. See Rafael Koskimies, "K. A. Tavaststjerna" in *Kirjallisuus* IV, pp. 257-58.

932. Ibid., p. 288. The long title poem of *Laureatus* is in eight-line stanzas with the rhyme scheme *a b b a a c c a*.

933. Ibid., p. 285.

934. Ibid., p. 288. A physician who was a close friend to Tavaststjerna described him in a letter as a "psychopathic and emotional personality, not to say an alcoholic." Quoted in Havu, "Miten K. A. Tavaststjerna kuoli?," p. 39. Cf. Erik Ekelund, *Tavaststjerna och hans diktning*, Skr SLSF 331 (Helsinki, 1950). Note that *psychopathic* is used here in the sense of *neurotic*.

935. Quoted in J. Salminen, *Levande och död tradition*, p. 37.

936. The lonely character under the cold stars was almost a cliché in the Swedish literature of Finland. We also find it in a short story by Runar Schildt and in one by Jarl Hemmer.

937. Tavaststjerna was also interested in Tolstoy although he could not accept his philosophy. Tolstoy's influence is notable in the conclusion of *Uramon torppa*. See Armo Nokkala, "Tavaststjerna ja Tolstoi" in *Juhlakirja Lauri Viljasen*, pp. 252-53 (French summary p. 378). Cf. E. N. Tigerstedt, *Det religiösa problemet i modern finlandssvensk litteratur*, Skr SLSF 272 (Helsinki, 1939), p. 229.

938. Warburton, *Femtio år*, p. 25.

939. Also under the title *Den starkaste.*

940. Rafael Koskimies, "Mikael Lybeck" in *Kirjallisuus* IV, p. 551, speaks of Maeterlinck in this connection. We think the atmosphere, the degenerate characters living in an old manor, the eroticism, and heavy symbolism are suggestive of Tennessee Williams.

941. Some texts on this subject now sound fantastic. The Swedes contended that they were of the Aryan or Nordic race, supposedly genetically superior to the Mongol race, in which they placed the Finns, and some of them pushed their conclusions to unpleasant extremes.

942. See Johannes Salminen, "Möte med dagdrivarna" in *Levande och död tradition*, pp. 53-55.

943. J. Salminen, "Varianter av utposttanken," pp. 39-47.

944. He was also proud to belong to the race of Aryan conquerors. He wrote, "Gobineau's and [Houston Stewart] Chamberlain's great shining visions appear to our eyes: we belong to the heroes of that epic." Quoted in J. Salminen, "Varianter av utposttanken," p. 42. Warburton, *Femtio år*, p. 80, discusses whether or not Gripenberg was a National Socialist, but Gripenberg was never part of a National Socialist or fascist organization.

945. Quoted in J. Salminen, "Varianter av utposttanken," pp. 43-44. In medieval Sweden, Finland was often called *Österland* (Eastland).

946. Warburton, *Femtio år,* pp. 71-3. Gripenberg in his poems is not necessarily the real Gripenberg. In his memoirs, *Det var de tiderna* ('Those Were the Times,' 1943), he tells of many gay parties at country estates.

947. Warburton, *Femtio år*, pp. 59-60.

948. Ibid., p. 61.

949. Ibid., p. 64. Warburton says that poets have lost their lives for less in later, more brutal times.

950. Ibid., p. 66.

951. The Swedes shared an attraction for the mysterious past reflected in the *Kalevala.* See Johannes Salminen, "Aspekter på inbördeskriget och finlandssvenskarna" in *Levande och död tradition*, pp. 74-76. Cf. Warburton, *Femtio år* p. 1.

952. Warburton, *Femtio år,* p. 34.

953. Doubts have been raised about Agricola's native tongue. See p. 11 this volume.

954. Warburton, *Femtio år,* p. 37.

955. Cf. Hellaakoski's poem about Koskenniemi p. 290 this volume.

956. See Warburton, *Femtio år,* pp. 46-47.

957. On Mörne's use of archaisms and popular dialects, see Ulla Olin, *Folkmålsord och arkaismer i Arvid Mörnes diktning,* Skr SLSF 299 (Helsinki, 1945).

958. Three have been translated into English, *The Melting Pot* (London, 1937), *Caribbean Symphony* (London, 1955), and *Slaves of the Sea* (London, 1956).

959. Warburton places Jarl Hemmer in a similar position. He states that Tegengren's poems are even read by people in the countryside (*folket i bygderna*). *Femtio år,* pp. 48-49.

960. Ibid., p. 53.

961. Ibid., p. 55.

962. Ibid., p. 151.

963. See p. 391 this volume.

964. Warburton, *Femtio år,* p. 150.

965. Ibid., p. 143.

966. J. Salminen, *Levande och död tradition,* p. 89. Cf. Warburton, *Femtio år,* pp. 146-47.

967. J. Salminen, *Levande och död tradition,* p. 91. A selection of the articles was published as *Herr X har ordet* ('Mr. X Has the Floor,' 1918). On Mörne's and Jansson's interest in socialism see P. O. Barck, "Arvid Mörne ja Ture Jansson. Kaksi ylioppilaspolvea työväenliikkeen alkuvaiheessa" in *Kiilan albumi* 7 (Helsinki, 1956), pp. 74-82.

968. Cf. Warburton, *Femtio år,* p. 137.

969. Ibid., p. 141.

970. Ibid., p. 159.

971. Ibid., pp. 159, 170. Cf. n. 486 this volume; Sillanpää wrote on Schildt in his memoirs, *Päivä korkeimmillaan* (Helsinki, 1956).

NOTES

972. "No writer has yet appeared to give us a deep description of Swedish-speaking common people in his time, of their psychology and character; only Runar Schildt's short stories from eastern Nyland are something more than an attempt." (Warburton, *Femtio år,* p. 15.) Note that Warburton's book was written before Leo Ågren had published.

973. Warburton, *Femtio år,* pp. 166-67, warns us against overestimating autobiographical elements in Schildt's work, but does not deny that they are there. See E. Kihlman, "Häxskogens diktare. Runar Schildt 1888-1925" in *Ord och Bild* (Stockholm, 1926), pp. 659-70. Schildt is called the "Writer of Witchwood."

974. Translated by Alarik Gustafsson in *Six Scandinavian Plays of the Twentieth Century* (Princeton, N. J., 1944). See George C. Schoolfield, "Runar Schildt and Swedish Finland," *Scandinavian Studies* 32 (1960): 7-17.

975. Warburton, *Femtio år*, p. 158.

976. *In the Wake of Ulysses* (New York, 1953), *In the Wake of Odysseus* (London, 1953), *In the Wake of a Wish* (London and New York, 1954), and *The Sun Boat* (London, 1957) (all trans. Alan Blair).

977. See n. 959.

978. On Hemmer's attitude toward war see A. L. [Agnes Langenskiöld], "Jarl Hemmers diktning," *Nya Argus*, 1946, pp. 3-6, 34-37.

979. Reviewed by A. M. Williams in *The Scandinavian Review* 2 (December 1939): 166, 168. See Warburton, *Femtio år*, p. 183.

980. Gunnar Castrén called *Över dunklet* "perhaps the most beautiful collection of poetry ever published in this country." See Johannes Salminen, "Uusi liikkeellelähtö," trans. Kyllikki Villa, in *Kirjallisuus* VI, p. 191.

981. Quoted in Hans Lindström, *Finlandssvensk nittonhundratalslitteratur* (Stockholm: Sveriges Finlandsföreningars Riksförbund, 1965), p. 64.

982. Warburton, *Femtio år,* pp. 191-92.

983. The Swedish poets have recognized their debt to them. See Lindström, *Finlandssvensk nittonhundratalslitteratur*, p. 76; Laitinen, *Suomen kirjallisuus*, pp. 57, 60, 71. Cf. Warburton, *Femtio år*, pp. 205-207; Walter Dickson and Hans Ruin, "Finlandssvensk modernism," *Svensk Litteraturtidskrift* 10, no. 2 (1947): 49-66, 138-42.

984. See Viljanen, "Tulenkantajat—Ultrasta Kiilaan," p. 297; Bo Carpelan, "Suomenruotsalaisen modernismin tausta," trans. Auli Tarkka, in *Kirjallisuus* VI, pp. 199-200. Carpelan remarks that expressionism had only slight influence, mainly on Södergran and Diktonius. Cf. Warburton, *Femtio år,* p. 206.

985. Viljanen, "Tulenkantajat—Ultrasta Kiilaan," p. 297; cf. Warburton, *Femtio år,* p. 275.

986. Johannes Salminen has devoted an entire essay to this question ("Så har ja åter fot mot jorden" in *Levande och död tradition*, pp. 118-34. The title is a quote from Diktonius.)

987. Thomas Warburton, "Moderni proosataide ja dramatiikka," trans. Rauni Puranen, in *Kirjallisuus* V, p. 240.

988. See Paavo Talasmaa, "Edith Södergranin lapsuudenrunous," *Nuori Suomi* 48 (1938): 42-47.

989. Warburton, *Femtio år*, p. 208.

990. Salminen, "Så har jag åter fot mot jorden," pp. 119-20.

991. Warburton, *Femtio år*, pp. 208, 210-11.

992. Especially the second collection. Warburton calls this "a shameful spot in the history of Swedish journalism in Finland" and says that she probably could not foresee in her first volume how revolutionary her art would appear. (Ibid., p. 214.)

993. Ibid., p. 210; cf. Gunnar Tideström, *Edith Södergran* (Helsinki, 1949).

994. Warburton, *Femtio år*, p. 217.

995. Ibid., p. 207. Cf. Bo Carpelan, "Edith Södergran," trans. Auli Tarkka, in *Kirjallisuus* VI, pp. 225-26.

996. Lindström, *Finlandssvensk nittonhundratalslitteratur*, p. 46; cf. Warburton, *Femtio år*, pp. 224-25.

997. Warburton, *Femtio år*, p. 227.

998. See Palmgren, *Työläiskirjallisuus*, pp. 208-210, n. 96; Olof Enckell, *Den unge Diktonius* (Helsinki, 1946), pp. 72-99, 145-46; Vesa Salminen, ed., *Nuori Otto Ville Kuusinen* (Jyväskylä, 1970), pp. 175-78, and T. Henrikson, *Romantik ou marxism* (Helsinki, 1971).

999. Lindström (*Finlandssvensk nittonhundratalslitteratur*, p. 49) and Warburton, (*Femtio år*, p. 231) give the date 1921; Bo Carpelan ("Elmer Diktonius," trans. Auli Tarkka, in *Kirjallisuus* VI, p. 227) gives December, 1920.

1000. Quoted in Carpelan, "Elmer Diktonius," p. 228. Carpelan calls it an "expressionistic idea."

1001. Warburton, *Femtio år*, p. 233; cf. Lindström, *Finlandssvensk nittonhundratalslitteratur*, pp. 50-51.

1002. Johannes Salminen used this line as the title of his essay on the "return to earth" of the radical poets of the 1920s, "Så har jag åter fot mot jorden." See n. 986.

1003. Warburton, *Femtio år*, pp. 237-38.

1004. See Laitinen, *Suomen kirjallisuus*, p. 186.

1005. Warburton, *Femtio år*, p. 246.

1006. In *Finlandssvensk nittonhundratalslitteratur*, p. 53.

1007. Quoted in Warburton, *Femtio år*, p. 251.

1008. Ibid. Note the idealistic personification of art and its goals, the almost Platonic "infinite" and "perfection." Cf. Lindström, *Finlandssvensk nittonhundratalslitteratur*, pp. 57-58.

1009. Cf. Warburton, *Femtio år*, p. 249.

1010. Laitinen, *Suomen kirjallisuus*, p. 70.

1011. Quoted in Warburton, *Femtio år*, p. 249.

1012. Laitinen, *Suomen kirjallisuus*, p. 69.

1013. Warburton (*Femtio år*, p. 250) says that Enckell wants to look at things from a distance and "preferably at his own feelings also." In our opinion Enckell constantly speaks of himself without using the personal pronoun.

1014. The first statements are quoted ibid., p. 253, the latter from *Essay om livets framfart* in Lindström, *Finlandssvensk nittonhundratalslitteratur*, pp. 58-59.

1015. Warburton, *Femtio år*, p. 254. In classical French poetry *un souffle d'airain*, the translation of *Andedräkt av koppar,* is a common phrase.

1016. The title is a good example of Enckell's taste for subdued humor. *Framfart* is a familiar Swedish word for progress; thus the title might be translated 'Essay on How Life Goes About It.'

1017. Lindström, *Finlandssvensk nittonhundratalslitteratur*, p. 60.

1018. Warburton, *Femtio år*, p. 273.

1019. See Lindström, *Finlandssvensk nittonhundratalslitteratur*, pp. 69, 71; Warburton, *Femtio år*, pp. 266-67.

1020. Warburton, *Femtio år*, p. 262, does call him "one of our most original and personal poets," but cf. p. 261.

1021. Lindström, *Finlandssvensk nittonhundratalslitteratur*, p. 71.

1022. "As a painter he is one of the most important in Finland in the twentieth century." (Ibid., p. 63.) The statement is an exaggeration.

1023. See Warburton, *Femtio år*, p. 281.

1024. *Asketernas väg* (1952) has been translated into English, *The Way of the Ascetics*, trans. K. Ferré, ed. R. M. French (London, 1960). *Taina, Förbarma dig, Grottan,* and *Fönster* have been translated into German, *Korståget* has been translated into German, Dutch and Norwegian, Repin's biography into Danish, French, and Norwegian, and *Asketernas väg* into Russian (probably not in the Soviet Union). There are also Finnish translations of many of his works.

1025. Edith Södergran had her last home there, and many writers who stayed there between the wars described it. See p. 381 this volume; cf. Laitinen, *Suomen kirjallisuus*, p. 109; Erik Ekelund, "Karelsk exotism," *Acta Academiae Aboensis Humaniora* 18 (1949): 96-108.

1026. See Warburton, *Femtio år*, pp. 292-93. Cf. Lindström, *Finlandssvensk nittonhundratalslitteratur*, p. 87; Laitinen, *Suomen kirjallisuus*, p. 110.

1027. Warburton, *Femtio år*, p. 291; Laitinen, *Suomen kirjallisuus*, p. 109.

1028. Laitinen, *Suomen kirjallisuus*, p. 109. The book has been translated into English, *The Bells of Rome*, trans. I. and F. McHugh (London, 1961), Dutch, French, German, Italian, Polish, and Spanish. *Hungergropen* has been translated into Danish, Dutch, German, and Finnish; *Fästningen* into Dutch and German; *Vatikanen* into Dutch, *Brödet och stenarna* into Dutch and German; *Från Rom till Rom* into German.

1029. In the eighteenth century two of his forefathers, Jaakko Stenius and Jaakko Stenius, Jr., were ministers of the Lutheran church in northern Karelia, but, like many of their colleagues (e.g., Browallius, Chydenius, and Mennander), they were also interested in practical pursuits, especially in the clearing of forests and watercourses. The local people nicknamed them Korpi-Jaakko (Forest Jim) and Koski-Jaakko (Rapids Jim).

1030. For this reason some critics have compared her to Diktonius (Lindström, *Finlandssvensk nittonhundratalslitteratur*, p. 79).

1031. J. Salminen, *Levande och död tradition*, pp. 135-36.

1032. Ibid., pp. 138-39.

1033. The word *offermänniska* (*människa* 'human being') is used by the author in *Besk brygd.* See Warburton, *Femtio år*, p. 296; Lindström, *Finlandssvensk nittonhundratalslitteratur*, p. 90.

1034. Mary Mandelin (b. 1918) and V. V. Järner (b. 1910) are among the few. Mrs. Mandelin has written a few light, absurd, satirical comedies. Järner is more serious and has been compared to Frisch and Dürrenmatt. Thomas Warburton, "Uusinta dramatiikkaa ja proosaa," trans. Rauni Puranen, in *Kirjallisuus* V, pp. 338-39.

1035. None of the authors we discuss, after Tavaststjerna, is really popular in translation among the Finnish-speaking population. *Kvinnan* has been translated into German, *Madame* into English, German, and Portuguese, *Systrarna* into English and German, *Ruoho* (first written in Finnish) into English, *Kattorna* into Danish, English, German and Norwegian. Several of his radio plays have also been translated into the latter languages. Finnish translations are even more numerous.

1036. Except the novel *Saltkaret* ('The Salt Cellar,' 1963).

1037. *Kirjallisuus* VI, pp. 630-31.

1038. See Lindström, *Finlandssvensk nittonhundratalslitteratur*, p. 91. Thomas Warburton, "Psykologeja ja hermoihmisiä," trans. Rauni Puranen, in *Kirjallisuus* V, p. 320, points out that in this respect his plays are better than his novels.

1039. Laitinen, *Suomen kirjallisuus*, p. 133.

1040. The English name for the little beings she created. No fewer than ten of her books were published in England between 1950 and 1963, several translated by Thomas Warburton.

1041. See Thomas Warburton, "Yksilö yhteiskuntaa vastaan," trans. Rauni Puranen, in *Kirjallisuus* V, p. 289. Another representative of this school is Harald Hornborg (b. 1890), who has written an entertaining and mildly spoofy series of novels on an imaginary German grand duchy, Flüstringen, in the seventeenth and eighteenth centuries.

1042. See Laitinen, *Suomen kirjallisuus*, pp. 71-72; cf. Nils-Börje Stormbom, "Nuori sukupolvi," trans. Mirjam Polkunen, in *Kirjallisuus* VI, p. 541. On recent prose, see George C. Schoolfield, "The Postwar Novel of Swedish Finland," *Scandinavian Studies* 34 (1962).

1043. He wrote a doctoral dissertation on Björling, *Studier i Gunnar Björlings diktning 1922-33* (Helsinki, 1960). See Bo Carpelan, "Tre Björling-synteser," *Ord och Bild* 64 (1957): pp. 239-47.

1044. See Lars Bäckström, "Hantverk för natten. Bo Carpelan" in *Under välfärdens yta* (Örebro, 1959), pp. 213-30; see also Jaakko Ahokas, "Two Poets."

1045. Quoted in Stormbom, "Nuori sukupolvi," pp. 540-41.

1046. Quoted in Lindström, *Finlandssvensk nittonhundratalslitteratur*, p. 96.

1047. The society has published since 1954 a periodical, *Horisont*, edited from 1954 through 1961 by Sven-Olof Högnäs, who also published some literary works.

1048. Stormbom, "Nuori sukupolvi," p. 542; cf. Lindström, *Finlandssvensk nittonhundratalslitteratur*, pp. 98-99. *Spöfågel* [*sic*], evidently coined by the author, is similar to the common Swedish *spefågel*, used to designate a disrespectful, mischievous person, which suggests 'The Whimp Bird' as the title.

1049. The FBT Group has also established contacts with the Finnish writers of Finland (Laitinen, *Suomen kirjallisuus*, p. 209). Thomas Warburton, often quoted here, has published three volumes of poetry, radio plays, and translations of British authors.

1050. Stormbom, "Nuori sukupolvi," p. 543.

1051. See Gunnar Castrén, "Wecksell och hans samtid. I. Finskan och svenskan" in *Humanister och humaniora*, p. 190.

Index of Names and Titles

According to American usage, but contrary to Finnish and Scandinavian, the letters a, ä, å and the digraph æ; o, ö, ø and the digraph œ; and u and ü are identified, whereas v and w are separated.

INDEX OF NAMES AND TITLES

527

INDEX OF NAMES AND TITLES

567